# Lecture Notes in Information Systems and Organisation

Volume 70

Lecture Notes in Information Systems and Organization—LNISO—is a series of scientific books that explore the current scenario of information systems, in particular IS and organization. The focus on the relationship between IT, IS and organization is the common thread of this collection, which aspires to provide scholars across the world with a point of reference and comparison in the study and research of information systems and organization. LNISO is the publication forum for the community of scholars investigating behavioral and design aspects of IS and organization. The series offers an integrated publication platform for high-quality conferences, symposia and workshops in this field. Materials are published upon a strictly controlled double blind peer review evaluation made by selected reviewers.

LNISO is abstracted/indexed in Scopus

Andrea Appolloni • Vikas Kumar •
Evgeny Kuzmin • Victoria Akberdina
Editors

# The Future of Industry

## Human-Centric Approaches in Digital Transformation

Springer

*Editors*
Andrea Appolloni
Department of Management and Law
University of Rome Tor Vergata
Rome, Italy

Department of Management
Minzu University of China
Beijing, China

Vikas Kumar
Faculty of Business, Law and Social Sciences
Birmingham City University
Birmingham, UK

Evgeny Kuzmin
Department of Regional Industrial Policy and Economic Security
Institute of Economics of the Ural Branch of the Russian Academy of Sciences
Ekaterinburg, Russia

Victoria Akberdina
Department of Regional Industrial Policy and Economic Security
Institute of Economics of the Ural Branch of the Russian Academy of Sciences
Ekaterinburg, Russia

ISSN 2195-4968 ISSN 2195-4976 (electronic)
Lecture Notes in Information Systems and Organisation
ISBN 978-3-031-66800-5 ISBN 978-3-031-66801-2 (eBook)
https://doi.org/10.1007/978-3-031-66801-2



This Springer imprint is published by the registered company Springer Nature Switzerland AG
The registered company address is: Gewerbestrasse 11, 6330 Cham, Switzerland

# About This Book

This book offers a selection of the best papers presented at the annual International Scientific Conference "Digital Transformation in Industry: Trends, Management, Strategies," held by the Institute of Economics of the Ural Branch of the Russian Academy of Sciences (Ekaterinburg, Russia) on October 25–27, 2023.

The main focus of the book is on Industry 5.0, a new paradigm for industrial development related to the humanization of technology and the sustainable development of industrial ecosystems. Industry 5.0 is not a technological revolution but a value-based initiative that drives technological transformation by establishing the primacy of human value and creating value for humans. Key topics include the cross-industry potential of Industry 5.0, the humanization of industrial technologies, the transition from Industry 4.0 ecosystems to Industry 5.0, the achievement of sustainability in the process of digital transition, assessing the impact of industrial digital transformation on society and the environment, regional practices for digital transformation, digital transformation strategies of industrial enterprises, and HR strategies for the digital transition of industry, among others.

Due to the scientific pluralism of the topics covered, the book is valuable to economists, researchers, and managers in industry and finance.

**Headliners**

- Provides an overview of the most recent studies in the digital economy
- Presents trends in digital transition to Industry 5.0
- Discusses the prospects of sustainable industrial digitalization
- Considers theoretical and practical aspects of the application of digital technologies

# Contents

## Part V Prospects for Digital Transformation Towards Industry 5.0

# About the Editors

**Andrea Appolloni** is Associate Professor of Sustainable Operations Management at the University of Rome Tor Vergata in Italy. He is also a visiting fellow at the Minzu University of China. His research areas and teaching activities are concentrated on operations, supply chain, and procurement management, focusing on sustainability and innovation. He is responsible for several national and international research projects and is linked with several research teams at the global level. At the University of Tor Vergata, he is the lead of the specialization on Supply Chain Management in the Master of Science in Business Administration, and he is the coordinator of the ESA_LAB@UNITOV, a research space center supported by the European Space Agency.

**Vikas Kumar** is Associate Dean for Research and Innovation and Professor of Operations and Supply Chain Management at the Faculty of Business, Law, and Social Sciences at Birmingham City University, UK. He serves on the editorial boards of several international journals and has published over 250 research papers and edited/co-authored several books in the operations and supply chain management domain. Prof. Kumar has worked on several international collaborative research projects with countries like Brazil, Turkey, Thailand, Indonesia, Vietnam, Jordan, Columbia, Hong Kong, and India. Prof. Kumar's current research focuses on sustainable supply chain management and Supply Chain 4.0.

**Evgeny Kuzmin** is a researcher at the Department of Regional Economic Policy and Economic Security at the Institute of Economics of the Ural Branch of the Russian Academy of Sciences. He has published numerous scientific papers and participated in the implementation of more than 10 scientific projects (grants) supported by the Russian Foundation for Basic Research, the Russian Humanitarian

Scientific Foundation, the Russian Science Foundation, and the Ministry of Education and Science of Russia. His research interests include risk, uncertainty, economic crises, sustainability, public–private partnerships, industrialization, industrial policy, industry markets, modeling, economic growth and development, and entrepreneurship.

**Victoria Akberdina** is Deputy Director of the Institute of Economics of the Ural Branch of the Russian Academy of Sciences and Head of the Department of Regional Industrial Policy and Economic Security. She conducts fundamental and applied research on problems concerning industrial policy formation, forecasting methodologies, and modeling the evolution of the economic and technological development of industrial complexes, as well as the structural dimensions of economic development. In 2019, she was selected as a Corresponding Member of the Russian Academy of Sciences.

# Editorial: Industry 5.0 Towards Human Value and Value for Human

**Evgeny Kuzmin, Andrea Appolloni, Vikas Kumar, and Victoria Akberdina**

**Abstract** The chapter summarizes the best studies published in the Proceedings of the International Scientific Conference "Digital Transformation in Industry: Trends, Management, Strategies" (DTI2023). The conference was organized by the Institute of Economics of the Ural Branch of the Russian Academy of Sciences and held on October 25–27, 2023. 'From Industry 4.0 to Industry 5.0: Challenges and Perspectives' was chosen as the central topic for discussion. The editors delve into the context and background that underlie research in this area. The chapter analyzes the major results and conclusions presented at the conference with a special focus on the human factor playing a strategic role in industrial digitalization. The key challenges and risks enterprises face amid global technological changes are identified, and opportunities for sustainable innovative development within the new industrial paradigm of Industry 5.0 are discussed. In conclusion, we provide a brief overview of the chapters' contributions to the book and emphasize their significance for exploring the conference's topic. This overview allows the readers to appreciate the diversity of research approaches presented. The editors highlight the importance of the authors' managerial recommendations for adapting industrial enterprises to new values in the context of Industry 5.0.

**Keywords** Industry 4.0 · Industry 5.0 · Human values · Digital economy · Sustainable innovative development

---

E. Kuzmin (✉) · V. Akberdina
Department of Regional Industrial Policy and Economic Security, Institute of Economics of the Ural Branch of the Russian Academy of Sciences, Ekaterinburg, Russian Federation
e-mail: kuzmin.ea@uiec.ru; akberdina.vv@uiec.ru

A. Appolloni
Department of Management and Law, University of Rome Tor Vergata, Rome, Italy

Department of Management, Minzu University of China, Beijing, China
e-mail: andrea.appolloni@uniroma2.it

V. Kumar
Faculty of Business, Law and Social Sciences, Birmingham City University, Birmingham, UK
e-mail: Vikas.Kumar@bcu.ac.uk

 
A. Appolloni et al. (eds.), *The Future of Industry*, Lecture Notes in Information Systems and Organisation 70, https://doi.org/10.1007/978-3-031-66801-2_1

Technological change is rapidly transforming the economy and society. In this context, there is a growing need to reconsider the approaches to organizing production processes and establishing guidelines for sustainable development pursued along the path [1–3]. Industry 5.0 is not only the new stage of industrial evolution and the continuation of the automation and digitalization of production initiated during Industry 4.0; it also emphasizes the human factor as a key value in technological processes [4–6].

The Industry 5.0 approaches discussed in the book are an attempt to synthesize the achievements of the previous industrial paradigms and the new interpretation of production organization concentrated on social aspects. We aim to analyze how integrating technological innovations within Industry 5.0 can contribute to creating Human Value and Value for Humans. The authors scrutinize various aspects of the Industry 5.0 technologies implementation, ranging from production process adjustments to regulations and ethics changes. They stress that the successful integration of Industry 5.0 principles requires the active participation of all stakeholders, which is highly important in building a more harmonious and sustainable future where technology encourages economic growth and an improved quality of life.

The emphasis on social impact and the human factor within Industry 5.0 reflects the wide range of opportunities for transforming individual enterprises, whole industries, and the entire society [7–11]. The role of humans is being actively transformed. This transformation implies deep social responsibility and a commitment to social well-being, which serves as the basis for long-term sustainable industrial development [12, 13]. At the same time, new challenges are emerging.

The existing prerequisites underlie the relevance of the conference's topic "From Industry 4.0 to Industry 5.0: Challenges and Perspectives." The International Scientific Conference DTI2023 provided participants with a platform to formulate their views on the current socio-economic shifts and explore new trends.

The book presents the best scientific reports divided into five sections covering various aspects of the conference topic. *Part I: Transition to Industry 5.0* addresses the specificity of the Industry 4.0-to-Industry 5.0 transition and its impact on society from the perspective of economic theory, politics and law. This section summarizes the debates on the dilemma between technological change and social well-being, the co-evolutionary development of Industry 4.0 and Industry 5.0, and the emerging challenges and future prospects. *Part II: Mechanisms, Methods, and Models of Digitalization* presents business models based on methodological approaches to assessing the impact of digitalization on the socio-economic development of countries and regions and revising the economic concept of enterprises within Industry 5.0. It also studies new economic phenomena arising against the background of Industry 4.0 and the transition to Industry 5.0. This section provides the readers with a vision of how digital innovation can drive progress and what strategic approaches can be practical in the new economic reality. *Part III: Digital Transformation in Industry* covers examples of digital transformation in various industries and examines the impact of digitalization on the reindustrialization of cities. This section also discusses innovative practices and strategies for introducing digital technologies into traditional and new sectors of the economy. Particular attention is given to the role of digitalization in sustainable business development and creating value for companies and society as a whole. *Part IV: Human Capital in the Digital Economy* discusses HR management strategies in the context of the digital economy, the impact of digitalization on the development of human capital, and the role of educational systems in training personnel for Industry 5.0. *Part V: Prospects for Digital Transformation Towards Industry 5.0* investigates various aspects of strategic planning and risk assessment for industrial regions, including the adaptation of production systems to new technological conditions and research aimed at increasing labor productivity. Each section of the book provides the readers with an in-depth review of the existing studies and presents a comprehensive summary of the distinguishing features of digitalization and its impact on society and the economy.

The conference fostered a collaborative exchange of ideas, allowing the participants to delve deeper into the implications of integrating advanced technologies into industrial systems.

Look at the authors' findings in more detail.

The studies emphasize that the implementation of Industry 5.0 principles requires the active involvement of human not only as a subject, but also as a central element of the innovation process. This implies creating jobs that promote creativity and innovation. The authors point out the need to devise new approaches to education and training that would form the skills needed for effective work in the digital economy. They also focus on using technologies to improve working conditions and increase safety.

The researchers formulate strategies for developing regulatory frameworks that ensure the ethical use of technologies. They highlight the importance of monitoring and evaluating technological innovation to avoid negative social impacts. Ethical considerations of using artificial intelligence, robots, and automated systems in industry often involve liability issues. These aspects need to be examined to develop a framework ensuring fair and safe use of technology that considers all stakeholders' interests. The authors analyze how necessary the measures are to mitigate the negative effects of technology on employment, including strategies for retraining and upskilling workers.

Research results demonstrate the importance of actively integrating the principles of social responsibility and sustainability into all aspects of production. This means not only reducing the negative man-made impact on the environment but also ensuring that technological development enhances prosperity and quality of life. The authors substantiate the need to integrate sustainable development strategies into corporate and national policies, which includes compliance with environmental standards and ensuring social justice.

The authors described approaches to the development of highly adaptable production systems. They emphasized the importance of integrating energy-efficient technologies and resource-saving practices, which help both increase production efficiency and reduce the environmental footprint. The experts also develop strategies for harmonizing technology standards and regulations, which can strengthen global cooperation. These strategies imply adopting unified approaches and procedures that facilitate international collaboration and knowledge sharing in key technology areas.

The authors' conclusions illustrate the importance of an interdisciplinary approach in developing and applying Industry 5.0 technologies. They point to the need for collaboration to devise technologies that consider both technical and social aspects. This collaboration helps produce solutions that promote sustainable development and social well-being by integrating scientific knowledge and practical experience from various disciplines.

Research results show that countries and companies investing in developing and applying Industry 4.0 and Industry 5.0 technologies often attain a significant competitive advantage. This highlights the role of innovation and technology development strategies. Success in this field requires the state to offer targeted support, including investments in R&D, education, and the environment conducive to enterprises' innovative activities. The authors stress the importance of supporting local initiatives, which allows technologies to be adapted to local conditions. This promotes deeper integration and strengthens innovation ecosystems.

The final chapters deal with technology development's long-term prospects and impact on global economic and social systems. The authors reflect on a future where technology and human values converge, creating a new era of innovative and responsible approaches to sustainable development.

These are just a few conference conclusions indicating the complexity and multifaceted nature of the transition from Industry 4.0 to Industry 5.0. Studies also highlight the relevance of the dilemma between technological development and the need to ensure human well-being. The transition to Industry 5.0 should be accompanied by meticulous attention to the social aspects of development, where technologies improve the quality of life. The presented works examine the transition as a process of interaction between technical and social aspects, where the key role is assigned to integrating innovative technologies and management practices to achieve a better personalization and sustainability of production. At the same time, we can talk about the co-evolution of Industry 4.0 and Industry 5.0, which mark the rise of a techno-social revolution. The authors investigate the role of Industry 5.0 in rethinking global economic relations and the balance of power in technological leadership. The specific problems and opportunities associated with implementing the Industry 5.0 principles in various countries and regions are analyzed. The particular focus is on developing digital infrastructure and training staff. Some of the papers analyze the effect of digitalization on the development and management of human capital, especially in terms of productivity management and adaptation of the workforce to new technological requirements. The methodological aspects of developing sustainable business models driven by digital technologies are explored, emphasizing the importance of innovation for long-term development. The articles analyze the risks associated with the transformation of industrial enterprises and regions, pointing to the need for strategic planning and assessment of the potential consequences of the transition to Industry 5.0.

These findings and results provide the basis for in-depth discussion and understanding of how Industry 5.0 can transform modern manufacturing and society. The results highlight the importance of balancing technological progress and human values. This approach helps create a more sustainable society. The studies demonstrate a multidimensional approach to examining the impact of digital technologies, emphasizing the importance of a comprehensive analysis of technological, economic, and social changes associated with the transition from Industry 4.0 to Industry 5.0.

These and other relevant issues were discussed at the International Scientific Conference "Digital Transformation in Industry: Trends, Management, Strategies" (DTI2023) held by the Institute of Economics of the Ural Branch of the Russian Academy of Sciences.

The book invites readers to consider how we can use modern technology to create a society in which technological progress establishes the primacy of Human Value and creates Value for Humans. Researchers, industrial enterprise managers, economists, financial experts, and managers alike can benefit from the results of the topics covered.

## References

1. Maddikunta, P. K. R., Pham, Q. V., Prabadevi, B., Deepa, N., Dev, K., Gadekallu, T. R., et al. (2022). Industry 5.0: A survey on enabling technologies and potential applications. *Journal of Industrial Information Integration, 26*, 100257. https://doi.org/10.1016/j.jii.2021.100257
2. Xu, X., Lu, Y., Vogel-Heuser, B., & Wang, L. (2021). Industry 4.0 and Industry 5.0—Inception, conception and perception. *Journal of Manufacturing Systems, 61*, 530–535. https://doi.org/10.1016/j.jmsy.2021.10.006
3. Zizic, M. C., Mladineo, M., Gjeldum, N., & Celent, L. (2022). From industry 4.0 towards industry 5.0: A review and analysis of paradigm shift for the people, organization and technology. *Energies, 15*(14), 5221. https://doi.org/10.3390/en15145221
4. Grabowska, S., Saniuk, S., & Gajdzik, B. (2022). Industry 5.0: Improving humanization and sustainability of Industry 4.0. *Scientometrics, 127*(6), 3117–3144. https://doi.org/10.1007/s11192-022-04370-1
5. Mourtzis, D., Angelopoulos, J., & Panopoulos, N. (2022). A literature review of the challenges and opportunities of the transition from industry 4.0 to society 5.0. *Energies, 15*(17), 6276. https://doi.org/10.3390/en15176276
6. Raja Santhi, A., & Muthuswamy, P. (2023). Industry 5.0 or industry 4.0S? Introduction to industry 4.0 and a peek into the prospective industry 5.0 technologies. *International Journal on Interactive Design and Manufacturing (IJIDeM), 17*(2), 947–979. https://doi.org/10.1007/s12008-023-01217-8
7. Adel, A. (2022). Future of Industry 5.0 in society: Human-centric solutions, challenges and prospective research areas. *Journal of Cloud Computing, 11*(1), 40. https://doi.org/10.1186/s13677-022-00314-5
8. Kovari, A. (2024). Industry 5.0: Generalized definition, key applications, opportunities and threats. *Acta Polytechnica Hungarica, 21*(3), 267–284. https://doi.org/10.12700/aph.21.3.2024.3.17
9. Paschek, D., Luminosu, C. T., & Ocakci, E. (2022). Industry 5.0 challenges and perspectives for manufacturing systems in the society 5.0. In *Sustainability and innovation in manufacturing enterprises: Indicators, models and assessment for industry 5.0* (pp. 17–63). https://doi.org/10.1007/978-981-16-7365-8_2

10. Saikia, B. (2023). Industry 5.0–its role toward human society: Obstacles, opportunities, and providing human-centered solutions. In *Fostering sustainable businesses in emerging economies: The impact of technology* (pp. 109–126). Emerald Publishing Limited. https://doi.org/10.1108/978-1-80455-640-520231008
11. Saniuk, S., Grabowska, S., & Straka, M. (2022). Identification of social and economic expectations: Contextual reasons for the transformation process of Industry 4.0 into the Industry 5.0 concept. *Sustainability, 14*(3), 1391. https://doi.org/10.3390/su14031391
12. Alves, J., Lima, T. M., & Gaspar, P. D. (2023). Is Industry 5.0 a human-centred approach? A systematic review. *Processes, 11*(1), 193. https://doi.org/10.3390/pr11010193
13. Žižek, S. Š., Mulej, M., & Potočnik, A. (2021). The sustainable socially responsible society: Well-being society 6.0. *Sustainability, 13*(16), 9186. https://doi.org/10.3390/su13169186

# Part I
# Transition to Industry 5.0

# The Dilemma Between Industry 4.0 and Society 5.0: A Technological Evolution of Digital Transformation or a Humanitarian Revolution of Well-being?

**Grigorios L. Kyriakopoulos**

**Abstract** Nowadays social cohesion and humanity prosperity are the issues directly linked to the evolution of traditional humanitarian ethics and the rethinking of indigenous cultural morals. In this context, the investigation of the entities of Society 5.0 and Industry 5.0 can be reviewed in terms of improving humanitarian values and ensuring sustainable development at an Industry 4.0 meta-epoch. Subsequently, humans and machines symbiosis is actually considered as a debate of Industry 5.0 vs. (evolving from) Industry 4.0, or (shifting) Industry 4.0 vs. (towards) Society 5.0. In this review study, a critique has raised of how digital transformation could actually identify and characterize an unstable era of threatening social cohesion, being considered as a global human-centricity issue by adopting production planning and suitable control systems towards Industry 5.0. Additionally, in the study an integrated approach of Industry 4.0 and Society 5.0 was structured and valued in alignment with sustainable development goals' (SDGs)-authorized/-driven sustainable societies. Conclusively, the main constraints, the prevalent challenges and the future research considerations of such a humanitarian (r)evolution towards a future well-being have been demonstrated.

**Keywords** Industry 4.0 · Society 5.0 · Digital transformation · Humanitarian revolution · Literature review · Sustainable Development Goals (SDGs) · Industry 4.0 vs. Society 5.0 debate

---

**Supplementary Information** The online version contains supplementary material available at https://doi.org/10.1007/978-3-031-66801-2_2.

---

G. L. Kyriakopoulos (✉)
School of Electrical and Computer Engineering, National Technical University of Athens, Athens, Greece
e-mail: gregkyr@chemeng.ntua.gr



A. Appolloni et al. (eds.), *The Future of Industry*, Lecture Notes in Information Systems and Organisation 70, https://doi.org/10.1007/978-3-031-66801-2_2

# 1 Introduction

In the existing literature, there are sparsely published studies in the field of Society 5.0 (S5.0). Therefore, it is quite challenging to explore the existence of S5.0 in alignment with Industry 4.0 (I4.0) the effectiveness of evaluating the applicability of United Nations Development Goals (SDGs) in this transition. In the relevant studies it was demonstrated that SDG9, SDG10, SDG11, SDG12, SDG13, and SDG14 were loosely linked to the application of I4.0 and S5.0. Moreover, a critical methodological constraint is the bias of participants who are actually not neutral or pathetic receptors of S5.0 but they provide biased/subjective responses when questioned on S5.0 and I4.0. This fact makes it necessary to use modern methodological tools to examine S5.0 and I4.0 while avoiding the employment of outdated processes [1].

The concepts of S5.0 and I5.0 are not simply chronological situations or alternatives to Industry 4.0. S5.0 places humans at the midpoint of innovation, demonstrating how technological innovations and I4.0 can support technological integration having the improvement of quality of life as ultimate goal, in alignment with social responsibility and sustainability. Such a perspective sustains common characteristics with the objectives of the United Nations SDGs, but it also extends its scopes to university transformations. Indeed, strategic goal of universities is to produce knowledge for new technologies and social innovation. Nowadays, digitalization can further envisage new perspectives for universities, playing a decisive role in their change. In this context, S5.0 and I5.0 assumptions can activate the university practices and policies enabling both universities and societies to benefit from digital transformation. University can trademark the human-oriented innovation towards developing new cooperative models for the development of new forms and channels of education, research and innovation within in the S5.0 context [2, 3].

In a similar study, it was stressed out that the achievement of SDGs can be directed towards sustainable development. In this context, there is the technological potential to attain the SDGs through disruptive technologies. For this, the critical aspects of SDGs 3, 8, 9 and 11 are predominately determined by product development, health care transformation, pandemic case studies, nature-inclusive business models, smart cities and villages. Additionally, to better understand the ways in which the SDGs are influenced by disruptive technologies, it is noteworthy that I5.0 and S5.0 could play a decisive role to support the development and underpin the efforts towards SDGs achievement. Such a methodology is capable in smart cities and villages showing the most advantageous prospects of achieving SDGs due to the integrated framework and the SDGs' interactions. Subsequently, an integrated framework contains new age technologies of smart cities and villages, conceptualizing I5.0 and S5.0 and supporting industrialists, policymakers and researchers to commit the technological perspectives of SDGs [4].

From an operational perspective, the transition from I4.0 towards the latest I5.0 and S5.0 prerequisites the re-evaluation of the ways in which manufacturing industries can embody the generation of digital production equipment in their plans. In such a way human worker inclusion can be prioritized thus demonstrating decision-making activities or physical actions that can be undertaken at the automated process flow of the so-called I5.0. In this context, the Japanese Society 5.0 concept was studied to address wider social and environmental problems, through the latest advantages of digital system, Artificial Intelligence (AI) and automation solutions [5]. I5.0 can be considered as a managerial tool to support infrastructural resilience, handle employees and environmental concerns in industrial settings, especially in the EU territory. Environmental problems of special provision should also be related to carbon output at production, considering carbon emissions overall the lifecycle steps of manufacturing products, including the disassembly procedure of products together with intelligent products subjected to a sustainable reuse of components and materials. In such a context, net zero carbon and circular economy goals are primary targets towards net zero production, conceiving the arbitration power over information and decisions, jointly with intelligent products utility [5].

S5.0 has been proposed by Japan Cabinet to balance economic advancement with the resolution of social problems in the highly industrialized Japanese society. For this, the revolutions of industry and society have associated with each other since the First Industrial Revolution. In the relevant literature, several approaches attempted to jointly evaluate the I4.0 and S5.0 convergence. Among them, the Large-Scale Optimization is applicable to supply chain and smart manufacturing, particularly exploring the role of Large-Scale Optimization in I4.0 and S5.0 regarding the digitalization and networking the manufacturing-operational with social sectors [6]. This methodological logic involved the futuristic industry and society of increasing attention, that is, on I5.0 and S5.0. Even more, the European Commission (EC) announced the sustainability, human-centricity, and resilience of European industry towards I5.0. At this point it is noteworthy that the coexistence of I5.0 and S5.0 can generate confusions that have to be clarified and resolved. Therefore, I5.0 and S5.0 can foremost address the corresponding foundational argument, comparison, complementation, and co-evolution about I5.0 and S5.0, inspiring the future investigation and the subsequent development of I5.0 and S5.0 [7].

The scope of this review study is to examine how Industry 4.0 features and enabling technologies can support the transition to Society 5.0 and to investigate the roles of clustered classification (as described in the Methodology section) to value the dominant literature aspects of achieving this transition. The conceptual framework of this review is to jointly consider all 4.0 s' and 5.0 s' concepts in the fields of: Industry, Society, or even Construction-Technology-Innovation, which are all challenging issues that firms or public and private organization must cope with nowadays. In addition, scholars and practitioners, managers and business owners could profit from these insights to design ad-hoc strategies in order to benefit from the opportunities emerging from this transition and overcome the main related challenges. This multifaceted and multi-parametric outlook also resides in similar and widely approved studies [8, 9]. It is anticipated that, as with all past industrial revolutions, Industry 4.0 is a confident tool to support the transition to a different society, i.e., Society 5.0. In this transition, all clustered classifications can play an important role, depending on each time context of analysis (such as business engineering, industry 4.0, and society 5.0 for SMEs food manufacturing especially in product innovation) being based on the changing of an industrial environment among manufacturing SME industries [10, 11].

## 2 Materials and Methods

As an aftermath of the Fourth Industrial Revolution at the beginning of the twenty-first century, emerging methodologies and technologies in both industry and society are linked to I4 improvements with technological and human characteristics, such as age, advances in information and computing technologies (ICT) coupled with new capabilities in modeling and solving algorithms (MSA) and mechatronics (MEC). At the same time technological hallmarks can also be related to business and managerial contexts, in which innovative industrial design, operation, and manufacturing control in logistics and supply chains are of utmost significance. Globally, the rise of crowd-sourcing towards operational cost reduction can be followed by the widespread information and communication capabilities gradually transforming the primitive norms of today's societies [12]. Moreover, in our high-tech era the Covid-19 pandemic is unavoidably reshaping the formal or even informal modes of education and simultaneously prioritizing the ways under which individuals share, connect, and communicate a collection of workloads, expertise, follow-ups. Therefore, the dawn of the I5.0 manages differently capabilities, readiness, and preparedness, than that of I4.0, thus, the I4.0–I5.0 interplay in the fields of industry and society, research and development (R&D) is the key-factor of a successful coordination of an I4-S5.0 pairing [12].

Following the aforementioned theoretical and practical background of research approaches, in this study a bibliometric analysis was conducted based on keywords from the Scopus database and classifying the research reports into the following five clusters. The research reports covered the period of analysis 2018–2024 and they are presented in alphabetical order of last name of first authors, followed by the descending order of publication: from the newest to the oldest. All clusters results have been presented in the form of Tables 1–5 of the Research Dataset [13], having also the calculated subtotals presented in alignment with the years of publication per cluster:

- Cluster 1: Industry 4.0 and Society 5.0, Table 1.
- Cluster 2: Industry 4.0 and Technologies with applications in 3D printing and Blockchain, Table 2.
- Cluster 3: Industry 4.0 and Human and Robots collaboration, Table 3.
- Cluster 4: Industry 4.0 and Industry 5.0, Table 4.
- Cluster 5: Industry 4.0 and Multi-parametric Approaches, Table 5.
  - Cluster 5A: Combination of Technologies.
  - Cluster 5B: Combination of Technologies with Society 5.0.

Based on Cluster 1, the allocation of documents per year of publication per year is: 2024: 0, 2023: 5, 2022: 9, 2021: 12, 2020: 3, 2019: 2, 2018: 0, having a subtotal of 31 documents in Cluster 1. In addition, the conceptual convergence of I4.0 with S5.0 has been widely studied. Among those paradigms it is that of Enhanced Living Environments (ELE) which are a kind of paradigm for life, well-being and social inclusion. Improving an environment implies the development of processes that, based on people needs and conditions, make pertinent adjustments, so that the feeling of comfort and security arises when the interaction takes place. Finally, the viability of I4.0 and S5.0 integration paradigms enabled an ELE ecosystem centered on patients and elderly people in extrahospitalary environments, implying the promotion of technological increase actions, favoring the adaptation of individual life conditions to improve the living conditions, while ensuring the autonomy and the independence of peoples' daily functions under disability or elderly living situations [14].

Based on Cluster 2, the allocation of documents per year of publication per year is: 2024: 0, 2023: 6, 2022: 2, 2021: 0, 2020: 1, 2019: 0, 2018: 0, having a subtotal of 9 documents in Cluster 2. Moreover, in jointly approaching contemporary governing principles, together with multidisciplinary corporate social responsibility (CSR) initiatives among organizations, it was proven that the coordination of technology CSR models are grounded to tackle individuals' social problems but also change the environmental, social and economic dimensions of CSR's under S5.0. The optimization of CSR practices in organizations also demands new possibilities for interest-based usage of human-centered society among individuals and organizations. An integral modelling of CSR can further approach social problems and circumstances of S5.0 by simultaneously employing advanced technologies [15].

Based on Cluster 3, the allocation of documents per year of publication per year is: 2024: 0, 2023: 10, 2022: 0, 2021: 0, 2020: 0, 2019: 0, 2018: 0, having a subtotal of 10 documents in Cluster 3. Regarding the overview of Cluster 3 it can be reported the research inevitability of I4.0, with two versions of I5.0—human-robot collaboration and bioeconomy should recognize technological comforts only as opportunity, not as a thread. The third dimension of inclusive and human-centric growth brought in by S5.0 should be overviewed especially among densely populated developing economies, focusing on how bioeconomy can play a decisive role in an international context. In the Indian context, it demonstrates suggestions for bioeconomy to gain prominence in balancing at a sustainable manner the proverbial 3 Ps viz. People, Planet and Profits [16].

Based on Cluster 4, the allocation of documents per year of publication per year is: 2024: 3, 2023: 70, 2022: 51, 2021: 9, 2020: 2, 2019: 2, 2018: 1, having a subtotal of 138 documents in Cluster 4. As it is shown in Cluster 4, there is a wide literature production on the I4.0–I5.0 coordination. At this point, it is noteworthy that in recent years enterprises and information societies confront crucial challenges, while Industry 4.0 becomes important in the global manufacturing industry and S5.0 should promote a super-smart society, being facilitated with high-tech sectors, as well as advanced healthcare services of employing digital platforms at monitoring physical activity and, subsequently improving the healthcare status of patients with diabetes and other lifestyle-related diseases. In this context, profitability can be ensured for health technology companies, also helping costs control in the healthcare ecosystem [17].

Based on Cluster 5 the allocation of documents per year of publication per year is: 2024: 0, 2023: 32022: 1, 2021: 1, 2020: 0, 2019: 0, 2018: 0, having a subtotal of 5 documents in Cluster 5. While it may be not a straightforward or powerful causality, in Cluster 5 the I4.0 can be productively coordinated with open data (OD) under a wide geographical dispersion. Indeed, the main role of OD performance expectancy is to support users' technology acceptance models for future implementation OD in I4.0, also highly impacting S5.0. Therefore, it is scientifically challenging to identify trends and leading terms that make ODs usable in both I4.0 and S5.0. It is also important to promote the use of OD in I4.0 and S5.0. Such contexts that can be benefited are the digital OD products and services, applications, websites and platforms of real time information on public issues, primarily in areas such as transport, education, culture and sport, economics and finance, health, as well as specialized geo-data of national and local interest. It is also notable that European countries can envisage and promote relevant OD-driven products and services of Western, Northern, Southern and Eastern Europe [18].

## 3 Results and Discussion

In addition to the aforementioned allocation of documents per cluster and per year, it is also important to obtain a time- and classification- outlook of the documents collected. Subsequently, Fig. 1 shows the relative literature dynamics considering the documents allocation per cluster. In particular, based on the analysis above, it can be noted that almost 48,2% of the collected documents were published in 2023, followed by 32,5% of documents released in 2022, and 11,7% of documents published in 2021. Moreover, less than 5% of collected documents were published in 2018, 2019 and 2024. This chronological finding is an indicator of an ongoing interest in studying the Industry 4.0 conceptualizations with the other co-evaluated terms/clusters from the year 2021 onwards, while in older times this research can be

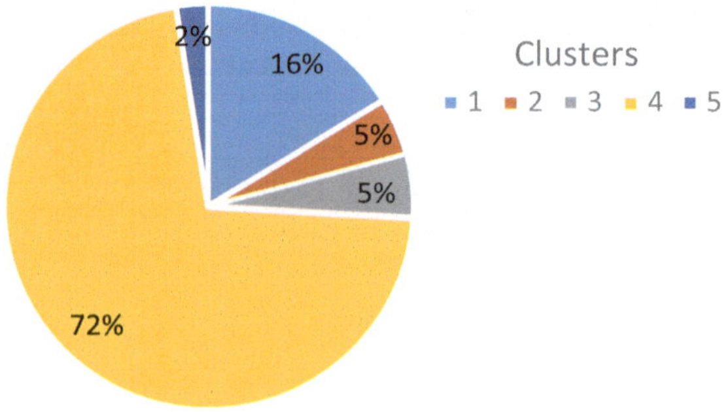


**Fig. 1** Profile of documents allocation per cluster developed

considered at its early developmental phase, being sparsely investigated and immature.

Based on Fig. 1, it is noteworthy that the most referencing cluster was Cluster 4, referring to the interplay between Industry 4.0 and Industry 5.0 (72%), showing a dynamic 4.5 times higher than that of the secondly ordered Cluster 1, referring to the associations and convergence developed between Industry 4.0 and Society 5.0. The dynamics of Clusters 2, 3, and 5 are weak, counting for 5% or less. The thematic dynamics of Clusters 1 and 4 reveal a priority investigation of shifting and evolving Industry 4.0 into Industry 5.0, but also an indicator of an ongoing interest in studying the society reflections and approval, or opposition of the socializing "attributes" of such an operational, technological and (actually) cultural and institutional evolution from Industry 4.0 to Society 5.0. These research outcomes are on their infancy and near future studies could also be systematically reported and considered, thus, achieving a more mature and transparent developmental phase of analysis, accordingly.

Based on the bibliometric data it can be argued that while I5.0 and S5.0 are capable of addressing distinct and separate technological and societal issues or solving problems in these two contexts, the critical aspect is the coupling synergies of I5.0 and S5.0 that have to be developed in a spectrum of today applications with innovation, socio-cultural, operational, and characteristics. In response to this challenge, there is a literature production that has been focused on smart environments, as an example for I5.0 and S5.0 purposes. At this point, it is vital to signify the necessity of systemic vision of the elements, which act and are acted within a given geo-spatial context. Therefore, the synergies activated by the system are actually the end-product of the applying particular knowledge-based open innovation strategies that are prone to transform theoretical assumptions into concrete and innovative operational paths/choices. Such synergies can also suggest the optimal solutions at implementing the new human-centric perception of I5.0, analyzing their cost-benefits for the ecosystem, and promoting novel technological changes and managerial visions. Knowledge circulation, adaptive technologies and entrepreneurial operational strategies should be overviewed as good practices and decision-making processes for smart, sustainable, and inclusive solutions [2, 3]. In similar studies, I4.0 focuses on the reordering of industrial components in alignment with strong digital support. For this, the successfulness of the Fourth Industrial Revolution caused among others the stirring revolution, the efficient extraction of advanced informatics analytics, the inter-networking machines all complementing the digital platform. Contrarily to technological revolution of I4.0, S5.0 involves a human-centric evolution in which community is balancing between the economic growth and the resolution of societal liabilities by the core combination of cyber and physical space. Additionally, S5.0 encourages mundane life to leap towards a digital revamp expanding across different tiers of the community. In this context, ICT can serve as a credible and mutually supportive "interface" along with the portrayal of S5.0, underscoring the wider significance of the Science and Technology Basic plan in synergistically approaching S5.0 and I5.0 [19]. Moreover, it cannot be undermined that, when investigating the benefits of value-driven ecosystems, human engagement behaviour through richer data can be foundational in enabling the reality of the Society 5.0 vision. Therefore, a deeper understanding of how organizations are spreading intelligence from the core to the edge to turn data into action and action into value should be accomplished by learning from the existing Society 4.0 together with social and economic deficiencies exposed during the Covid-19 outbreak and those solutions created during that time [20].

I4.0 is principally designed to ensure the sustainability and improve the efficiency of production systems. In its developmental stages, I4.0 was endorsed with digitization of systems and the technological evolution of the system/machine interactions. Therefore, I5.0 is able to support societal transformation and the transition to a new S5.0 society, thus emerging the social-humanity-technological aspects and human-centric aspects as critical ancestors of the early I4.0 framework. In this respect, sustainability and human well-being shape the future of I5.0 as a subset of S5.0. Apart from I5.0, keeping the I4.0 foundations can emphasize human-centered, resilient, and sustainable design. The research challenges facilitating the transition from I4.0 to S5.0 are linked to the coexistence of industry and the emerging societal trends and needs, considering I5.0 as a framework of such a research philosophy that can be further built up into S5.0 norms and forms [21].

## 4 Conclusion

In recent years, along with the technology development, new theoretical concepts are born continuously. Given today's climate and digitalization challenges, societies should make a conscious agreement on the meaning of concepts they want to build their societies on. Living in Industry 4.0, the future society will be grounded on two new conceptual perspectives: Society 5.0 and Industry 5.0. However, the level and common-shared characteristics of these two new terms are not clear. Except for the synonym meaning, some differences are also evident, as Society 5.0 seems to be related more to the human sphere, while Industry 5.0 seems to be more industrial-centered. Therefore, clarification on definitions is deemed mandatory. In addition to S5.0 and I5.0 definitions, future researches have to employ a comparable analysis on the prevailing similarities over differences between the two concepts, activating researchers to take stock of the actual society and propose final indications on which studies are needed in the future [22].

Industry 4.0 has focused on digitalization in the industry with smart factories making various promises to businesses. Society 5.0 trend offers promising integration of versatile environments, such as cyber and physical systems for individual or common use. Subsequently, Industry 4.0 and Society 5.0 trends are firstly conceptualized and co-evaluated in detail by handling the positive and the negative aspects of these concepts. It is notable that whether the concepts have superiority over each other or not, it remains critical to guide future academic and sectoral studies of the prevalence of Industry 4.0, or Society 5.0. In this way, literature can raise awareness of societies dealing with different dimensions of both concepts [23].

When approaching the concepts of Society and Industry in their latest available status (Society 5.0 (S5.0) and Industry 5.0 (I5.0)), it can be stressed out that they are relatively new and emerging domains since researchers all over the world are still striving to explore their influence within distinct contexts. However, studies should be able to investigate the impact of these two major models of industrialization, S5.0 and I5.0, in order to obtain a more comprehensive understanding of the insights into how it triggers the firms' sustainable development from the perspective of empirical examinations from national industrial sectors. Some researches found a positive affection of the I5.0 model with that of sustainable performance. Moreover, a positive association of the S5.0 model towards sustainable performance asserted a positive linkage between I5.0 and S5.0 from a social perspective, having also promising positive consequences in the environmental factors between I5.0 and S5.0 [24, 25].

However, future studies equipped with both I- and S- contexts that empirically conduct the contextual examination show insights into certain policy implications. For instance, while both I5.0 and S5.0 can support innovative ecosystems, it is crucial to encourage ethical and sustainable practices, effective infrastructure, empowerment of citizen participation, and supportive work for a societal well-being. The engagement of managerial and theoretical recommendations for the industries together with possibilities of future research directions for scholars all over the world [24, 25] is proposed under the versatile interplay of I4.0 to I5.0, or I5.0 to S5.0, which can be realistically and plausibly characterized as a radical "revolution" among industry, society, humanity, processes, products and services, either in local- and global- scales of investigation.

## References

1. Zengin, Y., Naktiyok, S., Kaygın, E., Kavak, O., & Topçuoğlu, E. (2021). An investigation upon Industry 4.0 and Society 5.0 within the context of sustainable development goals. *Sustainability, 13*(5), 2682. https://doi.org/10.3390/su13052682
2. Carayannis, E. G., Dezi, L., Gregori, G., & Calo, E. (2022a). Smart environments and techno-centric and human-centric innovations for Industry and Society 5.0: A quintuple helix innovation system view towards smart, sustainable, and inclusive solutions. *Journal of the Knowledge Economy, 13*(2), 926–955. https://doi.org/10.1007/s13132-021-00763-4
3. Carayannis, E. G., & Morawska-Jancelewicz, J. (2022b). The futures of Europe: Society 5.0 and Industry 5.0 as driving forces of future universities. *Journal of the Knowledge Economy, 13*(4), 3445–3471. https://doi.org/10.1007/s13132-021-00854-2
4. Kasinathan, P., Pugazhendhi, R., Elavarasan, R. M., Ramachandaramurthy, V. K., Ramanathan, V., Subramanian, S., Kumar, S., Nandhagopal, K., Raghavan, R. R. V., Rangasamy, S., Devendiran, R., & Alsharif, M. H. (2022). Realization of sustainable development goals with disruptive technologies by integrating Industry 5.0, Society 5.0, smart cities and villages. *Sustainability, 14*(22), 15258. https://doi.org/10.3390/su142215258
5. Turner, C., Oyekan, J., Garn, W., Duggan, C., & Abdou, K. (2022). Industry 5.0 and the circular economy: Utilizing LCA with intelligent products. *Sustainability, 14*(22), 14847. https://doi.org/10.3390/su142214847

6. Granrath, L. (2019). Large scale optimization is needed for Industry 4.0 and Society 5.0. *Optimization and Its Applications, 152*, 3–6. https://doi.org/10.1007/978-3-030-28565-4_1
7. Huang, S., Wang, B., Li, X., Zheng, P., Mourtzis, D., & Wang, L. (2022). Industry 5.0 and Society 5.0—Comparison, complementation and co-evolution. *Journal of Manufacturing Systems, 64*, 424–428. https://doi.org/10.1016/j.jmsy.2022.07.010
8. Aquilani, B., Piccarozzi, M., Abbate, T., & Codini, A. (2020). The role of open innovation and value co-creation in the challenging transition from Industry 4.0 to Society 5.0: Toward a theoretical framework. *Sustainability, 12*(21), 8943. https://doi.org/10.3390/su12218943
9. Elim, H. I., & Zhai, G. (2020). Control system of multitasking interactions between Society 5.0 and Industry 5.0: A conceptual introduction & its applications. *Journal of Physics: Conference Series, 1463*, 012035. https://doi.org/10.1088/1742-6596/1463/1/012035
10. Rahman, A., Pasanbu, E., Nugraha, Y., Khair, F., Soebandrija, K. E. N., & Wijaya, D. I. (2020). Industry 4.0 and Society 5.0 through lens of condition based maintenance (CBM) and machine learning of artificial intelligence (MLAI). *IOP Conference Series: Materials Science and Engineering, 852*(1), 012022. https://doi.org/10.1088/1757-899X/852/1/012022
11. Saptaningtyas, W. W. E., & Rahayu, D. K. (2020). A proposed model for food manufacturing in smes: Facing Industry 5.0. Proceedings of the International Conference on Industrial Engineering and Operations Management, (August).
12. Menezes, B., Yaqot, M., Hassaan, S., Franzoi, R., Alqashouti, N., & Al-Banna, A. (2022). Digital transformation in the era of Industry 4.0 and Society 5.0: A perspective. 2022 2nd International *Conference on Emerging Smart Technologies and Applications*, eSmarTA 2022. https://doi.org/10.1109/eSmarTA56775.2022.9935399.
13. Kyriakopoulos, G. (2024). DATASET. The dilemma between Industry 4.0 and Society 5.0: A technological evolution of digital transformation or a humanitarian revolution of well-being? (Version 1). https://doi.org/10.6084/m9.figshare.25472395.v1.
14. Caro Anzola, E. W., & Mendoza Moreno, M. Á. (2021). Enhanced living environments (ELE): A paradigm based on integration of Industry 4.0 and Society 5.0 contexts with Ambient Assisted Living (AAL). In *Lecture notes in bioengineering* (pp. 121–132). https://doi.org/10.1007/978-3-030-72567-9_12
15. Potočan, V., Mulej, M., & Nedelko, Z. (2021). Society 5.0: Balancing of Industry 4.0, economic advancement and social problems. *Kybernetes, 50*(3), 794–811. https://doi.org/10.1108/K-12-2019-0858
16. Chaudhari, P., Utgikar, R., Kelkar, B., & Borse, P. (2021). A novel approach: Bioeconomy Industry 5.0 enhanced version. *2021 IEEE Pune section international conference*, PuneCon 2021. https://doi.org/10.1109/PuneCon52575.2021.9686495.
17. Masuda, Y., Zimmermann, A., Shepard, D. S., Schmidt, R., & Shirasaka, S. (2021). An adaptive enterprise architecture design for a digital healthcare platform: Toward digitized society – Industry 4.0, Society 5.0. In *IEEE International Enterprise Distributed Object Computing Workshop, EDOCW proceedings* (pp. 138–146). https://doi.org/10.1109/EDOCW52865.2021.00043
18. Sołtysik-Piorunkiewicz, A., & Zdonek, I. (2021). How Society 5.0 and Industry 4.0 ideas shape the open data performance expectancy. *Sustainability, 13*(2), 917. https://doi.org/10.3390/su13020917
19. Nair, M. M., Tyagi, A. K., & Sreenath, N. (2021). The future with Industry 4.0 at the Core of Society 5.0: Open issues, future opportunities and challenges. In *2021 international conference on computer communication and informatics, ICCCI 2021* (p. 9402498). https://doi.org/10.1109/ICCCI50826.2021.9402498
20. Koumpan, E., & Topol, A. W. (2021). Promoting economic development and solving societal issues within connected industries ecosystems in Society 5.0. *Lecture Notes in Networks and Systems, 271*, 174–183. https://doi.org/10.1007/978-3-030-80624-8_22
21. Mourtzis, D., Angelopoulos, J., & Panopoulos, N. (2022). A literature review of the challenges and opportunities of the transition from Industry 4.0 to Society 5.0. *Energies, 15*(17), 6276. https://doi.org/10.3390/en15176276

22. Dautaj, M., & Rossi, M. (2022). Towards a new society: Solving the dilemma between Society 5.0 and Industry 5.0. In *IFIP advances in information and communication technology, 639 IFIP* (pp. 523–536). https://doi.org/10.1007/978-3-030-94335-6_37
23. Polat, L., & Erkollar, A. (2021). Industry 4.0 vs. Society 5.0. In *Lecture notes in Mechanical Engineering* (pp. 333–345). https://doi.org/10.1007/978-3-030-62784-3_28
24. Zhang, C., Wang, Z., Zhou, G., Chang, F., Ma, D., Jing, Y., Cheng, W., Ding, K., & Zhao, D. (2023a). Towards new-generation human-centric smart manufacturing in Industry 5.0: A systematic review. *Advanced Engineering Informatics, 57*, 102121. https://doi.org/10.1016/j.aei.2023.102121
25. Zhang, Y., & Li, Y. (2023b). Society 5.0 versus Industry 5.0: An examination of industrialization models in driving sustainable development from a normative stakeholder theory perspective. *Sustainable Development, 31*(5), 3786–3795. https://doi.org/10.1002/sd.2625

# Transitioning from Industry 4.0 to Industry 5.0: An Overview of Co-Evolution

**Evgeny Kuzmin, Guzalbegim Rakhimova, Ulugbek Nurmanov, and Kamolakhon Nasurova**

**Abstract** Our inquiry into the transition from Industry 4.0 to Industry 5.0 commences by tracing the technological progression from preceding industrial revolutions. Through comparative analysis, we show that while Industry 4.0 and Industry 5.0 share a foundational technological framework, they diverge in their approaches to production processes and human involvement. Industry 4.0 laid the groundwork for significant changes in manufacturing through automation and digitization, while Industry 5.0 expands this approach by integrating human elements into technological processes and prioritizing social goals such as enhancing quality of life and reducing environmental impact. This conceptual shift does not seek to replace Industry 4.0 but rather complements and reinterprets it, presenting new challenges and opportunities. Our research identifies both contradictions and points of convergence between these technological paradigms, highlighting the need for further exploration of the relationship between technological advancement and social factors in industrial innovation. Looking forward, Industry 6.0 represents the next stage, which is expected to deepen the integration of digital technologies into the physical world. The study outlines avenues for the exploration of the co-evolution of industrial paradigms and our findings can be used to formulate strategies for sustainable development in the context of global socio-economic and environmental challenges.

**Keywords** Industry 4.0 · Industry 5.0 · Industry 6.0 · Techno-social revolution

---

E. Kuzmin (✉)
Institute of Economics of the Ural Branch of the Russian Academy of Sciences, Ekaterinburg, Russian Federation
e-mail: kuzmin.ea@uiec.ru

G. Rakhimova
National Research University "Tashkent Institute of Irrigation and Agricultural Mechanization Engineers" (TIIAME National Research University), Tashkent, Uzbekistan

U. Nurmanov · K. Nasurova
Tashkent State University of Economics, Tashkent, Uzbekistan



A. Appolloni et al. (eds.), *The Future of Industry*, Lecture Notes in Information Systems and Organisation 70, https://doi.org/10.1007/978-3-031-66801-2_3

## 1 Introduction

The history of technological development is a journey through successive stages of industrial revolutions, marked by significant changes in production, society, and the economy [1]. This journey begins with Industry 1.0 (Fig. 1), characterized by the transition from manual production methods to machine-based methods, using steam and water power. The Second Industrial Revolution, based on electrification and mass production, ushered in the modern era of automobile manufacturing and the chemical industry [4]. The Third Industrial Revolution, or Industry 3.0, introduced information and communication technologies, leading to computerization and automation. Industry 4.0 is characterized by even greater automation with an emphasis on the merging of physical and information systems [5]. It has opened up new technological possibilities and led to the widespread digitization of production, giving rise to "smart factories" [6–10].

In recent decades, the concept of Industry 4.0 has had a significant impact on production processes and management approaches, mostly due to the strong integration of digital technologies into traditional business processes, and human-machine symbiosis in industry [11]. However, constantly growing demands for sustainability and flexibility create sufficient grounds for the transition to the next phase, which promises to rethink previous accomplishments [12].

Industry 5.0 signifies a new stage of development: it complements the existing paradigm of Industry 4.0, emphasizing socio-innovations as the driving force behind the transition to a sustainable, human-centered industry [1]. The fifth generation of industry prioritizes the collaboration between humans and machines, humans and technology. Industry 5.0 harnesses the fusion of human creative potential and technological capabilities to address increasingly complex tasks while prioritizing social development in alignment with core values.

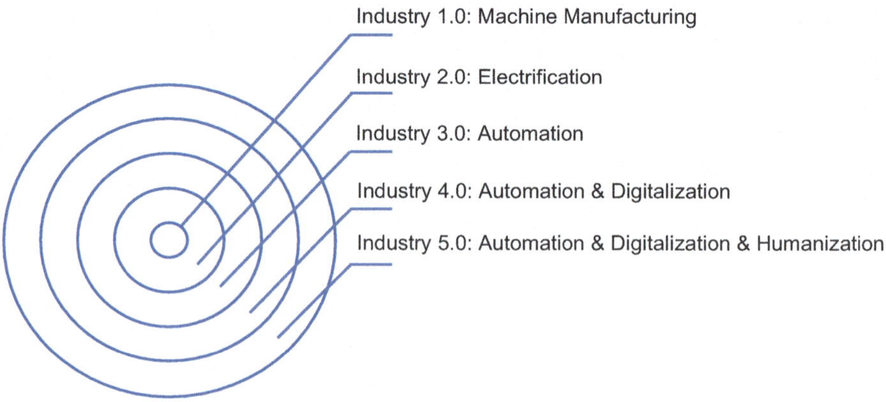


**Fig. 1** The evolution of industry: Industry 1.0, 2.0, 3.0, 4.0, and 5.0. Source: compiled by the authors based on [2, 3]

Industry 5.0 isn't a replacement or extension of Industry 4.0; rather, Industry 5.0 stems from social trends and needs and, therefore, complements Industry 4.0 [11]. Sustainable development is a key driving force behind Industry 4.0 within the industry initiative, transforming traditional production into a "smart" one through the adoption of digital technologies [13]. The shift to Industry 4.0 doesn't necessarily mean fewer jobs or sidelining the workforce's vital role in innovation and sustainability efforts driving this transition. While some sustainable practices are integrated, the primary focus of Industry 4.0 on technological progress may overlook all the implications of its adoption. Industry 5.0 is more focused on sustainability, highlighting the need to consider the social implications of technological changes.

These and other differences have led us to review the trends and technologies that define the transition from Industry 4.0 to Industry 5.0. In our study, we examine how technological progress reflects not only a shift in industrial paradigms but also social innovations, as significant adjustments are made to production and management approaches. A key aspect of Industry 5.0 is the pursuit of sustainability and human-centered development, where technologies not only contribute to efficiency but also to the common good. The review highlights the significance of technological innovations and their impact on the future of industrial production, outlining pathways for development and potential transformations that will be shaped by the next concept of industrialization. The study outlines the future prospects of industrial development, focusing on the next phase—Industry 6.0. This phase envisions a deeper integration of digital technologies with the physical realm. We intend to provide a general description of Industry 6.0, anticipate the challenges and opportunities along this path, and explore how the world can prepare for the next major leap in the industrial-technosocial revolution.

## 2 Industry 4.0

The term 'Industry 4.0' refers to the contemporary trend of automation and data exchange in manufacturing processes. Its implementation is largely enabled by widespread digitization, Internet development, virtual reality, and the capacity to collect and process vast amounts of data in real-time. Innovations in Industry 4.0 are linked to technological and managerial aspects. Tay et al. note that the concept of Industry 4.0 is based on such categories as cyber-physical systems (CPS), Internet of Things (IoT), big data analytics (BDA), cloud computing, fog and edge computing, augmented and virtual reality (AR/VR), robotics, cybersecurity, semantic web technologies, and additive manufacturing (AM) to enhance products, processes, services, and business models [14]. Production technologies are upgraded through digital solutions. In other words, the entire concept of Industry 4.0 can be viewed as a transition from individual, isolated computer systems to an integrated and closely interconnected network, where individual objects can interact with each other.

The fundamental model of Industry 4.0 can be divided into digital or computational technologies combined with systems of the physical world [15]. While artificial intelligence, machine learning, Big Data, cloud computing, and cybersecurity are part of the core computational technologies, other technologies such as automation and robotics, IoT, CPS, and AM constitute the physical aspect. Together, these technologies unlock the benefits of Industry 4.0, providing dynamic and flexible "on-demand" manufacturing, which is an integral part of smart industries.

In many respects, the current understanding of Industry 4.0 still remains ambiguous, especially concerning key aspects such as data processing and the application of new technologies [16]. The resolution of these issues will not only determine the future of individual enterprises but also the overall competitiveness of the economy as a whole. Therefore, there still remains ample scope for further academic discussion. Achieving sustainable development necessitates the delicate balance of technological advancements with social responsibility and environmental integrity, which requires not just state-of-the-art technologies, but also novel managerial strategies and business paradigms.

The integration of systems across both horizontal and vertical dimensions is a key aspect of Industry 4.0. Industry 4.0 is a multidimensional value creation system, uniting various managerial, organizational, technological, and production elements [17]. These factors interact with each other, forming clearly traceable and classifiable connections.

Saniuk et al. [18] systematized the barriers of Industry 4.0, dividing them into social and market categories and attributing them to various groups of stakeholders. These studies are complemented by an analysis of the barriers to the operation and development of enterprises within the new industrial paradigm, bringing to light the practical complexity of implementing Industry 4.0 technologies.

The key technologies of Industry 4.0 encompass a wide range of innovative solutions and approaches [19, 20], including the Internet of Things (IoT) and the Industrial Internet of Things (IIoT)—a concept that connects physical objects with network technologies, enabling them to exchange data; Big Data—technologies related to the processing and analysis of vast amounts of data generated and used in industry; 3D printing—additive manufacturing technology that allows the creation of complex objects with high precision; cloud computing and data storage systems (Cloud)—providing various services related to computing power provision and data storage; autonomous robots—robots capable of performing tasks automatically without direct human intervention; virtual and augmented reality (AR/VR)—technologies creating simulated or augmented environments for various purposes, including training and design; cyber-physical systems (CPS) and cyber-physical-social systems (CPSS)—the integration of intelligent algorithms and physical processes; artificial intelligence (AI)—the creation of algorithms capable of simulating human thinking and learning. These technologies can be categorized into several functional groups, including systems and automation, network technologies and communication, data, manufacturing technologies, robots, and information technologies.

Research also highlights four main areas in Industry 4.0: smart manufacturing, smart products and services, smart supply chains, and smart labor. Each of them reflects key aspects of the transformations in the industry. Smart manufacturing is at the core of Industry 4.0, integrating physical and cybernetic technologies to enhance productivity, quality, controllability, management, and precision of production processes [7, 21, 22]. Smart products and services refer to the development of goods capable of interacting with the environment, consumers, and other devices, providing increased functionality and adaptability. Smart supply chains focus on the application of the IoT, advanced robotics, and big data analytics in managing flows, which helps create more flexible supply chain management systems [23]. The efficiency of supply chains is increased through the automation of processes. Smart labor implies the use of digital technologies to improve working conditions and workforce productivity, as well as to integrate workers into more intelligent and automated production processes [19, 24]. These four areas underpin the transformation of manufacturing within Industry 4.0, combining technological innovations with new approaches to production management, products, supply chains, and labor resources.

The concept of Industry 4.0 is criticized by many researchers and experts. Despite numerous advantages, it has several drawbacks, which prompts calls for reconsideration. The concerns mainly revolve around the fact that the concept of Industry 4.0 focuses solely on technologies ignoring its impact on society and the environment. Industry 4.0 entails significant capital investment, management challenges, integration difficulties, cyberattack risks, and data leaks. Additionally, its primary focus on process automation raises concerns about the potential exclusion of humans from various areas of activity. A problem for the economy has become the disruption of employment: it is necessary to retrain and upskill employees to work with new technologies, which requires time and resources. There are challenges associated with the qualification of employees, their organizational, and production adaptation [25]. Moreover, increased dependence on complex technological systems heightens the risk of failures and disruptions in production processes. The above-described challenges of Industry 4.0 are significant hurdles.

## 3 Industry 5.0

The term Industry 5.0 has been introduced in several research fields and is considered the next industrial revolution. However, this is not a revolution per se but rather a systematic transformation that affects not only economic and industrial aspects but also society. Industry 5.0 should not be seen as a chronological continuation or alternative to the existing paradigm of Industry 4.0. Industry 5.0 is often described as the "era of harmonious expansion," in which humans and machines achieve mutual understanding and collaborate in symbiotic relationships. In this era, the focus shifts from purely technological automation to the integration of human creativity and innovation. This shift makes manufacturing processes not just more efficient but also better suited to individual requirements. This reconsideration of industry leads to the creation of jobs where human potential is enhanced by advanced technologies. It fosters a deeper fusion of technical capabilities with human skills, abilities, and talents, thus enhancing human capital.

By prioritizing social goals, Industry 5.0 transcends traditional understandings of production. This concept isn't limited solely to jobs and economic growth but also aims to create points of sustainable development for society as a whole [26]. The well-being of workers becomes a central element of the production process. This philosophy emphasizes the harmonious combination of the human factor and technology, striving to create a work environment where innovations and technologies serve to improve quality of life.

Industry 5.0 redefines the human-technology interaction. It is assumed that the true potential for progress and innovation lies in harmonious collaboration between humans and machines, where technologies are used to enhance human capabilities rather than replace them. Attention shifts to hybrid models—the driving forces behind Industry 5.0. This approach aims to initiate more social and inclusive production processes, where human skills and technological innovations complement each other to achieve sustainability [27].

Therefore, Industry 5.0 can be envisioned as a cybersocial ecosystem, where interacting actors and machines function symbiotically within a particular environment [28]. In this environment, collective intelligence emerges through the fusion of human abilities with the capabilities of AI. In this model, Industry 5.0 goes beyond traditional production systems, offering deeper interaction and integration between technological and social elements, resulting in the creation of human-centered solutions. The result will be the emergence of new global networks based on cyber-physical social systems. Further development will lead to the active involvement of cobots, collaborative robots designed to work alongside employees, which interact with employees [29–31]. This symbiosis is aimed at creating autonomous production that relies on corporate social networks for information exchange.

Our review has shown a broader understanding of Industry 5.0 and its key technologies compared to Industry 4.0. The main difference lies in the fact that Industry 5.0 is oriented towards the development of simultaneously innovative, flexible, and human-centric manufacturing systems [32]. The human-centred approach aims to reintegrate people's interests into the production process, which signifies a significant departure from the concept of Industry 4.0. Although some of these technologies are employed in both Industry 4.0 and Industry 5.0, we consider it necessary to specify the technologies that are more characteristic of Industry 5.0.

As was mentioned earlier, the technologies of Industry 5.0 include collaborative robots (cobots)—robots designed to interact with workers in the manufacturing environment; smart sensors—devices collecting data for use in digital systems, enabling more precise and automated process control; digital twins—virtual copies of physical objects or systems used for simulation, analysis, and improvement of real operations; Internet of Everything (IoE) and Artificial Intelligence of Things (AIoT)—a system that integrates things, data, processes, and people, incorporating integration with artificial intelligence for more advanced interaction and automation; blockchain—a distributed ledger technology providing security, transparency, and reliability of data and transactions; edge and fog computing—distributed computing

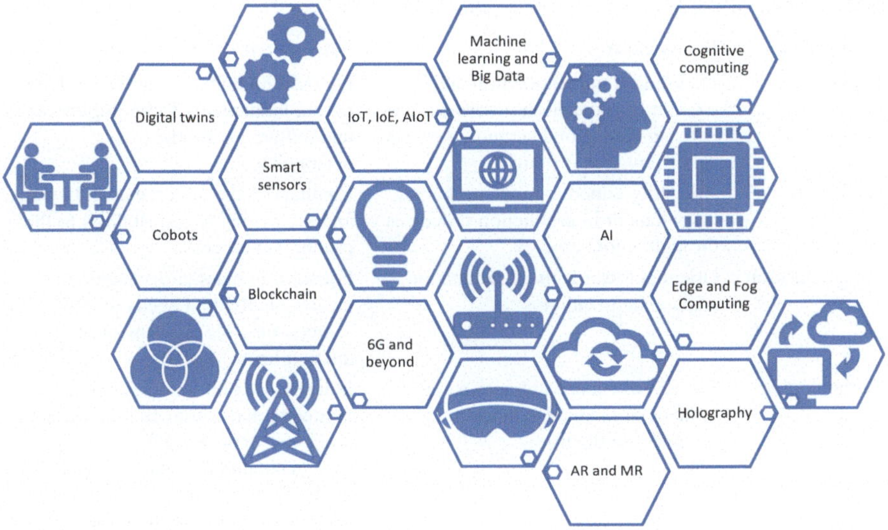


**Fig. 2** Key technologies of Industry 4.0 and Industry 5.0

platforms processing data closer to the source to accelerate processing and analysis, as well as to reduce the overall load on computational systems; cognitive computing—part of the development direction of artificial intelligence, its task is to provide a process of natural interaction between humans and digital objects and robots, similar to interaction among people; 6G and beyond—the next generation of network technologies promising even greater speed, reliability, and connectivity capabilities for devices, data transmission; augmented reality (AR), mixed reality (MR), and holography—technologies that enhance the perception of the real world by adding digital content or creating entirely virtual images.

All these technologies continue the trend started by Industry 4.0, complementing and expanding it within the framework of the next technological paradigm (Fig. 2), which creates opportunities not only to improve technological efficiency but also to ensure a higher level of product personalization and process sustainability.

## 4 Industry 4.0 Vs. Industry 5.0

The concepts of Industry 4.0 and Industry 5.0 have become key directions in the development of modern industry. These two paradigms, although closely related, represent different approaches to the use of technologies and the understanding of the human role in production processes. While Industry 4.0 marked the beginning of mass digitization and automation, Industry 5.0 deepens these trends, emphasizing the importance of harmonious coexistence between humans and the digital world.

**Table 1** Comparison of Industry 4.0 and Industry 5.0

| Characteristic | Industry 4.0 | Industry 5.0 |
|---|---|---|
| Focus | Focused on the automation and digitization of production processes, the IoT, big data, cloud technologies, and cyber-physical systems | Focused on human-machine collaboration, humanizing technologies, sustainability, and product personalization |
| Human factor | Allegedly aimed at reducing human involvement in production processes through automation | Emphasizes the importance of humans and their creative contribution to the production process. |
| Personalization | Oriented towards mass production and standardization. | Focused on mass customization, meeting individual needs of consumers. Flexible adjustment of production lines |
| Technologies | The use of robots and automated systems to increase efficiency and optimize production | Industry 4.0 laid the foundation for digitizing and automating production processes. Industry 5.0 expands on these technologies, placing emphasis on deeper human-machine integration. The use of cobots, which work in tandem with humans, as well as technologies promoting environmental sustainability |
| Sustainability | Sustainability is deemed secondary, taking a back seat to technological innovations | Active promotion of environmental sustainability and responsible consumption as key elements of production processes |
| Environmental aspect | Environmental considerations are not considered top priority | Environmental aspect is included into production processes to minimize the environmental damage |

Summarizing the positions of both industries, we compare them to reveal contradictions and potential points of intersection (Table 1).

The contradictions between Industry 4.0 and Industry 5.0 are largely related to differences in their focuses and goals. Both are oriented towards innovation and improvement of manufacturing processes. However, Industry 4.0 prioritizes automation, which may lead to job cuts and reduced human involvement in production, while Industry 5.0 prioritizes collaborative interaction between humans and machines, humans and the digital world, thus emphasizing the importance of human labor. Industry 4.0 favors centralized control and management, while Industry 5.0 leans towards decentralization and local management or self-organization. Industry 4.0 tends to see technological solutions as an end goal, while Industry 5.0 strives to humanize these technologies, placing significant focus on the social and ethical aspects of technological advancement. The concept of Industry 4.0 often implies competition, whereas Industry 5.0 emphasizes cooperation, partnership, and collaborative efforts among various stakeholders to achieve the best results. These and other differences highlight the shifts in approaches and values during the transition from Industry 4.0 to Industry 5.0, reflecting the changing understanding of the roles that technology and human involvement play in industrial production.

## 5 Problems and Challenges of Industry 5.0

Rather than merely increasing efficiency and productivity, Industry 5.0 aims to make people's lives better and minimize environmental harm. Despite the promises of integrating new technologies and innovations in Industry 5.0, various obstacles—technical, economic, social, and ethical—could hinder its widespread adoption [1]. In order to devise strategies to overcome these obstacles, further analysis is needed. Let us consider the main impediments to Industry 5.0.

*Diversity of values and degree of innovation acceptance.* The diversity of cultural and value orientations in society can complicate the implementation of new technologies, as it demands a special focus on social adaptation and inclusivity. In these circumstances, it is important to consider the expectations of various social groups to ensure broader adaptation and support for innovations. It is, therefore, necessary to devise measures to build public consensus on innovations. Additionally, it should be noted that employees at enterprises may also resist change as they are apprehensive about job losses due to automation. In this light, technological changes require additional efforts to retrain and educate the workforce. The widespread implementation of technologies that can replace humans in certain aspects of work raises questions about social justice, resource distribution, and the ethical aspects of using robots and AI in traditionally "human" roles.

*The integration of human creativity with AI and the collaborative participation of humans and machines in product creation remain challenging tasks.* Despite significant progress in the development of cobots and adaptive systems, it is still difficult to achieve their effective symbiosis with humans. Therefore, a new vision for designing workplaces and processes is needed to ensure safe and, at the same time, productive interaction between humans and robots, humans and artificial intelligence. It is also important to develop systems that can adapt to the individual characteristics of workers, thereby increasing their satisfaction and work efficiency.

*Technological maturity and the costs of technologies.* Many of the technologies linked to Industry 5.0 are still in their early development stages and haven't matured enough, which means that they might be too costly or demand substantial financial investments for broad application, especially in developing countries. This poses a significant challenge for the expansion of Industry 5.0. To address these issues, strategies are required to develop economically feasible technological solutions and accelerate the advancement of innovations towards technological maturity. These measures can assist in technological adaptation and enable broader implementation of Industry 5.0 principles.

*Interdisciplinarity and complexity of systems.* These aspects highlight the need to combine knowledge and methods from diverse scientific and technological domains to solve intricate challenges and make innovative advancements. In Industry 5.0,

It should be noted that although the main focus in Industry 4.0 is on technology, this concept is gradually reconsidered as questions of sustainability, human-centeredness, and resilience come to the fore. Furthermore, although automation and its subsequent robotization contribute to reducing the role of humans, this doesn't detract from Industry 4.0's efforts to create safer and more comfortable working conditions for people [46]. The introduction of adaptive equipment and interfaces, fostering human-machine interaction, aims to enhance operators' convenience and decrease the amount of physical labor. Undoubtedly, automation and robotization also help enhance system resilience [47–49]. Sustainability in Industry 4.0 is manifested through resource optimization and the reduction of production waste [50–52]. Hence it can be concluded that Industry 4.0 draws from the principles of Industry 5.0 to some extent; however, its approach still remains predominantly techno-centric. The tools of Industry 4.0 can be adapted and used to achieve some goals of Industry 5.0, but to fully align with the new ideals, the development of advanced technologies and approaches is necessary. This synergistic combination of old and new solutions will determine the success of future industrial innovations.

The study of the coevolution of Industry 4.0 and Industry 5.0, as well as the analysis of the transition from one industrial paradigm to another, can raise a number of important questions that will deepen the understanding of the nature of these phenomena and identify potential directions for further research. We can outline several key questions pertinent to this topic, including the following: What organizational and managerial changes are necessary for a smooth transition to Industry 5.0? How do changes in technologies impact the role and position of humans in production processes? What are the social and environmental consequences of the transition from Industry 4.0 to Industry 5.0? What new theoretical frameworks may be required to analyze future industrial changes? The answers to these questions can deepen our understanding of current industrial trends and help shape strategies and policies for sustainable development in technology and society.

## 7 Prospects of Industry 6.0

The recent industrial evolution is a remarkable example of rapid technological transformation that deeply impacts economic, social, and environmental spheres.

As we mentioned earlier, the journey towards Industry 4.0 and further towards Industry 5.0 is characterized by the integration of new technologies, changes in management approaches, and a rethinking of the role of humans in production processes. This path can be divided into several key stages, each of which contributes to the transformation of the industrial landscape. The first stage marks the establishment of the technological foundation in line with the principles of Industry 4.0. This stage corresponds to active implementation of automation, digitization, and robotics, use of technologies like the IoT, Big Data, cyber-physical systems, and others. On the second stage, there is a close digital integration of systems, improvement of interfaces, and methods of interaction between humans and machines, humans and AI. The final stage embodies the transition to Industry 5.0, where the focus shifts towards technologies that support and enhance human capabilities instead of merely replacing humans. Policies and strategies are being developed to promote social justice, improve working conditions, and engage society in industrial processes.

The rising socio-economic challenges require a constant reassessment of the prevailing development model. While previously Industry 4.0 was at the center of discussion, now many are beginning to ponder what lies ahead with Industry 5.0, which has yet to establish itself as a reality in the industrial world.

The concept of Industry 6.0 is currently surrounded by much debate and the ideas about its possible directions are beginning to emerge in academia. High-tech solutions are expected to take center stage, including advanced AI of the next generation, quantum computing, enhanced cyber-physical systems, and the full integration of digital technologies with the physical world. It is anticipated that there will be a strong focus on advancements that span various aspects of life—global technologies that promote sustainable development [53, 54], laying the foundation for the creation of more adaptable and autonomous industrial systems [55].

Although the contours of Industry 6.0 have not yet been fully defined, it can be inferred that Industry 6.0 will not only enhance the existing parameters of Industry 5.0 but also establish new frameworks for human-machine interaction, considering the increasing complexity of systems and the need to manage them in real-time. Industry 6.0 represents a fresh look at these concepts through the lens of progressive technologies. In this regard, AI and machine learning will play a central role in Industry 6.0 as it unfolds, while quantum technologies will become its revolutionary stronghold.

At the moment, the concept of Industry 6.0 has not yet been defined and established in the academic community. We found only a few publications that outline the future industrial paradigm and its distinctive features [55–58]. Clearly, the transition from Industry 5.0 to Industry 6.0 will signify a significant stage in the development of industry, where the boundaries between human intelligence and machine efficiency will not just blur but disappear altogether, thus granting artificial intelligence carte blanche in addressing emerging challenges. The transition from Industry 5.0 to Industry 6.0 will require not only technological innovations but also social changes, for example, new approaches to education, employment, and overall government policy. The ethics of implementing new technologies into society's life will be a critical concern.

## 8 Conclusion

The transition from Industry 4.0 to Industry 5.0 represents a significant step in the evolution of industrial paradigms, which not only continues technological development but also brings about significant social innovations. This shift emphasizes the importance of blending human creativity with innovative technologies, with the priority being given to the humanization of production processes. This study of the key aspects of Industry 4.0 and Industry 5.0 shows that, despite a common technological foundation, these two paradigms offer different visions of manufacturing process principles and slightly differ in their perspective on human involvement. Industry 4.0, with its emphasis on automation and digitization, laid the foundation for revolutionary changes in manufacturing, while Industry 5.0 aims to complement and expand upon this approach by incorporating a focus on integrating the human factor into technological processes.

Importantly, Industry 5.0 does not replace Industry 4.0 but complements and expands it. This reimagining of industry involves reconsidering the role of human workers and the ways they interact with technology, creating new types of jobs where technology enhances human abilities instead of replacing them. Industry 4.0 provides powerful tools and technologies that contribute to increased efficiency, while Industry 5.0 adds a framework of social responsibility to this. It is crucial to understand that the transition from Industry 4.0 to Industry 5.0 is not a replacement of one paradigm by another, but rather a coevolutionary development where both paradigms can coexist and complement each other, providing a comprehensive approach to sustainable industrial development in the future.

## References

1. Xu, X., Lu, Y., Vogel-Heuser, B., & Wang, L. (2021). Industry 4.0 and Industry 5.0—Inception, conception and perception. *Journal of Manufacturing Systems, 61*, 530–535. https://doi.org/10.1016/j.jmsy.2021.10.006
2. Thangaraj, J., & Narayanan, R. L. (2018). *Industry 1.0 to 4.0: The evolution of smart factories*. APICS. https://doi.org/10.17140/CSMMOJ-4-125
3. Saak, A. E., & Pakhomov, E. V. (2020). Kljuchevye tehnologii Industrii 4.0, Obshhestva 5.0, Jekonomiki 3.0 [key technologies of Industry 4.0, Society 5.0, Economy 3.0.]. *Inzhenernyj vestnik Dona, 2*(62), 6.
4. Yin, Y., Stecke, K. E., & Li, D. (2018). The evolution of production systems from Industry 2.0 through Industry 4.0. *International Journal of Production Research, 56*(1–2), 848–861. https://doi.org/10.1080/00207543.2017.1403664
5. Jiang, Z., Yuan, S., Ma, J., & Wang, Q. (2022). The evolution of production scheduling from Industry 3.0 through Industry 4.0. *International Journal of Production Research, 60*(11), 3534–3554. https://doi.org/10.1080/00207543.2021.1925772
6. Hozdić, E. (2015). Smart factory for industry 4.0: A review. *International Journal of Modern Manufacturing Technologies, 7*(1), 28–35.
7. Mittal, S., Khan, M. A., Romero, D., & Wuest, T. (2019). Smart manufacturing: Characteristics, technologies and enabling factors. *Proceedings of the Institution of Mechanical Engineers, Part B: Journal of Engineering Manufacture, 233*(5), 1342–1361. https://doi.org/10.1177/0954405417736547
8. Osterrieder, P., Budde, L., & Friedli, T. (2020). The smart factory as a key construct of Industry 4.0: A systematic literature review. *International Journal of Production Economics, 221*, 107476. https://doi.org/10.1016/j.ijpe.2019.08.011
9. Büchi, G., Cugno, M., & Castagnoli, R. (2020). Smart factory performance and industry 4.0. *Technological Forecasting and Social Change, 150*, 119790. https://doi.org/10.1016/j.techfore.2019.119790

10. Chung, S., & Kim, M. (2023). How smart is a "smart factory"?: An organizational view. *Industrial and Corporate Change*, dtad070. https://doi.org/10.1093/icc/dtad070
11. Longo, F., Padovano, A., & Umbrello, S. (2020). Value-oriented and ethical technology engineering in Industry 5.0: A human-centric perspective for the design of the factory of the future. *Applied Sciences, 10*(12), 4182. https://doi.org/10.3390/app10124182
12. Mourtzis, D., Angelopoulos, J., & Panopoulos, N. (2022). A literature review of the challenges and opportunities of the transition from Industry 4.0 to Society 5.0. *Energies, 15*(17), 6276. https://doi.org/10.3390/en15176276
13. Braccini, A. M., & Margherita, E. G. (2019). Exploring organizational sustainability of Industry 4.0 under the triple bottom line: The case of a manufacturing company. *Sustainability (Switzerland), 11*(1), 36. https://doi.org/10.3390/su11010036
14. Tay, S. I., Lee, T. C., Hamid, N. Z. A., & Ahmad, A. N. A. (2018). An overview of industry 4.0: Definition, components, and government initiatives. *Journal of Advanced Research in Dynamical and Control Systems, 10*(14), 1379–1387.
15. Sony, M. (2020). Pros and cons of implementing Industry 4.0 for the organizations: A review and synthesis of evidence. *Production & Manufacturing Research, 8*(1), 244–272. https://doi.org/10.1080/21693277.2020.1781705
16. Culot, G., Orzes, G., Sartor, M., & Nassimbeni, G. (2020). The future of manufacturing: A Delphi-based scenario analysis on industry 4.0. *Technological Forecasting and Social Change, 157*, 120092. https://doi.org/10.1016/j.techfore.2020.120092
17. Nosalska, K., Piątek, Z. M., Mazurek, G., & Rządca, R. (2019). Industry 4.0: Coherent definition framework with technological and organizational interdependencies. *Journal of Manufacturing Technology Management, 31*(5), 837–862. https://doi.org/10.1108/JMTM-08-2018-0238
18. Saniuk, S., Grabowska, S., & Gajdzik, B. (2020). Social expectations and market changes in the context of developing the Industry 4.0 concept. *Sustainability, 12*(4), 1362. https://doi.org/10.3390/su12041362
19. De Assis Dornelles, J., Ayala, N. F., & Frank, A. G. (2022). Smart working in Industry 4.0: How digital technologies enhance manufacturing workers' activities. *Computers & Industrial Engineering, 163*, 107804. https://doi.org/10.1016/j.cie.2021.107804
20. Azizi, A., & Barenji, R. V. (Eds.). (2022). *Industry 4.0: Technologies, applications, and challenges*. Springer. https://doi.org/10.1007/978-981-19-2012-7
21. Kang, H. S., Lee, J. Y., Choi, S., Kim, H. J., Park, J. H., Son, J. Y., Kim, B. H., & Noh, S. D. (2016). Smart manufacturing: Past research, present findings, and future directions. *International Journal of Precision Engineering and Manufacturing-Green Technology, 3*, 111–128. https://doi.org/10.1007/s40684-016-0015-5
22. Kusiak, A. (2023). Smart manufacturing. In S. Y. Nof (Ed.), *Springer handbook of automation* (pp. 973–985). Springer International Publishing. https://doi.org/10.1007/978-3-030-96729-1_45
23. Alicke, K., & Rachor, J. (2016, October 27). Supply Chain 4.0—The next-generation digital supply chain. McKinsey & Company. https://www.mckinsey.com/capabilities/operations/our-insights/supply-chain-40%2D%2Dthe-next-generation-digital-supply-chain
24. Angelici, M., & Profeta, P. (2023). Smart working: Work flexibility without constraints. *Management Science, 70*(3), 1680–1705. https://doi.org/10.1287/mnsc.2023.4767
25. Abu-Rumman, A., & AlSha'ar, H., Alqhaiwi, L. A., & Al Shraah, A. (2023). Exploring the challenges and opportunities of implementing Industry 4.0 in Jordan: Public shareholding manufacturing companies perspective. *Wireless Personal Communications*, 1–19. https://doi.org/10.1007/s11277-023-10169-x
26. European Commission, Directorate-General for Research and Innovation. (2020). *Industry 5.0: Human-centric, sustainable and resilient.* Publications Office of the European Union. https://op.europa.eu/en/publication-detail/-/publication/aed3280d-70fe-11eb-9ac9-01aa75ed71a1/language-en/format-PDF/source-search

27. Adel, A. (2022). Future of industry 5.0 in society: Human-centric solutions, challenges and prospective research areas. *Journal of Cloud Computing, 11*(1), 1–15. https://doi.org/10.1186/s13677-022-00314-5
28. Babkin, A. V., Shkarupeta, E. V., & Plotnikov, V. A. (2021). Intellektual'naja kibersocial'naja jekosistema Industrii 5.0: Ponjatie, sushhnost', model' [Intelligent cybersocial ecosystem of Industry 5.0: Concept, essence, model]. *Jekonomicheskoe vozrozhdenie Rossii, 4*(70), 39–62. https://doi.org/10.37930/1990-9780-2021-4-70-39-62
29. El Zaatari, S., Marei, M., Li, W., & Usman, Z. (2019). Cobot programming for collaborative industrial tasks: An overview. *Robotics and Autonomous Systems, 116*, 162–180. https://doi.org/10.1016/j.robot.2019.03.003
30. Faccio, M., Granata, I., Menini, A., Milanese, M., Rossato, C., Bottin, M., Minto, R., Pluchino, P., Gamberini, L., Boschetti, G., & Rosati, G. (2023). Human factors in cobot era: A review of modern production systems features. *Journal of Intelligent Manufacturing, 34*(1), 85–106. https://doi.org/10.1007/s10845-022-01953-w
31. Djuric, A. M., Urbanic, R. J., & Rickli, J. L. (2016). A framework for collaborative robot (CoBot) integration in advanced manufacturing systems. *SAE International Journal of Materials and Manufacturing, 9*(2), 457–464. https://doi.org/10.4271/2016-01-0337
32. Rajumesh, S. (2023). Promoting sustainable and human-centric Industry 5.0: A thematic analysis of emerging research topics and opportunities. *Journal of Business and Socio-economic Development, 4*(2), 111–126. https://doi.org/10.1108/JBSED-10-2022-0116
33. Kuzmin, E., Suvorova, A., Lavrikova, Y., & Sang, Y. (2023). Editorial: What is GLASS? And what prospects does it open for sustainable urban development? In *E3S Web Conf. Volume 435, 2023. VII international scientific conference cities of new age: GLASS (REC-2023)*. EDP Sciences. https://doi.org/10.1051/e3sconf/202343500001
34. Klein, D., Carazo, M. P., Doelle, M., Bulmer, J., Higham, A., & (Eds.). (2017). *The Paris agreement on climate change: Analysis and commentary*. Oxford University Press.
35. *Goal 10: Reduce inequality within and among countries*. (2015). Sustainable Development Goals. https://www.un.org/sustainabledevelopment/inequality
36. Osborn, D., Cutter, A., & Ullah, F. (2015). Universal sustainable development goals. Understanding the transformational challenge for developed countries. Stakeholder Forum. https://sustainabledevelopment.un.org/content/documents/1684SF_-_SDG_Universality_Report_-_May_2015.pdf
37. Stafford-Smith, M., Griggs, D., Gaffney, O., Ullah, F., Reyers, B., Kanie, N., Stigson, B., Shrivastava, P., Leach, M., & O'Connell, D. (2017). Integration: The key to implementing the Sustainable Development Goals. *Sustainability Science, 12*(6), 911–919. https://doi.org/10.1007/s11625-016-0383-3
38. Bagstad, K. J., Berik, G., & Gaddis, E. J. B. (2014). Methodological developments in US state-level genuine progress indicators: Toward GPI 2.0. *Ecological Indicators, 45*, 474–485. https://doi.org/10.1016/j.ecolind.2014.05.005
39. Guan, C., Yang, P., Yang, H., & Zhang, J. (2024). Is the genuine progress indicator a better policy goal for sustainable development? An empirical study based on the environmental Kuznets curve. *Social Indicators Research, 171*(1), 47–86. https://doi.org/10.1007/s11205-023-03237-z
40. Llena-Nozal, A., Martin, N., & Murtin, F. (2019). *The economy of well-being: Creating opportunities for people's well-being and economic growth*. OECD Statistics Working Papers 2019/02. OECD Publishing. https://one.oecd.org/document/SDD/DOC(2019)2/En/pdf
41. Mizobuchi, H. (2014). Measuring world better life frontier: A composite indicator for OECD better life index. *Social Indicators Research, 118*, 987–1007. https://doi.org/10.1007/s11205-013-0457-x
42. Nikolaev, B. (2014). Economic freedom and quality of life: Evidence from the OECD's your better life index. *Journal of Private Enterprise, 29*(3), 61–96.
43. Patil, A. R., Thakur, K., Gandhi, K., Savale, V., & Sayyed, N. (2022). A review on Industry 5.0: The techno-social revolution. *International Journal of Mechanical Engineering, 7*(5), 1–5.

44. Skoff, G., & Rollo, S. (2022). Techno-social futures: Trapped or transformative. *Digital Debates, 9*, 67.
45. Breque, M., De Nul, L., & Petridis, A. (2021). *Industry 5.0: Towards a sustainable, human-centric and resilient European industry*. European Commission, Directorate-General for Research and Innovation. https://data.europa.eu/doi/10.2777/308407
46. Salimi, M. (2015). Work 4.0: An enormous potential for economic growth in Germany. *ADAPT bulletin, 16*. https://englishbulletin.adapt.it/wp-content/uploads/2015/12/work4.0_sam.pdf
47. Farsi, M. A., & Zio, E. (2019). Industry 4.0: Some challenges and opportunities for reliability engineering. *International Journal of Reliability, Risk and Safety: Theory and Application, 2*(1), 23–34. https://doi.org/10.30699/IJRRS.2.1.4
48. Bragança, S., Costa, E., Castellucci, I., & Arezes, P. M. (2019). A brief overview of the use of collaborative robots in industry 4.0: Human role and safety. In P. Arezes, J. Baptista, M. Barroso, P. Carneiro, P. Cordeiro, N. Costa, R. B. Melo, A. S. Miguel, & G. Perestrelo (Eds.), *Occupational and environmental safety and health. Studies in systems, decision and control* (pp. 641–650). Springer. https://doi.org/10.1007/978-3-030-14730-3_68
49. Masood, A. B., Hasan, A., Vassiliou, V., & Lestas, M. (2023). A Blockchain-based data-driven fault-tolerant control system for smart factories in industry 4.0. *Computer Communications, 204*, 158–171. https://doi.org/10.1016/j.comcom.2023.03.017
50. Amjad, M. S., Rafique, M. Z., & Khan, M. A. (2021). Leveraging optimized and cleaner production through industry 4.0. *Sustainable Production and Consumption, 26*, 859–871. https://doi.org/10.1016/j.spc.2021.01.001
51. Rajput, S., & Singh, S. P. (2020). Industry 4.0 model for circular economy and cleaner production. *Journal of Cleaner Production, 277*, 123853. https://doi.org/10.1016/j.jclepro.2020.123853
52. Nascimento, D. L. M., Alencastro, V., Quelhas, O. L. G., Caiado, R. G. G., Garza-Reyes, J. A., Rocha-Lona, L., & Tortorella, G. (2019). Exploring Industry 4.0 technologies to enable circular economy practices in a manufacturing context: A business model proposal. *Journal of Manufacturing Technology Management, 30*(3), 607–627. https://doi.org/10.1108/JMTM-03-2018-0071
53. Chourasia, S., Tyagi, A., Pandey, S. M., Walia, R. S., & Murtaza, Q. (2022). Sustainability of Industry 6.0 in global perspective: Benefits and challenges. *Mapan, 37*(2), 443–452. https://doi.org/10.1007/s12647-022-00541-w
54. Žižek, S. Š., Mulej, M., & Potočnik, A. (2021). The sustainable socially responsible society: Well-being Society 6.0. *Sustainability, 13*(16), 9186. https://doi.org/10.3390/su13169186
55. Duggal, A. S., Malik, P. K., Gehlot, A., Singh, R., Gaba, G. S., Masud, M., & Al-Amri, J. F. (2022). A sequential roadmap to Industry 6.0: Exploring future manufacturing trends. *IET Communications, 16*(5), 521–531. https://doi.org/10.1049/cmu2.12284
56. Das, S., & Pan, T. (2022). A strategic outline of Industry 6.0: Exploring the future. SSRN Electronic Journal. https://papers.ssrn.com/sol3/papers.cfm?abstract_id=4104696
57. Almusaed, A., Yitmen, I., & Almssad, A. (2023). Reviewing and integrating AEC practices into Industry 6.0: Strategies for smart and sustainable future-built environments. *Sustainability, 15*(18), 13464. https://doi.org/10.3390/su151813464
58. Heilala, J., & Singh, K. (2023). Evaluation planning for artificial intelligence-based Industry 6.0 metaverse integration. In T. Ahram, W. Karwowski, P. Di Bucchianico, R. Taiar, L. Casarotto, & P. Costa (Eds.), *Intelligent Human Systems Integration (IHSI 2023): Integrating People and Intelligent Systems. AHFE (2023) International conference*. AHFE International. https://doi.org/10.54941/ahfe1002892

# Industry 5.0: Quo Vadis? Challenges and Concerns for Future Development

**Olga Buchinskaia**

**Abstract** The movement towards a new socio-technological order within Industry 5.0 is determined by the acceleration of scientific and technological progress and the development of new computer technologies. It focuses on the interaction of man and machine and implements the UN Sustainable Development Goals (SDGs), including improving the welfare of the population and caring for the environment. This study addresses the challenges arising in the transition to Industry 5.0 and identifies the consequences that humanity may face if these challenges are ignored. The author uses ecosystem and value analysis, analytical tools of economic theory, political economy, and narrative analysis of papers related to Industry 5.0. As a result, we identified ten basic challenges that arise within the transition to Industry 5.0 and defined possible negative scenarios that appear as part of these challenges. Those scenarios may not increase but instead reduce human welfare within Industry 5.0. We suggest that a careful revision of the strategy for the transition towards Industry 5.0 is needed in order to eliminate the negative effects of changes in employment, wealth, education, medical services, ecology, etc. arising from the impact of new technologies. We need to enforce processes that increase the well-being of all members of society, with an emphasis on ethics, respect for property relations, and the prevention of a rise in various types of inequality.

**Keywords** Industry 5.0 · Regional inequality · Digital inequality · Ethics · Property

## 1 Introduction

The issues surrounding the onset of the Fifth Industrial Revolution are widely considered by the modern scientific community from the viewpoint of the foundations, prospects, and achievements of the new socio-economic structure. Hu [1]

---

O. Buchinskaia (✉)
Institute of Economics of the Ural Branch of the Russian Academy of Sciences, Ekaterinburg, Russian Federation

 
A. Appolloni et al. (eds.), *The Future of Industry*, Lecture Notes in Information Systems and Organisation 70, https://doi.org/10.1007/978-3-031-66801-2_4

highlights several concepts developed by various countries: Society 5.0 (Japan), Industry 5.0 (EU), and Made in China 2025 (China).

A significant number of publications analyzing the results of society's entry into Industry 5.0 are essentially optimistic, anticipating how artificial intelligence and human-robot interaction will solve the pressing problems of achieving sustainability. Barata and Kayser [2], in a meta-analysis of publications on Industry 5.0, mention such hopes of researchers as achieving the goals of sustainable development in general, improving the wellbeing of individuals, communities, society, and the whole planet, decarbonization, solving food supply and social problems, improving healthcare, etc. Gasanov [3] argues that "empathic machines should actively cooperate with people based on artificial intelligence's understanding of human intentions and be consistent with long-term human aspirations and motives throughout the entire production activity".

Despite such optimism, some researchers approach the perception of the Industry 5.0 more cautiously. Xu et al. [4] suggest there are several challenges for society associated with the transition to a new industrial revolution:

- Social heterogeneity in terms of values and acceptance;
- Issues of measuring the creation of environmental and social values;
- Integration from customers across all value chains to small and medium-sized enterprises;
- Interdisciplinary research and system complexity;
- Large amount of investments required for expected performance.

This is not an exhaustive list of issues that society faces as part of the transition to Industry 5.0. In this study, we have tried to identify a number of additional challenges that human society must solve in order to get the results that modern visionaries expect.

## 2 Literature Review

Regarding the future development of Industry 5.0, researchers highlight various concerns that society in the near future may experience. Chin [5] believes that the major problem that society will face while building Industry 5.0 are people who must have both technical and soft skills, noting also the importance of investments. Saniuk et al. [6] state that the population complains about such aspects of the framework of Society 5.0 as technological unemployment, alienation of people with low qualifications, control over society by artificial intelligence (AI), the growth of virtualization of professional and private life, dehumanization of society through the use of AI, as well as a decrease in the sense of security because of cyberattacks, pollution issues, and a lack of resources. The problem of unemployment is stressed by Mitchell and Guile [7], as they present data that about 800 million jobs will disappear because of automation, and also 375 million employees will need to be relocated and retrained. Thus, the threat of increasing unemployment and property stratification is recognized as relevant right now. Elangovan [8] draws attention to the need to develop technical skills and the aggravation of competition to adapt to customer requirements in terms of mass product customization. Narkhede et al. [9] are concerned about the fate of small and medium-sized businesses because of the high cost of technologies. Stef and Draghici [10] describe a set of challenges in Industry 5.0, including the discrepancy between the development of technology, social evolution, and the business environment, giving rise to legal problems, demographic problems, "overproduction, lack of transparency", which is implemented in many processes and industries, the use of inadequate tools, technologies, or machine tools for the production of goods and services, an increase in dependence on the infrastructure of information technology and power supply, the general reluctance of stakeholders to change and to introduce new ideas.

Nahavandi [11] expresses concern that productivity growth caused by new technologies may provoke overproduction crises and draws attention to the lack of elaboration on ethics issues in autonomous systems. Barinova and Barinov [12] note the importance of moral, ethical, legal, personal, and other human norms, according to which the personal safety of an individual in the information space should be respected. Khan et al. [13] are much more optimistic, as they believe that all the above-mentioned problems are inherent in Industry 4.0 and will be successfully solved within the framework of the next industrial revolution because of the development of advanced technologies. On the other hand, Alves et al. [14] show robot-human interaction as the problem, since there is a doubt that joint technologies will help the operator and do not replace him/her. Minculete [15] refers to the opinions of experts that, in the conditions of Industry 5.0, shorter and more complex business cycles are likely to appear and that both wages and costs will increase.

## 3 Research Method

Considering the issues highlighted in the preceding section, we aim to outline a more extensive array of challenges that will confront human society during the shift to Industry 5.0, many of which are already being manifested. To identify problems in Industry 5.0, we searched scientific literature, news sites, blogs, and organization websites. Therefore, we have pinpointed ten most critical issues highlighted in this study. Through the application of narrative analysis, we can discern the viewpoints of researchers and business representatives on Industry 5.0. By comprehending narratives, we could address issues related to knowledge-intensive services and questionable rhetoric on "social waste". By employing the dialectical method of political economy, we were able to detect contradictions between narratives and economic reality, and uncover the interconnections among the challenges of Industry 5.0. Since the study, as well as the analysed sources, is based on the use of foresight, we consider Industry 5.0 from the point of view of scenario uncertainty proposed by Magruk [16] when the forecast is based on the current level of understanding of the world order. We project that the problems not solved in the framework of Industry 4.0 will acquire new significance in the framework of Industry 5.0.

## 4 Results

Despite the significant enthusiasm of society for the onset of Industry 5.0, it is necessary to analyse the failures that have already developed within the framework of Industry 4.0 and have not yet found their solution, so they will be inherited and aggravated by the next stage of industrial development. We have identified several such problems presented in Fig. 1.

The hollow arrows in Fig. 1 show the perils of the highlighted challenges to the society within Industry 5.0. The dotted lines indicate the internal relationship between the challenges that we identified during the analysis. Next, we will consider the selected factors in descending order of importance for the future socio-economic development of society.

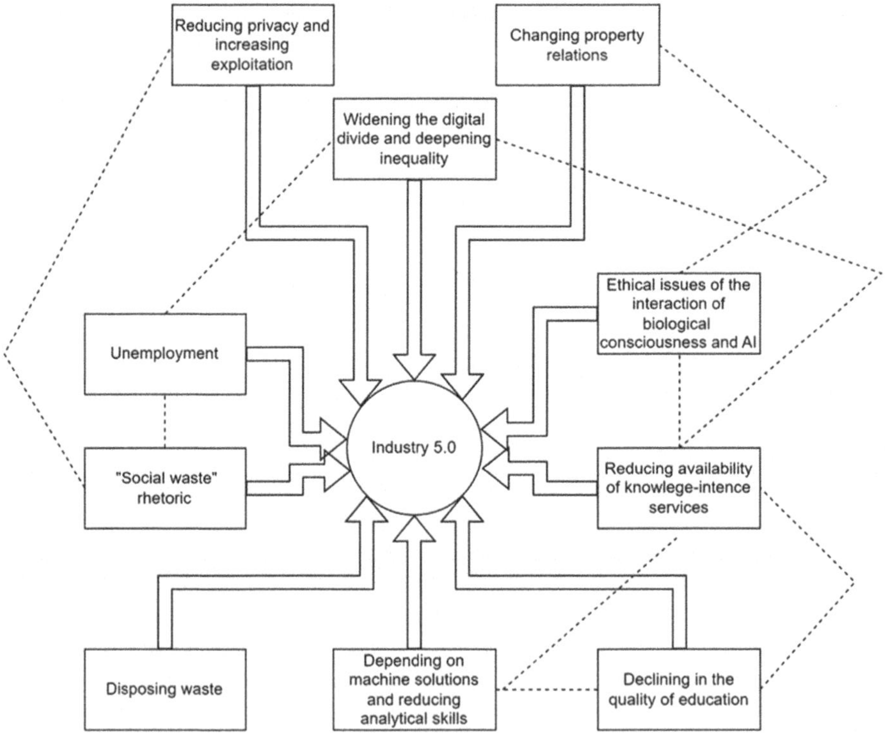


**Fig. 1** Complex of Industry 5.0 challenges

## 4.1 Unemployment

The growth of unemployment, as noted above, is the most troubling and rather strongly researched problem within the transition to Industry 5.0. Hammershøj [17] offers three scenarios of progressive unemployment. According to the first scenario, the growth of unemployment will be because job replacement with new technologies will outpace the development of relevant skills, which will lead to an increase in the rejection of low-skill labour forces. According to the second scenario, the polarization of the labour market is predicted, when the highly educated elite and inexpensive labour will be in demand, but the medium level of "white collars" will be replaced by electronic systems. The third, most optimistic scenario assumes the possibility of outstripping the speed of human capital growth over technological development, provided that the educational system and curriculum are radically changed. However, this scenario also has a dark side because, in this case, the increase in unemployment will occur at the expense of older and middle-aged workers. Like many other researchers in the field of Industry 5.0, we do not assume the implementation of these scenarios, predicting the overflow of labour into the creative industry. Still, we should not forget that not all categories of workers can adapt to the environment of the creative economy. The creative economy (based on arts, cultural goods and services, research and development), imposes specific requirements on employees that differ from the requirements for production personnel, and the demand for the products of the creative economy requires a high-income population [18]. This specificity of the creative economy, with the inflow of spare human resources into it first, will inevitably lead to an increase in unclaimed workers. Second, as the experience of the gig economy has shown, the high workforce supply, caused by increased labour mobility amid the digital economy, will naturally lead to a drop in prices for the relevant activities and, thus, to a decline in the income of workers whose competencies are unclaimed in the digital economy. As a result, the growth of low-paid jobs may become an alternative to unemployment.

## 4.2 Reducing Privacy and Increasing Exploitation

Concerns caused by the possibility of reducing privacy and increasing exploitation are already manifesting themselves. The publication of the European Commission expert group recognizes the use of AI as a new competitor to human labour. It also recognizes the fact that capital inevitably weakens the bargaining positions of workers, especially those who perform tasks at high risk of automation. As an advantage of Industry 5.0, the concept of so-called "good jobs" is put forward, having a rather vague definition, claiming that these jobs "tend to go beyond the static observation of the individual state of the employee, focusing on human prosperity and the gradual renewal of human capital" [19]. The development of means of communication and Internet networks has allowed people not only to simplify their work but also work from home and on a flexible schedule. But the opportunity to stay in touch 24/7 can erase the boundaries between work and personal time. This puts a person in the position of having to be in touch around the clock to solve emerging problems (which can negatively affect the quality of life and human health).

The second feature of the new internet systems is the use and analysis of human behaviour as a tool for modelling business and social processes. According to Zhiganov [20], there are software systems that apply to analyse human behaviour and calculate the list of goods and services and their value that should be displayed to the Internet user. Zhiganov believes that this is a way to ensure the constant assessment of human capital. In fact, along with human capital, an increasing proportion of human life will be increasingly digitized and evaluated, reducing freedom of will and human development. The third part of the strengthening of exploitation is the need for regular retraining and advanced training, which are directly embedded in the concept of Industry 5.0 [21]. If the EU considers investment in educational services through the process of creating a number of funds to finance the creation of educational courses, then the issue of financial and time costs paid by employees to acquire new knowledge remains open. In particular, if the professional development takes place in the worker's spare time, the need for a constant study in order to avoid the unemployment will reduce human free time, increasing the substantial burden on the employee.

## *4.3 Widening the Digital Divide and Deepening Inequality*

The widening of the digital divide and the aggravation of inequality against this background will be significant both internationally and sub-nationally. At the international level, inequality is primarily expressed by the continuation of the monopolization of digital technology developers and the strong separation of the largest economies, which accumulate leading technologies and personnel from other countries. These countries will be seen as primarily consumers rather than producers of digital products. An additional factor in strengthening the divergence may be the "Digital Cold War" predicted by Akimova [22], which will establish bans and restrictions on the distribution of digital products and technologies to undesirable countries and companies that will reduce availability of some knowledge-intensive services. Thus, developing countries will be blocked from technological development in order to prevent the possibility of any competition with world leaders.

At the subnational level, the problem of aggravating inequality through the un-even development of regions because of new technologies remains unsolvable. The regions with developed complex activities accumulate self-reinforcing regional potential, while less developed regions are trapped in the lack of accretion of opportunities, as shown on empirical data by Pinheiro et al. [23]. There are, of course, assumptions that this situation can be corrected through implementing a state policy of promotion and revision of labour training schemes, as Pal [24] suggests, or developing the digital infrastructure as shown in Wan et al. [25]. However, these measures can only partially tackle the ongoing trends associated with the migration of human resources and capital towards large cities, where both current specialists and high-performing students seek higher salaries and benefits, and where companies find it more profitable to operate. Thus, the self-sustaining nature of regional inequality will continue, both within the framework of population flow to the leading regions and agglomerations and the depopulation of smaller settlements.

### 4.4 "Social Waste" Rhetoric

The rhetoric of Industry 5.0 proponents on the concept of "social waste" is questionable. In earlier articles not related to Industry 5.0, social waste was recognized as unproductive behaviour and a waste of resources [26], e.g., on advertising and promotion [27], to find or avoid rent [28]. Within Industry 5.0, social waste includes certain categories of people. The meaning of social waste differs from the relatively mild and related to the concept of unemployment like "people willing to work but having no opportunity and people who are not willing" [29] or "number of people that want to work but do not have the knowledge to be employee" [10] and "people willing to work but having no opportunity, ineffective recruiting & employees retaining policies, assisted population unwilling to work" [30] to the radical, including such a definition as "people and animals cut from 'meaningful life' or kept serving the best dead as food stock" [31] or "relating to cultural practices" [32]. In any of these cases, social waste is on a par with physical trash, urban waste, and process waste, levelling a person with the state of debris. Industry 5.0 research does not show how social waste will be reduced, apart from the assumption that "we need to invest more in those who deserve it, while reducing unnecessary social waste" [33]. Such an attitude towards a person is rather weakly linked to the "human-oriented" direction proclaimed within Industry 5.0. Based on such rhetoric, a situation may arise when the programs of waste reduction, including "social waste", can harm the well-being of a person and society or increase the exploitation of human being.

### 4.5 Declining in the Quality of Education

The trends of digitalization in education also raise questions. Its current development, unfortunately, is not going to be human-centred but rather machine-centred. Trofimova [34] notes that Industry 5.0 concentrates on combining cognitive technologies with human intelligence and ingenuity, but modern education is aimed at templating cognition, and not developing original thinking patterns. The focus on distance learning leads to a deterioration in the quality of education because of the loss of feedback from the teacher, an emphasis on test-type tasks that are easier to automate. There is also an increased possibility of opportunistic behaviour by students in completing home tasks and examinations through the use of networks and ChatGPT. Such formats of training weaken the development of a person's cognitive potential and increase their dependence on machine solutions. Another challenge is the fact that proprietary educational technologies, software, and simulators based on digital tweens are playing an increasingly important role. However, the purchase and use of these technologies are quite expensive, which accordingly affects the cost of training. Thus, the already existing inequality in gaining a proper education may worsen. Graduates of the largest metropolitan universities have the greatest career opportunities, while there will be a shortage of qualified personnel on the periphery that will lead to a decrease in availability of knowledge-intensive services.

## 4.6 Reducing Availability of Knowledge-Intensive Services

A decrease in the availability of knowledge-intensive services is considered an un-obvious consequence of introducing new technologies. This can be most clearly seen in the example of medicine. AIs can be, and are already being, used in data processing. Their potential is extremely important for conducting four-dimensional medical research, 4D printing, the use of sensors, the development of new materials, etc. [35]. But rather ambiguous attempts are being made to replace knowledge-intensive professions with new technologies, for example, in medicine.

Supporters of the rapid implementation of Industry 5.0 tools largely agree with Bill Gates, who claims that "many people in those countries never get to see a doc-tor, and AIs will help the health workers they do see be more productive. (The effort to develop AI-powered ultrasound machines that can be used with minimal training is a great example of this.) AIs will even give patients the ability to do basic triage, get advice about how to deal with health problems, and decide whether they need to seek treatment" [36]. In fact, however, this will lead to a deterioration in the quality of medical services provided because:

1. AI is following the patterns laid down in training and the data already obtained in making diagnoses. This is fraught not only with the possibility of incorrect diagnosis, but also with the omission of emergency situations when new, potentially dangerous cases of diseases that have arisen, will not be noticed and identified in time;
2. Incorrect diagnosis is possible, as well as the creation of dangerous combinations of treatment regimens and new drugs because of the "hallucination" of AI, when it gives data not based on reality;
3. The absence of a human factor will negatively affect the mental state of the patient;

4. A decrease in the quality of training for medical specialists, when their training will be reduced to working with digital technologies, and not with a person;
5. A further flow of migration to large agglomerations in search of a more "human" level of health care;
6. Additional dependence of the provision of medical services on software and equipment provided by large multinational companies.

Thus, inequality in obtaining high-quality knowledge-intensive services will expand when a live specialist will be available for a high fee, and low-income segments of the population will have to use template solutions from AI.

## *4.7 Depending on Machine Solutions and Reducing Analytical Skills*

Being too dependent on machines and not being able to think critically can be a big problem in management. According to the results of Polyakova et al. [37], although analytical skills are among the most wanted by employers after communication skills, they are significantly inferior to the requirements for basic and advanced digital skills. People's critical thinking abilities are declining in a society that values narratives and has an excess of information. Users of computer systems usually trust the results obtained during data processing, but often they do not understand how to interpret the program output or how the machine analysis was performed. As a result, there may be a tendency to overemphasize the calculations without considering the real situation and related factors. Generally, forecasts based on the analysis of incomplete models cannot have high reliability, but there is a high probability that people will perceive these forecasts as correct and use them in their activities. As Saniuk and Grabowska note, "Currently, the focus on the development of basic research in a dynamically changing environment is becoming useless and overdue" [38]. This quote illustrates the danger of humanity falling into a cognitive deadlock, when research will be conducted purely on the terms of machine data analysis, which will limit their potential to expand human knowledge. Therefore, it is extremely important to develop analytical skills and the ability to interpret, verify, and sometimes check the falsifiability of the results, to develop such human skills as abstract thinking and creativity.

## *4.8 Disposing Waste*

Waste disposal is a significant problem that humanity faces in Industry 4.0 and that will undoubtedly be enhanced in Industry 5.0, given the trends towards the expansion of waste generation projected by the World Bank [39]. At the moment, the ideology of the new industrial revolution is guided by the narrative that "adoption of clean energy, reduction of waste, and judicial use of resources will become the industry standard" [40]. Modern additive technologies, replacing traditional subtractive ones, will somewhat reduce the loss of material resources, but the development of additive technologies is impossible for all industries. Certain amounts of waste can be utilized within the framework of the recycling, infra-cycling, reusing, or infra-using concept [41]. Some researchers propose to use plastic from electronic waste in construction as a substitute for sand in the cement production [42]. Others state that the use of e-waste can replace 7–10% of traditional materials without compromising the quality of the material [43]. Thus, the importance of the problem of e-waste disposal will increase. To date, there is no complete and environmentally friendly technology for the disposal of e-waste. Some valuable components are extracted from it, but the remaining components accumulate in rubbish or are disposed of in environmentally harmful ways, in particular by burying, burning, or dissolving in acids, as shown by Jain et al. [44]. In this situation, there is an urgent need to use more environmentally friendly materials for the creation and utilization of electronics, but this trend is currently not evolving.

## *4.9 Changing Property Relations*

A serious challenge from the viewpoint of economic theory is the transformation of property relations, which is becoming widespread because of the development of digital technologies. Modern technologies can significantly change the relationship between the manufacturer and the owner. This is happening not only due to the development of a platform business that allows the use of rental forms of goods and services instead of acquiring them, but also to the abundance of digital products that need constant support, updating, and upgrading. Those goods and services put the buyer in a situation where their ability to use the acquired products is limited and depends on the manufacturer, who can extract excess profits by unilaterally raising the cost of their services. The manufacturer has the possibility of limiting the use of benefits by cancelling the account of the product owner at any moment for the manufacturer's own reasons. More and more products with limited functionality appear, when the necessary functions can be unlocked for an additional fee (and, accordingly, blocked if desired by the manufacturer). AI development creates the possibility for cars to self-evacuate from the owner by the manufacturer's decision, e.g., the "repossession system", patented by Ford [45]. Thus, the ownership rights of the end user are becoming significantly limited. In addition, a significant amount of electronic products collect personal data about end users, effectively alienating personal data from people. Modern EU legislation [46] allows free flows of personal data for producers with the permission of the personal data subject. However, the issue of using the collected personal data is quite sensitive, given the possibilities of creating digital human twins (DHT) that are already emerging. Nowadays, we are discussing DHT through the means of telemetry, which allows us to identify physical and behavioural patterns of human thinking. With the development of technology, we can also use DHT, with the possibility of digitizing and analysing the cognitive processes of a biological individual. This can lead to the loss of freedom of choice for a person, since his choice will be predetermined by the analysed data. As Wei [47] points out, DHT is ideal for managing the full life cycle of a person. Now, according to the data of Miller and Spatz [48] technologies of the DHT are more studied in manufacturing industries than in medicine, biomechanics, and sports. The next issue in this group of challenges in Industry 5.0 may be the problem of AI ownership in the case of developing AI self-awareness. This issue is borderline between the questions of property and ethics, given the capabilities that AI can possess.

## *4.10 Ethical Issues of Interaction of Biological Consciousness and AI*

Ethical issues arising from the interaction of biological consciousness and AI are considered to some extent by modern researchers not purely as theoretical and futuristic research but also as an analysis of the existing experience. Chen [49] investigates the possibility of harmful use of large language models, such as GPT-3, to manipulate individuals or spread misinformation via programming unreliable answers through bias in training data. Although Fiordi et al. [50] recognize the risks of excessive use of AI, such as a decrease in the importance of human skills, a decline in human control, a denial of human responsibility, and a decrease in the possibilities of human self-determination, they note that "AI should be created in such a way as to reduce inequality and expand social opportunities while respecting human autonomy and increasing benefits that are fairly distributed among all". This is an extremely naive approach, since inequality is inherent in human society, and in order to program something, people already need to understand how to reduce inequality, as well as understand and accept life under given conditions. However, until now, human society has not built an equitable socio-economic system that would prove its effectiveness. Further, the authors [50] propose the development of various bureaucratic and financial add-ons that allow "regulating" the activities of AI. But this raises a new problem about the effectiveness of such add-ons and the objectivity of evaluating their performance. Recent events, such as the COVID-19 epidemic, have shown the disunity and inefficiency of the institutions of the world community in the fight against the global threat. In view of this, the use of AI for opportunistic purposes is much more likely than solving global challenges via it. And, in order to have an idea about the ethics of the interaction between humans and AI, it is necessary to pay attention to the ethics of the first one of these components.

## 5 Conclusion

Industry 5.0 is not a sudden revolutionary leap towards radical new principles of the organization of industry and society, but rather represents an expansion of Industry 4.0 with the use of new technologies and is aimed at achieving the UN SDGs. Even as many scientific papers state that new technologies will assist in reaching the objective, the real trends allow us to make rather pessimistic forecasts. Instead of solving the problems of human development, society will face a scenario where the basic problems of humanity will worsen and the untreated problems of Industry 4.0 may deepen within Industry 5.0. We do not aim to stop technological progress, but we ask humanity to pause and ponder: are we really moving in the right direction to actually achieve the SDGs? In this paper, we have noted ten challenges that can significantly worsen the human-oriented prospects of Industry 5.0 and predicted some consequences that are likely if those challenges are ignored. Although this list of issues is not exhaustive, it is necessary to work out realistic scenarios for solving the problems of inequality, ecology, respect to property rights, human and machine ethics, what will be the focus of our further research. It is necessary to draw the attention of businesses and authorities to the potential danger of the challenges we have identified related to the development of Industry 5.0. Otherwise, humanity has every chance of encountering serious failures that significantly slow down its development potential.

**Acknowledgments** The work was performed by the Research Plan of the Institute of Economics of the Ural Branch of the Russian Academy of Sciences.

## References

1. Hu, T. (2022). Review of national strategies for the transition to Industry 5.0. *Economics and innovation management, 3*, 28–38. https://doi.org/10.26730/2587-5574-2022-3-28-38
2. Barata, J., & Kayser, I. (2023). Industry 5.0–Past, present, and near future. *Procedia Computer Science, 219*, 778–788. https://doi.org/10.1016/j.procs.2023.01.351
3. Gasanov, E. A. (2022). A new form of human-machine connection in the industrial production model 5.0. *Economics and Management, 3*, 39–49. https://doi.org/10.26730/2587-5574-2022-3-39-49
4. Xu, X., Lu, Y., Vogel-Heuser, B., & Wang, L. (2021). Industry 4.0 and Industry 5.0—Inception, conception and perception. *Journal of Manufacturing Systems, 61*, 530–535. https://doi.org/10.1016/j.jmsy.2021.10.006
5. Chin, S. T. S. (2021). Influence of emotional intelligence on the workforce for Industry 5.0. *Journal of Human Resources Management Research, 2021*, 882278. https://doi.org/10.5171/2021.882278
6. Saniuk, S., Grabowska, S., & Straka, M. (2022). Identification of social and economic expectations: Contextual reasons for the transformation process of Industry 4.0 into the Industry 5.0 concept. *Sustainability, 14*(3), 1391. https://doi.org/10.3390/su14031391

7. Mitchell, J., & Guile, D. (2021). Fusion skills and Industry 5.0: Conceptions and challenges. In *Insights into global engineering education after the birth of Industry 5.0* (p. 100096). *Intech Open*. https://doi.org/10.5772/intechopen.100096
8. Elangovan, U. (2021). *Industry 5.0: The future of the industrial economy*. CRC Press. https://doi.org/10.1201/9781003190677
9. Narkhede, G., Pasi, B., Rajhans, N., & Kulkarni, A. (2023). Industry 5.0 and the future of sustainable manufacturing: A systematic literature review. *Business Strategy & Development, Wiley, 6*, 1–20. https://doi.org/10.1002/bsd2.272
10. Stef, D., & Draghici, G. (2022). Manufacturing processes automation and their intelligent monitoring. In *Sustainability and Innovation in Manufacturing Enterprises: Indicators, Models and Assessment for Industry 5.0* (pp. 89–113). https://doi.org/10.1007/978-981-16-7365-8_4
11. Nahavandi, S. (2019). Industry 5.0—A human-centric solution. *Sustainability, 11*(16), 4371. https://doi.org/10.3390/su11164371
12. Barinova, N. V., & Barinov, V. R. (2022). Digital economy, artificial intelligence, Industry 5.0: Challenges of our time. *Bulletin of the Plekhanov Russian University of Economics, 5*, 23–34. https://doi.org/10.21686/2413-2829-2022-5-23-34
13. Khan, M., Haleem, A., & Javaid, M. (2023). Changes and improvements in Industry 5.0: A strategic approach to overcome the challenges of Industry 4.0. *Green Technologies and Sustainability, 1*(2), 100020. https://doi.org/10.1016/j.grets.2023.100020
14. Alves, J., Lima, T. M., & Gaspar, P. D. (2023). Is Industry 5.0 a human-Centred approach? A systematic review. *Processes, 11*(1), 193. https://doi.org/10.3390/pr11010193
15. Minculete, G., Bârsan, G., & Olar, P. (2021). Conceptual approaches of Industry 5.0. Correlative elements with supply chain management 5.0. *Revista de Management Comparat International, 22*(5), 622–635. https://doi.org/10.24818/RMCI.2021.5.622
16. Magruk, A. (2020). Uncertainty, knowledge and future options in foresight research (using the example of Industry 4.0). *Foresight, 14*(4), 20–33. https://doi.org/10.17323/2500-2597.2020.4.20.33
17. Hammershøj, L. G. (2019). The new division of labor between human and machine and its educational implications. *Technology in Society, 59*, 101142. https://doi.org/10.1016/j.techsoc.2019.05.006
18. Kloudova, Y. (2010). The impact of the development of the creative economy on economically backward regions. *Journal of the New Economic Association, 5*(5), 109–124.
19. Dixson-Declève, S., Dunlop, K., Renda, A., Charveriat, C., Christophilopoulos, E., Balland, P.-A., Isaksson, D., Martins, F., Mir Roca, M., Pedersen, G., Schwaag Serger, S., Serger, S., Soete, L., Stres, Š., Gołębiowska-Tataj, D., Walz, R., & Huang, A. (2023). Industry 5.0 and the future of work: Making Europe the Centre of gravity for future good-quality jobs. https://publica.fraunhofer.de/entities/publication/7ce85b8e-b72f-4dd0-8f56-a860dea01443/details
20. Zhiganov, V. P. (2023). Human capital in Industry 5.0 *first. Economic Journal, 3*, 51–59. https://doi.org/10.58551/20728115_2023_3_51
21. Industry 5.0. (n.d.). European Commission. https://research-and-innovation.ec.europa.eu/research-area/industrial-research-and-innovation/industry-50_en
22. Akimova, K. E. (2022). The development of the digital economy in the context of global challenges. In *Economics and Industry 5.0 in the new reality (INPROM-2022)* (pp. 79–82). https://doi.org/10.18720/IEP/2022.1/18
23. Pinheiro, F. L., Balland, P. A., Boschma, R., & Hartmann, D. (2022). The dark side of the geography of innovation: Relatedness, complexity and regional inequality in Europe. *Regional Studies*, 1–16. https://doi.org/10.1080/00343404.2022.2106362
24. Pal, S. (2023). A comparative study of inter-regional intra-industry disparity. SSRN Electronic Journal. https://doi.org/10.2139/ssrn.4410800.
25. Wan, W., Wang, J., & Jiang, W. (2023). Does COVID-19 exacerbate regional income inequality? Evidence from 20 provinces of China. *Sustainability, 15*(15), 11894. https://doi.org/10.3390/su151511894

26. Bischoff, I., & Blaeschke, F. (2016). Performance budgeting: Incentives and social waste from window dressing. *Journal of Public Administration Research and Theory, 26*(2), 344–358. https://doi.org/10.1093/jopart/muv013
27. Guhathakurta, S. (1992). Regulation of firm size in industrial development: The experience of two manufacturing sectors in India. *Berkeley Planning Journal, 7*(1), 76–97. https://doi.org/10.5070/BP37113103
28. Appelbaum, E., & Katz, E. (1986). Transfer seeking and avoidance: On the full social costs of rent seeking. *Public Choice, 48*(2), 175–181. http://www.jstor.org/stable/30024590
29. Paschek, D., Mocan, A., & Draghici, A. (2019). Industry 5.0—The expected impact of next industrial revolution. In *Thriving on future education, industry, business, and society, proceedings of the MakeLearn and TIIM International Conference* (pp. 15–17), Piran, Slovenia. http://www.toknowpress.net/ISBN/978-961-6914-25-3/papers/ML19-017.pdf
30. Simion, L. C., Avasilcai, S., & Alexa, L. E. (2021). Transition Industry 4.0 to 5.0-renaissance of human driven approach adding value to people & management performance. Strategica shaping the future of business and economy, 897–917. https://strategica-conference.ro/wp-content/uploads/2022/04/68-2.pdf
31. Eco Amet Solutions. (n.d.). https://ecoametsolutions.com/industry-5-0/
32. America Alliance—Key Challenges for Waste Reduction in the Americas. (n.d.). https://eutec.org/past-events-db/america-alliance-key-challenges-for-waste-reduction-in-the-americas/
33. Ding, Y. (2022). Correlation analysis model of social capital and innovation performance based on knowledge mapping. *Computational Intelligence and Neuroscience, 2022*, 2138200. https://doi.org/10.1155/2022/2138200
34. Trofimova, N. N. (2023). Industry 5.0: Integration of human potential into Industry 4.0. *Economics and Management: Problems Solutions, 4*(1), 34–39. https://doi.org/10.36871/ek.up.p.r.2023.01.04.004
35. Haleem, A., & Javaid, M. (2019). Industry 5.0 and its expected applications in medical field. *Current Medicine Research and Practice, 9*(4), 167–169. https://doi.org/10.1016/j.cmrp.2019.07.002
36. Gates, B. (2023). The age of AI has begun. Artificial intelligence is as revolutionary as mobile phones and the Internet. https://www.gatesnotes.com/The-Age-of-AI-Has-Begun?WT.mc_id=20230321100000_Artificial-Intelligence_BG-TW_&WT.tsrc=BGTW
37. Poláková, M., Suleimanová, J. H., Madzík, P., Copuš, L., Molnárová, I., & Polednová, J. (2023). Soft skills and their importance in the labour market under the conditions of industry 5.0. *Heliyon, 9*(8), e18670. https://doi.org/10.1016/j.heliyon.2023.e18670
38. Saniuk, S., & Grabowska, S. (2022). Development of knowledge and skills of engineers and managers in the era of Industry 5.0 in the light of expert research. *Zeszyty Naukowe. Organizacja i Zarządzanie/Politechnika Śląska, 158*, 537–547. https://doi.org/10.29119/1641-3466.2022.158.35
39. World Bank. (n.d.). Trends in solid waste management. https://datatopics.worldbank.org/what-a-waste/trends_in_solid_waste_management.html
40. Sindhwani, R., Afridi, S., Kumar, A., Banaitis, A., Luthra, S., & Singh, P. L. (2022). Can Industry 5.0 revolutionize the wave of resilience and social value creation? A multi-criteria framework to analyze enablers. *Technology in Society, 68*, 101887. https://doi.org/10.1016/j.techsoc.2022.10188
41. Vefago, L. H. M., & Avellaneda, J. (2013). Recycling concepts and the index of recyclability for building materials. *Resources, Conservation and Recycling, 72*, 127–135. https://doi.org/10.1016/j.resconrec.2012.12.015
42. Kumar, N., & Jaglan, A. (2022). A review on utilization of E-waste in construction. In V. S. Kanwar, S. K. Sharma, & C. Prakasam (Eds.), *Proceedings of International Conference on Innovative Technologies for Clean and Sustainable Development (ICITCSD—2021)* (pp. 33–48). Springer. https://doi.org/10.1007/978-3-030-93936-6_4
43. Dixit, S., Arora, R., Kumar, K., Bansal, S., Vatin, N., Araszkiewicz, K., & Epifantsev, K. (2022). Replacing E-waste with coarse aggregate in architectural engineering and

construction industry. *Materials Today: Proceedings, 56*, 2353–2358. https://doi.org/10.1016/j.matpr.2021.12.154

44. Jain, M., Kumar, D., Chaudhary, J., Kumar, S., Sharma, S., & Verma, A. S. (2023). Review on E-waste management and its impact on the environment and society. *Waste Management Bulletin, 1*(3), 34–44. https://doi.org/10.1016/j.wmb.2023.06.004
45. Holderith, P. (2023). Ford applies to patent self-repossessing cars that can drive themselves away the drive. https://www.thedrive.com/news/future-fords-could-repossess-themselves-and-drive-away-if-you-miss-payments
46. Hadzovic, S., Mrdovic, S., & Radonjic, M. (2023). A path towards an internet of things and artificial intelligence regulatory framework. *IEEE Communications Magazine, 61*(7), 90–96. https://doi.org/10.1109/MCOM.002.2200373
47. Wei, S. (2021). Is human digital twin possible? *Computer Methods and Programs in Biomedicine Update, 1*, 100014. https://doi.org/10.1016/j.cmpbup.2021.100014
48. Miller, M. E., & Spatz, E. (2022). A unified view of a human digital twin. *Human-Intelligent Systems Integration, 4*, 23–33. https://doi.org/10.1007/s42454-022-00041-x
49. Chan, A. (2022). GPT-3 and InstructGPT: Technological dystopianism, utopianism, and "contextual" perspectives in AI ethics and industry. *AI and Ethics, 3*, 53–64. https://doi.org/10.1007/s43681-022-00148-6
50. Floridi, L., Cowls, J., Beltrametti, M., Chatila, R., Chazerand, P., Dignum, V., Luetge, C., Madelin, R., Pagallo, U., Rossi, F., Schafer, B., Valck, P., & Vayena, E. (2021). An ethical framework for a good AI society: Opportunities, risks, principles, and recommendations. In *Ethics, governance, and policies in Artificial Intelligence* (pp. 19–39). https://doi.org/10.1007/s11023-018-9482-5

# From Industry 4.0 to Industry 5.0: Challenges and Opportunities of Evolutionary Transition in Russia

**Olga Romanova and Evgeny Kuzmin**

**Abstract** The evolutionary transition from Industry 4.0 to Industry 5.0 inevitably influences all the aspects in the socio-economic life. It requires stakeholders not only to reconsider approaches to production and management, but also to form new strategic developmental directions on principles of sustainability, innovativeness, and human centricity. With regard to these challenges, an analysis of a development trajectory for Industry 5.0 in Russia is getting particularly important, taking into account the unique national socio-economic and political context. The authors explore key aspects in the development of Industry 4.0, including digital transformation, outline dominating patterns and principles of Industry 5.0. The review of research papers, expert reports, and cases of manufacturers' practice has shown that the new economic model is being actively established in Russia. The aspiration towards technological sovereignty is its descriptor. Despite external and internal challenges, Russia has a significant potential to implement Industry 4.0 and Industry 5.0 concepts. This includes both production and introduction of innovations, and human capital development. The authors identify the prevailing challenges that might slow down or complicate the transition to Industry 5.0. At the same time, they outline the opportunities related to more active involvement of internal resources and the development of new forms of cooperation. One of key findings is that the governmental industrial policy plays a critical regulatory role to encourage the technological development and support the transition to Industry 5.0. Authors point out to the need for strategic planning taking into account today's global trends, investments in research and education, as well as creating conditions for innovative entrepreneurship development. The research contributes to understanding of the prospects and challenges that Russia faces on its path to Industry 5.0. The research emphasizes the importance of coordinated efforts that all the stakeholders make in this process and a clear strategic direction that the government provided.

O. Romanova (✉) · E. Kuzmin
Institute of Economics of the Ural Branch of the Russian Academy of Sciences, Ekaterinburg, Russian Federation
e-mail: romanova.oa@uiec.ru; kuzmin.ea@uiec.ru



A. Appolloni et al. (eds.), *The Future of Industry*, Lecture Notes in Information Systems and Organisation 70, https://doi.org/10.1007/978-3-031-66801-2_5

**Keywords** Digital transformation · Industrial policy · Industry 4.0 · Industry 5.0 · Sustainable development

## 1 Introduction

Today, the global economy and industry are experiencing significant transformations driven by rapidly developing technology and new production paradigms that emerge [1–3]. In this process, the key stage was the transition from the concept of Industry 4.0 [4, 5] (which had been marked by the digitalization era) to the more advanced stage of Industry 5.0 that assumes the synthesis of technological innovations and human capital [6–9]. However, the industrial evolution does not occur in isolation from the national socio-economic context, which makes it important to explore the specifics of such a transition in terms of various geopolitical scenarios.

In the first two decades of the twenty-first century, Russia faced a series of economic crises and numerous challenges. Therefore, for Russia the issue of trial sector adjustment and development in compliance with global trends is getting particularly relevant. Four serious recent crises experienced by Russia have caused the ongoing change in the economic policy. The first crisis of 2008 was caused by the global systemwide crisis and the beginning of the sanctions war with Russia. The crisis of 2020 was caused by the COVID pandemic, while the other two of 2014 and 2022 were due to large-scale anti-Russian sanctions. Each of these crises had its own specifics that caused serious consequences. To overcome the crises of 2008, 2014, and 2020, Russia had to transform its macroeconomic policy, while the crisis of 2022 provided a rationale for a serious transformation of the established model of the Russian economy in general. These challenges do not only encourage a search for the ways, with which it is possible to keep national technological sovereignty, but also form the sustainable economic model that might be effectively integrated into the changing global production landscape.

The new economic model being established in Russia is a current result of this transformation. The model keeps certain transparency typical for the system of market freedoms. Various protective measures also complement it showing a more active role of the government not only in global economic relations, but also in its aspiration to a balance between public, corporate, and private interests. Thus, in Russia, the new economic model is emerging. It is a partially transparent economy of the independent type, and the achievement of technological sovereignty is its formal trait [10]. The paramount importance of its achievement in current Russia predetermines the need for the new technological basis for the economy that meets principles and criteria of both Industry 4.0 and Industry 5.0.

These and other reasons predetermined this research purpose as identifying Industry 4.0 development challenges and conceptual opportunities for Industry 5.0 introduction in the context of new economic and political priorities in Russia. An important aspect of the research is the analysis of a role of the government in creating conditions to encourage industrial innovations and the achievement of technological sovereignty in terms of global competition and geopolitical restrictions. The main assumption of the research is that the Russian economy despite multiple challenges that the sanctions regime causes is sufficiently capable to support of Industry 4.0 development and the initial stage of its evolutionary transition to implementation of Industry 5.0 concept.

The achievement of this goal involves a number of objectives to be addressed, including:

- Analyse Industry 4.0 current state and development potential in Russia,
- Identify essential features of Industry 5.0 concept as the next stage in the technological and socio-economic development,
- Identify challenges and opportunities associated with the evolutionary transition to implementation of Industry 5.0 concept,
- Develop proposals to make the efficient industrial policy to support such a transition.

The research is based on a review of research papers, statistical data, regulatory, and legal documents on strategic planning, as well as cases provided by leading Russian and overseas enterprises. Thus, the research aims at the development of conceptual and practical recommendations to encourage Industry 5.0 development in Russia, taking into account its specifics and current economic challenges.

## 2 Industry 4.0: Implementation Potential

Industry 4.0 as a term appeared in Germany in 2011 at the Hannover Messe. It refers to transformation of global value chains, the development of such technologies, as smart factories, not only smart and interconnected machines, but also entire systems, etc. However, Industry 4.0 as a term only came into wide-scale use in 2016 as a synonym to the term "the fourth industrial revolution" after the publication of the same-name book by Schwab, which quickly became a global bestseller [11]. So far, the conceptual framework of Industry 4.0 has been developed in detail. Theoreticians have identified the technologies typical for it and scales of their application in the economy of the developed and developing countries. They have also found that convergence of cognitive and operational technologies is one of the most important components of Industry 4.0 as a concept [12–16].

The global community generally agree that Industry 4.0 potential is still far from its full implementation [17–19]. Even the developed countries have great opportunities for its further use. As mentioned before, reproduction of the real world in the digital environment is one of the main, but not so far achieved goal of Industry 4.0. For example, numerous research papers claim that the global market of digital twins in 2019–2025 will have more than 9-time increase (from USD 3.8 billion to USD 35.8 billion) [20]. At the same time, many overseas enterprises are far from the achievement of the abovementioned goal. According to Gartner's study "IoT Digital Twin Adoption Proliferates Across Many Sourcing Options" [21], only 26% of the survey respondents say they have already created digital twins. At the same time, more than a half of respondent companies (59%) mentions that they are either starting to use digital twins in their practice or planning to introduce them next year.

Thus, even the developed countries have a large-scale and currently unused potential of Industry 4.0. This potential in Russia is much lower, but we can see its intensive development. Introducing the new technological basis based on large-scale application of critical and end-to-end technologies, that is key technologies of Industry 4.0, is the most important goal in the today's government science and technology policy. When implementing such a policy, special attention is paid to the fact that in the achievement of national technological sovereignty we should consider the most important trends and technologies of Industry 4.0. Moreover, it is getting more and more relevant and important that technologies transform into the added value making factor at national and corporate levels.

At the same time, severe anti-Russian sanctions primarily are aimed at restraining the development and learning key technologies of Industry 4.0, high-tech sectors, strategic sectors, primarily, the defence sector. The sanctions war against Russia has excluded the opportunity to reproduce technological innovations based on their import and imported mechanic engineering products. And this is a serious challenge, solution to which does not only assume intensified import substitution processes, but also the achievement of such import substitution, quality indicators of which must meet Industry 4.0 criteria. Today, there is a significant overrun (more than four times) of imported machinery, equipment, and vehicles over exported ones [22, 23]. There is almost similar situation in other sectors. Although new supply chains are primarily built with the friendly countries, a poor number of national manufacturers of high-tech production is a threat to the formation of the new technological basis for the Russian economy based on the development of less advanced technologies.

To mitigate such a threat and develop the new technological basis for the Russian economy, corresponding to Industry 4.0, both critical technologies (to address the most important current challenges in the technological and socio-economic development), and the end-to-end technologies must be developed that determine an image of both the future economy in general, and its most important high-tech sectors in particular. Today, with regard to the formation of the new technological basis, the development and application of advanced production technologies (APT) is of particular importance. By the end of 2022, Russia had developed 2621 technologies, which is 30% higher than the same figure in 2020 [24]. At the same time, the number of industrial computing and big data technologies had increased by 1.7 times by 2020, while technologies of production information systems and production management automation — by 1.8 times. In general, about a third of Russian enterprises use APT. This means that there is a large-scale unused potential driven by Industry 4.0. But a much more serious threat to formation of Russia's technological sovereignty and compliance with Industry 4.0 requirements today is not so much the small share of enterprises that use APT, as the insufficient activity of APT developers. Even among the most technologically advanced manufacturing enterprises, the share of APT developers is less than 2% [25].

The industry digital transformation plays a special role when we evaluate whether the Russian industry complies with Industry 4.0 criteria and addresses the objective of technological sovereignty achievement. The share of manufacturing enterprises that use such technologies, as industrial robots, RFID, cloud services, as well as special-purpose software, primarily ERP, MES, CAD/CAE/CAM/CAO, is larger than in other sectors of the Russian economy. In general, such digital technology, as the broadband Internet access is quite widespread in the Russian industry (more than 90% of enterprises have it) [26, 27]. But recent digital technologies are not so widespread. Thus, according to Rosstat, only about 30% of enterprises use ERP systems and cloud services, while less than 20% of enterprises use electronic sales, and only 12% of enterprises use RFID technologies.

In 2021, the industry digital maturity index was only 21% [28]. But there is a positive trend clear in this regard. In particular, in 2020, the demand of manufacturers for advanced digital technologies was, according to the expert survey by the Higher School of Economics, at the level of 41.5 billion roubles, while as early as by 2030, the need for these technologies will have amounted to 587.5 billion roubles, that is, the demand will have had its 14-time increase. According to this survey results, in the industry there is a high demand for such digital technologies, as artificial intelligence and neurotechnology, robotics and sensors, wireless communication and new production technologies. Virtual and augmented reality, distributed registry systems, and quantum technologies are in medium and low demand. The latter is of particular concern because as early as in 2025–2030, we expect intensive introducing of quantum computers which will make beyond-quantum technological leadership impossible. This literally condemns Russian enterprises to take part in the global quantum race, without which the achievement of technological sovereignty is beyond thought.

Creating such institutional conditions that might ensure smooth interaction [29, 30] between research institutions, universities, large tech businesses, including those with public ownership, small and medium-sized innovative businesses is important for successful digital transformation in the industry. But the need to restore applied research institutions is a particular issue in Russia both for the achievement of technological sovereignty and the growth of Industry 4.0 potential. Today, the main potential of applied and engineering research and development is distributed between 44 government-funded research centres, which quantitatively only makes 1% of enterprises working in this field [31–33]. At the same time, they account for 20% of national spending on applied research and development. Large state corporations and enterprises with public ownership also run such research projects. Nevertheless, in terms of some most important directions for research and technological development, for instance, microelectronics, space and energy technologies, etc., there is a serious lag in terms of compliance with Industry 4.0.

To eliminate this lag, a special role is assigned to Russian-based world-class research and educational centres. As a kind of innovative platforms which bring together educational and research organizations and businesses, such Centres might make the basis to build the up-to-date research and development pattern to ensure national technological sovereignty and wider use of the available potential of

Industry 4.0. Within this pattern, joint research and production initiatives are of increasing importance based on new organizational forms for their cooperation to meet specific technological priorities set for by Industry 4.0 criteria, as well as tasks of the achievement of technological sovereignty in Russia. More than RUB1.8 billion will be spent to support such Centres in 2023 in the form of grants to 15 research and educational centres located in 36 regions of the country [34].

## 3 Major Aspects the Industry 5.0 as a Concept

Research projects on identification of a new mega stage of such development are leaders in the field of promising areas for the technological and socio-economic development of the mankind. Its essential traits and principles are largely formed within Industry 5.0 framework [6, 35, 36]. The basics of this concept have been widely discussed at both European and Russian forums, main participants of which were representatives of technological, academic, research, and educational organizations. The presentations were mostly focused on discussions on Industry 5.0 supporting technologies [37–40].

However, it seems that the issue of work on the conceptual framework of Industry 5.0 goes far beyond technology with the human-cantered approach at the forefront [41]. Rajesh points out to the fact that the regulation issue seems to be the most important as it requires priority attention in terms of introduction and implementation of Industry 5.0 as a conceptual framework [42]. This is due to the need to create an effective regulatory framework as the basis for adjustment to innovative technologies and production methods. This aspect becomes key as we strive to harmonize new technologies with ongoing processes and regulatory frameworks. Issues of integration with previous generation technologies are the next in importance. In order of importance, on the third place, there are ethical issues that relate to the use and development of Industry 5.0 technologies, including issues of privacy, data security, and impact on labour processes. These aspects require a careful analysis and development of appropriate ethical codes and regulations to ensure a balance between technological progress and socio-ethical values.

Of course, introducing new technologies into industry, in particular Wi-Fi 6, 5G, and active sensors production are key factors for essential transformations in the industry [43, 44]. At the same time, the most important problem of its effective development is still unsolved (creating such a cross-functional solution that would make it possible to combine worlds of information and operational technologies) [45]. Each of those worlds has its own goals, competencies, and budgets. The question remains open (which must be solved within the framework of Industry 5.0) on the innovations to make such combining true, on convergence of cognitive and operational technologies, on achieving sustainable development and higher resilience of the economy, especially its industrial sector.

A significant step to solve abovementioned issues is the consensus reached by the global academic community on two conceptual directions to understand the meaning of Industry 5.0. It is important that in each of them the human-cantered approach is central. Brent Kedzierski, author of the first direction, based his concept on the idea of integration of Industry 4.0 connected technologies and Industry 5.0 humanitarian practices. Having supported these stands, his statement of Industry 5.0 as a concept makes it possible for us to expect that within its framework, we will find a path towards harmonious interaction of human intelligence with cognitive computations based on combined capabilities of Industry 4.0 connected technologies with the human-centred approach of Industry 5.0 [46].

Saritas provided a slightly different interpretation of the Industry 5.0 concept, saying that human and machine intelligences are to be combined to create a shared intelligence. Such intelligence, as the concept justifies, will make it possible to avoid technological singularity in the future being the basis for human's improvement in the context of the simultaneous development of technologies [47, 48].

We believe that research projects run by teams at Immanuel Kant Baltic Federal University and Peter the Great Saint Petersburg Polytechnic University are of significant interest [49, 50]. Having taken into account results of the abovementioned research initiatives and combined the views of various authors, the team is working on the shared research platform, on the basis of which it will be possible to develop the new concept for the development of high-tech industry called Industry 5.0. The same research platform might be the basis for the development of an applied toolkit to build new types of socio-economic, cyber-social, neuro-digital, and other ecosystems. So far, this team has proposed the understanding of Industry 5.0 as a cyber-social system that makes it possible to combine human and machine intelligences to create a shared super-intelligence, which will be a source of the harmonious technological development of the human civilization [48].

Despite the importance of the technological aspect of Industry 5.0, it is worth paying attention to the interpretation of Industry 5.0 most important goals agreed upon by the global community: sustainable development, human-centeredness, and resistance to external influences [51]. The implementation of these development goals should contribute to the formation of the new image of the industry. The main assessment criterion for such an industry will not be productivity and efficiency (although these indicators' role cannot be overestimated), but its contribution to the society development. The ethical aspect in the formation and development of Industry 5.0 precisely meets this goal. It is ethics and mutual trust of economic agents that should be among other most important factors in its formation and a criterion for economic behaviours of business entities in Industry 5.0. Improved social welfare will be a determinant basis for such a criterion.

## 4 Challenges and Opportunities of the Evolutionary Transition in the Russian Economy to Implementation of Industry 5.0

In discussions on the most likely scenario for the transition from Industry 4.0 to Industry 5.0, the prevailing opinion is the opinion (that we share) of the evolutionary nature of the transition [6, 40]. It seems inappropriate to consider Industry 5.0 independently of Industry 4.0. Certainly, when we set problems within emerging Industry 5.0 as a concept, a time horizon for their solution is getting significantly wider and this assumes the evolutionary approach to consideration of shared and unique traits that are typical for Industry 4.0 and Industry 5.0 respectively. There must be a natural transition between them. Consideration of this transition from the evolutionary theory point of view is still relevant as the theory aims at research of future uncertainty and states irreversibility of changes [52]. It is clear that the transition will be step-by-step.

Bonnaud and Didier [53] provides the rationale for the first stage of the evolution from the concept of Industry 4.0 to the concept of Industry 5.0. They point out to the fact that convergence of cognitive and operational technologies (and this is one of the most important components of Industry 4.0 as a concept that describes what these concepts share) makes it possible to create a fundamentally new neuro-digital meta-technology. Those authors together with other researchers [48] believe that managing cognitive production and industry on the bases of the neuro-digital meta technology is the first stage in the evolutionary transition from the concept of Industry 4.0 to the concept of Industry 5.0.

However, in the context of new geopolitical realia, there are significant adjustments to the milestones set for Russia's long-term development. Research on the conceptual framework of Industry 5.0 and opportunities for its implementation is still relevant. But the priority is now the achievement of technological sovereignty, which requires strengthening and implementation, first of all, of the potential of Industry 4.0. We are talking about the development of not only the latest, in particular, digital technologies, acceleration of institutional transformations, but also about consolidation of the human-centred and environmentally friendly economic development.

What opportunities are there in Russia in this regard? So far, Russia has introduced the coherent system to ensure accelerated digital transformation of the economy as a key direction to achieve national technological sovereignty. In terms of financial support to the IT sector, the most significant measures are preferential loans provided at a reduced rate, zero income taxes in 2022–2024 for a number of entities in the sector, large-scale grant support, establishment of industrial competence centres in key sectors of the economy, the main task of which is to substitute overseas digital solutions, as well as competence centres to develop Russian cross-system and application software. There is the intensive development of the mechanisms to protect the national digital market. They are also introducing experimental legal regimes in the field of digital innovations. Particular attention is paid to personnel training for the IT sector. To this end, in 2023–2024, there are more government-funded places for students at the universities that provide staff training for the digital economy. 115 Russian universities established "digital departments." This makes it possible for university students of other specialties to receive additional IT qualification in the period of their study [54].

Many experts claim that by the 2040s the global industry will have had such descriptors as sustainable development, and efficient energy and resource consumption [55–57]. Much more attention is paid to sustainable development and climate agenda and "ecology is becoming the economy of the 21st century" [58]. Not only actual data on the volume of emissions that pollute the environment, but also Russia's environmental sustainability rating in the Global Innovation Index confirm that the situation in Russia is much more complicated. If in terms of the innovative development level, in 2022, Russia was ranked the 47th among 132 countries in the mentioned index, then in terms of environmental sustainability it was ranked the 122nd. Moreover, serious deterioration of the situation is clear as in 2018 Russia was ranked the 95th in terms of this indicator [59].

The need to achieve resource, environmental, economic, and social efficiency of the industrial development within the framework of Industry 4.0 while at the same time observing a balance of interests between the government, business, and the society emphasizes the importance of compliance with ESG standards in each economic activity. This is also a prerequisite for successful formation of Industry 5.0. Of course, today's geopolitical realia will have a serious negative impact on the entire development of Industry 5.0 in Russia. At the same time, the most important task that the government and business face is to prevent a drastic relief in the requirements for compliance with ESG standards. Although such requirements of the countries friendly to Russia are currently significantly less strict than that set by the unfriendly ones, Russian businesses must not only maintain the levels already achieved in this field, but also must work towards further toughening of ESG standards compliance requirements. According to statements made at the Eastern Economic Forum (2023), Russia might become a leader with regard to new ESG standards among BRICS countries. The Far Eastern Centre for Artificial Intelligence, established by Sberbank of Russia and the Far Eastern Federal University, runs its own anchor ESG projects. Not only business structures, but also regional authorities are paying more attention to compliance with ESG standards. Thus, at the abovementioned forum, Sberbank of Russia signed agreements on strategic ESG cooperation with six regions of the Russian Federation.

One of the significant opportunities that makes it possible not to ignore the implementation of Industry 5.0 as a conceptual framework is the desire of the largest Russian corporations to follow the global trends related to the achievement of carbon neutrality. For example, Gazprom has approved its corporate Climate Strategy for the period until 2050 [60]. It was based on Gazprom's sustainable development scenarios for the period until 2050. The above-mentioned strategy takes into account the national goals saying that we will have achieved the balance between emissions and absorption of greenhouse gases by 2060. A positive aspect is that the company has introduced the Climate Strategy in the corporate planning system. To achieve the low-carbon development, the company's priorities are to promote the transition of transport to natural gas and further gasification in Russian regions. As of the end of 2022, gasification led to the reduction in greenhouse gas emissions by 1.446 million tons of CO2 equivalent. There is even more significant result from the transition of vehicles to the natural gas motor fuel—2.8 million tons of CO2 equivalent. An important distinctive feature in Gazprom's Climate Strategy is not only the company's commitment to participating in various climate-related initiatives aimed at its carbon footprint reduction, but also its support to research and educational projects in this field.

Without the achievement of carbon neutrality, it seems impossible to talk about the formation of Industry 5.0. In Russia, not only business structures, but also regional authorities have intensive discussions on the carbon neutrality achievement and take implementation efforts that are more or less efficient. We might consider Moscow one of the leaders in this field as in Moscow this issue is discussed and solved from different angles like greening in industrial production, energy sector, infrastructure, etc. For example, the metropolis of Moscow is consistently working on greening of public transport vehicles, in particular, on the development of electric transport [61]. Currently, more than a half of passenger rides in Moscow is done by electric transport. These efforts lead to the 5-thousand-ton reduction in pollutant emissions produced by transport in 2022 compared to 2021.

Intensified research in Russia on the development of new solutions and their implementation, primarily in the field of industry digital transformation and greening, associated with the achievement of technological sovereignty, will facilitate a wider use of the potential of Industry 4.0. However, ever-increasing variability in the environment, a speed of these changes, and attention of the world's community to Industry 5.0 challenges predetermine the need for well-timed consideration of these trends in the national economy.

The restricted use of the world's latest solutions has intensified a search for Russian solutions in the field of import phaseout and consolidated the government support to national high-tech developers. There are necessary starting conditions for such a development available in Russia. This includes available research, technological, and production facilities, certain elements of which have a serious development potential. Being rich with natural resources, the national industry might launch production of the most-in-demand metals, including rare earth ones. Increased attention to training programs for highly qualified professionals, establishment of advanced engineering schools that do not only support, but mainly develop the most in-demand competencies, will contribute into the solutions to the most important recruiting problem for the successful development of Industry 5.0. A serious form of support to Industry 5.0 in the civil industry might be the possibility of close cooperation with the enterprises that are a part of the military-industrial complex and that have broad competencies in high-tech production.

Our findings make it possible to claim that in Russia, despite the new geopolitical realia, such matter as the development of Industry 5.0 in the context of sustainability is still relevant. However, the new realia have led to significant adjustments to long-term planning benchmarks. The need for significant reduction of a planning period and the order of priority for solutions to short-term socio-economic objectives is getting more and more clear. The clear decline in dynamics of the global economic development, the wider use of long-established technical solutions in Russia, and less strict environmental standards are forming the new reality. Within its framework, as we have previously mentioned, the priority is the task to achieve national technological sovereignty, which in many respects is a guarantee of Russian national security. But the current situation, when strategic planning gives way to the manual type of management "under conditions of a narrow horizon planning" [62], is dangerous as long-term priorities of the Russian economy development are ignored. The scale of the sanctions that make the technological and economic development of Russia much more difficult, should not, to our mind, be a reason for cancelled consideration of generally significant directions of Industry 5.0 as a concept. The well-structured industrial policy with clearly stated strategic long-term developmental goals for Russia might play a significant role to reduce such a danger.

## 5 Industrial Policy as a Control Tool for Industry 5.0 Development

We believe that among the important problems, the solution of which is advisable not to be postponed for later, there is the development of the theoretical platform for Industry 5.0. Its development will make it possible in the future to offer the tools and mechanisms that encourage an interest in this matter among research and education-related communities, businesses and authorities.

The quality of the industrial policy able to launch the development of Industry 5.0 upon the development of its theoretical platform, will depend on research rational of its goals and objectives, effective implementation mechanisms, content, clear and logical sequence of procedures envisaged by an official government program document on the points that has been agreed between the government, businesses and the society and that declares Industry 5.0 priorities.

It is worth mentioning that a role of the government, in accordance with its mission, is not a compensation for market failures, but the development of the agreed national policy for main areas of technological and socio-economic development, among which the support to the development of Industry 5.0 will play an increasingly important role. It is the government who is responsible for organization of its interaction with businesses and society to draft strategic directions for such development (Industry 5.0) and their implementation in the most effective way to ensure a balance of interests of present and future generations of the Russians.

Numerous papers present various approaches to the development of theoretical foundations for the industrial policy. The paper [63] provides a rational for symbiosis of main provisions of the theories of institutional economics, long-term technical and economic development, economic synergetics as a theoretical basis for the industrial policy. Numerous authors, such as Simachev [64], Tolkachev [65],

Romanova [66, 67], Kuzmin [68], Dementyev [69], et al., deal with changing priorities in the industrial policy in the context of globalization. Tambovtsev [70] proposed the understanding of the industrial policy as a kind of art that does not require any theoretical justification. However, it seems that the industrial policy success at each stage of the national economic development largely depends on availability of its reliable theoretical platform that is a match for the given stage. Such a platform is based on the theories that have proven their viability and that have gone through some adjustments to take into account today's reality that mirror the development specifics of corresponding stages in the development of the national economy and the world economy in general.

In the context of the development of Industry 5.0, the up-to-date basis for the industrial policy theoretical platform, in our opinion, should look like the synthesis of main provisions of the theory of sustainable development, regulation theory, theory of functional economic systems, and economic synergetics. Below there are a few fragments from each of them. They explain why we need to use their basic conceptual provisions as mandatory elements in the new theoretical framework for the industrial policy to develop necessary procedures and tools to support Industry 5.0.

Theory of sustainable development. Consequences of the energy, raw-materials, and environmental crises of the 1970-ies made it possible for us to understand to the full extent that the global economic system has gone beyond tolerated limits of environmental pollution, that such going beyond means a direct threat to the further development of the Earth's civilization. The need to form the model of sustainable development was inevitable. Fundamental provisions of the new model of sustainable development, widely discussed by numerous publications, are totally consistent with the concept of Industry 5.0. To support the development of Industry 5.0 effective measures developed within the framework of the sustainable development model might be involved. It is important to emphasize that the ideology of Industry 5.0 as well as that of the model of sustainable development, is based on essential understanding of available growth thresholds in the global economic system with no limits to its development.

Regulation theory. French economists believe that the main purpose of the regulatory theory is theoretical understanding of the most important aspects in the human civilization development [71]. The regulation theory, in contrast to the neoclassical idea that assumes that an ideal company can always ensure sustainable economic dynamics, highlights that there are various ways to regulate economic systems. A special role is assigned to the government as the most important regulatory actor, which might define and consider long-term prospects for the country's development, protect positive social relations, and provide other shared services. It is difficult to overestimate the role of the government as a regulatory actor in supporting the development of Industry 5.0.

It seems that theoretical understanding of the Industry 5.0 role in economic development based on a number of provisions from the theory of regulation will contribute to consolidation of the research platform for the development of the industrial policy, first of all because it highlights major channels via which the government influences the economy. Direct government regulation is the most important of them with legislative, administrative, and redistribution activities. In the context of Russia, the government property management channel and the society influence channel seem no less important [72]. Considering comprehensive opportunities of the government influence on business and society, implementation of main ideas, advantages, and need for the Industry 5.0 development should take its place in the research basis of the industrial policy.

Theory of functional economic systems. For the purposes of this research, the possible interpretation of the theory of functional economic systems as a new research systemwide paradigm is of particular interest as it explores interaction between economy, policy, sociology, culture, ideology, etc., that is, interaction between various spheres of the society [73]. As the phenomenon of Industry 5.0 considerably assumes its interdisciplinarity, from these positions the theory of functional economic systems might become a full supplement to the new theoretical platform to develop the industrial policy as a tool to support the development of Industry 5.0. As open and self-regulating structures (that bring together various institutions and organizations), the functional economic systems that involve both hierarchical and network management principles make the entire economic system more sustainable and effective. Let us emphasize once again that functional economic systems do not only share central management centre, but also have regular relationships between constituent elements of the structure, that is, the network management principle is fully involved, which is of particular importance for the successful development of Industry 5.0.

Economic synergetics. We assume that the significance of methodological ideas (that synergetics provides and that is also interpreted as the theory of self-organization) for the development of the theoretical platform for the industrial policy largely depends on these ideas' focus on research of imbalances, development thresholds, and qualitative transitions. Economic synergetics emphasizes that the economy is full of subjective activities, which is especially important for the development of the industrial policy that implements principles of Industry 5.0. It is management and economic entities who prioritize directions and a chance for effective implementation of the industrial policy. It is important that the current stage in the social development is described as communicative and as based on the cooperation science. Therefore, it is impossible to achieve Industry 5.0 developmental goals without the co-evolutionary development of its technological base, as well as socio-cultural, ethical, psychological, and political aspirations. Within the synergetics framework, coevolution is referred to as an interactive relationship between individuals in the structure of social organizations and the human society in general. Such development, viewed by Industry 5.0 as basic, fully corresponds to synergetics logics that appear in the dialogue, in the dispute of arguments, in agreed definitions of goals for social and economy development, in a search for new connection principles between levels of economy. Coevolution synergistic principles might be involved for the purpose of efficient management. They are focused on the long-term future, in our case on Industry 5.0 development, which is almost impossible to build on the basis of the mainstream industrial policy.

We believe that a synthesis of the abovementioned theoretical provisions in the field of sustainable development, control, functional economic systems, and economic synergy might form a reliable theoretical and methodological basis to make the theoretical platform for the current industrial policy for successive step-by-step implementation of Industry 5.0 in Russia.

## 6 Conclusion

The research projects conducted have showed that in the latest conditions under which the Russian economy is functioning, unprecedented large-scale international economic sanctions are a kind of the bifurcation point, beyond which a correct choice of a preferred development vector becomes especially important. Therefore, it is necessary to implement the valid industrial policy into the macroeconomic policy, which in Russia has been traditionally reduced to fiscal and monetary policies.

To justify its implementation priorities, the imperative is to take into account the following:

- Strategic long-term development goals of Russia must fully comply with global trends in the technological and socio-cultural development, which in many ways form the basis for the development of Industry 5.0,
- Tactical goals for the near future depend on the need for further sovereignization of the Russian economy and consistent efforts to achieve industrial, structural, and technological sovereignty.

The findings confirm our hypothesis that the development of Industry 5.0 in Russia, although with a significant sanction-driven delay, will inevitably gain impetus following the implementation of the potential of Industry 4.0, achieved national technological sovereignty, establishment of international relations with the friendly states and new and more reliable technological chains.

**Acknowledgments** The article was written in accordance with the state assignment of the Ministry of Education and Science of the Russian Federation for the Institute of Economics of the Ural Branch of the Russian Academy of Science for 2024, "Methodology for assessing and forecasting the socio-economic effects of industrial transformation in industrial regions in the context of the formation of digital platform markets and industrial ecosystems", № 0327-2024-0010.

## References

1. Matyushok, V., Krasavina, V., Berezin, A., & Sendra García, J. (2021). The global economy in technological transformation conditions: A review of modern trends. *Economic Research-Ekonomska Istraživanja, 34*(1), 1471–1497. https://doi.org/10.1080/1331677X.2020.1844030
2. Alojaiman, B. (2023). Technological modernizations in the Industry 5.0 era: A descriptive analysis and future research directions. *PRO, 11*(5), 1318. https://doi.org/10.3390/pr11051318

3. Barata, J., & Kayser, I. (2023). Industry 5.0–Past, present, and near future. *Procedia Computer Science, 219*, 778–788. https://doi.org/10.1016/j.procs.2023.01.351
4. Pozzi, R., Rossi, T., & Secchi, R. (2023). Industry 4.0 technologies: Critical success factors for implementation and improvements in manufacturing companies. *Production Planning & Control, 34*(2), 139–158. https://doi.org/10.1080/09537287.2021.1891481
5. Pierli, G., Murmura, F., & Bravi, L. (2023). Digital transformation and sustainability. A systematic literature review. In V. Kumar, G. L. Kyriakopoulos, V. Akberdina, & E. Kuzmin (Eds.), *Digital transformation in industry. DTI 2022* (*Lecture notes in information systems and organization*) (Vol. 61). Springer. https://doi.org/10.1007/978-3-031-30351-7_8
6. Ghobakhloo, M., Iranmanesh, M., Tseng, M. L., Grybauskas, A., Stefanini, A., & Amran, A. (2023). Behind the definition of Industry 5.0: A systematic review of technologies, principles, components, and values. *Journal of Industrial and Production Engineering, 40*(6), 432–447. https://doi.org/10.1080/21681015.2023.2216701
7. Khan, M., Haleem, A., & Javaid, M. (2023). Changes and improvements in Industry 5.0: A strategic approach to overcome the challenges of Industry 4.0. *Green Technologies and Sustainability, 1*(2), 100020. https://doi.org/10.1016/j.grets.2023.100020
8. Maciaszczyk, M., Makieła, Z., & Miśkiewicz, R. (2023). Industry 5.0: A new reality, new challenges. In *Innovation in the digital economy* (pp. 51–61). Routledge. https://doi.org/10.4324/9781003384311-5
9. Mourtzis, D., Angelopoulos, J., & Panopoulos, N. (2022). A literature review of the challenges and opportunities of the transition from Industry 4.0 to Society 5.0. *Energies, 15*(17), 6276. https://doi.org/10.3390/en15176276
10. Afanasyev, A. A. (2022). The main directions of the formation of a limited open economy of the sovereign type. *Issues of Innovative Economics, 12*(3), 1869–1886.
11. Schwab, K. (2016). *The fourth industrial revolution*. Eksmo.
12. Babkin, A. V. (2017). *Digital economy and Industry 4.0: Problems and prospects: Proceedings of the research and practical conference with international participation*. Polytech.
13. Tarasov, I. V. (2018). Industry 4.0 technologies: Impact on increasing the productivity of industrial companies. *Strategic Decisions and Risk Management, 2*, 62–69. https://doi.org/10.17747/2078-8886-2018-2-62-69
14. Andieva, E. Y., & Filchakova, V. D. (2016). Digital economy of the future. Industry 4.0. *Applied Mathematics and Fundamental Computer Science, 3*, 214–218.
15. Javaid, M., Haleem, A., Singh, R. P., Suman, R., & Gonzalez, E. S. (2022). Understanding the adoption of Industry 4.0 technologies in improving environmental sustainability. *Sustainable Operations and Computers, 3*, 203–217. https://doi.org/10.1016/j.susoc.2022.01.008
16. Morgan, J., Halton, M., Qiao, Y., & Breslin, J. G. (2021). Industry 4.0 smart reconfigurable manufacturing machines. *Journal of Manufacturing Systems, 59*, 481–506. https://doi.org/10.1016/j.jmsy.2021.03.001
17. Hofmann, E., & Rüsch, M. (2017). Industry 4.0 and the current status as well as future prospects on logistics. *Computers in Industry, 89*, 23–34. https://doi.org/10.1016/j.compind.2017.04.002
18. Balland, P. A., & Boschma, R. (2021). Mapping the potentials of regions in Europe to contribute to new knowledge production in Industry 4.0 technologies. *Regional Studies, 55*(10–11), 1652–1666. https://doi.org/10.1080/00343404.2021.1900557
19. Czvetkó, T., Honti, G., & Abonyi, J. (2021). Regional development potentials of Industry 4.0: Open data indicators of the Industry 4.0+ model. *PLoS One, 16*(4), e0250247. https://doi.org/10.1371/journal.pone.0250247
20. MarketsandMarkets. (2023). Digital twin market size, share, industry Report, revenue trends and growth drivers. https://clck.ru/39xCFi
21. Gartner Research. (2021). *Survey analysis: IoT digital twin adoption proliferates across many sourcing options*. https://www.gartner.com/en/documents/3969712
22. Degotkova, I. (2023). Trade reduces surplus. *RBC Daily Business Newspaper, 144*(3814), 1511. https://www.rbc.ru/newspaper/2023/11/15/65532b479a79471209aab87e

23. MFD. (2024). *In 2023 Russia increased imports of machinery and equipment, exports of raw materials decreased.* https://mfd.ru/news/view/?id=2615115
24. HSE. (2023). *Technological development of production: Contribution of research organizations and universities.* https://issek.hse.ru/news/835863126.html
25. HSE. (2021). *Development of advanced production technologies in Russia.* https://issek.hse.ru/mirror/pubs/share/486647907.pdf
26. *Internet in Russia.* (2023). Design Studio RE-FORM.
27. *Information Society in the Russian Federation.* (2020). Statistical book. Rosstat; Higher School of Economics. https://rosstat.gov.ru/storage/mediabank/lqv3T0Rk/info-ob2020.pdf
28. Abdrakhmanova, G. I., Vasilkovsky, S. A., Vishnevsky, K. O., Gershman, M. A., Gokhberg, L. M., et al. (2022). *Digital transformation: Expectations and reality: Report at the 23rd Yasinsk (April) international Research Conf. On problems of economic and social development.* Publishing House of the Higher School of Economics. https://issek.hse.ru/mirror/pubs/share/603838492.pdf
29. Brunetti, F., Matt, D. T., Bonfanti, A., De Longhi, A., Pedrini, G., & Orzes, G. (2020). Digital transformation challenges: Strategies emerging from a multi-stakeholder approach. *The TQM Journal, 32*(4), 697–724. https://doi.org/10.1108/TQM-12-2019-0309
30. Gegenhuber, T., Logue, D., Hinings, C. B., & Barrett, M. (2022). Institutional perspectives on digital transformation. In *Digital transformation and institutional theory* (Vol. 83, pp. 1–32). Emerald Publishing Limited. https://doi.org/10.1108/S0733-558X20220000083001
31. Sytnyak, Y. A., & Tsvetkova, I. V. (2014). Analysis of the activities of state scientific centres of The Russian Federation. *News of the Institute of Engineering Physics, 3*(33), 85–88.
32. Klepach, A. N., Vodovatov, L. B., & Dmitrieva, E. A. (2022). Russian science and technology: Rise, or progressive lag (part I). *Problems of Forecasting, 6*(195), 76–93. https://doi.org/10.1134/S1075700722060077
33. Klepach, A. N., Vodovatov, L. B., & Dmitrieva, E. A. (2023). Russian science and technology: Rise, or progressive lag (part II). *Problems of Forecasting, 1*(196), 6–15. https://doi.org/10.1134/S1075700723010070
34. RIA Novosti. (2023). More than 1.8 billion Roubles will be allocated to Russian Research and Educational Centres. https://na.ria.ru/20230814/nauka-1889904859.html
35. Ordieres-Meré, J., Gutierrez, M., & Villalba-Díez, J. (2023). Toward the Industry 5.0 paradigm: Increasing value creation through the robust integration of humans and machines. *Computers in Industry, 150*, 103947. https://doi.org/10.1016/j.compind.2023.103947
36. Raja Santhi, A., & Muthuswamy, P. (2023). Industry 5.0 or Industry 4.0S? Introduction to Industry 4.0 and a peek into the prospective Industry 5.0 technologies. *International Journal on Interactive Design and Manufacturing (IJIDeM), 17*(2), 947–979. https://doi.org/10.1007/s12008-023-01217-8
37. Huang, S., Wang, B., Li, X., Zheng, P., Mourtzis, D., & Wang, L. (2022). Industry 5.0 and Society 5.0—Comparison, complementation and co-evolution. *Journal of Manufacturing Systems, 64*, 424–428. https://doi.org/10.1016/j.jmsy.2022.07.010
38. Maddikunta, P. K. R., Pham, Q. V., Prabadevi, B., Deepa, N., Dev, K., Gadekallu, T. R., & Liyanage, M. (2022). Industry 5.0: A survey on enabling technologies and potential applications. *Journal of Industrial Information Integration, 26*, 100257. https://doi.org/10.1016/j.jii.2021.100257
39. Xu, X., Lu, Y., Vogel-Heuser, B., & Wang, L. (2021). Industry 4.0 and Industry 5.0—Inception, conception and perception. *Journal of Manufacturing Systems, 61*, 530–535. https://doi.org/10.1016/j.jmsy.2021.10.006
40. Leng, J., Sha, W., Wang, B., Zheng, P., Zhuang, C., Liu, Q., et al. (2022). Industry 5.0: Prospect and retrospect. *Journal of Manufacturing Systems, 65*, 279–295. https://doi.org/10.1016/j.jmsy.2022.09.017
41. Pizoń, J., & Gola, A. (2023). Human–machine relationship—Perspective and future roadmap for Industry 5.0 solutions. *Machines, 11*(2), 203. https://doi.org/10.3390/machines11020203

42. Rajesh, R. (2023). Industry 5.0: Analysing the challenges in implementation using grey influence analysis. *Journal of Enterprise Information Management, 36*(5), 1349–1371. https://doi.org/10.1108/JEIM-03-2023-0121
43. Adel, A. (2022). Future of Industry 5.0 in society: Human-centric solutions, challenges and prospective research areas. *Journal of Cloud Computing, 11*(1), 40. https://doi.org/10.1186/s13677-022-00314-5
44. Akundi, A., Euresti, D., Luna, S., Ankobiah, W., Lopes, A., & Edinbarough, I. (2022). State of Industry 5.0—Analysis and identification of current research trends. *Applied System Innovations, 5*(1), 27. https://doi.org/10.3390/asi5010027
45. Borchardt, M., Pereira, G. M., Milan, G. S., Scavarda, A. R., Nogueira, E. O., & Poltosi, L. C. (2022). Industry 5.0 beyond technology: An analysis through the lens of business and operations management literature. *The Organ, 55*(4), 305–321. https://doi.org/10.2478/orga-2022-0020
46. Aveva World. (2024). https://www.avevaworld.com/
47. HSE. (2021). *Industry 5.0: Chimeras, test-tube food, symbiosis of machines and humans and "the Death of the Death."* https://issek.hse.ru/news/463657895.html
48. Babkin, A. V., Fedorov, A. A., Liberman, I. V., & Klachek, P. M. (2021). Industry 5.0: Concept, formation and development. *Industrial Economics, 14*(4), 375–395. https://doi.org/10.17073/2072-1633-2021-4-375-395
49. Fedorov, A. A., Koryagin, S. I., Liberman, I. V., Klachek, P. M., & Polupan, K. L. (2021). *Fundamentals of creating neuro-digital ecosystems. Hybrid Computational Intelligence*. IKBFU named after I. Kant.
50. Fedorov, A. A., Liberman, I. V., Koryagin, S. I., & Klachek, P. M. (2021). Technology for designing neuro-digital ecosystems to implement the Industry 5.0 concept. *Scientific and Technical Bulletins of SPbSPU. Economic Sciences, 3*, 19–39. https://doi.org/10.18721/IE.14302
51. Wheeler, M. (2021). Industry 5.0—An evolving concept. https://www.idexpert.ru/reviews/Industriya-5-0%2D%2D-razvivayushchayasya-kontseptsiya
52. Akberdina, V., Kumar, V., Kyriakopoulos, G. L., & Kuzmin, E. (2023). Editorial: What does industry's digital transition hold in the uncertainty context? In V. Kumar, G. L. Kyriakopoulos, V. Akberdina, & E. Kuzmin (Eds.), *Digital transformation in industry. DTI 2022* (*Lecture notes in information systems and organisation*) (Vol. 61). Springer. https://doi.org/10.1007/978-3-031-30351-7_1
53. Bonnaud, S., & Didier, C. *Industrie 4.0 & fabrication cognitive. Cas d'usage, patterns d'architecture*. IBM Corporation. https://www.Ibm.com/downloads/cas/N8DLLD6A
54. Ministry of Education and Science of Russia (2022). *115 Russian Universities are opening enrolment of students for "Digital Departments."* https://minobrnauki.gov.ru/press-center/news/nauka-i-obrazovanie/51479/
55. Terentyev, N. E. (2019). "Green" economy and tasks of innovative development. *Proceedings of the International Banking Institute, 3*(29), 107–130.
56. Rissman, J., Bataille, C., Masanet, E., Aden, N., Morrow, W. R., III, Zhou, N., et al. (2020). Technologies and policies to decarbonize global industry: Review and assessment of mitigation drivers through 2070. *Applied Energy, 266*, 114848. https://doi.org/10.1016/j.apenergy.2020.114848
57. Ghasemian, S., Faridzad, A., Abbaszadeh, P., Taklif, A., Ghasemi, A., & Hafezi, R. (2020). An overview of global energy scenarios by 2040: Identifying the driving forces using cross-impact analysis method. *International Journal of Environmental Science and Technology, 21*(11), 1–24. https://doi.org/10.1007/s13762-023-05220-0
58. Polyakov, L. V., Ankudinov, I. A., Egorov, V. Y., Lyatsos, A. D., & Ryzhkin, E. N. (2022). Green Russia of the future: Economic problems and political prospects. *Business. Society. Power, 46*, 87–116.
59. HSE. (2022). Global Innovation Index 2022. https://issek.hse.ru/news/777572032.html

60. Gazprom. (2023). *Gazprom Board of Directors Approved the Climate Strategy until 2050.* https://www.gazprom.ru/press/news/2023/october/article568673/
61. RBC. (2023). *Eco-friendly cleaning: How Moscow is developing municipal electric transport.* https://www.rbc.ru/technology_and_media/26/10/2023/653957749a7947721aaf57c8
62. Kadomtseva, M. E. (2023). The concept of sustainable development: The evolution of theoretical approaches and modern vision. *Alter Economics, 20*(1), 166–188. https://doi.org/10.31063/AlterEconomics/2023.20-1.9
63. Romanova, O. A., & Ponomareva, A. O. (2019). Theoretical, institutional and ethical foundations for the implementation of modern industrial policy. *Part I. Regional Economics, 15*(1), 13–28. https://doi.org/10.17059/2019-1-2
64. Simachev, Y. V., Fedyunina, A. A., & Kuzyk, M. G. (2022). Russian industrial policy in the context of transformation of the world production system and severe restrictions. *Questions of Economics, 6*, 5–25. https://doi.org/10.32609/0042-8736-2022-6-5-25
65. Tolkachev, S. A. (2018). Network industrial policy in the era of the new industrial revolution. *Journal of the New Economic Association, 3*(39), 155–161. https://doi.org/10.31737/2221-2264-2018-39-3-9
66. Romanova, O. (2019). Evolution of institutions for new industrial policy implementation. *Upravlenets / The Manager, 10*(3), 14–25. https://doi.org/10.29141/2218-5003-2019-10-3-2
67. Romanova, O. A., & Ponomareva, A. O. (2020). Multi-vector industrial policy of Russia in the conditions of the formation of a new industrial landscape. *Journal of Economic Theory, 17*(2), 276–291. https://doi.org/10.31063/2073-6517/2020.17-2.3
68. Romanova, O. A., & Kuzmin, E. (2021). Industrial policy: A new reality in the context of digital transformation of the economy. In V. Kumar, J. Rezaei, V. Akberdina, & E. Kuzmin (Eds.), *Digital transformation in industry* (*Lecture notes in information systems and organization*) (Vol. 44). Springer. https://doi.org/10.1007/978-3-030-73261-5_2
69. Dementiev, V. E. (2006). *"Catching-up post-industrialization" and industrial policy*. CEMI.
70. Tambovtsev, V. L. (2017). Industrial policy: Towards a new understanding. *News of USUE, 5*(73), 54–67. https://doi.org/10.29141/2073-1019-2017-17-5-5
71. Boyer, R. (1997). *Regulation theory: A critical analysis. Science for Society*. Russian State Humanitarian University.
72. Kleiner, G., & Petrosyan, D. (2005). Interaction of state and society in the formation of economic policy. *Society and Economy, 4*, 48–69.
73. Andrianov, V. (2005). Evolution of basic concepts of economic regulation (from the theory of mercantilism to the theory of functional economic systems). *Society and Economy, 4*, 3–47.

# Part II
# Mechanisms, Methods, and Models of Digitalization

# Theoretical Research on Sustainable Business Model Innovation Driven by Digital Technology

**Anastasia Yu. Nikitaeva and Zhaoqiang Yan**

**Abstract** The transformation of Industry 4.0 has not yet ended, and Industry 5.0 has increasingly gained in popularity. As an extension and upgrade of Industry 4.0, Industry 5.0 places a greater emphasis on people-oriented and sustainable development, aiming to achieve efficient integration and collaboration between people and advanced digital technology. Manufacturing enterprises, as the main actors in the market economy, need to introduce the Industry 5.0 idea to implement sustainable development by effectively utilizing advanced digital technology in the current dynamic and complex environment. Therefore, the article divides digital technology capabilities into four dimensions and sustainable business model innovation into five dimensions for measurement based on relevant theoretical research and practical experience. On this basis, a research framework of "digital technology capabilities – digital opportunity discovery, digital opportunity creation – sustainable business model innovation" is constructed.

**Keywords** Manufacturing enterprise · Sustainable development · Business model innovation · Digital technology capability · Industry 5.0

## 1 Introduction

### *1.1 Research Background*

With the proposal of the Industrial 5.0 concept, digital technology has become a catalyst for industrial development and a new driving force for economic growth, and also brings great competitive pressure and unprecedented challenges to enterprises' survival, especially in traditional manufacturing industry [1]. Currently, digital technologies are at the heart of many innovations of business models of enterprises [2].

---

A. Y. Nikitaeva · Z. Yan (✉)
Southern Federal University, Rostov-on-Don, Russian Federation
e-mail: aunikitaeva@sfedu.ru



A. Appolloni et al. (eds.), *The Future of Industry*, Lecture Notes in Information Systems and Organisation 70, https://doi.org/10.1007/978-3-031-66801-2_6

At the same time, sustainable development has become an important theme of theoretical research and social progress. Manufacturing enterprises possess and use a large amount of social resources, leading the main economic activities of society. Therefore, their production and operation activities will profoundly affect the development of the economy, society, and environment. Enterprises should also shoulder the responsibility of promoting sustainable social development [3]. The increasing awareness of environmental protection among consumers and various government policies also require enterprises to pay more attention to sustainable development. In response to the demand for sustainable development, manufacturing enterprises need to integrate sustainable development concepts into business model innovation activities [4].

Gaining profitability is a basic requirement for the survival and development of enterprises [5]. A well-designed sustainable business model could enable manufacturers to create additional social and environmental value on the premise of ensuring profitability [6]. By conducting sustainable business model innovation, enterprises can efficiently integrate internal and external resources, achieve higher risk adaptability and stronger core competitiveness, and meet the interests and requirements of multiple parties, which promote coordinated and sustainable development of society and the environment [7]. Therefore, how to transform traditional business models into sustainable business models has become crucial for manufacturing enterprises.

### *1.2 Research Objective*

The current research takes manufacturing enterprises in the digital economy environment as the research object. Through a certain amount of literature reading and theoretical exploration, we summarize four characteristics of digital technology capabilities and extract the sustainable business model theoretical framework that have five coupled elements. By introducing the digital opportunity theory as a mediating factor, a theoretical model of "Digital Technology - Digital Opportunity - Sustainable Business Model Innovation" was constructed. Subsequently, based on the existing research findings, the article preliminarily explores the underlying mechanisms of the interaction between digital technology capabilities, digital opportunity theory and sustainable business model innovation, and proposes a series of hypotheses on this basis. The study enriches the relevant research in the field of sustainable business models and provides a theoretical basis for empirical testing and practical production of manufacturing enterprises that use digital technology to drive innovation in sustainable business models.

## 2 Literature Review

At present, scholars have not fully reached a consensus on the definition and constituent elements of business models. Research on business model innovation has also been conducted from different perspectives. Most research on business model innovation starts from the innovation of one or more constituent elements of the business model, while few studies focus on the overall and systematic aspects of business model innovation elements. Timmer [8] first proposed that business models have systematic characteristics, so business model innovation needs to cover the entire process of enterprise business activities, including products and services, production operations, and profit distribution. Osterwalder [9] constructed a business model canvas, which includes nine constituent elements including value proposition, core resources, key business, etc. The innovation of business models can be an innovation in one of these nine elements. Zott and Amit [10] proposed that the process of business model innovation involves changes in one or more elements of the business model, including products and services, target markets, key resources, business processes, and profit models. Secondly, many studies have focused on the impact of technological innovation and enterprise resource capabilities on business model innovation. However, with the changing environment, both technology and enterprise capabilities have changed, and research on business model innovation also needs to keep up with the times. In this regard, there is currently limited empirical research on how enterprises can combine new technologies in the digital economy era and utilize their own resource capabilities to innovate business models [11].

As a topical research field in recent years, sustainable business models are constantly being enriched and improved, and have achieved certain preliminary research results. The theory of sustainable development was first established in 1987 as meeting current survival needs without compromising the survival and development of future generations. Stubbs and Cocklin [12] are researchers who have clearly defined the concept of sustainable business models. They define it as "sustainability business models" and advocate that sustainability is the core connotation of this concept. They propose that sustainable business models can construct a "triple bottom line approach" to define company goals and measure sustainable performance based on systems theory and enterprise level perspectives. Sosna et al. [13] defined sustainable business models from the perspective of factors. A sustainable new business model is a combination of transaction content, structure, and governance system that businesses can propose and create value for themselves and all stakeholders simultaneously. Porter and Kramer [14] argue that sustainable business model innovation essentially integrates a company's social responsibility strategy orientation into the business model innovation framework, actively embedding social opportunities into the company's strategic formulation and business model design while achieving economic sustainability, and creating greater social and environmental value for multiple stakeholders. Geissdorfer et al. [15] also proposed from a stakeholder perspective that sustainable business models aim to adopt proactive stakeholder management, seek business solutions that simultaneously achieve both economic and sustainable development goals, and effectively reduce the negative impact of business activities on the environment and society.

Drawing on the value related definitions of business models, this study defines sustainable business models as those that can help businesses sustainably create, transmit, and acquire. A management system that efficiently integrates internal and external resources of an enterprise based on economic, social, and environmental values. It can bring additional social and environmental benefits while helping enterprises maintain basic profitability, meet the needs of more stakeholders, and promote the sustainable development of the entire economy, society, and environment [3].

# 3 Materials and Methods

## *3.1 Bibliometric Analysis*

Considering the ongoing digital transformations of the economy, a significant number of researchers in recent years have devoted their works to the business model innovations of industrial companies due to digital technologies. An equally significant trend in the research of industrial dynamics is devoted to the sustainable development of manufacturing enterprises and industries. This is due to the fact that enterprises are forced to reinvent their business models to maintain competitiveness and survival while simultaneously facing the need to take into account the requirements of sustainable development. A significant potential for business model innovation lies in new digital technologies.

Keyword search publication in the scientometric system Lens.org allowed identifying 7139 scholarly works (Sustainable AND (Business AND (Model AND (Innovation AND (Digital AND Technology))). Narrowing the search specifically for industrial enterprises made it possible to identify 1602 Scholarly Works (Sustainable AND (Business AND (Model AND (Innovation AND (industrial AND (enterprise AND (Digital AND Technology)))))). Moreover, the dynamics of the number of scientific publications on the subject under consideration has been significantly increasing in recent years (Fig. 1).

Clustering of terms was carried out for 1000 of the publications sorted by relevance and a network map of keywords was built using the VOSviewer software (Fig. 2). The analysis of the network map made it possible to determine that the digital business model innovations of industrial enterprises are manifested in a large number of terms, and all clusters are closely interconnected. The research covers a wide range of issues in the field under study, but due to the novelty of the ongoing processes, the level of uncertainty is still high. Additional research is required to form a clear conceptual understanding of how to implement sustainable development through the innovation of business models in industrial enterprises, the driver of which is digital technology. A more in-depth content analysis of the most significant publications on the topic is needed to build the author's theoretical model, which this study is aimed at.

In this case, we are talking about the need for a more detailed and substantive consideration of each of the three components: innovation of business models; sustainable development; and the potential of digital technologies applied to manufacturing enterprises, since each industry has its own specifics.

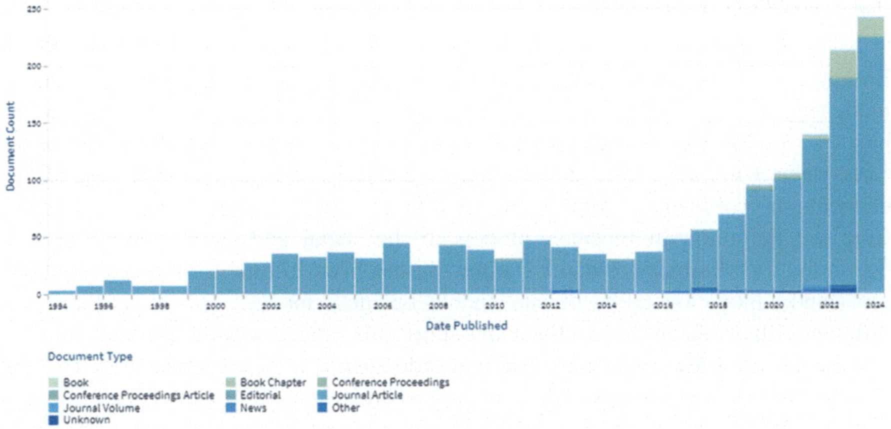


**Fig. 1** Dynamics of the number of publications on sustainable innovations of industrial enterprises' business models based on digital technologies according to Lens.org

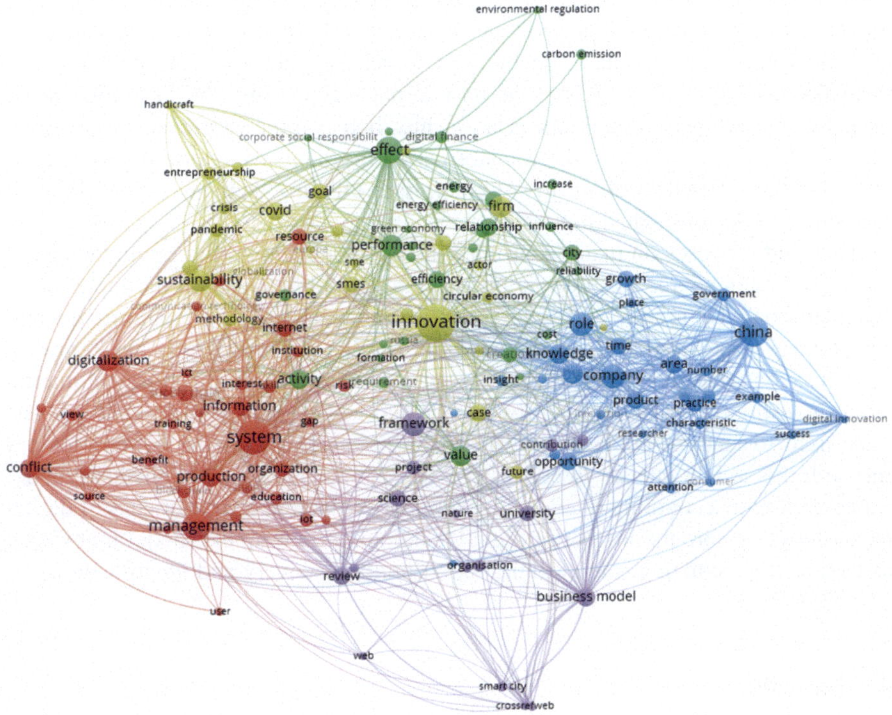


**Fig. 2** Network map of keywords of publications on sustainable business model innovations of industrial enterprises based on digital technologies. Source: developed based on data of Lens.org by using VOSviewer

### 3.2 Research Method

Based on the previous research status and results, research in the field of business model innovation is relatively rich and mature, while research on how traditional business models can be transformed into sustainable business models is still in its early stage. Currently, most definitions of sustainable business models extend the elements of "value proposition, value creation and transmission, value acquisition" from the definition of business models to the social and environmental levels. Secondly, a preliminary research framework has been formed for the development tools and innovation paths of sustainable business models. However, there are differences in research perspectives and applicable objects among different studies, and there is no consensus among scholars and experts on the constituent elements of sustainable business models. The existing research on sustainable business models mainly focuses on innovation paths, dimensions, and constituent elements, while there is relatively little research on the correlation between dimensions. Some domestic and foreign scholars have begun to study the application of digital technology in sustainable business model innovation, but current research mostly proposes the impact and application of digital technology on sustainable business models from a theoretical perspective. There is still relatively little research on how enterprises can use digital technology to achieve their own sustainable transformation and upgrading, as well as its internal mechanisms. In the future, more in-depth research is needed on the relationships between the various components of sustainable business models, the transformation mechanisms among the three benefits, and the internal mechanisms of enterprises utilizing their own capabilities to combine new technological innovation business models.

This study focuses on manufacturing enterprises in the digital economy environment. The main source of information is scientific publications on the topic under consideration. To search and select publications, the leading bibliometric and scientometric databases were used, including Scopus, ScienceDirect, and Lens.org, as well as materials directly from top scientific publishers. Methods of scientometric analysis (using the VOSviewer software), categorical analysis, and content analysis were used to analyze publications. Based on the synthesis of the hypotheses put forward, this article intends to construct a five-element sustainable business model framework with a coupling relationship, summarize the four characteristics of digital technology, explore the impact of digital technology on business model innovation as well as the mediating role of digital opportunity discovery and identification.

## 4 Results

### 4.1 Capability Dimensions of Digital Technology

Digital technology, as an enabling technology, can change the development mode of traditional industries, promote industrial upgrading and reshape the enterprise ecosystem [16]. In order to enable digital technology to innovate and develop business models more quickly and smoothly, the manuscript combines the existing research analysis of Yoo et al. and Otio et al. to summarize the four capability dimensions presented in the process of digital technology application [17], that is: evolutionary capability, integration capability, united capability, and empowerment capability.

Firstly, digital technology has the ability to evolve and integrate. Evolutionary capability refers to the dynamic and reshaping nature of digital technology, which can add new features after the product is completed, such as the iterative innovation of apps. Integration capability means the combination between digital technology and traditional products, such as embedding digital technology into automobiles and home appliances, in order to break industry boundaries and achieve cross industry integration. Secondly, the united capability of digital technology mainly includes two aspects: openness and transfer ability. Big data platform technologies enable suppliers, users, and competitors to participate more efficiently in the innovation process. Enterprises innovation place a greater emphasis on the concepts of multi-agent cooperation and ecology. In addition, on the basis of highly interconnected and collaborative internal networks, the level of information sharing and production collaboration among various business entities has been greatly improved. Thirdly, the empowerment of digital technology is mainly reflected in the collection, summary, and analysis of various types of data, which greatly improves the ability of collecting and processing information as well as provides reference basis for management decision-making and strategic planning.

The combination of digital technology and traditional manufacturing has effectively boosted the work efficiency of enterprises, creating more customer value and enterprise value. Combining the characteristics of digital technology and effectively applying it to every link of business model innovation will help enterprises better realize and implement digital transformation and sustainable development.

## *4.2 Elements of a Sustainable Business Model*

In recent years, many scholars have conducted research based on the paradigm constructed by Boons and Lüdeke-Freund [18], which has good effectiveness and achievement. Therefore, drawing on the research results proposed by Teece [19] and Richardson [20], this article ultimately constructs a sustainable business model framework that consists of five coupled elements, that is: sustainable value proposition, sustainable value creation, sustainable value network, sustainable financial model, and sustainable customer interface.

**Sustainable Value Proposition** For manufacturing enterprises, having their own unique value proposition and focusing on more precise target customers and markets can effectively maintain their core competition and continuously improve economic profits, which could gather and incorporate more stakeholders into the scope of their value proposition.

**Sustainable Value Creation** Sustainable value creation activities require manufacturing enterprises to consider how to meet social and environmental benefits through the rational allocation of core resources and the effective integration of key business processes. At the same time, they also need to guide the collaborative efforts of stakeholders to create social and environmental value.

**Sustainable Value Network** Manufacturing enterprises should incorporate collaborative partners into effective sustainable value network management, and simultaneously achieve the goals and requirements of sustainable development. A sustainable value network requires the entire industry and industry chain to work together to form a cooperative team of promoting synergetic development of economy, society and environment.

**Sustainable Financial Model** A scientific and reasonable sustainable financial model can not only enable manufacturing enterprises to more efficiently integrate resources and capabilities across the entire value network, but also bring positive social and environmental benefits. In addition, enterprises should also consider how to stimulate customers' awareness of social and environmental responsibility, and transform it into meeting customers' environmental and social needs.

**Sustainable Customer Interface** Sustainable customer interfaces should not only have the practicality, convenience and affinity of ordinary customer interfaces, but also fully reflect the sustainable management and development philosophy of enterprises as well as stimulate consumers' awareness of environmental protection and social services. In recent years, products or services that are non-profit and environmentally friendly are often more likely to attract consumers' interest and favor.

## *4.3 Theoretical Analysis on Sustainable Business Model Innovation Driven by Digital Technology*

### Evolutionary Capability and Sustainable Business Model Innovation

Program code itself can be reprogrammed, which endows digital technology with the characteristics of continuous improvement and evolution [21]. The evolutionary ability of digital technology is mainly reflected in its dynamism and plasticity, that is, it can continuously add new functions and attributes to products. This characteristic of digital technology can quickly obtain users' feedback after the release of new products and make the interaction between enterprises and users closer.

In addition, manufacturing enterprises can provide intelligent, personalized, and customized products and services relying on a large amount of customer feedback and real-time interaction, promote innovation at the level of enterprise value proposition and customer interface and make them better serve each other, and obtain more economic and customer value for the enterprise. In summary, this article hypothesizes that:

H1a: The evolutionary capability of digital technology has a positive impact on sustainable value proposition innovation.
H1b: The evolutionary power of digital technology has a positive impact on sustainable customer interface innovation.

### Integration Capability and Sustainable Business Model Innovation

Digital technology has increased the scalability of the existing enterprise technologies [22]. Manufacturers can use digital technology to redefine the available technological paradigms and integrate current technology types through adopting various digital infrastructure and platforms. For example, the emergence of smart home appliances and industrial internet platforms is the expansion and innovation of digital technology on the existing technology of enterprises.

Based on the current industry development trend, manufacturing enterprises can break the constraints of traditional value network systems, integrate and create unprecedented new value networks. It can also use digital technology to break the traditional business models and the existing industry boundaries, incorporate stakeholders from other industries into their own value network, and design solutions that satisfy customers' diversified requirements through cross industry integration. This not only enhances the adaptability to the external market environment, but also effectively reduces the company's own costs and changes the cost structure, thereby further improving the profit model and playing a decisive role in improving the innovation ability of the company's business model [7]. In summary, this article proposes that:

H2a: The integration ability of digital technology has a positive impact on sustainable value proposition innovation.
H2b: The integration ability of digital technology has a positive impact on sustainable value network innovation.
H2c: The integration ability of digital technology has a positive impact on sustainable financial model innovation.

### United Capability and Sustainable Business Model Innovation

Due to the emergence of digital platforms, business model innovation has become a collective behavior, and the innovation subject is no longer single, but has the characteristics of decentralization and diversification. Suppliers, customers, and even competitors can participate more efficiently in the innovation process. This feature can significantly reduce the cost of information search and sharing [23], making information, resource sharing, and cooperation among all parties more efficient.

At the same time, based on the optimization of resource allocation on digital platforms, the level of information sharing and operational collaboration among various innovative entities has been significantly enhanced, and the relationship network between enterprises and partners has been continuously strengthened, gradually forming a highly collaborative value co-creation system centered on the enterprise itself or digital platforms. This to some extent also reduces the costs of enterprise business processes and enhances the space and ability of enterprises to create value.

Furthermore, customer value can also be directly or indirectly transmitted to other partners or stakeholders, helping them unify customer interface design concepts and ideas, jointly develop and optimize customer interfaces, and provide customers with more targeted products and services [24]. In summary, we hypothesize that:

H3a: The united capability of digital technology has a positive impact on sustainable value creation innovation.
H3b: The united capability of digital technology has a positive impact on sustainable value network innovation.
H3c: The united capability of digital technology has a positive impact on sustainable financial model innovation.
H3d: The united capability of digital technology has a positive impact on sustainable customer interface innovation.

### Empowerment Capability and Sustainable Business Model Innovation

Entering the Industrial 5.0 era, manufacturing enterprises need the support of relevant big data in various aspects such as strategic formulation, strategic decision-making, operational management, and product sales. The empowerment capability of digital technology is mainly reflected in its ability to improve the extensive collection and efficient analysis of information and data by enterprises, thereby helping them make strategic and business decisions, achieving efficient communication and coordination among various stakeholders and provide enterprises with a wide range of resource sharing opportunities and value network governance capabilities. The introduction and embedding of digital technology in the production and manufacturing process supports enterprises in achieving a balance between customized and large-scale production, promoting precise production, and reducing product backlog. This greatly improves the production efficiency and resource utilization and improves the controllability and connectivity of the production process [25]. In summary, this article proposes that:

H4a: The empowerment capability of digital technology has a positive impact on sustainable value creation innovation.
H4b: The empowerment capability of digital technology has a positive impact on sustainable value network innovation.
H4c: The empowerment capability of digital technology has a positive impact on sustainable customer interface innovation.

### The Mediating Role of Digital Opportunity Discovery Between Digital Capability Dimensions and Sustainable Business Model Innovation

Manufacturing enterprises with strong digital capabilities can focus more on the application and development of digital technology, better grasp digital opportunities in the market and identify the ecological and social benefits of the existing products and services [26]. That is to say, digital capabilities are discovered through digital opportunities to make influence on sustainable business model innovation.

Specifically, manufacturing enterprises can use digital opportunities to discover and acquire new knowledge, cultivate new products, enhance their innovation and adaptation capabilities, and help them better and faster seize opportunities and achieve value creation, transmission, and acquisition, promoting business model innovation. Besides, digital capabilities can improve the efficiency of information search and enable manufacturing enterprises to guide resource reconstruction and optimization based on discovered digital opportunities [27]. In summary, we propose that:

H5: The dimension of digital ability has a positive impact on digital opportunity discovery.

H6: Digital opportunity discovery has a positive impact on sustainable business model innovation.

H7: Digital opportunity discovery plays a mediating role between the dimension of digital capabilities and sustainable business model innovation.

### The Mediating Role of Digital Opportunity Creation Between Digital Capability and Sustainable Business Model Innovation

Industry 5.0 requires companies to be good at taking the initiative to create digital opportunities and trigger disruptive changes through the use of new technologies, raw materials, and knowledge, thereby driving enterprise development. This proactive process of matching opportunities, resources, and environment promotes the creation of new value, thereby triggering business model innovation. That is to say, digital capabilities can influence a company's business model innovation through the process of creating digital opportunities.

Firstly, digital capabilities could enhance deep interaction between enterprises, stakeholders, and customers, thereby promoting the process of creating digital opportunities [28]. Secondly, the process of creating digital opportunities emphasizes cooperation and communication between enterprises and various economic activity entities through, which helps the better understand existing achievements and development directions in market preferences, thereby providing guidance for the design and implementation of business models. Finally, digital opportunities creation will build a value network that can enable enterprises to collaborate with different entrepreneurial entities. This process also continuously adjusts the enterprise's own value creation model and value proposition, enabling them to better adapt to the entire value creation network, thereby achieving business model innovation. In summary, out hypotheses are:

H8: The digital capability dimension has a positive impact on digital opportunity creation.
H9: Digital opportunity creation has a positive impact on sustainable business model innovation.
H10: Digital opportunity creation plays a mediating role between the dimension of digital capabilities and sustainable business model innovation.

#### The Continuous Mediation Role of Digital Opportunity Discovery and Creation Between Digital Capability Dimension and Sustainable Business Model Innovation

In the dynamic development of enterprises, opportunity discovery will gradually shift towards opportunity creation, and opportunity discovery can promote and enhance the creation of new opportunities.

Firstly, in order to survive and develop, manufacturing enterprises need to re-pick-up and redistribute digital or non-digital resources and generate new ways of utilizing opportunities, namely digital opportunity creation. Secondly, based on the results of digital opportunity discovery, manufacturing companies need to re-examine whether the value of the existing resources matches market demand. This enables them to better clarify the value, scope of use, and conversion costs of the existing resources and have the potential to become part of multiple value paths simultaneously, thereby enhancing the effectiveness of digital opportunity creation as well as promoting their innovative business models. In summary, this article proposes:

H11: Digital opportunity discovery has a positive impact on digital opportunity creation.
H12: Digital opportunity discovery and creation play a continuous mediating role between the digital capability dimension and sustainable business model innovation.

### 4.4 Integrated Research Model for Sustainable Business Model Innovation Driven by Digital Technology

Based on the previous explanation and summary of the relationships between various elements and variables, we divide digital technology capabilities into four dimensions and sustainable business models innovation into five dimensions for measurement based on relevant theoretical research and practical experience. On this basis, a research framework of "digital technology capabilities - digital opportunity

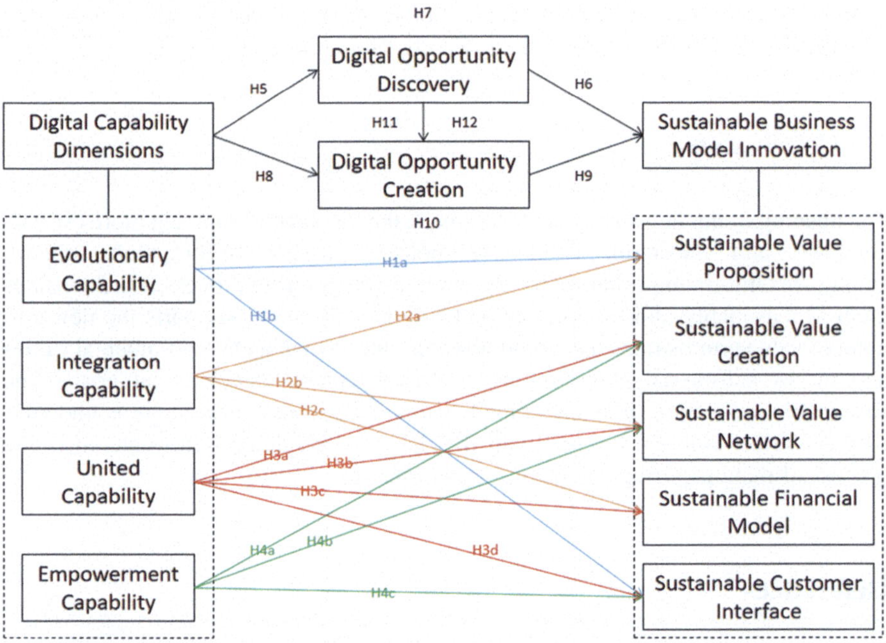


**Fig. 3** Theoretical research model for sustainable business model innovation driven by digital technology

discovery, digital opportunity creation - sustainable business model innovation" is constructed, as shown in Fig. 3.

## 5 Discussion

This article explores the mechanism of digital technology driving sustainable business model innovation and constructs a preliminary theoretical research model. However, there are also some shortcomings. The following suggestions for future research directions are proposed:

1. This study focuses on manufacturing enterprises as the research object, and the conclusions and suggestions obtained are only more applicable to manufacturers.
2. On the basis of studying the existing literature, the theoretical model proposed in the article is a cycle of hypotheses and still needs further empirical research. It is necessary to introduce some moderating variables and analyze the coupling mechanism between various elements to further improve the model.
3. We propose a sustainable business model framework composed of five elements with coupling relationships, but this article only uses qualitative methods to analyze the impact of coupling relationships between sustainable business

model elements on sustainable value. Future work can deepen research through quantitative methods to make the research results more convincing.

## 6 Conclusion

The opening of the Industrial 5.0 era has made the market environment more diverse, complex, and uncertain. Digital technology provides information support, strengthens information sharing for the entire manufacturing process, which enables them to reasonably allocate internal and external resources, supports the development of value propositions that integrate economic, social, and environmental values and makes substantial contributions to the sustainable development goals. The sustainable innovation of business models driven by digital technology is undoubtedly a feasible solution to cope with the risks and challenges encountered in the process of manufacturing enterprises transformation.

## References

1. Cheng, Y., & Sun, J. (2013). Theoretical model of business models: Elements and their relationships. *Journal of China's Industrial Economy, 1*, 143–155.
2. Wu, Y., & Du, M. (2019). Business model innovation: Research review and prospects. *Journal of Business Economics Research, 767*(04), 103–106.
3. Zhu, M., & Lin, Z. (2015). Conceptualization and research prospects of sustainable business models. *Journal of Shanghai University of International Business and Economics, 22*(02), 39–48.
4. Jin, L. (2019). *Research on sustainability oriented business models*. East China Normal University.
5. Hou, S., & Jin, L. (2019). Research on sustainability oriented business model innovation. *Journal of Xuzhou University of Engineering, 34*(04), 43–50.
6. Schaltegger, S. (2011). Sustainable entrepreneurship and sustainability innovation: Categories and interactions. *Business Strategy and the Environment, 20*(4), 222–237.
7. Sun, X. (2018). The impact of the internet environment on enterprise business model innovation. *Economic Research Guide, 22*, 10–17.
8. Timmers, P. (1998). Business model for electronic markets. *Electron Markets, 8*(2), 3–8.
9. Osterwalder, A., & Pigneur, Y. (2005). Clarifying business models: Origins, present, and future of the concept. *Communications of the Association for Information Systems, 15*(5), 1–25. https://doi.org/10.17705/1cais.01601
10. Zott, C., & Amit, R. (2010). Designing your future business model: An activity system perspective. *Long Range Planning, 43*(3), 216–226.
11. Wu, Y., & Du, M. (2019). Business model innovation: Research review and prospects. *Business Economics Research, 767*(04), 103–106.
12. Stubbs, W., & Cocklin, C. (2008). Conceptualizing a "sustainability business model". *Organization & Environment, 21*(2), 103–127. https://doi.org/10.1177/1086026608318042
13. Sosna, M., Trevinyo-Rodriguez, R. N., & Velamuri, S. R. (2010). Business model innovation through trial-and-error learning: The Naturhouse case. *Long Range Planning, 43*(2–3), 383–407. https://doi.org/10.1016/j.lrp.2010.02.003

14. Porter, M. E., & Kramer, M. R. (2011). The big idea: Creating shared value. *CFA Digest, 42*(1), 12–13. https://doi.org/10.2469/dig.v41.n1.28
15. Geissdoerfer, M., Vladimirova, D., & Evans, S. (2018). Sustainable business model innovation: A review. *Journal of Cleaner Production, 198*, 401–416. https://doi.org/10.1016/j.jclepro.2018.06.240
16. Teece, D. J. (2018). Profiting from innovation in the digital economy: Enabling technologies, standards, and licensing models in the wireless world. *Research Policy, 47*(8), 1367–1387. https://doi.org/10.1016/j.respol.2017.01.015
17. Yoo, Y., Boland, J. R. J., & Lyytinen, K. (2012). Organizing for innovation in the digitized world. *Organization Science, 23*(5), 1398–1408. https://doi.org/10.1287/orsc.1120.0771
18. Boons, F., & Lüdeke-Freund, F. (2013). Business models for sustainable innovation: State-of-the-art and steps towards a research agenda. *Journal of Cleaner Production, 45*, 9–19. https://doi.org/10.1016/j.jclepro.2012.07.007
19. Teece, D. J. (2009). Business models, business strategy and innovation. *Long Range Planning, 43*(2–3), 172–194.
20. Richardson, J. (2008). The business model: An integrative framework for strategy execution. *Strategic Change, 17*(5–6), 133–144.
21. Autio, E., Nambisan, S., & Thomas, L. D. W. (2018). Digital affordances, spatial affordances, and the genesis of entrepreneurial ecosystem. *Strategic Entrepreneurship Journal, 12*(1), 72–95. https://doi.org/10.1002/sej.1266
22. Adner, R., & Kapoor, R. (2015). Innovation ecosystems and the pace of substitution: Re-examining technology S. *Strategic Management Journal, 37*(4), 625–648. https://doi.org/10.1002/smj.2363
23. Felin, T., & Zenger, T. R. (2014). Closed or open innovation? Problem solving and the governance choice. *Research Policy, 43*(5), 914–925. https://doi.org/10.1016/j.respol.2013.09.006
24. Wang, Y. (2013). Research on business model innovation in the era of big data. *Journal of Nanjing University of Finance and Economics, 6*, 47–51.
25. Zhang, F., & Tao, J. (2016). Research on the relationship between internal element collaboration and innovation performance of enterprises. *Research Management, 37*(2).
26. Cai, L., Yang, Y., & Lu, S. (2019). Review and outlook on the impact of digital technology on entrepreneurship activities. *Academic Research, 37*(10), 1816–1824.
27. Peng, X., Cai, L., Chen, J., & Yu, H. (2016). From opportunity discovery to opportunity creation: Strategic choices for entrepreneurship enterprises select. *Journal of Management, 13*(9), 1312–1320.
28. Nambisan, S. (2017). Digital entryship: Forward a digital technology perspective of entryship. *Entrepreneurship Theory and Practice, 41*(6), 1029–1055.

# Economic Passionarity: Formation Peculiarities in the Digital Age

**Oksana Butorina and Yulia Karpovich**

**Abstract** The paper substantiates the relevance of passionarity research in the economic aspect. Based on the allocation of its socio-cultural peculiarities, its main characteristics are determined depending on the level of economic development. Digital transformation has become the basis for the formation of intellectual and informational passion that acts as a driver taking on large technological, production, and investment risks to achieve their goals mainly associated with personal success and/or public recognition. The results of a comparison of methods for analyzing economic passionarity made it possible to identify the existing limitations. Taking them into account, methodological provisions were developed for systematizing indicators for the quantitative assessment of economic passionarity in the conditions of the transition to a digital economy: (1) the presence of a close relationship between the processes of formation of economic passionarity and technological transformations; (2) the priority of scientists, their close relationship with business elites and representatives of government bodies; (3) recognition of the high level of importance of economic passionaries in the progressive dynamics of development of economic systems at different levels; (4) the study of cause-and-effect dependencies between the existing conditions for the formation of economic passionarity, its quantity, as well as the resulting influence on economic processes; (5) the focus on the existing features of the statistical base presented in statistical yearbooks. These methodological provisions became the basis for systematizing indicators for a comprehensive analysis of the dynamics of economic passionarity in the context of the transition to a digital economy.

**Keywords** Passionarity · Passionaries · Economic passionarity · Methods for assessing economic passionarity

---

O. Butorina · Y. Karpovich (✉)
Perm National Research Polytechnic University, Perm, Russian Federation



A. Appolloni et al. (eds.), *The Future of Industry*, Lecture Notes in Information Systems and Organisation 70, https://doi.org/10.1007/978-3-031-66801-2_7

# 1 Introduction

In modern conditions that are viewed as a crisis of civilization by sociologists, as an unprecedented structural crisis by economists, and as a period of changing historical eras by historians and social scientists, there is a significant increase in the interest in passionarity as a factor that determines the past, current and subsequent development of social processes.

The most common interpretations of passionarity presented in the literature, as well as descriptions of its relationships with social processes in general and socio-economic ones in particular at the present stage of social transformation actualize research into the characteristics of economic passionarity and its influence on subsequent progressive development.

In the published studies, passionarity is predominantly characterized as a cultural and social phenomenon; its significance in predetermining the historical development of individual ethnic groups and nations is considered.

The transformation processes associated with the transition to the digital economy have updated the study of various types of passionarity and their impact on social development. Currently, the emerging and aggravating contradictions in economic development, the growing need to modernize the economy, to increase its innovativeness as we see it underlie the formation of a "new"—passionate—group of people who have energy redundancy and are able to act as a driving force in ensuring the future progressive development of both the economy and the entire society.

The study of the relationship between the formation and development of "new passionaries" with objective technological transformations of the modern stage can be considered as the basis for identifying a new vector of research within the technological approach. It seems that this approach will allow identifying the distinctive features of economic passionarity and its components amid the transition to the digital economy, as well as the significance of each component in the context of technological and business transformations.

Thus, the purpose of this work is to identify the peculiarities of economic passionarity and its specifics in the conditions of the formation of the digital age.

This purpose defined the structure of the article. Section 1 highlights the distinctive features of economic passionarity. Section 2 compares the methods of its assessment and discusses the limitations of their use for analyzing the processes of its formation and development. Finally, Sect. 3 outlines the conceptual foundations of systematization of indicators reflecting their level of development of economic passionarity during the transition to the digital economy.

## 2 Research Methods

Analysis and systematization of literary data on problems of passionarity and observation of the research results obtained by other scientists were the theoretical methods used in the given study. The choice of this methodology is due to the fact that it is focused on the correlation of passionarity with cultural and social features of the society, which determines peculiarities of its economic behavior. The results of a comparison of methods for analyzing economic passionarity made it possible to identify the existing limitations. These methodological provisions are supposed to become the basis for systematizing indicators for a comprehensive analysis of the dynamics of economic passionarity in the context of the transition to a digital economy. The assumption of the study is that stimulation of the economic passionarity development pushes the technical progress forward and eliminates its technical limits. Some limitations of the current research are the consequences of participants lacking knowledge of economic relations, which breaks down the evolution of passionarity in the society.

Based on the review of the results of scientific research on methods for analyzing political, economic and intellectual elites in relation to economic passionarity, we believe it necessary to note the following:

- The predominance of meritocratic, technocratic and communicative approaches to quantitative assessment, which focus primarily on a differentiated analysis of economic and intellectual elites, which requires their subsequent adaptation in relation to the previously identified distinctive features of economic passionarity;
- Lack of clear boundaries for specifying signs of belonging to political, economic, and intellectual elite groups;
- Limited research into the effectiveness of the activities of political, economic, and intellectual elites from the position of the progressive and sustainable development of economic systems at different levels (the country, its regions, specific enterprises);
- The absence of a single characteristic that determines whether individuals or groups of individuals belong to political, economic, and intellectual elites in the conditions of technological transformations;
- The presence of a functional relationship between intellectual and economic elites, ensuring the progressive development of the national economy;
- Limited information sources for analyzing processes related to the identity of elites in the development of the national economy, which are based on sociological surveys conducted by scientific communities, as well as ratings of the leading analytical agencies.

# 3 Background

## *3.1 Passionarity as a Cultural and Social Phenomenon*

Despite almost a century of research, there is still no clear definition of passionarity. Thus, Kravchenko [1] defines passionarity as "... mainly a biological feature of an ethnic group... as a collective subject of history and an agent of group socialization". Focusing on the biosocial nature of passionarity, Shvachko and Duranov [2] define it as " ... excessive biochemical energy of living matter providing the ability to super-stress both an individual and an ethnic group as a whole, and its associations...". Lobankova [3] believes that passionarity is a biosocial phenomenon that accumulates the potential of human behavior at the collective and individual levels, the desire to change the environment, the effect of the geobiochemical energy of the biosphere living substance at the level of an ethnic group, the desire for a goal they risk their lives for, and the impulse of the subconscious nervous activity, the opposite of the instinct of self-preservation". Savelyeva and Maslova [4] support the concept of passionarity as a specific genetic allele, a set of traits encoded in DNA and transmitted in a hereditary way. Dawkins [5], when contrasting the altruism gene (a passionate behavior model) and the egoism gene (the opposite is a subpassional behavior model), comes to the conclusion that all eusocial behaviors are characterized by not altruism, but 'reasonable egoism' as "... a justified exclusive desire of animals to spread their genome, which implies sacrificing something, including self-sacrifice, to save a genetically close and reproductively active individual". In this regard, the reflections of Kraeva and Pestretsov [6] on the influence of passionarity on the formation of a national community are very interesting. Contrasting the Eastern and Western communities, based on the theory of passionarity, they justify the ruinous priority of the principle of personal gain proclaimed as the highest form of human freedom and the welfare of society. Sergeev and Kulesh [7] and Atambaev [8] reduce the essence of passionarity to energy excess, which forms in certain people the ability to actively influence the behavior and mental state of people, the ability to impose their own rules of behavior on others, to force them to excessive activity, generating a passion field characterized by tension.

The phenomenon of passionarity as a socio-economic phenomenon determines the subsequent social development and can be found in the works of Mukulov [9], who considers it as "... a socio-historical phenomenon characterized by a large number of passionate personalities emerging in a very limited space". According to Sedova [10], they display a "passionate" type of perception of the world, which in modern conditions makes them the social group capable of supporting social optimism and attitudes towards development in society, promote and disseminate life planning practices, demonstrate implementation of these plans even in times of crisis. As noted by Sergeev and Kulesh [7], it is the economic nature that underlies the internationalization of culture, the priority of interstate standardization of education and unification of international language communication on the English-language basis, the emergence and strengthening of planned labor and uncontrolled non-labor migration of the population leading to the mixing of ethnic communities, the totality of which can be considered as initial manifestations of a single-mentality humanity and on its basis the global hyperethnic system. The authors point out that these socio-cultural processes are based on the rapid development of transnational corporations, the flourishing of a common market internationalizing the economic life of the planet, the emergence of a single global information space through the development of information technologies, the spread of the World Wide Web, telecommunications networks, satellite television, fast-evolving international transport communications, and the strengthening of uneven socio-economic development of states and the formation of the "hunger belt". These factors taken into account in the process of social development of individual states, groups of states and the world increase the relevance of identifying the relationships between the passionarity of socio-cultural development and economic processes.

Mukulov [9], having compared the historical aspects of the formation and development of the main ethnic groups, established a direct dependence between a strong economy and society's passionarity, while emphasizing that passionarity is less noticeable in the economy than in revolutionary actions, wars and conquests. At the same time, the author believes that a high level of passionarity implies the purposefulness of all the life efforts of an individual, which can ultimately affect the environment as a whole, and the national economy development in particular.

Dymchenko [11] notes that historical evolution largely depends on changes in productive forces and production relations as a consequence of the organization of society. At the same time, passionarity in the course of the historical process allows considering short causal sequences which are regular at their own level, but random for processes of the highest rank.

The most common interpretations of passionarity presented above, as well as its interrelations with social and socio-economic processes at the present stage of society transformation make it especially relevant to examine the special features of economic passionarity and its impact on the subsequent progressive development.

## 3.2 *Economic Passionarity*

The formation and promotion of a nation's passion is known to be spontaneous. At the same time, the presence of an ethnic dominant, which organizes the development of passionarity, is not denied [12]. Kravchenko [1] identifies the political elite and the economic elite as the ethnic dominant. Thus, we can assume that among numerous types of passionarity, the most distinguished ones are political, economic, and mixed (political-economic and/or economic-political, depending on the element prevailing in social development—either economics or politics).

Economic passionarity (the economic elite) is obviously characterized by general signs of individual passionarity highlighted by Lev Gumilev [13]. Among them, we consider it appropriate to outline the following characteristics, which are more pronounced in the economic sphere:

- Activity of individuals of the group aimed at changing the environment, disrupting the aggregate state of the environment;
- The priority of high goals that they are ready to spend their lives on;
- Continuous activity of individuals and/or groups of individuals aimed at changing the established traditions, customs, and norms;
- Latent energy in the form of a passion impulse affecting others and forming their passionarity-imitating behavior;
- The ability of an individual to break the inertia of the social system's given movement;
- The impossibility for the bearer of passionarity to objectively assess the consequences of their actions for themselves, their family and loved ones, the people, the country, and the world.

At the same time, identifying the peculiarities of economic passionarity can be based on revealing the distinctive features of the energy surplus manifestation in different economic epochs (or systems based on dominant technologies and production methods). This approach is possible due to the findings by Atambayev [8], who, referring to the research by Kondratiev and Zhuglyar, proves the possibility of comparing the cycles of socio-cultural changes and social upheavals (the passion cycle) with cyclical changes in technologies that determine the dominant way of management and, as a consequence, the essence of the economic system.

The analysis of the main forms of economic passionarity in relation to the level of technological development shows that [14]:

- There is a relationship between the passionarity of society, economic passionarity and the specific features of economic systems development;
- The emergence of economic passionaries is based on objective processes of economic development, the exhaustion of opportunities for enhancing the efficiency of the economy as a whole and production in particular, as well as growing return on capital most often manifested in systemic economic crises;
- Economic passionaries play the role of a driving force taking on greater technological, production, and investment risks than all other members of society. It is them who unwinds the spiral of a new (subsequent) economic system in the context of the previous one still functioning;
- The speed of unwinding the spiral is determined by the extent to which society members are involved in the passion field being formed and their receptivity to innovations implemented by passionaries;
- At each stage of development, the emerging economic elite represented by passionaries creates comfortable conditions for the implementation of their goals, which are mainly associated with personal success and/or public recognition;
- Public recognition of the transformational significance predetermines a set of effects: first of all, those of a technological nature associated with the scientific and technological advances introduced to both production and the life of each subject, which forms the basis for capacity building;

- In the period of the post-industrial economic system being formed, in accordance with the need to overcome objective economic contradictions, creators, innovators, intellectuals (the intellectual and information elite) can be considered as passionaries, whose aspirations can largely determine the development vector of modern society, the country's economy, as well as the gradual transformation of sociological processes and the transition to a new system of social values;
- The exclusive role of passionaries in socio-economic development associated with their ability to take on technological, production, investment risks, as well as the presence and implementation of their own intellectual capital, which can be considered as a justification for their elitism.

Thus, economic passionarity is a type of passionarity in which a group of people translates its intellectual efforts to ensure the development of the transformational potential of the country's economy, while taking on technological, production and investments risks, and ultimately shaping the technological, economic, social and cultural effects of social development.

In accordance with the identified distinctive features, the concept of economic passionarity can be further specified in terms of its functions performed by political and economic elites discussed in the literature with the subsequent adaptation to the peculiarities of economic passionarity. Among the fundamental ones, we have identified the following [14]:

- Strategic function, which consists in forming ideology, concepts, doctrines, and programs for the development of society through generating new ideas that reflect its needs and affect its intellectual and cultural potential;
- Management function, in which management consists in regulating the processes of adaptation of subjects to innovative changes in socio-economic and ethical-cultural systems;
- Integrative function, which involves overcoming contradictions and disagreements between social groups and subjects based on common values and ideals formulated by the elite;
- Communicative function forming conditions and means for effective social, professional and cross-cultural communications in time and space aimed at harmonizing and stabilizing the processes unfolding in society;
- Axiological (value-normative) function associated with the ability to generate a stable scale of values according to the challenges of the time, ensuring the value-normative stability of society;
- Innovative function based on the creation of intellectual products and innovative technologies forming the value motivation of subjects of innovative activity and determining the behavior of consumers of innovative products in modern dynamically developing societies;
- Stabilization function, which involves balancing the cultural heritage and innovative development aimed at harmonizing them and forming a single vector of intellectual development.

Recognizing the importance of the selected functions, we consider the innovative function to be the essential one for each of them. It determines the general vector of development of society by generating new ideas (strategic function), creating effective social, professional and cross-cultural communications in time and space (communicative function), generating a stable scale of values (axiological function) for adapting social actors to innovative changes in the social system (managerial function), overcoming intergroup contradictions and disagreements between social groups and subjects (integrative function) and harmonizing the cultural heritage and the revolutionary achievements of the present and future (stabilization function).

## 4 Results

Today, amid a new format of public life being formed, which is based on highly developed information technologies and open access to information, a new social community is emerging that is the carrier of economic passionarity. They are the bearers of knowledge about production processes and mechanisms of social progress. Traditionally, such terms as "technocrats" (Touraine), "intellectual workers" (Mahlup), "meritocrats" (Bell), "experts" (Castells), intellectual elite (Markov, Aksenov), "cultural bourgeoisie" were used to define a new social community (Gouldner) [15].

The analysis of these terms allowed us to identify the criteria of economic passionarity during the transition to the digital economy:

- Meritocratic (traditional cultural and educational) criterion: the most capable representatives of various strata who meet the highest standards of the ongoing processes of intellectualization of economic development can be considered as economic passionaries in the digital era (Burnham) [16];
- Priority of qualification, professional experience and knowledge (Burnham) [16], as well as outstanding communication skills, high level of mobility and adaptability (Schiller) [17];
- Ability and readiness to implement economic and political management in society (Burnham) [16];
- High intellectual potential and the ability to create new knowledge (Bell), while the freedom of creativity is considered as a conscious necessity (Marcuse), as well as the basis of well-being (which becomes the basis for a new type of knowledge capital [18]);
- Creativity as the ability to produce new forms can be considered as individual capital aimed at commercializing the results of a particular activity [13].
- A high social status determined by socially recognized personal achievements and the authority of an expert, specialist (Bell) underlies a high level of conversion of social capital acquired in the network;

- Availability of resources for creating and replicating values, ideas, images, meanings as a system of reference points forming a lifestyle, stereotypes and behavioral patterns affects identification mechanisms [19];
- Access to the latest IT developments (Schiller) [17], which, according to Bard and Zoderquist [20] and Castells [21] is the basis of a new hierarchy of the elite in the information society;
- The ability to form an entrepreneurial culture as a set of values [21] focused on the culture of money, which makes it possible to extract profit from the development of network technologies focused on knowledge and entertainment;
- A high level of activism in the network characterized by Hauben [22] as the highest level of altruism, i.e., the desire and opportunity to "devote time and energy to creating the Network as a new part of our world, a better place" [23];
- Awareness of the decisive role in the formation and broadcast of mass culture based on the ability to predict the mass audience's demands with the subsequent successful commercialization of the mass culture elements underlying the subsequent legitimation of the high social status of economic passionaries in society [24].

Thus, economic passionarity in the context of the transition to a digital economy is a special group of people with a high level of individual intellectual potential and social activity for implementing innovations, which provides this group with the opportunity to broadcast their own value systems within the mass culture and capable of transforming ideological positions and behavioral norms of economic entities in society as a whole.

The presented interpretation defined the boundaries of the subsequent inquiry into methodological developments related to the analysis of economic passionarity in the transition to the digital economy.

It should be particularly noted that methods for analyzing economic passionarity in the literature are based on the specifics of the formation and development of economic and intellectual elites, which requires them to be critically reconsidered.

According to Galitsa [25], the achievement of the best intellectual and innovative results is among the features of the intellectual and innovative elite, which determine the level of innovation activity, competitiveness, and investment attractiveness of systems at various levels (countries, regions, enterprises).

Gorshkov [26] highlights the presence of economic culture as the main criterion of elitism formed by elite economic education, received specialty and position. The author suggests assessing the elitism of education using the following indicators:

- University rating;
- Diploma convertibility (equivalent to world standards);
- Elitism of a specialty;
- A competition for admission (the number of applicants per place);
- A variety of future jobs to choose from;
- The cost of the specialist's labor in the market, for elite positions—the size of personal income.

In Gorshkov's opinion, the public good growth dynamics (and the population living standards based on it) is a criterion of the truth of the national economic elite.

Zhiganova [12] defines elites as carriers of intellectual and social capital, which are inevitably integrated into the economic potential of the subject. Among the main peculiarities of the intellectual elite are:

1) Higher education and highly qualified intellectual work;
2) Relatively high material status (incomes are not lower than the middle class);
3) A stable system of values, attitudes and behavioral stereotypes;
4) Self-organization, established structural structure;
5) Intellectual results.

Zhiganova also focuses on the professional heterogeneity of the intellectual elite. The author identifies the upper class, i.e., state and municipal employees, entrepreneurs and managers of raw materials-producing industries, finance and services, as well as new middle-class carriers of values and lifestyle of the information society (researchers, doctors, teachers, managers and owners of innovative business enterprises).

Starostin [23] notes that the formation of innovative development of the world economy largely depends on the interaction of three elites: the political, business and intellectual elites, while the latter two he recognizes as the most important in the conditions of modernization of the national economy. Each of them, while performing its own functions and pursuing its own interests (technocrat intellectuals are responsible for knowledge about technological progress, entrepreneurs in charge of the process of their successful commercialization), solve the main task, namely ensuring the country's leading global position in the innovative world.

According to Yusim, when determining the boundaries and composition of the economic (corporate, business) elite for its subsequent characterization, it is necessary to identify the largest enterprises acting as the organizational basis of the elite, as well as to determine the circle of those individuals who have a decisive influence on the functioning of these enterprises. According to Scott, the latter can include those who exercise strategic control, which involves solving such issues as "... sources, level and distribution of investment funds; rate of profit of the enterprise and its divisions; appointment of senior managers; acquisitions and mergers, etc.". These are the shareholders who own large blocks of shares enterprises, senior managers, as well as financiers, which according to Kolesnik and Tev [27], can be considered as the basis for expanding the interpretation of the economic elite, which includes vice-presidents, senior and executive vice-presidents, and company presidents and chairmen. This approach to the quantitative assessment of the economic elite involving the analysis of the top management of a certain range of enterprises was developed by Gulbrandsen, Burris, Barton, and Davis.

When testing this approach in relation at the national level, the work by Kolesnik and Tev [27] is of special interest. In their study of the economic elite of large regions, the authors note, firstly, the limited regional information base for this kind of research; secondly, when determining enterprises, whose management forms the economic elite of the region, it is advisable to use a multidimensional indicator that includes the following criteria:

1) Sales volume (the ratio of profit from products sold to the total cost of products sold);
2) Tax deductions to the regional budget;
3) The number of employees in this enterprise (industry);
4) The company's monopoly position.

Thirdly, when selecting the economic elite as a social community, it is necessary to have mutually exclusive positions, based on which they included general directors (heads) of enterprises or their deputies, owners, presidents, chairmen of the board of directors, and chairmen of the management board [27].

Based on the presented generalizations, it is possible to identify the peculiarities of economic passionarity, which must be taken into account when developing methods for its quantitative assessment.

Firstly, in the conditions of the transition from the industrial to the digital economy, the following actors can be identified as carriers of economic passionarity: scientists (intellectual elite); heads of large enterprises of socially significant industries (business elite); high-ranking civil servants (political elite).

Secondly, among the signs of the formation and development of economic passionarity in the digital era are the level of: education (the sign applies to the economic, intellectual, political elites); entrepreneurial activity (this characteristic is more relevant to the economic elite); civic activity with high social responsibility (attribute applies to economic, intellectual, political elites).

Thirdly, the formation and development of economic passionarity is determined by a system of factors that can be divided into three groups: (1) infrastructural factors associated with the functioning of educational and medical institutions, as well as organizations performing scientific research; (2) economic factors associated with the sectoral structure of the economy, distribution of investment, labor, and information resources in it; (3) institutional factors, which include various forms of government participation and regulation of investment, labor, information and innovation flows. At the same time, it is the infrastructural factors that are of paramount importance, the institutional factors are of a formative nature, which may be associated with the need for accelerated development of the digital economy in modern conditions.

Among the resulting processes formed under the influence of economic passionaries, it is worth highlighting the progressive dynamics in production volumes, including innovative goods, changes in the structure of exports and imports, as well as state budget revenues, investment support.

These conclusions can be considered as a justification for the author's methodology for assessing economic passionarity amid the transition to the digital economy.

The author's systematization of the indicators is based on the following methodological provisions (Fig. 1):

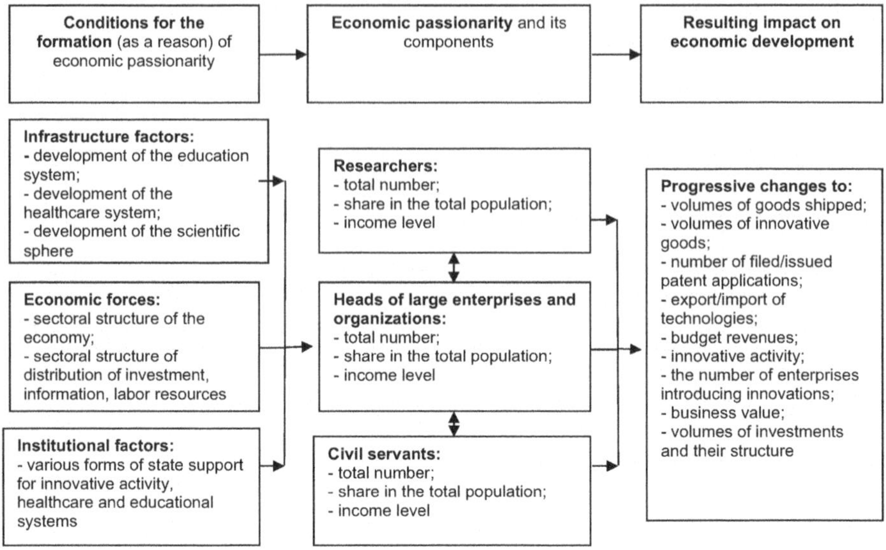


**Fig. 1** General provisions for systematizing indicators for assessing economic passionarity in the digital era

- The presence of a close relationship between the formation of economic passionarity and technological transformations: the development of digital technologies has created a stable environment for the emergence of new ways of management, commercialization and transmission of innovations that change all aspects of the life of individuals and social groups;
- Priority of scientific workers among economic passionaries, their close relationship with business elites and representatives of government authorities;
- High importance of economic passionaries in the progressive dynamics of economic systems development at different levels (countries, regions, territories and enterprises), which is associated with their ability to take on technological, production, investment risks, as well as the presence and implementation of their own intellectual capital;
- Study of cause-and-effect dependencies between the existing conditions for the formation of economic passionarity, its quantity (differentiated by groups), and the resulting influence primarily on economic processes. The influence of economic passionarity on social processes seems to be mediated by economic development, based on which we can assume the presence of long-time lags between them. This aspect can become the avenue for further research;
- Focus on the existing features of the statistical data presented in Rosstat's official statistical yearbooks.

The highlighted general provisions for systematizing indicators can become the basis for a comprehensive analysis of the dynamics of economic passionarity in the context of the transition to a digital economy.

Figure 1 shows three components of a comprehensive assessment of economic passionarity.

The first group, the conditions of formation, includes: (1) infrastructural factors associated with the functioning of educational and healthcare institutions, as well as organizations performing scientific research; (2) economic factors associated with the sectoral structure of the economy, the distribution of investment, labor, and information resources in it; (3) institutional factors, including various forms of state participation and regulation of investment, labor, information and innovation flows.

The second group, economic passionarity and its components, is based on a study of the dynamics of the total number, share in the total population, income level of scientists, managers of large enterprises and organizations, government officials.

The third group is a system of indicators that reflect the resulting impact on economic development and are manifested in the positive dynamics of the volume of goods shipped, the volume of innovative goods, the number of filed/issued patent applications, changes in the structure of technology exports/imports, budget revenues, innovation activity, the number of enterprises implementing innovation, business value, investment volumes and their structure.

In general, the proposed comprehensive assessment of economic passionarity:

- Allows conducting a more differentiated study of the phenomenon of the economic elite and the conditions;
- Carries out interregional and cross-country comparisons by groups of indicators in accordance with the available statistical base;
- Suggests possible additions in accordance with the specification of the issues to be resolved within further research on economic passionarity;
- Combines quantitative and qualitative indicators for each component of a comprehensive assessment;
- Allows identifying disproportions between the groups of indicators, suggests the authors' grouping of regions by the level of economic passionarity development, as well as conducts research on the impact of passionarity on subsequent economic and social development.

Thus, the authors interpret economic passionarity as a special type of passionarity, in which a group of people broadcasts their intellectual efforts to ensure the growth of the transformation potential of the country's economy, taking on technological, production, investment risks, and ultimately forming the vectors of progressive technological, economic, sociocultural transformations of social development as a whole. Based on the highlighted features of technological transformations, the concept of economic passionarity in the context of the transition to a digital economy has been specified, which can be understood as a special group of people with high levels of individual intellectual potential and social activity for the implementation of innovative activities, which provides this group with the opportunity to broadcast their own value systems within the mass culture, which are capable of transforming ideological positions and norms of behavior of economic entities in society as a whole.

The comparison of the methods for analyzing economic and intellectual elites allows obtaining the following limitations: the lack of a unified methodology for quantitative assessment, limited information sources for analyzing processes related to the identity of elites in the development of the national economy, which are based on sociological surveys conducted by scientific communities, as well as ratings of the leading analytical agencies, the presence of a functional relationship between the intellectual and economic elites, ensuring the progressive development of the national economy.

## 5 Conclusion

Based on the identified limitations, a system of indicators was proposed that reflects the level of development of economic passionarity in the context of the transition to a digital economy, which are based on the following methodological provisions:

1) The presence of a close relationship between the formation of economic passionarity and technological transformations: the development of digital technologies has created a stable environment for the emergence of new ways of management, commercialization and transmission of innovations that change all aspects of the life of individuals and social groups;
2) The priority of scientists among economic passionaries, their close relationship with business elites and representatives of government authorities;
3) Recognition of the high importance of economic passionaries in the progressive development dynamics of economic systems at different levels (countries, regions, territories and enterprises), which is associated with their ability to take on technological, production, investment risks, as well as the presence and implementation of their own intellectual capital;
4) Study of cause-and-effect dependencies between the existing conditions for the formation of economic passionarity, its quantity (differentiated by groups), as well as the resulting influence, primarily on economic processes. The influence of economic passionarity on social processes is mediated by economic development, which assumes the presence of long-time lags between them;
5) Focus on the existing features of the statistical data presented in Rosstat's official statistical yearbooks.

The highlighted general provisions for systematizing indicators can be the basis for a comprehensive analysis of the economic passionarity dynamics amid the transition to a digital economy. The proposed system of indicators can underlie the methodology of quantitative assessment of economic passionarity in the authors' subsequent research.

## References


1. Kravchenko, A. I. (2019). The biosocial concept of passionarity of L. Gumilyov. *Sociology, 6*, 48–63.
2. Shvachko, E. V., & Duranov, M. E. (2019). Issues of passion push and problems of socio-cultural education of youth in the era of digital transformation of society. *Pedagogical Science and Practice, 4*(26), 152–159.
3. Lobankova, I. P. (2016). Passionarity: A philosophical and anthropological aspect (on the example of the culture of the proto-city of Arkaim). *Society and Power, 2*, 132–137.
4. Savelyeva, O. V., & Maslova, M. V. (2007). Passionarity as a measure of human and society activity. *Ethnosocium and Interethnic Culture, 6*, 210–215.
5. Dawkins, R. (2013). *Egoistic gene*. CORPUS.
6. Kraeva, O. L., & Pestretsov, A. F. (2006). Passionarity as an integrating factor of national community. *Bulletin of the Lobachevsky University of Nizhny Novgorod. Series: Social Sciences, 1*, 105–114.
7. Sergeev, Y. N., & Kulesh, V. P. (2013). Global ethnogenesis and cyclical development of civilization. *Earth Science, 4*, 128–134.
8. Atambayev, K. (2015). *The awakening of nations*. Turar.
9. Mukulov, K. A. (2018). The influence of passionarity on the development of the country's economy in various time intervals. *Forum of Young Scientists, 6-2*(22), 201–205.
10. Sedova, N. N. (2016). Life goals and strategies of Russians: The context of passionarity. *Journal of Sociology, 2*(22), 73–91.
11. Dymchenko, M. E. (2012). The concept of passionarity in the concept of L. N. Gumilyov: Socio-philosophical aspect. *Izvestiya vuzov. The North Caucasus Region. Series: Social Sciences, 3*, 23–31.
12. Zhiganova, T. M. (2009). On approaches to the study of the intellectual elite of Russia. *The North Caucasus Region. Series: Social Sciences, 2*, 65–72.
13. Gumilev, L. N. (2001). *Ethnogenesis and the Earth's biosphere*. AST Publishing.
14. Butorina, O. V., & Karpovich, Y. V. (2023). Economic passionarity: Features of formation in the digital age. *Innovative Development of the Economy: Trends and Prospects, 2*, 64–76.
15. Markov, V. I. (2009). The creator in the system of culture. *Science. Philosophy. Society: Proceedings of the 5th Russian Philosophical Congress, 2*, 306–307.
16. Burnham, J. (1993). *Managerial revolution*. Yuridicheskaya literatura Publishing.
17. Buryakova, O. S. (2010). On the question of the subjects of the information and knowledge revolution. *The Humanities and Social Sciences, 4*, 98–107.
18. Orlov, M. I. (2010). Social functions of the intellectual elite. *Proceedings of the Saratov University. Series: Philosophy. Psychology. Pedagogy, 10*(4), 26–30.
19. Zotkin, A. A. (2015). Information domination of elites in the conditions of weakening of national states. *Power and Elites, 2*, 73–92.
20. Bard, A., & Zoderquist, Y. (2004). *Netdemocracy: The new ruling elite and life after capitalism*. Stockholm School of Ekonomics Publishing.
21. Castells, M. (2004). *The internet galaxy: Reflections on the internet, business and society* (p. 14). U-Factory Publishing House Humanit. Univ.
22. Hauben, M. (1997). *Netizens: On the history and impact of usenet and the internet*. Los Alamitos.
23. Starostin, A. M. (2016). Intellectual elites of modern Russia: Waiting mode or degradation? *Kommunikologiya, 6*, 201–208.
24. Girenok, F. I. (1998). Culture as virtuality: Event and meaning. *Virtual Realities, 4*, 23–31.
25. Galitsa, I. A. (2014). Intra-firm intellectual elites and anti-elites, competitiveness and economic security. *International Journal of Experimental Education, 1*, 132–136.

26. Gorshkov, A. V. (1999). The phenomenon of the economic elite in the Russian society. *Bulletin of Chelyabinsk State University, 1*, 44–55.
27. Kolesnik, N. V., & Tev, D. B. (2008). Economic elite in the Russian region: Methodological experience in determining the sample population. *Journal of Sociology and Social Anthropology, 1*, 67–75.

# Value-Based Vs Pragmatic Approach to the Sustainable Development of Energy Sector Companies in the Context of Industry 5.0

**Maria Vetrova, Tatyana Solovey, Igor Arenkov, and Dinara Ivanova**

**Abstract** The sustainable development has become acutely relevant in the last decade, and countries are allocating resources to decarbonization of energy and carbon-intensive production and technological processes. Since the signing of the Paris Agreement in 2015, the fourth energy transition has become a key challenge to achieving the goal of keeping global warming to 1.5 °C. This is primarily due to the dominant role of energy sector in the emission of climate-active gases, which accounts for more than 75% of greenhouse gas emissions worldwide, what causes the interest in studying the involvement of energy companies in ESG-agenda (environmental, social and governance). Therefore, in the context of the formation of Industry 5.0, along with achieving economic goals, digital transformation is aimed at solving social and environmental problems of sustainable development. Companies around the world set ambitious goals, which are published annually in non-financial reports; however, setting goals does not mean achieving them, but only improving their image in the eyes of counterparties, clients, and the state. The relevance of this article is due to the ongoing discussion of experts are the principles of sustainable development integrated into the business model of companies (strategic approach) or is ESG-agenda still about greenwashing (pragmatic approach). In this regard, the research assumption is that companies, despite the ongoing development of Industry 5.0, take a more pragmatic approach to sustainable development. Presumably, with negative changes in external business environment, companies can abandon or change their sustainable development goals to less ambitious ones without explaining their position to stakeholders. The selection of the energy companies is due to the fact that they have a significant environmental and social impact, are one of the leaders in integration principles of Industry 5.0 and they also publish non-financial reporting according to international standards that allow comparing the data. To confirm the assumption, the largest companies in the energy sector and their public non-financial reports in the area of social and environmental

M. Vetrova (✉) · T. Solovey · I. Arenkov · D. Ivanova
Saint-Petersburg University, Saint Petersburg, Russian Federation
e-mail: m.a.vetrova@spbu.ru; i.arenkov@spbu.ru; d.v.ivanova@spbu.ru



A. Appolloni et al. (eds.), *The Future of Industry*, Lecture Notes in Information Systems and Organisation 70, https://doi.org/10.1007/978-3-031-66801-2_8

goals were analyzed in the period from 2017 to 2022. Non-financial reports of energy companies were examined over time according to such criteria as goal-setting in the field of social and environmental aspects of sustainable development, their changes over the analyzed period, the availability of quantitative data confirming the implementation of the goals, the nature of changes in the goal-setting area (more ambitious goals or, on the contrary, refusal or relaxation of previously set goals). The results of the study confirm the assumption and the need for government regulation and the formation of an institutional environment for the development of a value-based approach to sustainable development by business structures.

**Keywords** Industry 5.0 · Climate agenda · Sustainable development · Fuel and energy sector

## 1 Introduction

The COVID-19 pandemic, large-scale digital transformation, deglobalization and increased geopolitical tension have failed to distract public attention from the urgent relevance of the climate agenda and sustainable development. The energy sector traditionally remains the key source of greenhouse gas emissions, accounting for about 73% of emissions worldwide [1]. Therefore, the basis of low-carbon development is the fourth energy transition associated with the decarbonization of the fuel and energy sector. According to the UN, the fourth energy transition should be accompanied by phasing out fossil fuels [2]. At the same time, the transition to alternative energy sources conceals a number of risks associated with the low technological readiness of production and infrastructure solutions, potential disruptions in energy supply, and a decrease in income in countries exporting fuel and energy resources.

Economic decarbonization and the fourth energy transition must be balanced considering the capabilities and priorities of certain regions to maintain business competitiveness and ensure equitable access to clean energy. At the same time, the decarbonization requirements put forward by the international community to the energy sector cannot be ignored by business structures, therefore, fuel and energy companies increasingly often declare strategic priorities such as the achievement of climate neutrality, targets for reducing greenhouse gas emissions, as well as the transformation of business processes with the orientation on sustainable development and people. Despite all the claims and efforts of states and businesses, the volume of greenhouse gases from anthropogenic activities is constantly growing. According to the UN Emissions Gap Report 2022, states are making insufficient efforts into transition to a low-carbon economy, for example, keeping global warming to 1.5 °C requires reducing global greenhouse gas emissions by 45% by 2030 [3]. Of particular relevance in this regard is the evolutionary transition to Industry 5.0, which implies solutions of large-scale challenges of sustainable development.

The developing Industry 5.0 incorporates the smart technologies of Industry 4.0 and adds cooperation and collaboration between humans and robots. Human needs become the center of the production process, and the production process itself is built with a focus on the principles of sustainable development. If Industry 4.0 focused not so much on the original principles of social justice and sustainability, but on automation and technologies for increasing production efficiency, then Industry 5.0 aims to create sustainable, ethical, environmentally friendly production and business processes to reduce waste and environmental impact. Thus, social and environmental values become fundamental elements of a successful transition to Industry 5.0.

Social values imply a person- and society-oriented approach that views employee-related expenses as investments rather than costs. Industry 5.0 enterprises create safe and inclusive work environments prioritizing physical and mental health, well-being and protection fundamental worker rights [4]. Environmental values are about reducing the negative anthropogenic impact on the environment. Industry 5.0 enterprises must develop closed-loop processes that reuse and recycle natural resources, reduce waste, and decarbonize production processes and achieve carbon neutrality, reducing environmental impact and ultimately conducting activities with higher resource and energy efficiency [5].

In the last decade, ESG transformation of enterprises, in which social and environmental values are of primary importance, has been actively developing. Fuel and energy enterprises are increasingly faced with technological, social and regulatory pressure requiring changes in production and technological processes, and real investments in changing processes are too high and are characterized by a long payback period, so greenwashing helps to maximize profits in the short term. This is perhaps the key shortcoming of the ESG concept today, in which a promise to reduce greenhouse gas emissions or other companies' statements about social and environmental goals, not proved by specific tasks with targets and deadlines, already help a company to improve its ESG profile and increase share price, achieve access to preferential financing, etc. The transition to Industry 5.0 should presumably reduce the gap between promises and real actions of companies, as it promotes economic, environmental, and social goals achievement. However, the development of Industry 5.0 has its limitations, among which trust in technologies and their adaptation to humans [6]. Issues of security, confidentiality, lack of qualified personnel, and significant investments complicate the evolutionary transition from Industry 4.0 to 5.0. Therefore, the question about continuing a pragmatic approach to the sustainable development of companies in the conditions of Industry 5.0 remains.

In this regard, this study is aimed, firstly, at systematizing factors for assessing the social and environmental values of energy sector enterprises; secondly, at assessing the value-based or pragmatic approach to the sustainable development of energy sector companies; thirdly, at analyzing the possibilities and limitations of introducing Industry 5.0 in fuel and energy enterprises for an effective energy transition. The purpose of this study is to identify trends in the field of goal-setting in the field of sustainable development of companies in the energy sector, namely how the external economic environment influences the activities of companies in the field of sustainable development. Does the deterioration of the external environment lead to the abandonment of previously set social, environmental, and climate goals or their weakening, or does the change in the external environment not have a significant impact on the companies' goals in the field of sustainable development? Permanence in sustainability goals might indicate a strategic, value-based approach for companies, while responding to a deteriorating or changing environment by abandoning or relaxing social and/or environmental goals might indicate a pragmatic, reactive approach.

Solving the set tasks is based on tools and methods within the framework of the theory of sustainable development and the modern concept of energy transition, institutional, sectoral and cross-country analysis.

## 2 Literature Review

Global problems, including environmental pollution, greenhouse gas emissions, depletion of natural resources, and the growing scale of landfills attracted the attention of society, scientists, governments of different states and entrepreneurs already in the second half of the twentieth century. At the 2nd UN World Conference on Environment and Development in 1992 in Rio de Janeiro, a declaration to achieve the principles of sustainable development based on the idea of combining environmental protection with the achievement, along with environmental, economic and social goals was adopted [7]. On 25 September 2015, at UN headquarters in New York, world leaders, including heads of states and governments, endorsed the post-2015 development agenda. They promised to lift humanity out of poverty and 'heal' the planet by adopting 17 economic, environmental and social goals [8]. In the 2000s, the concept of sustainable development was enriched with new ideas, including the task of transitioning to the principles of green and inclusive economy (with a special emphasis on improving the quality of life and reducing inequality between people, the environmental orientation of innovation and structural reforms) [9]. The inclusive economy and the value of human life in the context of sustainable development are being emphasized especially during the COVID-19 pandemic, with a new wave of research prioritizing the social aspects of doing business. All this laid the foundation for research in the field of climate and decarbonization of economic growth, as well as the development of social aspects and ESG business transformation.

Issues of decarbonization in the field of technological solutions, business strategies, sustainable economic development are being studied by scientists around the world [10–14], leading companies are investing into new low-carbon technologies, states are developing strategies for low-carbon socio-economic development [15]. At the same time, the tasks of the climate agenda in the field of reducing greenhouse gas emissions remain unresolved [16]. It is clear that the current tools are

**Table 1** Focuses of Industry 5.0 definitions

| Authors | Years | Focus of the definition |
|---|---|---|
| Masood & Sonntag [17] | 2020 | Smart factory with social networks for interaction between robots and people |
| Martos, Ahmad, Cartujo, & Ordoñez [18] | 2021 | Robots that help people work faster by using advanced technologies such as big data analytics |
| Ocicka & Turek [19] | 2021 | Forced acceptance and integration of human factor and technologies in production processes |
| Imoize, Adedeji, Tandiya, & Shetty [20] | 2021 | A revolution in which man and machine find ways to work towards increasing the efficiency of industrial production |
| Ietto, Ancillai, Sabatini, Carayannis, & Gregori [21] | 2022 | An industrial revolution centered on human and sustainable development |

insufficient to overcome the dependence of emissions of climate-sensitive gases on economic growth.

Therefore, Industry 5.0, often called the Fifth Industrial Revolution, is a new development model promoted by the European Commission and described in the report 'Industry 5.0 – Towards a sustainable, human-centric and resilient European industry'. Today there is no single definition of Industry 5.0 (Table 1).

Thus, Industry 5.0 is an innovative production model that combines machines, technologies and people to achieve sustainable development goals with a priority on social and environmental values.

The issue of values has been highlighted in philosophy, economics, and sociology. The literature discusses the relation between values and preferences [22], and environmental values in turn are associated with the formation or expression of preferences by which we care about something or believe that one thing better than another. Of particular interest in this context are the studies of Aguilar-Luzon et al. [23], which demonstrate the connection of personal values with environmental behavior.

If biosphere values, which are associated with caring for non-human species and the biosphere as a whole, and socio-altruistic values associated with caring for other people, are highly developed, then efforts will focus on environmental protection and human care, while individualistic values, which are associated with self-care, will negatively affect the environmental protection and human care [23].

Despite the large body of research in the field of sustainable development and Industry 4.0 and 5.0, there is a gap in assessing the social and environmental values of companies in the conditions of Industry 5.0. Therefore, this study aims to fill this gap by the example of companies in the energy sector.

In recent years creating shared value has become an imperative for corporations. The legitimacy of business has been called into question, with companies seen as prospering at the expense of the broader community. Examples include major corporate scandals, which received great resonance in news and society (VW, Enron, WorldCom). At the same time many global problems, from inequality and poverty to climate change, imply that solutions require the expertise and scalable business models of the private sector. Even corporations once known for a hard-nosed approach have embarked on significant shared value initiatives [24–27]. However, some companies continue to only create the appearance of integrating the principles of sustainable development (greenwashing, bluewashing), the characteristic features of such companies are only single social or environmental projects, the lack of a strategy, sustainable development goals, and the company's responsible person for ESG-agenda [28, 29].

## 3 Materials and Methods

First mention of the term 'Industry 4.0' was in Germany in 2011 [30], in 2013 the German government used the term Industry 4.0 in terms of the complete computerization of the country's manufacturing industry [31]. In June 2017, the President of Russia, speaking at the St. Petersburg International Economic Forum, gave priority to the development of the digital economy in the country [32]. Therefore, 2017 will determine the choice of starting point for our study of public non-financial reporting of companies from 2017–2022. For the empirical study, authors selected ten energy companies, four of which are the world's largest energy companies (CHN Energy, British Petroleum, Chevron Corporation, E.on), and six are the largest Russian ones (Inter RAO, RusHydro, EN+ GROUP, Rosseti, SUEK, T Plus). This is due to the significant social and environmental impact of energy companies, the ongoing process of digitalization of their activities, as well as the presence of accountability for the period under review.

Next, we will analyze the dynamics of changes in the goal setting of these companies in the field of social and environmental aspects of sustainable development for each reporting year according to the criteria presented in Table 2.

The following system of metrics was used to evaluate the factors:

0—the factor is absent or unchanged, i.e., 0 the assessment can also be used in cases where there has been no adjustment of goals or no information is provided about adjustments of goals or reduction/increase in disclosure of information about progress towards achieving goals or the use of technologies in environmental and social aspects;

1—is given if the company's report contains information about compliance with the stated factor, even if the factor is negative;

2—is given if in the year following the previous one there is a positive trend, for example, an adjustment of goals for the better or more detailed disclosure of information about the achievement of previously set goals;

−1—is given if in the year following the previous one there is a negative trend, for example, an adjustment of goals for the worse or reduction of disclosed information about the achievement of set goals.

Next, we analyzed the information collected from 2017 to 2022 in order to try to make conclusions about a pragmatic or value-based approach to companies'

**Table 2** Factors for assessing environmental and social aspects of sustainable development

| No. | Factors | Value-based approach | Pragmatic approach |
|---|---|---|---|
| 1 | Reflection of environmental goals in the strategy | Environmental goals have been set and digitized | No environmental goals |
| 2 | Reflection of social goals in the strategy | Social goals have been set and digitized | There are no social goals |
| 3 | Statements and facts regarding environmental goals | The goals set for previous years have been achieved | The goals are not achieved |
| 4 | Statements and facts regarding social goals | The goals set for previous years have been achieved | The goals are not achieved |
| 5 | Adjustment of environmental goals in response to environmental changes | The goals are adjusted for the better or remain unchanged | The goals are adjusted for the worse |
| 6 | Adjustment of social goals in response to environmental changes | The goals are adjusted for the better or remain unchanged | The goals are adjusted for the worse |
| 7 | Digital technologies in an environmental aspect | Digital technologies are used for environmental projects and achieving goals | Digital technologies are not used for environmental projects and achieving goals |
| 8 | Digital technologies in a social aspect | Digital technologies are used for social projects and achieving goals | Digital technologies are not used for social projects and achieving goals |

activities in the field of sustainable development. The value-based approach involves the formulation of strategic environmental and social goals, the dynamic disclosure of information about the process of their implementation, reasonable adjustment of goals, if necessary, as well as the phased introduction of digital technologies to achieve the goals. The pragmatic approach involves the formulation of qualitative goals without time limits, the disclosure of quality information about the progress towards achieving sustainable development goals.

# 4 Results

## *4.1 Environmental Pillar of Sustainable Development*

In 2017, the majority of the analyzed companies (7 out of 10 companies) had set environmental goals at a strategic level, but only a minority had quantitative and time-limited goals (3 out of 10 companies). At the same time, in their reports for 2022, 9 out of 10 companies formulated and digitized environmental goals in the field of sustainable development (Table 3).

It is also important that during the analyzed period, 7 out of 10 companies adjusted their environmental goals in a 'positive way', i.e., detailed them or decomposed into subgoals or added new ones, for example, formulated goals for

**Table 3** Reflection of environmental goals in the strategy

| Companies | Countries | 2017 | 2018 | 2019 | 2020 | 2021 | 2022 |
|---|---|---|---|---|---|---|---|
| CHN Energy | China | 1 | 0 | 0 | 0 | 0 | 2 |
| British Petroleum | Great Britain | 1 | 0 | 2 | 2 | 0 | 0 |
| Chevron Corporation | USA | 1 | 0 | 0 | 0 | 2 | 0 |
| E.on | Germany | 1 | 0 | 0 | 0 | 0 | 2 |
| Inter RAO | Russia | 0 | 0 | 0 | 0 | 0 | 0 |
| RusHydro | Russia | 1 | 0 | 0 | 0 | 0 | 0 |
| EN+ GROUP | Russia | 1 | 2 | 2 | 2 | 1 | |
| Rosseti | Russia | 1 | 2 | 2 | 0 | 0 | 0 |
| SUEK | Russia | 1 | 0 | 0 | 2 | 2 | |
| T Plus | Russia | 0 | 0 | 1 | 0 | 0 | 2 |
| *Total* | | 8 | 4 | 7 | 6 | 5 | 6 |

**Table 4** Statements and facts regarding environmental goals

| Companies | Countries | 2017 | 2018 | 2019 | 2020 | 2021 | 2022 |
|---|---|---|---|---|---|---|---|
| CHN Energy | China | 1 | 0 | 0 | 2 | 0 | 2 |
| British Petroleum | Great Britain | 1 | 2 | 2 | 2 | 2 | 0 |
| Chevron Corporation | USA | 1 | 0 | 2 | −1 | 2 | 0 |
| E.on | Germany | 1 | 2 | 0 | 0 | 1 | 2 |
| PJSC Inter RAO | Russia | 1 | 0 | 2 | 2 | 2 | 2 |
| PJSC RusHydro | Russia | 1 | 0 | 0 | 2 | 2 | 0 |
| MKPAO EN+ GROUP | Russia | 1 | 2 | 2 | 2 | | |
| PJSC Rosseti | Russia | 0 | 1 | 2 | 0 | 2 | 2 |
| SUEK | Russia | 1 | 1 | 0 | 0 | 2 | 2 |
| T Plus | Russia | 1 | 0 | 2 | 0 | 2 | 2 |
| *Total* | | 9 | 8 | 12 | 9 | 15 | 12 |

minimizing greenhouse gas emissions divided by Scopes and with deadlines to achieve carbon neutrality. Only one company adjusted its goal to a less ambitious one because of the current situation of the market (Table 4).

All analyzed companies have improved the disclosure of information about the environmental aspect, including minimizing the negative impact on the environment and their contribution to the fight against climate change, however, it is interesting that more detailed disclosure of qualitative and quantitative information does not imply a revision of strategic environmental goals (Table 5).

Thus, we can conclude that companies are cautious in setting ambitious environmental goals, while the details of disclosed information about the environmental pillar of sustainable development may be determined by dynamically changing legislation in this area and requests from stakeholders.

The reports for 2017 of all studied international companies contained information on the use of digital technologies to achieve their environmental goals of sustainable development (Table 6).

**Table 5** Adjustment of environmental goals in response to changes in the external environment

| Companies | Countries | 2017 | 2018 | 2019 | 2020 | 2021 | 2022 |
|---|---|---|---|---|---|---|---|
| CHN Energy | China | 0 | 0 | 0 | 0 | 0 | 2 |
| British Petroleum | Great Britain | 0 | 0 | 2 | 2 | 0 | 0 |
| Chevron Corporation | USA | 0 | 0 | 1 | | | 0 |
| E.on | Germany | 0 | 0 | 1 | 1 | 0 | 0 |
| PJSC Inter RAO | Russia | 0 | 0 | 2 | 0 | 0 | |
| PJSC RusHydro | Russia | 0 | 0 | 0 | 0 | 0 | 0 |
| MKPAO EN+ GROUP | Russia | | 0 | −1 | | | |
| PJSC Rosseti | Russia | 0 | 2 | 0 | 0 | 0 | 0 |
| SUEK | Russia | 0 | 1 | 1 | 2 | 2 | |
| T Plus | Russia | 0 | 0 | 1 | 0 | 0 | 2 |
| *Total* | | 0 | 3 | 7 | 5 | 2 | 4 |

**Table 6** Digital technologies in the environmental aspect

| Companies | Countries | 2017 | 2018 | 2019 | 2020 | 2021 | 2022 |
|---|---|---|---|---|---|---|---|
| CHN Energy | China | 1 | 0 | 0 | 2 | 0 | 2 |
| British Petroleum | Great Britain | 1 | 0 | 0 | 2 | 0 | 2 |
| Chevron Corporation | USA | 1 | 0 | 0 | −1 | 2 | 0 |
| E.on | Germany | 1 | 0 | 0 | 1 | 2 | 0 |
| PJSC Inter RAO | Russia | | | | | | |
| PJSC RusHydro | Russia | 0 | 0 | 0 | 0 | 0 | 0 |
| MKPAO EN+ GROUP | Russia | | 2 | 2 | | | |
| PJSC Rosseti | Russia | 1 | 2 | 0 | 0 | 2 | 0 |
| SUEK | Russia | 0 | 2 | 2 | 1 | 1 | |
| T Plus | Russia | 0 | 0 | 1 | 0 | 2 | 2 |
| *Total* | | 5 | 6 | 5 | 5 | 9 | 6 |

During the analyzed period, 4 out of 6 studied Russian energy companies also began to reveal successful cases of using digital solutions and technologies to achieve their environmental goals, including software products for calculating greenhouse gases, modernization of equipment for the automatic collection and consolidation of environmental indicators, use of technological solutions to minimize the company's negative impact on the environment. During the 2017–2022, only one company disclosed information about the refusal to use one technological solution in the office due to the transition to a remote work format caused by the COVID-19 pandemic.

## 4.2 *Social Pillar of Sustainable Development*

In 2017, 7 out of 10 companies set social goals in the field of sustainable development, but almost all the goals of both international and Russian companies were rather declarative without specifying target indicators and deadlines. Only social

**Table 7** Reflection of social goals in the strategy

| Companies | Countries | 2017 | 2018 | 2019 | 2020 | 2021 | 2022 |
|---|---|---|---|---|---|---|---|
| CHN Energy | China | 0 | 0 | 0 | 0 | 0 | 2 |
| British Petroleum | Great Britain | 1 | 0 | 2 | 2 | 0 | 0 |
| Chevron Corporation | USA | 1 | 0 | 0 | −1 | 0 | 2 |
| E.on | Germany | 1 | 2 | 0 | 0 | 0 | 2 |
| PJSC Inter RAO | Russia | 0 | 0 | 0 | 0 | 0 | 0 |
| PJSC RusHydro | Russia | 0 | 0 | 0 | 0 | 0 | 0 |
| MKPAO EN+ GROUP | Russia | 1 | 2 | −1 | 2 | | |
| PJSC Rosseti | Russia | 1 | 2 | 2 | 0 | 0 | 0 |
| SUEK | Russia | 1 | 0 | 0 | 2 | 2 | |
| T Plus | Russia | 0 | 0 | 1 | 0 | 0 | 2 |
| *Total* | | 6 | 6 | 4 | 5 | 2 | 8 |

goals in the field of labor protection and industrial safety were digitized and sounded like 'achieving zero injuries at work, no deaths at work, etc.' Social goals regarding inequality issues are mostly written as 'preventing all types of inequality in the company' without providing specific examples or metrics to measure progress towards the goal. In 2022, 9 out of 10 companies formulated rather clear social goals for sustainable development, affecting both internal (employees, labor union) and external aspect (interaction with the local community, social investments, interaction with educational institutions, etc.) (Table 7).

Absolutely all companies in 2022 disclosed information about the social pillar of sustainable development, including gender and age composition, male and female share, the share of employees of different age by position, gender wage ratio, information on employee training, social investments, programs for interaction with the local community and educational institutions, etc.

All companies improved the quality of disclosure of information about the social pillar of sustainable development during the period under review (availability of comparable information for three periods, specification of the disclosed information, explanation of the calculation methodology and reporting on each social indicator) (Table 8).

All companies revised their social sustainability goals 'for the better' during the analyzed period, with 6 out of 10 companies have done this since 2020, which may be due to the COVID-19 pandemic and the current geopolitical situation (Table 9).

In 2017, all international companies disclosed information about the use of digital technologies to achieve social goals of sustainable development, while none of the Russian companies disclosed such information (Table 10).

During the period under review, all Russian companies began to disclose information about the digital solutions they use (portals for collecting feedback, various internal educational portals, programs for searching and hiring employees using artificial intelligence, video surveillance systems and recognition of potentially unsafe actions in terms of violations of labor protection rules and industrial safety, etc.)

**Table 8** Statements and facts regarding social goals

| Companies | Countries | 2017 | 2018 | 2019 | 2020 | 2021 |
|---|---|---|---|---|---|---|
| CHN Energy | China | 1 | 0 | 0 | 2 | 0 |
| British Petroleum | Great Britain | 1 | 2 | 2 | 2 | 2 |
| Chevron Corporation | USA | 1 | 2 | 0 | 0 | 0 |
| E.on | Germany | 1 | 2 | 2 | 1 | 1 |
| PJSC Inter RAO | Russia | 1 | 2 | 2 | 0 | 2 |
| PJSC RusHydro | Russia | 1 | 0 | 0 | 2 | −1 |
| MKPAO EN+ GROUP | Russia | 1 | 2 | 2 | 2 | |
| PJSC Rosseti | Russia | 0 | 1 | 2 | 0 | 0 |
| SUEK | Russia | 1 | 1 | 0 | 0 | 1 |
| T Plus | Russia | 0 | 0 | 1 | 0 | 2 |
| *Total* | | 8 | 12 | 11 | 9 | 7 |

**Table 9** Adjustment of social goals in response to changes in the external environment

| Companies | Countries | 2017 | 2018 | 2019 | 2020 | 2021 | 2022 |
|---|---|---|---|---|---|---|---|
| CHN Energy | China | 0 | 0 | 0 | 0 | 0 | 2 |
| British Petroleum | Great Britain | 0 | 0 | 2 | 2 | 0 | 0 |
| Chevron Corporation | USA | 0 | 0 | 2 | 0 | 0 | 0 |
| E.on | Germany | 0 | 0 | 0 | 1 | 0 | 0 |
| PJSC Inter RAO | Russia | | | | | | |
| PJSC RusHydro | Russia | 0 | 0 | 0 | 0 | 0 | 0 |
| MKPAO EN+ GROUP | Russia | | 0 | | | | |
| PJSC Rosseti | Russia | 0 | 2 | 2 | 0 | 2 | 0 |
| SUEK | Russia | 0 | 1 | 1 | 0 | 0 | |
| T Plus | Russia | 0 | 0 | 1 | 0 | 2 | 2 |
| *Total* | | 0 | 3 | 8 | 3 | 4 | 4 |

**Table 10** Digital technologies in the social aspect

| Companies | Countries | 2017 | 2018 | 2019 | 2020 | 2021 | 2022 |
|---|---|---|---|---|---|---|---|
| CHN Energy | China | 1 | 0 | 0 | 2 | 0 | 2 |
| British Petroleum | Great Britain | 1 | 0 | 0 | 2 | 0 | 2 |
| Chevron Corporation | USA | 1 | 0 | 0 | −1 | 0 | 0 |
| E.on | Germany | 1 | 0 | 0 | 0 | 1 | 0 |
| PJSC Inter RAO | Russia | | | | | | |
| PJSC RusHydro | Russia | 0 | 0 | 0 | 0 | 0 | 0 |
| MKPAO EN+ GROUP | Russia | | 2 | | | | |
| PJSC Rosseti | Russia | 0 | 1 | 2 | 0 | 0 | 2 |
| SUEK | Russia | 0 | 2 | 2 | 1 | 1 | |
| T Plus | Russia | 0 | 0 | 1 | 0 | 2 | 2 |
| *Total* | | 4 | 5 | 5 | 4 | 4 | 8 |

## 5 Discussion

In the context of the Industry 5.0 formation, the social pillar is becoming an integral part of the sustainable development of companies. Energy sector companies, under pressure from the climate agenda to reduce greenhouse gas emissions, are improving their performance on environmental goals without neglecting social ones. At the same time, there is no stable improvement in performance and proactive actions of companies; improvements occur in response to changes in government policy, and today a pragmatic approach to the environmental and social pillars of sustainable development still prevails. In the context of large-scale development of Industry 5.0, social and environmental pillars should be on a par with economic goals; only this approach may provide companies with long-term competitiveness. Otherwise, as advanced companies adopting the principles of Industry 5.0 separate from companies pursuing only commercial short-term goals, the negative reaction of society will contribute to an even greater lag.

Due to the scale of the coming changes, it is important to move to a higher level, where not the enterprise plays the key role in achieving sustainable development goals, but society as a whole. Therefore, the term Industry 5.0 should be replaced by Society 5.0, in which digital technologies are aimed at harmonizing the goals of companies, the state and humans for sustainable development. The conducted research showed the ineffectiveness of large-scale digital transformation without social and environmental objectives, at the same time the goals of sustainable development, including goals in the area of the climate agenda, have not been achieved despite all the efforts made by states and business structures. Thus, the transition to Society 5.0 should be aimed primarily at shifting the emphasis from commercial goals of digitalization to the harmonious achievement of social and environmental goals and objectives.

## 6 Conclusion

The results of this study confirm the hypothesis that companies in the energy sector in the period 2017–2022 take a more pragmatic approach to social and environmental values, improving targets primarily in response to legislative changes. At the same time, digital technologies can significantly improve the harmonization of economic, environmental and social goals, which is the main priority of Society 5.0. At the same time, the state should play the role of a regulator and create a favorable institutional environment.

The conducted study has certain limitations that give rise to future areas of research. Thus, only one sector of the economy (energy) was considered, and therefore for future research and valid conclusions it is important to study other sectors of the national economy, as well as expand the list of analyzed countries in which Industry 5.0 is already being formed and there are strategic tasks for the formation of the Society 5.0.

**Acknowledgements** This work was supported by Saint-Petersburg State University research grant pr. No GZ_MDF_2024-2, pure ID 103905601.

## References

1. Ritchie, H., & Roser, M. (2022). Emissions by sector. https://ourworldindata.org/emissions-by-sector#direct-industrial-processes-5-2.
2. UNEP. (2022). Adaptation gap report 2022. https://www.un.org/ru/climatechange/reports
3. IEA. (2022). World Energy Outlook 2022. https://www.iea.org/reports/world-energy-outlook-2022
4. Lu, Y., Adrados, J. S., Chand, S. S., & Wang, L. (2021). Humans are not machines—Anthropocentric human–machine symbiosis for ultra-flexible smart manufacturing. *Engineering, 7*, 734–737. https://doi.org/10.1016/J.ENG.2020.09.018
5. Breque, M., & De Nul, L. (2021). *Petridis Industry 5.0: Towards a sustainable, human-centric and resilient European industry*. European Commission, Directorate-General for Research and Innovation. https://doi.org/10.2777/308407
6. Haleem, A., & Javaid, M. (2019). Industry 5.0 and its applications in orthopaedics. *Journal of Clinical Orthopaedics and Trauma, 10*(4), 807–808. https://doi.org/10.1016/j.jcot.2018.12.010
7. UN. (1992). *United Nations Conference on Environment and Development, Rio de Janeiro.* https://www.un.org/ru/documents/decl_conv/declarations/riodecl.shtml#a1
8. UN. (2015). *Resolution adopted by the General Assembly. Transforming our world: The* 2030 *Agenda for Sustainable Development* https://www.un.org/sustainabledevelopment/ru/about/development-agenda/
9. Corrado, G., & Corrado, L. (2017). Inclusive finance for inclusive growth and development. *Current Opinion in Environmental Sustainability, 24*, 19–23. https://doi.org/10.1016/j.cosust.2017.01.013
10. Creutzig, F., Agoston, P., Goldschmidt, J. C., Luderer, G., Nemet, G., & Pietzcker, R. C. (2017). The underestimated potential of solar energy to mitigate climate change. *Nature Energy, 2*(9), 17140. https://doi.org/10.1038/nenergy.2017.140
11. Hilaire, J., Minx, J. C., & Callaghan, M. W. (2019). Negative emissions and international climate goals—Learning from and about mitigation scenarios. *Climatic Change, 157*, 189–219. https://doi.org/10.1007/s10584-019-02516-4
12. Pakhomova, N., Richter, K. K., & Vetrova, M. (2022). Global climate challenges, structural shifts in the economy and business development of proactive strategies to achieve carbon neutrality. *Bulletin of St. Petersburg University. Economics, 38*(3), 331–364. https://doi.org/10.21638/spbu05.2022.301
13. Way, R., Ives, M., & Mealy, P. (2022). Empirically grounded technology forecasts and the energy transition. *Joule, 6*(9), 2057–2082. https://doi.org/10.1016/j.joule.2022.08.009
14. Xiao, M., Junne, T., Haas, J., & Plummeting Klein, M. (2021). Costs of renewables—Are energy scenarios lagging? *Energy Strategy Reviews, 35*, 100636. https://doi.org/10.1016/j.esr.2021.100636
15. IPCC. (2023). *Sixth assessment report of the IPCC.* https://op.europa.eu/en/publication-detail/-/publication/468a892a-5097-11eb-b59f-01aa75ed71a1/
16. Masood, T., & Sonntag, P. (2020). Industry 4.0: Adoption challenges and benefits for SMEs. *Computers in Industry, 121*, 103–261. https://doi.org/10.1016/j.compind.2020.103261
17. Martos, V., Ahmad, A., Cartujo, P., & Ordoñez, J. (2021). Ensuring agricultural sustainability through remote sensing in the era of agriculture 5.0. *Applied Sciences, 11*(13), 5911. https://doi.org/10.3390/app11135911

18. Imoize, A. L., Adedeji, O., Tandiya, N., & Shetty, S. (2021). 6G enabled smart infrastructure for sustainable society: Opportunities, challenges, and research roadmap. *Sensors, 21*, 1709. https://doi.org/10.3390/s21051709
19. Ocicka, B., & Turek, J. (2021). Supply chain sustainability risk management in a digitally VUCA changing world. In *The economics of sustainable transformation* (pp. 167–190).
20. Ietto, B., Ancillai, C., Sabatini, A., Carayannis, E. G., & Gregori, G. L. (2022). The role of external actors in SMEs' human-centered industry 4.0 adoption: An empirical perspective on Italian competence centers. *IEEE Transactions on Engineering Management, 71*, 1057–1072. https://doi.org/10.1109/tem.2022.3144881
21. Luzón, M. D. C. A., Martínez, M. A. G., Sánchez, A. M., & de Lecea, J. M. S. M. (2006). El modelo del valor, las normas y las creencias hacia el medio ambiente en la predicción de la conducta ecológica. *Medio ambiente y comportamiento humano: Revista Internacional de Psicología Ambiental, 7*(2), 21–44.
22. Crites, S. L., Fabrigar, L. R., & Petty, R. E. (1994). Measuring the affective and cognitive properties of attitudes: Conceptual and methodological issues. *Personality and Social Psychology Bulletin, 20*(6), 619–634. https://doi.org/10.1177/0146167294206001
23. Aguilar-Luzón, M. C., Calvo, A., & Berrios, M. P. (2008). Responsible ecological behavior: An analysis based on biospheric, social-altruistic and egoistic values. *Revista electrónica de Investigación y Docencia, 1*, 11–25.
24. Figge, F., & Hahn, T. (2004). Sustainable value added – Measuring corporate contributions to sustainability beyond eco-efficiency. *Ecological Economics, 48*(2), 173–187. https://doi.org/10.1016/j.ecolecon.2003.08.005
25. Figge, F., & Hahn, T. (2005). The cost of sustainable value of companies. *Journal of Industrial Ecology, 9*(4), 47–58.
26. Kramer, P., & Pfitzer, M. (2016). The ecosystem of shared value, Harvard Business Review. https://hbr.org/2016/10/the-ecosystem-of-shared-value
27. Rasheed, T. (2021). Value based sustainability development. *Journal of US-China Public Administration, 18*(4), 147–151. https://doi.org/10.17265/1548-6591/2021.04.001
28. Free, C., Jones, S., & Tremblay, M.-S. (2024). Greenwashing and sustainability assurance: A review and call for future research. Journal of Accounting Literature, Vol. ahead-of-print No. ahead-of-print. https://doi.org/10.1108/JAL-11-2023-0201.
29. Santos, C., Coelho, A., & Marques, A. (2023). A systematic literature review on greenwashing and its relationship to stakeholders: State of art and future research agenda. *Management Review Quarterly*. https://doi.org/10.1007/s11301-023-00337-5
30. Digital Transformation Monitor Germany: Industrie 4.0. (2017, January). https://ati.ec.europa.eu/sites/default/files/2020-06/DTM_Industrie%204.0_DE.pdf
31. FU and Acatech. (2013). Securing the future of Germany manufacturing industry—Recommendations for implementing the strategic initiative INDUSTRIE 4.0—Final report.
32. Digital Transformation of Key Industries. SPIEF, 2017. https://forumspb.com/en/news/news/digital-transformation-of-key-industries-to-be-discussed-at-spief/

# Institutional Environment of the Information Economy: A Method for Assessing the Contribution to the Socio-Economic Development

**Alexander Baranov**

**Abstract** The research examines the role of institutional factors in the development of the information economy and its impact on economic growth. The central practical thesis of the study posits that institutional factors, including public expenditures on national endeavors, the efficacy of the judiciary, law enforcement, and security services, the efficiency of public administration and regulatory frameworks, the protection of property rights, the prevalence of corruption, and the overall business climate play a pivotal role in the development of the information economy and exert a significant influence on economic growth, in addition to the conventional drivers of economic growth, such as advancements in the number of Internet users, e-government and scientific innovation. Based on the combination of different institutional indicators, the Aggregate Index of Institutional Development of the Republic of Belarus for 2002–2021 is created and its impact on the country's information economy is assessed. The author's methodological contribution lies in developing a multiple regression model to identify the institutional factors that most strongly influence economic growth in the context of the information economy. The study's findings can contribute to macroeconomic policymaking by providing a systematic and comprehensive approach to understanding the complex interactions between institutions and economic outcomes.

**Keywords** Information economy · Institutional environment · Information and transaction costs · Economic growth · Innovation

## 1 Introduction

The main hypothesis of the practical part of the research is that institutional factors, such as public spending on national activities and the judiciary, law enforcement and security, efficient public administration and regulatory quality, property rights protection, the level of corruption and the overall business environment play a

A. Baranov (✉)
Francisk Skorina Gomel State University, Gomel, Belarus

 
A. Appolloni et al. (eds.), *The Future of Industry*, Lecture Notes in Information Systems and Organisation 70, https://doi.org/10.1007/978-3-031-66801-2_9

significant role in the development of the information economy and have an impact on economic growth in addition to the traditional drivers of economic growth, such as the number of Internet users, e-government and scientific innovation. By examining the interactions between institutional factors and economic growth in the context of the information economy, the study aims to provide a comprehensive understanding of the complex dynamics of the proposed Aggregate Index of Institutional Development at play in shaping the future of the information economy.

The researches in that field highlights the critical role that institutional factors have in the development of the information economy and its impact on socio-economic development. Scientific contributions related to other studies in the field of the institutional environment of the information economy and its influence on the socio-economic development involve examining the impact of various institutional factors on the development and functioning of the information economy, such as regulatory frameworks, intellectual property rights protection, access to information, and government policies. Researchers analyze how these factors influence innovation, investment, competitiveness, and overall economic growth in the context of the information economy, providing valuable insights for policymakers, businesses, and other stakeholders seeking to enhance the socio-economic benefits of information technology and digital innovation.

But the main conclusions of the authors' method differ from the existing methodology in that it justifies the necessary steps for a balanced macroeconomic policy in relation to individual factors of institutional development and a harmonious combination of the proportions of state influence on information, scientific and innovative potentials, the optimal choice of which is confirmed by the multiple regression model built by the author. The choice of model key figures is determined in the result-cost system, which provides the most reliable variables.

This methodological contribution adds to the body of knowledge by providing a systematic and comprehensive approach to understanding the complex interactions between institutions and economic outcomes.

The study's findings can serve as the basis for further development of the method of the transformation of the institutional infrastructure and the operation of key areas of macroeconomic regulation of the information economy in order to achieve balanced and sustainable economic development.

The first part of the article is an introduction that provides background of the topic. The second part presents the theoretical aspects of the research and an overview of the relevant literature, the genesis of the views on dependence of institutional factors of information economy and economic growth. The third part is devoted to the analysis of empirical data of institutional infrastructure development of information economy of Belarus in accordance with different international indices and sub-indices. The fourth part is devoted to the creation of multiple regression to identify the factors of institutional infrastructure development that influence the economic growth of the Republic of Belarus. The fifth part is a discussion that reflects and interpret the results in the light of previous studies and points out their limitations. The sixth part is a conclusion that summarizes and outlines further prospects for research in this area.

## 2 Theoretical Aspects and Literature Review

In our view, in the context of the information economy being formed, it is most justified to use the *theory of endogenous growth*, which substantiates the impact of innovation, knowledge and investment in human capital on economic growth. That concept was refined by Romer [1], Mankiw, Romer and Weil [2], Lucas [3], Barro and Sala Martin [4] and other prominent scientists. At the same time, it is obvious that an important aspect of the theory is the focus on positive externalities in the knowledge economy and government involvement in its formation. For example, subsidies for science and education speed up the rate of economic development in certain endogenous growth patterns by increasing incentives for innovation.

In accordance with the Neoclassical and Keynesian methodology of economic growth (the Solow model, the Harrod-Domar model), the rate of scientific progress is a determining exogenous parameter of economic development. However, Solow's [5] model characterizes the economic growth of the industrial economy, where the main role was played by physical capital and high capital-labor ratio. Barro and Sala Martin [4] developed an empirical econometric model that tested the Solow model and its influence on the convergence of growth rates of different countries and regions. According to Krinichansky and Lavrentiev [6], the core concept of this model revolves around examining the hypothesis concerning the convergence of economic growth rates and the levels of economic development among different countries.

New theories of economic growth, including the concepts developed by Barro and Sala Martin [7], are based on the accumulation of innovative and anthropogenic capital: not only new technologies, but also awareness of their practical application contribute to saving labor resources and enhancing their efficiency [4]. According to Akaev [8], the validity of increasing returns is mainly observed in those sectors of the economy that rely on knowledge and high technologies, where human capital plays a crucial role. So, based on an analysis of more than a hundred countries performed by Kolosnitsyna and Ermolina [9], *the quality of human capital and the adoption of innovative technologies, including IT, are essential factors in driving economic growth.*

However, the correlation between education spending and economic growth depends on the level of the country's development. Mobilization of highly qualified anthropogenic resources requires special attention. This implies the formation of a fairly complete and consistent system of indirect and direct financial incentives, such as targeted grants for the launch of high-tech products, R&D, and the promotion of demand for highly qualified personnel.

The elements of the description of endogenous growth are based on Schumpeter's [10] ideas that innovation is an endogenous factor determining economic growth in the region. The formulation of the model corresponds to the traditional models of catch-up endogenous growth. Obviously, the model can be extended to cover indicators that characterize regional or national development.

These conclusions are also confirmed by the knowledge flow model of Odretch and Feldman [11]. Their research was primarily focused on the hypothesis that economic activity tends to cluster in industries and regions where active knowledge generation processes occur. However, the authors considered the flow of knowledge from the position of spatial economics taking into account the impact of geographic proximity in the field of science and innovation on economic growth. Similar conclusions are confirmed by Bernard and later by Prokop, Steiskal, Klimova and Zitek [12]. Finally, Marocco, Paci and Usai [13], Ermak et al. [14] completed the production function of knowledge as a new factor of homogeneity, namely the institutional and organizational ones.

According to Malerba [15] and Fagerberg [16], to determine the priorities of economic development, one should apply *the theory of national innovation systems,* using factorial and regression analyses in order to determine the main advantages or opportunities of the countries. The indicators can be grouped *according to technical and institutional criteria.*

Golichenko and Samovoleva [17] adhere to the methodology for assessing national innovation systems from the standpoint of functional analysis, which involves the research of not only the object, but also its economic environment, performance efficiency, as well as the search and definition of the determinants of the object's efficiency; in this case, an important element of the study is the analysis of institutional conditions for innovative development.

The inquiry into the institutional environment's characteristics and components, the issues of institutional dynamics are reflected in the works of the classics of neo-institutionalism, such as Akaev [8], Mankiw, Romer, and Weil [2], Williamson [18], North [19], etc.

However, in the scientific works of most modern scientists, institutional infrastructure is used as a general theoretical term, while the methodological aspects of its impact on economic growth are poorly studied. The influence of institutions on economic growth and its quality are examined by Akemoglu, Johnson, Robinson, Thayicharoen [20], Barro [21], Eltisa [22], Robinson [23], Rodrik [24], Scully [25], Uzawa [26], Eggertsson [27], etc.

Eggertsson [27] developed the fundamentals of the methodology of economic growth factors by introducing the transaction opportunities and the social opportunity curves. In his opinion, the interaction of these curves determines the qualitative impact of institutions on minimizing transaction costs. In his studies, Eggertsson proves that the improvement of the institutional system makes it possible to activate the growth of the country's economy, since the curves of social and transactional opportunities approach each other. Malerba [15] considers the influence of political institutions on economic growth. Similar views are shared by Paul and Knack [28], who present the model of general equilibrium growth depending on social, economic and institutional conditions. This concept is also adhered to by modern scientists Xiaoliang, Yiameng, and Xiaochen [29], who consider the links between the influence of social trust on corporate innovation in information economy, and Trittin-Ulbrich and Böckel [30], investigating the institutional factors influencing digital innovation and the effects of corporate digital responsibility on economic growth.

According to *Koshkin*, institutional factors are the primary determinant of economic growth in the modern information system [31]. Dominguez [32], Simon [33], Gundyrina [34], and Sytnik [35] propose expanding the institutional infrastructure by combining the market subsystem and legal, organizational and managerial institutions.

Within the general methodological aspects of dynamic models of endogenous growth, the dependence of behavioral and institutional parameters on the impact of the state's macroeconomic policy is partially considered. Improving the institutional environment ensures the unlocking of the country's potential and creates conditions for boosting the business and social efficiency of the entire economic complex. However, both the policy of creating such a favorable institutional environment and the mechanism of influence of some institutions in the information economy remain a serious problem for science. If we consider the real economy, or models as close to it as possible, it turns out that institutional changes play a big role [36].

At the same time, according to Motorina [37], the main methodological problem is the search for a variable measured quantitatively and characterizing the level of institutions' development. In accordance with the research of Lemeshchenko and Gaponenko [38], one of the ways to analyze and assess the quality of institutions is the rating approach used by international organizations. All institutions are divided into groups depending on the chosen criterion. We believe that legal, administrative and regulatory institutions, institutions for human potential development, for anthropogenic capital production, for IT potential development, etc., can be distinguished as the key ones.

## 3 Materials and Methods

The main hypothesis of the practical part of our research is that institutional factors in the development of the information economy have an impact on economic growth in addition to the information-technological and scientific ones. The hypothesis is tested in two stages. The first stage is to compile an aggregate index of the country's institutional development (using the case of the Republic of Belarus). The second stage is to construct a mathematical model of the influence of institutional, information-technological and scientific factors on the country's economic growth.

The choice of the variables in the model for assessing the impact of the institutional environment of the information economy on the country's economic development is justified as follows. The Institutional Development Index is a key indicator that points to the quality of the country's institutions and legal system, which has a direct impact on economic activity and investment climate. The average budget expenditures for national activities make it possible to assess the level of state expenditures and the efficiency of using budget funds, which may reflect the amount of state support for the information economy. The E-Government Index shows the degree of development of electronic services and the availability of public services via the Internet, which is one of the key factors in the progress of the information economy. The number of Internet users is an important indicator of the availability and distribution of information technologies in the country, which may indicate the potential of the information economy. The dynamics of budget expenditures on the informatization of public authorities and on scientific and technical activities reflects the priorities of the state in the advancement of information technologies and science, which can affect the development of the information economy and innovative activity of the country.

On the first stage, to conduct the institutional analysis of the legal environment of the information economy we can take the *property rights component of the Index of Economic Freedom* [39]. Property rights are the basic institution of the economic system, which determines both the level of costs associated with the redistribution of resources and the effectiveness of this redistribution. The indicator of the property rights development has a *direct impact on the country's information economy* as it *characterizes the level of intellectual property and data rights protection*. According to the research data of Clague et al. [40] and Gagliardi [41], who studied the impact of institutions on economic development, institutions that primarily protect property rights and control the fulfillment of contractual obligations are significantly associated with economic growth.

The next institutional factor that can influence the development of the country's information economy is *the level of corruption*. In the field of information economy, it can lead to a *restriction of competition* and hinder the development of new technologies and innovations; corruption can lead *investors to be wary of investing in a country* because of the high risks, this may limit access to capital and slow down the information economy.

The effectiveness of the country's legal system is assessed by *Transparency International,* an international non-governmental anti-corruption organization. The index of this organization is compiled on the basis of expert assessments of lawyers and business representatives received by the World Bank and the Asian Bank. Countries are ranked on a scale from 0 to 100 points, where 0 indicates the highest level of perceived corruption, and 100 indicates the lowest [42].

Indicators of curbing corruption are ones of the quality of the legal system and public administration. The next group of factors influencing the institutional environment of the information economy refers to regulatory institutions. Obviously, the division into legal and regulatory institutions is conditional and many indicators characterizing the quality of the legal system are similar to those of the quality of the state's regulatory impact. However, this group should include institutions that create a favorable innovative and entrepreneurial climate in the country, facilitate the access of business structures to the resource potential, including anthropogenic and information resources, and also provide preferential treatment for priority projects in the field of information development.

In this regard, the effectiveness of government regulation (*Government Integrity*) of the *Index of Economic Freedom* is an extremely important indicator in institutional terms for analyzing the effectiveness of the business environment [43].

The relationship between the effectiveness of public administration and the digital economy are discussed by Dixhit and Sinha [44]. Transparency and openness of state bodies allow businesses and investors to get access to information about the political and economic situation in the country. This can increase investment confidence and promote the development of the information economy. The quality of public administration affects the level of corruption in the country, which can adversely influence the information economy. *Good governance* can stimulate the development of digital infrastructure such as *high-speed internet connections and access to digital services*. This can create a favorable environment for the information economy and e-commerce. Public administration can also regulate the information economy, for example, by creating laws and policies in the field of data protection and privacy, which can increase trust in digital services and stimulate their use.

Although the dynamics of institutional development in Belarus is positive, the country lags far behind other developed nations. According to Sidorchuk, Okhrimenko and Krys [45], improving the legal institutions can raise the level of the country's institutional development. These, in particular, include not only technical, but also educational areas: regulation of activities for the creation and development of state digital platforms, information systems and resources; participation in providing the content of educational programs of higher, additional adult education and advanced training of personnel in the field of digital development.

Economic growth depends on many factors, such as technological progress, investment, educational level, etc. However, the costs of these factors are also an important aspect that must be taken into account when analyzing economic growth. In addition, effective management of these costs can be a key aspect of achieving sustainable economic growth in the long term. *General government spending* can influence economic growth through several mechanisms researched by modern scientists at the national and regional levels (for example, by Olaoye and Afolabi [46]).

A number of scientists have studied the impact of spending on science on economic growth, starting from Robert Solow, an American economist who received the Nobel Prize for developing the model of economic growth that included investment in scientific and technological progress [5]. Romer [1] studied the theory of economic growth, in which he substantiated the priority role of investment in innovation and technological development. Political scientist Attali [47] focused on the importance of investment in science and technology for economic growth.

*Number of Internet Users and E-Government Index* can improve the efficiency of public administration, speed up decision-making processes and provide faster access to information. The Internet has a powerful impact on economic development. Marketing and the service industry have changed under the influence of the Internet and its unique capabilities: expanding the geographical opportunity to target an Internet audience and form organizational relationships with partners. The Internet helps small and medium-sized businesses achieve high performance, focuses on new sales and service channels, and also provides novel business models.

According to the research results, as the number of users increases, the demand for information products and services, such as online stores, social networks, cloud technologies, video streaming services, etc., grows, which in turn stimulates the development of infrastructure in the information sphere and creates new opportunities for business. Investing in scientific activities can attract extra investment in the economy, as companies will be interested in using new technologies and innovations. The emergence of scientific and innovative activities can lead to the creation of new jobs, as new technologies may require additional labor resources.

In general, the *Index of Institutional Development* can have an impact on economic growth, as it reflects the quality of the institutions that regulate economic activity in the country. Sustainable and transparent institutions can create an enabling environment for investment and business development. Thus, all these factors are interconnected and can affect the economic growth in the country.

*Economic growth* is a long-term phenomenon that occurs due to the accumulation of human capital and technological progress. The E-Government Index, the number of Internet users and spending on innovation can have a positive impact on economic growth, but this process does not happen instantly. For example, the e-government can accelerate economic growth, but it will take time to devise and implement appropriate technologies, train staff and create new services for citizens. Likewise, increasing the number of Internet users can improve access to information and enhance business opportunities, but it will also take time to develop infrastructure, improve education, and so on. In addition, innovation processes require significant investment and time to research and implement new technologies. Only then we can start using innovations which can affect economic growth.

We can compile an aggregate index of the legal environment for the development of the information economy of the Republic of Belarus (*Legal Field Index)* by combining *the Corruption Perceptions Index, property rights component of the Index of Economic Freedom* and *the Index of the Quality of State Regulation.* Its dynamics is presented in Fig. 1.

In the 2021 Corruption Perceptions Index, the Republic of Belarus was ranked 82nd out of 180 countries [42].

To evaluate the efficiency of public administration and government regulation, we can utilize the key components of the Worldwide Government Indicators Project.

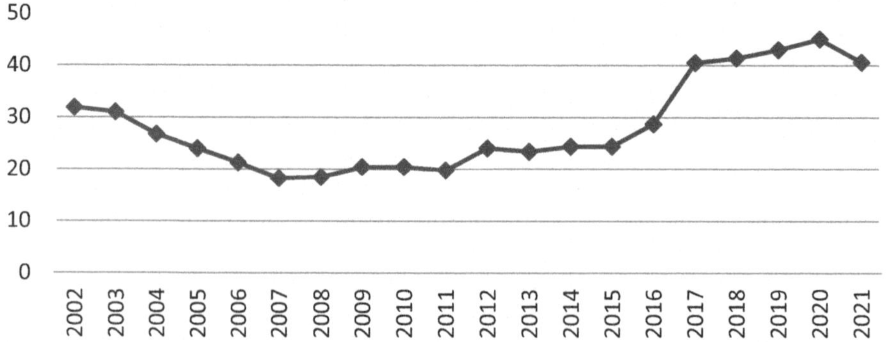


**Fig. 1** Dynamics of the Legal Field Index of the Republic of Belarus, 2012–2022

This project was created by experts from the Governance, Regulation and Finance Group at the World Bank Institute [43] (Fig. 2).

Assessing the sub-index components, it should be noted that the indicators of Freedom of Business and Freedom of Labor Relations for the Republic of Belarus for the period 2012–2021 were at a very high level (70.0–79.9) [43].

At the next stage of our research, we combine all the indicators in the *Index of Institutional Development* of the Republic of Belarus. As seen from Fig. 3, the overall dynamics of the Index of Institutional Development shows an increase in almost the entire period until 2019, when a slight decrease in the indicator was recorded.

Dynamics of public spending on national activities and the judiciary, law enforcement and security is presented in Fig. 4. It is obvious that in our model we need to

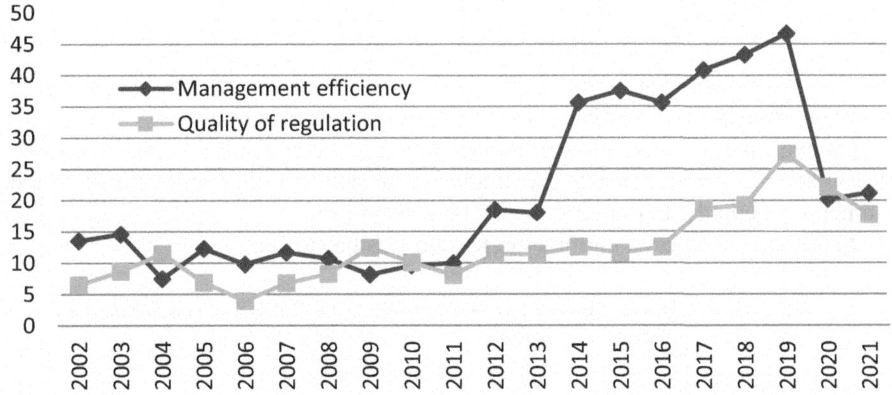


**Fig. 2** Dynamics of sub-indices Efficiency of Public Administration and Quality of State Regulation of the Republic of Belarus, 2002–2021

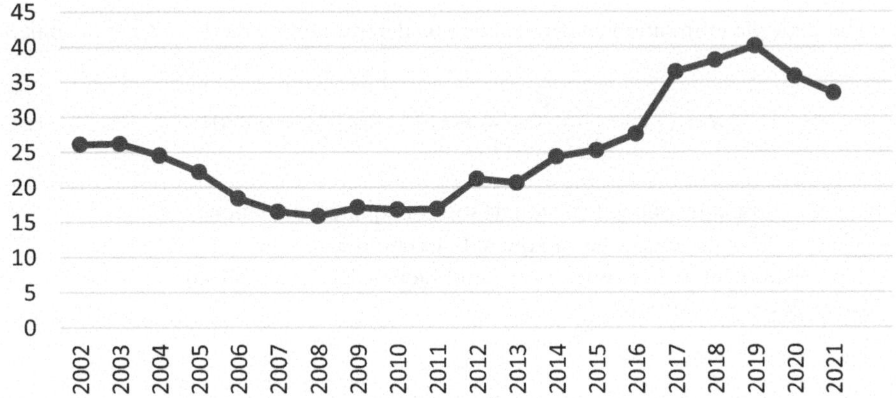


**Fig. 3** Dynamics of the Index of Institutional Development of the Republic of Belarus, 2002–2021

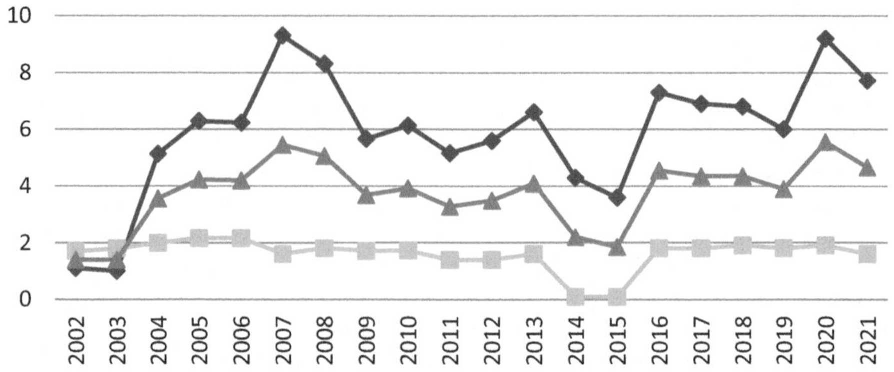


**Fig. 4** Dynamics of public spending on national activities and the judiciary, law enforcement and security in Belarus, in % of GDP, 2002–2021. Source: [48]

compare *the E-Government Index with government spending on informatization of government bodies* in accordance with the Government Programs.

However, these factors cannot immediately affect economic growth, as it takes time to achieve positive results. Such a lag corresponds to the methodology of the cliometrics methods. In our case, it will be 2 years [49].

On the second stage, a multiple regression was calculated:

$$Y = 42,5173 - 0,9805X1 + 0,2129X2 + 21,7488X + 0{,}427X4 + 307,8399X5 - 1,0894X6 \quad (1)$$

Let us build a multiple regression of the basic indicators of the institutional development of the information economy and economic growth in the Republic of Belarus. We determine the estimation vector of the regression coefficients. According to the least squares method, the vector *s* is obtained from the expression: *s = (XTX)-1XTY.*

The multiple correlation coefficient can be determined by the following formula:

$$R = \sqrt{1 - \frac{S_e^2}{\sum (y_i - \bar{y})^2}} = \sqrt{1 - \frac{27.849}{717.67}} = 0.9804, \quad (2)$$

where $S_e^2$ is the unexplained (residual) sum of squared deviations;

$\sum (y_i - \bar{y})^2$ is the total sum of squared deviations.

The relationship between feature Y and factors Xi is very strong.

Determination coefficient:

$$R^2 = 0.9804^2 = 0.9612 \tag{3}$$

The closer this coefficient is to 1, the more the regression equation explains the behavior of *Y*. Let us test the hypothesis about the general significance—the hypothesis about the simultaneous equality to zero of all regression coefficients with explanatory variables: $H0: R2 = 0; \beta 1 = \beta 2 = \ldots = \beta m = 0. H1: R2 \neq 0.$

To determine the value of the model in general, the Fisher criterion, or F-criterion, is used, it is equal to the ratio of the total variance to the residual:

$$F = \frac{R^2(n-m-1)}{1-R^2 m} = \frac{0.9612}{1-0.9612}\,\frac{17-6-1}{6} = 41.284, \tag{4}$$

where *n* is the number of observations;

*m* is the number of factors in the equation, including the resultant one.

Table value at degrees of freedom $k_1 = 6$ and $k_2 = nm - 1 = 17 - 6 - 1 = 10$, $F_{kp}(6; 10) = 3.22$.

Since the actual value of $F > F_{kp}$, the coefficient of determination is statistically significant and the regression equation is statistically reliable (i.e., the coefficients *bi* are jointly significant).

We calculate the observed values of *t-statistics* for $rx_n$ by formula:

$$T_v = rx\sqrt{\frac{n-m-1}{1-rx^2}} \tag{5}$$

where $m = 1$ is the number of factors in the regression equation.

Based on *Student's table*, we find $T_{table}(n - m - 1; \alpha/2) = (15; 0.025) = 2.49$ $T_{v1} = 4.02$; $T_{v2} = 5.349$; $T_{v3} = 4.02$; $T_{v4} = 4.44$; $T_{v5} = 3.39$; $T_{v6} = 4.52$. Since $T_v > T_{cr}$, for all $r_{xn}$, we reject the hypothesis that the correlation coefficient is equal to 0. In other words, the correlation coefficient is statistically significant.

*Goldfeld-Quandt test.* In this case, it is assumed that the standard deviation $\sigma_i = \sigma(\varepsilon_i)$ is proportional to the value $x_i$ of the variable *X* in this observation, i.e., $\sigma 2i = \sigma 2x2i$, $i = 1, 2, \ldots, n$. Let us sort all the values by X. Find the subsample size $k = (17 - 4)/2 = 7$, where $c = 4n/15 = 4^{*}17/15 = 4$. Estimate the regression for the first subsample.

*We find the parameters of the equation by the least squares method.* The system of least squares equations:

$$\begin{aligned} a_0 n + a_1 \sum x &= \sum y \\ a_0 \sum x + a_1 \sum x_2 &= \sum y \cdot x \end{aligned} \tag{6}$$

For our data, the system of equations takes the form:

$$\begin{aligned} 7a_0 + 102.54a_1 &= 379.62 \\ 102.54a_0 + 1517.8a_1 &= 5556.06 \end{aligned} \quad (7)$$

We express $a_0$ from the first equation and substitute it into the second equation.

We get $a_0 = -0.32$, $a_1 = 58.92$

Here $S_1 = 74.97$. Let us evaluate the regression for the third subsample. We find the parameters of the equation by the least squares method. For our data, the system of equations takes the form:

$$\begin{aligned} 7a_0 + 203.38a_1 &= 388.22 \\ 203.38a_0 + 6106.38a_1 &= 11432.51 \end{aligned} \quad (8)$$

We express $a_0$ from the first equation and substitute it into the second equation.

We get $a_0 = 0.78$, $a_1 = 32.92$..

Here $S_3 = 132.85$. Number of degrees of freedom $v1 = v2 = (n - c - 2m)/2 = (17 - 4 - 2^*1)/2 = 5.5$. $f_{kp}(5.5, 5.5) = 5.99$. Building F-statistics: $F = 132.85/74.97 = 1.77$. Since $F < Fkp = 5.99$, the *hypothesis of the absence of heteroscedasticity is accepted.*

*Checking the normality of the residual component distribution.* Unbiased estimate of the standard deviation:

$$S_e = \sqrt{\frac{\sum e^2}{n-1}} = \sqrt{\frac{27.848}{17-1}}1.319, \quad (9)$$

The calculated value of the RS-criterion:

$$RS = \frac{E_{max} - E_{min}}{S_e} = \frac{2.112 - (-2.762)}{1.319} = 3.695, \quad (10)$$

where $\varepsilon max = 2.1124$ is the maximum value of residues;

$\varepsilon min = -2.7621$ is the minimum level of a series of residues;

$S\varepsilon$ is the standard deviation.

The calculated value of the *RS-criterion* falls within the interval (2.7–3.7), therefore, the normal distribution property is fulfilled. Thus, the model is adequate in terms of the normality of the distribution of the residual component.

The statistical significance of the equation was confirmed through the coefficient of determination and Fisher's test. These tests revealed that in the specific research scenario approximately 96.12% of the total variability in Y can be explained by changes in the factors Xj.

As a result of testing our hypothesis, the Aggregate Index of the country's institutional development was formed and the influence of institutional factors (in addition to information technological and scientific ones) on the country's economic growth was mathematically proved.

## 4 Results

The Institutional Development Index is a key indicator that shows the quality of the country's institutions and legal system, which has a direct impact on economic activity and investment climate. The average budget expenditures on national activities make it possible to assess the level of state expenditures and the efficiency of budget funds, which may reflect the degree of state support for the information economy. The E-Government Index displays the degree of electronic services development and the availability of public services via the Internet, which is one of the key factors for the progress of the information economy. The number of Internet users is an important indicator of the availability and distribution of information technologies in the country, which may indicate the potential of the information economy. The dynamics of budget expenditures on informatization of public authorities and scientific and technical activities highlights the priorities of the state in the advancement of information technologies and science, which can affect the development of the information economy and the innovative activity of the country.

Our hypothesis on the correlation of institutional, scientific and informational factors of economic development is supported by our researches for the various countries. Thus, in Japan, the average information economy development index corresponds to the level of institutional capacity, which meets the institutional conditions created to form an information economy. In China, research and development and the average information economy index are significantly inferior to the institutional level, which is explained by the peculiarities of the institutional and legal regulation of the information economy. In the United States, there is a correlation between the level of development of the institutional environment and the research sector of the economy, as well as the information sphere. In fact, the United States is the leader in most indicators. For the EU countries, the indicators of institutional, scientific and information potentials are relatively uniform and show the similar dynamics. In Belarus, there is a relative correlation of all the three indicators [49].

An economic interpretation of the model parameters suggests that changes in the independent variables have different effects on the dependent variable. Specifically, an increase in the *Index of institutional development* (X1) by 1 unit is associated with a decrease in *GDP* (Y) by an average of 0.98 units. On the other hand, an increase in the *Average expenditures of the republican budget for general state activities and the judiciary, law enforcement and security* (X2) by 1 unit leads to an increase in GDP by an average of 0.213 units. Furthermore, an increase in the *E-Government Index* (X3) by 0.1 units is associated with an increase in GDP by an average of 2.1749 units. Similarly, an increase in the *Number of Internet users* in % of the population (X4) by 1 unit leads to an increase in GDP by an average of 0.427 units. In addition, an increase in the *Dynamics of public spending on the development of e-government and informatization of public administration, judicial and executive authorities* (X5) by 0.01 units results in an increase in GDP by an average of 3.0784 units. Finally, an increase in the *Dynamics of expenditures of the republican budget for scientific, scientific-technical and innovative activities* (X6) by 1 unit leads to a decrease in GDP by an average of 1.089 units.

An increase in the *Index of institutional development* can cause a decrease in economic growth for several reasons: the transition to more advanced institutions may take time and resources. In the process of adapting to new institutions, subjects of the information economy may face uncertainty and inefficiency, which may slow down economic growth; tightening the rules and norms of institutional development may entail large costs for the subjects of the information economy (for example, the introduction of new requirements for compliance with information security standards or labor relations rules may entail additional costs for equipment, staff training, etc.); an increase in the Institutional Development Index may cause an increase in the bureaucratic burden, increase the time it takes to obtain permits and licenses, which can slow down economic growth; with a rise in the Institutional Development Index, there may be more competition in the market.

An *increase in spending on scientific, technical and innovative activities* can lead to a decrease in economic growth for several reasons: growing spending on science and innovation does not always guarantee the efficient use of resources. If the funds are not properly directed and do not achieve their goals, then they can be wasted; successful implementation of scientific and innovation projects requires a developed innovation infrastructure, including clusters, technology parks, venture companies, etc. If such an infrastructure is missing or underdeveloped, then additional spending on science and innovation may not bring the desired results; successful scientific and innovative activities require highly qualified specialists who can develop and implement new technologies. If such specialists are unavailable or scarce, then additional spending on science and innovation may not produce the desired results; if the market is not ready to accept new innovations, then additional spending on science and innovation may not bring economic growth.

In general, increasing *R&D spending can be beneficial for economic growth,* but only if resources are used properly, *institutional infrastructure is developed,* highly skilled people are available, and innovations are demanded.

## 5 Discussion

Despite the applied methodical rigor, this study has some limitations that need to be taken into account when interpreting its findings and conducting future research.

Various approaches have been utilized to explore the impact of institutional factors on economic growth, including quantitative analyses that examine the relationship between specific institutional variables (such as property rights protection, rule of law, and regulatory quality) and economic outcomes. Comparative case studies are also employed to assess how different institutional frameworks influence growth trajectories in various countries or regions. Additionally, the endogenous growth theory approach, which considers knowledge and innovation as key drivers of economic growth, has been widely used to study the impact of science and IT factors on economic growth. This approach emphasizes the role of human capital, research and development, and technological progress in fostering economic growth and advancement. Overall, these diverse methodological approaches contribute to a comprehensive understanding of how institutional and innovative factors affect economic growth and provide valuable insights for policymakers seeking to design effective strategies for sustainable development.

The link between institutional quality and economic growth seems to be the most well-established in the literature as well as the link between information and science factors and their influence on the economic development of the state. But there is no approach similar to the author's that can unite all the established factors in the mode of "expenses-results".

The idea is that the institutional framework lays the foundation for the economic development, the success of which depends also on the factors of the e-government, IT industry and the research sector.

When evaluating the impact of institutional infrastructure on economic growth, it is important to adopt a balanced approach. This entails avoiding excessive regulation of the economy while understanding the dynamics of its effects. To achieve this, the assessment model should consider the expansion of costs associated with institutional, innovative and informatization activities. These indicators should be increased in accordance with the country's macro-level anthropogenic policy, with a prior focus on enhancing the development of information and technological infrastructures.

In addition, it is necessary to solve the number of problems, related to combining the institutional, innovation and information factors of economic growth through the prism of its conceptual and theoretical classification. Besides, the mathematical methods for measuring the institutional and innovation factors of economic growth requires justification.

Vision of solving these problems by offering the methods for assessing the contribution of the institutional environment of the information economy to the socio-economic development on the case Belarus is considered.

Indeed, the research suggests some limitations related to the use of the author's method. There is no enough connection between researchers and practitioners in this field. However, empirical data on institutional infrastructure of the information economy of the Republic of Belarus make it possible to note patterns confirming the main hypotheses.

## 6 Conclusion

An important group of factors determining the institutional development of the information economy includes mechanisms for the interaction of society and the state through modern technological infrastructure. Analysis of conditions affecting economic growth rates shows that the increase in production is inextricably linked to socio-technological and anthropogenic macroeconomic policies. Thus, in order to improve the methodological aspects of assessing the contribution of the institutional infrastructure of the information economy to the socio-economic development, it is primarily necessary to increase in institutional terms the average expenditures of the republican budget for national activities, judicial power and security, public spending on the development of the e-government and informatization of state bodies. As a result, we will develop a social and information infrastructure. At the same time, it is necessary to pursue a balanced macroeconomic policy regarding the Institutional Development Index and the dynamics of budget expenditures on scientific, technical and innovative activities, since their increase without changing the existing institutional conditions can have a negative impact on economic growth.

One of the possible areas of research on the impact of institutional infrastructure on the information economy may be the study of the role of state bodies and legal norms in creating a favorable environment for the development of information technologies. Researchers can analyze what laws and policies contribute to attracting investment, protecting intellectual property, and driving innovation in information technology. The impact of the financial system on the information economy can also be investigated, including the role of banks and investors in financing startups and the development of information technology. Another area of research is the role of education and scientific inquiry into the development of the information economy. Researchers can study what education programs and scientific research contribute to the advancement of human resources and innovative activities in IT industry. Researchers can also focus on examining the influence of cultural and social factors on the development of the information economy, including the analysis of various values, norms and customs that can affect supply and demand in the field of information technology.

In general, research on the impact of institutional infrastructure on the information economy can contribute to a deeper understanding of the factors influencing the progress in this area and help to provide effective policies and strategies for its development.

However, inherent limitations in data availability and the complexity of institutional interactions may pose challenges in fully capturing the nuances of these relationships and limit the generalizability of findings. Future extensions of this research could focus on conducting longitudinal studies to track changes over time, exploring the cultural dimensions that influence the institutional environment, and setting practical frameworks to guide policymakers in fostering sustainable socio-economic development within the context of the information economy.

## References

1. Romer, P. M. (1986). Increasing returns and long-run growth. *Journal of Political Economy, 94*, 1002–1037.
2. Mankiw, N. G., Romer, D., & Weil, D. N. (1992). A contribution to the empirics of economic growth. *Quarterly Journal of Economics, 107*, 407–437. https://doi.org/10.2307/2118477

3. Lucas, R. E. (1988). On the mechanics of economic development. *Journal of Monetary Economics, 22*, 3–42. https://doi.org/10.1016/0304-3932(88)90168-7
4. Barro, R. J., & Sala Martin, H. (2004). *Economic growth. The MIT Press*. http://piketty.pse.ens.fr/files/BarroSalaIMartin2004Chap1-2.pdf
5. Solow, R. M. A. (1956). Contribution to the theory of economic growth. *The Quarterly Journal of Economics, 70*, 65–94. https://doi.org/10.2307/1884513
6. Krinichansky, K. V., & Lavrentiev, A. S. (2017). Analysis of the priorities of the structural policy of regions using estimates of the parameters of Barro regressions. *Regional Economics: Theory and Practice, 15*, 1233–1250. (In Russ.). https://doi.org/10.24891/re.15.7.1233
7. Barro, R. J., & Sala Martin, H. (1995). Capital mobility in neoclassical models of growth. *The American Economic Review, 85*, 103–115. https://doi.org/10.3386/w4206
8. Akaev, A. A. (2015). Models of AN-type innovative endogenous economic growth and their rationale. *Modernization. Innovations. Development, 6*, 70–79. (In Russ.). https://doi.org/10.18184/2079-4665.2015.6.2.70.79
9. Kolosnitsyna, M. G., & Ermolina, Y. E. (2021). Public spending on education and economic growth: A cross-country analysis. *Questions of statistics, 28*(3), 70–85. (In Russ.). https://doi.org/10.34023/2313-6383-2021-28-3-70-85
10. Schumpeter, J. A. (2003). *Capitalism, socialism, and democracy*. Rout-ledge.
11. Odretsch, D. B., & Feldman, M. P. (1996). R&D spillovers and the geography of innovation and production. *American Economic Review, 86*(4), 253–273.
12. Prokop, V., Stejskal, J., Klimova, V., & Zitek, V. (2021). The role of foreign technologies and R&D in innovation processes within catching-up CEE countries. *PLoS ONE, 16*(4), 2–23. https://doi.org/10.1371/journal.pone.0250307
13. Marroco, E., Paci, R., & Usai, S. (2013). Proximity, networking and knowledge production in Europe: What lessons for innovation policy? *Technological Forecasting and Social Change, 80*, 1484–1498. https://doi.org/10.1016/j.techfore.2013.03.004
14. Ermak, S., Kuznetsov, P., Tolmachev, D., & Yurovskikh, P. (2022). *The inner universe of university science*. Research division of the EXPERT media holding. (In Russ.). https://expert-ural.com/analytics/ratings/reyting-publikacionnoy-i-izobretatelskoy-aktivnost.html
15. Malerba, F. (2006). *Sectoral systems: How and why innovation differs across sectors*. Oxford University Press.
16. Fagerberg, J. (2018). *Innovation, economic development and policy: Selected essays*. Edward Elgar Publishing.
17. Golichenko, O. G., & Samovoleva, S. A. (2014). State policy in the national innovation system: Theory and practice. *Innovations, 10*(192), 83–94. (In Russ.).
18. Williamson, O. (1987). Economic institutions of capitalism. Firms, markets and relational contracting. *Australian Journal of Management, 12*, 125–137. https://doi.org/10.1177/031289628701200
19. North, D. (1997). *Institutions, institutional changes and the functioning of the economy. Nachala*. (In Russ.).
20. Acemoglu, D., Johnson, S., Robinson, J., & Thaicharoen, Y. (2003). Institutional causes, macroeconomic symptoms: Volatility, crises and growth. *Journal of Monetary Economics, 50*, 49–123. https://doi.org/10.1016/S0304-3932(02)00208-8
21. Barro, R. (1998). *Human capital and growth in cross-country regressions*. Harvard University.
22. Eltis, W. (1973). *Growth and distribution*. Macmillan.
23. Robinson, J. (1962). *Essays in the theory of economic growth*. Macmillan.
24. Rodrik, D. (1997). *Controversies, institutions and economic performance in East Asia. NBER Working Paper 5914*. National Bureau of Economic Research, Inc.
25. Scully, G. W. (1988). The institutional framework and economic development. *Journal of Political Economy, 96*, 652–662.
26. Uzawa, H. (1965). Optimal technical change in an aggregative model of economic growth. *International Economic Review, 6*, 18–31.

27. Eggertsson, T. (1990). *Economic behavior and institutions: Principles of neoinstitutional economics. Cambridge University Press.*
28. Zak Paul, J., & Knack, S. (2001). Trust and growth. *The Economic Journal, 111*, 295–321. https://doi.org/10.1111/1468-0297.00609
29. Xiaoliang, L., Jiameng, M., & Xiaochen, Z. (2023). Social trust and corporate innovation: An informal institution perspective. *The North American Journal of Economics and Finance, 64*, 101–117. https://doi.org/10.1016/j.najef.2022.101829
30. Trittin-Ulbrich, H., & Böckel, A. (2022). Institutional entrepreneurship for responsible digital innovation: The case of corporate digital responsibility. *Creativity and Innovation Management, 31*(3), 2–13. https://doi.org/10.1111/caim.12513l
31. Mullakhmedova, S. S., Shakhpazova, R. D., & Omarov, Z. Z. (2016). Institutional factors of economic growth: Theoretical and methodological aspect. *Fundamental Research, 8-2*, 356–360. (In Russ.).
32. Dominguez, G. (1978). *Marketing in a regulated environment. Wiley*. https://doi.org/10.2307/1250765
33. Simon, H. A. (1972). *Theories of bounded rationality*. North-Holland Publishing Company.
34. Gundyrina, T. O. (2011). Institutional innovations as a form of institutional changes. *Industry: Economics, Management, Technologies, 4*, 9–14. (In Russ.).
35. Kurpayanidi, K. (2021). National innovation system as a key factor in the sustainable development of the economy of Uzbekistan. *E3S Web of Conferences, 258*, 1–13. https://doi.org/10.1051/e3sconf/202125805026
36. Tereshchenko, D. S. (2016). Institutional factors of economic growth: Identification, evaluation and identification of the nonlinearity of influence. *Bulletin of the National State University of Economics, 3*, 299–314. (In Russ.).
37. Motorina, O. (2022). Assessment of the level of development of the business environment in the Republic of Belarus and other countries (based on data from Enterprise Surveys). *Bankauski Vesnik, 12*(713), 44–52. (In Russ.).
38. Lemeshchenko, P. S., & Gaponenko, N. G. (2019, February 28). The institutional structure of the Republic of Belarus: An introduction to dynamic analysis. In *Trends in economic development in the XXI century: Int. sci. conf* (pp. 95–99).
39. Interactive Heat Map. (2023). *Index of economic freedom.* https://www.heritage.org/index/heatmap
40. Clague, C., Keefer, P., Knack, S., & Olson, M. (1999). Contract-intensive money: Contract enforcement, property rights and economic performance. *Journal of Economic Growth, 4*, 185–211.
41. Gagliardi, F. (2008). Institutions and economic change: A critical survey of the new institutional approaches and empirical evidence. *The Journal of Socio-Economics, 37*(1), 416–430.
42. Corruption Perceptions Index. (n.d.). Transparency international. https://www.transparency.org/en/cpi/2022/index/blr
43. Worldwide Governance Indicators. (n.d.). The World Bank Group of indicators. https://info.worldbank.org/governance/wgi/Home/Reports
44. Dixit, R., & Sinha, V. (2023, May 12). Promoting knowledge management in public sector enterprises for sustainability. In *Governance as a catalyst for public sector sustainability* (pp. 222–241). https://doi.org/10.4018/978-1-6684-6966-8.ch011
45. Sidorchuk, I. P., Okhrimenko, A. A., & Krys, E. G. (2022). Institutional environment of the digital economy and stages of digital development of Belarus. *Law and Economics, 13*, 233–241. (In Russ.).
46. Olaoye, O., & Afolabi, O. (2021). Government spending and economic growth: A trivariate causality testing. *African Journal of Economic and Management Studies, 12*(2), 250–268. https://doi.org/10.1108/AJEMS-07-2020-0334
47. Attali, J. (2023). *Le monde, modes d'emploi*. Su Kindle Scribe.

48. Law of the Republic of Belarus of December 31, 2021 No. 142-Z On the republican budget for 2022 *Official Internet portal of the Ministry of Finance of the Republic of Belarus*. https://www.minfin.gov.by/upload/bp/act/zakon_311221_142z.pdf
49. Baranov, A. M. (2023). *Information economy: Evaluation methodology and institutional development mechanisms*. Pravo i ekonomika. (In Russ.).

# Agile Methodology Catalyzing Digital Transformation: Implementation Objectives and Evaluation Criteria in Organizational Settings

**Andrei Plotnikov, Kursat Demiryurek, Alla Plotnikova, Olga Andreeva, and Gulnaz Suzdaleva**

**Abstract** The paper evaluates the impact of Agile implementation within organizations focusing on enhancing project delivery, customer satisfaction, team collaboration, productivity, and a culture of innovation. It seeks to determine Agile's effectiveness through criteria such as customer contentment, team efficiency, delivery velocity, quality, adaptability, and stakeholder involvement, utilizing a survey of 1161 participants across various sectors. The analysis identifies four pivotal factors: work clarity and quality, business-IT alignment, risk and cost reduction, and management optimization. Agile's success correlates with internal process and culture ratings, development methodologies, and interdepartmental teamwork, yielding benefits like heightened motivation, superior product quality, increased productivity, and cost savings. The essence of Agile transformation lies in improving team dynamics and product results, contingent on an organization's inherent culture and processes. By endorsing collaboration, communication, and flexibility principles, Agile practices such as stand-ups and retrospectives foster continuous improvement and efficient problem-solving. The organizational culture's perception significantly influences Agile's successful adoption, with a transparent and empowering environment enhancing its integration. It leads to a virtuous cycle of productivity and improved product support. Moreover, Agile methodologies enhance resource efficiency via team and departmental coordination, with frameworks like Scrum and Kanban facilitating cost reduction and expedited delivery, ensuring business goals and development efforts are well-aligned.

A. Plotnikov (✉)
Ondokuz Mayıs University, Samsun, Türkiye

Perm National Research Polytechnic University, Perm, Russian Federation

K. Demiryurek · A. Plotnikova
Ondokuz Mayıs University, Samsun, Türkiye

O. Andreeva · G. Suzdaleva
Perm National Research Polytechnic University, Perm, Russian Federation



A. Appolloni et al. (eds.), *The Future of Industry*, Lecture Notes in Information Systems and Organisation 70, https://doi.org/10.1007/978-3-031-66801-2_10

**Keywords** Agile methodology · Information technology · Project management · Agile software development · Digital transformation

## 1 Introduction

The pivotal role of Agile methodology in digital transformation within a company is that it facilitates a more adaptive, responsive approach to change. Agile methodology, characterized by the principles of flexibility, iterative development, and stakeholder collaboration, is integral in enabling organizations to navigate the complexities of digital transformation.

Agile is a product management [1, 2] and project management [3–5] methodology that has gained widespread popularity in recent years due to its ability to improve project outcomes. However, implementing Agile in an organization can be challenging, as it requires significant changes in the organization's culture, processes, and mindset. Therefore, it is crucial to identify the principal objectives of Agile and the primary criteria for evaluating its effectiveness in organizations.

Agile methodology significantly impacts the manufacturing industry directly by developing manufacturing-specific software and indirectly influencing operational practices and strategies. Initially designed for software development, Agile's principles—such as continuous improvement, customer feedback, and flexibility—are perfectly suited to address the dynamic challenges of the manufacturing sector [6, 7].

Directly, Agile fosters the creation of software closely aligned with the ever-evolving needs of manufacturing processes. This alignment is achieved through iterative development, which allows for rapid adjustments in software functionality to match new requirements or technological advancements. Collaborative efforts between developers, users, and stakeholders ensure that the software meets the technical specifications and is user-friendly and tailored to the unique ecosystem of the manufacturing industry. The customer-centric approach guarantees that feedback from the manufacturing floor can directly influence software updates, ensuring that tools remain relevant and practical [8].

Indirectly, the Agile methodology influences the manufacturing industry by enhancing operational efficiency and innovation. Software developed under Agile principles supports streamlined operations, reduces waste, and promotes productivity by offering solutions for resource management, inventory control, and production scheduling [9]. The iterative nature of Agile encourages ongoing innovation in software functionalities, providing manufacturers with competitive advantages through advanced analytics, optimization algorithms, and other cutting-edge features. Moreover, Agile's flexibility allows manufacturers to adapt to market changes swiftly, maintaining relevancy and competitiveness. The emphasis on collaboration and communication fosters a teamwork culture and openness within manufacturers, enhancing the integration and effectiveness of software tools.

The principal Agile implementation objectives in organizations include improving project delivery, increasing customer satisfaction, enhancing team collaboration and productivity, and fostering a culture of innovation and continuous improvement. These objectives are often interrelated and may vary depending on the organization's industry, size, and goals.

Evaluating the effectiveness of Agile in organizations requires identifying the primary criteria that measure the extent to which Agile practices achieve their objectives. The primary criteria for evaluating Agile effectiveness typically include customer satisfaction, team productivity, project delivery speed, quality, flexibility, and stakeholder engagement (criteria following by goal).

The paper aims to explore the principal groups of Agile implementation objectives in organizations and the primary criteria for evaluating the effectiveness of Agile in organizations. By identifying these objectives and criteria, organizations can understand how to implement Agile practices more adequately and assess their effectiveness in achieving their objectives.

## 2 Literature Review

Initially conceptualized for software development projects, the Agile Methodology has seen widespread adoption across various domains due to its flexibility, responsiveness to change, and focus on stakeholder satisfaction. This literature review delves into the multifaceted dimensions of Agile practices, drawing on seminal works and recent studies that highlight its application, effectiveness, and areas necessitating further inquiry. We begin by examining the foundational principles of Agile outlined by Bose [10], who revisits 12 case studies on the successful implementation of distributed Agile software projects. The synthesis of these cases offers a comprehensive understanding of Agile's practical benefits and sets the stage for discussing its theoretical underpinnings. Further exploration by Maruping et al. [11] draw on control theory to reveal the conditions under which agile practices are most effective in improving software project quality. Owing to the ever-increasing demand for agile approaches, Qureshi [12] addresses the problem of Extreme Programming's (XP) ability to handle medium and large projects. There is a need for a methodology which merges Lean and Agile into a holistic unit. Altameem [13] explains various ways the Agile Methodology impacts software development. As proposed, the combination of Agile development and modelling is a new concept that requires further data gathering and investigation to determine if it will improve productivity and risk reduction without losing the benefits of the Agile Methodology [14].

Azanha et al. [15] analyzed the benefits of the Agile Project Management (APM) framework compared to the traditional waterfall model, aiming to understand how it can help companies add value and gain a competitive advantage. Combining building information modelling with the Agile Management Approach was suggested because it helps reduce time and cost and improve quality. Agile's flexibility, iterative development, and stakeholder engagement starkly contrast the rigid, linear approach of traditional Software Development Life Cycle (SDLC), making Agile more suited to the rapid innovation and adaptability required in digital transformation [16]. Ahmed et al. [17] aim to ascertain the status of using Building Information Modeling (BIM) and Agile Project Management (APM) in Iraq and to shed light on the merging of this integration, explaining the benefits, difficulties, and workflow practices, finding the most influencing factors on the time, cost and quality of the project. The proposed research model for evaluating how the Agile Methodology uses factors that influence project performance [18]. A current study in industrial practice reveals that out of 23 objectives that are expected when introducing Agile Development Processes to technical systems, the three objectives mentioned above show the most significant negative deviations from expected benefit to realized benefit. Riesener et al. [19] addressed the shortcomings by developing a methodological approach to the Agile development of technical systems. A risk management framework is necessary to succeed in such teams. Esteki et al. [20] proposed a risk management framework in Scrum using the PRINCE2 Methodology, which includes the perceived risks in distributed Scrum projects and their causes and roots for managing these risks.

Survey data from 316 project managers and product owners across different industries reveal that the impact of control on innovation project performance depends on the design of control systems and the emphasis on different control levers used by top managers [21]. Khan et al. [22] introduce the AUTOSAR Driven Agile Development (AUTILE) Framework as a new methodology to develop automotive software to reduce the number of defects and their severity. The existing literature needs concrete guidelines for practitioners to define such a strategy systematically. Maro et al. [23] address this gap by defining a Traceability Introduction Methodology (TracIMo) for systematically designing, implementing, and evaluating software traceability in practice. The research identified studies with reported application practices of Agile Methodologies in the global and Brazilian public administration scenarios. By exploring the research, studies address ways to start a project, its difficulties, and its benefits [24].

As we can see, there are a large number of relevant studies, and below we highlight those focusing on digital transformation.

Ayaz and Shaukat [25] note that, although Agile methodologies address barriers and challenges effectively, many organizations need help implementing technological changes as part of their digital transformation efforts. The paper categorizes barriers into several groups, such as organization-related barriers, people-related barriers, process-related barriers, technology-related barriers, project-related barriers, adoptive/capacity-related barriers, and behavior-related barriers. Each category encompasses specific challenges that organizations encounter during the digital transformation process. For example, organization-related barriers include resistance to change, a lack of Agile culture, or unsuitable organizational structures for Agile methodologies. Technology-related barriers involve integrating new digital tools and platforms, while people-related barriers focus on the skills and mindset of the workforce. The thesis utilizes contingency theory and Kotter's change management model to explore these barriers further and proposes a framework for addressing them. Contingency theory is applied to understand how external and internal factors influence the adoption of agile methodologies. At the same time, Kotter's model provides a step-by-step approach to managing change effectively during the digital transformation. In conclusion, the critical barrier identified in the paper revolves around the complex interplay of organizational, technological, and human factors that challenge the effective implementation of Agile methodologies in digital transformation initiatives. Addressing these barriers requires a comprehensive approach that considers the specific context and needs of the organization, as well as the adoption of suitable change management strategies to facilitate the transition.

Fuchs and Hess [26] consider that firms must embrace Agile practices prioritizing flexibility, responsiveness, and customer focus to stay competitive in a fast-evolving digital landscape. This shift is not just technological but requires significant organizational and social changes, including a cultural shift towards agility and restructuring organizational hierarchies. Their study, based on qualitative research and case studies, identifies the episodic and socio-technical nature of Agile transformation, which involves overcoming numerous challenges through specific strategic actions. These actions facilitate the transition through various phases of Agile integration, highlighting the complex interplay between technological advancements and organizational dynamics in achieving successful digital and Agile transformation. Key to navigating this transformation is Agile leadership, which integrates critical factors such as workforce transformation, dynamic capability, and strategic flexibility into the organizational context [27].

Another study [28] emphasizes the change of information systems development into strategic, customer-centric, iterative, and experimental processes to meet the accelerating rates of technological change and continuously shifting customer behavior and markets. It points out that while Agile methods have shown positive effects in smaller projects, there needs to be more knowledge about their application in more extensive, complex organizational settings where interdependencies increase significantly.

Alruwaili et al. [16] comprehensively analyses how Agile development methodologies such as Scrum, Kanban, Extreme Programming, and Agile tools support digital transformation initiatives. Scrum is noted for its high flexibility in project implementation, focusing on incremental product delivery and team adaptability to changes during system implementation. Scrum as the framework is beneficial for digital transformation as it allows for rapid adaptation to evolving digital landscapes and customer needs, ensuring products are developed in alignment with current market demands. Scrum's roles (Product Owner, Development Team, Scrum Master) and processes (Development and Release) are structured to support collaborative work and continuous improvement, which is essential for the dynamic nature of digital transformation projects. Kanban's emphasis on visualizing work, limiting work in progress, and managing flow aligns with the need for agility and responsiveness in digital transformation efforts. XP emphasizes dividing processes into smaller, manageable parts for easier and quicker processing, facilitating project completion. This methodology enhances clarity, simplifies role distribution, and boosts team responsiveness and communication—critical aspects for successfully executing digital transformation strategies. XP's roles (Customer, Coach,

Programmer, Tracker, Tester) and processes (Planning, Exploration, Iterations, Maintenance) focus on constant feedback, adaptability, and quality, aligning well with the iterative nature of digital transformation.

Gurusamy et al. [29] consider strategic integration of Design Thinking and Agile methodology to drive digital transformation, highlighting the importance of adapting innovative approaches to rapidly changing customer needs. Design Thinking, with its human-centric, iterative process, fosters innovation by emphasizing a deep understanding of user needs, desirability, feasibility, and viability. At the same time, the Agile methodology caters to dynamic project environments by delivering value early and encouraging continuous feedback. Combining Design Thinking's thorough exploration of problems and solutions with Agile's flexible and iterative delivery model, the proposed framework effectively balances each methodology's strengths and weaknesses. This integration facilitates the faster delivery of solutions that closely align with customer needs, ultimately reducing costs, waste, and time and marking a significant advancement in how businesses approach digital transformation.

The papers discuss Agile methodologies' role, benefits, challenges, and nuances in software development and other technical projects. They are drawn from academic research, case studies, and industrial insights.

Key findings from the literature review:

- Building Information Modeling (BIM) in Iraq is quite low, but this does not directly relate to Agile methods. However, when Agile is employed, it has been found to significantly reduce development time, enhance team motivation, and improve final product quality.
- Distributed Agile development can be particularly challenging due to differences in time zones, work cultures, and communication barriers. However, it has been embraced for its potential benefits, including cost reduction and increased flexibility. Various solutions to the inherent challenges have been discovered through case studies.
- A framework integrating Scrum and PRINCE2 methodology has been proposed for managing risks in distributed Agile projects. The framework has proven effective in identifying and mitigating risks in case studies.
- A new framework called AUTILE has been introduced for automotive software development that leverages Agile methodologies for higher-quality outputs.
- Control mechanisms adapted to Agile projects can substantially impact the project's success. Research using data from 316 project managers revealed that the impact of control on project performance varies based on the control mechanisms employed.
- A methodology named TracIMo has been developed to improve software traceability in Agile environments, showing promising results in case studies.
- Extreme Programming, an Agile methodology, has limitations in medium and large projects due to issues like weak documentation and lack of solid architecture. Modifications to XP have been proposed to address these issues.

- Attempts are being made to adapt Agile methodologies for developing technical systems, primarily to improve customer orientation, flexibility, and time-to-market.
- Design Thinking is the approach to problems and solutions with Agile's adaptable and progressive delivery approach, achieving a harmonious balance between the strengths and weaknesses of each methodology.

Hence, the papers cover various facets of the Agile methodology in software development, focusing on its advantages, limitations, and application in different contexts such as distributed settings and various sectors like automotive and finance. The Agile methodology is noted for producing high-quality software efficiently while enhancing team motivation and stakeholder engagement. However, challenges arise in distributed environments, involving issues related to communication, time zones, and cultural differences. PRINCE2 and AUTILE have been proposed to mitigate these risks for specific contexts. The papers also explore the impact of Agile on innovation, proposing that management control mechanisms must be adapted to reap its benefits fully. Recent research reveals that Agile practices are not uniformly beneficial, and their effectiveness can be contingent on various factors such as project scale and control modes. However, Agile methodologies play a critical role in digital transformation, offering the flexibility, collaboration, and iterative development essential for navigating organisations' rapid technological changes. Studies highlight the challenges of implementing Agile, including organizational, technological, and human factors, and suggest comprehensive strategies for overcoming these barriers, such as integrating change management models. Agile's adaptability and focus on stakeholder engagement contrast with the rigidity of traditional SDLC methods, underscoring its superiority in supporting the dynamic requirements of digital transformation initiatives. Finally, the papers suggest that Agile principles are being adapted beyond software development into areas like technical systems, albeit with mixed results.

## 3 Materials and Methods

### *3.1 Data Description*

The survey was conducted in 2020 and involved 1161 participants from various cities (mainly in Russia). The respondents answered questions about the organization they work for. Thus, the results obtained make it possible to analyze the peculiarities of Agile practices in the following organizational groups: the IT industry (482 participants, 42%), the financial sector (206, 18%), telecommunications (56, 5%), and other sectors (417, 35%).

ScrumTrek conducted the survey in partnership with the Project Management Institute® in the Moscow Branch and with the participation of Grass and Xsolla companies. In recent years, Agile in Russia has been the largest annual study of flexible management approaches compared to Agile studies in individual countries and the global State of Agile study from Digital.ai.

The data gathering, conducted from December 20, 2019 to December 11, 2020 was a collaborative effort with the Project Management Institute® Moscow, Grass, and Xsolla. Importantly, the respondents participated voluntarily and had the freedom to suspend their involvement at any point. This ethical approach ensured no personal data was collected, enhancing the credibility of the study.

The data are relevant today; firstly, they represent the period that fell during the COVID-19 pandemic. Thus, the data were collected in unique conditions that are difficult to reproduce, which means the data remains relevant and valuable to the scientific community. Secondly, the data contain significant theoretical information—a value that confirms or refutes the existing hypotheses and theories—which makes them relevant regardless of the time of collection. Thirdly, researchers can compare the available data with recent data in future studies.

The survey included individuals occupying various roles in their respective organizations, ranging from top managers and company owners to developers. The distribution of employees by the primary type of activity (positions in the organization) varied among enterprises in different industries. IT organizations had a significantly higher representation of project managers (26%) than organizations in other industries. Financial sector organizations had a significantly higher representation of analysts and product owners (23%) than organizations in other industries. The highest percentage of Scrum Masters and Agile Coaches was observed in telecommunications (25%) and financial sector organizations (22%).

The survey included employees from enterprises of various sizes—from small ones (less than 50 employees) to large ones (more than 500 employees).

The key clients of most organizations whose employees participated in the survey are the B2B category (business and other companies, 61%), followed by B2C (end consumers, 20%), and then B2G (internal clients, 16%).

## 3.2 Methods

Agile has become increasingly popular as a project management methodology in recent years, but how do we determine its effectiveness? One approach is to identify the main criteria for evaluating Agile's effectiveness from the perspective of employees within a company. In this regard, a factor analysis was conducted on responses to the question "What benefits have been obtained in your company from implementing Agile?". This analysis aimed to identify the key factors that influence Agile's effectiveness. Moreover, the hypothesis was tested that there are several main groups of criteria for Agile effectiveness, including social and technical. The following sections will delve into the results of this analysis and their implications for Agile implementation in companies.

Principal Component Analysis (PCA) is a statistical technique used to reduce the number of variables in a dataset while retaining as much variance as possible [30]. In

PCA with Kaizer normalization [31], the input data is standardized by dividing each variable by its standard deviation, known as normalization. The Kaizer normalization method ensures that all variables contribute equally to the analysis by weighting them based on their variance.

Varimax rotation is an orthogonal rotation used to simplify the interpretation of principal component analysis by maximizing the variance of the squared loadings of each variable onto a single factor [31]. Varimax rotation aims to create factors with high loadings on only a few variables, which can aid in identifying underlying factors in the data. It rotates the axes of the factors to produce a new set of uncorrelated factors, making it easier to interpret the results.

PCA is an excellent tool for reducing dimensionality in a complex dataset, allowing for a more focused and meaningful interpretation. Given that Agile methodologies can have a wide range of effects, spanning social to technical benefits, this technique enables researchers to zero in on critical criteria that genuinely matter. By retaining maximum variance while minimizing the number of variables, PCA helps identify which aspects of Agile contribute most significantly to its effectiveness, as employees perceive.

Kaiser normalization standardizes the dataset by weighting variables based on their variance. It ensures that each variable contributes equally to the analysis. In the context of Agile, where benefits can range from the nuanced (like team morale) to the more overt (such as reduced project costs), all the variables must be considered equally. This normalization process ensures that conclusions are not skewed by variables that may inherently have higher variance.

Varimax rotation complements PCA by simplifying the interpretation of the analysis. It maximizes the variance of squared loadings for each variable on a single factor, aiding in identifying underlying factors or criteria that define Agile's effectiveness. Given that the hypothesis suggests that there may be different main groups of criteria for Agile's effectiveness, such as social and technical, Varimax rotation serves as a crucial tool to confirm or disprove this hypothesis by making the results more interpretable.

## 4 Findings

### *4.1 The Main Objectives Groups of Agile Implementation in Organizations*

To determine how employees group the goals of Agile implementation in their organizations, a factor analysis was conducted on the respondents' answers to the question "What are the goals of Agile implementation in your company?". Four of the thirteen items have a positive or negative correlation with Factor 1 prior to rotation of 0.5 or more, while the rest have a low correlation coefficient of less than 0.5. Thus, it is reasonable to acknowledge a low relationship among the questionnaire items. However, due to Varimax rotation, four factors (components) were identified that group Agile goals into categories (Table 1). Nonetheless, the total percentage of explained variance was 46.4%, indicating the identified groups' weak stability.

The objectives groups are denoted as follows (Table 2):

1-. Clarity and quality of work to ensure company success in the long term;
2-. Alignment of business and IT to increase speed and predictability of work;
3-. Reducing risks and costs;
4-. Management optimization.

The rotated component matrix from factor analysis is a statistical technique used to identify underlying factors that explain patterns of variance in a set of variables. In this case, the variables are the Agile goals of a company, and the factors are the components that explain the variance in those goals.

The first component, Clarity and quality of work to ensure company success in the long term, includes the Agile objectives of increasing team motivation, improving product quality, improving engineering culture, simplifying product support, and improving project management transparency. These objectives are associated with the long-term success of the company and represent a common theme of improving the quality and efficiency of work.

The second component, aligning business and IT to increase speed and predictability of work, includes the Agile objectives of ensuring coordinated work between business and IT, increasing delivery predictability, and accelerating product delivery to market. These goals are related to the need for businesses to align their IT strategies with their overall objectives to increase efficiency and speed of work.

The third component, reducing risks and costs, includes the Agile implementation objectives of reducing project costs and risks. These objectives are associated with companies' need to manage costs and risks related to their projects to ensure their long-term success.

The fourth component, management optimization, includes the goals of better managing distributed teams and better managing changing priorities. These aims are connected to companies' need to optimize their management practices to ensure that their teams are working effectively and efficiently.

Overall, the rotated component matrix provides a valuable framework for understanding Agile implementation's different goals and components. It can help companies identify areas where they need to focus their efforts to achieve success.

## *4.2 The Main Criteria for Evaluating Agile Effectiveness in Organizations*

The main criteria for evaluating Agile effectiveness in organizations were identified by conducting a factor analysis of responses to the question "What benefits have

**Table 1** Explained variance (objectives of Agile implementation in organizations)

| Component | Initial eigenvalues | | | Sums of squares of extraction loads | | | Sums of squares of rotational loads | | |
|---|---|---|---|---|---|---|---|---|---|
| | Total | % Variance | Cumulative % | Total | % Variance | Cumulative % | Total | % Variance | Cumulative % |
| 1 | 2.680 | 20.616 | 20.616 | 2.680 | 20.616 | 20.616 | 1.801 | 13.852 | 13.852 |
| 2 | 1.252 | 9.631 | 30.247 | 1.252 | 9.631 | 30.247 | 1.534 | 11.799 | 25.651 |
| 3 | 1.093 | 8.411 | 38.658 | 1.093 | 8.411 | 38.658 | 1.493 | 11.484 | 37.135 |
| 4 | 1.008 | 7.751 | 46.409 | 1.008 | 7.751 | 46.409 | 1.206 | 9.274 | 46.409 |
| 5 | .948 | 7.293 | 53.703 | | | | | | |
| 6 | .874 | 6.720 | 60.423 | | | | | | |
| 7 | .860 | 6.617 | 67.040 | | | | | | |
| 8 | .808 | 6.214 | 73.254 | | | | | | |
| 9 | .786 | 6.045 | 79.299 | | | | | | |
| 10 | .764 | 5.878 | 85.177 | | | | | | |
| 11 | .714 | 5.489 | 90.666 | | | | | | |
| 12 | .638 | 4.906 | 95.571 | | | | | | |
| 13 | .576 | 4.429 | 100.000 | | | | | | |

Note: Extraction method: Principal Component Analysis

**Table 2** Rotated Component Matrix (objectives of Agile implementation in organizations)

| | Components | | | |
|---|---|---|---|---|
| | Clarity and quality of work to ensure company success in the long term | Alignment of business and IT to increase speed and predictability of work | Reducing risks and costs | Management optimization |
| Increase team motivation | .689 | | | |
| Improve product quality | .656 | | | |
| Increase productivity | .520 | | .359 | |
| Improve engineering culture | .455 | | | |
| Simplify product support | .431 | | | |
| Improve project management transparency | .349 | | | |
| Ensure coordinated work between business and IT | | .680 | | |
| Increase delivery predictability | | .623 | | |
| Accelerate product delivery to market | | .584 | | |
| Reduce project costs | | | .825 | |
| Reduce project risks | | | .730 | |
| Better manage distributed teams | | | | .687 |
| Better manage changing priorities | | | | .621 |

Note: Extraction method: Principal component analysis. Rotation method: Varimax with Kaiser normalization. Convergence was achieved after five iterations of rotation

been obtained in your company from implementing Agile?". Additionally, the hypothesis was tested that there are several main criteria for Agile effectiveness, including social and technical.

Social and technical factors can be divided based on the nature of the criteria used to evaluate the effectiveness of Agile implementation.

Social factors typically focus on Agile implementation's social aspects, such as employee satisfaction, team collaboration, and organizational culture. These factors are often subjective and based on personal experiences and perceptions of employees and stakeholders.

On the other hand, technical factors focus on more objective and measurable aspects of Agile implementation, such as project delivery speed, quality, flexibility, team productivity, and stakeholder engagement. These factors are often quantifiable and can be objectively measured using various performance indicators and metrics.

Thus, the division between social and technical factors depends on the nature of the criteria used to evaluate the effectiveness of Agile implementation. While social and technical factors are essential in assessing Agile effectiveness, they differ in the focus and methods used to measure their impact.

The results of the factor analysis are presented in Tables 3 and 4. The criteria for evaluating the benefits of Agile implementation are divided into two groups (Table 3). However, the total percentage of explained variance is only 40.7%, indicating a weak level of stability in the identified groups. Nevertheless, using Varimax rotation, two factors (components) were identified that combine Agile benefits across groups and can be designated as social and technical (Table 4).

Therefore, employees associate Agile practices in their organizations with two main benefits: social and technical. Social benefits include the organization's flexibility, such as improving project management transparency, effectively managing changing priorities, increasing delivery predictability, and achieving business and IT alignment. Technical benefits include improving product quality and support, reducing costs and project risks, and optimizing team management.

The notion that employees associate the implementation of Agile practices with social and technical benefits offers a comprehensive understanding of the multi-faceted impact of Agile methodologies.

## Social Benefits

One of the fundamental tenets of Agile is transparency, which enables every team member to understand project goals, responsibilities, and progress. It fosters an environment of trust and facilitates better decision-making.

Agile methodologies are designed to be flexible, allowing teams to adapt to changing requirements quickly. This adaptability is crucial in today's fast-paced business environment and is a social benefit that promotes organizational resilience.

Through iterative cycles and regular reviews, Agile practices help to make delivery timelines more predictable. It fosters a sense of reliability and stability within the team and the organization.

Agile practices promote a collaborative approach where business stakeholders and IT teams work closely. This alignment is not merely operational but also cultural, helping to break down silos and promote organizational unity.

## Technical Benefits

Through practices like Test-Driven Development (TDD) [32] and Continuous Integration [33], Agile methodologies contribute to higher product quality. Agile also enables quick iterations, allowing for timely product support and updates.

**Table 3** Explained variance (criteria for evaluating Agile effectiveness in organizations)

| | Initial eigenvalues | | | Sums of squares of extraction loads | | | Sums of squares of rotational loads | | |
|---|---|---|---|---|---|---|---|---|---|
| Component | Total | % Variance | Cumulative % | Total | % Variance | Cumulative % | Total | % Variance | Cumulative % |
| 1 | 4.082 | 31.399 | 31.399 | 4.082 | 31.399 | 31.399 | 2.898 | 22.291 | 22.291 |
| 2 | 1.213 | 9.329 | 40.728 | 1.213 | 9.329 | 40.728 | 2.397 | 18.437 | 40.728 |
| 3 | .937 | 7.209 | 47.937 | | | | | | |
| 4 | .874 | 6.726 | 54.663 | | | | | | |
| 5 | .849 | 6.532 | 61.195 | | | | | | |
| 6 | .760 | 5.849 | 67.044 | | | | | | |
| 7 | .736 | 5.660 | 72.704 | | | | | | |
| 8 | .715 | 5.501 | 78.206 | | | | | | |
| 9 | .619 | 4.759 | 82.964 | | | | | | |
| 10 | .593 | 4.562 | 87.526 | | | | | | |
| 11 | .565 | 4.344 | 91.870 | | | | | | |
| 12 | .558 | 4.291 | 96.161 | | | | | | |
| 13 | .499 | 3.839 | 100.000 | | | | | | |

Note: Extraction method: Principal component analysis

By emphasizing the delivery of small, functional pieces of a project and obtaining frequent feedback, Agile helps to identify and mitigate risks earlier in the project lifecycle, often leading to cost savings.

Agile practices such as Scrum and Kanban provide frameworks for optimizing team workflows and resource allocation. This results in better task delegation, smoother project execution, and, ultimately, more effective team management.

## Interplay Between Social and Technical Benefits

It is essential to note that social and technical benefits are often intertwined. For instance, improving project management transparency (a social benefit) can lead to better risk identification and mitigation (a technical benefit). Similarly, managing changing priorities (social) can reduce costs due to less time spent on unnecessary features or rework (technical).

Employees often perceive the advantages of Agile implementation as falling into two broad categories: social and technical. The social benefits enhance organizational culture and flexibility, while the technical benefits focus on tangible outcomes like product quality and cost reduction. The interplay between these benefits can be a powerful catalyst for comprehensive organizational improvement.

Notably, the benefit of increased productivity has a relatively high correlation coefficient value in both factors (Table 4). In the respondents' minds, both social and technical benefits of Agile are associated with increased productivity.

**Table 4** Rotated Component Matrix (criteria for evaluating Agile effectiveness in organizations)

| | Components | |
|---|---|---|
| Indicator | Social benefits | Technical benefits |
| Project management transparency has improved | .685 | |
| Better management of changing priorities | .661 | |
| Delivery predictability has increased | .655 | |
| Product delivery to market has accelerated | .612 | |
| Productivity has increased | .513 | .514 |
| Coordinated work between business and IT has been ensured | .511 | |
| Team motivation has increased | .464 | |
| Engineering culture has improved | .373 | |
| Product support has been simplified | | .755 |
| Project costs have decreased | | .728 |
| Product quality has improved | | .641 |
| Project risks have decreased | | .525 |
| Distributed teams are better managed | | .366 |

Note: Extraction method: Principal component analysis. Rotation method: Varimax with Kaiser normalization. Convergence was achieved after three iterations of rotation

Correlation analysis of employees' responses to the questions "What benefits have been obtained in your company from implementing Agile?" and "How do you rate the current state of affairs in your company (compared to other companies in the industry) in terms of . . .?" allowed us to identify several trends. We are discussing trends, not stable interdependencies, as the correlation coefficients do not exceed 0.3 (Table 5).

**Table 5** Trends between the benefits of implementing Agile and the rating of the current state of affairs in a company

| | How do you rate the current state of affairs in your company (compared to other companies in the industry) in terms of . . . | | | |
|---|---|---|---|---|
| What benefits have been obtained in your company from implementing Agile? | Internal processes and culture that make it pleasant to work | Development processes: fast delivery and flexible adaptation to customer needs | Coordinated work of teams and departments, business and development alignment | Creating new products that make money and satisfy customers |
| Better management of changing priorities | .174** | .185** | .202** | .123** |
| Distributed teams are better managed | .189** | .155** | .155** | .162** |
| Coordinated work between business and IT has been ensured | .165** | .172** | .235** | .148** |
| Product support has been simplified | .208** | .243** | .208** | .195** |
| Team motivation has increased | .257** | .127** | .191** | .098** |
| Delivery predict-ability has increased | .125** | .182** | .121** | .131** |
| Productivity has increased | .197** | .254** | .189** | .146** |
| Product quality has improved | .249** | .246** | .188** | .169** |
| Project costs have decreased | .156** | .228** | .242** | .217** |
| Project risks have decreased | .152** | .226** | .221** | .198** |
| Engineering culture has improved | .180** | .205** | .142** | .155** |
| Project manage-ment transparency has improved | .171** | .157** | .147** | .131** |
| Product delivery to market has accelerated | .184** | .275** | .207** | .136** |

So, the state of the company's affairs is interrelated in the minds of employees with the benefits of implementing Agile in the following way.

The higher employees rate their company's current state of affairs in terms of "internal processes and culture that make it pleasant to work," the more they often note Agile benefits such as increased team motivation and improved product quality.

The higher employees rate their company's current state of affairs in terms of "development processes: fast delivery and flexible adaptation to customer needs," the more they often note Agile benefits such as increased productivity and more direct product support.

The higher employees rate their company's current state of affairs in terms of "coordinated work of teams and departments, business and development alignment," the more they often note Agile benefits such as reduced project costs.

When employees rate their company highly regarding positive work culture and efficient internal processes, they are more likely to notice benefits such as increased team motivation and improved product quality after implementing Agile methodologies. This linkage can be explained by aligning company culture with Agile values such as collaboration, communication, and adaptability. When the existing culture already promotes these values, implementing Agile processes can catalyze noticeable improvements in motivation and product quality.

Similarly, when employees rate their organization highly regarding quick delivery and flexible adaptation to customer needs, they often attribute increased productivity and more direct product support to Agile adoption. In a company already focused on customer and speed, Agile serves as an accelerator. It formalizes these attributes into a structured approach, making it easier for employees to see direct correlations between Agile practices and productivity gains or better product support.

Lastly, employees who rate their company highly regarding coordinated work among teams and departments and business and development alignment are likelier to notice benefits such as reduced project costs upon Agile adoption. It is likely because Agile methodologies like Scrum and Kanban promote transparency and collaboration across different units and functions. When there is a pre-existing culture of coordination and alignment, the resource allocation efficiency brought by Agile can easily translate into cost savings, reinforcing employees' positive perceptions.

It is crucial to understand that this is a reciprocal relationship. While positive perceptions of the company can lead to a more noticeable appreciation of Agile benefits, the successful implementation of Agile can also improve employees' perceptions of the company's state of affairs. Thus, it creates a virtuous cycle: better perceptions lead to more successful Agile implementation, improved company metrics and even better perceptions.

## 5 Conclusion

The causes of these observations can be attributed to the fact that Agile methodologies are designed to improve how teams work together and collaborate, ultimately leading to improved product quality and higher team motivation. Employees who perceive a positive internal culture and efficient processes are more likely to adopt Agile principles and practices after digital transformation, leading to further productivity and product support improvements. Additionally, coordinated work among teams and departments and alignment between business and development can lead to more efficient use of resources and reduced project costs, key benefits of the Agile methodology. Positive perceptions of the company's internal culture and processes can foster a more conducive Agile implementation and success environment during digital transformation.

The idea posits that Agile methodologies enhance product quality and bolster team motivation, ultimately creating a virtuous cycle of continuous improvement within an organization. Below is an expanded development of the concept:

Agile methodologies place strong emphasis on collaboration, communication, and flexibility. By adopting Agile principles, teams can adapt to changes more swiftly and effectively, creating higher-quality products. It is due to various Agile practices such as regular stand-ups, retrospectives, and cross-functional collaboration that focus on problem-solving and continual improvement.

A pivotal factor in the success of Agile implementation is employees' perception of the organization's internal culture. When employees recognize a culture that values transparency, empowerment, and respect, they are more inclined to adopt Agile principles and practices. This positive reception of Agile can improve individual productivity and the quality of support provided for the product, thereby creating a mutually reinforcing cycle of improvement.

Coordinated work among teams and across departments is another strength of Agile methodologies. Agile frameworks like Scrum and Kanban facilitate this by making work transparent and breaking it down into manageable units that can be prioritized. This efficient management of resources leads to reduced project costs and quicker delivery. Moreover, aligning business objectives with development efforts ensures that all team members work towards a common goal, thus optimizing the resource use.

The alignment of a positive internal culture with efficient processes creates an environment conducive to successfully implementing Agile methodologies. Employees in such an environment are not just foot soldiers following orders; they become stakeholders deeply invested in the product and the Agile process. It fosters a culture of continuous improvement and learning, which is central to the Agile philosophy.

Agile methodologies improve team collaboration and product quality by instilling a strong focus on efficient, transparent, and adaptable processes. It attracts positive perceptions from employees, further encouraging the adopting of Agile practices. Coordinated work and business-development alignment then contribute to the efficient use of resources and cost reduction. Thus, a positive internal culture combined with efficient processes sets the stage for a more prosperous and sustainable Agile implementation.

In conclusion, the implementation of Agile practices in organizations is perceived by employees to yield significant benefits that can be broadly categorized into social and technical dimensions. On the social front, Agile fosters an environment of transparency, adaptability, and alignment, strengthening the organizational culture and making it more resilient. It improves project management transparency, efficiently handles changing priorities, and promotes predictability in project deliveries. Moreover, Agile facilitates a symbiotic relationship between business and IT units, fortifying the company's internal cohesion.

On the technical side, Agile methodologies contribute to elevating product quality through practices such as Test-Driven Development and Continuous Integration. They enable timely risk identification and mitigation, reducing costs and project risks.

Notably, the social and technical benefits are not mutually exclusive but are closely interlinked. For example, greater project management transparency leads to more effective risk identification, and adaptability in managing priorities can result in cost reduction. The synergy between the social and technical benefits makes Agile methodologies a holistic approach to organizational excellence, not just a project management tool. Thus, the multi-faceted impact of Agile practices is a compelling argument for their broader adoption in organizations aiming during digital transformation for cultural and operational optimization.

**Acknowledgments** We thank ScrumTrek LLC (www.scrumtrek.ru): IT-Product Manager Aleksei Evdokimov, Agile-coach and Agile Transformation Expert Sergei Rogachev for the data.

The study was supported by the Scientific and Technological Research Council of Türkiye (TÜBİTAK), The Department of Science Fellowships and Grant Programs (BİDEB), 2221—Fellowship Program for Visiting Scientists and Scientists on Sabbatical Leave (2022/3).

## References

1. Tkalich, A., Ulfsnes, R., & Moe, N. B. (2022, June). Toward an agile product management: What do product managers do in agile companies? In *International conference on agile software development* (pp. 168–184). Springer International Publishing.
2. De Carvalho, B. V., & Mello, C. H. P. (2011). Scrum agile product development method-literature review, analysis and classification. *Product: Management and Development, 9*(1), 39–49. https://doi.org/10.4322/pmd.2011.005
3. Fernandez, D. J., & Fernandez, J. D. (2008). Agile project management—Agilism versus traditional approaches. *Journal of Computer Information Systems, 49*(2), 10–17.
4. Highsmith, J. (2009). *Agile project management: Creating innovative products*. Pearson Education.
5. Stare, A. (2014). Agile project management in product development projects. *Procedia-Social and Behavioral Sciences, 119*, 295–304. https://doi.org/10.1016/j.sbspro.2014.03.034

6. Kumar, R., Singh, K., & Jain, S. K. (2020). An empirical investigation and prioritization of barriers toward implementation of agile manufacturing in the manufacturing industry. *The TQM Journal, 33*(1), 183–203. https://doi.org/10.1108/tqm-04-2020-0073
7. Jadoon, G., Ud Din, I., Almogren, A., & Almajed, H. (2020). Smart and agile manufacturing framework, a case study for automotive industry. *Energies, 13*(21), 5766. https://doi.org/10.3390/en13215766
8. Weichbroth, P. (2022). A case study on implementing agile techniques and practices: Rationale, benefits, barriers and business implications for hardware development. *Applied Sciences, 12*(17), 8457. https://doi.org/10.3390/app12178457
9. Reichwein, J., Vogel, S., Schork, S., & Kirchner, E. (2020). On the applicability of agile development methods to design for additive manufacturing. *Procedia CIRP, 91*, 653–658. https://doi.org/10.1016/j.procir.2020.03.112
10. Bose, I. (2008). Lessons learned from distributed agile software projects: A case-based analysis. *Communications of the Association for Information Systems, 23*(1), 34. https://doi.org/10.17705/1cais.02334
11. Maruping, L. M., Venkatesh, V., & Agarwal, R. (2009). A control theory perspective on agile methodology use and changing user requirements. *Information Systems Research, 20*(3), 377–399. https://doi.org/10.1287/isre.1090.0238
12. Qureshi, M. R. J. (2012). Agile software development methodology for medium and large projects. *IET Software, 6*(4), 358–363. https://doi.org/10.1049/iet-sen.2011.0110
13. Altameem, E. A. (2015). Impact of agile methodology on software development. *Computer and Information Science, 8*(2), 9. https://doi.org/10.5539/cis.v8n2p9
14. Osvalds, G., & Lempia, D. L. (2015, October). Do teams using agile methodology need modeling? *In INCOSE international symposium* (Vol. 25, No. 1, pp. 634–647).
15. Azanha, A., Argoud, A. R. T. T., Camargo Junior, J. B. D., & Antoniolli, P. D. (2017). Agile project management with scrum: A case study of a Brazilian pharmaceutical company IT project. *International Journal of Managing Projects in Business, 10*(1), 121–142.
16. Alruwaili, F., Alrajihi, M., & Saeedi, K. (2018). How agile development and its tools support digital transformation. *International Journal of Computers & Technology, 18*, 7440–7450. https://doi.org/10.24297/ijct.v18i0.8060
17. Ahmed, G. A., & Altaie, M. R. (2021). Investigation the opportunity of BIM with agile management approach in Iraqi construction projects. In *E3S web of conferences* (Vol. 318, p. 02001). EDP Sciences. https://doi.org/10.1051/e3sconf/202131802001
18. Moloto, M., Harmse, A., & Zuva, T. (2021, October). Agile methodology use factors that influence project performance in South African banking sector-a case study. In *2021 international conference on electrical, computer, communications and mechatronics engineering (ICECCME)* (pp. 1–6). IEEE.
19. Riesener, M., Doelle, C., Schloesser, S., & Schuh, G. (2019, August). Prototype design in agile product development processes for technical systems. In *International design engineering technical conferences and computers and information in engineering conference* (Vol. 59278, p. V007T06A001). American Society of Mechanical Engineers. https://doi.org/10.1115/detc2019-97008
20. Esteki, M., Gandomani, T. J., & Farsani, H. K. (2020). A risk management framework for distributed scrum using PRINCE2 methodology. *Bulletin of Electrical Engineering and Informatics, 9*(3), 1299–1310. https://doi.org/10.11591/eei.v9i3.1905
21. Lill, P. A., & Wald, A. (2021). The agility-control-nexus: A levers of control approach on the consequences of agility in innovation projects. *Technovation, 107*, 102276. https://doi.org/10.1016/j.technovation.2021.102276
22. Khan, A. M., & Blackburn, T. D. (2020). AUTILE framework: An AUTOSAR driven agile development methodology to reduce automotive software defects. *IEEE Systems Journal, 15*(3), 3283–3290.
23. Maro, S., Steghöfer, J. P., Bozzelli, P., & Muccini, H. (2022). TracIMo: A traceability introduction methodology and its evaluation in an agile development team. *Requirements Engineering, 27*(6), 1–29. https://doi.org/10.1007/s00766-021-00361-5

24. Rosa, M. R. D., & Pereira, E. N. (2021). Metodologias ágeis no contexto da administração pública: análise de estudos de caso de implementação ágil. *Revista Do Serviço Público, 72*, 479–497. https://doi.org/10.21874/rsp.v72.i2.4310
25. Ayaz, M. S., & Shaukat, Z. (2021). Use of agile methodologies in digital transformation barriers. Master's thesis.
26. Fuchs, C., & Hess, T. (2018). Becoming agile in the digital transformation: The process of a large-scale agile transformation.
27. Delioğlu, N., & Uysal, B. (2023). A review on agile leadership and digital transformation. *Yıldız Social Science Review, 8*(2), 121–128.
28. Mikalsen, M., Moe, N. B., Stray, V., & Nyrud, H. (2018). Agile digital transformation: A case study of interdependencies. In *In proceedings of the 39th international conference on information systems (ICIS)*. Association for Information Systems (AIS).
29. Gurusamy, K., Srinivasaraghavan, N., & Adikari, S. (2016). An integrated framework for design thinking and agile methods for digital transformation. In *Design, user experience, and usability: Design thinking and methods: 5th international conference, DUXU 2016, held as part of HCI international 2016, Toronto, Canada, July 17–22, 2016, proceedings, part I 5* (pp. 34–42). Springer International Publishing. https://doi.org/10.1007/978-3-319-40409-7_4
30. Ringnér, M. (2008). What is principal component analysis? *Nature Biotechnology, 26*(3), 303–304.
31. Kaiser, H. F. (1958). The varimax criterion for analytic rotation in factor analysis. *Psychometrika, 23*(3), 187–200. https://doi.org/10.1007/bf02289233
32. George, B., & Williams, L. (2004). A structured experiment of test-driven development. *Information and Software Technology, 46*(5), 337–342. https://doi.org/10.1016/j.infsof.2003.09.011
33. Shahin, M., Babar, M. A., & Zhu, L. (2017). Continuous integration, delivery and deployment: A systematic review on approaches, tools, challenges and practices. *IEEE Access, 5*, 3909–3943. https://doi.org/10.1109/access.2017.2685629

# New Forms of Capital in the Context of Digitalization of the Industrial Sector

**Oksana Butorina and Yulia Starodumova**

**Abstract** In the study, digital transformation of the industrial sector is considered as an adjustment the internal processes of an enterprise based on the use of digital technologies, which aimed at ensuring innovation to increase competitive advantages, profitability, and the efficiency of resource management. The objectivity of this process serves as the basis for creating new forms of capital. Informatization as a conjunctural process of digital transformation and the transition to the next megacycle underlie of the author's interpretation of the monetary and information forms of capital. Based on a bibliographic analysis of the digital transformation of the industrial sector and information and intellectual forms of capital, a close relationship was proven between the creation of new forms of capital, primarily in the industrial sector, ICT development and intellectualization of economic activities. The distinctive features of the monetary-information form of capital were determined. It is necessary to highlight the close relationship with the ICT sector and the intellectualization of economic activity, which underlie the formation of a new system of socio-economic relations that transform the system of traditional resources for production, as well as a new self-increasing value for income rise, structurally including knowledge capital, human capital, organizational capital and other minor components of intangible capital. The results obtained can become the basis for further research into the processes of capital transformation in modern conditions.

**Keywords** Digital transformation · Industrial sector · Intellectualization · Opportunism · Capital

## 1 Introduction

The formation of new business conditions within the digital economy development is one of the determining factors in the transformation of all sectors of the economy, primarily of the industrial sector. According to Polozhentseva, Sogacheva, and

---

O. Butorina (✉) · Y. Starodumova
Perm National Research Polytechnic University, Perm, Russian Federation



A. Appolloni et al. (eds.), *The Future of Industry*, Lecture Notes in Information Systems and Organisation 70, https://doi.org/10.1007/978-3-031-66801-2_11

Byankin [1], the prospects for digital transformation of industry are related to the use of customer experience management systems. Istomina [2] considers that this process is also closely connected with the introduction of blockchain technologies, machine learning, and big data. Shituhina [3] combines it with the strengthening of the roles of digital ambassadors in companies.

In relation to the industrial sector, the greatest activity of enterprises in the digital transformation processes is observed in the field of robotization of production, introduction of end-to-end integration and automation technologies, digital workplace, RFID and sale of industrial goods via the Internet, as well as open production technologies and additive technologies. Their extensive use is aimed at improving the efficiency of the industrial sector, which has a number of limitations:

1) Overall insufficient level of digital literacy of the population;
2) Technical and technological backwardness of industrial enterprises;
3) Possible job cuts;
4) Lack of sufficient multidirectional funding for the development and subsequent heavy use of digital technologies to ensure innovation.

Zvereva and Deputatova [4] consider the predominance of investment in intangible assets (software, R&D, etc.) as an integral condition for ensuring this process.

The development of ICT highlighted by Chulkov et al. [5] and Kablashova et al. [6] in conjunction with society and economic entities being aware of the importance of intellectual capital and the need to preserve and develop it are defined as the basis for creating new forms of capital, such as intellectual and informational. At the same time, Bushuev and Lezhenina [7] note the lack of a unified interpretation of each of the forms, as well as studies of their relationships with the subsequent differentiation of essential characteristics has become the basis for a more comprehensive research into new forms of capital inherent in the digital transformation of the production sector.

In the given study, the authors offer their own interpretation of the monetary and information form of capital (MIFC) as a new form of capital in the era of digital transformation of the manufacturing sector. Achieving this purpose involves covering the following issues:

- Theoretical aspects of studying the industrial sector's digital transformation;
- New forms of capital in the context of digital transformation of the industrial sector.

In conclusion, the article provides limitations of the study and discusses opportunities for future research.

# 2 Background

## *2.1 Theoretical Aspects of the Study of Digital Transformation in the Industrial Sector*

Digital transformation is considered in terms of two aspects: in relation to the functioning of both the national economy and a particular enterprise. Peculiarities of digital transformation of economic entities are most fully examined by Mugutdinov and Gorovoy [8], Ananyin [9], et al.

According to Astratova [10], digital production can be considered not only as one of the basic components of the concept of digital enterprise, but one of the leading components of virtual modeling of various systems and processes, so they define digital production as a process of transformation of socio-economic relations at all levels of government based on the use of digital technologies. Kirichenko [11] adds that this process involves the transfer of all types of resources to a digital format. This may be considered as a condition for increasing the competitiveness and innovativeness of industrial enterprises. This interpretation is mostly based on the priority of the technological basis of enterprise functioning, assuming a description of the mechanism for creating an information network within the framework of digitalization and the organization's participation in it.

The priority of network interaction as an integral part of the digital transformation of enterprises can be traced in the works by Zvereva and Deputatova [4]. They argue that digital transformation of an industrial enterprise is "a continuous process of transformation of the company's entire ecosystem, including employees, customers, suppliers, and partners". As its goals, the authors note optimization and/or improvement of the existing business model in order to obtain additional sources of profit and optimize costs based on advanced business technologies. Kablashova, Logunova, and Salikov [6], when describing an enterprise as a complex self-developing system, note its need to integrate internal technical and socio-economic subsystems through the formation of spaces of the Internet of Things, the Internet of People, and the Internet of Services. Based on this interpretation, they identified the main trends in the development of the industrial enterprise management system in the context of digital transformation. According to Zyablyuk and Titova [12], digital transformation of capital helps expand the area where employee' and enterprise's interests intersect, thus reducing the effectiveness of control over personnel performance and strengthening employee self-control, encouraging the development of horizontal communications, as well as the formation and development of flexible network structures with horizontal communications and project teams as a mechanism for adapting to changes in the need of the market.

The priority of the organizational component within the enterprise as the most important element of digital transformation of industry is noted by Ananyin [9]. It is this component that underlies changes in business processes, organizational structures, and management practices implemented within the enterprise.

**Table 1** Key processes of digital transformation of industrial enterprises

| Highlighted processes and their orientation | Effectiveness | Author |
|---|---|---|
| Large-scale implementation of computer systems and adaptive technologies with a focus on the principles of the Internet of Things in all areas of an industrial enterprise | Optimization of resource flows, increasing efficiency and improving the business model | Sakaya [13] |
| Making strategic, tactical and operational decisions based on a continuous information flow in real time | Increasing the enterprise's adaptability to changes in the external environment and reducing the parameters of the innovation life cycle | Ostrik & Balko [14] |
| Virtualization of the enterprise as digital twin systems used for a set of products and/or business processes | Improving the quality of forecasting economic results, risks, and production efficiency growth | Bashin [15] |
| Strengthening the dynamism of the organizational structure enterprises, primarily internal business processes | Constant updating of functions and services to changing market parameters and changes in the external environment | Mikhneva [16] |
| Development and implementation of new enterprise cybersecurity systems based on automated collection, storage, processing and analysis of information, improvement of analog control and distributed digital control over all components of enterprise development | Risk and threat reduction | Kirshin [17] |
| Automation of manual labor in the context of basic technological processes and document flow, which involves reducing the pattern of manual labor | Leveling production risks and increasing the speed of translation of production processes | Zyablyuk & Titova [12] |

In other words, the authors of the above studies reasonably prove that the digitalization of industrial production is a subjective condition, forming a set of processes within itself. Table 1 shows the main processes of digital transformation of industry and their purpose/effectiveness for the functioning of industrial enterprises.

Based on the identified processes, it can be argued that the digital transformation of industrial enterprises involves the large-scale introduction of computer systems and adaptive technologies into all functional areas of an industrial enterprise, which contribute to the growth of the organization's adaptability to changes in the external environment, increase the innovativeness of its activities and profitability, optimize costs, and reduce risks and losses.

Based on the bibliographic analysis we have identified the key processes and their purpose/effectiveness in the functioning of industrial enterprises that do not contradict the advantages of digital production presented in the literature, which are:

- Cost reduction at all stages of production and sales of product;
- Improving the efficiency and management of resource flows;
- Ensuring the reliability of production lines and technical and technological configurations of production systems [18];

- Faster creation of innovative products at all stages;
- Optimization of speed and management in decision-making;
- Increasing the efficiency of organization and interaction of all counterparties of an industrial enterprise [19];
- Strengthening the sustainability of producers in the context of rapid changes in the external environment of their functioning [2].

Thus, the digital transformation of the industrial sector can be considered as an adjustment process of the enterprise's internal processes (according to Norton's classification, these include: (1) sales; (2) production; (3) innovation; (4) procurement; (5) finance; (6) personnel; (7) management) based on the use of digital technologies aimed at ensuring innovation to increase competitive advantages, profitability, and efficiency of enterprise resource management.

This process is ensured by a system of factors. The conditions of digital transformation identified by researchers and management practitioners can be divided into two groups. The first group, according to Starostin [20], combines the conditions "formed from the bottom", i.e., the level of the enterprise itself, and includes primarily changes in the principles of business structures functioning for effective adaptation to changing market requirements. The second group includes factors "formed from the top", or environmental factors affecting the activities of industrial enterprises. The second group may encompass:

1) The state of human potential and science [1];
2) The general level of business development as its readiness to generate fixed and current production assets to ensure increasing innovation [8];
3) The formation and development of relevant institutions [1];
4) The predominance of investment in intangible assets (software, R&D, etc.) [8].

At the same time, the latter becomes the basis for the formation of new forms of capital, which seems to have an accumulative effect of all other factors in the process of digital transformation of the production sector.

## 2.2 New Forms of Capital in the Context of Digital Transformation of the Industrial Sector

According to Korechkov and Leznina [21], intellectual capital is singled out as a new form of capital in the conditions of digital transformation. They consider its main manifestation to be the information formula, which implies the accumulation and extensive use of knowledge in the digital economy. It focuses on the creation and implementation of intellectual, and as a consequence, innovative potentials of society as a whole and specific organizations. Bauchenkov [22], while considering information capital as a specific form of economic relations in the new economic conditions, identifies its commodity, functional, and reproductive nature, only the totality of which underlies the transformation of investments and existing "...

institutional and social conditions for providing a stock of knowledge, abilities, professional skills and abilities, health and culture of each subject and society as a whole".

The new form of capital is interpreted more broadly by Brooking [23], Edvinsson [24], and Sweiby [25]. They write about its intellectual nature, defining its structural components: human, infrastructure, and market assets, as well as intellectual property, and structural capital (customer and organizational capital [23], internal and external structures of the company [25]).

Arkhipova and Rodionov [26] described the concept of digital capital as a capital based on digital technologies that are able to integrate the existing sources of labor and capital to create new more successful and competitive business models.

At the same time, according to Kulagina [27], digitization as an objective process of using information in various forms creates new systems of production relations that undelie further development of new forms of capital.

According to Koreshkov and Lezhenina [21] and Boyko [28], the key distinguishing characteristic of the informational capital at the present stage is the ability to generate a self-increasing value based on the intellectualization of production. Thus, among the conditions that ensure the self-growth of information capital they distinguish: the strengthening competition between enterprises that launch innovative products; the growing importance of the ICT sector in the functioning of enterprises; and the improvement of the system of enterprises' institutional regulation in the changing conditions of digital transformation.

## 3 Results and Discussion

### *3.1 The Impact of Digital Transformation on Forms of Capital*

The processes of digitalization in general and the manufacturing sector in particular, as well as their interrelation with the formation of new forms of capital, are mostly based on the technological component of the digital economy development, which, in our opinion, may not be sufficient to characterize the transformational essence of modern capital.

Hence, to identify the specific features of new forms of capital, we propose to compare the processes of transformation of the socio-economic system and investment within the development of the digital economy (Table 2).

The methodological peculiarities of its compilation are the following.

First, the priority is the recurrent approach in the study of modern transformation processes, which is based on the assumption that each process has relationships with previous and subsequent development (genetic inheritance) and is directly and inversely dependent on other basic processes that determine the transformational essence of modern macroeconomic development.

**Table 2** Interrelations with the value characteristics of the digital transformation of the current stage and the processes of formation and development of new forms of capital

| Basic transformation processes | Subprocesses reflecting the essence of the basic transformation process | Investment priorities |
|---|---|---|
| ***That form the basis of digitalization processes*** | | |
| Informatization transformation | Development of communication networks and data storage and processing infrastructure | Investment in information resources as the most important productive force of both the economy and economic entities |
| | Socialization of information | |
| Technological transformation | Automation to the level of digital ecosystem | Investing in an intelligent resource with the ability to generate self-increasing value |
| | Ubiquitous robotization | |
| | Intelligent behavior automation (AI) | |
| Innovatization transformation | Mastering borrowed innovations | Investing in the infrastructure for the transition to creative and intellectual work [29] |
| | Creating own innovations | |
| Investment transformation | Venture investment | Increasing investment in the information content of a new product |
| | Public investment ICT sectors | |
| ***That characterize the basis of digitalization processes*** | | |
| Production transformation | Improving production efficiency | Investing in information and intellectual resources that ensure increasing efficiency application of all other factors of production |
| | New type of economic growth | |
| ***Resulting from digitalization processes*** | | |
| Structural transformation | Changes in the sectoral structure of the national economy | Investment in knowledge that determines the growth of their value and the value of their creator [30] |
| | Industry 4.0 and 5.0 | |
| | Knowledge industry | |
| Social transformation | Capitalization of professional abilities | Investment in a person capable of generating new knowledge and broadcast it [31] |
| | Intellectualization of labor | |

Second, within the framework of the recurrent approach (based on the results of previously published works), the digital economy as an independent phase of the modern macroeconomic cycle can have a unique two-fold nature: it is formed within the regression of industrial development and is the basis for subsequent (information and innovation) development in the progression phase of the subsequent post-industrial megacycle [32].

Third, considering the highlighted features of the digital economy, it can be argued that there emerge the processes of knowledge-intensive industrialization, the scaling of the economy's own innovative achievements, the transition to new business models, structural changes in the manufacturing sector, increasing 'traditional' incomes and expanding opportunities for obtaining income from intellectual property.

Fourth, the above interpretation allowed us to specify the most significant transformational (informational, technological, innovative, industrial, social, structural) processes in the formation and development of the digital economy, which, according to the recurrent approach, are also characterized by interconnections and interdependencies.

Fifth, the dual nature of the digital economy allowed us to specify the processes of intellectualization and informatization of the transformational transition to the next megacycle as opportunistic ones.

Sixth, the identified key processes of informatization and intellectualization form the specific features of information, innovation, technology, innovation, investment transformations that determine the production, social and structural processes of subsequent development. All of them taken together underlie the uniqueness of digital transformation of the economy as a whole and the manufacturing sector in particular.

Based on the basic transformation processes identified in Table 1 and the investment priorities corresponding to them, it can be argued that the formation and development of new forms of capital is based on the processes of investing in informatization processes, which involve not only the creation of infrastructure, but also increasing the intellectualization of all spheres of life of economic entities to ensure subsequent progressive development.

## 3.2 The Monetary and Information Form of Capital

The previously identified informatization as an opportunistic process within the digital transformation and transition to the next megacycle became the basis for the author's interpretation of the monetary and information form of capital.

The conducted bibliographic analysis, as well as differential analysis of the main components of this category allowed us to highlight its distinctive features:

- A close relationship with the development of the ICT sector, which allows increasing the level of informatization in society as a whole and economic entities;
- Close interdependence with the intellectualization of economic activity;
- The integration of intellectualization and informatization is the basis for a new socio-economic system that transforms the interrelationships of traditional production resources;
- The basis for its growth is a new self-increasing value based on intellectualization, which determines the growth of income;
- Information scaling can be considered a material manifestation of the intellectualization of economic activity;
- The need to change the organization of production processes through intellectualization and informatization underlies the transformation of organizations into self-learning systems;

- The dual nature of information resources, which simultaneously act as both a capitalized stock and a flow. This nature underlies the formation of consumer and commercial values, bringing their income to their owners and/or producers.
- Knowledge capital, human capital, organizational capital and other less significant components of intangible capital can be considered structural components of the monetary and informational form of capital.

In general, new forms of capital can contribute to the digitalization of the manufacturing sector through:

- Knowledge increments and information scaling as the main factors in ensuring digital transformation at the current stage;
- Ensuring the stability of the reproduction process and increasing its efficiency at each level of the economic system;
- Forming new global investment flows with a different range of participants' functions.

However, scant attention is paid to the possible impact of the processes on labor relations and employment in the industrial sector, as well as the possible risks and challenges. They will inevitably change the labor market and work methods and transform the character of work and employment. Serious social consequences of digital industrial transformation include increased unemployment, reduced labor force, the disappearance of companies, cybercrime, and anomie. In this case government should also use preventive measures to eliminate these problems.

## 4 Conclusion

New forms of capital are manifestations of the transformational essence of modern capital formed under the influence of intellectualization and informatization as opportunistic processes in the development of the digital economy at the present stage. As its main distinguishing features, it is necessary to highlight the close relationship with the ICT sector and the intellectualization of economic activity, which underlie the formation of a new socio-economic system that transforms the interrelationships of traditional production resources and generate a new self-increasing value for increasing income, structurally including knowledge capital, human capital, organizational capital and other minor components of intangible capital.

The interrelation of digital transformation and innovative activity of industrial enterprises is very strong. Digital transformation can allow industrial enterprises to increase their innovation potential. Innovation activity can strengthen competitive advantages in the digital eco-environment by optimizing business processes, as well as the production of innovative products.

It should be particularly noted that new forms of capital and the speed of their development can help accelerate the transition from the industrial era to the information and innovation phase of the post-industrial megacycle, as well as ensure the progressiveness of digital transformation.

## References


1. Polozhentseva, Y. S., & Klevtsova, M. G. (2021). Transformation of industrial complex development in the digital economy. *Bulletin of the University, 2*, 71–79.
2. Istomina, E. A. (2018). Assessment of industrial digitalization trends. *Bulletin of the Chelyabinsk State University, 12*, 108.
3. Shitukhina, N. (2018). Information capital: The essence and key properties. *Scientific Bulletin of the Southern Institute of Management, 2*, 17–21. https://doi.org/10.31775/2305-3100-2018-2-17-21
4. Zvereva, A. O., & Deputatova, E. Y. (2019). Trade service transformation in digital economy. *Vestnik of the Plekhanov Russian University of Economics, 4*(106), 156–163. https://doi.org/10.21686/2413-2829-2019-4-156-163
5. Chulkov, V. O., Rakhmonov, E. K., Kasyanov, V. F., & Gusakova, E. A. (2012). Infographic modeling of the hierarchical structure of the management system in the context of innovative conflict. *Bulletin of MGSU, 12*, 282–287.
6. Kablashova, I. V., Logunova, I. V., & Salikov, Y. A. (2019). The innovative development of the enterprise management system in the conditions of digital transformation. *Production Organization, 27*(2), 46–58. https://doi.org/10.25987/VSTU.2019.92.57.005
7. Bushuev, A. V., & Lezhenina, L. A. (2012). Information capital in the knowledge economy. *Science Studies, 4*(35).
8. Mugutdinov, R. M., & Gorovoy, A. A. (2022). Features of digital transformation in industry. *Bulletin of the Academy of Knowledge, 1*(48), 33–41. https://doi.org/10.24412/2304-6139-2022-48-1-216-226
9. Ananyin, V. I. (2018). Digital enterprise: Transformation into a new reality. *Business Informatics, 2*(44), 45–54. https://doi.org/10.17323/1998-0663.2018.2.45.54
10. Astratova, G. V., Burnasheva, E. P., & Shupletsova, V. S. (n.d.). Information capital and its assessment. Company marketing research. Library of key performance indicators. http://www.kpilib.ru/article.php?page=325
11. Kirichenko, D. A. (2019). Digital transformation: Impact on the activity of a modern enterprise. *Academic Bulletin of the Rostov Branch of the Russian Customs Academy, 4*, 55–59.
12. Zyablyuk, R. T., & Titova, N. I. (2016). Neoindustrialization of the Russian economy: Necessity and opportunity (review of materials of the round table on neoindustrialization of the Russian economy). *Vestnik Moskovskogo universiteta. Series 6: Economics, 2*, 119–135.
13. Sakaya, T. (1999). The value created by knowledge, or the history of the future. In *New industrial wave in the west: Anthology* (pp. 337–371). Academia.
14. Ostrik, V. Y., & Balko, S. V. (2021). Digital transformations of modern personnel management systems. *Innovative Economics Development, 4*, 23–33.
15. Bashin, Y. B. (2009). Information and intellectual capital as factors of information system evaluation. *Bulletin of the Moscow State University of Instrument Engineering and Informatics. Series: Social and economic sciences, 18*.
16. Mikhneva, S. G. (2003). Intellectualization of the economy: Innovative production and human capital. *Innovations, 1*, 37–48.
17. Kirshin, I. A., & Izmailov, A. E. (2018). Industry 4.0: Creation of a digital enterprise and transformation of the world industry. *Scientific works of the Center for Advanced Economic Research, 14*, 65–73.
18. Butorina, O. V. (2023). Conceptual foundations of quantitative measurement of digital economy development in modern conditions. In *Perm region. Strategy in global uncertainty. From*

*mining plants to future technologies: Proceedings of the 7th Perm Economic Congress (Perm, February. 2–3)* (pp. 26–35). Perm State National Research University.
19. Ermakova, M. G. (2006). Intellectualization of labor as a factor of sustainable economic growth. *Russian Entrepreneurship, 7*(10), 146–149.
20. Starostin, V. A. (2020). Digitalization of labor relations and employment in a technogenic society. *Bulletin of PAGS, 5*, 59–66.
21. Korechkov, Y. V., & Lezhenina, L. A. (2018). Information capital as a new form of intellectual capital in economic models of the digital economy. *The Eurasian Scientific Journal, 3*(10).
22. Bauchenkov, V. A. (2014). Features of the formation of intellectual and informational capital at the macro and micro level. *Proceedings of the Saratov University. The Economics series. Management. Law, 8*, 12–20.
23. Brooking, A. (1996). *Intellectual capital: Core asset for the third millennium enterprise*. International Thomson Business Press.
24. Edvinsson, L., & Malone, M. S. (1997). *Intellectual capital. Realizing your company's true value by finding its hidden roots*. Doubleday, Cuzzency.
25. Sveiby, K. E. (1997). *The new organizational wealth: Managing and measuring knowledge-based assets*. Berrett-Koehler.
26. Arkhipova, N. I., & Rodionov, I. I. (2015). Changing the content and role of production factors as a source of competitiveness in the modern world. *Series Economy. Management. Right, 4*(147), 44–52.
27. Kulagina, N. A., Mikheenko, O. V., & Rodionov, D. G. (2019). Technologies for the development of methods for evaluating an innovative system. *International Journal of Recent Technology and Engineering, 8*(3), 5083–5091. https://doi.org/10.35940/ijrte.C5714.098319
28. Boyko, A. N. (2020). The place and role of intellectualization of labor in ensuring world innovative development. *Bulletin of the North Caucasus Federal University, 6*(81).
29. Dyatlov, S. A., & Selishcheva, T. A. (2018). *Transformation of capital in the context of growth of informatization of the economy. Series: Economics,* 103-1.
30. Fedchenko, A. A. (2018). *Transformation of social-labor relations in the digital economy* (Vestnik VSU. Series: Economics and Management) (p. 3).
31. Golubev, S. S., & Shcherbakov, A. G. (2018). The impact of information technologies on the activities of defense industrial enterprises in Russia. *Bulletin of the Moscow Region State University. Series: Economics*, 3.
32. Buleev, E. I., Ryabykina, N. I., & Revva, A. N. (2017). Intellectualization of labor as the highest form of its division at the present stage of economic development. *Strategy and Mechanisms for Regulating Industrial Development, 9*.

# Developing an Agent-Based Model for Intelligence Transformation of a Regional Industrial Complex

**Andrey Shorikov, Grigoriy Korovin, and Dmitry Sirotin**

**Abstract** The industrial complex with its production, economic, and social connections is a complex object for research and modeling. The tasks of managing such structures are complicated by new challenges associated with Industry 5.0, technology humanization, and sustainable development requirements. The paper aims to develop an agent-based model for managing the industrial complex of a separate region. Three-level management architecture is proposed, including government authorities at the federal and regional levels, as well as the management level of enterprises (united by type of activity). The model is implemented as a software package for assessing industrial development scenarios and involves expansion in the form of a module for calculating the optimal step-by-step control of the industrial complex. Scenario calculations (detailed by the sector of industrial activity) were based on the proposed scenario of control actions according to the data from a region of the Russian Federation. The model and its software implementation can be used by regional authorities and scientific organizations for model calculations and conceptual assessment of the influence of individual control factors. The shortcomings of the model include the limited statistical base in the Russian Federation, which lacks indicators of industry development humanization.

**Keywords** Industry · Agent-based model · Industrial management

## 1 Introduction

The industrial complex is a management object with a multi-level subject-object structure and a multidimensional system of material, control, and information connections. In addition, the industrial system is constantly influenced by technological, social, and economic changes and by random external factors. The management model for the industrial complex of a region must take into account the

A. Shorikov · G. Korovin (✉) · D. Sirotin
Institute of Economics of the Ural Branch of the Russian Academy of Sciences, Ekaterinburg, Russian Federation
e-mail: shorikov.af@uiec.ru; korovin.gb@uiec.ru; sirotin.dv@uiec.ru

 
A. Appolloni et al. (eds.), *The Future of Industry*, Lecture Notes in Information Systems and Organisation 70, https://doi.org/10.1007/978-3-031-66801-2_12

difficulties associated with the correct understanding of the composition of its objects, with the targets of management subjects and the criteria for its optimal management.

When creating a model, one should consider the new challenges the industry faces, which are associated with Industry 5.0: the need for technology humanization, resilience, and sustainable development of the industrial ecosystem. The values aimed at increasing the well-being of the population of the regions and the country as a whole are to be taken into account as guidelines influencing industry development.

The paper develops previous research by the authors [1, 2] on the construction of a deterministic economic-mathematical model for forecasting the state and optimizing industrial management based on a three-level hierarchical agent-based model.

Agent-based models were first formally proposed in the early 1990s. Now they are reaching a point of acceptance as a social sciences research tool. The major forces behind the increased interest in agent-based modeling can be attributed to a notable shift in the available computing and information technologies, the increase in individual-level data and improvements in agent-based modeling software [3].

Now the agent-based modeling (ABM) methodology, widely used to model socio-economic systems, allows considering the economic system as a community of agents with their connections, resources, individual strategies, and behavior algorithms. The attitude to the economic system as a collection of heterogeneous agents and their coordination using the example of industry was described by Cimoli and Stigliz, justifying it with decentralized behavior and radically different goals of heterogeneous agents [4]. A review of the research shows that ABM models are an efficient tool for managing of industry transformation, taking into account market dynamics, decisions of individual enterprises and the application of various government policies [5–8].

The present study aims to develop an agent-based three-level model for managing a regional industrial complex. The paper is structured as follows. Section 2 provides a review of research on the agent-based modeling of socio-economic systems. Section 3 presents concept of the agent-based model of industrial complex. Section 4 provides results of model development, including structure, statistical base, calculating the model parameters and software implementation. Section 5 summarizes the main conclusions.

## 2 Literature Review

For industrial modeling, methods of simulation modeling, extrapolation, and expert assessments are widely used [9–12]. Among the most significant Russian models based on these methods are the macroeconomic model *RUSEC* and its development in models of economic equilibrium [13], a set of models based on the RIM model, including the regional socio-economic model NORM (Institute of National Economic Forecasting RAS), and some others. The creators of this model point to the need to take into account the structural sectoral parameters of the economy, resource and other constraints, inter-industry interactions, and the behavior of key economic agents. These parameters are estimated on the basis of econometric equations, and economic policy parameters act as external factors [12].

Makarov et al. [13] identified the state, market, banking sectors, households, governments at various levels (including extra-budgetary funds), and the outside world as seven economic agents. More modern models include the agent-oriented model of regional socio-ecological-economic development [14]; systems for simulating the functioning of public procurement mechanisms [10]; model for regulating industrial emissions based on optimizing the emissions trading system [14]. ABM is used to model the industrial complex in the context of individual types of activity [15–17]. For the correct use of such models, it is necessary to adequately formalize the properties of agents; to calibrate parameters; to specify strategies and behavior algorithms for agents, etc. [18].

The significant agent-based model *Eurace* [19] formalizes the market interaction of the main sectors of the economy of the European Union countries on the basis of real economic mechanisms. The simulation of the economic environment of the European Union is created by influencing the dynamics of economic development of various regimes and instruments of macro-economic policy.

To develop individual elements of ABM models, the most innovative methods of data analysis are used, such as machine learning [20] and neural networks [21].

Agent-based models have a high potential for application in a number of practical areas of economic analysis and management: forecasting economic crises, bankruptcy, systemic risks [22, 23], assessing the possible effectiveness of the ongoing monetary and fiscal policies [24], studying the features of the diffusion of innovations [7, 25–27], the impact of digital technologies on economic sectors [28]. As a rule, ABM is based on the theory of complex systems which explains the formation of special properties and structures by the interaction of simple agents [21, 29]; on the game theory [30, 31]; on the theory of diffusion of innovations in the field of shaping agents' attitudes towards new technologies [32, 33].

In general, the feasibility of using ABM for modeling socio-economic systems is predetermined by the complexity of the relationships between agents; heterogeneity of agents; nonlinear behavior, learning ability of agents.

## 3 Agent-Based Model Concept

ABM is proposed to model the industrial complex of a territory, identifying as agents the types of industrial activities and the federal and regional government agents influencing them in case of risks and constraints. The constructed model includes three levels of management: federal, regional, and the level of enterprises grouped by type of activity. The totality of enterprises belonging to the same class of industrial activity will be considered a management object. In the hierarchy of control actions, the federal level of management is dominant; the regional managing agent and,

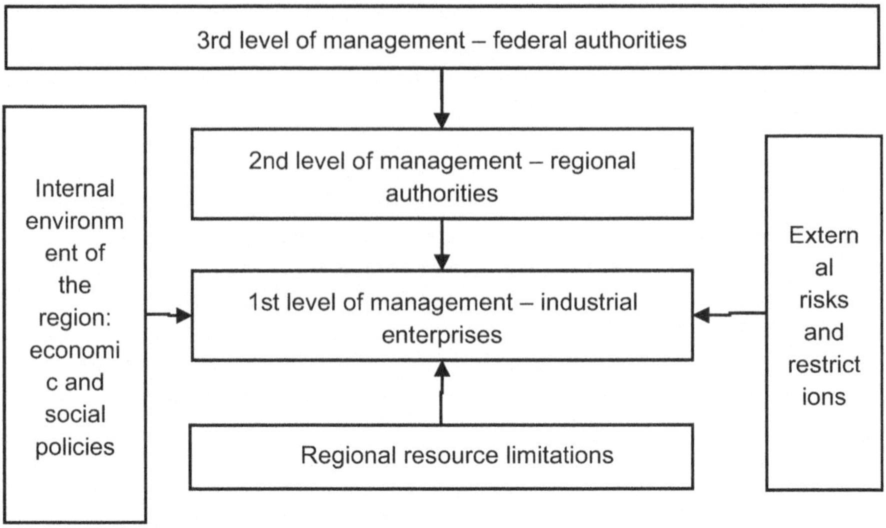


**Fig. 1** Enlarged agent-based model of management of a regional industrial complex

further, agents—types of industrial activity of the region are subordinate. Using economic activities as separate objects controlled by appropriate agents will allow modeling the dynamics and structure of the industrial complex and the response to control influences more accurately.

Types of activities possess certain features that are characteristic of ABM agents: independence, own strategies and reactions to managerial influences, horizontal interactions, etc. To determine the parameters of the model, data from the statistical bodies of the Russian Federation and individual regions were collected and structured (gks.ru). The maximum possible detail of industry, for which complete reliable data can be found in the statistics of the Russian Federation, was adopted (Fig. 1). The information base for testing the approach was prepared based on the data from the Sverdlovsk Region for 28 types of economic activities related to industrial production for 2005–2021. At the same time, a model of the main indicators' dynamics and their exposure to control influences and risks is identified for each object of industrial activity in the region.

# 4 Results

## *4.1 Model Structure*

In the general structure of the model, federal and regional authorities are designated as corresponding control agents P and E; focusing on the state of the regional industrial complex, they form their own control actions. Agents E*i* are the enterprises of the $i$-th type of activity, subordinate to agents P and E; they manage regional industrial enterprises of the $i$-th type of activity. The characteristics of the socio-economic and production parameters of each type of activity are presented in the form of the vector $X^{(i)}(t)$. Agents at each level have their own strategies and corresponding objective functions.

At this stage of model development, for each period $t$, the dynamics of the types of activities of the regional industrial complex $I_i$, controlled by the agents $E_i$, is described as follows:

$$X^{(i)}(t+1) = A^{(i)}(t) \cdot X^{(i)}(t) + B^{(i)}(t) \cdot U(t) + C^{(i)}(t) \cdot U^{(i)}(t) + D^{(i)}(t) \cdot V^{(i)}(t) \quad (1)$$

$$X^{(i)}(0) = X_0^{(i)}, i \in = \overline{1, n}.$$

where

$X^{(i)}(t)$ are the socio-economic parameters (presented in the form of a phasor) of the object $I_i$, $X_0^{(i)}$ is the initial value of the phasor;

$U(t)$ is the general vector of the control influence of regional and federal authorities—agents $E$ and $P$;

$U^{(i)}(t)$ is the vector of the control influence of the bodies managing a particular type of activity—agent $E_i$;

$V^{(i)}(t)$ is the vector of risks affecting the object;

$A^{(i)}(t)$ is the real matrix of mutual influence coefficients of indicators of the state of the phasor of the $i$ -th sector of the regional industrial complex;

$B^{(i)}(t)$ is the real matrix of influence coefficients of control actions of government authorities—agents $E$ and $P$ on the $i$ -th sector of the regional industrial complex;

$C^{(i)}(t)$ is the real matrix of influence coefficients of control actions of bodies managing the $i$ -th sector of the regional industrial complex—agent $E_i$;

$D^{(i)}(t)$ is the real matrix of influence coefficients of uncontrolled disturbances (risks) on indicators of the state of the sector of the regional industrial complex.

At this stage, it is assumed that the parameters of the main object are formed as a set of all the considered sectors of the industrial complex of the region.

In the implemented algorithm, it is assumed that the goal of each agent is to maximize (minimize) its own objective function by choosing its optimal control, taking into account the possible worst risks and control actions of higher-level agents.

For computer implementation, an algorithm for the model was developed, including adaptive optimization of control of a regional network industrial complex. In a simplified form, the algorithm can be represented as follows:

*Stage 1.* Forming the initial data: determining the number of management periods, the number of types of industrial activities in the region; determining the socio-economic parameters of the regional industrial complex, which are to be taken into account.

*Stage 2*. Generating the calculated data: creating coefficient matrices, which characterize the mutual influence of individual model parameters, regional and federal control actions, disturbances in the form of real coefficient matrices.

*Stage 3*. Solving the problem of forming a set U of optimal (minimax) controls of agent E (regional authorities) during the working cycle of the model, for each period and for a fixed initial control action of agent P (federal authorities).

Next, the problem of forming a set W of optimal (minimax) controls for agent P corresponding to the target function of agent P is solved.

Then, for each object I*i* of the *i*-th type of activity of the industrial complex of the region and for the fixed controls of agents P and E, the problems of forming sets of optimal (minimax) controls of agents Ei are solved.

*Stage 4*. The final results of solving the problem are generated—a set of acceptable options for phasors of objects I and Ii and a set of optimal (minimax) control actions of agents P, E and Ei.

## 4.2 Preparing the Statistical Base and Calculating the Model Parameters

An important issue while developing the model is determining the quantitative criteria (target functions) for assessing the quality of problem-solving in managing industrial complex facilities in case of risks (disturbances). A key target quantitative criterion is financial efficiency, which takes into account indicators of profit, profitability, and investment attractiveness of the regional industrial complex. Another important quantitative criterion is the assessment of production quality, for example, indicators of production efficiency, product quality, and its innovation. However, one needs to take into account the level of production digitalization and its environmental friendliness. Taking into account the degree of detail of the model—down to the level of types of economic activities, a target function for the regional level of management is proposed, including the following indicators: Goods shipped, million RUR, Investments in fixed capital, million RUR, Costs of digital technologies, million RUR, Profit (loss), million RUR. These indicators are part of the phasor of the model; they are calculated for the forecast period and have a retrospective statistical base. In the future, as the statistical base expands, it is envisaged for upper-level agents to expand the elements of the target function with indicators of technological efficiency and humanization of production.

Next, the coefficients matrices for the unknown parameters of the agent-based model for managing the development of industry in the region were calculated for the main matrix-vector control (1), based on statistical data from the Sverdlovsk Region. The estimated parameters characterize the dependencies between the socio-economic characteristics of the industrial complex and their response to control influences at the regional and industry levels. To solve the problem of identifying the parameters of a dynamic model, linear regression equations were generated. For this purpose, a number of indicators were selected, considered in the context of individual industries related to industrial production in the Sverdlovsk Region in 2005–2021. The sample included the following indicators:

(1) shipped goods of own production, performed work and services using own resources, million RUR; (2) investments in fixed assets, million RUR; (3) costs of implementation and use of digital technologies, million RUR; (4) profit (loss) before tax, million RUR; (5) payroll fund, million RUR; (6) number of organizations according to state registration, units. The payroll fund indicator was calculated manually as the product of the average number of employees per organization and the average monthly nominal accrued wages per employee.

The volumes of the attracted budget funds, as well as the attracted funds other than the budget ones, were used as control factors. The latter include bank loans and borrowed funds from other organizations, extra-budgetary funds, funds from organizations and the population for shared construction, and other sources other than own.

## 4.3 *Software Implementation of the Model*

Based on the previously developed architecture of a three-level model for managing a regional industrial complex, relying on the generated databases and constructed matrices of regression coefficients, a software package was developed and implemented programmatically in the AnyLogic Personal Learning Edition environment. The software package implements an agent-based model of hierarchical management of a regional industrial complex. From the created database, indicators of 30 types of economic activities of regional industrial enterprises are imported, forming: the initial phasor; the matrix of phasor dynamics coefficients; the matrix of influence coefficients for control actions; scenarios for implementing control actions by year for each type of activity. The program calculates the trajectory of indicators of the regional industrial complex and the target function in accordance with the management scenario. The data in the software implementation of the model is structured in several main blocks (Table 1).

The software package created as a result of the project helps carry out calculations based on scenarios for developing a regional industrial complex. This framework is to be supplemented with modules that allow making calculations for a wide range of scenarios and selecting the optimal scenario from the standpoint of the objective function, of the ratio of resources spent on supporting industry (by type of activity) and the result obtained. The calculated scenarios will allow formulating substantiated and detailed proposals for adapting regional industrial policy, taking into account the opportunities and risks of digital transformation of the industrial complex (Fig. 2).

The main task in developing the model will be constructing a module for calculating optimal control actions from the standpoint of bringing industry to the target state in case of uncertainty. Implementation of the model provides for the most

**Table 1** Data structure of an agent-based model for managing a regional industrial complex

| Blocks of data | Data structure |
|---|---|
| General data of the model | n—number of industrial activities types;<br>T—number of periods for model calculation;<br>k—number of phasor parameters;<br>m—number of control actions of federal and regional authorities;<br>q—number of disturbances |
| Parameters of the regional industrial complex (phasor) | X(t)—phasor of object I |
| Phasor constraints | $X_*(t)$—vector of phasor constraints for object I |
| Coefficient matrices for each industry sector | For each type of activity, matrices for Eq. (1) are calculated $A^{(i)}$ (t), (k × k); $B^{(i)}$ (t), (k × m); $C^{(i)}$ (t), (k × p); $D^{(i)}$ (t), (k × q) |
| Parameter constraint vectors for each industry sector | $X^{(i)}{}_*(t)$—vector of phasor constraints for object $I_i$ |
| Control actions of federal and regional authorities | Depending on the model mode, it can be initial control values or control scenarios over the entire period T;<br>U(t)—vector of control actions of regional and federal authorities for object I;<br>$U_*(t)$—vector limiting the change in vector U(t);<br>$U^{(i)}$ (t)—vector of control actions of regional and federal authorities for object $I_i$;<br>$U^{(i)}{}_*(t)$—vector limiting the change in vector $U^{(i)}(t)$ |
| Data on the risks and constraints of the model | V(t)—vector of uncontrollable risks and disturbances; can be probability—or scenario-based;<br>$V_*$ (t)—vector limiting the change in vector V(t) |
| Objective functions of model agents | $\Phi_t$—the target function of agent P—The federal body managing the industrial complex;<br>$F_t$—the target function of agent E—The regional body managing the industrial complex;<br>$F_t^{(i)}$—the target function of agent $E_i$ $E_i$ managing the type of industrial activity *i* |

flexible architecture that allows changing the number and composition of sectors, parameters, control actions, disturbances, and risks when calculating scenarios. At the moment, the model is implemented in software and allows calculating the development trajectories of the industrial complex of the region based on prepared management scenarios (Fig. 3).

An aggregated indicator was adopted as the target function, consisting of a set of indicators normalized relative to the initial values: Goods shipped, million RUR, Investments in fixed capital, million RUR, Costs of digital technologies, million RUR, Profit (loss), million RUR. The weight of each indicator was taken at 0.25. The calculations carried out according to the base scenario showed an increase in the objective function by more than 5 times over the calculation period of 20 years. This shows that the structure of the indicators under consideration and the calculated coefficients of the model, allowing for the complexity of the object under consideration, require additional assessment and calculation (identification).

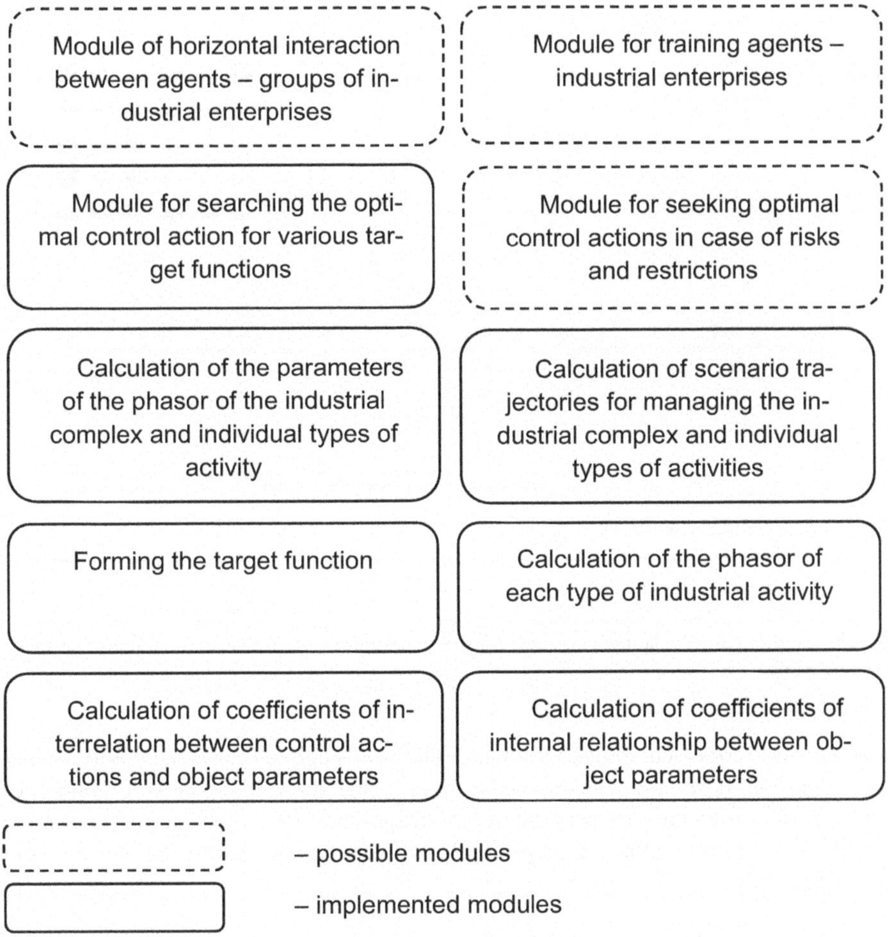


**Fig. 2** Implemented and possible modules of the industrial complex management model

## 5 Conclusion

The structure of the software package allows detailed calculations by class of economic activity, based on a scenario of control actions formed in the same context. At the moment, the software package is being tested based on the identified parameters of the model, taking into account the studied parameters of development and optimization of management of the state of objects and processes of the network industrial complex. The model and its software implementation can already be used by regional authorities and scientific organizations to implement model calculations and assess the influence of control factors. The disadvantages of the model and its implementation include the incomplete statistical base for calculating coefficients and the relative reliability of the resulting statistical models and, accordingly, of the

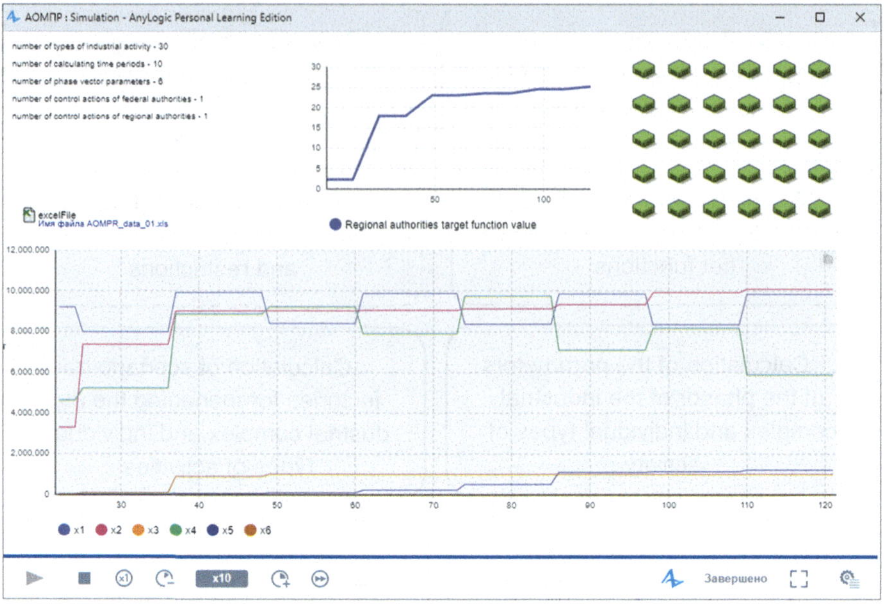


**Fig. 3** Example of calculating a scenario for the development of an industrial complex for given control actions

matrices used for calculating coefficients. The next stage of the research will expand the statistical base, the object and managing agents and develop a system of formalized horizontal information relationships between agents. The modeling results will offer adaptable and expandable software tools for industrial management at the regional level.

**Acknowledgements** The study was carried out in accordance with the state task for the Institute of Economics of the Ural Branch of the Russian Academy of Sciences.

## References

1. Akberdina, V. V., & Shorikov, A. F. (2022). Hierarchical agent-oriented model of industrial complex management. *Upravlenets = The Manager, 13*(6), 2–14. https://doi.org/10.29141/2218-5003-2022-13-6-1. (In Russ.).
2. Shorikov, A. F., Korovin, G. B., & Sirotin, D. V. (2023). Methodology for regional industrial complex management: Architecture of an agent-based model. *Upravlenets = The Manager, 14*(6), 63–76. https://doi.org/10.29141/2218-5003-2023-14-6-5. EDN: CQLXNE.
3. Heppenstall, A. J., Crooks, A., Malleson, N., Manley, E., Ge, J., & Batty, M. (2020). Future developments in geographical agent-based models: Challenges and opportunities. *Geographical Analysis, 53*, 76–91. https://doi.org/10.1111/gean.12267

4. Cimoli, M., Dosi, G., Nelson, R., & Stiglitz, J. E. (2006). Institutions and policies shaping industrial development: An introductory note. Initiative for Policy Dialogue. https://doi.org/10.1093/acprof:oso/9780199235261.003.0002.
5. Cooper, R., & Jarre, A. (2017). An agent-based model of the South African offshore hake trawl industry: Part I model description and validation. *Ecological Economics, 142*, 268–281. https://doi.org/10.1016/j.ecolecon.2017.06.026
6. Pu, Z., Shao-Chao, M., & Haizhong, A. (2024). Market-driven transformation policy for mobility electrification: An agent-based modelling approach. *Transportation Research Part D: Transport and Environment, 129*, 104148. https://doi.org/10.1016/j.trd.2024.104148
7. Scheller, F., Johanning, S., & Bruckner, T. (2019). A review of designing empirically grounded agent-based models of innovation diffusion: Development process, conceptual foundation and research agenda. Preprint submitted to Technological Forecasting and Social Change. https://doi.org/10.13140/RG.2.2.29711.94887.
8. Yin, S., & Zhao, Y. (2024). An agent-based evolutionary system model of the transformation from building material industry (BMI) to green intelligent BMI under supply chain management. *Humanities and Social Sciences Communications, 11*, 468. https://doi.org/10.1057/s41599-024-02988-5
9. Maaouane, M., Zouggar, S., Krajačić, G., & Zahboune, H. (2021). Modelling industry energy demand using multiple linear regression analysis based on consumed quantity of goods. *Energy, 225*, 120270. https://doi.org/10.1016/j.energy.2021.120270
10. Makarov, V. L., Bakhtizin, A. R., Sushko, E. D., & Abramov, V. I. (2017). Computer situational modeling in economic management. *Gosudarstvennyj audit. Pravo. Ekonomika = State Audit. Law. Economy, 3–4*, 31–40. (In Russ.).
11. Mashkova, A. L., Savina, O. A., Mamatov, A. V., & Novikova, E. V. (2018). Computer modeling of economic dynamics processes in the sectoral context. *Izvestiya Yugo-Zapadnogo gosudarstvennogo universiteta = Proceedings of the Southwestern State University, 22*(5), 96–108. https://doi.org/10.21869/2223-1560-2018-22-5-96-108. (In Russ.).
12. Shirov, A. A., & Yantovsky, A. A. (2017). Intersectoral macroeconomic model RIM – Development of tools in modern economic conditions. *Problemy prognozirovaniya = Problems of Forecasting, 3*, 3–19. (In Russ.).
13. Makarov, V. L., Bakhtizin, A. R., & Bakhtizina, N. V. (2005). *CGE model of the socio-economic system of Russia with embedded neural networks*. CEMI RAS. (In Russ.).
14. Makarov, V. L., Bakhtizin, A. R., & Sushko, E. D. (2020). Agent-oriented model as a tool for regulating the ecology of the region. *Zhurnal Novoj e'konomicheskoj associacii = Journal of the New Economic Association, 1*(45), 151–171. https://doi.org/10.31737/2221-2264-2020-45-1-6. (In Russ.).
15. Gorchakova, D. A., & Shabalov, V. A. (2017). On the application of simulation modeling for forecasting demand for metallurgical industry products. *Ekonomika i upravlenie v XXI veke: Nauka i praktika = Economics and Management in the XXI century: Science and Practice, 4*, 108–112. (In Russ.).
16. Kislitsyn, E. V., & Gorodnichev, V. V. (2021). Simulation modeling of the development of individual branches of heavy industry. *Biznes-informatika = Business Informatics, 15*(1), 59–77. https://doi.org/10.17323/2587-814X.2021.1.59.77. (In Russ.).
17. Medvedev, S. N., & Aksenov, K. A. (2012). Analysis of the applicability of simulation and multi-agent modeling in the planning tasks of machine-building production. *Sovremennye problemy nauki i obrazovaniya = Modern Problems of Science and Education, 5*, 101–106. (In Russ.).
18. Samkov, T. L., Shvetsov, Y., & P. (2017). About some problems in the construction of agent-oriented models of economic processes. *Biznes. Obrazovanie. Pravo. Vestnik Volgogradskogo instituta biznesa = Business. Education. Law. Bulletin of the Volgograd Institute of Business, 2*(39), 85–87. (In Russ.).

19. Cincotti, S., Raberto, M., & Teglio, A. (2010). Credit money and macroeconomic instability in the agent-based model and simulator Eurace. *Economics, 4*, 2010–2026. https://doi.org/10.5018/economics-ejournal.ja.2010-26
20. Turgut, Y., & Bozdag, C. E. (2022). A framework proposal for machine learning-driven agent-based models through a case study analysis. *Simulation Modelling Practice and Theory, 123*, 102707. https://doi.org/10.1016/j.simpat.2022.102707
21. Bonabeau, E. (2002). Agent-based modeling: Methods and techniques for simulating human systems. *Proceedings of the National Academy of Sciences, 99*(3), 7280–7287. https://www.pnas.org/doi/abs/10.1073/pnas.082080899
22. Delli Gatti, D., Gallegati, M., Greenwald, B., Russo, A., & Stiglitz, J. E. (2010). The financial accelerator in an evolving credit network. *Journal of Economic Dynamics and Control, 34*(9), 1627–1650. https://doi.org/10.1016/j.jedc.2010.06.019
23. Raberto, M., Teglio, A., & Cincotti, S. (2012). Debt, deleveraging and business cycles: An agent-based perspective. *Economics, 6*, 1–49. https://doi.org/10.5018/economics-ejournal.ja.2012-27
24. Dosi, G., Fagiolo, G., & Roventini, A. (2010). Schumpeter meeting Keynes: A policy-friendly model of endogenous growth and business cycles. *Journal of Economic Dynamics and Control, 34*(9), 1748–1767. https://doi.org/10.1016/j.jedc.2010.06.018
25. Jensen, T., & Chappin, É. J. L. (2017). Automating agent-based modeling: Data-driven generation and application of innovation diffusion models. *Environmental Modelling & Software, 92*, 261–268. https://doi.org/10.1016/j.envsoft.2017.02.018
26. Stummer, C., Kiesling, E., Günther, M., & Vetschera, R. (2015). Innovation diffusion of repeat purchase products in a competitive market: An agent-based simulation approach. *European Journal of Operational Research, 245*(1), 157–167. https://doi.org/10.1016/j.ejor.2015.03.008
27. Zhangqi, Z., Zhuli, C., & Lingyun, H. (2022). Technological innovation, industrial structural change and carbon emission transferring via trade. An agent-based modeling approach. *Technovation, 110*, 102350. https://doi.org/10.1016/j.technovation.2021.102350
28. Chanias, S., Myers, M. D., & Hess, T. (2019). Digital transformation strategy making in pre-digital organizations: The case of a financial services provider. *The Journal of Strategic Information Systems, 28*(1), 17–33. https://doi.org/10.1016/j.jsis.2018.11.003
29. Tsvetkov, V. Y. (2017). Emergence. *Mezhdunarodny'j zhurnal pri-kladny'x i fundamental'ny'x issledovanij = International Journal of Applied and Fundamental Research, 2-1*, 137–138. (In Russ.).
30. Cullen, A. C., Alpcan, T., & Kalloniatis, A. C. (2022). Adversarial decisions on complex dynamical systems using game theory. *Physica A: Statistical Mechanics and its Applications, 594*, 126998. https://doi.org/10.1016/j.physa.2022.126998
31. Tian, Y., Govindan, K., & Zhu, Q. (2014). A system dynamics model based on evolutionary game theory for green supply chain management diffusion among Chinese manufacturers. *Journal of Cleaner Production, 80*, 96–105. https://doi.org/10.1016/j.jclepro.2014.05.076
32. Greenhalgh, T., Robert, G., Macfarlane, F., Bate, P., & Kyriakidou, O. (2004). Diffusion of innovations in service organizations: Systematic review and recommendations. *The Milbank Quarterly, 82*(4), 597–598. https://doi.org/10.1111/j.0887-378x.2004.00325.x
33. Kiesling, E., Günther, M., Stummer, C., & Wakolbinger, L. M. (2011). Agent-based simulation of innovation diffusion: A review. *Central European Journal of Operations Research, 20*(2), 183–230. https://doi.org/10.1007/s10100-011-0210-y

# Part III
# Digital Transformation in Industry

# The New Industry 5.0 Paradigm: An Investigation in the Italian Automotive Sector

**Federica Murmura, Laura Bravi, and Giada Pierli**

**Abstract** Today, companies are experiencing a paradigm shift that sees the conceptual and cultural evolution from the highly techno-centric principles of Industry 4.0 to those of Industry 5.0 focusing on three drivers: human-centricity, sustainability, and resilience. Guided by these three elements, the 5.0 paradigm not only considers technologies as tools for bringing the efficiency of and improvement in production processes, but also recognises the importance of using these solutions with respect for people and the planet. The study aims to figure out the possible orientation towards the new principles of Industry 5.0 in Italian companies, with a particular focus on the automotive sector given its strong propensity for innovation. To this end, a quantitative survey was conducted using a survey questionnaire distributed among a sample of Italian automotive companies in May 2023. A total of 78 companies contributed to the study. The results show that Italian automotive companies have fully integrated Industry 4.0 solutions into their production processes (59%). Likewise, a change of perspective towards Industry 5.0 principles can be perceived, especially about the driver of human-centricity (mean 4.46). Managers and institutions should thus make greater efforts to enable companies to complete the digital and sustainable transition by defining proper strategies and measures.

**Keywords** Industry 4 · Industry 5.0 · Automotive sector · Technology · Industrial revolution

## 1 Introduction

In January 2021, the European Commission published the Policy Brief relating to the field of Research and Innovation (R&I), in which the concept of Industry 5.0 was introduced for the first time [1, 2]. On this occasion, the debate sees the future of

F. Murmura · L. Bravi (✉) · G. Pierli
Department of Economics, Society, Politics, Carlo Bo University of Urbino, Urbino, Italy
e-mail: federica.murmura@uniurb.it; laura.bravi@uniurb.it; g.pierli@campus.uniurb.it



A. Appolloni et al. (eds.), *The Future of Industry*, Lecture Notes in Information Systems and Organisation 70, https://doi.org/10.1007/978-3-031-66801-2_13

European industry as the protagonist and how it is closely related to innovation and technological progress.

The new Industry 5.0 paradigm will mainly achieve social, sustainable, and resilient objectives [3, 4]. It acts as a stimulus towards a technological transition, already underway for some time, paradoxically more humane, but also sustainable and resilient. With its essence and its values, it invites European industrial realities to "act" and "behave" not only because "to compete we need to keep up with", but because "as part of the world I can contribute to making it better". In the document, there is also a strong reference to Society 5.0, that is a concept closely linked to that of Industry 5.0 introduced in Japan in 2016 by the largest Japanese business association *Keidanren* [5, 6]. The philosophy of Society 5.0 encourages citizens to "merge" together with intelligent technologies while maintaining a certain balance between the achievement of economic objectives and those linked to the resolution of social and environmental problems [7, 8]. Technology in this sense becomes man's tool in actively carrying out the most varied activities ranging from those of daily life to those, for example, performed within one's own company [9].

Subsequently, in January 2022 the European Commission published Policy Brief n. 3 drawn up by the Expert Group on the Economic and Societal Impact of Research and Innovation (ESIR), dedicated to the future vision of European industry from the 5.0 perspective. This vision, updated compared to the first official document, views the commitment made by companies, industrial players, and industrial innovation as a fundamental lever in providing more sustainable and circular solutions, of fundamental importance for increasing the "competitive sustainability" that Europe sees in its strategy [10, 11].

In essence, the industry is given the role of driving the regeneration of the planet considering the recent pandemic crisis. This requires, according to the ESIR, changes not only in business models, but also in the mentality of acting and a new political and governance approach. The pure vision of Industry 4.0 is essentially not suitable for transforming Europe in the context of climate crisis and planetary emergency, nor it addresses the present social tensions [12].

Even though Industry 4.0 is insufficient to drive the transition to a more sustainable Europe, it is essential to emphasise that this paradigm is closely related to Industry 5.0. This relationship stems from the presence of advanced and smart technologies that constitute a fundamental element of both paradigms [13, 14]. Given the correlation between the two paradigms, it is believed that investing in 4.0 technologies is a necessary condition to talk about Industry 5.0 and therefore through this study we tried to verify whether this approach is already present in the vision of Italian companies, making reference to the specific automotive sector, for which the analysis of the literature shows how companies are already active in introducing the principles and enabling technologies of Industry 4.0 into their business processes. The objective of this research work is therefore twofold, that is, (i) to verify how much companies in a specific sector invest in 4.0 technologies, and (ii) to determine whether there is the possibility of identifying within one's own vision some of the inspiring principles of the Industry 5.0 concept. Therefore, the research questions that emerge from this study are the following:

*RQ1: How much do companies in the Italian automotive sector invest in 4.0 technologies?*
*RQ2: Is it possible to identify the principles of Industry 5.0 in the vision of Italian automotive companies?*

The paper is organized as follows: Sect. 2 describes the methodology used to collect the quantitative data of the research; Sect. 3 illustrates the results; and Sect. 4 provides the main conclusions and future research directions.

## 2 Theoretical Background

According to the National Institute of Standards and Technology (NIST), smart factories are characterized by almost completely automated production in which production systems are integrated, collaborative and interconnected and respond in real time to the complexities of the factory and all the actors that they revolve around it [15–17].

What the Fourth Industrial Revolution brings with it within industrial and manufacturing companies is certainly a much more flexible production environment, in which production can be managed through highly performing "Smart Technologies" with large processing and storage capacities of large quantities of data and access to knowledge. Literature identifies nine Industry 4.0 enabled technologies, namely 3D printers, tools related to digitalization, vertical/horizontal integration, the Internet of Things (IoT), Cloud Computing, Big Data and Analytics, Cyber-security Systems, Automation and Cyber-physical Systems [18–20]. Another aspect is linked to the growing interest in issues relating to the environment and sustainability, seen as opportunities to be more productive and efficient.

Industry 4.0 is a model that creates technological monopolies and increases wealth inequality and therefore, precisely by its nature, it is not the ideal paradigm to address recent global issues and challenges [12]. The 5.0 paradigm is instead considered a new transformative model that reflects the evolution of thinking following the Covid-19 health crisis. The vision proposed in the document goes beyond the traditional focus on technology and economic growth based on production and consumption typical of capitalism, to embrace a more transformative one that incorporates the Industry 4.0 approach, but at the same time broadens its horizons surrounded by human well-being, from new sources of sustainable, circular and resilient value creation. The drivers of Industry 5.0 incorporated into European policies contribute to shaping the industrial policy necessary for a more equitable and profound transition [21]. European policies, in essence, must be accompanied at an operational level by a long-term industrial strategy that prepares the industry and the companies that are part of it to embrace digitalization, to achieve zero emissions, to deal more with social issues (in particular of workers but not only) and to regenerate the environment and biodiversity.

## 3 Methodology

Data were collected using a questionnaire survey performed on a sample of Italian companies which operate in the automotive industry.

To detect companies belonging to this sector, it was chosen to use the ATOKA database (https://atoka.io/). This platform allows finding various information on Italian companies by setting up a search strategy based on specific criteria. The criteria used for the strategy covered by this investigation are mainly three:

1) The companies must be located in Italy;
2) The companies must belong to the same automotive sector;
3) Companies must have at least one e-mail address in the database.

In the search for companies belonging to the Italian automotive sector, it was decided to use the ATECO 2007 code, in use since January 1, 2008 in Italy. The ATECO Code is a type of classification of economic activities adopted by the Italian National Institute of Statistics (ISTAT) and it is equal to the European NACE classification, in order to have an equal comparison of sectors all around Europe. Among the manufacturing activities indicated in the classification with the "C" letter, the automotive sector is identified with code 29 (Manufacture of motor vehicles, trailers and semi-trailers) which also includes the subcodes: manufacture of motor vehicles (29.10.00), manufacture of bodywork for motor vehicles, trailers and semi-trailers (29.20.00), manufacture of parts and accessories for motor vehicles and their engines (29.30.00) with the relevant sub-categories manufacture of electrical and electronic equipment for motor vehicles and their engines (29.31.00), manufacture of seats for motor vehicles (29.32.01) and manufacture of other parts and accessories for motor vehicles and their engines nec (29.32.09). These are the codes that made up the database of companies to which the questionnaire was administered in a subsequent phase.

The total number of companies identified with the ATOKA platform, which also have a valid e-mail address to subsequently send the survey, is 1192.

Based on a preliminary analysis of the 1192 companies belonging to the Ateco 29 code in Italy, it is possible to draw up some general information. In the database, 42.4% (506 companies) deal with the manufacture of other parts and accessories for motor vehicles and engines, 38% (453 companies) are engaged in the manufacture of bodywork for motor vehicles, trailers and semi-trailers, 9.7% (116 companies) manufacture motor vehicles, 7.6% (90 companies) manufacture electrical and electronic equipment for motor vehicles and their engines, 1.7% (20 companies) produce seats for motor vehicles, and finally 0.4% (5 companies) manufacture parts and accessories for motor vehicles and their engines. As regards the location of the companies, the largest number is in the north-west and north-east regions of Italy (in total 72.6%, 865 companies) compared to 12.6% (150 companies) in central Italy and 14.8% (176 companies) in Southern Italy and the Islands.

The questionnaire was structured and sent using the Computer Assisted Web Interviewing (CAWI) methodology during the first week of May 2023. It is made up of three sections. Section one is dedicated to identifying the survey sample and therefore the profile of the responding companies. Section two investigates how much companies in the automotive sector invest in Industry 4.0 technologies. Section three is aimed at understanding whether or not there are traces of the three characteristics of the Industry 5.0 paradigm within the companies considered.

After the first sending, a second sending was made as a reminder, 2 weeks later, to remind those who had not yet participated in the survey of the possibility of contributing. Companies whose e-mail returned even after a second sending or those without a second e-mail were not considered in the sample. Furthermore, seven companies indicated their unwillingness to participate in the survey. The total sample was thus reduced to 1159 companies, among which 78 participated in the study.

As for data analysis, descriptive analysis was performed to describe the sample profile of respondent companies. A five-point Likert scale was used to evaluate the questionnaire items.

Non-response bias was assessed by verifying that early and late respondents were not significantly different [22]. A set of tests compared respondents who answered to the questionnaire during the first administration and those who answered when the survey was submitted for the second time. All possible t test comparisons between the means of the two groups showed insignificant differences ($p < .1$ level).

# 4 Results

## *4.1 Company Profile*

Most of the companies investigated (58.0%) produce parts and accessories for motor vehicles, trailers, and their engines, falling within ATECO code 29.30.00. 15.0% and 10.0% of the sample respectively manufacture motor vehicles (ATECO 29.10.00) and bodies for motor vehicles, trailers, and semi-trailers (ATECO 29.20.00), while the remaining 17.0% carry out activities that combine two of the codes between 29.10.00, 29.20.00 and 29.30.00 or belonging to subcategories such as production of electrical and electronic equipment for motor vehicles and their engines (29.31.00), seats for motor vehicles (29.32.01) and other parts and accessories for motor vehicles and their engines (29.32.09). The companies analyzed operate for more than 11 years and mainly serve the national and European market (51.3%). Regarding company size in terms of the number of employees and the amount of turnover, micro and small enterprises make up 74.4% of the sample, while 21.8% are medium-sized and only 3.8% are large; furthermore, 70.5% are family-owned. The companies surveyed are mostly located in Northern Italy (83.3%), especially in the regions of Lombardy (26.9%), Piedmont (16.7%), Emilia-Romagna (14.1%) and Veneto (14.1%). This is followed by Trentino Alto-Adige, Friuli-Venezia Giulia, and Liguria (6.5% overall). Finally, 10.3% work in Southern Italy and the Islands, and 6.4% in the Centre.

## *4.2 Investments in 4.0 Technologies*

The second section of the questionnaire focuses on investments in 4.0 technologies by automotive companies, investigating the motivations for their adoption, the number and type of enabling technologies introduced, the benefits and problems arising from the use of smart technologies. To this end, the first aspect investigated concerns the presence or absence of investments in 4.0 technology in the company, as this element is a necessary condition for subsequently exploring a possible development path towards Industry 5.0 paradigms. The results show that 59.0% of the responding companies have invested in 4.0 in recent years, while 41.0% have not taken any action. Those who answered negatively were not included in this study.

Stimulating the companies surveyed in their decision to invest in 4.0 technologies are mainly reasons related to the need of increasing or maintaining competitive advantage (mean 3.96), cost containment (3.63) and automation of production processes (3.61). The automotive industry is characterised by a high degree of innovation and competition [23] that pushes companies to face continuous challenges in order to create a distinctive value proposition. Therefore, making their production systems more efficient through technology becomes a key element to successfully compete in the current market [24, 25]. Less importance, on the other hand, was attached to motivations such as the use of quality raw materials, environmental protection and needs of key customers, with mean values of 2.59, 2.54 and 2.20, respectively.

Afterwards, the companies were asked to indicate how many and which enabling technologies they are investing in. In general, it can be seen that an average of 3 technologies are implemented. Among the companies that invest, 65.2% allocate their resources to a maximum of three technologies, of which 13.0% adopt three, 37.0% two and 15.2% only one of them. The remaining 34.8% implement four or more technologies, with the highest percentage of 15.2% using four technologies. None use all nine Industry 4.0 technologies. Regarding the type of solution introduced, the investments that attracted the most interest were in the categories of automation (3.48) and vertical and horizontal information integration (3.39). Indeed, advanced robotics and remote monitoring systems, autonomous robots and machine-to-machine communication enable companies to automate their production processes [26], responding to the growing competitiveness of automotive markets. Similarly, Programmable Logic Controller (PLC), Supervisory Control and Data Acquisition (SCADA), Manufacturing Execution System (MES) and Enterprise Resource Planning (ERP) systems allow greater control of the entire business system [27], increasing the efficiency and effectiveness of management processes. As opposed to what can be observed in the general framework of the Italian automotive sector, Big Data and Analytics (2.41), the Internet of Things (2.30) and Cloud Computing (2.24) are not particularly attractive to the companies in the sample. Cyber-physical systems are the technology that attracted the least interest, presenting a mean value of 1.78.

Moving towards digital technology allows not only boosting performance in the short and long term, but also improving plant monitoring and track all components of the supply chain. Specifically, the companies surveyed indicated the following as the main benefits of adopting 4.0 solutions: improved productivity (3.72), increased efficiency (3.65), easier access to real-time information (3.61), better corporate image (3.54), and higher product and process quality (3.50). Even though the potential of these technologies for reducing the environmental impacts generated by the company's activities has been widely emphasized in the literature [28–30], the sample does not appear to perceive this type of benefit, attributing relatively low values to the items related to lower production waste (2.91) and more efficient use of natural and energy resources (2.70).

Along with the undeniable advantages associated with the use of enabling technologies, there are also potential critical issues that should not be underestimated when pursuing corporate digitization. Just think of the implications that Industry 4.0 has on the workplace, on privacy and on social and ethical issues [31]. Therefore, the sample was asked to indicate the challenges associated with the adoption of 4.0 technologies. Interestingly enough that none of the responding companies perceived any difficulties or dangers. The most relevant data concerns the opinion expressed on unemployment, which is not perceived as an imminent threat (1.67), contrary to the major pessimistic currents that see further technological progress as a risk to jobs [32, 33]. However, companies emphasize the lack of qualified personnel (3.15); this is in line with the findings in the literature about the increasing demand for workers who are skilled and competent in new digital technologies [34]. Issues related to IT security (2.41), technological lock-ins (2.39), privacy (2.26), data ethics (2.07), alienation between staff and product (2.00) and a potential organizational misalignment between objectives, strategies, roles, tasks and duties (1.98) are also low.

### *4.3 Elements of Industry 5.0*

The third section seeks to understand the orientation of Italian automotive companies towards the principles of Industry 5.0. In this perspective, it was primarily investigated the degree of adoption of the technologies belonging to this new paradigm. In general, none of the proposed 5.0 solutions raised particular interest within the sample studied. Predictive maintenance (3.22), technologies related to energy efficiency, renewable energy, energy storage (3.17), autonomy and decision support systems (3.13) received the most attention. Each of these technologies represents a good solution to the main challenges for the automotive sector today [35], such as proactivity and changing orientation, sustainable mobility, and responsiveness to the turbulent dynamics of the external environment.

The focus then shifted to the approach of automotive companies towards the three drivers of Industry 5.0 [21], namely human-centricity, sustainability, and resilience. As regards human-centricity in business processes, the results show that companies

**Table 1** Level of human-centricity in the sample (Likert scale 1–5)

| Parameter | Mean | SD |
|---|---|---|
| The company safeguards workers' fundamental rights (e.g., autonomy, human dignity, and prestige) | 4.30 | 0.963 |
| The company considers the workers as an investment that enables the company to grow (they are trained, empowered, and involved in the design and implementation of new technologies) | 4.20 | 0.934 |
| The company creates a safe and inclusive working environment to prioritise physical and mental health and Well-being | 4.02 | 0.906 |
| The company applies new technologies correctly, increasing employee satisfaction and Well-being and overcoming fear of job loss | 3.61 | 1.000 |
| The company sees collaboration between humans and robots giving rise to new professional figures. | 3.50 | 1.130 |
| The company believes that the demand for the "human touch" will grow in the future because consumers will seek to express their individuality through the products they buy | 3.48 | 1.225 |
| | Mean | SD |

place a high value on the role that people play within the business system (4.46). Although there is a consensus that humans should not adapt their needs to technology (2.96), technology is still considered the key element for being more efficient and productive (4.26). Furthermore, the responding companies appear to be quite sensitive to the protection and enhancement of their human capital. As shown in Table 1, the sample is rather attentive to the protection of workers' fundamental rights (4.30) and considers the worker not a cost but an investment that can contribute to the company's growth (4.20), in line with the studies of Xu et al. [36]. Creating a safe and inclusive work environment to prioritize people's physical, mental health and well-being (4.02) is also something that companies are working on. Likewise, they are committed to the proper application of new technologies, thus increasing employee satisfaction, and avoiding fears of job loss (3.61).

Thanks to technological development and the IoT, it is therefore possible to contribute to the achievement of important ergonomic results and to foster human-machine collaboration [21]. Regarding this last aspect, the sample is willing to facilitate interaction between workers and robots (3.50), thus promoting the creation of new professional figures. For instance, collaborative robots called *cobots* are designed precisely to combine "the strength, repeatability and accuracy of robots with the high-level cognition, flexibility and adaptability of humans to achieve ergonomic working environment with better overall productivity" [37, p. 199]. The synergy between humans and intelligent systems generates undeniable benefits for companies. Among these, the main advantages identified by the surveyed automotive companies are fewer accidents (fatal and non-fatal) in the workplace (69.6%), the reduction of work requiring physical force (67.4%) and the introduction of skilled and unskilled employees (45.7%).

Sustainability, the second driver of Industry 5.0, has become increasingly important within the automotive industry. Therefore, it was decided to verify the possible

**Table 2** Level of environmental sustainability in the sample (Likert Scale 1–5)

| Parameter | Mean | SD |
|---|---|---|
| Waste prevention and recycling | 3.70 | 1.171 |
| Reduction of pollutant emissions into the atmosphere | 3.59 | 1.326 |
| Recycling of materials used in production | 3.35 | 1.386 |
| Use of renewable energy sources | 3.02 | 1.437 |
| Circular economy | 3.00 | 1.193 |
| Energy-efficient data storage, transmission, and analysis | 2.46 | 1.130 |
| Intelligent and energy autonomous sensors | 2.26 | 1.124 |

contribution of the companies investigated with respect to the pursuit of the 17 Sustainable Development Goals defined by the United Nations within the UN 2030 Agenda. 56.6% of the companies stated that they do not work towards these goals, 26.1% plan to do so, and only 17.4% responded positively. Among the latter, the main ones are GOAL 8 (Decent work and economic growth) and GOAL 12 (Responsible consumption and production). Building a sustainable business model requires redesigning value chains, optimizing the life cycle of each product or service and reducing the impact that industrial production has on people and the environment [38]. Despite the complexity of the issue, more than half of the companies surveyed (56.5%) have not developed a clear sustainability strategy consistent with their business and value chain. Furthermore, 78.6% of the responding companies have not produced a sustainability report in recent years, which is a fundamental tool for communicating not only economic results, but also the social and environmental performance achieved [39]. The actions implemented mainly concern the prevention and recycling of waste (3.70) and the reduction of pollutant emissions into the atmosphere (3.59) (Table 2). Less adopted are measures such as energy-efficient data storage, transmission, and analysis (2.46) and the use of intelligent and energy-independent sensors (2.26). Also, the implementation of circular processes (3.0) does not appear to be widespread within the sample surveyed, despite the enormous potential of the circular economy to reduce waste and, consequently, environmental impacts [40, 41]. It is evident, therefore, that the orientation towards sustainability is not yet well embedded among the companies in the sample. However, the increasing pressure from the external environment necessarily requires a change of direction. Industry 5.0 may represent a major opportunity for the automotive sector as the adoption of Artificial Intelligence and additive manufacturing enable a more efficient use of resources while ensuring the preservation of the planet and social welfare [42].

The last driver considered is therefore resilience, which is a decisive factor in responding promptly to sudden internal or external changes to the company, without suffering permanent consequences [43]. In this regard, it can be observed that companies readily face to promptly cope with internal events (3.72), such as changes in the organizational asset, deficiencies in the information system or the use of outdated technologies (Table 3). By contrast, they appear less resilient to changes occurring outside the company such as alterations in geopolitical balances (3.30), economic, energy and other crises (3.02), natural disasters (3.00) and cyber-attacks

**Table 3** Level of resilience in the sample (Likert Scale 1–5)

| Parameter | Mean | SD |
|---|---|---|
| Internal company changes (e.g., organisational set-up, technological failures, etc.) | 3.72 | 0.981 |
| Geopolitical changes (e.g., Brexit, wars between nations etc.) | 3.30 | 1.209 |
| Crises (e.g., economic, energy, employment etc.) | 3.02 | 1.043 |
| Changes and natural disasters (e.g., pandemic, effects of climate change, etc.) | 3.00 | 1.011 |
| External changes (e.g., cyber-attacks, trade wars etc.) | 2.89 | 1.140 |

or trade wars (2.89). These results highlight the need for companies in the sample to improve their response to unforeseen traumatic events, especially external ones, by developing greater resilience. As indicated by Xu et al. [36], the industry of the future will need to be resilient enough to quickly navigate through change. Therefore, it will be crucial to develop a more robust and proactive industrial production to ensure business continuity and to deal quickly with crisis situations [44]. The companies surveyed seem to be quite clear on this issue, stating that they could ensure products and/or services (3.87), business continuity (3.78), robustness in production/supply (3.76), adaptability of production capacity (3.74) and flexible business processes (3.74).

## 5 Discussion

In the manufacturing sector, a change in direction seems to be taking place [45], with a conceptual and cultural evolution from the principles of Industry 4.0 strongly linked to a techno-centric vision, to those embodied by the new paradigm of Industry 5.0 promoting a human-centric, sustainable, and resilient perspective. However, the 5.0 paradigm should not be seen as a chronological continuation nor as an alternative to Industry 4.0 [36]. To approach Industry 5.0, indeed, it is necessary that the company has already carried out a process of technological and digital transformation in a 4.0 direction. The aim of the study was thus to verify the possible orientation towards the principles of Industry 5.0 by Italian automotive companies, after determining their current level of adoption of 4.0 technologies. To this end, a quantitative analysis was carried out by means of a survey questionnaire, shared among companies in the Italian automotive sector.

As for the degree of deployment of 4.0 technologies (RQ1), the results indicate that a large majority of the responding companies (59.0%) invest in these solutions. The need to preserve competitive advantage, cost containment and automation of production processes are the main reasons why the companies surveyed have embraced technological change. Indeed, the high levels of innovation and competitiveness that characterize the automotive sector make investment in enabling technologies a necessary condition for long-term success in the market [24, 25]. To meet these challenges, the companies implement an average of three enabling technologies, preferring tools related to automation and vertical and horizontal information integration. The companies also seem to be aware of the benefits and challenges of introducing these technologies. In line with what was indicated by Machado et al. [46], the most relevant benefits noted concern an increase in productivity and efficiency, smoother access to information and an improvement in corporate image. Among the difficulties, companies have prioritized the lack of qualified employees; in contrast to some of the current thinking [32, 33] job losses are not perceived as a danger associated with the use of enabling technologies.

If Industry 4.0 solutions are now an integral part of production processes within automotive companies, similar considerations cannot be made for 5.0 ones. The companies' interest in the tools of this new paradigm is still low and does not appear to be widespread within the sample. Although to a limited extent, the greatest attention appears to be paid towards predictive maintenance. Nevertheless, it is possible to perceive a change of perspective towards the principles of Industry 5.0 (RQ2), especially with respect to the driver of human-centricity. The companies recognize the centrality of the human figure in business processes, showing particular attention to the protection and enhancement of human capital. Workplaces become inclusive and safe, and the worker is seen as an investment that can significantly contribute to the company's growth [36].

Concerning the sustainability driver, full maturity on the topic is not yet visible from the companies analyzed. They mostly focus on the prevention and recycling of waste and the reduction of pollutant emissions into the atmosphere. Most lack the definition of a well-structured sustainability strategy consistent with their value chain. As the companies in the sample are predominantly micro and small, the absence of a clear sustainability strategy plan may be due to the difficulties typically encountered by these enterprises in terms of financial resources, proper technological infrastructure, and skilled human resources [47]. However, public opinion is increasingly attentive to the environmental and social impacts of industrial activity, necessarily requiring companies to adopt a more sustainable approach. Finally, the automotive companies interviewed appear to be quite ready to deal with internal changes, while less responsiveness was found in the event of external adverse events. Given the turbulence of the external environment, the need to develop plans and actions which can also counter possible changes outside the company context becomes evident [48].

## 6 Conclusions and Future Research

Italian automotive companies are gradually facing a transition to the principles of the new Industry 5.0 paradigm. This change is still primordial, with the leading efforts focused on the human-centric driver. Given the increasing market dynamism and the greater focus on sustainability issues, supporting automotive companies in this transformation process becomes crucial. Industry 5.0 requires a profound cultural and organizational re-thinking to enhance interaction between people and emerging technologies while developing a sustainable and proactive approach to business management.

The study contributes to enriching the literature on the topic by providing interesting pointers on the motivations, benefits, and difficulties of introducing 4.0 technologies in business processes and by outlining a preliminary overview of the transition path towards the new 5.0 paradigm principles, which is still empirically poorly investigated [49]. Useful insights for practitioners and policy makers are also provided. Managers should make further efforts to use their technologies to achieve sustainability goals by defining a clear strategy that combines production efficiency with environmental protection and social welfare. It is also important to increase responsiveness to external changes through the formulation of targeted actions and the use of appropriate technological tools, avoiding serious effects on business operations. At the same time, public institutions should outline suitable measures and provide proper incentives to support companies' investments in new technologies, promoting and facilitating their digital and sustainable transition path.

The paper is not without some limitations. Firstly, the number of responding companies is small and confined to Italy. Furthermore, the focus is on companies that invest in enabling technologies, excluding from the analysis those that do not adopt such solutions. Future research could not only expand the sample of automotive companies, but also extend the study to more sectors of the manufacturing industry and explore contexts other than national ones. It would also be interesting to investigate the factors that determine the decision not to invest in new technologies, thus obtaining a more comprehensive framework of the difficulties encountered and the necessary support actions.

## References

1. Özdemir, V., & Hekim, N. (2018). Birth of industry 5.0: Making sense of big data with artificial intelligence, "the internet of things" and next-generation technology policy. *Omics: A Journal of Integrative Biology, 22*(1), 65–76.
2. Breque, M., De Nul, L., & Petridis, A. (2021). *Industry 5.0: Towards a sustainable, human-centric and resilient European industry*. European Commission, Directorate-General for Research and Innovation.
3. Renda, A., Schwaag Serger, S., Tataj, D., Morlet, A., Isaksson, D., Martins, F., & Giovannini, E. (2022). *Industry 5.0, a transformative vision for Europe: Governing systemic transformations towards a sustainable industry*. European Commission, Directorate-General for Research and Innovation. https://doi.org/10.2777/17322
4. Ghobakhloo, M., Iranmanesh, M., Morales, M. E., Nilashi, M., & Amran, A. (2023). Actions and approaches for enabling Industry 5.0-driven sustainable industrial transformation: A strategy roadmap. *Corporate Social Responsibility and Environmental Management, 30*(3), 1473–1494. https://doi.org/10.1002/csr.2431
5. Banholzer, V. M. (2022). From "Industry 4.0" to "Society 5.0" and "Industry 5.0": Value-and mission-oriented policies. Technological and social innovations–aspects of systemic transformation. *IKOM WP, 3*(2).
6. Lu, Y., Zheng, H., Chand, S., Xia, W., Liu, Z., Xu, X., Wang, L., Qin, Z., & Bao, J. (2022). Outlook on human-centric manufacturing towards Industry 5.0. *Journal of Manufacturing Systems, 62*, 612–627. https://doi.org/10.1016/j.jmsy.2022.02.001

7. Deguchi, A., Hirai, C., Matsuoka, H., Nakano, T., Oshima, K., Tai, M., & Tani, S. (2020). What is society 5.0. *Society, 5*(0), 1–24. https://doi.org/10.1007/978-981-15-2989-4_1
8. Narvaez Rojas, C., Alomia Peñafiel, G. A., Loaiza Buitrago, D. F., & Tavera Romero, C. A. (2021). Society 5.0: A Japanese concept for a superintelligent society. *Sustainability, 13*(12), 6567. https://doi.org/10.3390/su13126567
9. Nair, M. M., Tyagi, A. K., & Sreenath, N. (2021, January). The future with Industry 4.0 at the core of Society 5.0: Open issues, future opportunities and challenges. In *2021 international conference on computer communication and informatics (ICCCI)* (pp. 1–7). IEEE.
10. Owen, R., Macnaghten, P., & Stilgoe, J. (2020). Responsible research and innovation: From science in society to science for society, with society. In *Emerging technologies* (pp. 117–126). Routledge.
11. Ivanov, D. (2022). The Industry 5.0 framework: Viability-based integration of the resilience, sustainability, and human-centricity perspectives. *International Journal of Production Research, 61*(5), 1–13. https://doi.org/10.1080/00207543.2022.2118892
12. Jankelova, N., & Súkeník, N. (2023). The impact of the crisis as an accelerator of changes in managerial decision-making on corporate culture in the era of Industry 4.0. *Industry 4.0, 8*(4), 135–139.
13. Maddikunta, P. K. R., Pham, Q. V., Prabadevi, B., Deepa, N., Dev, K., Gadekallu, T. R., et al. (2022). Industry 5.0: A survey on enabling technologies and potential applications. *Journal of Industrial Information Integration, 26*, 100257. https://doi.org/10.1016/j.jii.2021.100257
14. Golovianko, M., Terziyan, V., Branytskyi, V., & Malyk, D. (2023). Industry 4.0 vs. Industry 5.0: Co-existence, transition, or a hybrid. *Procedia Computer Science, 217*, 102–113. https://doi.org/10.1016/j.procs.2022.12.206
15. Lu, Y., Morris, K. C., & Frechette, S. (2016). Current standards landscape for smart manufacturing systems, National Institute of Standards and Technology. Report No. NISTIR 8107. https://doi.org/10.6028/NIST.IR.8107.
16. Shi, Z., Xie, Y., Xue, W., Chen, Y., Fu, L., & Xu, X. (2020). Smart factory in Industry 4.0. *Systems Research and Behavioral Science, 37*(4), 607–617. https://doi.org/10.1002/sres.2704
17. Grabowska, S. (2020). Smart factories in the age of Industry 4.0. *Management Systems in Production Engineering, 2*(28), 90–96. https://doi.org/10.2478/mspe-2020-0014
18. Bigliardi, B., Bottani, E., & Casella, G. (2020). Enabling technologies, application areas and impact of Industry 4.0: A bibliographic analysis. *Procedia Manufacturing, 42*, 322–326. https://doi.org/10.1016/j.promfg.2020.02.086
19. Forcina, A., & Falcone, D. (2021). The role of Industry 4.0 enabling technologies for safety management: A systematic literature review. *Procedia Computer Science, 180*, 436–445. https://doi.org/10.1016/j.procs.2021.01.260
20. Sigov, A., Ratkin, L., Ivanov, L. A., & Xu, L. D. (2022). Emerging enabling technologies for industry 4.0 and beyond. *Information Systems Frontiers*, 1–11. https://doi.org/10.1007/s10796-021-10213-w
21. Zizic, M. C., Mladineo, M., Gjeldum, N., & Celent, L. (2022). From Industry 4.0 towards Industry 5.0: A review and analysis of paradigm shift for the people, organization and technology. *Energies, 15*(14), 5221. https://doi.org/10.3390/en15145221
22. Armstrong, J. S., & Overton, T. S. (1977). Estimating nonresponse bias in mail surveys. *Journal of Marketing Research, 14*(3), 396–402. https://doi.org/10.2307/3150783
23. Lopes, A. P., Ferrarese, A., & Carvalho, M. M. D. (2019). Collaboration, competition and innovation: A consortium of tribology in the automotive sector. *Production, 29*, e20180106. https://doi.org/10.1590/0103-6513.20180106
24. Mehrpouya, M., Dehghanghadikolaei, A., Fotovvati, B., Vosooghnia, A., Emamian, S. S., & Gisario, A. (2019). The potential of additive manufacturing in the smart factory Industrial 4.0: A review. *Applied Sciences, 9*(18), 3865. https://doi.org/10.3390/app9183865
25. Sira, M. (2022). Efficient practices of cognitive technology application for smart manufacturing. *Management Systems in Production Engineering, 2*(30), 187–191. https://doi.org/10.2478/mspe-2022-0023

26. Rane, S., Shah, P., & Sekhar, R. (2022, August). Survey of technologies for Industry 4.0. In *2022 6th international conference on Computing, Communication, Control and Automation (ICCUBEA)* (pp. 1–6). IEEE.
27. Chehri, A., Zimmermann, A., Schmidt, R., & Masuda, Y. (2021). Theory and practice of implementing a successful enterprise IoT strategy in the industry 4.0 era. *Procedia Computer Science, 192*, 4609–4618. https://doi.org/10.1016/j.procs.2021.09.239
28. Wen, H., Lee, C. C., & Song, Z. (2021). Digitalization and environment: How does ICT affect enterprise environmental performance? *Environmental Science and Pollution Research, 28*(39), 54826–54841. https://doi.org/10.1007/s11356-021-14474-5
29. Sharma, M., Kamble, S., Mani, V., Sehrawat, R., Belhadi, A., & Sharma, V. (2021). Industry 4.0 adoption for sustainability in multi-tier manufacturing supply chain in emerging economies. *Journal of Cleaner Production, 281*, 125013. https://doi.org/10.1016/j.jclepro.2020.125013
30. Javaid, M., Haleem, A., Singh, R. P., Suman, R., & Gonzalez, E. S. (2022). Understanding the adoption of Industry 4.0 technologies in improving environmental sustainability. *Sustainable Operations and Computers, 3*, 203–217. https://doi.org/10.1016/j.susoc.2022.01.008
31. Wang, W., & Siau, K. (2019). Industry 4.0: Ethical and moral predicaments. *Cutter Business Technology Journal, 32*(6), 36–45.
32. Heinrich, T., & Witko, C. (2021). Technology-induced job loss and the prioritization of economic problems in the mass public. *Review of Policy Research, 38*(2), 164–179. https://doi.org/10.1111/ropr.12418
33. Braxton, J. C., & Taska, B. (2023). Technological change and the consequences of job loss. *American Economic Review, 113*(2), 279–316. https://doi.org/10.1257/aer.20210182
34. van Laar, E., van Deursen, A. J., van Dijk, J. A., & de Haan, J. (2019). Determinants of 21st-century digital skills: A large-scale survey among working professionals. *Computers in Human Behavior, 100*, 93–104. https://doi.org/10.1016/j.chb.2019.06.017
35. Ebrahimi, M., Baboli, A., & Rother, E. (2019). The evolution of world class manufacturing toward Industry 4.0: A case study in the automotive industry. *Ifac-Papersonline, 52*(10), 188–194. https://doi.org/10.1016/j.ifacol.2019.10.021
36. Xu, X., Lu, Y., Vogel-Heuser, B., & Wang, L. (2021). Industry 4.0 and Industry 5.0—Inception, conception and perception. *Journal of Manufacturing Systems, 61*, 530–535. https://doi.org/10.1016/j.jmsy.2021.10.006
37. Wang, L. (2022). A futuristic perspective on human-centric assembly. *Journal of Manufacturing Systems, 62*, 199–201. https://doi.org/10.1016/j.jmsy.2021.11.001
38. Goni, F. A., Gholamzadeh Chofreh, A., Estaki Orakani, Z., Klemeš, J. J., Davoudi, M., & Mardani, A. (2021). Sustainable business model: A review and framework development. *Clean Technologies and Environmental Policy, 23*, 889–897. https://doi.org/10.1007/s10098-020-01886-z
39. Gazzola, P., Ratti, M., & Amelio, S. (2017). CSR and sustainability report for nonprofit organizations. An Italian best practice. *Management Dynamics in the Knowledge Economy, 5*(3), 355–376. https://doi.org/10.25019/mdke/5.3.03
40. Gusmerotti, N. M., Testa, F., Corsini, F., Pretner, G., & Iraldo, F. (2019). Drivers and approaches to the circular economy in manufacturing firms. *Journal of Cleaner Production, 230*, 314–327. https://doi.org/10.1016/j.jclepro.2019.05.044
41. Li, J., Song, G., Cai, M., Bian, J., & Mohammed, B. S. (2022). Green environment and circular economy: A state-of-the-art analysis. *Sustainable Energy Technologies and Assessments, 52*, 102106. https://doi.org/10.1016/j.seta.2022.102106
42. Coronado, E., Kiyokawa, T., Ricardez, G. A. G., Ramirez-Alpizar, I. G., Venture, G., & Yamanobe, N. (2022). Evaluating quality in human-robot interaction: A systematic search and classification of performance and human-centered factors, measures and metrics towards an Industry 5.0. *Journal of Manufacturing Systems, 63*, 392–410. https://doi.org/10.1016/j.jmsy.2022.04.007
43. Muhammad, H., Latief, F., Widiawati, A., Asbara, N. W., & Zaeni, N. (2021). Factors supporting business and its distribution to business resilience in new normal era. *Journal of Distribution Science, 19*(11), 5–15.

44. Graham, J., & Loke, H. Y. (2022). Theory rewritten: Business continuity and crisis management in the wake of the Covid-19 pandemic. *Journal of Contingencies and Crisis Management, 30*(3), 231–233. https://doi.org/10.1111/1468-5973.12415
45. Huang, S., Wang, B., Li, X., Zheng, P., Mourtzis, D., & Wang, L. (2022). Industry 5.0 and Society 5.0—Comparison, complementation, and co-evolution. *Journal of Manufacturing Systems, 64*, 424–428. https://doi.org/10.1016/j.jmsy.2022.07.010
46. Machado, C. G., Winroth, M., Carlsson, D., Almström, P., Centerholt, V., & Hallin, M. (2019). Industry 4.0 readiness in manufacturing companies: Challenges and enablers towards increased digitalization. *Procedia CIRP, 81*, 1113–1118. https://doi.org/10.1016/j.procir.2019.03.262
47. Álvarez Jaramillo, J., Zartha Sossa, J. W., & Orozco Mendoza, G. L. (2019). Barriers to sustainability for small and medium enterprises in the framework of sustainable development—Literature review. *Business Strategy and the Environment, 28*(4), 512–524.
48. Zamoum, K., & Gorpe, T. S. (2018). Crisis management: A historical and conceptual approach for a better understanding of today's crises. In *Crisis management-theory and practice*. IntechOpen.
49. Leng, J., Sha, W., Wang, B., Zheng, P., Zhuang, C., Liu, Q., Wuest, T., Mourtzis, D., & Wang, L. (2022). Industry 5.0: Prospect and retrospect. *Journal of Manufacturing Systems, 65*, 279–295. https://doi.org/10.1016/j.jmsy.2022.09.017

# Operational Management of Production for Car Maintenance and Repair Using Digital Twin Technology

**Evgeniy Kozin**

**Abstract** The article discusses approaches to creating a digital twin of a car service station. Given the six levels of evolution of digital twins identified by experts, the work proposes ways for implementing the first three levels. The first level of the digital twin is directed to reflect a piece of information about the actual state of the production area by analyzing the flow of frames from a video camera installed in the area and a neural network that makes it possible to detect cars and mechanics in these frames. The second level is a virtual model of the production zone. The model allows one to visually evaluate the current state of the technological operations performed by mechanics and the quality of the work performed. The third level of the digital twin allows predicting the technological route of mechanics, taking into account the established list of influencing factors, among which are the need for work indicated by the client, the probability of related work occurring, etc. The research applied computer vision methods using convolutional neural networks, simulation modeling and technology for creating digital twins of production facilities. The developed neural network model allows determining key points of the technological route and binding them to time markers. As an efficiency criterion, it is proposed to use the current production losses of the enterprise associated with the ineffective organization of the production process and the incorrect choice of technological routes for mechanics. The developed methodology is presented in the form of an algorithm for using a neural network to determine a technological route, which can be applied to develop a software product for the operational management of production for vehicle maintenance and repair. The practical significance of the findings lies in the development of a methodology for using neural networks to assess the efficiency of the car maintenance and repair process, which can be used by automobile manufacturers.

**Keywords** Service station · Digital twin · Production management · Automobiles · Maintenance and repair · Optimization

---

E. Kozin (✉)
Industrial University of Tyumen, Tyumen, Russian Federation



A. Appolloni et al. (eds.), *The Future of Industry*, Lecture Notes in Information Systems and Organisation 70, https://doi.org/10.1007/978-3-031-66801-2_14

## 1 Introduction

The development of digital twins of transport infrastructure facilities is indicated as one of the directions for the digital transformation of transport in the transport strategy of many countries [1–3]. Currently, digital twins of urban transport infrastructure and transport frameworks of large cities are being actively created, and transport flows are being modeled. The goal is to identify ways to improve the efficiency of the road network, as well as the organization and methods of transport management [4–6]. This direction relates to the field of operation of road transport. But at the same time, the field of technical operation of road transport, which is aimed at maintaining and restoring the performance of vehicles owned by individuals and organizations, also has a great potential for digitalization [7–10]. This area has greater inertia in terms of the use of innovative approaches and is more inclined to use traditional technology and organization of vehicle maintenance and repair [11–14]. At the same time, the car is a source of a large amount of data that can be used to improve the efficiency of motor transport enterprises. In our work, a motor transport enterprise refers to both organizations that have their own fleet of vehicles and a production base for its maintenance or repair, as well as enterprises specializing in the maintenance and repair of cars on a commercial basis. The latter include service stations, the main production element of which is a post, determined by a location with a production building, equipped with technological equipment and mechanics to carry out work on the car [15]. It is obvious that with the intensive digitalization of cars happening today, it is necessary to digitalize related areas, which include the motor transport enterprise. The purpose of the study is to determine the structure of the digital twin of a motor transport enterprise and determine methods for its formation.

## 2 Materials and Methods

According to a number of research works, there are several levels of digital twin generation [16]. The levels under consideration are presented in Fig. 1.

Level one corresponds to the introduction of sensors and systems into the enterprise that are capable of providing the operator with characteristics of the current state of the production facility [17–19]. The second level allows one to structure the information obtained using data collection systems and organize its presentation in a flexible form according to user requests. This type includes systems equipped with Business Intelligence technology that visualize information depending on the request in the convenient form of dashboards and interactive graphs. The third level allows making predictions based on datasets collected at the previous stages using machine learning technologies [20–23]. At the fourth level, mathematical and simulation models can be used for optimization problems, allowing one to "play out" several options for the development of events and use

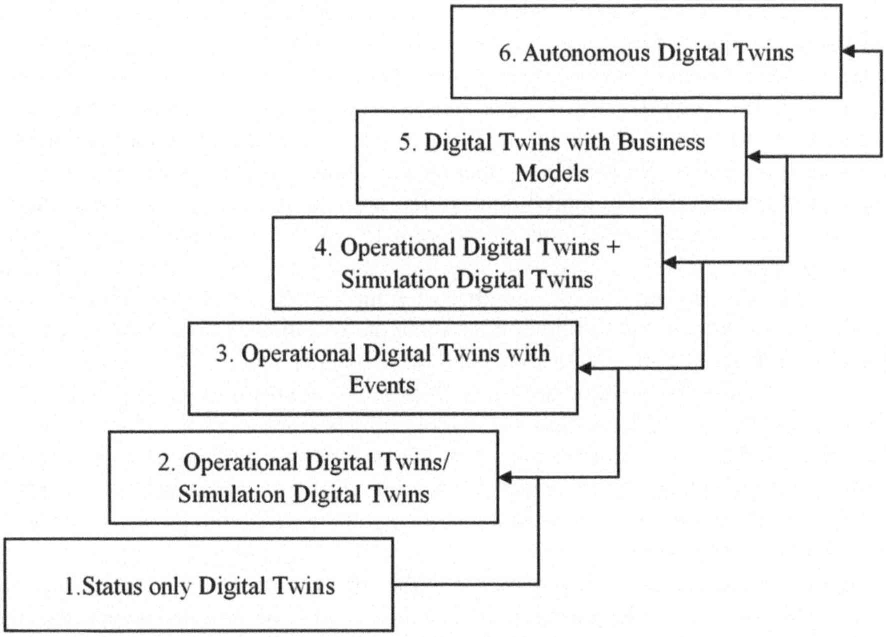


**Fig. 1** Stages of evolution or levels of development of digital twins

the result to help in the process of management decision-making. Levels five and six combine the capabilities of operational twins and simulation, as well as increase the degree of autonomy in decision-making. All this makes it possible to use digital twins for forecasting based on current information and searching for optimal options for implementing business processes in enterprises.

The structure presented above is quite universal and can serve as the basis for the development of a digital twin in the field of technical operation of automobiles. Next, the structure of the digital twin of the production area of a car service station will be considered.

The laboratory of the Institute of Transport of the Tyumen Industrial University with the car located there was used for experiment. A video camera was installed in front of the car, which recorded the actions of the mechanic within the boundaries of the post area [24–28]. For the experiment, not a complete technological process was used, but a conditional list of operations to inspect the engine compartment and all four wheels of the car by a mechanic lasting no more than 2 min. The mechanic approached the car, opened the hood from the passenger compartment, then inspected the engine for a few seconds, after which he moved to the front right wheel area, carried out the inspection for a few seconds and performed the same operations with the other wheels, walking around the car clockwise.

The resulting video was processed using the YOLOv3 neural network to detect a mechanic and a car within the borders of the post area [29–31]. In addition, the space of the post was marked out at key points corresponding to the stages of the technological process under consideration: the areas of the hood and all the wheels of the car were allocated to rectangles. Detection of objects of the "person" and "car" classes was recorded by rectangles with inscriptions of class names in the upper left corner [32, 33]. The system was implemented in the Python programming language using weights of a neural network pre-trained to recognize the specified objects, the computer vision library OpenCV, numerical calculations numpy, data visualization matplotlib and the statistics module stats of the scipy library. The result of the neural network was the class label and the coordinates of the rectangle describing the detected object. As a metric for assessing the accuracy of object recognition by the model, we used the ratio of the number of frames with objects identified by the model to the total number of frames containing the specified objects. As an indicator for assessing the presence of a mechanic on a specific section of a technological route, for example, in the hood area, it is proposed to use the intersection over union metric, which allows determining the area of correspondence between the bounding box of the target zone and the object [34]. Thus, the model allows us to assess the compliance of the actual sequence of technological operations performed by a mechanic with the normative one, i.e., indirectly characterize the quality of vehicle maintenance and repair.

However, the presence of a mechanic in the specified area for a given period of time does not answer the question of whether or not the required technological operations were actually performed. To solve this problem, a neural network was used to detect the required objects and segment the image pixels into those that belong to the desired object and those that do not. The model was tested on an annotated dataset of oil filters for a Renault Duster. When replacing an oil filter during maintenance, a mechanic is expected to remove the old filter and install a new one. In this case, the neural network must record the oil filter twice at different, predetermined time intervals. If detection occurs, it is concluded that the oil filter was replaced by a mechanic during the work. To implement the segmentation model, the basic pre-trained neural network mobilenet_v2, located in the tf.keras.applications library, was used. As a superstructure, the U-net model with the pix2pix generative adversarial network discriminator was utilized [35]. The size of the dataset was 40 images of an oil filter made by the author and taken freely from the Internet; marking was done using the online program CVAT.

One of the main tasks when managing a car service enterprise is predicting a specific technological route for the client's car [36]. For example, if there is a declared need for maintenance at a certain mileage, during the work, related faults may be identified that increase the planned time for the work. Some jobs may require ordering spare parts that were not pre-scheduled in stock, which can also disrupt the job schedule. These factors can be taken into account by the model, which will improve the accuracy of the technological route forecast.

The technological process of vehicle maintenance and repair represents a set of $K = \{k{:}k = 1, K\}$ pre-established standard combinations of technical influences or technological routes (TR). In this regard, the target function of the study can be represented by an additive expression characterizing the current production losses:

$$C_{\sum in} = \left(C_{\sum fl} + C_{\sum vl} + C_{\sum opt}\right)N_v \rightarrow \min \quad (1)$$

where $C_{\sum in}$ is generalized in-production losses of a car service enterprise, c.u.; $C_{\sum fl}$ is enterprise losses caused by errors in the distribution of mechanics along technological routes, c.u.; $C_{\sum vl}$, is losses of the enterprise associated with violation of the normative technological process by personnel, c.u.; $C_{\sum opt}$ is losses caused by insufficient optimization of existing technological routes and inefficient organization of production, c.u.; $N_v$ is production program of the enterprise, units/year.

Moreover, each of the TRs represents a certain subset $\{i\}_k$ of technical operations, the entire set $R = \{r{:}r = 1, R\}$ of which is necessary and sufficient for the maintenance and repair of any car from among the clients of this enterprise.

In the general case, the number of TRs during the maintenance and repair of cars is set by a previously known value *Z*, and *X* is a combination of vehicle and production parameters that must be classified. *X* is the collection of these parameters, i.e., $X = \{S_1, \ldots, S_M\}$. Each specific technological route *Y* is some derivative of *X*, i.e., the neural network must classify $X \rightarrow Y$, and then distribute mechanics into TRs depending on the set of parameters: $Y \rightarrow Z$, where $y \in Y$ and $z \in Z$.

The set of parameters of *X* was presented in the form of a matrix of factors influencing the determination of an effective technological route and is summarized in Table 1.

List of factors that determine the technological route of production personnel of a car service center:

$S_1$—car maintenance or repair work requested by the client.
$S_2$—need for additional related work on the car.
$S_3$—need for cleaning and washing work on the car.
$S_4$—need for spare parts or consumables for work.
$S_5$—mechanic qualification.
$S_6$—need for technological equipment and tools for work.
$S_7$—actual load level of the production area.
$S_8$—make and model of the car, defining specific technological operations.

To solve the problem of choosing a technological route depending on the values of the influencing factors, a fully connected neural network was used with three hidden layers containing 32, 64 and 128 neurons each, the input layer contained eight input values corresponding to the number of factors determining the technological

**Table 1** Example of a matrix for determining a technological route for production personnel of a car service center

| No. | Combinations of factors | | | | | | | | |
|---|---|---|---|---|---|---|---|---|---|
| 1 | $S_{1,1}$ | $S_{1,2}$ | $S_{1,3}$ | $S_{1,4}$ | $S_{1,5}$ | $S_{1,6}$ | $S_{1,7}$ | $S_{1,8}$ | $S_{1,M}$ |
| 2 | $S_{2,1}$ | $S_{2,2}$ | $S_{2,3}$ | $S_{2,4}$ | $S_{2,5}$ | $S_{2,6}$ | $S_{2,7}$ | $S_{2,8}$ | $S_{2,M}$ |
| ... | ... | ... | ... | ... | ... | ... | ... | ... | ... |
| N | $S_{N,1}$ | $S_{N,2}$ | $S_{N,3}$ | $S_{N,4}$ | $S_{N,5}$ | $S_{N,6}$ | $S_{N,7}$ | $S_{N,8}$ | $S_{N,M}$ |

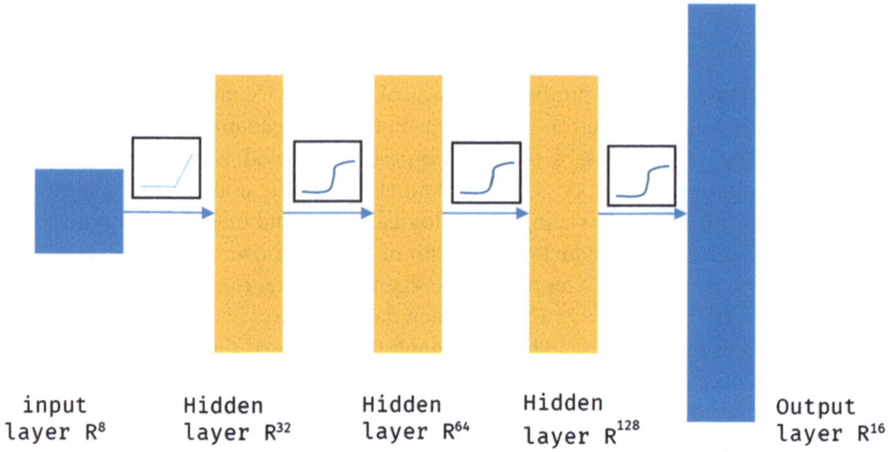


**Fig. 2** Architecture of a fully connected neural network for predicting a technological route

process. The output layer consisted of the coordinates of eight key points corresponding to the stages of the technological process, as well as the binding of each point to time, i.e., had a dimension equal to 16. "Relu" was used as the activation function of the first layer, and the "tanh" function was used for the remaining layers. The model was trained for 50 epochs with a batch size of 20. The neural network was implemented using the Sequential module of the Tensorflow Keras framework in the Python programming language. The architecture of the developed neural network is presented in Fig. 2.

## 3 Results and Discussion

The first level of the digital twin of the production area of a car service station is represented by a video camera and software capable of processing information about the actual state of objects. For the experimental conditions, the YOLOv3 neural network showed sufficient accuracy in detecting a mechanic and a car, which for these objects was more than 90%. Thus, the neural network allows the operator to receive real-time information about objects in the production area of the car service center. Figure 3.1a shows the result of object detection on a marked video frame from the camera. There is a car and person object defined by the neural network, as well as bounding boxes for zones such as the hood, front left wheel, front right wheel, rear right and rear left wheel, which were manually specified for the selected technological process. The model also correctly determines the duration of the presence of a mechanic or a car in a selected area of the production zone using the iou metric. The high iou values in the graph in Fig. 3b indicate that the mechanic was in the hood area for 23 s.

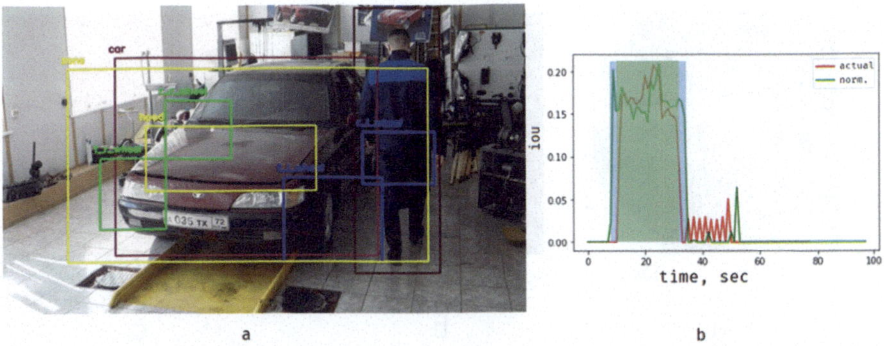


**Fig. 3** Video frame of a real object with marked technological work zones and objects of the "car" and "person" classes recognized by the YOLO v3 neural network

Figure 3b shows the result of comparing the actual value of the iou metric for the hood area with the standard value determined according to the stages of the technological process. For the conditions of the presented example, the mechanic had to be in the specified zone from 15 to 38 s (green line), which corresponds to the actual duration of his work in the specified zone. Due to the different size of the bounding boxes for the hood and mechanics areas, the metric value does not exceed 0.2. A rectangle was drawn around each graph using the gradient exponent of the function, after which the area of overlap of the two rectangles is determined. The correspondence between the normative and actual technological processes is higher, the closer the result is to unity, or the more the area of the rectangle for the actual technological process coincides with the area for the normative one. For the conditions of the example, the value of the "intersection over union" metric is 0.93. The user can determine the threshold values of the indicator to tighten the limits of compliance.

To assess the quality of vehicle maintenance and repair operations using video frame segmentation, a neural network was trained. Then the accuracy of image segmentation of a Renault car oil filter was assessed. The Sparse CategoricalCrossentropy indicator was used to assess the model error. According to the training results, by the end of the 50th epoch the model showed the accuracy of 0.996. Figure 4 illustrates a visualization of the original test image of an oil filter under the hood of a car, a labeled mask for the same image, and the result of image segmentation made by a trained neural network.

According to Fig. 4, we can conclude that the model is able to accurately determine the location of the object in the image and the boundaries of this object, separating it from the background. You can see that the neural network quite accurately indicated the area in which the oil filter is contained, especially since part of it is blocked by the cooling system pipes. The high accuracy of object recognition demonstrated the applicability of the approach under consideration. As directions for further research, the authors plan to train a neural network to detect all the main consumables for the selected technological process for the maintenance of

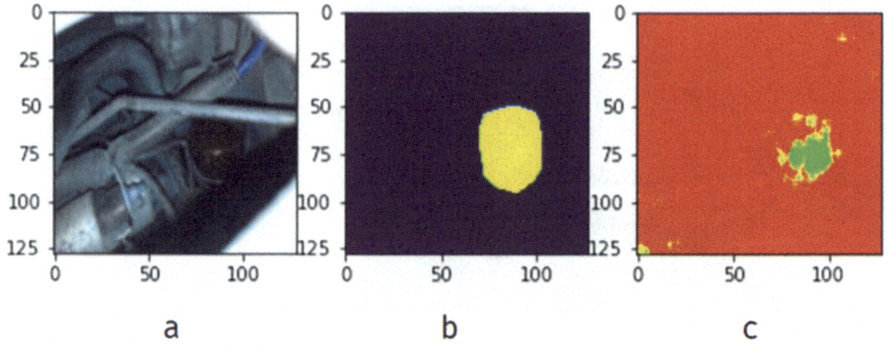


**Fig. 4** Assessing the quality of vehicle maintenance and repair operations using video frame segmentation. (**a**) test image of the Renault Duster oil filter; (**b**) labeled mask for the test image; (**c**) segmentation of a test image of an oil filter carried out by a trained neural network

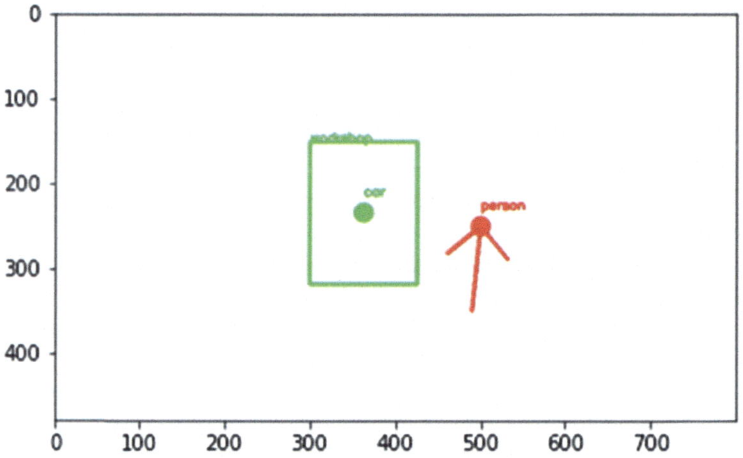


**Fig. 5** Video frame of a virtual model of a real object

a car: oil filter, air filter, cabin filter, as well as detecting containers for changing engine oil.

After this, a virtual model of the car service production area was developed. Figure 5 shows a video frame of a virtual model of a production area, where a circle represents a car (in the center of a post surrounded by a rectangle) and a mechanic who walks around the car on the right towards the rear left wheel. The arrow of the virtual model also points there.

The resulting model can serve not only as a virtual copy of the service area, but also for accumulating and analyzing information about the activities of the zone, thus acting as the implementation of the second level of the enterprise's digital twin. The model can be made more detailed by adding virtual copies of other objects of the production zone: people, cars, technological equipment, numerical parameters of

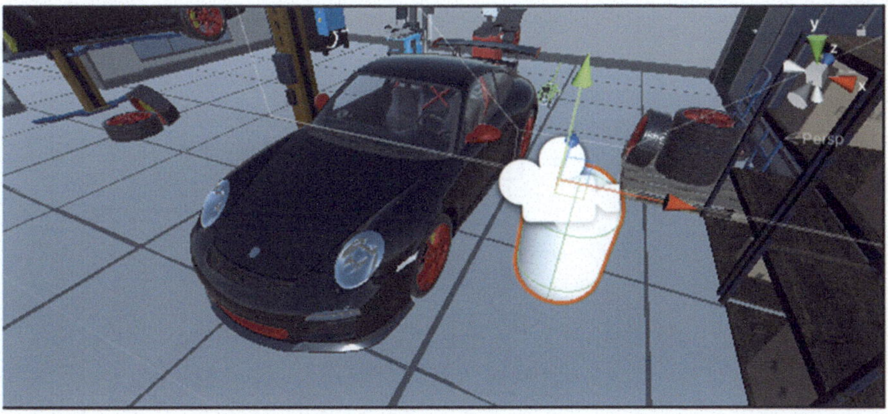

**Fig. 6** Potential for improving the virtual model of the production area of a motor transport enterprise using Unity game development environment

each of these objects, traffic routes and much more. The schematic view of the virtual model shown in Fig. 5 can be replaced by a more user-friendly one by connecting the model to one of the well-known 3D computer game development systems. Figure 6 shows an option for further development of the virtual car service model using the Unity engine.

The advantages of the proposed approach are the possibility of visual remote monitoring of the production process while maintaining the real spatial dimensions of objects, the distances between them, the arrangement of technological equipment, etc. In addition, the 3D interactive model is an important step in the design of a digital twin at level 3 and above, i.e., models capable of predicting the behavior of objects and the state of the production area as a whole.

As part of the implementation of the third level of the digital twin, it is proposed to use a fully connected neural network to predict the optimal technological route, taking into account minimizing the current production losses of the enterprise. Taking into account the input factors presented in Table 1 and characterizing the initial conditions, the neural network model makes it possible to determine the type of technological route, key waypoints and their time reference for control. Figure 7 shows an example of classification and selection of a technological route for experimental conditions.

For the presented conditions, the model determined a technological route consisting of eight key points, and also identified five zones for performing technological operations corresponding to the conditions shown in Fig. 2. The mechanic must start moving from the first key point "wp1", and then sequentially go through the rest, making stops in each technological zone for a given period of time. In the presented example, it is obvious that the mechanic began the execution of the technological route incorrectly, which should be recorded by the module presented within level 1 of the digital twin.

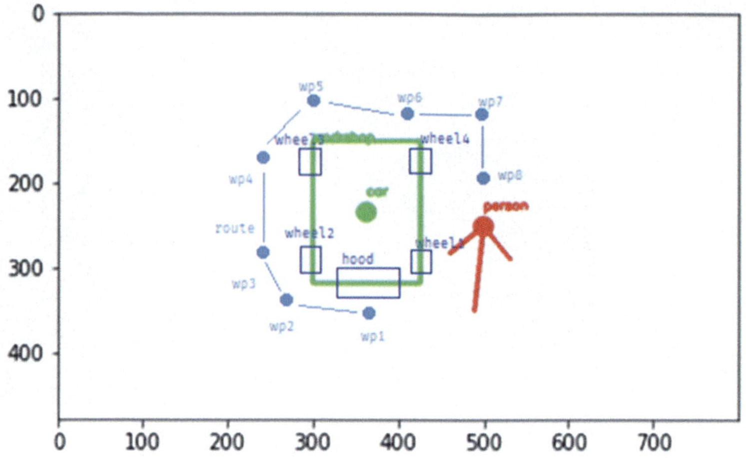


**Fig. 7** The route predicted by the ANN and the actual technological route for the test process

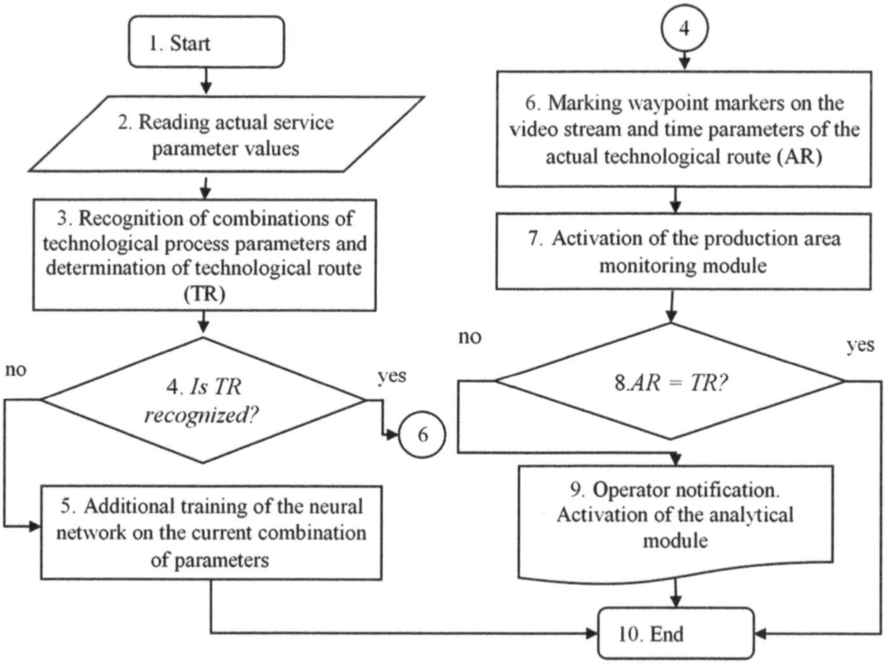


**Fig. 8** The algorithm for using ANN to determine the technological route

Based on the research carried out, a block diagram of an algorithm for using an artificial neural network was developed. It determines the optimal technological route for the mechanic and assess the quality of technological operations. The algorithm is shown in Fig. 8.

The block diagram of the algorithm for using an ANN to determine a technological route consists of ten main stages. Stages 1 and 10 are the beginning and the end, respectively. 2—reading the actual values of the service parameters presented in Table 1. These parameters determine the type of mechanic's technological route and the main key points. 3—recognition of combinations of process parameters and determination of a specific technological route, for example, maintenance number 1 with diagnosing the front suspension of the car. 4—condition for checking the fact of recognition of the technological route. If the route is recognized, then program goes to block 6. If it is not recognized, then program goes to block 5.5—a block for additional training of the neural network on the current combination of technological parameters for which the model's prediction gave results with low accuracy. 6—marking waypoint markers on the video stream of surveillance of the production area and determining the time parameters of the technological route. 7—activation of the module for monitoring the production area and assessing the quality of technological operations performed by the mechanic. 8—condition for checking the degree of compliance of the actual technological route with the normative one, i.e., determination of deviations from the execution of a sequence of actions or detection of the fact of failure to perform a number of technological operations. 9—notifying the operator about the violation of the technological process. Activation of the analytical module and management decision-making module. Simulation modeling of zone operation with current parameters. Forecasting the result and assessing the economic effect of its implementation.

## 4 Conclusion

Digital twins are actively developing for many industries. Within the framework of this study, the problem of creating the appearance of a digital twin for an automobile maintenance and repair enterprise was considered. This area has significant potential for digitalization as mentioned in the course of the study.

Thus, as a result of the research, approaches to the implementation of the first three levels of a digital twin of a motor transport enterprise were developed. The first level corresponds to obtaining information about the actual state of the enterprise's production area through video surveillance and object detection using a convolutional neural network. In addition, methods have been developed for assessing the quality of technological operations for the maintenance and repair of automobiles by assessing the sequence of actions performed by a mechanic and determining whether certain operations have been performed. Level 2 of the digital twin is implemented as a virtual model of the production area, capable of displaying the status of participants in the production process in real time. Approaches to the development of a three-dimensional functional model using the existing engines for creating computer games are presented. The third level of the digital twin is proposed to be implemented by predicting optimal production parameters, in particular, choosing a mechanic's technological route according to the list of input factors that can make changes to the standard technological process. It is proposed to evaluate the effectiveness of implementing a digital twin at a motor transport enterprise using a model of the enterprise's current production losses, which consist of losses generated by errors in the distribution of mechanics along technological routes, losses associated with personnel violation of the standard technological process, and losses caused by insufficient optimization of the existing technological routes and inefficient organization of production. A preliminary assessment of the effectiveness of the developed methodology using formula (1) allows us to talk about reducing the generalized in-production losses of a car service enterprise by 5–10% when using a system for monitoring and forecasting technological routes of repair personnel. For more accurate estimates, it is planned to conduct an experiment at a number of car service enterprises. The given algorithm for using a neural network to determine a technological route can serve as the basis for the development of software aimed at increasing the efficiency of management decision-making. The results obtained can be used to design software products for assessing the effectiveness of vehicle maintenance and repair, as well as to form higher levels of digital twins of a motor transport enterprise.

## References

1. Kossiakoff, A., Sweet, W. M., Seymour, S. J., & Biemer, S. M. (2014). *Systems engineering. Principles and practice* (2nd ed.). Wiley.
2. Lambiotte, R., Rosvall, M., & Scholtes, I. (2019). From networks to optimal higher-order models of complex systems. *Nature Physics, 15*(4), 313–320. https://doi.org/10.1038/s41567-019-0459-y
3. Stevens, A. L., & Collins, A. (2021). Multiple conceptual models of a complex system. In *Aptitude, learning, and instruction* (pp. 177–198). Routledge. https://doi.org/10.4324/9781003163145-20
4. Jbili, S., Chelbi, A., Radhoui, M., & Kessentini, M. (2018). Integrated strategy of vehicle routing and maintenance. *Reliability Engineering and System Safety, 170*, 202–214. https://doi.org/10.1016/j.ress.2017.09.030
5. Lu, C. C., Yan, S., Li, H. C., Diabat, A., & Wang, H. T. (2021). Optimal fleet deployment for electric vehicle sharing systems with the consideration of demand uncertainty. *Computers & Operations Research, 135*, 105437. https://doi.org/10.1016/j.cor.2021.105437
6. Militao, A. M., & Tirachini, A. (2021). Optimal fleet size for a shared demand-responsive transport system with human-driven vs automated vehicles: A total cost minimization approach. *Transportation Research Part A, 151*, 52–80. https://doi.org/10.1016/j.tra.2021.07.004
7. Bouvard, K., Tedie, H., & Lesobre, R. (2018). Joint dynamic scheduling of missions and vehicle: Value of on-line information vehicle: Value of on-line information. *IFAC PapersOnLine, 51*(24), 837–842. https://doi.org/10.1016/j.ifacol.2018.09.672
8. Dobromirov, V., Verkhorubov, V., & Chernyaev, I. (2018). Systematizing the factors that determine ways of developing the vehicle maintenance system and providing vehicle safety. *Transportation Research Procedia, 36*, 114–121. https://doi.org/10.1016/j.trpro.2018.12.052
9. Liu, G., Chen, S., Jin, H., & Liu, S. (2021). Optimum opportunistic maintenance schedule incorporating delay time theory with imperfect maintenance. *Reliability Engineering and System Safety, 213*, 107668. https://doi.org/10.1016/j.ress.2021.107668

10. Markudova, D., Mishra, S., Cagliero, L., Vassio, L., et al. (2021). Preventive maintenance for heterogeneous industrial vehicles with incomplete usage data. *Computers in Industry, 130*, 103468. https://doi.org/10.1016/j.compind.2021.103468
11. Prytz, R., Nowaczyk, S., Rögnvaldsson, T., & Byttner, S. (2015). Predicting the need for vehicle compressor repairs using maintenance records and logged vehicle data. *Engineering Applications of Artificial Intelligence, 41*, 139–150. https://doi.org/10.1016/j.engappai.2015.02.009
12. Rokhforoz, P., & Fink, O. (2022). Maintenance scheduling of manufacturing systems based on optimal price of the network. *Reliability Engineering and System Safety, 217*, 108088. https://doi.org/10.1016/j.ress.2021.108088
13. Semykina, A., Zagorodni, N., Novikov, I., & Novikov, A. (2021). Main directions of improving the maintenance and repair of vehicle units in the Far North. *Transportation Research Procedia, 57*, 611–616. https://doi.org/10.1016/j.trpro.2021.09.090
14. Wang, Y., Limmer, S., Nguyen, D. V., Olhofer, M., Bäck, T., & Emmerich, M. (2021). Optimizing the maintenance schedule for a vehicle fleet: A simulation based case study. *Engineering Optimization, 53*, 1258–1271. https://doi.org/10.1080/0305215X.2021.1919888
15. Monteiro Tavares, C. M., & Szpytko, J. (2016). Vehicles emerging technologies from maintenance perspective. *IFAC-PapersOnLine, 49*(28), 67–72. https://doi.org/10.1016/j.ifacol.2016.11.012
16. Kim, B. S., & Kim, T. G. (2019). Cooperation of simulation and data model for performance analysis of complex systems. *International Journal of Simulation Modelling, 18*(4), 608–619. https://doi.org/10.2507/ijsimm18(4)491
17. Garcia-Sanchez, A. J., Garcia-Sanchez, F., & Garcia-Haro, J. (2011). Wireless sensor network deployment for integrating video-surveillance and data-monitoring in precision agriculture over distributed crops. *Computers and Electronics in Agriculture, 75*(2), 288–303. https://doi.org/10.1016/j.compag.2010.12.005
18. Lee, C.-M. (2023). Development of an automated spare-part management device for ship controlled by raspberry-pi microcomputer based on Image-Progressing & Transfer-Learning. *Journal of Marine Science and Engineering, 11*, 1015. https://doi.org/10.3390/jmse11051015
19. Parameshwaran, R., Srinivasan, P. S. S., Punniyamoorthy, M., Charunyanath, S. T., & Ashwin, C. (2009). Integrating fuzzy analytical hierarchy process and data envelopment analysis for performance management in automobile repair shops. *European Journal of Industrial Engineering, 3*(4), 450–467. https://doi.org/10.1504/EJIE.2009.027037
20. Ahmed, U., Carpitella, S., & Certa, A. (2021). An integrated methodological approach for optimising complex systems subjected to predictive maintenance. *Reliability Engineering & System Safety, 216*, 108022. https://doi.org/10.1016/j.ress.2021.108022
21. El-Awady, A., & Ponnambalam, K. (2021). Integration of simulation and Markov chains to support Bayesian networks for probabilistic failure analysis of complex systems. *Reliability Engineering & System Safety, 211*, 107511. https://doi.org/10.1016/j.ress.2021.107511
22. Rohaan, D. (2022). Using supervised machine learning for B2B sales forecasting: A case study of spare parts sales forecasting at an after-sales service provider. *Expert Systems with Applications, 188*, 115925. https://doi.org/10.1016/j.eswa.2021.115925
23. Vlachas, P. R., Arampatzis, G., Uhler, C., & Koumoutsakos, P. (2022). Multiscale simulations of complex systems by learning their effective dynamics. *Nature Machine Intelligence, 4*(4), 359–366. https://doi.org/10.1038/s42256-022-00464-w
24. Akinyede, R. O., & Daramola, O. A. (2013). Neural network web-based human resource management system model. *International Journal of Computer Networks and Communications Security, 1*(3), 75–87. https://doi.org/10.47277/ijcncs/1(3)2
25. Alhoniemi, E., Hollmén, J., Simula, O., & Vesanto, J. (1999). Process monitoring and modeling using the self-organizing map. *Integrated Computer-Aided Engineering, 6*(1), 3–14. https://doi.org/10.3233/ica-1999-6102
26. Babiker, M., Khalifa, O., Htike, K., Hassan, A., & Zaharadeen, M. (2017). Automated daily human activity recognition for video surveillance using neural network. In *2017 IEEE 4th*

*international conference on smart instrumentation, measurement and application (ICSIMA)* (pp. 1–5). https://doi.org/10.1109/icsima.2017.8312024
27. Franklin, R. J., & Dabbagol, V. (2020). Anomaly detection in videos for video surveillance applications using neural networks. In *2020 Fourth International Conference on Inventive Systems and Control (ICISC)* (pp. 632–637). https://doi.org/10.1109/icisc47916.2020.9171212
28. Gonzaga, J. C. B., Meleiro, L. A. C., Kiang, C., & Maciel Filho, R. (2009). ANN-based soft-sensor for real-time process monitoring and control of an industrial polymerization process. *Computers & Chemical Engineering, 33*(1), 43–49. https://doi.org/10.1016/j.compchemeng.2008.05.019
29. Amato, A., Di Lecce, V., & Piuri, V. (2005). Neural network-based video surveillance system. *CIHSPS 2005*. In *Proceedings of the 2005 IEEE international conference on computational intelligence for homeland security and personal safety* (pp. 85–89).
30. Butt, U. M., Letchmunan, S., Hassan, F., Zia, S., & Baqir, A. (2020). Detecting video surveillance using VGG19 convolutional neural networks. *International Journal of Advanced Computer Science and Applications, 11*(2). https://doi.org/10.14569/ijacsa.2020.0110285
31. Jiang, P., Ergu, D., Liu, F., Cai, Y., & Ma, B. (2022). A review of Yolo algorithm developments. *Procedia Computer Science, 199*, 1066–1073. https://doi.org/10.1016/j.procs.2022.01.135
32. Patalas-Maliszewska, J., Halikowski, D., & Damaševičius, R. (2021). An automated recognition of work activity in industrial manufacturing using convolutional neural networks. *Electronics, 10*(23), 2946. https://doi.org/10.3390/electronics10232946
33. Trivedi, S., & Patel, N. (2021). Virtual employee monitoring: A review on tools, opportunities, challenges, and decision factors. *Empirical Quests for Management Essences, 1*(1), 86–99.
34. Tseng, T. Y., & Luo, Q. (2021). Company employee quality evaluation model based on BP neural network. *Journal of Intelligent & Fuzzy Systems, 40*(4), 5883–5892. https://doi.org/10.3233/jifs-189428
35. Huang, H. (2020). UNet 3+: A full-scale connected UNet for medical image segmentation. In *IEEE International Conference on Acoustics, Speech and Signal Processing* (pp. 1055–1059). https://doi.org/10.1109/ICASSP40776.2020.9053405
36. Muzaffar, S., & Afshari, A. (2019). Short-term load forecasts using LSTM networks. *Energy Procedia, 158*, 2922–2927. https://doi.org/10.1016/j.egypro.2019.01.952

# Industrial Digitalization as a Driver of City Reindustrialization: Evidence from Detroit

**Irina Turgel and Aleksandr Pobedin**

**Abstract** The paper delves into the problems of digital transformation and reindustrialization of an old industrial city. Detroit, one of the largest US industrial cities of the second echelon, was chosen as the object of the study. We analyze the city's economic development, problems and challenges typical of its current evolutionary stage, as well as the measures taken to overcome them. The paper provides some examples of modern technological solutions implemented by major enterprises in Detroit and details the ecosystem of Industry 4.0 in the city, which includes high-tech enterprises, digital platforms, educational organizations, scientific institutions, government support measures, market of qualified specialists and modern digital technologies. We examine the prospects for the industrial transition to Industry 5.0 in Detroit, which would involve human-machine collaboration and social innovations, and identify the main obstacles to such a transition.

**Keywords** Industrial digitalization · Deindustrialization · Old industrial city · Reindustrialization · Industry 4.0 · Industry 5.0 · Digital transformation

## 1 Introduction

The stages of industrial development resulting from both scientific/technological progress and socio-economic factors inevitably affect the structure of the interregional division of labor, creating prerequisites for an accelerated economic growth in certain territories, which can then be replaced just as rapidly by a long period of economic stagnation and decline. The risk of such a scenario is more likely to occur not in metropolitan areas, which are usually the leaders in adapting to

I. Turgel (✉)
Ural Federal University, Ekaterinburg, Russian Federation
e-mail: i.d.turgel@urfu.ru

A. Pobedin
Ural Institute of Management – Branch of the Russian Presidential Academy of National Economy and Public Administration (RANEPA), Ekaterinburg, Russian Federation
e-mail: pobedin-aa@ranepa.ru



A. Appolloni et al. (eds.), *The Future of Industry*, Lecture Notes in Information Systems and Organisation 70, https://doi.org/10.1007/978-3-031-66801-2_15

changing economic conditions, but in the so-called "second tier" or "second echelon" cities, located one level below in the hierarchy of economic centers. Such cities, despite the accumulated industrial potential, are often less adaptable to changing environmental conditions. Studies show that second-tier cities are more dependent on the deterioration of the macroeconomic environment and suffer more from the consequences of economic downturn [1, 2], especially if their economy is mainly characterized by mono-industrial patterns.

The city of Detroit, located in the state of Michigan (USA), can be a vivid illustration of these trends. From the 1920s to the 1940s, Detroit was one of the leaders of industrial development, having concentrated automobile manufacturing enterprises, one of the most technologically advanced industrial sectors at that time. Detroit's population was growing rapidly, reaching 1,850,000 by 1950, and making it the fifth largest city in the United States on this measure [3]. However, the second half of the last century was not that successful for Detroit. There was a redistribution of influence in the international automobile market, products from the USA began to be squeezed by manufacturers from other countries, primarily Germany and Japan. Economic problems that led to local budget deficits were accompanied by infrastructure degradation, increased crime, corruption, poor quality of education and racial problems [4]. As a result, in 2013 Detroit declared bankruptcy, the population of the city by that time already totaled 688.7 thousand people, i.e., it decreased by 62.77% compared to 1950. Nevertheless, by 2021, Detroit's GDP had already grown by 28.8% compared to 2013, amounting to 283.6 billion dollars [5]. The stabilization of the economic situation in the city was largely due to the developing processes of reindustrialization based on modern digital technologies. Although there are still a number of serious problems in modern Detroit. The experience of the city's socio-economic development is of significant interest, especially to industrial cities in Russia suffering from restructuring and facing the problems of reindustrialization, such as Togliatti and Naberezhnye Chelny, which, like Detroit, specialize in the automotive manufacturing.

The purpose of this paper is to study the model of reindustrialization implemented in Detroit. Using the case of Detroit, the authors attempt to answer the following questions: what measures can stimulate the city's industry after a long period of deindustrialization and economic decline, what problems an industrial city faces when reindustrializing in the context of global competition, how significant are the benefits of digitalization of the city's industry?

## 2 Literature Review

A significant number of scientific researches on the problems of reindustrialization and digital transformation of industry has been accumulated to date; Web of Science alone has indexed over a thousand publications on this topic, and more than 60% of them relate to the period after 2010.

The main factor that stimulates the interest of researchers in the issues under consideration is undoubtedly the accelerating development of the technological base. Most of the papers that analyze the processes of reindustrialization and digital transformation focus on technological solutions, the use of which can significantly affect the economic growth rate: cyber-physical systems, the Internet of Things in industry, use of Big Data, machine learning and artificial intelligence, smart cities, smart services, smart manufacturing, etc. Nadkarni and Prügl [6] analyzed 58 studies from 2001 to 2019 and identified the most significant trends of transformational changes at the macro and micro levels based on their review of sources. The researchers noted a radical change in the direction of implementation of digital innovations in the companies' activities: from ERP (enterprise resource planning) and CRM (customer relationship management), which improve internal business processes, enterprises are moving to the implementation of cross-border technological solutions, such as big data analytics [7–9], 3D printing [10], the Internet of Things devices [11], that causes radical changes in business models [12, 13].

Another part of the studies focuses on the economic consequences of reindustrialization and digital transformation, including production factor productivity, competitiveness (of both enterprises/industries and regions), income and employment of the population. Thus, Dweck et al. [14] considered reindustrialization through the lens of overcoming the problems caused by the pandemic. Prisecaru [15] considers digital transformation of industry as a tool for enhancing the competitiveness of European regions in the attraction of industrial investments and for counteracting the processes of transferring industrial capacities to East Asian countries. Stojčić et al. [16] using the case of Central and Eastern European countries proved the correlation between the processes of digital transformation in urban and rural areas with the inflow of investments and increase in the share of manufacturing in the structure of regional employment.

Of special interest are the papers that address the problems of regulation of reindustrialization processes and digital transformation by the state. Teixeira and Lehmann [17] provide a comparative analysis of both European and national level programs that stimulate the implementation of Industry 4.0 technological solutions. Zhao et al. [18] consider the project of low-carbon city, implemented in China, which includes state stimulation of the introduction of advanced digital technologies at industrial enterprises. The authors note a positive impact of transformational changes on the level of inter-sectoral and inter-regional differentiation. Jiang et al. [19] assess the impact of digital transformation processes on the sustainable development of territories.

A significant number of studies has been accumulated on the problems of socio-economic development of Detroit, for example, about 2.5 thousand papers on this subject have been indexed in the Web of Science database. Three basic directions of such studies may be distinguished. The first is the study of environmental problems that Detroit faces, including water management [20, 21], green spaces [22, 23], environmental pollution [24], and adaptation to climate changes [25]. The second direction, which attracts the attention of a significant number of researchers, is urban planning. The problems considered here are: spatial organization and zoning of urban environment [26, 27], functioning of public spaces [28], transport [29], options for renovation of abandoned buildings and structures [30], stimulation of cultural and creative activities of residents through the elements of urban infrastructure. The third area of researches is the study of Detroit's social environment, including such issues as demographic dynamics, population migration [31], racial and ethnic segregation [28, 32], income differentiation [32, 33], crime [30, 34], social and civic activity of residents, and the development of the city's human capital [29].

There are also numerous publications on the problems of digital transformation of industry and its impact on the development of territories [35–39], there are analytics on specific examples of digital transformation [40–46], but there is still a deficit of publications on successful cases of digital transformation as part of the process of reindustrialization of old industrial regions and cities, including those specializing in the automotive industry.

## 3 Materials and Methods

This study is based on the concept of digital transformation of the industry, which includes the use of digital technological solutions that create new or change the existing goods, services, business processes; integrating physical and digital systems on the basis of data processing automation; realization of a flexible customer-oriented approach in business management, development of digital culture, stimulation of creativity in relation to both employees and customers [47]. The transition to Industry 4.0 is associated with a number of advantages unavailable in the traditional industry. Firstly, the productivity of the used factors of production increases due to lower costs, higher production process rates and growth in production. Secondly, the quality of manufactured products is improved, as modern technological solutions ensure lower percentage of defective products and increase control over production processes. Thirdly, the flexibility of production operations increases with better ability to reconfigure and switch between the tasks performed. Fourthly, production efficiency enhances, as the use of materials, energy, time and space is optimized. Fifthly, Industry 4.0 contributes to the sustainable development of the territory where the enterprise is located, as negative environmental impacts are reduced, the safety of employees is increased, and the level of social responsibility of the business grows. Sixthly, the innovativeness of production increases, as R&D is stimulated, new technologies are used, new business processes are implemented, new ecosystems and platforms are formed [48]. At present, the relevant task is the transition to a new stage of industrial development, i.e., Industry 5.0, which implies a systematic solution to the weaknesses of Industry 4.0 in the social and environmental spheres. The main principles of Industry 5.0 should be human-centricity, integration, adaptability and sustainability [49].

In the present study, the processes of digital transformation and reindustrialization are explored using the case study approach.

Detroit was chosen as the object of analysis due to the following factors:

- One of the largest industrial cities in the United States;
- Mono-industrial pattern of the city's economy;
- Economic stagnation during the second half of the last century;
- Severe economic crisis of 2008–2014, which resulted in the bankruptcy of the city and mass shutdowns of enterprises;
- Signs of positive economic development and recovery of the city economy due to the application of new business models and introduction of advanced technological solutions.

According to the authors, Detroit is an extremely interesting case study, and its experience can be used to regulate the growing processes of digital transformation and reindustrialization in Russian old industrial territories.

The paper examined both aggregated information on the whole area under study and data on the development of the city's largest enterprises, which were selected by the following criteria: degree of integration of digital technologies into production processes, efficiency of economic activity, and presence of a digital transformation strategy.

The tools for data collection were: document analysis (study of official reports, forecasts and programs, information from official websites of authorities and enterprises) and statistical analysis (statistical data on the economic development of the city, including the size of the gross product, data on employment, investment and trade).

When forming the database of the study, the authors drew upon official statistical information, including data from the U.S. Federal Reserve System (https://fred.stlouisfed.org), the U.S. Census Bureau (https://www.census.gov/), the reports on the socio-economic development and planning documents of Detroit were taken from the official website of the city administration (https://detroitmi.gov/).

## 4 Results

Detroit's problems accumulated over several decades starting from the 1950s and significantly worsened in the first decade of the twenty-first century. The city faced a serious economic crisis caused both by the global recession of 2008 and the difficult situation in its main sector of specialization—the automotive industry. By 2009, Detroit's unemployment rate reached a 20-year high of 14.3%, many businesses were closing or relocating, real estate values plummeted, a significant number of buildings were abandoned, and the city's infrastructure was not functioning well (e.g., water supply disruptions). The population continued to dwindle, falling to 714,000 by 2010.

The following measures were taken to support the economic development of the city: stimulation of the gambling business (opening of three casinos), attempts to make large investments in the real estate of the city (in 1996, General Motors bought

**Table 1** Examples of the transition to Industry 4.0 of Detroit's largest enterprises

| Enterprise | Industry 4.0 elements | Investment amount |
|---|---|---|
| General motors | Electric vehicles, autonomous driving systems, connected mobility, cloud platform and DevOps, artificial intelligence and machine learning | 27 billion USD by 2025 for e-vehicles and autonomous vehicles |
| Ford Motor Company | Electric vehicles, advanced network architecture, cloud platform and DevOps, artificial intelligence and machine learning, digital approach to vehicle rollout, sales and after-sales service | 22 billion USD by 2025 for e-vehicles |
| DTE energy | Smart grid technologies, advanced metering infrastructure, renewable energy sources | 2 billion dollars by 2023 for smart grid technologies |
| American Axle & Manufacturing | Electric drive units, wheel end motors and e-beam axles for battery electric and plug-in electric vehicles, powered by digital technologies | Undisclosed information |

Note: compiled based on data retrieved from Michigan Economic Development Corporation (https://www.michiganbusiness.org/), Detroit Free Press (https://eu.freep.com/), Manufacturing in America (https://www.attendmia.com/), Ford Media Center (https://media.ford.com/), DTE Energy (https://www.dteenergy.com/), American Axle & Manufacturing (https://www.aam.com/)

a skyscraper complex in the city center and moved its headquarters there), infrastructure investments (including the construction of two new stadiums), development of the urban environment (green spaces, street installations, bicycle paths, community gardens on vacant lots and abandoned buildings). However, the measures taken did not lead to significant economic outcomes. As a result, the local budget faced serious problems [50]: the tax base plummeted and the debt load increased beyond the city's financial capacity, eventually leading to Detroit's bankruptcy in 2013.

Ideas of Detroit's reindustrialization emerged as far back as the turn of the 70–80 s of the last century. For example, Luria and Russell [51] propose the concept of a program for preservation and creation of new high-paying jobs in the city's industry through restructuring, i.e., the use of the existing industrial base for the organization of new product lines, including among others the production of energy equipment and mining machinery. However, the most significant changes in Detroit started only in the 2010s, being triggered, on the one hand, by the need to overcome the acute crisis of the city economy, and on the other, by the emergence and development of a new technological base, providing a new phase of industrial development—Industry 4.0. New business models, technological solutions and products were adopted by Detroit's major companies (see Table 1). A number of non-commercial organizations were established to stimulate the digital transformation processes—Automation Alley (scientific research and scientific-practical activities in the field of Industry 4.0), Detroit Technology Center at Wayne State University, Detroit Mobility Initiative and others. General Motors (GM) established an unmanned vehicle development center in Detroit in 2019, and Ford Motor Company opened an innovation center in Detroit in 2020. The successful Industry

4.0 Accelerator, which selects the best high-tech startups for further cooperation with manufacturing companies, is also working. Another tool for the development of digital technologies is LIFT, a non-profit organization that focuses on the development and implementation of advanced technologies for lightweight materials production, as well as the support of education and professional development programs.

The digital transformation processes of 2010–2023 in Detroit resulted in high economic growth, increase in employment (including industrial sector), multiple increase in investments and improvement of the city's competitive position in outside markets (see Table 2). The analysis of socio-economic indicators of Detroit's development for the period 2010–2022 shows that the crisis phenomena have been overcome and sustainable recovery growth achieved. The key indicator of positive dynamics is the dynamics of GRP, which after the recession in 2020, provoked by the COVID-19 pandemic and accompanied by a decline of 4.9%, in 2021 showed growth of 8.7%, which is a manifestation of the realization of the internal potential of the city's economy. The vector of labor market recovery is determined by a steady downward trend in the unemployment rate, decreasing from 13.4% in 2010 to 3.8% in 2022, correlating with the growth of total employment in non-agricultural industries from 1738.3 thousand people in 2010 to 2001.6 thousand in 2022. The increase in the number of people employed in manufacturing industries from 178.54 thousand people in 2010 to 247.74 thousand people in 2022 indicates the re-industrialization of the city and strengthening of its traditional specialization. A contributing factor to the revitalization of business activity is the increase in private investment from USD 1.4 billion in 2010 to USD 7.7 billion in 2022. The accompanying factor in the revitalization of business activity is the increase in the volume of private investment from USD 1.4 billion in 2010 to USD 7.6 billion in 2022, indicating the growth of the city's investment attractiveness. Export growth from $44.8 billion in 2010 to $83.5 billion in 2022 indicates an increase in the international competitiveness of manufactured products. The totality of the studied quantitative indicators gives grounds to assert that Detroit has overcome the systemic crisis and has entered the trajectory of sustainable socio-economic growth.

The crisis of 2019–2020 caused by the Covid 19 pandemic had a painful impact on the city's economy, but its consequences were overcome rather quickly in the following years. According to the forecast of Wayne State University, both employment and income growth will continue in Detroit up to 2028 [52].

## 5 Discussion

It can be said that Detroit has a stable ecosystem of Industry 4.0, including high-tech enterprises, modern technological solutions (see Table 1), educational and scientific organizations (the University of Michigan, Wayne State University), which both develop/adapt technological solutions and provide new highly qualified personnel

**Table 2** Detroit's key economic development indicators for 2010–2022

| Year | GDP value (billion USD) | Real GDP growth rate (%) | Unemployment rate (%) | Total nonfarm employment (thousand) | Manufacturing employment (thousand) | Total private investment (billion USD) | Total value of exports (billion USD) |
|---|---|---|---|---|---|---|---|
| 2010 | 192,776 | 6.5 | 13.40 | 1738.3 | 178.54 | 1.40 | 44.8 |
| 2011 | 202,095 | 4.1 | 11.00 | 1787.6 | 197.01 | 1.70 | 50.9 |
| 2012 | 214,466 | 3.4 | 10.00 | 1835.4 | 211.68 | 2.20 | 52.7 |
| 2013 | 222,516 | 1.9 | 9.70 | 1869.6 | 221.15 | 2.80 | 55.4 |
| 2014 | 229,738 | 1.3 | 8.10 | 1900.5 | 231.39 | 3.30 | 58.5 |
| 2015 | 240,956 | 1.5 | 5.80 | 1938.9 | 241.32 | 3.90 | 54.4 |
| 2016 | 248,635 | 1.8 | 5.20 | 1977.5 | 247.45 | 4.00 | 51.0 |
| 2017 | 253,36 | 0.8 | 4.50 | 2008.5 | 253.60 | 4.10 | 51.0 |
| 2018 | 261,792 | 1.8 | 4.30 | 2033.5 | 259.46 | 4.60 | 53.3 |
| 2019 | 266,537 | −0.3 | 4.20 | 2043.8 | 257.43 | 5.10 | 54.9 |
| 2020 | 257,19 | −4.9 | 11.50 | 1846.3 | 224.17 | 5.80 | 61.1 |
| 2021 | 283,66 | 8.7 | 6.10 | 1928.6 | 240.09 | 6.70 | n/a |
| 2022 | n/a | n/a | 3.80 | 2001.6 | 247.74 | 7.60 | 83.5 |

Note: compiled by the authors based on the data from Federal Reserve Bank of St. Louis (https://fred.stlouisfed.org/), The Observatory of Economic Complexity (OEC) (https://oec.world/)

and digital platforms connecting various market participants (for example, Detroit Mobility Lab).

Additionally, we would like to emphasize the availability of substantial assistance, including the financial one, from the public authorities to various participants of the Industry 4.0 ecosystem, first of all, business representatives, research teams and citizens wishing to improve their knowledge and skills. For example, the Michigan Economic Development Corporation (MEDC) within the framework of the Industry 4.0 initiative implements a program of grants for technology implementation, which provides reimbursement of 50% of technology costs [53], the financial resources for startups being distributed through the previously mentioned Industry 4.0 Accelerator and LIFT.

Another effective tool implemented in Detroit when incentivizing the digital transformation of industry is public-private partnerships, such as Detroit Smart City Initiative, Detroit Innovation District, and Detroit Future City. Detroit Smart City Initiative (result of cooperation between the city administration, the University of Michigan, Ford Motor Company and other partners) involves the development and implementation of technological solutions that improve the efficiency, safety, accessibility and sustainability of the city's transportation system. The Detroit Innovation District is a designated area in downtown Detroit where entrepreneurs, researchers, educators, and investors come together to create and grow innovative startups. The district is supported by a coalition of public and private partners, including the City of Detroit, Wayne State University, and TechTown Detroit. Detroit Future City is a nonprofit organization that works with various public and private partners to fully engage the city community in the development of strategic solutions for land use, economic growth, sustainable urban neighborhoods, and environmental issues.

Detroit is close to the transition to Industry 5.0, which implies a synergy between humans, artificial intelligence and robots based on the principles of digital transformation, networking and sustainable development, but this transition is difficult because of a number of objective problems. One such problem is the shortage of skilled workers whose competencies are sufficient to cooperate with smart machines. Currently, many Detroit residents still lack the prerequisite skills needed for Industry 5.0, only 18% of Detroit workers have a bachelor's degree or higher, compared to 36% of the national average [54]. This creates a gap between the supply and demand of Industry 5.0 jobs, especially such positions as data analysts, programmers, engineers, and technicians. The second problem is related to the high cost of implementing and supporting modern advanced technologies (artificial intelligence, Internet of Things, blockchain, digital twins and 6G systems), the challenge for the development of Detroit's industry is the need to upgrade its infrastructure and equipment. Moreover, these technologies require continuous maintenance, safety control, and upgrades, which are essential to their reliability and performance. These costs are often difficult to deal with, especially for small and medium-sized businesses.

## 6 Conclusion

The case of Detroit confirms that this city is an example of successful digital transformation and reindustrialization of an old industrial city that overcame a severe economic crisis and entered the track of sustainable economic growth. The main factors of Detroit's reindustrialization are the introduction of advanced technologies (such as electric cars, autonomous driving systems, smart grids, etc.) and new business models by the city's largest companies, as well as the development of a supporting ecosystem, including educational and scientific organizations, non-profit initiatives and public-private partnerships. However, in its transition to the Industry 5.0 stage, Detroit has faced a number of serious challenges, namely lack of qualified personnel, high cost of introduction and maintenance of modern technologies, and need to upgrade the infrastructure and equipment. Further competitiveness and sustainability of the city's development depend on how successfully and quickly these problems will be solved.

Based on the results of this research, which is based on the case study methodology, a few limitations should be stated, which are determined by the chosen research approach. Each industrial city experiencing deindustrialization and reindustrialization is characterized by a unique combination of prerequisites and conditions for digital transformation, which does not allow us to fully extrapolate the trends observed in Detroit to other territories. Nevertheless, the study of Detroit's experience has revealed a number of factors that may be of significant importance for other old-industrialized regions. These include the role of public policy in stimulating the processes of re-industrialization, the importance of attracting investment in new high-tech industries, the need to develop human capital and improve the skills of the workforce, as well as the importance of partnership between government agencies, business and scientific and educational institutions. These factors taken into account can contribute to more effective management of the digital transformation of industrial cities.

**Acknowledgements** The research was funded by the Russian Science Foundation (grant No. 22-18-00679, https://rscf.ru/project/22-18-00679/).

## References

1. Cardoso, R. V., & Meijers, E. J. (2017). Secondary yet metropolitan? The challenges of metropolitan integration for second-tier cities. *Planning Theory & Practice, 18*(4), 616–635. https://doi.org/10.1080/14649357.2017.1371789
2. Parkinson, M., Meegan, R., & Karecha, J. (2015). City size and economic performance: Is bigger better, small more beautiful or middling marvellous? *European Planning Studies, 23*(6), 1054–1068. https://doi.org/10.1080/09654313.2014.904998
3. Top 100 Biggest US Cities in The Year 1950. (n.d.). Retrieved October 01, 2023, from https://www.biggestuscities.com/1950

4. McDonald, J. F. (2014). What happened to and in Detroit? *Urban Studies, 51*(16), 3309–3329. https://doi.org/10.1177/0042098013519505
5. Federal Reserve Economic Data. (n.d.). *Total gross domestic product for Detroit-Warren-Dearborn.* Retrieved October 01, 2023, from https://fred.stlouisfed.org/series/NGMP19820
6. Nadkarni, S., & Prügl, R. (2021). Digital transformation: A review, synthesis and opportunities for future research. *Management Review Quarterly, Q71*, 233–341. https://doi.org/10.1007/s11301-020-00185-7
7. Dremel, C., Wulf, J., Herterich, M. M., Waizmann, J. C., & Brenner, W. (2017). How AUDI AG established big data analytics in its digital transformation. *MIS Quarterly Executive, 16*(2), 81–100.
8. Fosso Wamba, S., Akter, S., Edwards, A., Chopin, G., & Gnanzou, D. (2015). How 'big data' can make big impact: Findings from a systematic review and a longitudinal case study. *International Journal of Production Economics, 165*, 234–246. https://doi.org/10.1016/j.ijpe.2014.12.031
9. Guandalini, I. (2022). Sustainability through digital transformation: A systematic literature review for research guidance. *Journal of Business Research, 148*, 456–471. https://doi.org/10.1016/j.jbusres.2022.05.003
10. Rayna, T., & Striukova, L. (2016). From rapid prototyping to home fabrication: How 3D printing is changing business model innovation. *Technological Forecasting and Social Change, 102*, 214–224. https://doi.org/10.1016/j.techfore.2015.07.023
11. Ng, I. C. L., & Wakenshaw, S. Y. L. (2017). The internet-of-things: Review and research directions. *International Journal of Research in Marketing, 34*(1), 3–21. https://doi.org/10.1016/j.ijresmar.2016.11.003
12. Rêgo, B. S., Jayantilal, S., Ferreira, J. J., & Carayannis, E. G. (2022). Digital transformation and strategic management: A systematic review of the literature. *Journal of the Knowledge Economy, 13*(4), 3195–3222. https://doi.org/10.1007/s13132-021-00853-3
13. Schallmo, D., Williams, C. A., & Boardman, L. (2017). Digital transformation of business models — Best practice, enablers, and roadmap. *International Journal of Innovation Management, 21*(08), 1–17. https://doi.org/10.1142/S136391961740014X
14. Dweck, E., Bassetti Marcato, M., Torracca, J., & Miguez, T. (2022). COVID-19 and the Brazilian manufacturing sector: Roads to reindustrialization within societal purposes. *Structural Change and Economic Dynamics, 61*, 278–293. https://doi.org/10.1016/j.strueco.2022.02.018
15. Prisecaru, P. (2015). EU reindustrialization on the coordinates of scientific and technical progress. *Procedia Economics and Finance, 22*, 485–494. https://doi.org/10.1016/S2212-5671(15)00243-9
16. Stojčić, N., Aralica, Z., & Anić, I.-D. (2019). Spatio-temporal determinants of the structural and productive transformation of regions in central and east European countries. *Economic Systems, 43*(3–4), 100715. https://doi.org/10.1016/j.ecosys.2019.100715
17. Teixeira, J. E., & Tavares-Lehmann, A. T. C. P. (2022). Industry 4.0 in the European union: Policies and national strategies. *Technological Forecasting and Social Change, 180*, 121664. https://doi.org/10.1016/j.techfore.2022.121664
18. Zhao, S., Zhang, L., An, H., Peng, L., Zhou, H., & Hu, F. (2023). Has China's low-carbon strategy pushed forward the digital transformation of manufacturing enterprises? Evidence from the low-carbon city pilot policy. *Environmental Impact Assessment Review, 102*, 107184. https://doi.org/10.1016/j.eiar.2023.107184
19. Jiang, Z., Zhang, X., Zhao, Y., Li, C., & Wang, Z. (2023). The impact of urban digital transformation on resource sustainability: Evidence from a quasi-natural experiment in China. *Resources Policy, 85*(Part A), 103784. https://doi.org/10.1016/j.resourpol.2023.103784
20. Gaber, N., Silva, A., Lewis-Patrick, M., Kutil, E., Taylor, D., & Bouier, R. (2021). Water insecurity and psychosocial distress: Case study of the Detroit water shutoffs. *Journal of Public Health, 43*(4), 839–845. https://doi.org/10.1093/pubmed/fdaa157
21. Goodspeed, R., Van Eyl, A., & Vaccaro, L. (2018). Analyzing stakeholder's perceptions of uncertainty to advance collaborative sustainability science: Case study of the watershed

assessment of nutrient loads to the Detroit River project. *Environmental Impact Assessment Review, 72*, 145–156. https://doi.org/10.1016/j.eiar.2018.06.001
22. Draus, P., Haase, D., Napieralski, J., Roddy, J., & Qureshi, S. (2019). Wounds, ghosts and gardens: Historical trauma and green reparations in Berlin and Detroit. *Cities, 93*, 153–163. https://doi.org/10.1016/j.cities.2019.05.002
23. Hwang, K., & Papuga, S. A. (2023). COVID-19 pandemic underscores role of green space in urban carbon dynamics. *Science of the Total Environment, 859*(1), 160249. https://doi.org/10.1016/j.scitotenv.2022.160249
24. O'Leary, B. F., Hill, A. B., Akers, K. G., Esparra-Escalera, H. J., Lucas, A., Raoufi, G., Huang, Y., Mariscal, N., Mohanty, S. K., Tummala, C. M., & Dittrich, T. M. (2022). Air quality monitoring and measurement in an urban airshed: Contextualizing datasets from the Detroit Michigan area from 1952 to 2020. *Science of the Total Environment, 809*, 152120. https://doi.org/10.1016/j.scitotenv.2021.152120
25. Hughes, S. (2020). Principles, drivers, and policy tools for just climate change adaptation in legacy cities. *Environmental Science & Policy, 111*, 35–41. https://doi.org/10.1016/j.envsci.2020.05.007
26. Meerow, S., & Newell, J. P. (2017). Spatial planning for multifunctional green infrastructure: Growing resilience in Detroit. *Landscape and Urban Planning, 159*, 62–75. https://doi.org/10.1016/j.landurbplan.2016.10.005
27. Newell, J. P., Foster, A., Borgman, M., & Meerow, S. (2022). Ecosystem services of urban agriculture and prospects for scaling up production: A study of Detroit. *Cities, 125*, 103664. https://doi.org/10.1016/j.cities.2022.103664
28. Lee, J., Vojnovic, I., & Grady, S. C. (2022). What lies beyond the built environment? Exploring "walkability" across the Detroit region. *Applied Geography, 141*, 102670. https://doi.org/10.1016/j.apgeog.2022.102670
29. Bills, T. S., Twumasi-Boakye, R., Broaddus, A., & Fishelson, J. (2022). Towards transit equity in Detroit: An assessment of microtransit and its impact on employment accessibility. *Transportation Research Part D: Transport and Environment, 109*, 103341. https://doi.org/10.1016/j.trd.2022.103341
30. Kagawa, R., Calnin, B., Smirniotis, C., Cerdá, M., Wintemute, G., & Rudolph, K. E. (2022). Effects of building demolitions on firearm violence in Detroit, Michigan. *Preventive Medicine, 165*(A), 107257. https://doi.org/10.1016/j.ypmed.2022.107257
31. Herrmann, D. L., Shuster, W. D., Mayer, A. L., & Garmestani, A. S. (2016). Sustainability for shrinking cities. *Sustainability, 8*(9), 911. https://doi.org/10.3390/su8090911
32. Xie, Y., Gong, H., Lan, H., & Zeng, S. (2018). Examining shrinking city of Detroit in the context of socio-spatial inequalities. *Landscape and Urban Planning, 177*, 350–361. https://doi.org/10.1016/j.landurbplan.2018.03.002
33. Sanchez, L., & Reames, T. G. (2019). Cooling Detroit: A socio-spatial analysis of equity in green roofs as an urban heat Island mitigation strategy. *Urban Forestry & Urban Greening, 44*, 126331. https://doi.org/10.1016/j.ufug.2019.04.014
34. Lin, Y., Zhang, J., & Jiang, S. (2022). Spatial and temporal correlations of crime in Detroit: Evidence from spatial dynamic panel data models. *International Review of Law and Economics, 72*, 106100. https://doi.org/10.1016/j.irle.2022.106100
35. Liñeiro, A. B., Gómez-Cruz, N. A., & Pérez, C. J. V. (2023). Sustainability in the era of digital transformation and Industry 4.0: Key issues and further conceptual developments. In J. Molina-Muñoz (Ed.), *Sustainability and management: Sostenibilidad y dirección de empresas* (1st ed., pp. 1–32). Editorial Universidad del Rosario. http://www.jstor.org/stable/jj.3252821.4
36. Komarčević, M., Dimić, M., & Čelik, P. (2017). Challenges and impacts of the digital transformation of society in the social sphere. *SEER: Journal for Labour and Social Affairs in Eastern Europe, 20*(1), 31–48. http://www.jstor.org/stable/26379907
37. Lévesque, C., Fairbrother, P., & Roby, N. (2020). Digitalization and regulation of work and employment: Introduction. *Relations Industrielles / Industrial Relations, 75*(4), 647–659. https://www.jstor.org/stable/27016453

38. Stroud, D., Timperley, V., & Weinel, M. (2020). Digitalized drones in the steel industry: The social shaping of technology. *Relations Industrielles / Industrial Relations, 75*(4), 730–750. https://www.jstor.org/stable/27016457
39. Kim, K., Mithas, S., & Kimbrough, M. (2017). Information technology investments and firm risk across industries: Evidence from the bond market. *MIS Quarterly, 41*(4), 1347–1368. https://www.jstor.org/stable/26630297
40. Bin Hozaim, A., & Akre, V. L. (2017). A framework for transforming Dubai into a smart city. In M. Al-Mansoori, M. Al-Hammadi, & S. Al-Mulla (Eds.), *2017 fourth HCT information technology trends (ITT)* (pp. 1–6). IEEE. https://doi.org/10.1109/CTIT.2017.8259573
41. Dong, H., & Zhu, P. (2015). Smart growth in two contrastive metropolitan areas: A comparison between Portland and Los Angeles. *Urban Studies, 52*(4), 775–792. https://www.jstor.org/stable/26146006
42. Goetz, A. (2013). Suburban sprawl or urban Centres: Tensions and contradictions of smart growth approaches in Denver, Colorado. *Urban Studies, 50*(11), 2178–2195. http://www.jstor.org/stable/26145576
43. Akberdina, V. V., & Romanova, O. A. (2021). Regional industrial development: Review of approaches to regulation and determining of priorities. *Ekonomika regiona [Economy of Region], 17*(3), 714–736. https://doi.org/10.17059/ekon.reg.2021-3-1
44. Chernova, O. A., Liu, L., & Wang, X. (2023). Role of digitalization of logistics outsourcing in sustainable development of automotive industry in China. *R-Economy, 9*(2), 123–139. https://doi.org/10.15826/recon.2023.9.2.008
45. Akberdina, V. V., Kozonogova, E. V., & Dubrovskaya, Y. V. (2023). Digital platforms for regional economic research: A review and methodology proposal. *R-Economy, 9*(1), 52–72. https://doi.org/10.15826/recon.2023.9.1.004
46. Turgel, I., Pobedin, A., & Panzabekova, A. (2022). Digitalisation of the economy and regional development. *Lecture Notes in Information Systems and Organisation, 54*, 133–147. https://doi.org/10.1007/978-3-030-94617-3_11
47. Ardito, L., Cerchione, R., Mazzola, E., & Raguseo, E. (2022). Industry 4.0 transition: A systematic literature review combining the absorptive capacity theory and the data–information–knowledge hierarchy. *Journal of Knowledge Management, 26*(9), 2222–2254. https://doi.org/10.1108/JKM-04-2021-0325
48. Zhang, C., Chen, Y., Chen, H., & Chong, D. (2021). Industry 4.0 and its implementation: A review. *Information Systems Frontiers*, 1–11. https://doi.org/10.1007/s10796-021-10153-5
49. Ghobakhloo, M., Iranmanesh, M., Foroughi, B., Babaee Tirkolaee, E., Asadi, S., & Amran, A. (2023). Industry 5.0 implications for inclusive sustainable manufacturing: An evidence-knowledge-based strategic roadmap. *Journal of Cleaner Production, 417*, 138023. https://doi.org/10.1016/j.jclepro.2023.138023
50. Detroit. (n.d.). *2010–2011 Executive budget summary.* Retrieved October 01, 2023, from https://detroitmi.gov/departments/office-chief-financial-officer/ocfo-divisions/office-budget/detroit-budget-archives-information/2010-2011-executive-budget-summary
51. Luria, D., & Russell, J. (1981). *Rational reindustrialization: An economic development agenda for Detroit.* Widgetripper Press.
52. LSA. College of literature, science, and the arts. University of Michigan (n.d.). *City of Detroit Economic Outlook* 2022–2028. *August 2023.* Retrieved October 01, 2023, from https://lsa.umich.edu/content/dam/econ-assets/Econdocs/RSQE%20PDFs/Detroit_Forecast_(2023.08).pdf
53. Michigan Economic Development Corporation. (n.d.). Industry 4.0. Retrieved October 01, 2023, from https://www.michiganbusiness.org/industry4-0/
54. Lynch, E., & Nash, K. (2023). Growth occupations: Opportunities for more equitable participation in Detroit's growing economy. A publication of Detroit Future City's Center for Equity, Engagement, and Research in collaboration with Brookings Metro. Retrieved October 01, 2023, from https://detroitfuturecity.com/wp-content/uploads/2023/02/Growth-Occupations-Report.pdf

# Strategic Interventions: Navigating Industry Development Trends Through Digitalization for Enhanced Competitiveness of Italian Wood-Furniture Companies

**Fabio Musso, Laura Bravi, and Alessio Travasi**

**Abstract** The adoption of digital technologies has become a critical factor in innovation management, impacting the wood-furniture industry significantly. In today's highly globalized and interconnected economy, this industry relies on efficient, sustainable digital production for customized services. The study assesses Italian wood-furniture companies' digitalization level and strategies for digital transition through case study analysis. To this end, a comprehensive approach was taken, involving six semi-structured interviews, based on an interview protocol.

These interviews were conducted between October and November 2021, engaging a diverse array of respondents ranging from entrepreneurs and business managers to representatives of trade associations, consultancy firms, and suppliers of advanced services for the sector. The results show a transformation within the furniture industry, transitioning from its conventional industrial framework towards embracing the disruptive changes catalyzed by the advent of Industry 4.0. This transition represents a pivotal shift towards a more agile, technologically-driven landscape, wherein digital transformation emerges as not merely an option but an imperative for survival and success. Particularly in the realm of Business-to-Consumer (B2C) sectors, where brand recognition and consumer engagement are paramount, the role of digital tools cannot be overstated. Failure to capitalize on the opportunities afforded by digitalization can indeed imperil the very existence of a company in today's fiercely competitive marketplace, emphasizing the critical need for proactive adoption and integration of digital strategies across all facets of the business.

**Keywords** Digital transformation · Digital transition · Wood-furniture companies · Digital strategies

F. Musso · L. Bravi (✉) · A. Travasi
Department of Economics, Society, Politics, Carlo Bo University of Urbino, Urbino, Italy
e-mail: fabio.musso@uniurb.it; laura.bravi@uniurb.it; a.travasi@campus.uniurb.it



A. Appolloni et al. (eds.), *The Future of Industry*, Lecture Notes in Information Systems and Organisation 70, https://doi.org/10.1007/978-3-031-66801-2_16

## 1 Introduction

Over the past 20 years, digital transformation (hereafter DT) has revolutionized the way companies conduct businesses, build relationships with their consumers, suppliers, and other stakeholders [1] and promote business model innovation and customer value creation [2]. According to Becker et al. [3], the DT of business models is one of the most defining megatrends of the twenty-first century. Thus, DT is closely linked to the resulting innovation in companies' business models and represents the way in which a firm employs digital technologies to develop a new business model that helps to create superior value for the firm and its customers [4]. Hence, such transformation requires holistic changes to business models such as to influence the processes, operational routines, and organizational capabilities of companies [5, 6].

Furthermore, DT is also affecting the traditional interaction between consumers and businesses [7]. Nowadays, consumers have access to dozens of new digital channels through which they can communicate seamlessly with other businesses and consumers, conveying their messages through a rapidly growing number of touchpoints [8]. Consequently, it has become of primary importance for companies to control all marketing channels to ensure uniform and integrated communication to their target customers on the dictates of an increasingly omnichannel approach [9]. Therefore, the aim of this study is to evaluate, through multiple case study analysis, the level of digitalization of Italian companies in the wood-furniture sector and the efforts and strategies they are carrying out to strengthen the digital transition of the sector.

The paper is structured as follows: Sect. 2 defines the theoretical background on digital technologies and how they affect the wood-furniture industry; Sect. 3 describes the methodology used; Sect. 4 presents the results of the interviews carried out and finally Sect. 5 discusses the results obtained and draws the main conclusions and limitations.

## 2 Theoretical Background

In the early 2000s, the use of digital technologies by companies mainly involved the implementation of internal management information systems such as Enterprise Resource Planning (ERP) or Customer Relationship Management (CRM) [10]. DT was limited to the adoption of information systems aimed at improving business processes within organizational boundaries to achieve efficiency, both in terms of cost savings and business process optimization [11]. In recent years, then, new digital technologies—such as big data, artificial intelligence and systems related to Industry 4.0—have revolutionized the way companies conduct their business [12]. These new technologies have been able to improve operational efficiency through the process management optimization [13]. Today, companies are focused on applying cross-border digital technologies [6], aimed at transforming the way organizations and consumers interact and exchange value [14].

In particular, the adoption of digital technologies has become a critical factor in innovation management. The associated DT process enables concrete management improvements that promote innovation of the entire business model [15]. Such business model innovation is therefore a direct consequence of the use of these new technologies, which oblige companies to innovate far beyond the mere introduction of new products or services, to the point of having to adopt true digital business models [16]. Consequently, DT can be seen as the process of integrating digital technologies into all aspects of business processes, which entails the need for fundamental changes in the technology of creating new products and services, operations, and business culture [17].

Therefore, digitization changes the entire structure of a company's business model [18], including the value proposition and customer relationships [19]. This digital transformation has been further boosted by the spread of mobile devices [20]: apps, digital platforms, and overall any electronic media available to customers and businesses, have become elements of experimentation, seeking to intercept the emerging business opportunities associated with their use according to an increasingly omnichannel approach [21]. These digital tools have proven to be extremely useful for small and medium-sized enterprises (SMEs), helping them to overcome their size disadvantage. Indeed, these technologies enable content generation and communication, consumer interaction, and brand development, much faster and at a lower cost compared to physical channels. The adoption of these tools is increasingly important, especially for operating in international markets, where digital tools are becoming essential to engage new customers, build relationships and brand loyalty, sell products directly abroad, better understand consumer needs and change consumer orientations [22].

DT also affects the wood-furniture industry. In today's highly globalized and interconnected economy, the wood-furniture industry offers customized service-based products relying on resource-efficient and sustainable digital production systems. More specifically, Computer-Aided Design (CAD) or Building Information Modeling (BIM)based digital design platforms, which enable real-time, integrated design between companies and their suppliers and customers, are being adopted by an increasing number of companies [23]. Moreover, online 3D configurators, which are increasingly being used by interior design firms, guarantee integrated order management in accordance with customer preferences [24]. Lastly, modern additive manufacturing techniques, supported by 3D printing, make it possible to reduce the time taken to define technical product specifications, prototyping, and production [25]. These technologies, for companies capable of adopting and using them correctly, offer transformative business potential, both in terms of products and production processes. An even greater transformation can potentially result from the cumulative effect of the combination of some of these new technologies, most of which can be used by SMEs and large companies, making them suitable for a large share of the European wood-furniture industry [26].

The COVID-19 pandemic has further accelerated the digitization process of many companies [27], including those in the wood-furniture industry. The report Direzione Studi e Ricerche Intesa San Paolo [28] highlighted how several companies in the sector have implemented increasingly omnichannel marketing strategies, using both online and offline channels simultaneously, developing new products and systems functional to the new needs of smart working and co-living. The digitization of processes is seen as a strategic lever to acquire more customers globally. Thus, it is plausible to say that the rapid shift towards digital business models will have lasting effects, as organizations have acquired transformational capabilities that will remain and the digital trajectory, as a result, has changed forever [27].

## 3 Methodology

In order to understand the evolutionary trends of the wood-furniture sector a qualitative research methodology has been used, developing a multiple case study analysis based on semi-structured interviews done with privileged interlocutors, companies and stakeholders of the sector. The purpose was to represent future directions and changes taking place in the light of which outlining strategic guidelines for companies and policies to boost the development of this industry. The focus was on the Marche region, which hosts in its Pesaro-Urbino province one of the most important furniture districts in Italy.

According to Creswell [29, p. 97], a multiple case study method explores multiple bounded systems (cases) over time, through detailed, in-depth data collection involving multiple sources of information [29]. The chosen methodology of the multiple case-study is that of a descriptive type, as the research aims to delineate the general and particular features of a given phenomenon [30].

The respondents were entrepreneurs and business managers, representatives of trade associations, consultancy firms, and suppliers of advanced services for the sector. In particular, interviews were carried out with three final manufacturing companies, differentiated by size, type of production specialization, and adopted distribution channels; a research center and technological laboratory for the wood-furniture sector, a consultancy company that offers advanced services for the web, a consultancy company specialized in integrated corporate management systems, a project management company specialized in contract supplies for the furniture sector, and a trade association. This is in line with Yin's [31] guidelines, suggesting that the number of units to be analyzed in a multiple case study is between four and twelve.

The six semi-structured interviews, based on an interview protocol, were conducted between October and November 2021, and typically lasted 1 h.

The interviews covered the following topics: (i) main changes taking place in the wood-furniture sector following the digitalization of internal and external processes and organizational implications for companies in the sector; (ii) changes in channel relationships and in the role of intermediaries; (iii) level of online integration with suppliers in the supply chain (for transmission of orders, co-design of components, etc.); (iv) role and functionality of company websites, e-commerce and eventual adoption of a multi/omnichannel approach; (v) fronts of intervention and stimulus by public/institutional bodies.

Secondary data were gathered thanks to a review of the companies' websites and their profiles on different social networks to comply with the triangulation principle [32] and to validate the information collected through the semi-structured interviews.

# 4 Results

## *4.1 Digitalization in the Wood-Furniture Sector of the Marche Region: The Main Changes Underway*

The wood-furniture sector shows a partial lag in the adoption of digital technologies, especially with regard to the ability to fully exploit their potential. From this point of view, there is a substantial dualism. On the one hand, there are large and structured companies that have an approach to digital that has improved over time: their presence on the internet, both in terms of communication and the collection of information on customers and users, shows how quickly these companies are able to adapt to changes, making use of various applications linked to the web usage for demand analysis and customer relationship management. On the other hand, there are small and very small companies, often artisanal in nature and with a limited number of employees—less than 15/20—which are the overwhelming bulk of the sector. These have difficulty in making the transition to digital due to both lack of resources and an approach that is not always geared to change, for which training and support would be necessary.

These companies struggle to adopt advanced technologies and to adapt internal organizational processes. However, like all Italian manufacturing sectors, the wood-furniture sector is undergoing a process of evolution according to the principles of Industry 4.0, with the gradual adoption of solutions in various areas such as digital design, rapid prototyping with the use of 3D printers, robotics, engineering through digital technologies, and the use of electronic tools to make production phases interactive and flexible. On these aspects, the interviewees confirm the different level of digital development of companies in the sector, highlighting the above dualism.

An important stimulus to digitalization came from government incentives for Industry 4.0. However, this has resulted in a significant increase in the purchase of machinery only by the larger companies due to the high costs involved. In fact, although this funding was created mainly to incentivize small businesses, in the furniture sector it was mainly the larger companies that benefited from it, given their ability to make higher investments.

Furthermore, *"the use of machinery was very limited compared to its potential due to the lack of adequate training to deploy all the machinery functions that could help to connect the various company areas"*. In fact, what seems to be missing is the ability to accompany technical innovation with a corresponding evolution in organizational solutions for full integration within the company.

Public incentives for digital innovation have often been oriented towards supply chain aggregations, but not infrequently ephemeral aggregations have been formed, linked only to the single project in order to obtaining funding but unable to consolidate over time. The cause is to be found in the highly individualistic spirit typical of SMEs, even if cases where these are located in district networks in which vertical collaboration relationships are in the very nature of the district [33].

According to the respondents, it would be useful to finance projects that provide from the recruitment or retraining of human resources to join their organizations on a permanent basis in order to facilitate the digital transition, with the training activity acting as a "glue" to enable the growth of the enterprise as a whole. Projects must be company-wide, in the sense that it is not enough to introduce an innovation in a single department, but programs must be developed to integrate the project with other areas.

Compared to other sectors, the digitalization of industrial processes in the wood-furniture sector appears rather lagging behind. Most of the investments concerned the purchase of machinery and its interconnection. Other areas considered among Industry 4.0 technologies such as simulation systems, 3D printing, artificial intelligence, cyber security, and the Internet of Things (IoT) are touched upon only sporadically: *"the sector is in the phase preceding Industry 4.0, which is linked to the introduction into the company of computerized numerical control machines, CAD and CAM systems, configurators and other solutions which, although cutting-edge, have had isolated applications with respect to the entire process from conception to marketing of the product."*

In fact, innovations are mainly driven by machinery suppliers, whose presence has developed thanks to a strong specialization that has the district as its center of gravity. Machinery manufacturers have become the promoters of innovation for companies in the sector and are paving the way for advanced solutions based on interconnection, artificial intelligence and other technological developments that leverage the ability to process the vast amount of information that becomes available and that, in the future, can be linked between purely industrial activities and commercial and marketing activities.

On the other hand, one of the causes of this delay is the fact that the sector is particularly complex in terms of product design. More precisely, *"In the furniture sector we no longer talk about a product but about a system, with a strong component of modularity and customization, and this considers the involvement of external partners who have to be coordinated through interface solutions. ... Since the sector is not a simple system, it has difficulties in investing in Industry 4.0. For example, the use of configurators is quite widespread, because the configurator allows to present a product based on pre-design, i.e. on a series of rules already set in the program. Furniture companies can work well on configurators, as they connect the project to the machines. On the other hand, on simulators, which allow production to be programmed according to the delivery target, almost no one has developed the technology in the sector. Only a few are now starting experimental projects in this regard."*

For the future, according to the respondents, an increasing use of IoT devices and computer vision systems to obtain information from images for quality, production monitoring, material movements and warehouse management is conceivable. The use of smart devices, such as glasses with an egocentric vision system (e.g., for training or safety), which are increasing the use of artificial intelligence (machine learning and deep learning) to create internal (machine IoT) and market information, is likely to become more widespread.

## 4.2 Digitalization Projects of Leading Companies

Among the main projects developed by the interviewed companies, of particular importance for digital innovation is the initiative involving the Fab Lab Pesaro for the development of innovative digital furniture and product prototyping. Established in 2013, the company is a digital manufacturing laboratory, part of an international network of laboratories. The projects developed have involved companies from the Marche region in the wood-furniture sector, with a focus on the main living environments (i.e., living room furniture, night furniture, and office environment).

The innovations developed for the kitchen environment were based on the combination of functionality and technology, to the develop modular kitchens in which innovative materials and home automation devices could be used. As far as innovative materials are concerned, doors with an aluminum honeycomb core covered in wood were developed, with the advantage of being lightweight, allowing the sliding mechanisms to work efficiently. Furthermore, other projects developed within the Fab Lab area represent a testing ground for the application of home automation and IoT, better expressed, in this case, as Internet of Furniture (IoF), through the integration of Wi-Fi devices equipped with sensors communicating with each other that allow interaction with the home environment (waste detection, water leaks, air quality monitoring to identify leaks or fires). Innovative projects were also developed for lighting, with the kitchen equipped with intelligent LED lights that can minimize the intensity of the lights by using data provided by sensors to improve the energy efficiency of the environment. Furthermore, smart technologies have been developed to allow the "hand-free" opening of the various elements.

In the production of mattresses, the collaboration between Cosmob, the Italian Quality Laboratory for furniture testing, the Fab Lab Pesaro, and companies in the Marche region in the sector has made enabled the development innovative projects, such as an electronic system integrated into the mattress capable of communicating information to the user on his/her sleep quality. These systems allow monitoring the duration of the different sleep phases and relating them to the characteristics of the environment, such as the body/mattress interface temperature, the environment humidity, the pressure exerted on the body by the mattress, the bedroom characteristics, e.g., temperature, degree of relative humidity, brightness, noise and level of pollutants (Volatile Organic Compound, VOC).

The information is then transferred to a cloud platform via a Wi-Fi communication system and processed remotely, to be returned through the display of customizable graphs via both computer and smartphone. The system is also open to communication with other smart objects in the environment to interface with other devices within the home automation system, such as the possibility of adjusting the bedroom temperature based on the temperature of the body/mattress interface or send a command to open the shutter to accompany the user in his/her waking phase.

A second project developed by Cosmob, again in the sleeping area, aimed to develop a system for selecting the correct mattress based on individual morphological characteristics, allowing optimal posture of the spinal column in a lying position, without parts of the body being subjected to excessive pressure. The Laboratory's role was to validate the pressure detection system and the consequent transmission of data.

Finally, for the office environment, one of the leading companies in the Marche furniture district has developed a project to rethink the furniture to adapt it to an environment that requires evolution from a technological point of view. The office is in fact a place conceived in times when knowledge and technology were very different from those of today. The objective was therefore to rethink the spaces and accommodate the different requirements, which are those of safety, ergonomics, and healthiness of the working environment. The key element around which the project revolved was technological innovation applied to office furniture, in order to give the working environment functional characteristics for productivity and people's well-being. The company has realized various furnishings by intervening on aspects such as eco-sustainability (e.g., by using innovative and ecological panels obtained through the introduction of cellulose microfibres), healthiness, (e.g., by using innovative soundproof panels), and lighting (by providing the work environment with the right mix of light and aesthetic appeal. Furthermore, to ensure security, technological additions were made to preserve documents and valuables in the environment through the development of fingerprint recognition systems for opening doors and drawers. Although these technologies are already in use and on the market, when integrated into the furniture element they contribute to giving innovation to products that until were characterized by a generally low level of technological.

## *4.3 Digitalization in Supply Chain Management*

As regards the digitalization of upstream processes, for which supply chain partners are involved, the sector presents elements of complexity because while on the one hand there are leading companies that may be able to introduce innovative processes for supply chain management, on the other hand there is a very heterogeneous number of suppliers, sub-suppliers and contractors in terms of size, investment capacity, organizational capacity and level of culture and skills.

The peculiarity of the furniture sector is that the supply chain is directly involved in the preparation of orders for end customers, orders that are highly customized and for whose composition the suppliers of the individual components contribute.

The logic of the processes in these cases is based on production-to-order, rather than to-stock, with a mixed assembly-to-order system, whereby semi-finished products and basic furniture components are produces in the warehouse and then finished and/or assembled after receiving the order from the customer. Therefore, the supply chain is not only involved in the creation of a predefined catalogue offer, but acts as a network of players who have to respond flexibly to market demand in a rapid and coordinated manner: *"There is a host of relevant subcontractors and smaller contractors who carry out a large part of the production. Even if recently some of the large leading companies in the sector are bringing part of the production in-house, the bulk is done outside, outsourced"*.

This increases the difficulty relating to the adoption of digital technologies, because it is not enough to be efficient and organized internally, but the involvement of suppliers is needed, who must be ready to respond to all needs. According to one of the respondents *"digitalization is helping, but the one developed so far is not yet sufficient. At the moment, technology allows the supply chain to become more efficient, but the organizational capacity of companies is lacking."* IT service providers and consultancies continually adapt companies' information systems—both office and factory—to technological developments, but what is missing is a project that looks at the efficiency of the entire production chain. The lack of willingness of entrepreneurs to share the information in their possession with other companies plays a significant role in this: *"The problem is of coordination and transparency of information, because the standards are already there, and the systems are technically interfaceable"*. At the same time, the small, and often very small, size of supply chain partners does not facilitate the adoption of advanced technologies (e.g., RFID for supply control).

However, on the latter, new projects have been established. For example, one of the projects carried out by a kitchen company allowed preliminary studies to be carried out to analyze the feasibility of an innovative E-Supply Chain system. This was developed with a view to improving the entire value chain, believing that the inclusion of home automation technologies in the kitchen can be achieved with a strong bond and collaboration with suppliers, through sharing the project which goes from the choice of materials, to the control of supplies to guarantee constant quality and a rapid and efficient communication. This project, in addition to the electronic management of the order-receipt document, involved the development of a web portal for e-procurement. The project also involved the introduction of a software, Warehouse Management Service (WMS), which, operating with a radio frequency system, made it possible to carry out logistics more efficiently, from the preparation of production orders to the positioning of entry goods, the management of replacements and inventories.

## 4.4 The Website Role

The presence on the web and the use of digital tools to interact with suppliers and consumers are now part of business habits. Thinking about furniture companies, the greatest opportunities that the internet can offer concern, in addition to the possibility of finding both final and intermediate customers, communicating with distributors and entities involved in contract design circuit. Linked to these aspects there is also the theme of communication and image construction, which, thinking on the internet, means monitoring social networks.

According to the respondents', the web has always been seen by most companies in the wood-furniture sector as a classic showcase in which to display their products and collections. It has almost never been used as a collector of information. In fact, regarding the idea of putting the catalog online, there has often been the fear of being copied. Today, *"The Covid-19 pandemic has forced companies to review this idea of the web, leading to a forced evolution, both because it was no longer possible to have meetings with national or foreign customers, and because the fairs were interrupted"*.

Moreover, the acceleration in the use of web tools has recently been favored by public incentives offered in the second half of 2020 for the use of digital tools. Consultants and web service providers have also played an important role in guiding entrepreneurs in the digital evolution, making them understand the usefulness of using the Internet to collect data on end consumers, create contact with the customer, organize online meetings, and create 3D virtual showrooms to replace physical fairs. In some cases, digital showrooms have been released with access by invitation, using the showroom as a completion of a personalized conversation that the company has started with its customers. The virtual tour is accompanied by videos presenting the new collections which are sent as newsletters to customers, using them as real call to action tools, making a one-to-one relationship with the customer. Currently, the info-commerce phase, i.e. information on the products sold by the company thanks to an innovative and updated version of its website, is the most monitored phase by companies in the sector, even by SMEs. As regards the product purchasing phase, however, only a few companies—the larger and more organized ones—have invested in digital technologies to facilitate sales. In these cases, drive-to-store processes are implemented such as "make an appointment with the point of sale" processes, or more advanced tools such as geo-localized proximity marketing campaigns, through which if the consumer's profile is in line with what has been defined by the company and passes near a store, the relevant social media offers the consumer sponsored ads.

Regarding the role of social media there are still conflicting opinions as it is believed that, considering the type of products, which are durable goods, the use of social media as a weekly publication of news and photos regarding the company's products and the stories that may result are completely ineffective.

## The E-commerce as a Digital Sales Strategy

The e-commerce phase in the wood-furniture sector is considered by the respondents still to be in its infancy, even if *"the Covid-19 pandemic has brought an enormous boost, so much so that all the leading companies in the sector have planned to start selling their products online. The problem that emerges in the online sale of furniture products is linked to its configurability and complexity compared to products of other sectors, such as fashion"*. The complexity of wood-furnishing products is very high, also in relation to the fact that the concept of modularity has extended from the kitchen to other living environments. This makes e-commerce more viable for upholstered and accessories manufactures, whose catalog is based on individual products divided into a limited number of variants.

According to one of the respondents, *"the problem lies in the business model of companies in the sector, which still leads to designing the product according to the traditional channel, with the shopkeeper going to the end customer's home to take measurements, design the composition and send the project to the manufacturer who starts production. What companies should do is to review the product setup, in the form of the Ikea model, which conceives the independent transport and assembly by the end customer"*.

Configurators play a key role in these processes, but few are used in the wood-furniture sector, and they are often integrated into company's ERP for the development of orders. The use of configurators requires technical skills that often cannot be placed in the hands of the end user, thus making their implementation difficult. More precisely, *"The problem of configuration for furniture is an intrinsic problem in the sector since the product has always been intermediated by the distribution network. A furniture contract has always been thought of as a complex system, which could be managed by the technical experience of the retailer. It would be necessary to rethink the product so that it can pass through the digital chain without all its complexity; a product natively suitable for the digital distribution chain should be developed, without trying to bring a product born in a different system into the digital chain"*. Accordingly, the companies that report the best results from online sales are those that conceive their own offer for e-commerce, selecting only the products that are suitable for distance selling and optimizing the solutions proposed.

A front that is still underdeveloped by companies in the sector is the so-called *Digital Concierge*, i.e., an "online designer" who carries out a product configuration service. This service has been experimented with by micro-businesses that have set up tailor-made services.

Often the choice to start e-commerce passes through third-party marketplaces, which companies rely on by creating *ad hoc* product lines, with distinct brands, so that they do not conflict with the products distributed by traditional retailers, and this happens for both the Italian and foreign markets. It is a typically multi-channel approach, which is still far from that concept of omnichannel already widely established in other sectors. In some cases, companies manage to use the main brand. In these cases, what should be guaranteed is a uniform price for all channels.

One of the respondents who adopted this solution claims that *"price of online furniture is the same whether the product is sold through a traditional intermediary, whether it transits on marketplaces or whether it is sold from the company website, and this applies in Italy and abroad. What may vary from Italy to abroad are the transport costs."*

The potential conflict with the traditional channel is managed by making the retailer an ally rather than a competitor. This allows for better after-sales service and ensures greater loyalty. Accordingly, a responding company states that it *"sells throughout Italy through resellers. Today the company is also investing again in traditional retail, as the shopkeeper can use the company's website to advertise the product and can benefit from the company's logistics network for direct delivery of the product to the end customer. Furthermore, the shopkeeper is given the opportunity to intervene on the price list, enabling him to carry out promotional campaigns to have a further competitive advantage in attracting the customer."*

One of the critical variables for e-commerce in the sector is logistics, both for costs and the risk of breakages during transport, in addition to the fact that the product must be sent disassembled.

In general, within an omnichannel logic, e-commerce allows the last mile of the customer journey to be shortened as the customer can independently see the configurations of the furnishing solution, even if he/she then must go to the traditional physical store for the detailed specification of the order to the manufacturer.

## 5 Discussion

The scenario described above helps to contextualize the field of intervention for the development of strategies useful for relaunching the competitiveness of companies through the digitalization of processes. Interventions should be based on the following key elements.

*Structural and infrastructural actions*. Investment in digitalization requires planning from a medium-long term perspective aimed at creating an ecosystem-based supply chain approach. The level of adoption of digital technologies can occur in different stages, from the simple acquisition of hardware tools and software packages, up to the development of more complex organizational and technological solutions aimed at the competitive repositioning of companies. For this to happen more efficiently, the problem of completing the digital infrastructure and broadband connection across the entire national territory urgently arises. This is essential for attracting innovative investments and to allow local businesses to tackle advanced digitalization paths, using technologies connected to Industry 4.0.

*Focus on the supply chain as a fundamental element for the development of product and process innovations*. From this perspective, it is important to invest in making the supply chain of companies interconnected, aiming to achieve an e-Supply Chain—as some of the most important companies in the sector are attempting to do—with a view to improving the entire value chain through strengthening collaboration with suppliers and subcontractors, sharing project details with them.

*Defense and enhancement of technical knowledge, thanks to the investment in new digital technologies (such as 3D printers/scanners and augmented reality) which can constitute a differential element of Made in Italy.* Current professional figures are not sufficient to meet the new requirements of Industry 4.0. Therefore, it becomes essential to acquire digital and teamwork skills. Even in a traditional industry such as the wood-furniture sector, it is necessary to train professional figures who know how to combine artisan tradition with the ability to use latest digital tools. Furthermore, the current scenario highlights a significant training gap between the professional education and training programs and the needs arising from the digital transformation of companies. However, this is still not enough, as the wood-furniture sector is facing a new transition phase called Twin Transition, in which digitalization is accompanied by sustainable development, playing a crucial role for competitiveness. Therefore, it becomes necessary to launch innovative training programs that are able to enhance young people's skills also on green and environmentally sustainable issues.

*Promote innovation.* Without diminishing the importance of incremental and continuous innovation, which has always characterized the strengths of SMEs, it is necessary to introduce new technological knowledge and skills into businesses. A particular focus must be placed on research and development actions. The competition factors based on creativity, experience, and learning by doing should be integrated and strengthened by greater collaboration with the world of research, to make companies more aware of the evolution of innovation paths.

## 6 Conclusion

In conclusion, it can be said that the furniture industry is currently transitioning from being a traditional industrial sector to one that is opening up to the changes brought by Industry 4.0. The adoption of new digital technologies and the use of the web are considered one of the key drivers of current change and of the coming decades, together with the growing attention towards environmentally sustainable issues.

In a sector where corporate reputation, brand recognition, and customer relationships are key elements for success on the market, digital technologies undoubtedly represent an important tool. Digital transformation is a condition for the creation of value also at an international level, especially in Business-to-Consumer (B2C) sectors, where brand awareness is crucial and even more in a sector such as the furniture one which was defined by the respondents as Business-to-Business-to-Consumer (B2B2C), because the relationship with end customers is not purely Business-to-Consumer (B2C), but is intermediated by the retailer. Neglecting the use of digital tools can compromise the survival of the company. For this reason, in a highly globalized and interconnected economy, companies will have to aim to offer personalized products and services based on digitalized production systems capable of ensuring time efficiency, accuracy of workmanship, flexibility, timeliness, and reliability. Multi-channel and omni-channel represent demanding challenges for companies but necessary to sustain the pace of market evolution. As emerged from the interviews, the adaptation and full use of digital technologies is not without difficulties and requires companies' cultural and organizational changes.

Furthermore, the rapid pace of technological advancements presents challenges in terms of keeping up with evolving standards and practices. As the industry progresses towards Industry 5.0, which emphasizes greater collaboration between humans and machines, there will be a need for significant cultural and organizational changes. This transition requires a shift from a purely mechanized approach to one that prioritizes human creativity, emotional intelligence, and critical thinking. Companies must invest in training and development programs to cultivate these skills among their workforces.

Social media platforms play a crucial role in facilitating this transition by enabling companies to engage with customers directly and gather real-time feedback. However, leveraging social media effectively requires a nuanced understanding of consumer behaviour and preferences, as well as the ability to navigate potential risks such as negative publicity or misinformation. Cultural and organizational changes are paramount in transitioning from Industry 4.0 to what can be termed as Social 5.0 (S5.0). This involves not only integrating digital technologies into existing processes but also reimagining business models to prioritize social responsibility, sustainability, and ethical practices. Companies must foster a culture of innovation and adaptability to thrive in this evolving landscape.

The main limitation of the study derives from its qualitative nature which, although it allows for an in-depth investigation of the opinions of stakeholders within the sector, collects the opinion of few players. It would be relevant to strengthen this opinion with quantitative research, to evaluate if it is truly widespread among other actors in the sector. Therefore, future studies should consider developing quantitative research on these topics.

## References


1. Scuotto, V., Arrigo, E., Candelo, E., & Nicotra, M. (2019). Ambidextrous innovation orientation effected by the digital transformation. *Business Process Management Journal, 26*(5), 1121–1140. https://doi.org/10.1108/bpmj-03-2019-0135
2. Do Vale, G., Collin-Lachaud, I., & Lecocq, X. (2021). Micro-level practices of bricolage during business model innovation process: The case of digital transformation towards omni-channel retailing. *Scandinavian Journal of Management, 37*(2), 101154. https://doi.org/10.1016/j.scaman.2021.101154
3. Becker, W., Nolte, M., & Schuhknecht, F. (2023). The role of the chief financial officer in the digital transformation of business models. In I. Keimer & U. Egle (Eds.), *The digitalization of management accounting*. Springer. https://doi.org/10.1007/978-3-658-41524-2_21
4. Verhoef, P. C., Lemon, K. N., Parasuraman, A., Roggeveen, A., Tsiros, M., & Schlesinger, L. A. (2009). Customer experience creation: Determinants, dynamics and management strategies. *Journal of Retailing, 85*(1), 31–41. https://doi.org/10.1016/j.jretai.2008.11.001

5. Klos, C., Spieth, P., Clauss, T., & Klusmann, C. (2021). Digital transformation of incumbent firms: A business model innovation perspective. *IEEE Transactions on Engineering Management, 70*(6), 2017–2033. https://doi.org/10.1109/tem.2021.3075502
6. Li, L., Su, F., Zhang, W., & Mao, J. Y. (2018). Digital transformation by SME entrepreneurs: A capability perspective. *Information Systems Journal, 28*(6), 1129–1157. https://doi.org/10.1111/isj.12153
7. Taiminen, H. M., & Karjaluoto, H. (2015). The usage of digital marketing channels in SMEs. *Journal of Small Business and Enterprise Development, 22*(4), 633–651. https://doi.org/10.1108/jsbed-05-2013-0073
8. Santos, S., & Gonçalves, H. M. (2022). Consumer decision journey: Mapping with real-time longitudinal online and offline touchpoint data. *European Management Journal, 42*(3), 397–413. https://doi.org/10.1016/j.emj.2022.10.001
9. Palmié, M., Miehé, L., Oghazi, P., Parida, V., & Wincent, J. (2022). The evolution of the digital service ecosystem and digital business model innovation in retail: The emergence of meta-ecosystems and the value of physical interactions. *Technological Forecasting and Social Change, 177*, 121496. https://doi.org/10.1016/j.techfore.2022.121496
10. Boersma, K., & Kingma, S. (2005). From means to ends: The transformation of ERP in a manufacturing company. *The Journal of Strategic Information Systems, 14*(2), 197–219. https://doi.org/10.1016/j.jsis.2005.04.003
11. Besson, P., & Rowe, F. (2012). Strategizing information systems-enabled organizational transformation: A transdisciplinary review and new directions. *The Journal of Strategic Information Systems, 21*(2), 103–124. https://doi.org/10.1016/j.jsis.2012.05.001
12. Rothberg, H. N., & Erickson, G. S. (2017). Big data systems: Knowledge transfer or intelligence insights? *Journal of Knowledge Management, 21*(1), 92–112. https://doi.org/10.1108/jkm-07-2015-0300
13. Cenamor, J., Parida, V., & Wincent, J. (2019). How entrepreneurial SMEs compete through digital platforms: The roles of digital platform capability, network capability and ambidexterity. *Journal of Business Research, 100*, 196–206. https://doi.org/10.1016/j.jbusres.2019.03.035
14. Yadav, M. S., & Pavlou, P. A. (2014). Marketing in computer-mediated environments: Research synthesis and new directions. *Journal of Marketing, 78*(1), 20–40. https://doi.org/10.1509/jm.12.0020
15. Mies, Y. A., & Hausberg, J. P. (2023). Business model innovation in manufacturing firms: Exploring the driving forces of digital transformation. *International Journal of Innovation and Technology Management, 20*, 2350048. https://doi.org/10.1142/s0219877023500487
16. Rummel, F., Hüsig, S., & Steinhauser, S. (2022). Two archetypes of business model innovation processes for manufacturing firms in the context of digital transformation. *R&D Management, 52*(4), 685–703. https://doi.org/10.1111/radm.12514
17. Pronchakov, Y., Prokhorov, O., & Fedorovich, O. (2022). Concept of high-tech enterprise development management in the context of digital transformation. *Computation, 10*(7), 118. https://doi.org/10.3390/computation10070118
18. Savastano, M., Zentner, H., Spremić, M., & Cucari, N. (2022). Assessing the relationship between digital transformation and sustainable business excellence in a turbulent scenario. In *Total Quality Management & Business Excellence* (pp. 1–22). https://doi.org/10.1080/14783363.2022.2063717
19. Bouwman, H., Heikkilä, J., Heikkilä, M., Leopold, C., & Haaker, T. (2018). Achieving agility using business model stress testing. *Electronic Markets, 28*(2), 149–162. https://doi.org/10.1007/s12525-016-0243-0
20. Rachinger, M., Rauter, R., Müller, C., Vorraber, W., & Schirgi, E. (2018). Digitalization and its influence on business model innovation. *Journal of Manufacturing Technology Management, 30*(8), 1143–1160. https://doi.org/10.1108/jmtm-01-2018-0020
21. Zott, C., & Amit, R. (2017). Business model innovation: How to create value in a digital world. *Marketing Intelligence Review, 9*(1), 18–23. https://doi.org/10.1515/gfkmir-2017-0003

22. Matarazzo, M., Penco, L., Profumo, G., & Quaglia, R. (2021). Digital transformation and customer value creation in made in Italy SMEs: A dynamic capabilities perspective. *Journal of Business Research, 123*, 642–656. https://doi.org/10.1016/j.jbusres.2020.10.033
23. Ren, J., & Xiong, X. (2022). Digital design process and part family division of solid wood custom cabinet door based on multi-attribute overlapping clustering technology. *Bio Resources, 17*(3), 5393. https://doi.org/10.15376/biores.17.3.5393-5419
24. Zhang, S., Zhu, J., Wang, G., Reng, S., & Yan, H. (2022). Furniture online consumer experience: A literature review. *BioResources, 17*(1), 1627–1642. https://doi.org/10.15376/biores.17.1.1627-1642
25. Bravi, L., Murmura, F., & Santos, G. (2022). Additive manufacturing as a digital design technology in the wood-furniture sector: Benefits and barriers to its implementation. In V. Kumar, J. Leng, V. Akberdina, & E. Kuzmin (Eds.), *Digital transformation in industry* (*Lecture notes in information systems and organisation*) (Vol. 54). Springer. https://doi.org/10.1007/978-3-030-94617-3_18
26. DIGI-FUR. (2019). L'impatto della trasformazione digitale nel settore del legno-arredo. Retrieved November 16, 2021, from www.digit-fur.eu
27. Kronblad, C., & Pregmark, J. E. (2021). Responding to the COVID-19 crisis: The rapid turn toward digital business models. *Journal of Science and Technology Policy Management, (ahead-of-print), 15*(3), 451–467. https://doi.org/10.1108/jstpm-10-2020-0155
28. Direzione Studi e Ricerche Intesa Sanpaolo. (2021). L'industria e i distretti del mobile: tra tradizione e Innovazione. Retrieved November 16, 2021, from https://group.intesasanpaolo.com/content/dam/portalgroup/repository-documenti/newsroom/comunicati-stampa-it/2021/02/ricerca-industria-legno-arredo-in-italia.pdf
29. Creswell, J. W. (2013). *Qualitative inquiry and research design: Choosing among five approaches*. Sage Journals.
30. Bertazzaghi, E., Guerci, M., & Vinante, M. (2010). La valutazione stakeholder-based della formazione continua. In *Modelli, processi, strumenti, [The stakeholder-based assessment of continuing education. Models, processes, tools]*. Franco Angeli.
31. Yin, R. K. (1984). *Case study research: Design and methods*. Sage Publications.
32. Denzin, N. (1984). *The research act*. Englewood Cliffs.
33. Musso, F. (2003). Le relazioni con i mercati esteri delle imprese produttrici di mobili. In *Sistemi distrettuali e canali distributivi. [Relations with foreign markets of furniture manufacturing companies. District systems and distribution channels]*. Edizioni Goliardiche.

# Robotic Technological Processes Optimization in the Context of Digital Transformation of Industry

**Markel Melnichenko, Mikhail Gorkavyy, Yuri Ivanov, and Aleksandr Gorkavyy**

**Abstract** Modern industrial enterprises equipped with robotic production complexes rely on highly efficient models of technological processes, including energy consumption, to reduce production costs. The paper presents a method for enhancing the energy efficiency of robotic technological processes characterized by a limited class of complexes of movement trajectories, using the optimization algorithms developed by the authors. The presented studies were based on methods of identification, analysis and synthesis, as well as mathematical, in particular, simulation modeling to create models of energy consumption of robotic technological complexes. Automation of the proposed solutions was carried out using intelligent tools in the MATLAB environment. The study investigates robotic technological processes for laying blocks and mechanical processing, identifies the parameters of the processes under consideration, and develops reduced models of energy consumption of industrial robots as part of robotic technological complexes. We present algorithms for optimizing trajectory movements for processes with a predominance of long-stroke movements (cargo stowage) and with a predominance of short-stroke movements (mechanical processing) according to the criteria of minimizing energy consumption and time for performing a technological operation. The paper delivers the results of testing the proposed optimization solutions and the calculation of energy benefits from implementation in production.

**Keywords** Neural network model · Digitalization of production · Energy efficiency · Technological processes optimization · Trajectory movements

## 1 Introduction

One of the priority directions of modern production is the automation of technological operations based on robotic technological complexes (RTC), which definitely leads to an increase in energy consumption due to the replacement of a significant

M. Melnichenko (✉) · M. Gorkavyy · Y. Ivanov · A. Gorkavyy
Komsomolsk-on-Amur State University, Komsomolsk-on-Amur, Russian Federation



A. Appolloni et al. (eds.), *The Future of Industry*, Lecture Notes in Information Systems and Organisation 70, https://doi.org/10.1007/978-3-031-66801-2_17

share of manual labor with machine labor and an increase in the concentration of high-tech robotic equipment at manufacturing enterprises. In this regard, the issues of rational energy consumption and optimization of other RTK indicators in the conditions of the growing level of automation (robotization) of production are of particular relevance [1, 2].

Today a significant part of the algorithms for designing production technologies using industrial robots (IR) does not provide for ways to increase the efficiency by implementing an integrated approach, on the one hand, to the goals and objectives of the process and, on the other hand, to the required resources. Often, a systematic assessment of the feasibility and potential of automating operations with the use of robotic systems is impossible due to the lack of unified tools for optimizing technological processes (in particular, according to the criteria for minimizing energy consumption and/or time costs). The rejection of a complex of factors often demonstrates an imaginary overall positive effect of robotization—a reduction in labor costs against the background of increased energy consumption [3, 4].

The availability of methods, models and tools for assessing the energy saving potential of a robotic production process, as well as the ability to predict the energy costs of robotic systems (through the analysis of control programs) and automated output of optimization solutions using intelligent tools will ensure a comprehensive positive effect from the automation of the chain of operations and, as a result, increase the competitiveness of the enterprise.

This work proposes a solution to the problem of reducing the total energy and time costs in the implementation of robotic technological processes (RTP) of varying complexity due to the introduction of intelligent algorithms and control systems into the production process that allows optimizing the trajectory movements of an industrial robot. At the same time, changes in spatial displacements of the IR do not entail the need to change the key parameters reflected in the terms of reference.

Thus, the purpose of the study is to increase the efficiency of robotic technological complexes implementing a set of differentiated technological operations through the development of intelligent methods, models, algorithms and control systems in the conditions of modern requirements for reducing energy consumption.

## 2 Methodology

Ghobakhloo et al. [5] have compiled a diagram illustrating the key technologies of the Industry 5.0 paradigm (Fig. 1).

In accordance with Fig. 1, it seems possible to divide the position of the current research—the development of intelligent control systems.

According to [2], to achieve optimization goals, modern scientists mostly use the following broad classes of optimization tools: heuristic/meta algorithms (47%), math proof (18%), exact algorithms (12%), simulation algorithms (6%), proof-number search (4%), machine learning (2%).

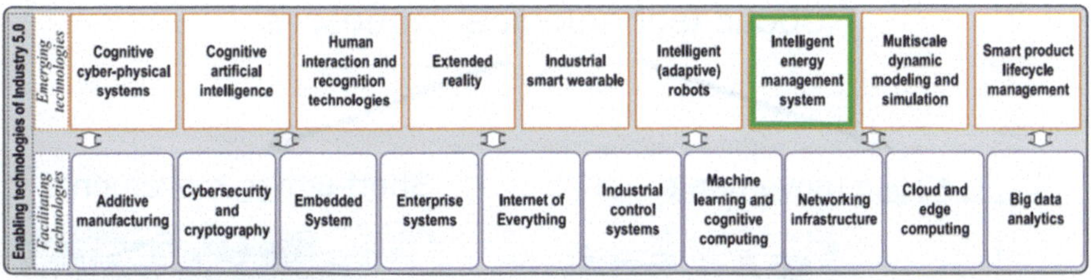


**Fig. 1** Scheme of key technologies of Industry 5.0. Source: Reproduced from [5]

The reduction of RTP energy consumption is possible due to digitization—an approach in which the control laws are previously predicted using the model. This approach to calculating optimal trajectories from the perspective of energy saving is classical and is characterized by high quality of the result obtained. However, at the same time, this approach is also quite complex and costly, since it implies the construction of a mathematical model, its analysis, verification of adequacy and the formation of control laws [6, 7].

It is worth noting that the task of the considered classical approach to reducing energy consumption may be complicated by the fact that modern robotic equipment is, as a rule, imported, and, moreover, the hardware and software parts of such equipment are constantly becoming more complicated and modified. At the same time, changes in the structures of technological processes are continuously taking place (new equipment is supplied, new complexes are being created) [8, 9].

Thus, the classical approach to reducing energy consumption is not always appropriate, especially in simple robotic processes with a limited set of trajectory movements, such as palletizing, moving and stowing loads, assembly. These technological operations are strictly deterministic, and their parameters greatly restrict the freedom of action of an industrial robot, therefore, it is proposed to develop a number of reduced models suitable for the processes under study and slightly inferior in performance and quality to classical digital models.

As part of the study, robotic technological processes are proposed to be divided into two classes: with the predominance of (1) long-stroke and (2) short-stroke movements (Fig. 2).

Each of the presented classes of robotic technological processes has its own specifics when carrying out optimization measures. At the same time, the long-stroke authors determined the movements with a length of more than 300 mm, and the short-stroke ones with a length of 300 mm or less.

To conduct current scientific research on optimization and intellectualization, the authors used methods of identification, analysis and synthesis, as well as simulation modeling to create models of energy consumption of robotic technological complexes [10, 11]. In the synthesis of control systems and control programs, methods of the theory of automatic control (including optimal and adaptive), methods of artificial intelligence (neural networks), as well as an object-oriented approach to the

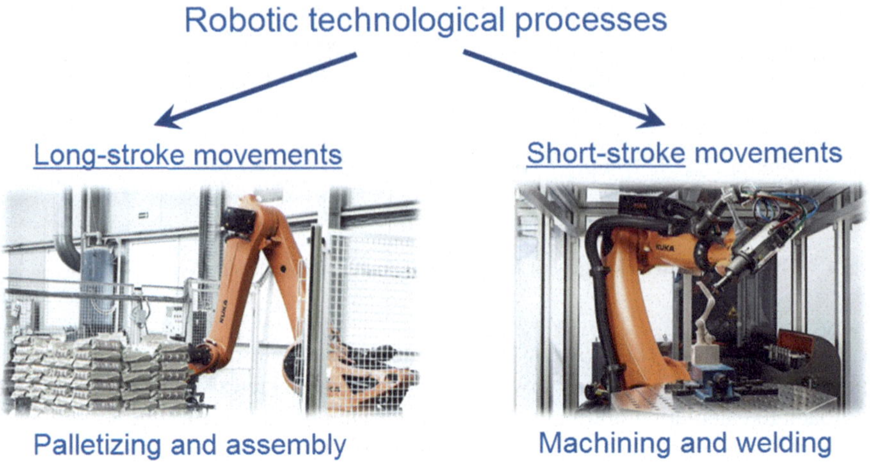


**Fig. 2** Fragment of RTP classification by types of movements

development of control programs in high-level languages (MATLAB, KRL, Java, C ++, Arduino C) were applied. Mathematical modeling methods in MATLAB and MATLAB/Simulink were used to solve simulation problems.

The energy consumption of industrial robots was measured by the devices developed by the authors.

## 3 Optimization of a Robotic Technological Process with a Predominance of Long-Stroke Movements Based on a Neural Network Simulation Model of Energy Consumption

### *3.1 Robotic Technological Complex of Cargo Stowage*

The first of the classes under consideration is characterized by the predominance of long-stroke movements. The robotic technological complex under study (Fig. 3) consists of an industrial robot [12] mounted on a steel pedestal, a conveyor with blocks (cargo), a set of pallets and a robotic trolley (RT) that can be adjusted in height and can be located in different places of the loading zone W [13].

Thus, when changing the position of the trolley in the loading zone, the complexes of the trajectories of movement of the industrial robot change, which are accompanied by a change in the time and energy spent on performing a complex of movements.

In production, this task is often not solved, due to the lack of appropriate tools and the apparent imaginary benefits of optimization measures. It is also quite difficult for the operator of a robotic complex to assess the most advantageous position in which

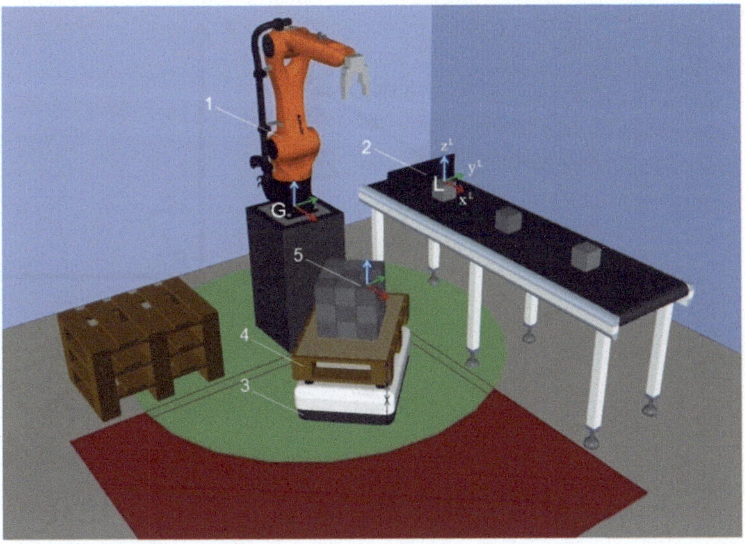


**Fig. 3** Virtual model of the robotic technological process of cargo stowage: 1—industrial robot manipulator KUKA KR10 R1100 sixx, 2—conveyor belt, 3—robotic trolley, 4—pallets, 5—base unit in the loading area

the minimum amount of energy is consumed. To solve this problem, the authors have developed such a model of IR energy consumption, which will allow determining the position of the flange as simply and quickly as possible and achieve the minimum level of electricity consumption.

As a result of the implementation of the proposed method on an operating robotic complex, the operator will have information about the exact location of the base point relative to which the cargo complex will be collected with minimal time and/or energy, as well as the exact values of these costs.

### 3.2 *Formation of a Complex of Trajectories of Movement of the End Effector*

Since all the features and attributes are known for the considered technological process, each trajectory in the complex of movements can be represented by template segments. The selected type of trajectory movement for loading blocks is shown in Fig. 4.

In this case, since the displacement complexes are quite limited, the load must be lifted, shifted forward or backward relative to the IR base, moved along a circular trajectory and lowered down to the level of the trolley.

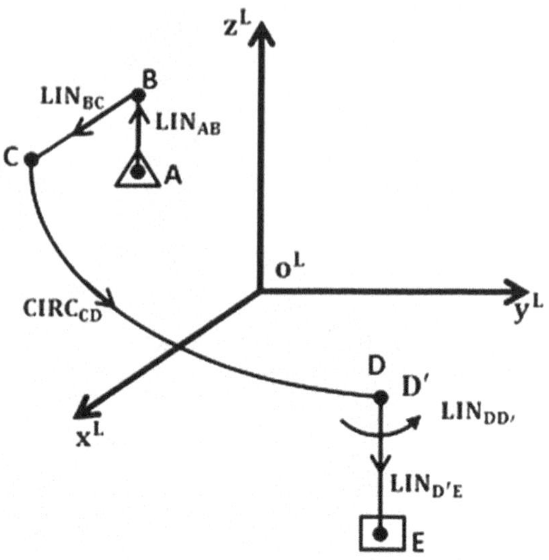


**Fig. 4** Typical trajectory of movement when loading on a robotic trolley

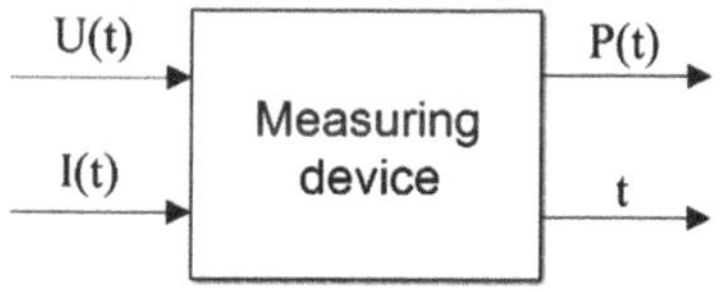


**Fig. 5** Scheme of the measuring device

Thus, if we form the entire permissible spectrum of the same type of movements within the working area of the robot, then we can experiment and restore (with a certain discreteness) for any trajectory the values of the coordinates of the points, as well as the values of instantaneous power and time, on the basis of which the energy expended can be calculated. The obtained data can be used as statistical information in the formation of a training sample for a neural network and further identification of nonlinear dependencies of energy consumption and/or time on the values of variables forming the trajectory of the movement [14]. This problem can also be solved with fuzzy systems tools.

### 3.3 Description of Measuring Equipment for the Experiment

For the experiment, a measuring device has been developed with the ability to remove and process instantaneous current and voltage values, as well as with the ability to receive signals from the digital outputs of the robot controller (Fig. 5).

The device designed and manufactured by the authors based on current and voltage sensors, as well as the Arduino UNO hardware platform meets the above requirements (Fig. 6).

**Fig. 6** Measuring device: 1—current sensor; 2—voltage sensor; 3—control board

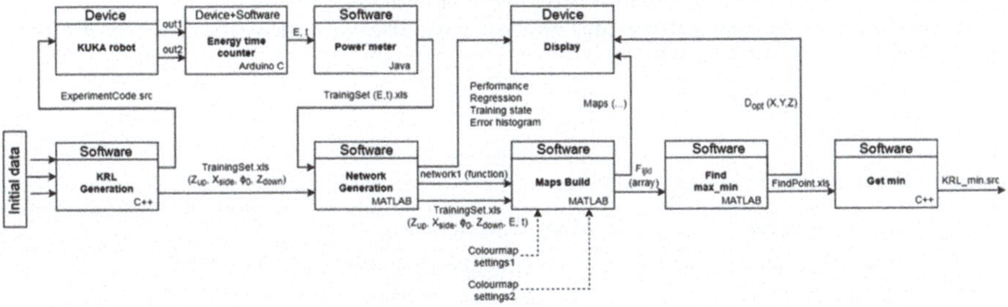


**Fig. 7** Block diagram of the developed software

## 3.4 Development of the Control Program for the Experiment

To form an algorithmized geometric model of displacement, data characterizing the trajectory of the shift, as well as the energy and time values for each shift are needed.

Knowing the types of trajectory movements, the process of forming a control program in the KUKA Robot Language (KRL) can be automated using a high-level programming language C++. In this case, when changing any parameters of the technological process, a new control program can be easily formed, after clarifying the data about the object being moved, the characteristics of the RT, the restriction zones and the robot's reach. The complete structure of the software automating the process of synthesis of the neural network model of energy consumption is shown in Fig. 7.

After setting the initial data in an automated mode, a control program for an industrial robot (ExperimentCode.src) can be formed in order to measure energy consumption for the execution of individual trajectories. The received data (Training set.xls) are used to form a neural network (Network Generation), which allows one to build color maps of energy consumption or time consumption (Maps build) in the automated mode, according to which, in turn, one can determine the optimal energy consumption point (Find max_min) and generate a new program (Get min) to assemble a complex of cargo with minimal energy consumption. The intermediate results of calculations and modeling with the support of a graphical interface are visible to the RTC operator on the monitor display.

Thus, the process of taking readings is automated. This approach is an unambiguous advantage in the final implementation for an engineer who is reconfiguring the model in production.

### 3.5 *Measurement Results on a Real Robotic Technological Complex of Cargo Stowage*

The experiment was carried out on a real robotic technological complex for stacking cargo subject to the experimental parameters specified in Table 1.

As a result, the values of time and energy costs for each movement were obtained (Table 2).

**Table 1** Geometric and physical parameters of the experimental objects

| No. | Name of parameter | Main characteristics |
|---|---|---|
| 1 | Coordinates of key points and coordinate systems | • Global coordinate system G {0;0;0};<br>• Local coordinate system L {600, 300, 200}, cos $R^{x'}{}_{L} = 1$, cos $R^{y'}{}_{L} = 1$, cos $R^{z'}{}_{L} = 1$<br>• Dimensions of the RT (l × w × h) = 0.58 × 0.376 × 0.14 (m)<br>• Dimensions of the pallet (l × w × h) = 0.6 × 0.4 × 0.145 (m)<br>• Dimensions of the block (l × w × h) = 0.05 × 0.05 × 0.05 (m)<br>• Dimensions of the packed cargo (l × w × h) = 0.15 × 0.15 × 0.15 (m) |
| 2 | Robot motion parameters | Linear speed υ = 1 m/s; linear acceleration a = 2 m/s$^2$; smoothing type—With smoothing; operating mode—AUT (automatic); time spent on executing the code to generate a training sample—3.5 h; energy spent on executing the code to form a training sample 1.36 kW·h |

**Table 2** A fragment of the table with the results of the experiment (cargo stowage)

| Rise index | Shift index | Turn index | Descent index | $z_{up}$ (mm) | $x_{side}$ (mm) | φ (°) | $z_{down}$ (mm) | E (W·h) | t (ms) |
|---|---|---|---|---|---|---|---|---|---|
| 1 | 1 | 1 | 1 | 400 | 400 | −86.87 | 200 | 1.059 | 8881 |
| 1 | 1 | 1 | 2 | 400 | 400 | −86.87 | 250 | 1.071 | 8725 |
| 1 | 1 | 1 | 3 | 400 | 400 | −86.87 | 300 | 1.023 | 8533 |
| 1 | 1 | 1 | 4 | 400 | 400 | −86.87 | 350 | 0.999 | 8318 |
| 1 | 1 | 2 | 1 | 400 | 400 | −76.87 | 200 | 1.07 | 8869 |

In the presented table, it is possible to highlight the values generated in automated mode, as well as the values obtained experimentally (columns E and t).

### 3.6 Neural Network Training in MATLAB

After obtaining experimental data and entering them into Table 1, it is possible to identify the dependence in the form of functions:

$$\begin{aligned} E &= f_1(z_{up}, x_{side}, \varphi, z_{down}), \\ t &= f_2(z_{up}, x_{side}, \varphi, z_{down}), \end{aligned} \tag{1}$$

showing the value of energy consumption and time depending on the configurations of the trajectory of movement.

At this stage, the mathematical processing of experimental data takes place. The generated table can be used as a training sample for neural or fuzzy systems [15, 16]. The paper proposes a neural network formed in the MATLAB environment using Neural Network tools.

As a result, two neural networks with one hidden layer were selected and trained. The error on the training sample for the neural network identifying the processes of energy consumption was $\approx 0.0003$, the time was $\approx 0.0009$, which indicates the high quality of training of the received networks.

### 3.7 Formation of an Optimization Algorithm for the Robotic Technological Process of Cargo Stowage

The proposed optimization algorithm consists in the fact that after the functional dependence (1) is established, an optimal complex of motion trajectories inside the working area can be obtained, providing loading of the required volume of blocks.

The quality functionality takes the following form:

$$E = f_1(z_{up}, x_{side}, \varphi, z_{down}); E \to \min; t = f_2(z_{up}, x_{side}, \varphi, z_{down}); t \to \min;$$

As a result of the algorithm implementation, a four-dimensional array V was obtained, each point of which has an index reference to real coordinates in the global coordinate system of an industrial robot.

$$V(i, j, k, :) = \{z_{up}, x_{side}, \varphi, z_{down}, E_{min}, \text{label}, E_{sum}\}.$$

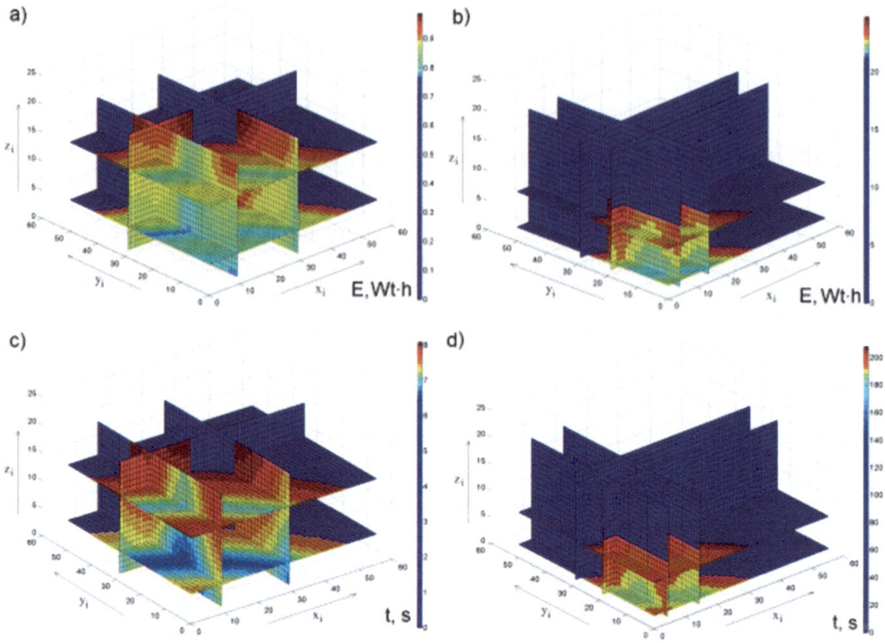


**Fig. 8** Maps of energy consumption (**a**, **b**) and Maps of time consumption (**c**, **d**)

At the same time, the first three indexes characterize the element of the array in which the vector is stored, reflecting the four coordinates $z_{up}$, $x_{side}$, φ, $z_{down}$, describing the trajectory of movement; $E_{min}$ is the minimum energy required to carry cargo along this trajectory; label is a label characterizing the possibility of carrying cargo to this point and taking the values 0 or 1; $E_{sum}$ is the total energy required to build a complex of loads relative to a given point. In exactly the same way, a vector containing the data necessary for optimizing time costs is formed.

The obtained values of energy consumption and time were reflected in the form of color maps. Figure 8 shows a map of energy consumption (a) and time spent (b) for a single movement without taking into account the assembly of the cargo complex, Fig. 8 (c, d)—taking into account the assembly of the cargo complex relative to the base point, respectively.

The values on the axes of the presented maps have an index format. These indexes correspond to real coordinates in the global coordinate system of an industrial robot.

According to the color map (Fig. 8a), the most energy-efficient ($E_1 = 0.803$ W·h) and least energy-efficient ($E_2 = 1.094$ W·h) trajectories are determined.

# 4 Development of a Method for Finding the Optimal Position of the Workpiece and Elements of the Equipping Equipment in the Workspace of an Industrial Robot Performing a Complex of Technological Operations with a Predominance of Short-Stroke Movements

## *4.1 Robotic Technological Complex of Mechanical Processing*

Since the robotic technological process of mechanical processing belongs to the class of processes with a predominance of short-stroke movements, the previously proposed optimization algorithm is not applicable due to a large number of trajectories and their high density [17]. Therefore, in order to improve the efficiency of technological processes of this class, it is necessary to develop a different optimization algorithm.

The robotic machining cell (Fig. 9) is a complex of an industrial robot, an additional external axis (positioner), a control controller, tooling, a milling table and security systems. The workpiece of the product can be installed on the desktop of the IR, and, depending on the selected position of the workpiece, the energy value required for its processing will change. Thus, the task of positioning the workpiece within the desktop is an optimization one.

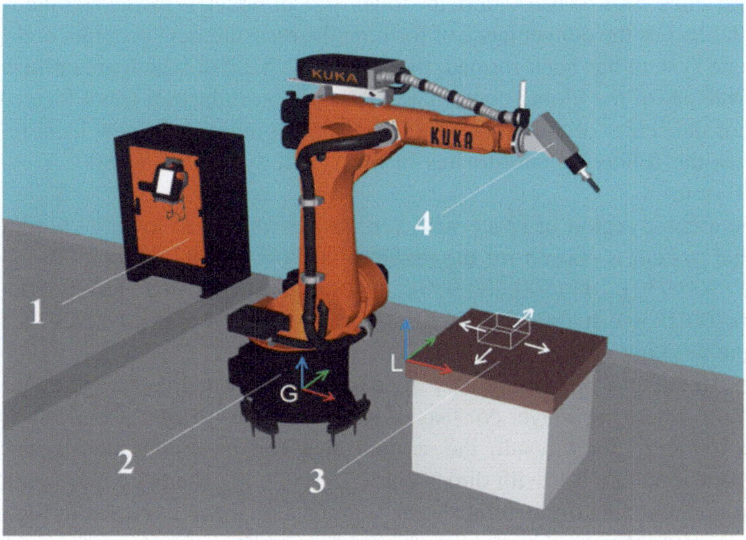


**Fig. 9** Robotic technological complex of mechanical processing: 1—robot controller KUKA KRC4; 2—industrial robot manipulator KUKA KR60-3; 3—milling table; 4—electric spindle with cutting tool

The authors have suggested that, depending on the position of the product's workpiece within the workspace, the value of the energy consumed by an industrial robot for machining operations will change. In this regard, when carrying out optimization measures considering the specifics of the robotic machining complex, in order to ensure energy efficiency it is necessary to adhere to an algorithm that consists of the following main stages:

1) Dividing the working space of an industrial robot into individual areas of cubic shape and fixed size;
2) Measuring energy consumption when performing an identical set of technological operations in each area (processing of a conditional product);
3) Training of a neural network using a sample obtained as a result of experiments. In this case, the input data are the coordinates of the areas of the divided space, and the output data are the values of energy consumption for processing the required product;
4) Calculating the optimal position of the workpiece in the working space under study using the obtained neural network (with the support of energy consumption maps) and solving the optimization problem.

## *4.2 Separation of the Workspace of an Industrial Robot*

Measuring the entire workspace is difficult due to the large amount of time. Therefore, it was decided to study and take readings from the working area bounded by a cube with sides 700x700x700 mm, the lower side of which is located on the working milling table. For the convenience of forming the measurement program code, a new coordinate system has been formed, the vectors X, Y, Z of which are collinear with similar vectors of the global coordinate system of an industrial robot located at the bottom of the center of the robot base [18]. The beginning of a new local reference frame has the following coordinates in the global system: $X = 800$; $Y = -500$; $Z = 930$ (mm).

Thus, a cubic region of space with vertices having the following coordinates in the global system is chosen for the research: **a** (800;-500;930), **b** (1500;-500;930), **c** (1500;200;930), **d** (800;200;930), **e** (800;-500;1630), **f** (1500;-500;1630), **g** (1500,200;1630), **h** (800,200;1630). The investigated area of space is located above the working milling table.

The selected area is conditionally divided into horizontal layers with a thickness of 100 mm, where each layer consists of basic segments of space, i.e., cubes with a side of 100 mm. As a result, the studied area can be represented as an empty multidimensional array P with dimension i, j, $k = 7$. A schematic representation of the measurement area divided into basic segments of space is shown in Fig. 10.

As a result of the experiment, the values of energy consumption for processing a conditional product in each area of the studied space were measured. To carry out the measurements, a control program has been formed consisting of linear displacements that do not go beyond the established dimensions having a size of

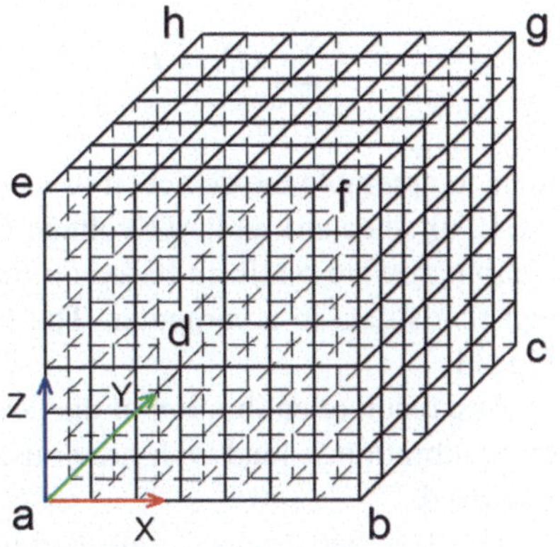


**Fig. 10** Schematic representation of the measurement area

100x100x100 mm. Thus, the study of energy consumption in each area is implemented using a set of basic movements presented in [19].

The control program is replicated for all segments studied within the allocated space (7x7x7 values) and sequentially launched for execution by an industrial robot. As a result of the measurements, arrays of data containing information about energy consumption in individual zones of the workspace were obtained.

## *4.3 Description of Measuring Equipment for the Experiment*

The research has solved the task of developing and assembling a measuring device capable of registering the values of currents and voltages in a three-phase network with a sufficiently high sampling rate and writing data to a file on a computer. The measuring device must be integrated into a robotic complex without changing the control system of the control system and the key parameters of the technological process.

Currently, most of the energy consumption measurement devices on the market are aimed at a wide range of tasks to be solved and have many functions, but they cannot receive a digital signal from an external device to provide signals about the beginning and the end of measurement [20]. Moreover, three-phase meters, as a rule, are not common due to the narrow specialization of such devices and have a high cost. In this regard, it was decided to create a device whose functionality will provide a solution to a specific task, namely registering and writing to a file the values of current forces (x3), voltages (x3), as well as the current time value during the execution of the control program by an industrial robot powered by a three-phase network.

In this study, the authors proposed to measure the energy consumption of all PR systems by installing an electric energy meter in the gap of the supply network.

Since the value of energy consumption in a three-phase network for a certain time interval can be found by the formula:

$$E = \sum_{t=0}^{T} (P_1 + P_2 + P_3) \cdot dt = \sum_{t=0}^{T} (U_1 I_1 + U_2 I_2 + U_3 I_3) \cdot dt$$

then, to assemble the device, it is necessary and sufficient to use AC sensors (Talema AC1030 selected) and AC voltage (ZMPT101B selected), as well as the Arduino Nano hardware platform based on the ATmega 328 microcontroller, which collects and sends data to a computer. The final view of the developed device is shown in Fig. 11.

As a result of calibration of the device, a scaling factor of the values was obtained. For calibration, a load with previously known reliable values of current and voltage was used.

The designed device is installed in the gap of the three-phase supply network. In this case, the ABC phases are connected to the measuring device, and the neutral and ground lines are connected directly to the IR controller.

Thus, the designed and manufactured device allows registering the current values of individual phases of a three-phase consumer (industrial robot). The advantages of the device are a high frequency of current values, low cost and ease of manufacture in compliance with the required measurement accuracy.

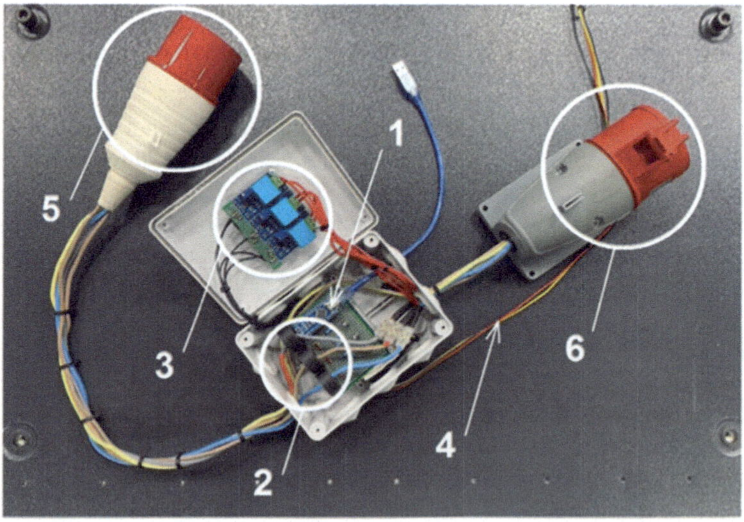


**Fig. 11** Three-phase power consumption meter: 1—Arduino Nano hardware platform; 2—Talema AC1030 current sensors; 3—ZMPT101B voltage sensors; 4—contacts for digital signals; 5—three-phase plug (for connecting to the power supply network); 6—three-phase socket (for connecting the controller IR)

## 4.4 Development of the Control Program for the Experiment

The control program in the KRL programming language for conducting an experiment to measure the energy consumption of an industrial robot for processing a conditional product within each section of the segmented space is formed in the automated mode using the high-level MATLAB language. The control program is based on a nested loop that iterates through the studied areas in the directions of the X, Y and Z axes.

## 4.5 Measurement Results on a Real Robotic Technological Complex of Mechanical Processing

The experiment was carried out on a real robotic technological complex of mechanical processing, subject to the experimental parameters specified in Table 3.

As a result of the execution of the developed control program, the following values of energy and time for processing the conditional product were obtained (Table 4).

According to the presented data, a map of the energy consumption zones of an industrial robot has been formed (Fig. 12).

The values indicated on the axes of the three-dimensional graph (Fig. 12) correspond to the real coordinates of the selected local system (milling table IR).

It is this stage, where, based on the results of the experiment, it is possible to specify the area of the workspace with the lowest energy consumption. In the example under consideration, the area with minimal power consumption (E = 5.536 W·h) has coordinates (500;500;300).

**Table 3** Geometric and physical parameters of the experimental objects

| No. | Name of parameter | Main characteristics |
|---|---|---|
| 1 | Coordinates of key points and coordinate systems | • Global coordinate system G {0;0;0};<br>• Local coordinate system L {800, −500, 930}, $\cos R^{x'}{}_{L} = 1$, $\cos R^{y'}{}_{L} = 1$, $\cos R^{z'}{}_{L} = 1$; |
| 2 | Dimensions of the working area / research areas of the working area | • Dimensions of the working area (l × w × h) = 0.7 × 0.7 × 0.7 (m);<br>• Dimensions of the research areas (l × w × h) = 0.1 × 0.1 × 0.1 (m). |
| 3 | Robot motion parameters | Linear speed υ = 2 m/s; linear acceleration a = 2 m/s$^2$; smoothing type—No smoothing; operating mode—AUT (automatic); time spent executing the code to generate a training sample—1.8 h; energy spent on executing the code to form a training sample 2.033 kW·h. |

**Table 4** A fragment of the table with the results of the experiment (mechanical processing)

| X (mm) | Y (mm) | Z (mm) | E (W·h) | t (s) |
|---|---|---|---|---|
| 0 | 0 | 0 | 6.738 | 18.54 |
| 100 | 0 | 0 | 6.460 | 18.53 |
| 200 | 0 | 0 | 6.221 | 18.53 |
| 300 | 0 | 0 | 6.049 | 18.54 |
| 400 | 0 | 0 | 5.921 | 18.50 |
| 500 | 0 | 0 | 5.809 | 18.52 |
| 600 | 0 | 0 | 5.764 | 18.53 |
| 0 | 100 | 0 | 6.587 | 18.54 |
| 100 | 100 | 0 | 6.367 | 18.53 |
| 200 | 100 | 0 | 6.152 | 18.54 |

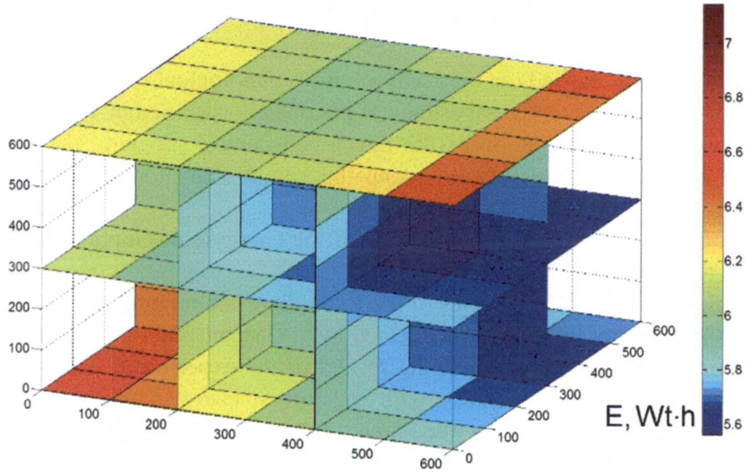


**Fig. 12** Industrial robot energy consumption zone map

The data obtained during the experiment constitute a training sample for a neural network, where the input data are the coordinates of the region (X, Y, Z), and the output data are the energy values for processing the conditional product.

## 4.6 Development of an Algorithm for Optimizing the Robotic Technological Process of Mechanical Processing

With the help of Neural Network MATLAB tools, a neural network with one hidden layer has been formed. The error on the training sample was ≈ 0.0027, which also indicates the high quality of the trained network.

The optimization algorithm for this class of RTP consists in the fact that after establishing a functional relationship between the coordinates of the workspace segment and the energy consumption for processing a conditional product in this segment, an optimal location of the workpiece of the product can be obtained providing a minimum of energy consumption without changing the time of the technological process.

The quality functionality has the following form:

$$E = f_3(X, Y, Z, t_{XYZ}); E \rightarrow \min; t = \text{const}.$$

As follows from the expression, the energy consumption of a robotic machining process depends on the coordinates of the workspace area (X, Y, Z) and the processing execution time ($t_{XYZ}$).

As a result of the algorithm implementation, a four-dimensional array N was obtained, each point of which has an index reference to real coordinates in the global coordinate system of an industrial robot.

$$N(i, j, k, :) = \{X, Y, Z, E\}.$$

At the same time, the first three indexes characterize an array element in which a vector containing three coordinates of a region of space (X, Y, Z) and the value of energy (E) necessary for processing a conditional product in this area is stored.

As a result, based on the results of the functional dependence described by the neural network, a map of the energy consumption zones of an industrial robot with high detail was built to visualize the nature of the distribution of energy-consuming zones and clarify the position of the workpiece (Fig. 13).

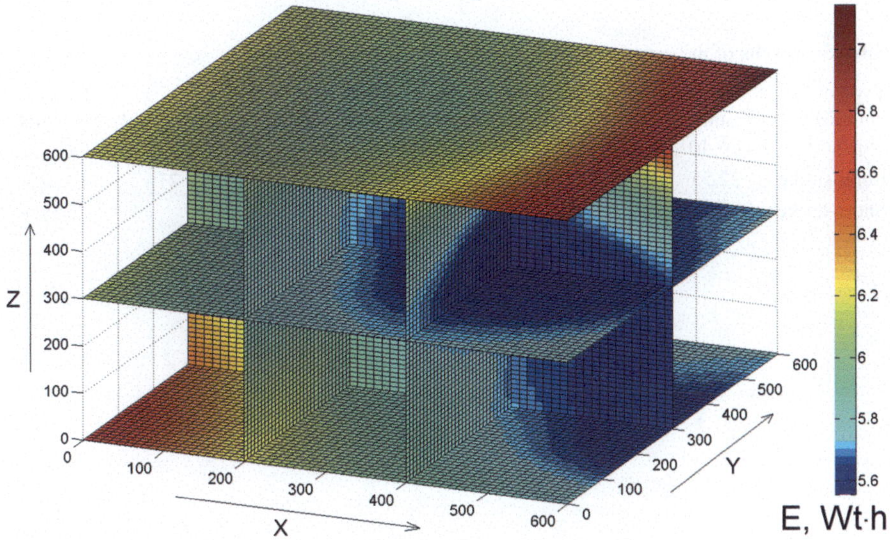


**Fig. 13** Industrial robot energy consumption zone map (high resolution)

According to the presented map, it is possible to most accurately determine the coordinates of the point for positioning the workpiece with minimal energy consumption. In the example under consideration, the minimum value of energy consumption during processing of the product $E_{min} = 5.53$ W·h is reached at the point with coordinates (510;530;330).

Thus, with the help of the developed algorithm, the optimization problem has been solved.

## 5 Economic Justification of the Feasibility of Integration and Using the Developed Optimization Solutions

To confirm the expediency of the developed methods for optimizing robotic technological processes with a predominance of long- and short-stroke movements, an experiment was conducted to determine energy costs using the proposed method and without using it (i.e., when choosing the optimal trajectory/position by the operator). The following results were obtained (Table 5).

Thus, as a result of the operations performed to improve the energy efficiency of robotic technological processes, a significant energy benefit was obtained. At the same time, RTP with the use of industrial robots with high load-carrying capacity, which implement the laying of larger loads (processing of harder materials), have the greatest potential for energy saving.

It should be noted that the downtime of the robotic complex for the time for conducting experiments was only 3 h.

**Table 5** Results of the experiment and calculations of energy benefits

| Type of optimized trajectories | Minimum value $E_{min}$ (W·h) | Maximum value $E_{max}$ (W·h) | Energy value by operator selection $E_{oper}$ (W·h) | Technological cycle time (s) | Energy benefits (%) |
|---|---|---|---|---|---|
| Long-stroke | 22.55 | 26.92 | 25.23 | 8·27 = 216 | 10.62% |
| Short-stroke | 5.53 | 7.144 | 5.92 | 18.52 | 6.59% |

## 6 Conclusion

In the current study, the authors have developed ways to increase the energy efficiency of robotic technological processes with a predominance of long- and short-stroke movements.

The conducted studies allow us to draw the following conclusions:

1) To solve optimization problems of reducing energy and/or time costs for the execution of RTP with a predominance of long-stroke/short-stroke movements, it is advisable to use reduced models constructed using intelligent RTP optimization methods;
2) The measuring devices developed by the authors on the basis of sensors of alternating current, alternating voltage and a control board based on the ATmega328 controller are able to provide a sufficient amount of data for forming training and test samples of neural networks underlying the simulation models of energy consumption, etc.;
3) As a result of the graphical analysis of the color maps of energy consumption for the execution of fragments of the final effector's movement trajectories, the most energy-efficient trajectory ($E_1 = 0.803$ W·h) and the least energy-efficient trajectory ($E_2 = 1.094$ W·h), as well as the most and least expensive complexes of trajectories of movement for the laying of the combined load were determined;
4) The analysis of the experimental data on the study of the areas of the working space of the IR without the use of a neural network model showed the presence of zones with high energy efficiency indicators, guided by which it is possible to conceptually form the most effective location of the workpiece to achieve the minimum energy consumption during the implementation of RTP. At the same time, the use of the developed neural network model of energy consumption makes it possible to clarify the position of the workpiece in the automated mode, as well as to provide the possibility of orientation by the operator of the workpiece, taking into account the nature of the distribution of the density of processing trajectories (the time the tool is in the area under consideration);
5) A technical and economic analysis of the results of using the developed neural network models demonstrated a significant benefit from the optimization procedures carried out, equal to 10.62% (with an energy saving potential of 16.23%—the difference between $E_{max}$ and $E_{min}$) for a class of long-stroke movements when comparing the optimal trajectory calculated by the model and an arbitrary trajectory chosen by the operator. For the class of short-stroke movements, the energy benefit when implementing the algorithm for finding the optimal position of the workpiece in the working space of the IR was 6.59% (with an energy saving potential of 22.59%).

Methods and models for optimizing industrial robots and complexes based on them usually require high development costs. The research results presented in the work demonstrate the feasibility of synthesizing reduced models based on modern neural network tools. The use of this approach will make it possible to develop models of industrial robots to optimize robotic technological processes and conduct scientific research in the field of robotics, which ultimately will significantly reduce the costs of performing a wide range of robotic operations and increase the economic sustainability of modern industrial enterprises.

**Acknowledgements** The work was supported by the Russian Science Foundation (project №22-71-10093 https://rscf.ru/project/22-71-10093).

## References


1. Ribeiro, J., Lima, R., Eckhardt, T., & Paiva, S. (2021). Robotic process automation and artificial intelligence in Industry 4.0. A literature review. *Procedia Computer Science, 181*, 51–58. https://doi.org/10.1016/j.procs.2021.01.104
2. Vaisi, B. (2022). A review of optimization models and applications in robotic manufacturing systems: Industry 4.0 and beyond. *Decision Analytics Journal, 2*, 100031. https://doi.org/10.1016/j.dajour.2022.100031
3. Soori, M., Arezoo, B., & Dastres, R. (2023). Optimization of energy consumption in industrial robots, a review. *Cognitive Robotics, 3*, 142–157. https://doi.org/10.1016/j.cogr.2023.05.003
4. Sinaga, N., Paryanto, P., Widyanto, S. A., Rusnaldy, R., Hetzner, A., & Franke, J. (2018). An analysis of the effect of gravitational load on the energy consumption of industrial robots. *Procedia CIRP, 78*, 8–12. https://doi.org/10.1016/j.procir.2018.09.043
5. Ghobakhloo, M., Iranmanesh, M., Foroughi, B., Tirkolaee, E. B., Asadi, S., & Amran, A. (2023). Industry 5.0 implications for inclusive sustainable manufacturing: An evidence-knowledge-based strategic roadmap. *Journal of Cleaner Production, 417*, 138023. https://doi.org/10.1016/j.jclepro.2023.138023
6. Borovkov, A. I., Ryabov, Y. A., Kukushkin, K. V., Maruseva, V. M., & Kulemin, V. Y. (2019). *Digital twins and digital transformation of defense industry enterprises. Vestnik vostochno-sibirskoy otkrytoy akademii*. Peter the Great St. Petersburg Polytechnic University.
7. Wenjun, X., Cui, J., Li, L., Yao, B., Tian, S., & Zhou, Z. (2021). Digital twin-based industrial cloud robotics: Framework, control approach and implementation. *Journal of Manufacturing Systems, 58, B*, 196–209. https://doi.org/10.1016/j.jmsy.2020.07.013
8. Siar, M. V. S., & Fakharian, A. (2018). Energy efficiency in the robot arm using genetic algorithm. In *8th conference of AI & Robotics and 10th RoboCup IRANOPEN International Symposium (IRANOPEN)* (pp. 14–20). https://doi.org/10.1109/RIOS.2018.8406625
9. Mahdavian, M., Shariat-Panahi, M., Yousefi-Koma, A., & Ghasemi-Toudeshki, A. (2015). Optimal trajectory generation for energy consumption minimization and moving obstacle avoidance of a 4DOF robot arm. In *3rd RSI International Conference on Robotics and Mechatronics (ICROM)* (pp. 353–358).
10. Kim, K. K., & Ivanov, S. N. (2019). Simulation of a combined electric drive. *Izvestiya vyshih uchebnikh zavedeniy. Elektromechanika, 62*(3), 44–50. https://doi.org/10.17213/0136-3360-2019-3-44-50
11. Mokritsky, B. Y., & Sitamov, E. S. (2021). Simulation modeling of the turning process. *Vestnik mashinostroeniya, 2*, 77–81. https://doi.org/10.36652/0042-4633-2021-2-77-81
12. KUKA KR AGILUS sixx V12 in variants of execution W and C. Manual guide, KUKA Roboter GmbH, 2015.
13. Egorov, O. D., Poduraev, Y. V., & Buynov, M. A. (2015). *Robotic mechatronic systems*. Moscow State Technological University "STANKIN".

14. Savelev, D. O., Chernyj, S. P., & Solovev, V. A. (2020). Improving the accuracy of compensation of nonlinear elements of control systems. *Izvestiya vysshih uchebnyh zavedenij, Priborostroenie, 63*(3), 213–221. https://doi.org/10.17586/0021-3454-2020-63-3-213-221
15. Kozhevnikov, V. V., Leont'ev, M. Y., Prihod'ko, V. V., Sergeev, V. A., & Fomin, A. N. (2019). Neural network technologies for building intelligent robot control systems. In *Scientific notes Ulyanovsk State University, Matematika i informacionnye tekhnologii* (pp. 36–53).
16. Vlasenko, M. A., Ivanov, D. A., Kuznecov, S. I., & Lauta, O. S. (2018). Ensuring the safety of control of robotic systems using neural networks. In *Actual problems of infotelecommunications in science and education, VII international scientific-technical and scientific-methodical conference (VII Mezhdunarodnaya nauchno-tekhnicheskaya i nauchno-metodicheskaya konferenciya)* (pp. 167–171).
17. Suhorukov, S. I., Chernyj, S. P., Buzikaeva, A. V., & Ovsyannikov, A. R. (2022). Control system for the wire feeding and positioning module for a robotic complex for three-dimensional printing of metal products. *Izvestiya vysshih uchebnyh zavedenij, Elektromekhanika, 65*(3), 66–73. https://doi.org/10.17213/0136-3360-2022-3-56-63
18. Golz, J., Wruetz, T., Eickmann, D., & Biesenbach, R. (2016). RoBO-2L, a Matlab interface for extended offline programming of KUKA industrial robots. In *11th France-Japan & 9th Europe-Asia congress on mechatronics (MECATRONICS) Compiegne* (pp. 64–67).
19. Uhlmann, E., Reinkober, S., & Hollerbach, T. (2016). Energy efficient usage of industrial robots for machining processes. *Procedia CIRP, 48*, 206–211. https://doi.org/10.1016/j.procir.2016.03.241
20. Ded, A. V., Sikorskij, S. P., & Rogozina, D. A. (2017). Overview of the modern market of measuring instruments for electricity quality indicators. *OHB, 5*(155).

# Driving Sustainable Growth: Leveraging Digital Transformation in Photovoltaic Manufacturing

**Magdalena Ramirez-Peña, Nieves Saborido Barba, Manuel Otero-Mateo, Andrés Pastor-Fernández, and Alberto Cerezo-Narváez**

**Abstract** The performance of photovoltaic modules in the field plays a crucial role in ensuring reliability, quality, and financing for photovoltaic installations. Recent years have witnessed exponential growth in the solar photovoltaic industry, potentially driven by the principles of Industry 5.0. In this digital transformation era, companies can enhance production efficiency, mitigate environmental impact, and transition towards a more sustainable and profitable manufacturing model. Therefore, it is imperative to examine the stress conditions encountered by photovoltaic modules during the manufacturing process, as they are a major contributing factor to field failures. The objective of the article is to prolong the lifespan of photovoltaic panels by addressing various stages of their manufacturing, aiming to identify enhancements that will result in prolonged durability. This extension is closely linked to the performance of photovoltaic modules where the article finds solutions such as a modification on the rigidity of the encapsulant to reduce stresses, cooling in different ways to reduce temperature or change the angle of inclination to avoid dust accumulation. Additionally, this phase presents an opportune moment to reduce greenhouse gas emissions, further aligning the process with sustainability goals. Furthermore, the article analyzes the advantages and disadvantages of different photovoltaic cell technologies. While the current market is dominated by c-Si technology, significant increases are expected in the adoption of other technologies highlighting the use of bifacial cells in the coming years.

**Keywords** Photovoltaic energy · Lifecycle product · Manufacturing process Industry 5.0 · Failure test

M. Ramirez-Peña (✉) · N. S. Barba · M. Otero-Mateo · A. Pastor-Fernández · A. Cerezo-Narváez
University of Cadiz, Higher School of Engineering, Cadiz, Spain
e-mail: magdalena.ramirez@uca.es; nieves.saborido@uca.es; manuel.otero@uca.es; andres.pastor@uca.es; alberto.cerezo@uca.es



A. Appolloni et al. (eds.), *The Future of Industry*, Lecture Notes in Information Systems and Organisation 70, https://doi.org/10.1007/978-3-031-66801-2_18

## 1 Introduction

Since the beginning of the first industrial revolution, fossil energy sources have been predominant. These types of energies are among the non-renewable and dirty, exist in limited quantities and are a source of pollution, however there are other types of energy called renewable and clean that do not produce pollution and exist in unlimited quantities, examples of which are solar, geothermal, wind, biomass, etc. [1]. Among those derived from the sun are solar-thermal and solar-photovoltaic, the latter has its beginnings based on the photovoltaic effect developed by Becquerel in 1839, giving rise, years later, to the first photoelectric cell developed by Fritts in 1883 [2].

Solar photovoltaic energy is the fastest growing renewable energy source in recent years, where China is significantly the country with the largest installed capacity so far as can be seen in Fig. 1, followed by the United States, Japan, Germany, and India. It can be said that it is one of the booming types of renewable energy in developing countries where the annual growth rate from 2016–2021 was

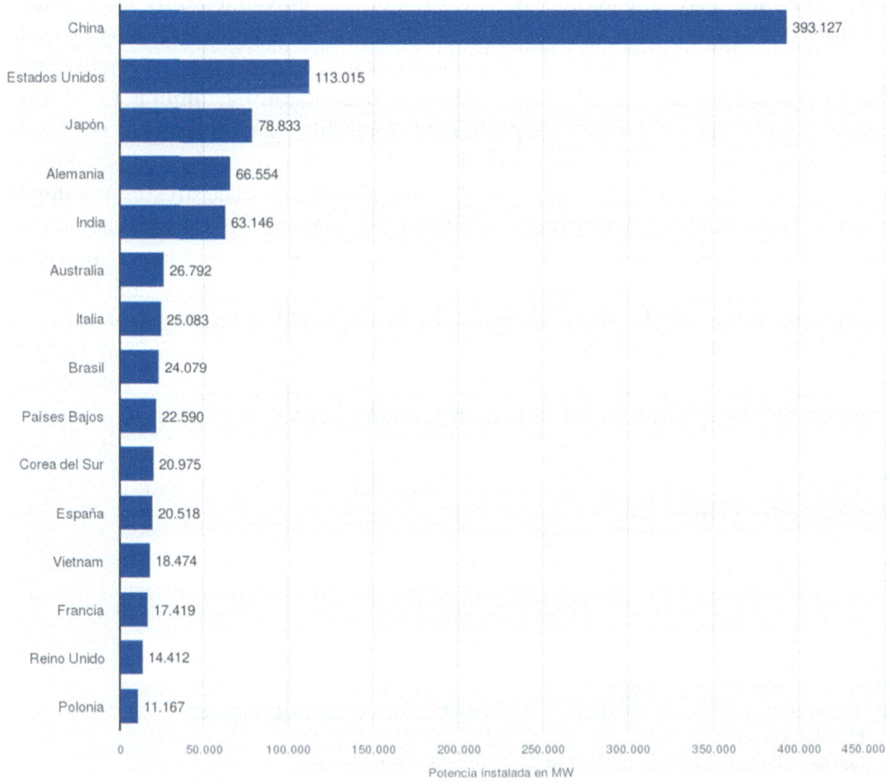


**Fig. 1** Ranking of countries with the highest installed solar photovoltaic capacity in MW by 2022 shows that it is one of the booming types of renewable energy in developing countries [3]

9.6% compared to 8.6% for the period of 2010–2015 as indicated by the United Nations in its SDG Progress Report, given that affordable and clean energy is one of the Sustainable Development Goals (SDGs) [4].

Of the different renewable energy sources, solar photovoltaic energy is the cleanest, abundantly available, can be used for the maximum number of days in a year and has low operating/maintenance costs for implementation [5].

Solar PV has become an important asset within renewable energies. According to the latest report of the International Energy Agency (IEA-PVPS), the demand for electricity covered by photovoltaic was 11.6% in 2022 compared to 8.2% in 2021 [6]. However, to be economically viable, the modules should operate reliably for 25 to 30 years. This means that the lifecycle of the photovoltaic panel must be long, or the energy mix must be poor, which means that as the energy mix becomes cleaner, as is the current trend, it takes longer to recover the initial investment. As an example, Fig. 2 shows the energy mix in the south of Europe, Spain, where it can be seen how the generation of renewable energy today is around 50% between the generation of energy from renewable and non-renewable sources, where solar photovoltaic energy is the second source of energy among the renewable ones.

Faced with this problem, for which there is hardly any literature on the subject, it is necessary to extend the lifecycle of the photovoltaic panel so that its investment is profitable in the shortest possible time, and it can continue to be one of the renewable energy sources.

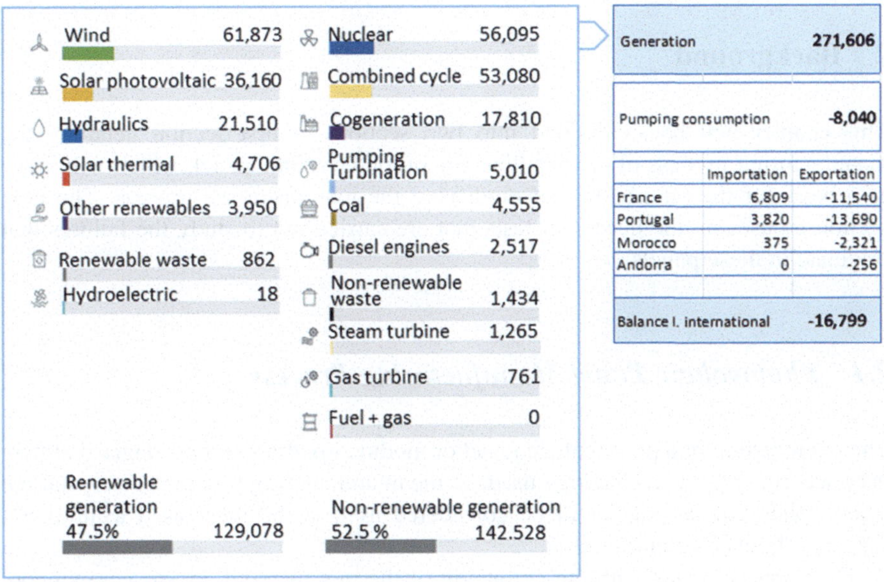


**Fig. 2** Electricity balance (GWh) 10/2022–10/2023 of the electricity system in Spain where the generation of renewable energy today is around 50% between the generation of energy from renewable and non-renewable sources [7]

The digital transformation in this context involves the integration of advanced digital technologies and data-driven processes to optimize production efficiency, improve product quality, and enhance overall sustainability. This transformation is driven by various factors: Industry 5.0 (I5.0) can play a crucial role in advancing efficiency and sustainability. In different ways photovoltaic panel manufacturing is related to I5.0, through the use of automation and advanced robotics [8], through the implementation of IoT devices to ensure quality by improving operational efficiency [9].

Focused on the idea that I5.0 promotes the development of advanced and sustainable manufacturing technologies, which includes the adoption of clean manufacturing processes, the aim of this article is to increase the lifecycle of the photovoltaic panel by addressing its manufacture in its various stages with the intention of finding improvements that allow conclusions focused on extending its useful life, directly proportional to the performance of the photovoltaic module and precisely at this stage where you can work on reducing the emission of greenhouse gases, thus trying to make the process more sustainable. Solutions will be analyzed to mitigate the effects of residual stress, the appearance of cracks, the complete aging of the module and how to improve the damage caused by temperature, humidity, wind, and dust accumulation. For this purpose, the different technologies used in the manufacture of photovoltaic panels will be described, as well as their manufacturing process and the different procedures and inspection processes carried out on these panels.

## 2 Background

This chapter will be subdivided into two sections, a first section detailing the manufacturing process of a crystalline silicon photovoltaic panel, which will serve as a basis for the possibilities of modifying the manufacturing process. The next section focuses on the necessary tests that are carried out to study the failures that originate in these panels.

### *2.1 Photovoltaic Panel Manufacturing Process*

The manufacture of a photovoltaic panel or module involves several stages that may vary according to the technology used, so the manufacturing process of a crystalline silicon photovoltaic panel will be considered as it is the most used technology. Figure 3 shows its configuration.

The process begins with the extraction of the raw material, in this case silicon, obtained from quartz sand and other materials. This is followed by the production of polycrystalline where the extracted silicon is melted and formed into polycrystalline silicon ingots, which are then cut into thin sheets called wafers or monocrystalline

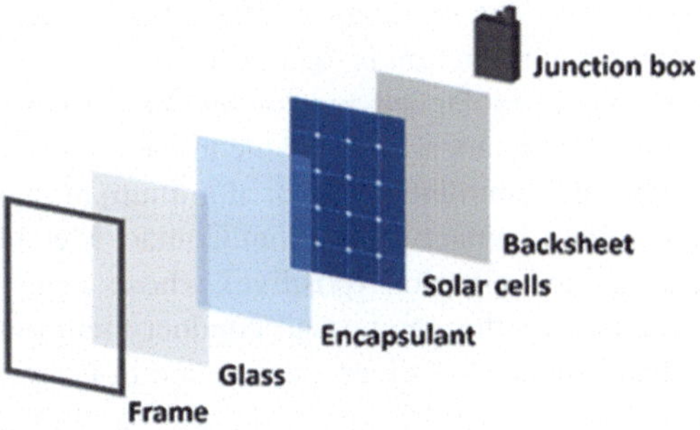


**Fig. 3** Common crystalline silicon module configuration adapted from [10]

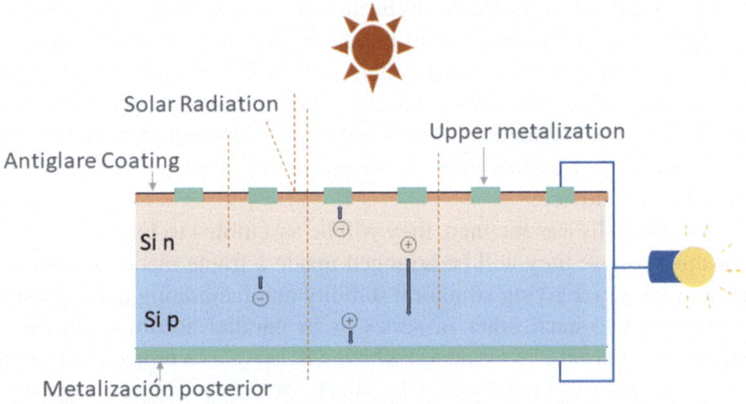


**Fig. 4** Structure and operation of the photovoltaic cell

silicon where a single silicon crystal is grown from a mono-crystalline ingot which is cut into individual wafers, a more expensive process, but with more efficient cell production [11].

These silicon wafers must be doped with materials such as phosphorus and boron to create a positive-negative (p-n) structure essential for electricity generation. A structure formed by the union of two different semiconductor regions in the crystalline structure of the semi-conductor must be achieved, one doped with p-type (positive) impurities, i.e. introducing "holes", spaces where an electron is missing, resulting in a positive charge so that the entire region becomes positively charged, and the other doped with n-type (negative) impurities, impurities that introduce additional electrons into the crystalline structure, which negatively charges the region due to the excess of electrons. In this way, solar cells are created where the p-n junction allows the conversion of solar energy into electricity. When photons of sunlight strike the solar cell, they generate electrons and holes, and the p-n junction facilitates the separation of these electrons and holes, which creates an electric current. Figure 4 shows the structure and operation of the photovoltaic cell.

Metal contacts are added to this structure to allow efficient collection of electrons generated by sunlight. These metal contacts are essential for the operation of the solar cells. The two main contacts that are added are, Back Contact Metal Contact whose main function is to collect the electrons that are generated in the n (negative) region of the solar cell and conduct them to the outside for further use in an electrical charge. In monocrystalline silicon solar cells and some polycrystalline silicon solar cells, a thin aluminum film or aluminum mesh is often used as the back contact. The other main contact is the Front Contact Metal Contact placed at the top of the solar cell, in the p-region (positive) whose main function is to collect the electrons generated in this region and conduct them out of the solar cell. Front contacts are usually made of a silver mesh or a thin layer of conductive metal, such as silver or tin [1].

In addition to these main contacts, there may also be other metallic contacts on the surface of the solar cell to facilitate uniform current distribution and reduce losses. These contacts are usually designed to minimize shading on the cell surface and to maximize solar energy conversion efficiency. Metallic contacts are critical to the operation of solar cells, as they allow the extraction of electrical energy generated by sunlight. The choice of materials and the design of these metal contacts are important aspects of solar cell manufacturing, as they can affect the overall efficiency and performance of the device.

Once the solar cells are obtained, they will be assembled to form the photovoltaic panel, for this purpose they will be arranged inside a frame made of aluminum that will surround the panel giving structural stability and facilitating the installation and will be connected to each other in series or in parallel according to the desired electrical design. A front glass is added which will serve as a protective front layer of the panel in addition to being sealed by sheets of encapsulating material, usually ethylene vinyl acetate (EVA) placed both in the front and in the back and that after the application of heat and pressure to melt the encapsulant and hermetically seal the cells, will protect the cells from moisture and other elements. The electrical connections will be made by soldering the metallic contacts on the back of the cells with the cables that will carry the energy out of the panel and in this way they will be ready to undergo quality tests and visual inspection to detect possible defects in the manufacture [12]. At this point, it will be necessary to mark the panels with relevant information such as power rating and date of manufacture. Labels with identification information and technical data are added to facilitate installation and tracking and are ready to be packaged so that they are protected during transport and can be stored until distribution and installation.

In this section, the manufacturing process of photovoltaic cells, the importance of choosing materials, as well as the metallic contacts that will give greater efficiency and performance of the photovoltaic module have been studied.

## 2.2 *Accelerated Aging Tests*

The IEC 61215 series determines whether modules of a given design will suffer known failures in the field. During testing, modules are subjected to accelerated stress tests that have been experimentally developed to separate failed or degraded modules from modules that behaved as predicted [13]. The main objective of these tests is to focus on failures in PV module quality and design to help find early failures and deficiencies. During these tests, PV modules are subjected to stresses (damp heat (DH), mechanical loading (ML), thermal cycling (TC), UV precondensing (UV), hot spot testing, humidity freezing (HF)), providing a "pass" or "fail" to a set of modules [14]. The different accelerated aging tests performed are described below.

Temperature test: Temperature is a major factor influencing all module degradation processes. To perform this test, oven-type thermal chambers are required. The standardized test temperature for photovoltaic is between 80 °C and 90 °C. Relative humidity test: To perform this test, climatic cabinets are required. This test called DH is performed at 85 °C and 85% RH for 1000 h according to IEC61215. This test has limitations when it is carried out in a real laboratory.

Ultraviolet test: To perform this test, metal halide or Xenon (Xe) lamps, fluorescent tubes or LED light are used. The IEC61215 standard defines that this test shall be performed at 15KWh/m$^2$ at 60 °C, which is comparable to a 3-month outdoor exposure in moderate climates. One of the shortcomings of this test is that different light sources provide different spectra. In a comparative study carried out in 13 laboratories, errors of up to 120% were found [15].

Thermal stress test: This test uses the temperature cycles established by the IEC 61215 standard, which uses temperature ramps from −40 °C to +85 °C and vice versa 50 or 200 times.

Corrosion test: Through this test the effects of corrosion will be known, and it will be possible to determine which type of material will be more suitable for different atmospheres. To perform this test, the modules are subjected to the corrosive effects produced by salt spray in climatic chambers. There are articles that show that there is no correlation between this test and the outside reality [16].

Mechanical testing: This test has significant weaknesses. The tests are divided into snow and wind loads. For the snow tests, static loads are applied, but at room temperature, therefore, the behavior may be different in the material when performed outdoors. For wind tests, loads are applied in different directions. The wind is produced in gusts. This is also not close to reality.

Finally, and with respect to the standardized tests on the effects of sunlight on power loss, these consist of causing defective states related to Light Elevate Temperature Induced Degradation, Boron Oxygen BO LID or Light and Elevated Temperature Induced Degradation LETID, the two defects differing mainly in the difference in temperature at which it occurs, LETID usually occurs above 50 ° C while LID at lower temperatures, and make them progress to a relevant condition for the field [17].

To study the failures caused to the photovoltaic modules, in this study the IEC 61215 standard has been considered. The different tests to which the photovoltaic modules are subjected have been analyzed under this standard, as well as the limitations of each of them. As can be seen, the limitations of the standard are many from the different aspects analyzed, which gives rise to the need to study what the scientific community is doing in this respect to find a solution to the limitations of the standard.

## 3 Methodology

The article will follow the Design science research (DSR) methodology whose main objective is to develop knowledge to the researcher while can be used to design solutions to the problem. The methodology focuses more on the search for possible alternative solutions rather than on analyzing existing alternatives. The DSR starts with a first descriptive stage of the problem in order to understand it in depth that will lead to the prescriptive stage, thus through analysis and design and development, allows, in a systematic and iterative way, the collaboration between researchers and professionals in the field to develop theories and design principles adapted to each case [18].

The problem is therefore addressed through the selection of a series of inspection procedures or processes that should be performed on photovoltaic modules to reach conclusions that will extend their useful life. These inspection procedures are precisely the factors included in the accelerated aging tests, described in the background, to which photovoltaic panels are subjected according to the IEC 61215 standard and which present limitations with the intention of seeking solutions provided by the scientific community to extend the life of the modules. The present study is based on a review of the literature published on the subject and on the professional experience of the authors in this field.

## 4 Results and Discussion

To show the results of the research in a clearer structure, they have been divided into different sections to evaluate the factors that have been studied from different perspectives.

### *4.1 Manufacturing Stages*

During the solar cell manufacturing process, three stages can be distinguished: firing process, soldering process, and lamination process. In the firing process, residual stresses can be induced inside the silicon cell, because the aluminum paste and the silver serially silver have different thermo-mechanical properties and reach very high temperatures to create electrical contacts. This can be solved by modifying the amount and chemistry of the paste and the firing conditions [19].

During the welding process, high thermomechanical stresses are produced. Due to the coefficients of thermal expansion (CTE), cracks can occur. These cracks are usually caused by physical contact of fragile C-Si cells using electrical heating of soldering iron. In order to avoid physical contact, infrared light [20] and laser heating technologies have been introduced [21].

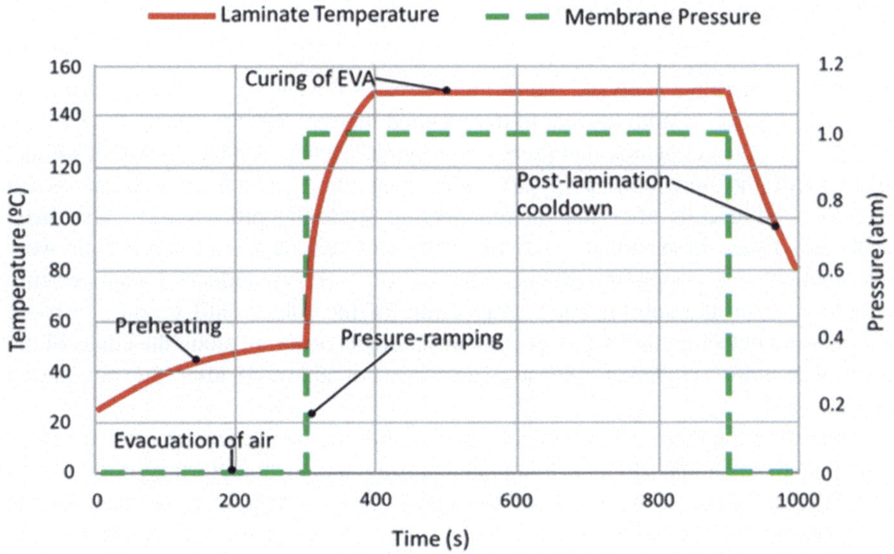


**Fig. 5** Variation of temperature and pressure difference during the lamination process [24]

During the lamination process, thermal stresses can be induced that can lead to micro-cracks in the solar cells and residual stress causing a deformation of the laminate due to the temperature variation that occurs from the curing temperature to the ambient temperature. To eliminate the cracks that can occur in this process, the stiffness of the encapsulant [22] and the thickness of the interconnect can be modified [23]. In [22], it was found that the stiffness of the encapsulant significantly influenced the residual stress of the silicon. The thickness of the interconnect is also involved [23], whereas the width of the interconnect decreases, the voltage at the back of the cell increases. All this will lead to greater or lesser reliability in the photovoltaic module. Figure 5 shows the variation of temperature and pressure difference during the rolling process. The lamination process is divided into three phases: Preheating and evacuation, pressure ramp and cooling process. During the first stage, the laminate is placed on lifting bars, heating it to 50 °C, extracting the air from the laminator chambers. During the second stage, the laminate is lowered down the heating plate and the upper chamber is ventilated. In this step the flexible membrane introduces atmospheric pressure to the entire laminate. At this moment the EVA is solid at 50 °C. Continuous contact with the heating plate causes the temperature of the laminate to reach 150 °C, liquefying the EVA and encapsulating the cells and interconnections. After 10 min the EVA has cured, and it is cooled from 150 °C to 25 °C.

## 4.2 Environmental Testing

Several authors have analyzed the residual stresses developed in Si cells during the fabrication process. With respect to the residual thermal stresses during the fabrication process, they conclude that there is a dependence between the thickness and the stiffness of the bimaterial strip [25]. Moreover, the mechanical problems when interconnecting cells after the interconnecting soldering process have also been analyzed. Three-dimensional (3-D) FE models of two adjacent quarter cells were interconnected by copper interconnections and stresses were induced by temperature reduction, from the solidification temperature of the solder until it cools to room temperature detecting that the largest stress gradients occurred along the edges of the interconnections. However, the stresses were not analyzed after the lamination process [26].

Regarding the thermo-mechanical stresses after the lamination process, it can be said that the residual stress accumulated during the manufacturing process of a photovoltaic panel is the result of the residual stresses in each segment of the manufacturing cycle, where the residual stresses caused at the end of one step are carried over to the next one [27].

Furthermore, after analyzing the stresses during the welding and lamination process with the modification of the use of lifting pins, it was found that the stresses on the rear surface of the cells were 80% higher than those on the front surfaces, and the critical moment was identified as the moment of pressure increase. Thinner cells were found to give rise to lower cell stresses than wider cells [28].

By analyzing residual stresses, but taking into account material properties and thermal cycling using the finite element method, it can be determined how the maximum residual stress occurs during the encapsulant curing cycle of the lamination process [24]. Using the same method, but in the study of microcracks, it is determined that the most critical cells are located near the weld region [29].

However, as it has been shown in the background, there are certain factors that cause the aging of the complete module, for example, a temperature increase of 30° causes a decrease of up to 1.23% in the module [30]. The literature consulted shows different alternatives in this regard, on the one hand the use of water as a cooling agent which can improve the efficiency of the panel by 3% [31]. Another option suggests the use of phase change material compositions, which can be solid-liquid, solid-gas, solid-solid, and liquid-gas, reducing the temperature up to 10.29 ° C [32, 33].

Among the options evaluated in relation to temperature, there is the placement of fins to disperse the heat, thus improving the photothermal conversion efficiency by 61.08% [34], or the passive photovoltaic cooling tower approach, which cools the air from 50 °C to 30 °C, improving the average annual efficiency of the photovoltaic panels by 6.83% [35]. Another system consists of jute fabric cooling applied to the back of the panel, reducing the average temperature by 18 °C and increasing the electrical efficiency by 10.31% [36].

Regarding humidity, the literature shows that it plays a synergistic role with UV rays in relation to the formation of surface cracks in the backsheets [37]. An important aspect within the humidity tests are the water vapor infiltrations in the photovoltaic modules, especially in the polymer components (backsheet and encapsulation materials), the influence of these infiltrations depends on the type of material used in the backsheet [38].

As mentioned above, the different types of degradation encountered and despite the tests indicated in the standards, make it very difficult to study them under real conditions, although there are models associated with such degradation that help to overcome the need for very long-term experiments to simulate real conditions [39].

With respect to mechanical tests, there are publications in which, through the analysis of the encapsulant discoloration rate and the study of UV stress tests at three simultaneous module temperatures and field climatic data, very similar results are obtained at different points [40]. Moreover, there are also studies that allow the development of an analytical model to simulate the effects of these mechanical tests [41].

With regard to LETID tests performed on bifacial modules in three different climates, the back of the module shows higher sensitivity than the front according to power measurements [14]. However, studies are located where changes to the IEC61215 standard are proposed, given that when these tests are performed at qualifying temperatures published in the 2016 version, LID and LELID reaction rates can give false results [42].

Finally, the tests that are performed on the photovoltaic module during the manufacturing process to obtain maximum performance of the panel, during the production stage are affected by environmental conditions that will influence the efficiency of the module. Among these environmental conditions is dust as a natural phenomenon that affects the module's performance in a negative way [43]. In order to obtain information on dirt, models based on Convolutional Neural Networks (CNN) have been developed for this purpose [44]. Dust is deposited on the module surface in the form of hidden, dry, or wet accumulation. It is understood as hidden accumulation, when the humidity in the fog, relative humidity or dew is on the surface of the module. Wind is one of the factors that can positively or negatively affect in the dust accumulation in the module depending on wind speed and direction [45]. A solution to reduce dust accumulation on the module is to install the modules at a greater angle of inclination due to the effect of gravity [46]. The presence of dust can reduce photovoltaic efficiency by 60% [47].

### 4.3 *Type of Cell*

Concerning the type of cell used, it is concluded that cut cells are more thermodynamically stable since they withstand less stress than full cells [48] and thus avoid the propagation of cracks and are more resistant to shading [49] improving their

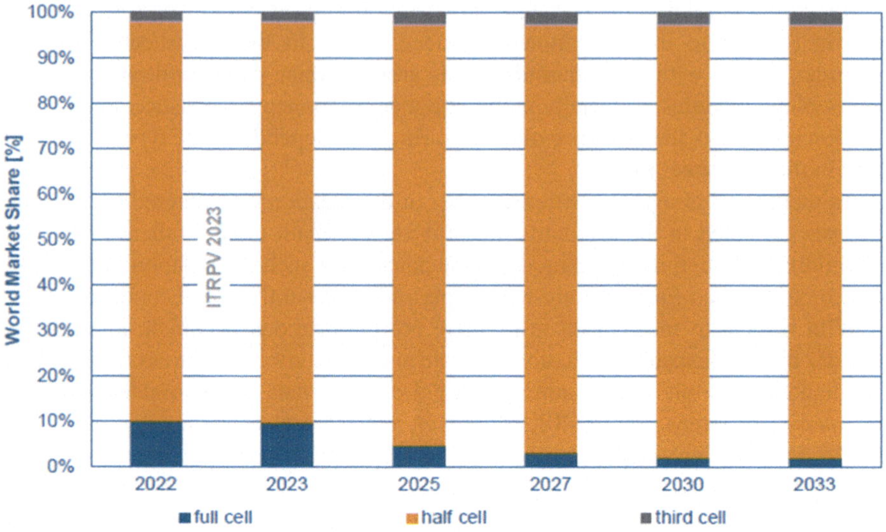


**Fig. 6** World market share of different cell sizes [50]

performance. Figure 6 shows the current market situation in relation to cell size differences.

Some authors are in favor of modifying the design of the modules by using multi-bar modules which, together with the use of round cables instead of rectangular tabs, reduces the contact between the metallization and the cell interconnections, thus reducing reflective losses [51].

## 4.4 New Technologies

The use of different technologies also offers opportunities for improvement, including Cadmium Telluride (CdTe) thin film panels deposited on a substrate, known for their good efficiency and low cost, Copper-Indium-Selenium (CIS) and Copper-Indium-Gallium-Selenium (CIGS), which use these semiconductor composite materials with high efficiency potential, and Amorphous Silicon (a-Si), which are less efficient than crystalline silicon panels, but offer advantages in terms of flexibility and special applications [52, 53].

Another emerging technology is perovskite solar cells, named after the crystalline material from which they are made, promising high efficiency and reduced costs. They are in a state of development and the advantages are attracting research attention [54]. Also among the advanced crystalline silicon technologies, there are advances such as bifacial silicon cells, where sunlight can be captured from both sides [55], Fig. 7 shows the bifacial cell in world market, or Passivated Emitter Rear

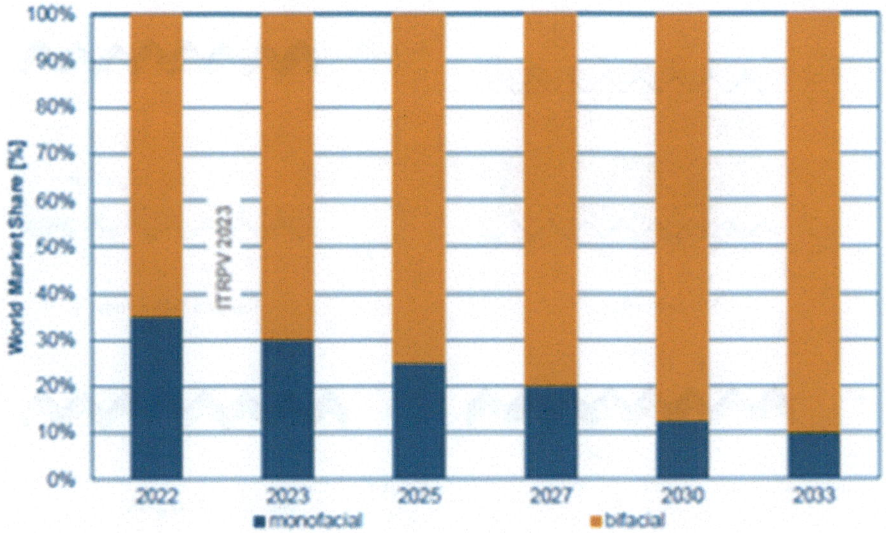


**Fig. 7** Bifacial cell in world market

Cell (PERC) solar cells, where the electrical contacts are at the rear, thus improving their efficiency [56].

Back Surface field (BSF) technology that introduces a layer highly doped with diffused aluminum on the back side of the wafer so that it changed from a flat n+/p diffused phosphorous bond to an n+/p/p + structure. The screen-printed aluminium and thermal alloying are used to obtain an Al back-surface field (Al-BSF) that can reduce the effective recombination rate of the back surface. The efficiency obtained is 6 to about 22% [57]. And the so-called "industrial tunnel oxide passivated contacts" (i-TOPCon) in which the structure, the wafer is not in contact with the metal, but tunnel oxide is deposited, and a layer of poly Si strongly doped with n or p comes into contact with the metal. The efficiency of this structure is 25.8% in the lab and about 24.5% in production [58]. Finally, Silicon heterojunction technology (SHJ) represents a very important efficiency, however, its production depends on rare materials such as indium and silver paste. Recent research proposes using tin oxide as an alternative material (SnOx), resulting in an efficiency of 24.91%. Currently, the rear cell (PERC) is the main technology for monocrystalline silicon solar cells due to its high efficiency and low process cost [59, 60]. Figure 8 shows the technologies mentioned.

Cracks in a photovoltaic panel will cause energy loss. To avoid this loss of energy during the manufacturing process, this section analyzes the different stresses caused during the cooking, welding, and lamination process of the photovoltaic module. Greater attention should be paid to the surface stresses on the back of each cell, these being 80% higher than those on the front, as well as the residual stresses induced near the welding region [29]. Another aspect to consider is the reduction of the module temperature which will lead to greater efficiency as well as the accumulation

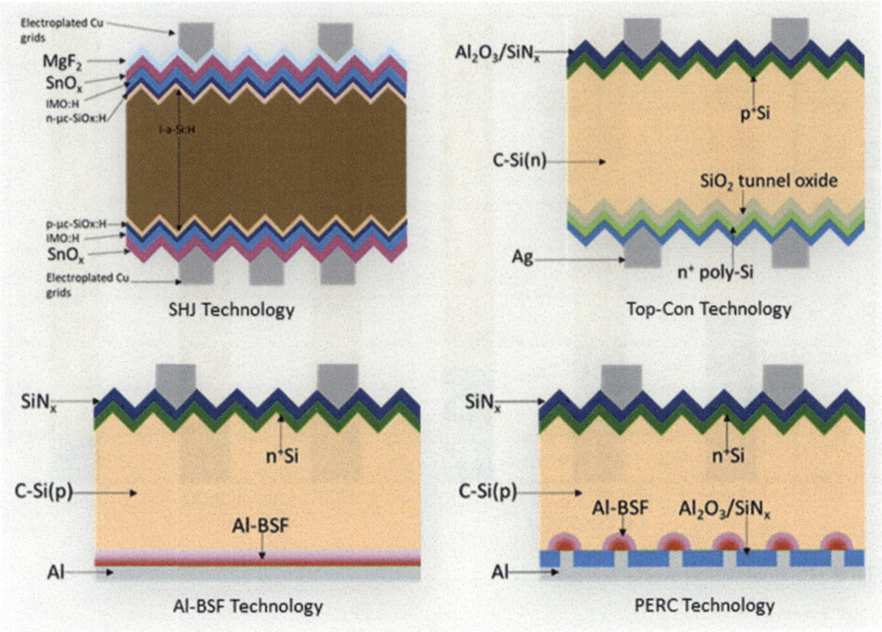


**Fig. 8** Emerging technologies

of dust. Regarding the type of cells, cut cells are more thermodynamically stable since they support less stress than complete cells [48], being also more resistant to shading [49].

## 5 Conclusion

The performance of PV modules in the field is a key factor in PV installations to ensure reliability, quality, and financing. The solar PV industry is growing exponentially in recent years potentially driven by the principles of Industry 5.0 in which companies can improve production efficiency, reduce their environmental impact, and move towards a more sustainable and profitable manufacturing model.

Thus, it is also necessary to study the stress conditions to which photovoltaic modules are subjected during the manufacturing process and to analyze the advantages and disadvantages of the different photovoltaic cell technologies. This raises a key point: How can an improvement in photovoltaic modules be improved and demonstrated? How can cracks be reduced during the manufacturing process?

To answer these questions, the tests defined in the IEC 61215 standard are followed; however, there is no correlation between the tests performed indoors and the conditions in the field.

The different parts in which a photovoltaic panel is formed are analyzed and the importance of choosing the metal contacts in the cells that will give rise to a uniform distribution of the current and reduce losses.

This study analyzes the different stresses to which silicon solar cells are subjected during the manufacturing process, reaching different conclusions. During the lamination process, tensions caused by temperature variation are created, finding that these can be eliminated by modifying the rigidity of the encapsulant.

Furthermore, the stresses on the rear surface of the cells are 80% higher than that of the front cells. The most critical cells are identified as those closest to the welding region.

Once in the field, the photovoltaic modules are affected by different factors such as the increase in temperature, where an increase of 30° decreases the efficiency of the photovoltaic module by 1.23%; different authors provide a solution to this problem. Another factor is dust, reducing the panel's efficiency by 60%. Different alternatives are analyzed to reduce the accumulation of dust in the module.

Different technologies are analyzed that offer improvements in the performance of the photovoltaic module.

95% of the PV market is covered by c-Si technology and 5% is thin film. Within c-Si technology, i-TOPCon is expected to grow by 60% over the next few years and SHJ by 25% over the next 10 years. However, BSF is expected to be eliminated by 2023 and PERC is expected to decrease by 10% in the next few years. However, due to its low process cost and high efficiency, PERC technology is currently the most used technology.

The advantages in the use of bifacial cells were analyzed, where the current market share is 70% and is expected to be 90% in the next 10 years.

Considering the points analyzed as a basis, strategies can be designed to improve the useful life of photovoltaic systems and extend their useful life.

However, it would be interesting to extend as lines of future research regarding the thickness of the interconnections because an increase of the thickness at the front interconnections of the PV module leads to an increase of the stresses at the back side of the cells. However, the narrower interconnection leads to increased cracking and fracture of the cells [23].

In addition, and based on the study using two types of soft and stiff materials to test the stresses produced during the lamination process [22], it would be important to go deeper to find a material that causes less stresses, resulting in higher feasibility of solar PV.

## References


1. Madrid Vicente, A. (2009). *Energía solar térmica y de concentración: Manual práctico de diseño, instalación y mantenimiento*. 1ª. (A. E. Madrid Vicente, Ed.). INO Reproducciones.
2. Fritts, C. E. (1883). New form of selenium cell. *American Journal of Science, 26*(156), 465–472.

3. Energy Institute. (2023). Statista. World ranking of countries with the largest installed solar PV capacity as of 2022 (in megawatts). https://es-statista-com.bibliouca.idm.oclc.org/estadisticas/641225/potencia-solar-fotovoltaica-instalada-por-paises/
4. Organización Mundial de las Naciones Unidas. (2023). Informe de los Objetivos de Desarrollo Sostenible. Plan de rescate para las personas y el planeta, pp. 1–80. https://unstats.un.org/sdgs/report/2023/The-Sustainable-Development-Goals-Report-2023_Spanish.pdf?_gl=1*arkxzk*_ga*MTc3ODI5OTYwMS4xNjE4MzU3NTMz*_ga_TK9BQL5X7Z*MTY5NDkwMzM3OS4xLjEuMTY5NDkwMzU1OS4wLjAuMA
5. Vinod, K. R., & Singh, S. K. (2018). Solar photovoltaic modeling and simulation: As a renewable energy solution. *Energy Reports, 4*, 701–712. https://doi.org/10.1016/j.egyr.2018.09.008
6. Helwig, N. E., Hong, S., & Hsiao-Wecksler, E. T. (2022). Photovoltaic power systems programme.
7. Red Eléctrica. (2023). Balance eléctrico Gwh del sistema electrico nacional. España. https://www.ree.es/es/datos/balance/balance-electrico
8. Hajiahmadi, F., Dehghani, M., Zarafshan, P., Moosavian, S. A. A., & Hassan-Beygi, S. R. (2023). Initial analysis and development of an automated maintenance system for Agrivoltaics plants. *Agricultural Engineering International: CIGR Journal, 25*(3), 130–145.
9. Abdallah, F. S. M., Abdullah, M. N., Musirin, I., & Elshamy, A. M. (2023). Intelligent solar panel monitoring system and shading detection using artificial neural networks. *Energy Reports, 9*, 324–334. https://doi.org/10.1016/j.egyr.2023.05.163
10. Cancelliere, P., Liciotti, C., Cardinali, M., & Puccia, V. (2014). Analysis of the combustion fumes and gases released during the burning of some C-Si PV modules. *29th Eur Photovolt sol energy Conf Exhib* (pp. 2259–2266). https://www.eupvsec-proceedings.com/proceedings?paper=27582
11. Fermín, R. J. (2019). De la arena a la oblea de silicio, *14*, 57–64. https://www.researchgate.net/publication/333421859_De_la_arena_a_la_oblea_de_silicio
12. Dintcheva, N. T., Morici, E., & Colletti, C. (2023). Encapsulant materials and their adoption in photovoltaic modules: A brief review. *Sustainability, 15*(12), 1–13. https://doi.org/10.20944/preprints202304.1165.v1
13. Runkle, L. D., & Dumas, L. N. (1980). Progress in the performance of terrestrial solar cell modules. In *Proceedings of the 1980 annual meeting of the American section of the international solar energy society* (pp. 1109–1113). Phoenix.
14. Gebhardt, P., Mülhöfer, G., Roth, A., & Philipp, D. (2021). Statistical analysis of 12 years of standardized accelerated aging in photovoltaic-module certification tests. *Progress in Photovoltaics: Research and Applications, 29*(12), 1252–1261. https://doi.org/10.1002/pip.3450
15. Barkhouse, D. A. R., Gunawan, O., Gokmen, T., Todorov, T. K., & Mitzi, D. B. (2015). Yield predictions for photovoltaic power plants: Empirical validation, recent advances and remaining uncertainties. *Progress in Photovoltaics: Research and Applications, 20*(1), 6–11. https://doi.org/10.1002/pip.1160
16. Eddine, D. (2021). Evaluation of the effect of backsheet properties on PV encapsulant degradation under ultraviolet-damp-heat conditions Djamel Eddine MANSOUR.
17. Niewelt, T., Schon, J., Warta, W., Glunz, S. W., & Schubert, M. C. (2017). Degradation of crystalline silicon due to boron-oxygen defects. *IEEE Journal of Photovoltaics, 7*(1), 383–398. https://doi.org/10.1109/jphotov.2016.2614119
18. da Assunção Moutinho, J., Fernandes, G., & Rabechini, R. (2024). Evaluation in design science: A framework to support project studies in the context of university research Centres. *Evaluation and Program Planning, 102*, 102366. https://doi.org/10.1016/j.evalprogplan.2023.102366
19. Popovich, V. A., van Maris, M. P. F. H. L., Janssen, M., Bennett, I. J., & Richardson, I. M. (2013). Understanding the properties of silicon solar cells aluminium contact layers and its effect on mechanical stability. *Materials Sciences and Applications, 04*(02), 118–127. https://doi.org/10.4236/msa.2013.42013

20. Sander, M., Dietrich, S., Pander, M., Ebert, M., Karra, B. M., Lippmann, R., et al. (2013). Influence of manufacturing processes and subsequent weathering on the occurrence of cell cracks in PV modules. *28th European Photovoltaic Solar Energy Conference and Exhibition, 53*(9), 1689–1699.
21. Schulte-Huxel, H., Blankemeyer, S., Bock, R., Merkle, A., Kajari-Schröder, S., & Brendel, R. (2012). Aging behaviour of laser welded Al-interconnections in crystalline silicon modules. *Solar Energy Materials and Solar Cells, 106*, 22–26. https://doi.org/10.1016/j.solmat.2012.06.021
22. Rengarajan, K. N., Radchenko, I., Illya, G., Handara, V., Kunz, M., Tamura, N., & Budiman, A. S. (2016). Low stress encapsulants? Influence of encapsulation materials on stress and fracture of thin silicon solar cells as revealed by synchrotron X-ray submicron diffraction. *Procedia Engineering, 139*, 76–86. https://doi.org/10.1016/j.proeng.2015.09.230
23. Song, W. J. R., Tippabhotla, S. K., Tay, A. A. O., & Budiman, A. S. (2018). Effect of interconnect geometry on the evolution of stresses in a solar photovoltaic laminate during and after lamination. *Solar Energy Materials and Solar Cells, 187*, 241–258. https://doi.org/10.1016/j.solmat.2018.07.026
24. Mathusuthanan, M., Narayanan, K. R., & Jayabal, K. (2021). In-plane residual stress map for solar PV module: A unified approach accounting the manufacturing process. *IEEE Journal of Photovoltaics, 11*(1), 150–157. https://doi.org/10.1109/jphotov.2020.3029226
25. Ridhuan, S. W. M., Tippabhotla, S. K., Tay, A. A. O., & Budiman, A. S. (2019). A simulation study of the stresses in crystalline silicon photovoltaic laminates during the soldering and lamination processes along the longitudinal direction. *Advanced Engineering Materials, 21*(5), 1800986. https://doi.org/10.1002/adem.201800986
26. Kraemer, F., Seib, J., Peter, E., & Wiese, S. (2014). Mechanical stress analysis in photovoltaic cells during the string-ribbon interconnection process. *15th Int Conf Therm Mech Multi-Physics Simul Exp Microelectron Microsystems, EuroSimE.*
27. Eitner, U., Kajari-Schröder, S., Köntges, M., & Brendel, R. (2010, September). Non-linear mechanical properties of ethylene-vinyl acetate (Eva) and its relevance to thermomechanics of photovoltaic modules. *The international photovoltaic science and engineering conference (PVSEC)* (pp. 4366–4368).
28. Song, W. J. R., Tippabhotla, S. K., Tay, A. A. O., & Budiman, A. S. (2018). Numerical simulation of the evolution of stress in solar cells during the entire manufacturing cycle of a conventional silicon wafer based photovoltaic laminate. *IEEE Journal of Photovoltaics, 8*(1), 210–217. https://doi.org/10.1109/jphotov.2017.2775158
29. Mathusuthanan, M., Gembali, M., Narayanan, K. R., & Jayabal, K. (2021). Analysis of micro-cracks evolution in silicon cell during entire solar photovoltaic module manufacturing process. *Solar Energy, 224*(June), 1160–1169. https://doi.org/10.1016/j.solener.2021.06.075
30. Idzkowski, A., Walendziuk, W., & Borawski, W. (2015). Analysis of the temperature impact on the performance of photovoltaic panel. In *Photonics applications in astronomy, communications, industry, and high-energy physics experiments 2015* (p. 96620J). https://doi.org/10.1117/12.2205241
31. Bin Wan Abdullah, W. A. F., Ping, C. S., Binti Radzuan, R. N., & Binti Mokhtar, A. S. N. (2021). The improvement on the efficiency of photovoltaic module using water cooling. In *IOP Conference Series: Earth and Environmental Science* (Vol. 721, No. 1).
32. Govindasamy, D., & Kumar, A. (2023). Effect of composite phase-change materials on improving the efficiency of solar photovoltaic panels. *Heat and Mass Transfer, 59*(10), 1949–1970. https://doi.org/10.1007/s00231-023-03366-8
33. Govindasamy, D., & Kumar, A. (2023). Experimental analysis of solar panel efficiency improvement with composite phase change materials. *Renewable Energy, 212*, 175–184. https://doi.org/10.1016/j.renene.2023.05.028
34. Zhao, Z., Zhu, L., Wang, Y., Huang, Q., & Sun, Y. (2023). Experimental investigation of the performance of an air type photovoltaic thermal collector system with fixed cooling fins. *Energy Reports, 9*, 93–100. https://doi.org/10.1016/j.egyr.2023.02.059

35. Abdelsalam, E., Alnawafah, H., Almomani, F., Mousa, A., Jamjoum, M., & Alkasrawi, M. (2023). Efficiency improvement of photovoltaic panels: A novel integration approach with cooling tower. *Energies, 16*(3), 1070. https://doi.org/10.3390/en16031070
36. Bhakre, S. S., Sawarkar, P. D., & Kalamkar, V. R. (2023). Evaporative cooling of photovoltaic panels in dry and hot climatic conditions. *Energy Sources, Part A: Recovery, Utilization, and Environmental Effects, 45*(4), 11259–11277. https://doi.org/10.1080/15567036.2023.2256687
37. Lin, C. C., Lyu, Y., Jacobs, D. S., Kim, J. H., Wan, K. T., Hunston, D. L., & Gu, X. (2019). A novel test method for quantifying cracking propensity of photovoltaic backsheets after ultraviolet exposure. *Progress in Photovoltaics: Research and Applications, 27*(1), 44–54. https://doi.org/10.1002/pip.3038
38. Mansour, D. E., Barretta, C., Bauermann, L. P., Oreski, G., Schueler, A., Philipp, D., & Gebhardt, P. (2020). Effect of backsheet properties on PV encapsulant degradation during combined accelerated aging tests. *Sustainability, 12*(12), 1–13. https://doi.org/10.3390/su12125208
39. Ndiaye, A., Charki, A., Kobi, A., Kébé, C. M. F., Ndiaye, P. A., & Sambou, V. (2013). Degradations of silicon photovoltaic modules: A literature review. *Solar Energy, 96*, 140–151. https://doi.org/10.1016/j.solener.2013.07.005
40. Sinha, A., Gopalakrishna, H., Bala Subramaniyan, A., Jain, D., Oh, J., Jordan, D., & TamizhMani, G. (2020). Prediction of climate-specific degradation rate for photovoltaic encapsulant discoloration. *IEEE Journal of Photovoltaics, 10*(4), 1093–1101. https://doi.org/10.1109/jphotov.2020.2989182
41. Hsu, S. T., & Wu, T. C. (2017). Simulated wind action on photovoltaic module by non-uniform dynamic mechanical load and mean extended wind load. *Energy Procedia, 130*, 94–101. https://doi.org/10.1016/j.egypro.2017.09.401
42. Repins, I. L., Kersten, F., Hallam, B., VanSant, K., & Koentopp, M. B. (2020). Stabilization of light-induced effects in Si modules for IEC 61215 design qualification. *Solar Energy, 208*, 894–904. https://doi.org/10.1016/j.solener.2020.08.025
43. Gholami, A., Saboonchi, A., & Alemrajabi, A. A. (2017). Experimental study of factors affecting dust accumulation and their effects on the transmission coefficient of glass for solar applications. *Renewable Energy, 112*, 466–473. https://doi.org/10.1016/j.renene.2017.05.050
44. Mehta, S., Azad, A. P., Chemmengath, S. A., Raykar, V., & Kalyanaraman, S. (2018). DeepSolarEye: Power loss prediction and weakly supervised soiling localization via fully convolutional networks for solar panels. In *Proc – 2018 IEEE Winter Conf Appl Comput Vision, WACV 2018* (pp. 333–342). IEEE. https://doi.org/10.1109/wacv.2018.00043
45. Adinoyi, M. J., & Said, S. A. M. (2013). Effect of dust accumulation on the power outputs of solar photovoltaic modules. *Renewable Energy, 60*, 633–636. https://doi.org/10.1016/j.renene.2013.06.014
46. Mekhilef, S., Saidur, R., & Kamalisarvestani, M. (2012). Effect of dust, humidity and air velocity on efficiency of photovoltaic cells. *Renewable and Sustainable Energy Reviews, 16*(5), 2920–2925. https://doi.org/10.1016/j.rser.2012.02.012
47. Asl-Soleimani, E., Farhangi, S., & Zabihi, M. S. (2001). The effect of tilt angle, air pollution on performance of photovoltaic systems in Tehran. *Renewable Energy, 24*(3–4), 459–468. https://doi.org/10.1016/s0960-1481(01)00029-5
48. Waqar Akram, M., Li, G., Jin, Y., Zhu, C., Javaid, A., Zuhaib Akram, M., & Khan, M. U. (2020). Study of manufacturing and hotspot formation in cut cell and full cell PV modules. *Solar Energy, 203*, 247–259. https://doi.org/10.1016/j.solener.2020.04.052
49. Papargyri, L., Papanastasiou, P., & Georghiou, G. E. (2022). Effect of materials and design on PV cracking under mechanical loading. *Renewable Energy, 199*, 433–444. https://doi.org/10.1016/j.renene.2022.09.009
50. ITPRV. (2022, March). International technology roadmap for photovoltaic (13th ed.), 53. https://itrpv.vdma.org/en/ueber-uns

51. Walter, J., Tranitz, M., Volk, M., Ebert, C., & Eitner, U. (2014). Multi-wire interconnection of busbar-free solar cells. *Energy Procedia, 55*, 380–388. https://doi.org/10.1016/j.egypro.2014.08.109
52. Madrid Vicente, A. (2009). *Curso de Energía Solar (fotovoltaica, Térmica y Termoeléctrica).* 1ª (A. E. Madrid Vicente, Ed.). INO REPRODUCCIONES.
53. Budea, S., & Safta, C. A. (2021). Review on modern photovoltaic panels – Technologies and performances. In *IOP Conference Series: Earth and Environmental Science* (Vol. 664, No. 1). https://doi.org/10.1088/1755-1315/664/1/012032.
54. Ramírez, D., & Jaramillo, F. (2021). Design of two-dimensional perovskite solar cells with superior efficiency and stability. *Revista Facultad de Ingeniería Universidad de Antioquia, 100*, 67–74. https://doi.org/10.17533/udea.redin.20210424
55. Libal, J., & Kopecek, R. (2018). *Bifacial photovoltaics: Technology, applications and economics.* Institution of Engineering and Technology.
56. Urdiroz, U., Itoiz, I., Sevilla, J., & Andueza, A. (2023). Combining radiative cooling and light trapping strategies for improved performance of PERC bifacial silicon solar cells. *Energy Reports, 10*, 1116–1125. https://doi.org/10.1016/j.egyr.2023.07.047
57. Verlinden, P., Young, D. L., Xiong, G., Reese, M. O., Mansfield, L. M., Powalla, M., et al. (2023). Photovoltaic device innovation for a solar future. *Device, 1*(1), 100013. https://doi.org/10.1016/j.device.2023.100013
58. Chen, D., Chen, Y., Wang, Z., Gong, J., Liu, C., Zou, Y., et al. (2020). 24.58% total area efficiency of screen-printed, large area industrial silicon solar cells with the tunnel oxide passivated contacts (i-TOPCon) design. *Solar Energy Materials and Solar Cells, 206*, 1–8. https://doi.org/10.1016/j.solmat.2019.110258
59. Catchpole, K. R., & Blakers, A. W. (2002). Modelling the PERC structure for industrial quality silicon. *Solar Energy Materials and Solar Cells, 73*(2), 189–202. https://doi.org/10.1016/s0927-0248(01)00124-6
60. Hsu, C. H., Wu, J. R., Lu, Y. T., Flood, D. J., Barron, A. R., & Chen, L. C. (2014). Fabrication and characteristics of black silicon for solar cell applications: An overview. *Materials Science in Semiconductor Processing, 25*, 2–17. https://doi.org/10.1016/j.mssp.2014.02.005

# Digital Twin Prototype Structure of Value, Demand and Supply Chain Management

**Alexey Tyapukhin, Andrey Yumatov, and Raisa Vidishcheva**

**Abstract** The article aims to substantiate the structure of a digital twin prototype, including the subject and objects of chain management, and to create methodological prerequisites for their digitalization. The research methodology includes the determination of qualitative attributes and dichotomies of the subject and objects of chain management, as well as the creation and study of binary matrices, which make it possible to clarify the structure of the digital twin prototype. The novelty of the research results lies in the differentiation of the competencies of the subject and objects of chain management, the determination of their components and relations, the use of a matrix approach to the transformation and digitalization of the subject and objects, as well as the justification of the possibility of using artificial intelligence in the management of non-physical objects of chain management. The results of the research make it possible to clarify the requirements for creating instances of the subject and management objects, as well as the digital twin aggregate for managing value, demand and supply chains in the implementation of the Industry 5.0 concept.

**Keywords** Digital twin · Prototype · Management subject · Non-physical management object · Management system · Chain

## 1 Introduction

Digitalization is a trend that has affected all areas of human activity [1]. However, while the results of digitalization have been impressive in some areas, such as engineering and technology, they have been more modest in others. These areas include the management of value [2], demand [3], and supply [4] chains (hereafter referred to as chain management). Solving this problem is hindered by: first, a significant number and variety of objects: enterprises [5], relationships [6], processes

A. Tyapukhin (✉) · A. Yumatov · R. Vidishcheva
Orenburg Branch of the Russian Presidential Academy of National Economy and Public Administration, Orenburg, Russian Federation



A. Appolloni et al. (eds.), *The Future of Industry*, Lecture Notes in Information Systems and Organisation 70, https://doi.org/10.1007/978-3-031-66801-2_19

[7], and flows [8] in their various combinations; second, the need for their constant adaptation to environmental factors; third, the lack of scales and tool measurements of non-physical subjects and objects of chain management; fourth, the limited computer processing capabilities of subjects and objects; fifth, the unique delimitation of powers of management decision makers and their interaction in the management system, including goals, objectives, principles, approaches, methods, and functions [9]; and, sixth, the orientation of the performer of works related to the digitalization of chain management to the subject and the management system of this subject. In other words, before developing an instance or an aggregate of a digital twin of chain management, as well as the external environment [10], it is advisable for the customer to create the digital twin prototype and, based on it, a technical assignment for the performer.

Taking into account the above aspects will make it possible to clarify and supplement the methodology of designing digital twins not only of chains but also of subjects and management systems of these chains that do not belong to the group of physical subjects and objects. The purpose of this article is to clarify the requirements for the digital twin prototype of chain management, as well as the interrelations of the subject and objects of management in the process of their digitalization. The objectives of the research are to substantiate a matrix approach to structuring and digitalization of subjects and objects of chain management; to study the features of digital twins of non-physical object management in business; to develop recommendations for creating the structure of the digital twin prototype of value, demand and supply chain management, as well as to clarify the technical assignment for its design. The article is presented in the following order: substantiation of the problem and the choice of research methodology; study of options for the subject and objects of chain management and the nature of their interaction; and the development of a sequence for creating a digital twin prototype of chain management.

## 2 Literature Review

Digital twins are increasingly being used in areas where the objects are physical objects. Regarding the digital twin of a logistics system [11], the following results can be obtained: first, this system includes a subject (who or what manages?) and an object (who or what is being managed?) of management, each of which consists of components, elements, and relations; second, the digital twin for managing non-physical objects contains real and virtual research objects, as well as horizontal and vertical, forward and backward connections between them [12]; third, the following types of digital twins are distinguished: prototype (DTP), instance (DTI), and aggregate (DTA), which operate in the digital environment (DTE) [9]; fourth, the DTP involves the design, analysis, and use of a specific research object [13]; fifth, the DTP requires unambiguous measurement of this object [14], creation of copies and virtual models corresponding to its real counterpart [15]; sixth, the DTP of non-physical objects must meet the requirements of the customer [16, 17];

and seventh, the DTP assumes regular, mass, and accurate measurements of the object research [18].

Thus, for the successful digitalization of chain management, it is necessary to take into account the specific features of non-physical objects of research; organize effective human (user) interaction with a computer; periodically update information that allows artificial intelligence to understand user actions and to achieve its goals; create specific software capable of developing management decisions with minimal loss of profits [19].

## 3 Methods

Since the subjects and objects of value, demand and supply chain management are mostly non-physical objects, a methodology of qualitative research should be chosen as a priority, which involves determining classification attributes and dichotomies relevant to a specific management situation, choosing their rational combinations, building binary matrices [20], making it possible to obtain “2” variants of these subjects and objects, where the digit “2” reflects the number of dichotomies, and x is the number of classification attributes of the subject and the object of management. These attributes and dichotomies are substantiated by analyzing literary sources and sociological surveys of specialists in the field of chain management. A feature of binary matrices is the possibility of moving from one subject, object, or component to another subject, object, or component and studying them when changing one or another of their attributes and/or dichotomies. This feature forms the basis for designing algorithms used by the software and contributing to the development of rational management decisions by the digital twin.

## 4 Results

To clarify the structure of the digital twin prototype of chain management as an aggregate consisting of a subject and objects of management, it is necessary to develop a classification of its options. To solve this problem, it is advisable to use the following qualitative attributes: “the subject of commodity-money relations”: the customer, symbol “0”, and the performer, symbol “1”, and “the function of creating a digital twin”: identification, symbol “0”, and modeling the object (subject) of management, symbol “1”. The joint use of these attributes and dichotomies makes it possible to identify four main options of subject and objects: a real object (subject), code “00”, its prototype, code “01”, the prototype of the digital twin of the object (subject) of management, code “10”, as well as their instances and aggregate, code “11” (Fig. 1).

Thus, prototypes of the subject and object of management, as well as the external environment, represent lists of actual quantitative parameters and qualitative

| Subject of relationships | Function of creating a digital twin: Identification of the object (subject) of management (0) | Function of creating a digital twin: Modeling the object (subject) of management (1) |
|---|---|---|
| Customer (0) | Real object (subject) of management (01) | Management object (subject) prototype (01) |
| Performer (1) | Digital twin prototype of the object (subject) of management (10) | Digital twin instance (aggregate) of the object (subject) of management (11) |

**Fig. 1** Classification of options of subject and object of management in the process of their digitalization

characteristics that make it possible to identify them and to choose the closest standard for each of them, the structure and content of which, if necessary, can be refined through additional parameters and characteristics. In turn, prototypes of digital twins of the subject and objects of management, as well as the external environment, represent options of prototypes that take into account their possible states after digitization. This aspect of the study is presented in more detail in Fig. 2.

This figure allows one to assert, first, that the prototype of the external environment is transformed into a prototype of its digital twin. This prototype provides for possible trends and forecasts of changes in the external environment, and also assumes the digitization of their options in manual or machine modes; second, the prototype of the subject and objects of chain management is the basis for creating their digital twins in the case of threats and opportunities predetermined by the external environment, determining the weaknesses and strengths of the subject and objects of management, as well as the digitization of their components and elements; third, prototypes of digital twins of the subject, objects, and environmental factors, as a rule, are created by the customer of instances and aggregates of the digital twin, primarily by persons performing strategic planning functions, and are necessary, on the one hand, to understand the situations in which the subject and objects of management are and will be located, and, on the other hand, for the execution of a technical assignment to the performer of instances and an aggregate of the digital twin, capable of using information products and technologies efficiently, operating with uniquely characterized components and elements of the subject and objects; fourth, the performer for the creation of instances and an aggregate of the digital twin of chain management, among other things, must understand the structure and relations of the subject, objects, and environmental factors, possess methods and technologies for their research, have the necessary information about the experience previously gained by the subject of management, and be able to identify reserves and potentials of management objects; fifth, in order to create the digital twin of chain management, the customer and performer must take into account risks, put forward ideas, design options for the subject and objects, calculate alternatives, use models and develop scenarios of behavior, create projects, and justify chain management strategies; and, sixth, the digital twin aggregate of chain management formed in this

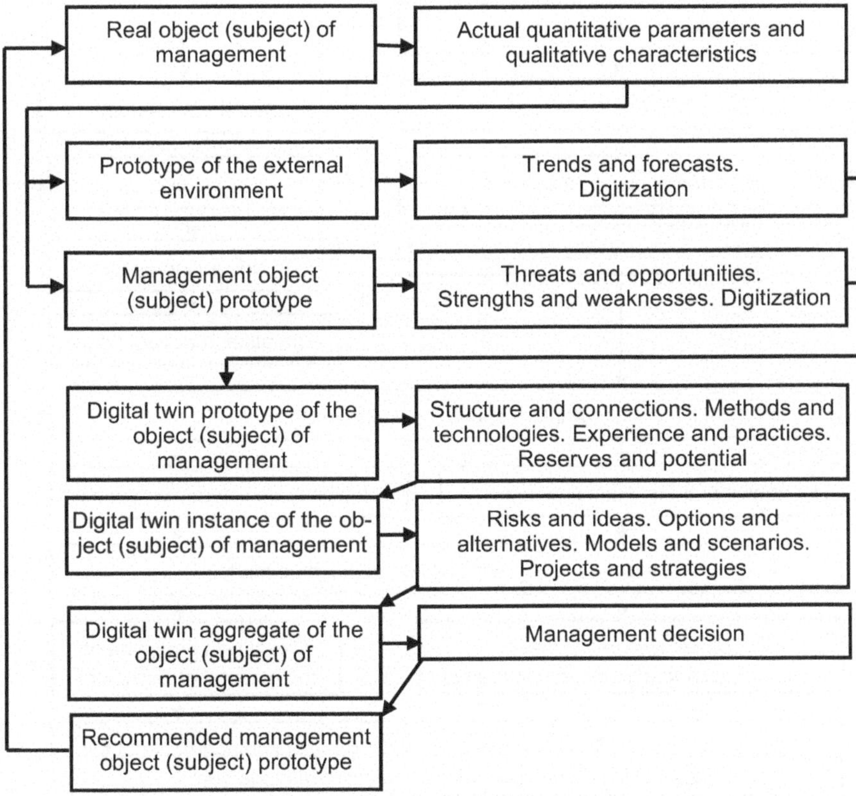


**Fig. 2** Process of transforming the options of the subject and objects of management

way should create prerequisites for the development of decisions that take into account possible decisions of the customer's competitors, their further structuring by levels of the management subject, delegation of authority, and establishment of responsibility up to those who create value for the end consumers of products and services.

The information in Fig. 2 makes it possible to draw the following conclusions (Fig. 3).

First, the creation of the digital twin of chain management requires the joint participation of the customer and the performer (software developer); second, the functions of the customer include monitoring and researching the external and internal environment of management facilities; identifying threats and opportunities; creating databases that include attributes, metrics, and standards of the subject, objects, and the external environment; development of their prototypes; execution of technical assignments for the design (application) of instances of the digital twin of the subject and objects of management and their timely correction; third, the functions of the performer of digital twin include the creation of instances and an aggregate, their periodic adjustment, as well as bringing to the attention of the

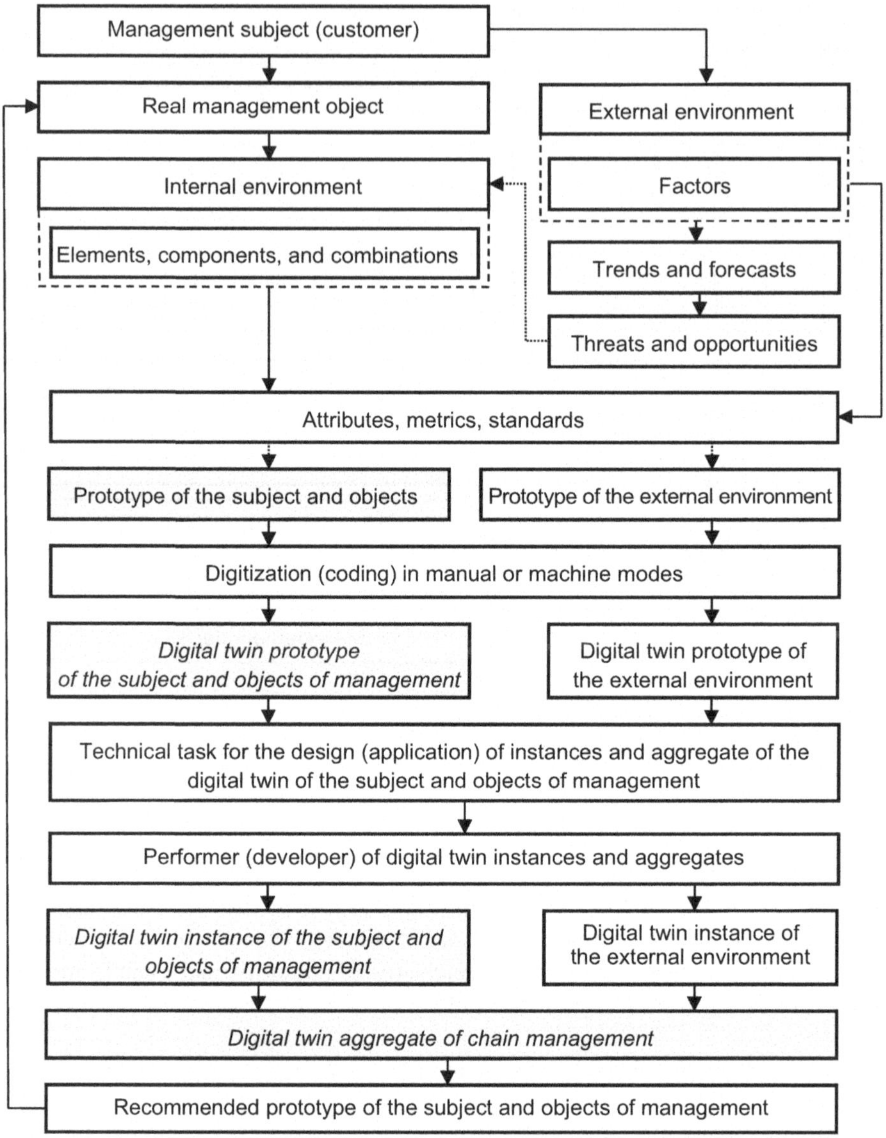


**Fig. 3** Refined process of transforming the options of the subject and objects of management

customer information about new technologies and software products that can improve the quality of management decisions made by the subject; and, fourth, the results obtained using the digital twin of chain management include options and the structure of the prototypes of the subject, objects, and external environment; their standards; as well as the decisions made, which can later be used in the study of new management situations.

**Table 1** Characteristic features of the digital twin prototype of chain management

| Classification attributes | | | |
|---|---|---|---|
| Time | Goal (mission) | Resources | Characteristic features of the digital twin prototype of the management subject and objects |
| 0 | 0 | 0 | Uncertainty |
| 0 | 0 | 1 | Uniqueness |
| 0 | 1 | 0 | Preventativenes |
| 0 | 1 | 1 | Instability |
| 1 | 0 | 0 | Responsiveness |
| 1 | 0 | 1 | Adaptability (dominance) |
| 1 | 1 | 0 | Innovativeness |
| 1 | 1 | 1 | Complexity |

An important aspect of this research is the substantiation of the characteristic features of the digital twin prototype of chain management, which are derived from the characteristic features of the external environment. The solution to this problem is presented in Table 1.

As follows from this Table, the qualitative attributes characterizing a specific situation are its duration: is taken into account, symbol "0", and is not taken into account, symbol "1"; the goal (mission): is taken into account, symbol "0", is not taken into account, symbol "1"; and the availability of resources: is taken into account, symbol "0", and is not taken into account, symbol "1". The joint use of these attributes and dichotomies makes it possible to substantiate the following characteristic features of the digital twin of the subject and objects of management: uncertainty, code "000", uniqueness, code "001", preventativeness, code "010", instability, code "011", responsiveness, code "100", adaptability or dominance, code "101", innovativeness, code "110", and complexity, code "111". Taking into account these features increases the efficiency of using the digital twin of chain management due to timely adjustments of its structure and content, including the identification of actual qualitative attributes and dichotomies of the subject, objects, and environmental factors of chain links of various types.

As was shown earlier, the objects of chain management include enterprises, relationships, processes, and flows, each of which involves the identification and study of the structure, not only at the level of the chain link but also at the level of the business channel, which includes two links: the consumer C, its supplier S and their corresponding management systems. The solution to this problem is shown in Fig. 4.

The basis for the formation of a business channel of the chain is the order of the consumer enterprise Cc of the consumer C. This order involves the involvement of the supplier S. In this case, as a rule, the sequence of several components characterizing a particular management object of the supplier enterprise is taken into account. Such components (not to be confused with chain management components: value, demand, and supply) are:

(a) For the enterprise-supplier S: its specialization; the potential for fulfilling the order (demands) of the consumer C; the utilization of the production capacity of

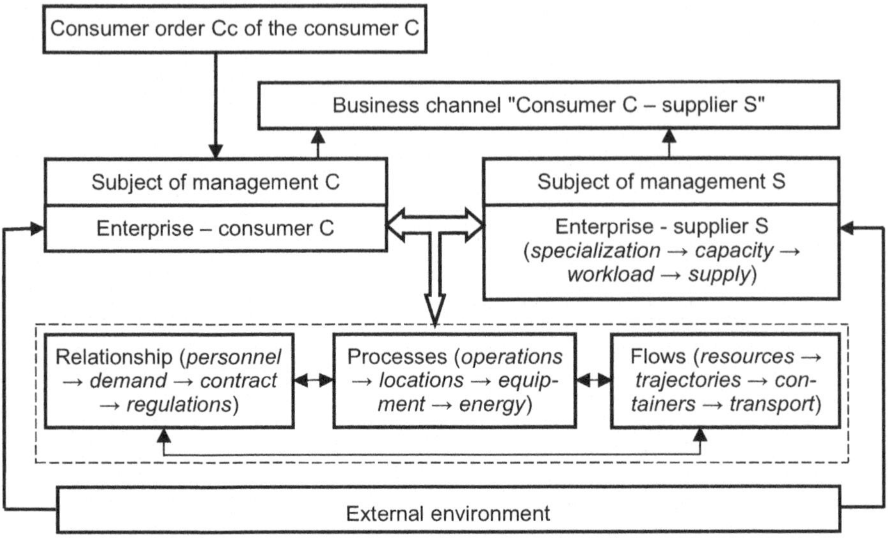


**Fig. 4** Components of business channel management objects

this enterprise and the compliance with the terms of delivery of the necessary consumer products and/or services;

(b) For relationships: the competence of the personnel of the enterprises C and S; the content of the consumer's requirement C; the specifics of the contract and regulations between these enterprises;

(c) For processes: the structure and content of operations performed by the supplier S; the locations of machines, equipment, warehouses, etc.; the quantitative parameters and qualitative characteristics of machines, equipment, warehouses, etc.; as well as the types of used energy; and.

(d) For flows: the totality of material, information, financial, and human resources; the trajectories of their movement; containers and transport.

The sequence of using components and, accordingly, prototypes of objects and components of the C—S business channel management is shown in Fig. 5, the features of which are: coordinated personnel management of the enterprises C and S; correspondence of the quantitative parameters and qualitative characteristics of the desired and actual deliveries; the possibility of not only sequential but also parallel impact on the components of management objects; ensuring a rational combination of these components and synchronization when using them. This sequence lays the foundation for creating the digital twin prototype of the business channel and then the digital twin prototype of an "n"-link chain, sequentially formed starting from the end consumer of products and/or services and ending with the initial supplier of resources.

Since the digital twin of chain management provides for making managerial decisions concerning not only objects but also the subject of management, when

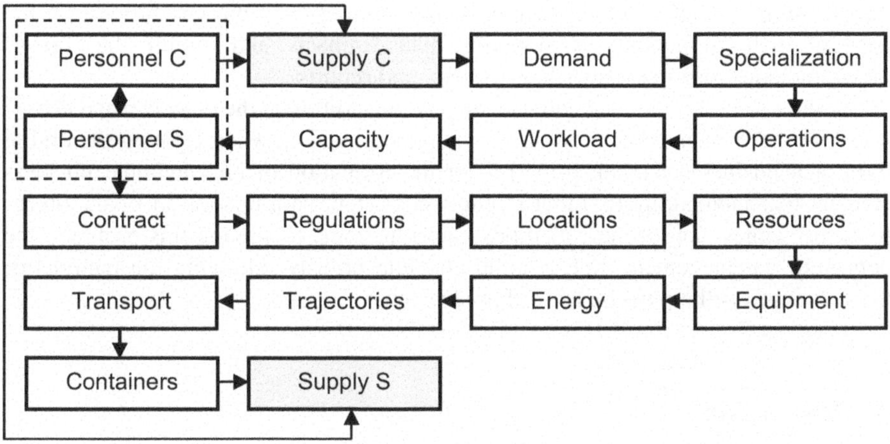


**Fig. 5** Sequence of using components and prototypes of C—S business channel management components

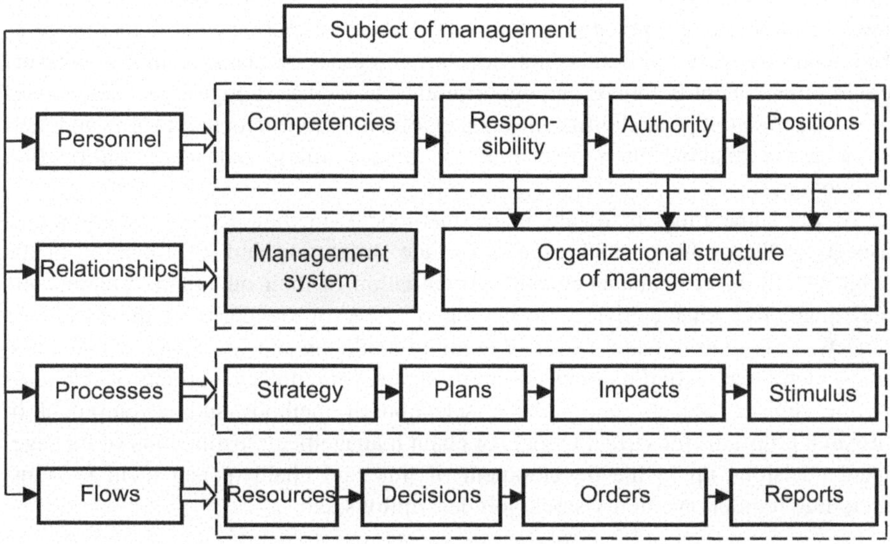


**Fig. 6** Components of the business channel management subject

creating it, it is necessary to take into account the components that also form a certain sequence. The solution to this problem is shown in Fig. 6.

As can be seen from the content of this figure, the formation of the structure of the management subject is also based on a typical set of objects with a few exceptions: instead of the "enterprise" object, the "personnel" object is used, the components of which are: its competencies, as well as responsibilities, authority, and positions. In turn, the "relationships" object extends to the management system, including the organizational structure of management; the "processes" object is formed on the basis of such components as strategies, plans, impacts, and stimuli; the "flows" object includes resources, decisions, orders, and reports.

As shown earlier, the management subject, in addition to the objects listed above, focuses on the "management system" component, which, when creating the digital twin of a business channel, provides for the formation of an integrated business channel management system that requires consistent coordination of goals, objectives, principles, approaches, methods, and functions. In solving this problem, the consumer's management system is an absolute priority. Studying the patterns of these changes is the purpose of further research.

## 5 Discussion

The problem of creating a digital twin is not just chain (values, demands, and supplies), namely chain management is extremely difficult [21], but it is quite solvable. To do this, it is necessary to identify the subject and objects of management, as well as environmental factors; clarify their structure, including components and relations; identify trends and develop forecasts of changes in the external environment, identify threats and opportunities, as well as strengths and weaknesses of management objects; digitize the subject, objects, environmental factors and their components, making them available for programming and using information technologies.

At the same time, there are many theoretical, methodological, and practical aspects of the problem. Such aspects include structuring and identification of the subject and object of management; substantiation of their quantitative parameters and qualitative characteristics; formation of a set of standards of these subject, objects, and environmental factors that allow modeling specific management situations; identification of directions for clarifying the structure and variants of standards of the subject, objects, and factors; selection of methods and development of research programs for virtual models of chain management; justification of management decisions up to the development of link and chain management systems, including regulations on divisions, job descriptions, etc.

## 6 Conclusion

The results obtained in this article create prerequisites for clarifying the essence and content of the digital twin of chain management of the type "consumer value – subject of management – management system – chain in statics – chain in dynamics – external environment". The creation of digital twins of this type is fully in line with the goals and objectives of the well-known Industry 5.0 concept, focused on effective user interaction with a computer that perceives and processes information in different ways, which is insufficiently taken into account when improving the theory and methodology of value, demand, and supply chain management.

In further research, it is planned to clarify the criteria for the effectiveness of the subject and the chain management system, to develop a classification of their components and elements, to justify the basic options of the subject and the management system with their subsequent digitization in manual mode, and to develop recommendations for the performer on their use to create a digital twin of various types of chain management.

## References


1. Aamer, A., Sahara, C. R., & Al-Awlaqi, M. A. (2023). Digitalization of the supply chain: Transformation factors. *Journal of Science and Technology Policy Management, 14*(4), 713–733. https://doi.org/10.1108/JSTPM-01-2021-0001
2. Porter, M. E. (1985). *Competitive strategy: Techniques for analyzing industries and competitors*. The Free Press.
3. Selen, W., & Soliman, F. (2002). Operations in today's demand chain management framework. *Journal of Operation Management., 20*, 667–673. https://doi.org/10.1016/S0272-6963(02)00032-3
4. Coyle, J. J., Langley, C. J., Novack, R. A., & Gibson, B. J. (2013). *Supply chain management: A logistics perspective*. South-Western Cengage Learning.
5. Oliver, R. K., & Weber, M. D. (1982). Supply-chain management: Logistics catches up with a strategy. In M. L. Christopher (Ed.), *Logistics: The strategic issues* (pp. 63–75). Chapman & Hall. https://doi.org/10.1007/978-3-642-27922-5_15
6. Christopher, M. (2011). *Logistics & Supply Chain Management* (4th ed.). Pearson Education Limited.
7. Wisner, J., Tan, K. C., & Leong, G. K. (2012). *Principles of supply chain management: A balanced approach* (3rd ed.). South-Western Cengage Learning.
8. Blackhurst, J., Cantor, D., & O'Donnell, M. (2012). *Sustainable supply chains: A guide for small – To medium-sized manufacturers*. Retrieved September 13, 2023, from https://www.hbs.edu/faculty/conferences/2015-strategy-research/Documents/Sustainable%20Supply%20Chains.pdf
9. Tyapukhin, A. P. (2022). A systematic approach to substantiating chain management structures in businesses. In W. D. Nelson (Ed.), *Advances in business and management, 20* (pp. 167–191). Nova Science Publishers, Inc. https://doi.org/10.52305/NGNY3123
10. Grieves, M., & Vickers, J. (2017). Digital twin: Mitigating unpredictable, undesirable emergent behavior in complex systems. In F.-J. Kahlen, S. Flumerfelt, & A. Alves (Eds.), *Transdisciplinary perspectives on complex systems: New findings and approaches* (pp. 85–113). Springer.
11. Busse, A., Gerlach, B., Lengeling, J. C., Poschmann, P., Werner, J., & Zarnitz, S. (2021). Towards digital twins of multimodal supply chains. *Logistics, 5*(25), 1–12. https://doi.org/10.3390/logistics5020025
12. Srai, J. S., Settanni, E., Tsolakis, N., & Aulakh, P. K. (2019). Supply chain digital twins: Opportunities and challenges beyond the hype, *23rd Cambridge International Manufacturing Symposium University of Cambridge*, 26–27 September 2019, 1–6.
13. Kim, Y. -W., Yoo, S., Lee, H., Kim, S. H., & Han, S. (2020). Characterization of digital twin, Research Gate. Retrieved September 13, 2023, from https://www.researchgate.net/publication/353930234_Characterization_of_Digital_Twin/link/634d4d466e0d367d91a5ca68/download

14. Söderberg, R., Wärmefjord, K., Carlson, J. S., & Lindkvist, L. (2017). Toward a digital twin for real-time geometry assurance in individualized production. *CIRP Annals, 66*(1), 137–140.
15. Tao, F., & Zhang, M. (2017). Digital twin shop-floor: A new shop-floor paradigm towards smart manufacturing. *IEEE Access, 5*, 20418–20427.
16. Wang, Z. (2020). Digital twin technology. In *Industry 4.0-impact on intelligent logistics and manufacturing*; London, UK, Intech Open. Retrieved September 13, 2023, from https://www.researchgate.net/publication/340055758_Digital_Twin_Technology. https://doi.org/10.5772/intechopen.80974.
17. Gerlach, B., Zarnitz, S., Nitsche, B., & Straube, F. (2021). Digital supply chain twins—Conceptual clarification, use cases and benefits. *Logistics, 5*(86), 1–24. https://doi.org/10.3390/logistics5040086
18. Parrott, A., & Warshaw, L. (2017). Industry 4.0 and the digital twin manufacturing meets its match. Retrieved September 13, 2023, from https://www2.deloitte.com/content/dam/Deloitte/kr/Documents/insights/deloitte-newsletter/2017/26_201706/kr_insights_deloitte-newsletter-26_report_02_en.pdf
19. Fawcett, S. E., Magnan, G. M., & McCarter, M. W. (2008). Benefits, barriers, and bridges to effective supply chain management. *Supply Chain Management, 13*(1), 35–48. https://doi.org/10.1108/13598540810850300
20. Bailey, K. D. (1994). *Typologies and taxonomies: An introduction to classification techniques*. Sage Publications, Inc.
21. Hendriksen, C. (2023). Artificial intelligence for supply chain management: Disruptive innovation or innovative disruption? *Journal of Supply Chain Management, 59*(3), 65–76. https://doi.org/10.1111/jscm.12304

# Green Warehouse 5.0

**Bernardo Nicoletti and Andrea Appolloni**

**Abstract** The traditional focus of sustainable logistics has been on transportation issues such as energy intensity, carbon footprint and supply chain sustainability. In this chapter, the focus shifts to digital transformation and the impact of warehousing on resources, the environment and the supply chain. From an environmental perspective, Warehousing 5.0 means integrating environmentally friendly practices into warehouse operations, primarily to reduce energy consumption, costs and greenhouse gas emissions. Initially, companies are focusing on energy resources and their use, including lighting systems, temperature control and specialized material handling equipment, and later increasingly on using advanced technologies. This chapter attempts to provide a comprehensive framework for resource-efficient and environmentally friendly warehousing practices in sustainable supply chains. By examining industry insights and analyzing real-world examples, the aim is to create a novel framework that uses Artificial Intelligence (AI) algorithms to support the potential of Warehousing 5.0. First, this chapter explores the fundamental concepts and theories of sustainability and green warehouses, highlighting their importance in the evolving business landscape and the key drivers for digital transformation. In particular, the chapter focuses on the use of artificial intelligence to facilitate the transition to green warehouses. The chapter develops an integrated framework for the use of artificial intelligence in warehouses 5.0. The final section of the chapter draws on interviews with stakeholders to examine the Italian warehousing industry, tracing its recent evolution and highlighting new trends and practices within the sector.

**Keywords** Warehouse · Artificial intelligence · Industry 5.0 · Sustainability · Supply chain innovation

B. Nicoletti (✉)
Temple University Rome, Rome, Italy

A. Appolloni
Department of Management and Law, University of Rome Tor Vergata, Rome, Italy

Department of Management, Minzu University of China, Beijing, China
e-mail: andrea.appolloni@uniroma2.it

 
A. Appolloni et al. (eds.), *The Future of Industry*, Lecture Notes in Information Systems and Organisation 70, https://doi.org/10.1007/978-3-031-66801-2_20

# 1 Introduction

Warehousing 5.0 means integrating environmentally friendly practices into warehouse operations, primarily to reduce energy consumption, costs and greenhouse gas emissions [1]. Initially, companies are focusing on energy resources and their use, including lighting systems, temperature control and specialized material handling equipment [2], and later increasingly on using advanced technologies [3].

A study by Oloruntobi et al. [4] has uncovered a surprising fact: manufacturing, logistics and warehousing together contribute to a whopping 23% of total greenhouse gas emissions in the US. This figure is echoed on a global scale: the World Economic Forum 2016 [5] reports that transportation and logistics alone are responsible for 13% of global emissions, with logistics facilities themselves accounting for a significant 11% [6].

While sustainable logistics research has traditionally focused on transportation and its impact on energy consumption, carbon footprint and overall supply chain sustainability [7], the environmental impact of warehousing remains largely unexplored. This knowledge gap raises a crucial question: How is it possible to effectively minimize the environmental impact of warehouses and, more importantly, how can innovative solutions such as artificial intelligence help to make warehouses more environmentally friendly?

This question is particularly relevant given the Industry 5.0 approach. Industry 5.0 is based on three factors: human-centricity, sustainability and resilience. The transformative technology that underpins it is artificial intelligence [8]. This chapter dives deep into the world of Warehousing 5.0 and explores the challenges facing Industry 5.0, best practices for implementation and exciting future directions for logistics functions related to warehousing, including the concept of achieving net zero emissions in warehousing [9].

Warehousing 5.0 means integrating and implementing environmentally friendly practices in a warehouse to minimize resource consumption, operational costs and greenhouse gas emissions [10]. Companies are beginning their journey to Warehousing 5.0 from an environmental perspective by focusing on energy optimization and considering lighting systems, temperature control and even dedicated material handling equipment. Building warehouses 5.0 from the ground up is a clear sign of a company's commitment to protecting the environment. By incorporating green considerations into the initial design phase, environmental concerns are taken into account from the outset [11].

This chapter looks at the specific actions required to adopt and maintain environmentally friendly warehousing practices, with a focus on how artificial intelligence algorithms can be used to achieve this goal. It begins with a general overview of sustainable warehouses before moving on to look at the specific measures influencing Warehousing 5.0 within green supply chains. The innovative application of artificial intelligence is at the center of the discussion. Finally, the chapter provides a detailed analysis of the state of warehousing in Italy and examines the various practices that have been introduced in the sector in recent years.

## 2 Literature Review

Warehouses and pollution go hand in hand. Building materials and processes used to construct and operate them release emissions. Daily operations emit greenhouse gasses and pollutants from equipment such as forklifts [3, 12–14]. Companies need to take a close look at their environmental footprint across all logistics stages to reduce these impacts [15, 16].

Reducing energy consumption in warehouses has become a top priority in recent years [17]. It is a crucial part of any Warehousing 5.0 strategy, and there are various methods to achieve this goal [1]. Researchers have investigated how picking methods, storage strategies and even the equipment used can impact energy consumption [18, 19].

The studies by Iancu and Moga [20] focused on the environmental impact of warehouse building materials. They found that warehouses built predominantly from concrete had the worst sustainability over their entire life cycle (construction and operation). This suggests that the use of environmentally friendly building materials significantly improves the environmental performance of a building [21].

Although there is no excellent traditional method for optimizing the energy consumption of warehouses, most studies emphasize the importance of efficient warehouse design [22]. This includes analyzing aspects such as lighting, ventilation, cooling and heating [23]. Energy-saving technologies such as temperature control systems and LED lighting can significantly reduce energy consumption [24]. Optimizing warehouse layout, picking methods and material handling equipment are other areas where improvements can be made.

Lighting is one of the most controllable aspects of warehouse operations and has an impact on energy consumption, costs and emissions [24]. Studies show that warehouses can significantly improve their energy efficiency by using LED lighting with intelligent control systems that adapt to occupancy and natural light [2, 25]. It is important that employees are comfortable with the temperature, but lowering the target temperature within a reasonable range can significantly reduce energy consumption [24, 26].

Creating a warehouse 5.0 requires a comprehensive approach [26]. This solution includes efficient energy use, a broader sustainability perspective and measures to address external environmental impacts. Optimizing energy consumption is the first step [27].

The choice between electric and LPG-powered forklifts is an example of a specific decision in Warehousing 5.0. Although LPG-powered forklifts may appear more energy efficient due to their lower $CO_2$ emissions per operating cycle, electric forklifts have a lower overall carbon footprint [2, 18]. Which option is the most environmentally friendly ultimately depends on the activity in each situation.

Picking, i.e. the removal of products for orders, is another area where efficiency improvements can benefit both operations and the environment. By optimizing picking routes and storage strategies, forklift truck travel distances are shortened and energy consumption is minimized [28]. The layout and design of aisles in a warehouse also play a crucial role. When these elements are strategically planned and aligned with the chosen materials management strategy, they have a significant impact on the company's energy and environmental performance.

Life cycle assessment (LCA) is a valuable tool for evaluating the environmental impact of warehouses throughout their life cycle [29]. Although LCA is not widely used in the logistics sector, it can help in analyzing the environmental impact of warehouse construction [20, 21]. Although the implementation of LCA for logistics systems can be complex, it enables comparisons between different scenarios [30].

Research on the application of artificial intelligence (AI) to warehousing 5.0 practices is still limited. Studies suggest that AI has the potential to further optimize warehouse operations and improve resource efficiency. For example, AI can be used to optimize warehouse layout and design, picking routes and storage strategies, resulting in lower energy consumption and reduced environmental impact. In addition, AI-powered warehouse solutions such as mobile robots and predictive maintenance can improve operational efficiency and reduce waste [31, 32].

Warehousing 5.0 is important to minimize the environmental impact of logistics processes and contribute to a more sustainable future. Therefore, it is crucial to explore the potential of AI in warehousing 5.0 and develop new frameworks for research trends in this area Azian and Yudi [31].

## 3 Methodology

This study looks at the current state and future prospects of green storage in Italy. To gain a comprehensive understanding, a three-pronged approach was adopted: a thorough literature review, in-depth interviews with carefully selected stakeholders and the definition of a framework for the use of artificial intelligence solutions.

The literature review provided a wealth of viewpoints that encompassed different perspectives and experiences within the industry. Following the literature review, the interviews complemented this analysis by providing valuable insights and exploring potential solutions to existing challenges. The interviews were mainly conducted face-to-face in the second half of 2023. The interviewed stakeholders responsible for or involved in warehouse management came from Italian logistics companies of different sizes and from domestic subsidiaries of large international companies.

After identifying critical potential actions, the authors developed a groundbreaking framework. This framework utilizes artificial intelligence algorithms to support these critical solutions, which encompass both the design and operation of Warehouse 5.0. This multi-layered approach has led to a nuanced understanding of the challenges facing the industry. The result is that academics are given a solid foundation for further investigation, while practitioners are equipped with an AI toolkit to pave the way to a greener future in Warehouse 5.0.

# 4 Factors Supporting Warehousing 5.0

The concept of a warehouse 5.0 goes beyond minimizing the environmental impact of internal operations. It also encompasses the entire life cycle of the facility itself, from construction to ongoing expansion [33]. Energy efficiency is a key aspect, but building warehouses with a sustainable mindset is equally important. Below is an overview of some key strategies and certifications that can help companies achieve this goal.

Sustainable warehouses favor renewable energy sources such as solar, wind, geothermal and biofuels to minimize emissions and achieve energy independence [34]. Options such as natural gas and biodiesel with a lower carbon footprint can also contribute. Choosing the optimal combination requires careful consideration of factors such as market conditions, costs and regulations.

Building features and architecture are increasingly being used as a means to achieve environmental goals [35]. In general, companies lack a long-term plan that links building operations to climate goals. To establish a baseline, companies should evaluate factors such as monthly energy consumption, equipment efficiency, and resulting carbon emissions. Continuous monitoring of the warehouse's environmental performance is essential. The final strategy should focus on reducing consumption and emissions, utilizing renewable resources whenever possible, and ensuring efficient building and operational practices.

Several non-mandatory certifications and programs provide incentives for companies to go beyond basic compliance and adopt green building practices [36]. These certifications evaluate factors such as recycled materials, construction processes, energy and water consumption, and resource management.

Two well-known rating systems, LEED (Leadership in Energy, and Environmental Design), and BREEAM (Building Research Establishment Environmental Assessment Method), assess the environmental performance of buildings [37, 38]. LEED uses a credit-based system that awards points for environmentally friendly measures in the development and operation of buildings. The increasing number of LEED registered and certified projects reflects the growing interest in sustainable warehouses [22].

LEED certification offers several benefits, including a positive environmental image and differentiation in the marketplace. Certification levels range from Platinum (highest level) to Certified (lowest level). By targeting specific levels, companies can prioritize their environmental initiatives. LEED-certified warehouses can identify opportunities for improvement, such as convenient location, minimizing paved areas or incorporating natural lighting, all of which help reduce the environmental footprint. The ultimate goal is to build net-zero buildings based on the generation or use of on-site renewable energy [39].

BREEAM, on the other hand, assesses building specifications, design and construction against performance criteria [40]. The standards cover areas such as energy, ecology, carbon emissions, sustainable design and biodiversity protection. Unlike LEED, BREEAM uses licensed assessors to verify compliance with the standards prior to accreditation. Quantitative methods are used rather than percentage thresholds.

Despite their differences, both certification systems have a significant impact on the market for warehouse properties [13, 41]. The market is increasingly prioritizing the minimization of operating costs and emissions over upfront investments and short-term leases, especially for new buildings.

The large space requirements and lengthy renovation cycles typical of the warehousing industry can hinder the implementation of sustainable practices [42]. The European Union (EU) emphasizes that most existing buildings are energy inefficient, rely on fossil fuels and use outdated technologies. To counteract this, the 2030 Climate Target Plan calls on organizations to reduce net greenhouse gas emissions in the EU by at least 55% compared to 1990 levels [42]. To achieve this goal, existing buildings must be made less carbon-intensive and more sustainable, as it is not enough to simply build new, environmentally friendly facilities. The current EU renovation rate of just 1% highlights the need for improvement [43]. Accreditation schemes that offer renovation certificates could incentivize owners to consider the environmental impact of existing buildings alongside new builds [44].

By implementing these strategies and certifications, companies in the warehousing industry can make significant progress towards a more sustainable future.

## 5 Artificial Intelligence Support

Artificial intelligence (AI) is changing the warehousing industry at a rapid pace Warehousing 5.0 is no exception [8, 45] AI applications in Warehousing 5.0 aim to achieve a dual objective: Minimizing environmental impact while maximizing efficiency and productivity (see Figs. 1 and 2 for the proposed framework). These applications can be broadly categorized based on their ideal implementation timeframes: Planning, Operations and Monitoring.

By using AI in the design, construction and operation of buildings, projects can achieve LEED certification, a globally recognized symbol of commitment to sustainable practices and resource efficiency [46]. AI contributes to the achievement of LEED points in various categories, e.g. energy and atmosphere (by optimizing energy and water efficiency), materials and resources (by selecting sustainable materials), indoor quality (by optimizing air quality), innovation in design (by optimizing sustainable design) [47].

AI plays a crucial role in optimizing energy efficiency, a key aspect for LEED certification. AI-powered building management systems reduce resource waste and costs, while AI-powered water management systems implement water-saving. Measures, detect leaks and optimize water consumption. Optimizing building design through AI-powered tools can further minimize resource consumption and environmental impact by creating layouts that prioritize efficiency, minimize energy waste and enable automated inventory tracking and management. All of these measures

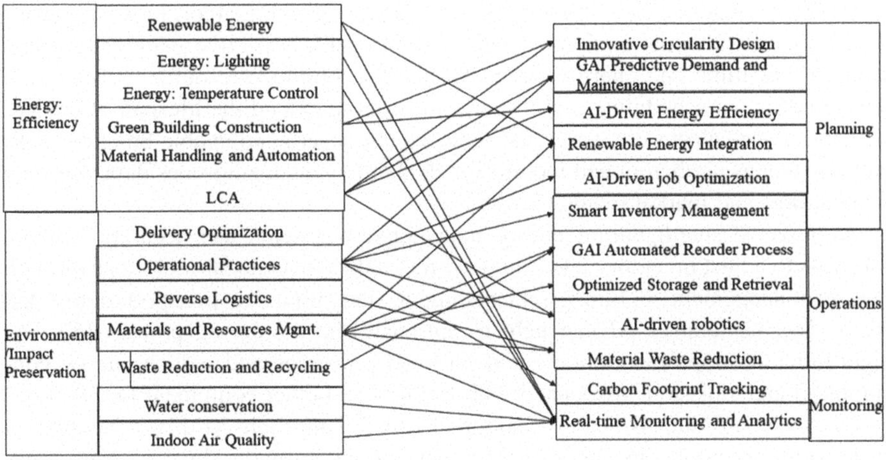


**Fig. 1** Green strategies at Warehouse sites and AI solutions

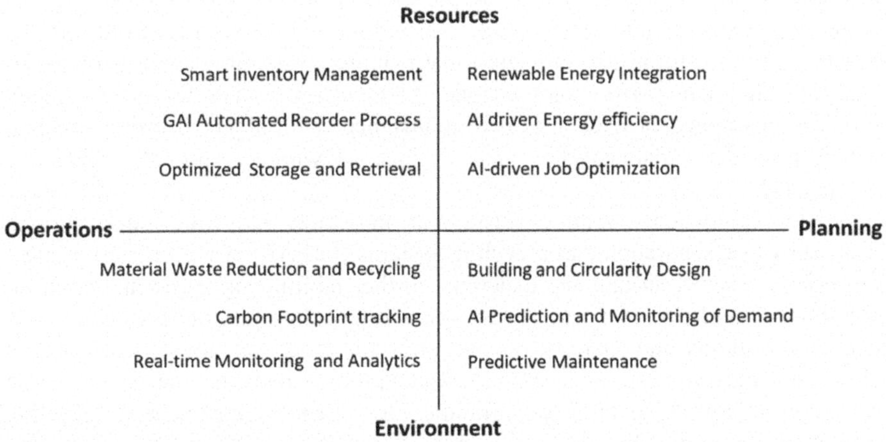


**Fig. 2** Framework of AI to support Warehouse 5.0

help to reduce manual errors and energy-intensive processes [48]. AI can also contribute to a more systemic circular economy in warehouse construction [49], integrate and manage hybrid renewable energy sources [50] and optimize workplace design [51].

AI is ideal for optimizing resource consumption, e.g. of energy or water, by analyzing consumption patterns and identifying areas for improvement. This can include controlling lighting, heating, cooling and refrigeration systems to minimize energy waste, optimizing energy and water consumption through efficient scheduling and resource allocation, and identifying opportunities to integrate renewable energy and store resources [52, 53].

Predictive maintenance through AI uses machine learning algorithms and sensor data to detect potential equipment failures and enable proactive maintenance that reduces downtime and energy waste. AI can also optimize resource consumption through efficient scheduling and resource allocation, extend the lifespan of devices (which reduces electronic waste and replacement costs), and enable broader applications such as predicting and monitoring demand by analyzing sales data, seasonal fluctuations, and market trends [54, 55].

AI-powered intelligent inventory management systems use accurate demand forecasts to adjust inventory levels in real time, reduce overstocks and waste through precise management, optimize replenishment, and minimize transportation emissions [56]. Generative AI can help to automate the reordering process [57]. AI algorithms also optimize storage and retrieval processes and reduce energy consumption and emissions associated with forklifts and other equipment [4, 58, 59].

AI can contribute to healthy indoor air quality through AI-driven ventilation systems and promote sustainable movement options through AI-driven transportation management systems that prioritize electric vehicles, forklifts, robotic systems, and alternative transportation methods [60]. AI algorithms can optimize putaway and retrieval processes by analyzing product demand and storage patterns to improve inventory placement and reduce energy consumption and emissions from forklifts and other equipment through efficient route planning. Real-time analysis of sensor data and equipment performance enables AI to identify areas for improvement, optimize operations, provide data-driven insights for strategic decision making, enable proactive maintenance, and reduce downtime through predictive analytics [61].

AI can significantly reduce waste and maximize recycling rates through AI-driven waste separation and recycling systems [62] AI-powered material selection tools can select sustainable materials, further minimizing waste and environmental impact. AI-powered waste reduction and recycling programs analyze waste generation patterns and identify opportunities for reduction, implement efficient sorting and recycling systems, monitor and optimize recycling rates, and waste prevention measures identify opportunities for waste reduction and recycling throughout the supply chain [63].

AI can provide real-time insights into warehouse operations and enable data-driven decisions to optimize efficiency and sustainability [64] and improve or automate manual activities [65]. Tracking the carbon footprint is particularly important [66].

## 6 Warehousing 5.0 in Italy

This section looks at the current state of Italian logistics, focusing on warehousing services and their link to environmentally friendly practices. This section focuses on Italian small and medium-sized enterprises (SMEs) that use sustainable warehousing solutions. Despite their dominance in the Italian market, SMEs have played a relatively minor role in the transition to green practices [67]. In this context, government intervention through regulation and support, alongside the concept of sustainable finance, appears to be crucial in promoting innovation in SMEs [68].

Bardi [69] provides a comprehensive examination of best practices and case studies that demonstrate the successful implementation of sustainable warehousing strategies in Italy. The book explores both the benefits and challenges of Warehousing 5.0 practices and emphasizes the importance of sustainable logistics and supply network management. This book is valuable for professionals, researchers and students who want to understand the future of sustainable warehousing in Italy.

Cavagnero [70] has written a detailed guide that provides an overview of sustainable logistics and warehousing in Italy and includes strategies and implementations for Warehousing 5.0. The author advocates the adoption of sustainable practices to reduce environmental impact and improve supply chain efficiency. This book is a useful resource for professionals and companies looking to adopt sustainable logistics and warehousing practices in Italy, covering topics such as green technology, renewable energy and sustainable transportation.

De Marco [71] examines the adoption of environmentally friendly warehousing practices in the Italian food industry and highlights the challenges and opportunities associated with sustainability. The author provides an in-depth analysis of the current state of sustainable warehousing in the food industry. He identifies the key drivers and barriers to implementation. The book includes detailed case studies showing the successful application of Warehousing 5.0 practices in different areas of the food industry. Recommendations are provided for policy makers, industry leaders and practitioners, outlining a roadmap for the adoption of sustainable warehousing practices in Italy.

Giannelli [72] presents a comprehensive approach for the implementation of Warehousing 5.0 and sustainable supply chain management in Italy. The author outlines a structured approach to introducing sustainable practices, covering topics such as green technology, renewable energy and sustainable transportation. It also presents case studies and best practices that demonstrate the successful implementation of Warehousing 5.0 and sustainable supply chain management strategies.

Ricciardi [73] provides an overview of green technologies and practices for sustainable warehousing in Italy, including case studies and best practices. The author examines the current state of sustainable warehousing and highlights the benefits and challenges associated with adopting green technologies and practices.

The current state of Italian companies with regard to Warehousing 5.0 is characterized by the following aspects [74, 75]. While interest in sustainable warehousing is increasing, there is a significant knowledge gap regarding the environmental performance of logistics centers. Few studies provide an in-depth analysis of the operational greenhouse gas emissions of these facilities.

In a first comparison, a benchmark for consumption and emission figures, broken down by characteristics of logistics centers, was established between Italy and Germany [76]. This comparison forms the basis for the definition of a set of relevant greenhouse gas emission indicators to assess the sustainability performance of

European logistics centers. This research builds on the GILA project (German-Italian-Latin American Consortium for Resource Efficient Logistics Centers and Transport), which is funded by the German Federal Ministry of Education and Research [77]. The logistics sector as a whole appears to have experienced growth after the pandemic, with warehousing services showing a particularly strong increase in 2022.

The Italian warehousing sector is showing a growing interest in environmentally friendly practices. A growing number of companies are introducing sustainable initiatives for their warehousing operations. The results of the Osservatorio Green Logistics Hub study show which measures are required, which practices are most commonly used and the extent to which companies in the manufacturing sector have made progress [78, 79].

The analysis of the Italian logistics and warehousing sector highlights the significant impact of global events on supply chains and the resulting challenges for companies.

This analysis looks at the factors influencing the adoption of green practices in Italian warehouses. National and European regulations play a central role, with environmental compliance playing an important role. Both consulting and construction companies as well as specialized 3PL warehousing companies confirm that customers are pushing for greener operations due to stricter regulations. Even small Italian companies confirmed this finding in the interviews.

Beyond regulations, a genuine interest in environmental and social responsibility motivates companies to adopt environmentally friendly practices. This is reflected in the offsetting efforts of various organizations, which resonate with their customers and generate additional customer inquiries. Large organizations in particular are increasingly striving for higher certifications and implementing sustainable measures that go beyond legal requirements.

Commonalities have emerged in the practices adopted by Italian warehouses. Initiatives on energy use and consumption, such as the installation of solar panels, the optimization of warehouse management and the use of sustainable packaging materials, are the most widespread strategies. These measures not only reduce environmental impact, but also lead to long-term cost savings and improved overall efficiency, also thanks to the support of AI-based control systems.

The interviews addressed the topic of green building certifications. The organizations in the sample confirmed that there has been a recent increase in demand for high-quality certifications that offer significant benefits for the development of the Warehousing 5.0 sector. These certifications provide specific, structured guidelines and protocols that establish common industry standards and improve comparability. Large companies use certifications, especially for new warehouse construction projects. However, smaller companies often lack the resources to invest in new facilities or advanced measures, which limits their role in this area. Nevertheless, the contribution of SMEs to the overall growth of Warehousing 5.0 in Italy should not be underestimated [80, 81].

The discussions have shown that Italy's current focus on Warehousing 5.0 prioritizes the development of new buildings. The renovation of existing warehouses and the use of brownfield sites, which could contribute significantly to environmental sustainability, remain largely unexplored [82]. The construction of warehouses on brownfield sites, i.e. abandoned or underutilized land, is in line with the principles of circular economy and sustainable land use. This approach preserves natural habitats and ecosystems while revitalizing previously polluted or abandoned areas. The use of brownfield sites can help the sector achieve a more comprehensive approach to environmental sustainability, which is particularly important given the growing demand for warehouse space and the development of the logistics industry.

Another interesting observation from the interviews concerns the profile of the organizations interviewed, with the exception of the small organizations. These organizations, which are all leaders in the green logistics industry, share a strong sense of responsibility towards their communities and the promotion of a green culture [83]. They help to promote a culture of sustainable logistics in Italy through various initiatives, such as research in the industry, collaboration with universities to reach students, development of projects with local associations to engage and add value to their communities. Their commitment also extends to relationships with their suppliers and subcontractors. They look for partners that adhere to green standards and align them with their vision to expand the green culture.

The interviews also highlighted the challenges that companies face when introducing Warehousing 5.0 processes. These challenges include the initial investment costs, dealing with complex regulatory requirements and ensuring a smooth transition from traditional to sustainable practices. Despite these obstacles, interviewees showed a strong commitment to continuous improvement.

The insights gained from the interviews underline the growing importance of Warehousing 5.0 in the Italian business landscape. By adopting environmentally friendly practices, companies can not only meet legal requirements and societal expectations, but also increase their competitiveness and contribute to a more sustainable future.

The results of the survey are consistent with those of [77], which examined four Italian companies that have implemented net-zero efforts in terms of Warehousing 5.0 solutions and emissions reduction. The cases showed significant emission reductions (between −3% and − 56%), depending on the facility and the solutions implemented. These results show that achieving net-zero logistics facilities requires a multi-dimensional approach where solutions are implemented in different strategic areas. Sustainable solutions can be implemented in existing buildings, not just new buildings. Flexibility and the ability to manage multiple energy sources is critical, with warehouses acting as "energy hubs" with self-generation and storage systems. A comprehensive view with strategic planning and advanced monitoring systems is essential for a successful transition to net-zero warehouses.

This analysis of the interviews provides valuable insights into Italy's current status and plans for green warehousing. It serves as a basis for further research and exploration. Continued knowledge sharing and collaboration between industry players is essential to drive the adoption of Warehousing 5.0 practices and promote a more sustainable logistics sector.

## 7 Extensions

This analysis looks at a model that uses artificial intelligence (AI) to support Warehousing 5.0 practices and provides an overview of the current state of this approach in Italy. While this research focuses on the role of AI in sustainability, future efforts could explore a holistic model that incorporates social, economic and management aspects of a fully sustainable warehouse. For example, examining the warehouse site through a social lens could provide valuable insight into community impact.

Another possible extension is to investigate a model for a fully automated warehouse, a trend that is particularly relevant for the storage of small to medium sized goods. This analysis would require a similar investigation of Robotic Process Automation (RPA) and Process Mining [84].

An interesting avenue for further research is the application of terotechnology to achieve net-zero storage [85, 86]. Terotechnology fits seamlessly into Warehousing 5.0 practices to minimize environmental impact and improve sustainability. This approach can include energy-efficient systems, optimized material handling and storage, reduced water consumption, waste reduction and recycling initiatives, optimized transportation, and logistically sustainable building design and maintenance. By adhering to the principles of terotechnology, Warehousing 5.0 can significantly reduce its environmental footprint, lower costs and achieve greater overall efficiency.

Examples of terotechnology applications include the installation of energy-efficient lighting, heating, ventilation and air conditioning (HVAC) systems and the use of renewable energy sources such as solar or wind power. In addition, efficient storage systems can minimize space and energy consumption, while environmentally friendly packaging materials can reduce packaging waste. Terotechnology offers a comprehensive range of strategies to improve the sustainability and environmental performance of warehouse operations.

## 8 Conclusion

This chapter deals with Warehousing 5.0 and its significant impact on the environment. Although warehouses contribute significantly to $CO_2$ emissions and energy consumption, many companies have not prioritized sustainability in this area. Recent research highlights the need for sustainable practices with a focus on environmental protection and resource utilization in Warehousing 5.0, thanks to the support of artificial intelligence.

The European Union is actively promoting sustainability in the supply chain and requires companies to adapt to evolving regulations in order to be successful in the long term. Building a warehouse 5.0 is all about energy efficiency, with improvements needed in lighting, ventilation, cooling and heating. In addition, optimized picking and storage strategies, order selection processes and material handling can significantly reduce emissions and costs.

The development of Warehouse 5.0 depends on sustainable design. To achieve sustainability, cycle time, costs and carbon footprint must be reduced throughout the entire life cycle—from the design phase onwards. Voluntary certifications such as LEED and BREEAM promote sustainable building practices and influence the warehouse real estate market. Renovation of existing buildings is also critical to achieving sustainability goals.

Several significant hurdles hinder the widespread adoption of AI for warehousing 5.0 [1, 3, 21] The high cost of implementation can be a major obstacle, especially for the many small and medium-sized enterprises (SMEs) that dominate the Italian warehouse landscape, for example. Many warehouses lack the robust data infrastructure required for AI, requiring retrofit investments. In addition, there is a potential skills gap due to limited expertise on AI and its application in logistics. Training programs may be necessary to ensure that operators can manage AI systems effectively. Integrating AI into existing warehouse management systems (WMS) can also be a challenge. Overcoming these challenges is crucial in many countries, such as Italy, to unlock the full potential of AI for Warehousing 5.0.

Appropriate strategies to engage SMEs in environmental policies and dedicated financial instruments can support the green transition [87]. Green finance can provide SMEs with access to funding for sustainable projects, expand market opportunities, improve brand image and increase their customer base. Further research is needed to analyze the barriers to full SME participation in green solutions across all industries, including logistics, in order to develop effective strategies.

Regardless of size or capabilities, every warehouse has the opportunity to become more sustainable with the help of numerous green initiatives—thanks to the support of artificial intelligence. Energy-efficient lighting, optimized storage and sustainable materials are all steps towards a Warehouse 5.0. This chapter highlights the importance of sustainable warehousing and encourages companies to use AI solutions to save resources such as water and energy, minimize environmental impact and contribute to a more sustainable future.

**Acknowledgements** The European Union funded this study - NextGenerationEU, in two projects: 1) the first project in the framework of the GRINS - Growing Resilient, Inclusive and Sustainable project (GRINS PE00000018 – CUP E83C22004690001); 2) the second project in the framework of the ECS 0000024 Rome Technopole – CUP B83C22002820006, NRP Mission 4 Component 2 Investment 1.5.

## References

1. Meixell, G. D., & Zartha, D. (2020). A review of green logistics practices: The drivers and barriers. *Transportation Research Part E: Logistics, Traffic and Transportation Planning, 142*, 101849.

2. Papinutto, M., Boghetti, R., Colombo, M., Basurto, C., Reutter, K., Lalanne, D., et al. (2022). Saving energy by maximising day-light and minimising the impact on occupants: An automatic lighting system approach. *Energy and Buildings, 268*, 112176. https://doi.org/10.1016/j.enbuild.2022.112176
3. Kamyabi, G. R., & Khoobfar, M. (2022). Green warehousing for sustainable supply chains: A critical review. *International Journal of Production Economics, 247*, 102339.
4. Oloruntobi, O., Mokhtar, K., Rozar, N. M., Gohari, A., Asif, S., & Chuah, L. F. (2023). Effective technologies and practices for reducing pollution in warehouses – A review. *Cleaner Engineering and Technology, 13*, 100622. https://doi.org/10.1016/j.clet.2023.100622
5. LEED. (2022, October). *Data trends from the past five years*. LEED.
6. Young Global Leaders. (2016). *World economic forum annual meeting 2016 mastering the fourth industrial revolution*. Weforum.org.
7. Herrmann, F. F., Barbosa-Povoa, A. P., Butturi, M. A., Marinelli, S., & Sellitto, M. A. (2021). Green supply chain management: Conceptual framework and models for analysis. *Sustainability, 13*(15), 8127. https://doi.org/10.3390/su13158127
8. Nicoletti, B. (2023). *Supply Network 5.0*. Springer International Publishing. https://doi.org/10.1007/978-3-031-22032-6_9.8
9. Perotti, S., & Dobers, K. (2023, June). Measuring environmental sustainability at logistics hubs: An international benchmark of greenhouse gas emissions. In *Proceedings of the Changeable, Agile, Reconfigurable and Virtual Production Conference and the World Mass Customization & Personalization Conference* (pp. 413–422). Springer International Publishing. https://doi.org/10.1007/978-3-031-34821-1_45
10. Valero-Gil, J., Rivera-Torres, P., & Garcés-Ayerbe, C. (2017). How is environmental proactivity accomplished? Drivers and barriers in organizations' pro-environmental change process. *Sustainability, 9*(8), 1327. https://doi.org/10.3390/su9081327
11. D'Angelo, V., Cappa, F., & Peruffo, E. (2022). Green manufacturing for sustainable development: The positive effects of green activities, green investments, and non-green products on economic performance. *Business Strategy and the Environment, 32*(4), 1–4. https://doi.org/10.1002/bse.3226
12. Balasubramanian, S., & Shukla, V. (2017). Green supply chain management: The case of the construction sector in The United Arab Emirates (UAE). *Production Planning & Control, 28*(14), 1116–1138. https://doi.org/10.1080/09537287.2017.1341651
13. Hashem, H. T., Jabbar, M. A., Sani, M. S., Rashid, A. F., & Abdullah, R. (2020). The role of green logistics practices in carbon dioxide emissions reduction: A review. *Journal of Cleaner Production, 273*, 122982.
14. Khan, S. A. R., Zhang, Y., & Nathaniel, S. (2020). Green supply chain performance and environmental sustainability: A panel study. *Log-Forum, 16*(1), 141–159. https://doi.org/10.17270/J.LOG.2020.394
15. Fichtinger, J., et al. (2015). Assessing the environmental impact of integrated inventory and warehouse management. *International Journal of Production Economics, 170*, 717–729. https://doi.org/10.1016/j.ijpe.2015.06.025
16. McKinnon, A., Browne, M., Whiteing, A., & Piecyk, M. (Eds.). (2015). *Green logistics: Improving the environmental sustainability of logistics*. Kogan Page Publishers.
17. Jaber, A., Jabbour, A. B., & Jabbour, S. (2020). Green logistics practices and corporate sustainability: A comprehensive literature review. *Corporate Social Responsibility and Environmental Management, 27*(1), 1–22.
18. Boenzi, F., Digiesi, S., Facchini, F., & Mummmolo, G. (2017). Electric and LPG forklifts GHG assessment in material handling activities in actual operational conditions. In *IEEE International Conference on Service Operations and Logistics, and Informatics*. https://doi.org/10.1109/SOLI.2017.8120982.
19. Li, D., Wu, Y., Wang, B., Liu, C., & Arıcı, M. (2020). Optical and thermal performance of glazing units containing PCM in buildings: A review. *Construction and Building Materials, 233*, 117327. https://doi.org/10.1016/j.conbuildmat.2019.117327
20. Iancu, I. E., & Moga, L. M. (2022, May). Life cycle analysis of warehouse-type constructions. In *CLIMA 2022* conference. Rotterdam, The Netherlands.

21. Amodeo, L., Azevedo, S., & Benedetto, G. B. (2021). Life cycle assessment of logistics centers: A review of methodological approaches and key impact factors. *Journal of Cleaner Production, 280*, 124348.
22. Lewczuk, K., Kłodawski, M., & Gepner, P. (2021). Energy consumption in a distributional warehouse: A practical case study for different warehouse technologies. *Energies, 14*(9), 2709. https://doi.org/10.3390/en14092709
23. Pathak, M., Slade, R., Pichs-Madruga, R., Ürge-Vorsatz, D., Shukla, R., & Skea, J. (2022). Climate change 2022 mitigation of climate change: Technical summary.
24. Carbon Trust. (2018). *Warehousing and logistics, energy efficiency opportunities for warehousing and logistics companies*. The Carbon Trust.
25. Füchtenhans, M., Grosse, E., & Glock, C. H. (2021). Smart lighting systems: State-of-the-art and potential applications in warehouse order picking. *International Journal of Production Research, 59*(12), 3817–3839. https://doi.org/10.1080/00207543.2021.1897177
26. Marchand, C. (2015). Reducing the environmental impact of warehousing. In *Green logistics, improving the environmental sustainability of logistics* (p. 167).
27. Bai, C., & Ng, S. (2016). A critical review of studies on green logistics practices and their impacts on corporate performance. *Transportation Research Part E: Logistics, Traffic and Transportation Planning, 92*, 38–50.
28. Đukić, G., Česnik, V., & Opetuk, T. (2010). Order-picking methods and technologies for greener warehousing. *Strojarstvo: časopis za teoriju i praksu u strojarstvu, 52*(1), 23–31.
29. Böckin, D., Goffetti, G., Baumann, H., et al. (2022). Business model life cycle assessment: A method for analysing the environmental performance of business. *Sustainable Production and Consumption, 32*, 112–124. https://doi.org/10.1016/j.spc.2022.04.014
30. Kumar, N., Agrahari, R. P., & Roy, D. (2015). Review of green supply chain processes. *Ifac-Papersonline, 48*(3), 374–381. https://doi.org/10.1016/j.ifacol.2015.06.110
31. Azian, I., & Yudi, F. (2023). Ten-year thematic review and future trends of green warehouse. *International Journal of Management Concepts and Philosophy, 16*(4), 400–412. https://doi.org/10.1504/IJMCP.2023.133800
32. Mathew, D., Brintha, N. C., & Jappes, J. W. (2023). Artificial intelligence powered automation for industry 4.0. In *New horizons for Industry 4.0. In modern business* (pp. 1–28). Springer International Publishing. https://doi.org/10.1007/978-3-031-20443-2_1
33. Dey, P. K., Malesios, C., Chowdhury, S., Saha, K., Budhwar, P., & De, D. (2022). Adoption of circular economy practices in small and medium-sized enterprises: Evidence from Europe. *International Journal of Production Economics, 248*, 108496. https://doi.org/10.1016/j.ijpe.2022.108496
34. Cuce, E., Harjunowibowo, D., & Cuce, P. M. (2016). Renewable and sustainable energy saving strategies for greenhouse systems: A comprehensive review. *Renewable and Sustainable Energy Reviews, 64*, 34–59. https://doi.org/10.1016/j.rser.2016.05.077
35. Kibert, C. J. (2016). *Sustainable construction: Green building design and delivery*. John Wiley & Sons.
36. Liu, Z., Yu, C., Qian, Q. K., Huang, R., You, K., Visscher, H., & Zhang, G. (2023). Incentive initiatives on energy-efficient renovation of existing buildings towards carbon-neutral blueprints in China: Advancements, challenges and perspectives. *Energy and Buildings, 296*, 113343. https://doi.org/10.1016/j.enbuild.2023.113343
37. Mohamed, M. (2020). *Green building rating systems as sustainability assessment tools: Case study analysis (Vol. 1)*. IntechOpen. https://doi.org/10.5772/intechopen.87135
38. Roderick, Y., McEwan, D., Wheatley, C., & Alonso, C. (2009). *Comparison of energy performance assessment between LEED*. BREEAM and Green Star.
39. Richter, M., Lombardi, P., Arendarski, B., Naumann, A., Hoepfner, A., Komarnicki, P., & Pantaleo, A. (2021). A vision for energy decarbonization: Planning sustainable tertiary sites as net-zero energy systems. *Energies, 14*(17), 5577. https://doi.org/10.3390/en14175577
40. Hirostov, I., Appolloni, A., Chirico, A., & Cheng, W. (2021). The role of the environmental dimension in the performance management system: A systematic review and conceptual

framework. *Journal of Cleaner Production, 293*, 126075. https://doi.org/10.1016/j.jclepro.2021.126075
41. Hossain, S. M., Van de Wetering, J., Devaney, S., & Sayce, S. (2023). UK commercial real estate valuation practice: Does it now build in sustainability considerations? *Journal of Property Investment & Finance, 41*(4), 406–428. https://doi.org/10.1108/JPIF-11-2022-0083
42. Sinha, G. K. (2022). Relationship between sustainable logistics practices and the organization's performance in automobile industry – An empirical study with logistic regression machine learning. *International Journal of Mechanical Engineering, 7*(1).
43. Economidou, M., Della Valle, N., Melica, G., & Bertoldi, P. (2024). The role of European municipalities and regions in financing energy upgrades in buildings. *Environmental Economics and Policy Studies, 26*(2), 369–401. https://doi.org/10.1007/s10018-023-00363-3
44. Chen, L., Ma, M., & Xiang, X. (2023). Decarbonizing or illusion? How carbon emissions of commercial building operations change world-wide. *Sustainable Cities and Society, 96*, 104654. https://doi.org/10.1016/j.scs.2023.104654
45. Nicoletti, B., & Appolloni, A. (2023). *Framework of IoT, Blockchain, digital twins, and Artificial Intelligence solutions in support of the digital business transformation of logistics 5.0. Paper 12*. IGI Global. https://doi.org/10.4018/978-1-6684-5747-4.ch012
46. Rane, N. (2023). Integrating leading-edge artificial intelligence (AI), internet of things (IoT), and big data technologies for smart and sustainable architecture, engineering and construction (AEC) industry: Challenges and future directions. *Engineering and construction (AEC) industry: Challenges and future directions* (September 24, 2023). https://doi.org/10.2139/ssrn.4616049.
47. Bibri, S. E., Krogstie, J., Kaboli, A., & Alahi, A. (2024). Smarter eco-cities and their leading-edge artificial intelligence of things solutions for environmental sustainability: A comprehensive systematic review. *Environmental Science and Ecotechnology, 19*, 100330. https://doi.org/10.1016/j.ese.2023.100330
48. Kalkha, H., Khiat, A., Bahnasse, A., & Ouajji, H. (2024). *Enhancing warehouse efficiency with time series clustering: A hybrid storage location assignment strategy*. IEEE Access. https://doi.org/10.1109/ACCESS.2024.3386887
49. Oluleye, B. I., Chan, D. W., & Antwi-Afari, P. (2023). Adopting artificial intelligence for enhancing the implementation of systemic circularity in the construction industry: A critical review. *Sustainable Production and Consumption, 35*, 509–524. https://doi.org/10.1016/j.spc.2022.12.002
50. Talaat, M., Elkholy, M. H., Alblawi, A., & Said, T. (2023). Artificial intelligence applications for microgrids integration and management of hybrid renewable energy sources. *Artificial Intelligence Review, 56*(9), 10557–10611. https://doi.org/10.1007/s10462-023-10410-w
51. Vyas, B. (2023). Java-powered AI: Implementing intelligent systems with code. *Journal of Science & Technology, 4*(6), 1–12.
52. Himeur, Y., Alsalemi, A., AlKababji, A., Bensaali, F., Amira, A., Sardianos, C., et al. (2021). A survey of recommender systems for energy efficiency in buildings: Principles, challenges and prospects. *Information Fusion, 72*, 1–21. https://doi.org/10.1016/j.inffus.2021.02.002
53. Honrao, Y., & Mantri, S. (2023, December). Artificial intelligence in trucking business operations-a systematic review. In *International conference on Information and Communication Technology for Competitive Strategies* (pp. 121–131). Springer Nature Singapore. https://doi.org/10.1007/978-981-99-9489-2_11
54. Hamdan, A., Ibekwe, K. I., Ilojianya, V. I., Sonko, S., & Etukudoh, E. A. (2024). AI in renewable energy: A review of predictive maintenance and energy optimization. *International Journal of Science and Research Archive, 11*(1), 718–729. https://doi.org/10.30574/ijsra.2024.11.1.0112
55. Langevin, A., Cheriet, M., & Gagnon, G. (2023). Efficient deep generative model for short-term household load forecasting using non-intrusive load monitoring. *Sustainable Energy, Grids and Networks, 34*, 101006. https://doi.org/10.1016/j.segan.2023.101006

56. Choudhury, D., & Gorantla, T. (2023). AI in supply chain, logistics and manufacturing. In *Artificial intelligence for business* (pp. 206–224). Productivity Press. https://doi.org/10.4324/9781003358411-13
57. van Steenbergen, M., Nouwens, H., & Eusterbrock, T. (n.d.). Survival fitting. www.lectoraatdigitalethics.nl/wp-content/uploads/2023/09/Sogeti-DYA-Survival_of_the_fitting.pdf
58. Onyeaka, H., Tamasiga, P., Nwauzoma, U. M., Miri, T., Juliet, U. C., Nwaiwu, O., & Akinsemolu, A. A. (2023). Using artificial intelligence to tackle food waste and enhance the circular economy: Maximising resource efficiency and minimising environmental impact: A review. *Sustainability, 15*(13), 10482. https://doi.org/10.3390/su151310482
59. Tsolakis, N., Zissis, D., Papaefthimiou, S., & Korfiatis, N. (2022). Towards AI driven environmental sustainability: An application of automated logistics in container port terminals. *International Journal of Production Research, 60*(14), 4508–4528. https://doi.org/10.1080/00207543.2021.1914355
60. Sethy, A., Shaik, N., Saravanan, V., & Karthika, S. (2023). 10 The future with AI and AI in action. *Toward Artificial General Intelligence: Deep Learning, Neural Networks, Generative AI*, 213. https://doi.org/10.1515/9783111323749-010.
61. Javaid, M., Haleem, A., Singh, R. P., & Suman, R. (2022). Artificial intelligence applications for industry 4.0: A literature-based study. *Journal of Industrial Integration and Management, 7*(01), 83–111. https://doi.org/10.1142/S2424862221300040
62. Nova, K. (2023). AI-enabled water management systems: An analysis of system components and interdependencies for water conservation. *Eigenpub Review of Science and Technology, 7*(1), 105–124.
63. Chung, S. H. (2021). Applications of smart technologies in logistics and transport: A review. *Transportation Research Part E: Logistics and Transportation Review, 153*, 10245. https://doi.org/10.1016/j.tre.2021.102455
64. Tseng, M. L., Tran, T. P. T., Ha, H. M., Bui, T. D., & Lim, M. K. (2021). Sustainable industrial and operation engineering trends and challenges toward Industry 4.0: A data driven analysis. *Journal of Industrial and Production Engineering, 38*(8), 581–598. https://doi.org/10.1080/21681015.2021.1950227
65. Daios, A., Xanthopoulos, A., Folinas, D., & Kostavelis, I. (2024). Towards automating stocktaking in warehouses: Challenges, trends, and reliable approaches. *Procedia Computer Science, 232*, 1437–1445. https://doi.org/10.1016/j.procs.2024.01.142
66. Anthony, L. F. W., Kanding, B., & Selvan, R. (2020). Carbontracker: Tracking and predicting the carbon footprint of training deep learning models. *arXiv preprint arXiv:2007.03051.*
67. Creazza, A. (2022, October). Green logistics survey, Logistica.
68. Prataviera, L. B., Creazza, A., & Perotti, S. (2023). A call to action: A stakeholder analysis of green logistics practices. *The International Journal of Logistics Management, 35*(3), 979–1008. https://doi.org/10.1108/IJLM-09-2022-0381
69. Bardi, A. (2022). *Green warehousing in Italy: A sustainable future*. Springer.
70. Cavagnero, S. (2021). *Sustainable logistics and warehousing in Italy: A guide to green practices*. Routledge.
71. De Marco, A. (2020). *Green warehousing in the Italian food industry: A study on sustainable practices*. Elsevier.
72. Giannelli, G. (2022). *Green warehousing and supply chain management in Italy: A framework for implementation*. CRC Press.
73. Ricciardi, F. (2021). *Sustainable warehousing in Italy: A review of green technologies and practices*. John Wiley & Sons.
74. Baglio, M. (2023). Dossier sul Green Warehousing, *Logistca.*
75. Cerved. (2022). *Rapporto Italia sostenibile 2022*. Cerved Rating Agency.
76. Lombardi, M., & Peterson, P. (2020). Greening warehouses: A definition and framework for decision-making. *International Journal of Production Research, 58*(10), 2994–3012.
77. Perotti, S., Coslovich, M., & Granata, E. (2023, June). Transitioning towards net-zero warehouses: Empirical insights and best practices in Italy. In *Proceedings of the 2023 9th*

*International Conference on e-Society, e-Learning and e-Technologies* (pp. 82–87). https://doi.org/10.1145/3613944.3613957
78. Creazza, A., Colicchia, C., & Evangelista, P. (2023). Leveraging shippers-logistics providers relationships for better sustainability in logistics: The perspective of SMEs. *The International Journal of Logistics Management, 35*(3), 1009–1039. https://doi.org/10.1108/IJLM-03-2022-0103
79. Serrano-García, J., Llach, J., Bikfalvi, A., & Arbeláez-Toro, J. J. (2023). Performance effects of green production capability and technology in manufacturing firms. *Journal of Environmental Management, 330*, 117099. https://doi.org/10.1016/j.jenvman.2022.117099
80. Green Jr, K. W., et al. (2012). Green supply chain management practices: Impact on performance. *Supply Chain Management: An International Journal, 17*, 290–305. https://doi.org/10.1108/13598541211227126
81. Vasileiou, E., Georgantzis, N., Attanasi, G., & Llerena, P. (2024). The role of innovation portfolio in green innovation decisions: A study of French and Italian firms. *Technovation, 130*, 102921. https://doi.org/10.1016/j.technovation.2023.102921
82. Kandrot, S., & Holloway, P. (2020). Applications of drone technology for sustainable development of the coastal zone: A literature review. *Project report.*
83. Sowl, M. (2017). *Green logistics and warehousing: A practical guide for reducing the environmental impact of logistics operations*. Kogan Page Publishers.
84. Lievano-Martínez, F. A., Fernández-Ledesma, J. D., Burgos, D., Branch-Bedoya, J. W., & Jimenez-Builes, J. A. (2022). Intelligent process automation: An application in manufacturing industry. *Sustainability, 14*(14), 8804. https://doi.org/10.3390/su14148804
85. Kiran, D. R. (2022). *Principles of Economics and Management for Manufacturing Engineering*. Butterworth-Heinemann.
86. Nicoletti, B. (1979). Maintenance strategies. *Terotechnica, 16*, 1–11.
87. Balin, A. I., & Sari, K. (2023). The effect of green purchasing practices on financial performance under the mediating role of environmental performance: Evidence from Türkiye. *Sustainability, 15*(4), 3617. https://doi.org/10.3390/su15043617

# Part IV
# Human Capital in the Digital Economy

# Digitalization of Manufacturing Enterprises: The Perspective of Employees and Employers

**Tatiana Stuken, Tatiana Lapina, and Olga Korzhova**

**Abstract** When digitizing a business, it is essential to understand the objectives set and achieved by management in organizations, as well as the barriers limiting the possibilities for effective implementation. The study aims to identify priority areas, outcomes, and barriers to digitization, using the case of industrial companies. The analysis is based on data from the manufacturing industry in one of Russia's regions with a well-developed industrial complex. Information was collected through semi-standardized interviews with top management and a questionnaire survey with specialists from functional departments. Data analysis was carried out using descriptive statistics. The main objectives of digitalization include increasing business efficiency, decision-making speed, and work performance. The analysis identified contradictions in the evaluation of the goals and obstacles of digitalization. Compared to employers, employees were more likely to identify software incompatibility and business process shortcomings as barriers. Both employees and employers noted the quality of the workforce as a significant obstacle to digitalization. Another significant outcome of digitalization, in addition to enhancing the speed and accuracy of work, is the reduction in labor input. Organizational reforms and the introduction of digital competence training programs can help reduce barriers and prevent conflicts between employees and employers.

**Keywords** Digital competencies · Digitalization · Barriers · Manufacturing industry

## 1 Introduction

The digitalization of the economy is, according to numerous researchers, a significant driver of socio-economic progress, presenting a range of possibilities for growth in production, reduction in costs, enhancement of product quality, and improved decision-making processes. It is unsurprising that the utilization of information and

T. Stuken (✉) · T. Lapina · O. Korzhova
Faculty of Economics, Psychology, Management, Dostoevsky Omsk State University, Omsk, Russian Federation
e-mail: Stuken@omsu.ru; LapinaTA@omsu.ru; KorzhovaOS@omsu.ru



A. Appolloni et al. (eds.), *The Future of Industry*, Lecture Notes in Information Systems and Organisation 70, https://doi.org/10.1007/978-3-031-66801-2_21

communications technologies has become the focus of attention for economists [1, 2]. Official statistics show general trends in digitalization, but a deeper study of the processes associated with the introduction of digital technologies and their consequences requires special research that should take into account industry specifics. Taking into account the significant role of the manufacturing industry and the traditionally high attention of the state [3], this paper deals with issues related to the digitalization of this industry from the positions of employees and employers. This makes it possible to identify not only the goals of digitalization, but also the features of the implementation of processes in this area.

The aim of the research is to identify trends and contradictions, as well as barriers, in the process of digitizing industrial enterprises. The objectives of the research are:

- to assess the goals, outcomes, and barriers of digitalization, from the perspectives of top management and industry specialists,
- to identify commonalities and differences in the assessments of digitalization by top management and industrial specialists,
- to determine key barriers to and opportunities for reducing barriers in digitalization.

## 2 Background

According to the available data, digitalization processes in the manufacturing industry are quite effective, and the level of its digitalization is characterized as medium or high [4, 5]. The countries of the Asia-Pacific region, the European Union, the USA, and Canada are recognized as world leaders in the digitalization of industry [4, 5].

Open data allow us to get a certain idea about the use of digital technologies in Russian industry.

According to the Russian Federal State Statistics Service, the manufacturing industry has higher indicators of digital infrastructure development compared to the average Russian indicators (Fig. 1).

In addition to the availability of technical means, it is important to understand what solutions and software products are used in the manufacturing industry. Since information about the share of organizations using special software tools is available only in the regional context, we calculated the Pearson correlation coefficients between the share of organizations using special software tools in the region, on the one hand, and the share of those employed in the manufacturing industry, on the other. The correlation coefficients of the average strength of the connection are noted between the share of people employed in manufacturing and the use of the following software products:

Software for design ($r = 0.503$, the average value for organizations of all types of economic activity is 9.9%);

Software for management of automated production and/or individual technical means and technological processes ($r = 0.481$ with an average value of 7.7%);

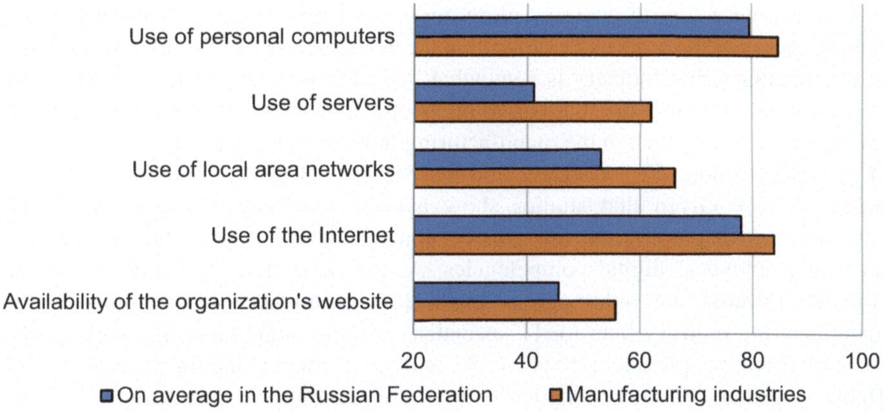


**Fig. 1** Indicators of digital infrastructure development in the Russian manufacturing industry (as a percentage of the total number of organizations, 2022). *Source*: authors' calculations based on [6]

Customer relationship management systems (r = 0.508 with an average value of 12.1%);

Enterprise resource planning systems (r = 0.477 with an average value of 13.0%);

Supply chain management systems (r = 0.522 with an average value of 4.8%).

Some available studies show that cloud technologies, enterprise resource planning systems, electronic sales, and radio frequency identification technologies are widely used in the Russian manufacturing industry. However, the pace of digitalization of the Russian economy is lagging behind the leading countries, and the Russian manufacturing industry according to the digitalization index is ranked 21st out of 27 countries for which relevant data are available. If the directions of digital development correspond to the world leaders, the gap from them is about 5–10 years [1]. At the same time, such comparisons are often carried out using best practices that do not allow assessing the average situation in an industry characterized by a sufficiently high dispersion.

There are even more difficulties when we try to assess the level of employees' digital competencies based on open data.

In the manufacturing industry, the share of specialists in the field of information and communication technologies in the total number of employed corresponds to the average for the economy—2.5% and 2.4%, respectively (authors' calculations based on [7]).

In general, it is possible to assess the level of digital competencies of other employees by analyzing the answers to the question of The Russia Longitudinal Monitoring Survey about whether the respondents had to use the Internet over the past 12 months and for what purposes. According to the 31st wave of research conducted in 2022, manufacturing workers use the Internet as often as other workers to communicate and solve various household issues, but less often—for work (52.0% vs. 78.8%) and training (8.0% vs. 15.6%) [8].

It is also necessary to note one more important circumstance. Microdata from a sample survey of the workforce shows that the age structure of IT workers employed in the manufacturing industry is somewhat biased towards older age groups. If on average in the economy the share of young people under 29 in the total number of IT specialists is 31.1%, then in the manufacturing industry it is 28.1%, and the shares of IT specialists under 39 are 71.7% and 66.7%, respectively (authors' calculations based on [7]). Given that studies show a correlation between age and digital competencies of employees, this can be considered as a factor that reduces the level of employees' digital competencies. At the same time, the shift of the age structure towards the older age is much less pronounced for workers in the manufacturing industry than for IT specialists. Among manufacturing workers, the share of young people under 29 is 14.5%, with an average value for the economy of 16.6%, the shares of workers under 39 are 44.6% and 46.4%, respectively.

Thus, from the review presented, we can only draw general conclusions based on indirect estimates.

## 3 Research

### *3.1 Concept of the Study*

The logic of the study is in line with the well-known concept of three levels of digital inequality [9–11].

The first level is characterized by access to information and communication technologies. Despite the widespread availability of the internet and computer technology, digital inequality at this level continues to be a concern, even in highly developed countries. This is because new technologies are continuously emerging requiring rapid adaptation [12].

The second level of digital inequality is the level of digital literacy. Increasingly, jobs require not only basic digital skills, but also more advanced ones. Due to a lack of these skills, employees are unable to effectively utilize information and communication technologies, which is considered a significant barrier to digital transformation [13–15]. Studies show that differences in the level of development of digital skills correlate with many characteristics of personnel: level of education, gender, age, place of residence, motivation, social environment, etc. [11, 16–19].

The third level of digital inequality is associated with obtaining specific benefits from the use of digital technologies in various fields of activity. There is a basis to assume that digitization is positively correlated with innovation. It assists in enhancing the quality of governance and reducing barriers to organizational innovation. This impact is particularly significant in high-technology and highly competitive sectors [20]. An important driving force behind digitalization is the desire of the company's management to increase control and ensure that information is received in real time [21].

At the same time, a number of important results of digitalization concerning both the organization as a whole and individual workplaces have not yet been sufficiently studied. These include, in particular, changes in organizational culture, working environment, and the activities of middle management [22].

Assessing the results of digitalization, it should be noted that its impact on the growth of economic indicators, and labor productivity in particular, is ambiguous. The absence of a positive correlation between investments in technology and labor productivity growth in developed countries was first noted in 1970–1980 and was called the productivity paradox. The growth of labor productivity in the 1990s allowed researchers to talk about the disappearance of this paradox [23, 24], however, since the mid-2000s, scientists have recorded a slowdown in labor productivity growth [25, 26]. This fact can be explained by organizational, technical and other barriers to digitalization, as well as false expectations, measurement errors, or time lags [26]. The barriers to digitalization in industrial enterprises have been extensively discussed in a number of foreign studies [27–29]. The researchers have found that developing countries face more organizational and technical barriers but also perceive more opportunities [27]. At the same time technological barriers are considered as the most significant category of challenges followed by financial challenges in adoption of digital manufacturing [28].

In accordance with this logic, we will analyze the available information on the digitalization of the Russian manufacturing industry.

## 3.2 *Methodology of Research*

The purpose of this study is to evaluate the directions of work and performance of manufacturing enterprises in the field of digital technologies.

We focused on answering the following questions:

What are the priority directions and goals of digitalization set by manufacturing enterprises?

What are the most common barriers to digitalization?

How do manufacturing enterprises evaluate the results of digitalization?

For each of the tasks, we studied the responses of representatives of top management (hereinafter referred to as employers), and representatives of employees.

The analysis of digitalization of industrial enterprises is carried out based on the Omsk region, which is one of the industrial regions in the Russian Federation. In the structure of the value added of the region, the share of manufacturing production is 30.4% with the share of employed 14.3% (in the total number of employed in the region). Similar indicators for the Russian Federation according to official statistics are 17.0 and 14.1%, respectively [30].

In terms of the volume of industrial products shipped in the region, coke and petroleum product production predominates, followed by rubber and plastic product production (65.7%), food, beverage, and tobacco product production (12.2%), finished metal product, electronic, and optical product production, electrical equipment production, machinery and equipment production (10.0%) and chemical and chemical product production (8.6%) [30].

A sufficiently high level of labor productivity in the manufacturing industry of the region, combined with a diversified production structure, suggests that the situation with the digitalization of industrial enterprises in the region will be quite typical for other Russian regions. Given that the level of adoption of digital technologies is linked to the specifics of production processes, we have chosen to focus our analysis on the implementation of digital solutions in functional areas of organizations, such as accounting and finance, marketing and sales, procurement and human resources, legal affairs, information technology, technical support, process management including planning and control.

Research data were collected in three stages.

At the first stage, using SPARK data, we compiled a register of manufacturing enterprises and determined a sample. A total of 92 organizations participated in the study. In order to obtain information about the goals, directions, barriers and results of digitalization, we conducted an expert survey of top managers/employees in charge of digitalization processes representing large and medium-sized enterprises. This part of the study was carried out in September-October 2022.

At the second stage, we surveyed 960 employees of these enterprises (quota sample). The purpose of the survey is to collect information about employees' readiness for digital innovations, their understanding of the goals of implementing digital technologies and assessing the consequences of digitalization and about the development of digital competencies among employees and their need for companies. The assessment of employees' digital competencies was performed using the European methodology DigComp 2.0 [31]. This part of the study was conducted in September-October 2023.

## 4 Research Results

According to the survey results, employers implement various digitalization projects. The most frequently cited projects are in the areas of enterprise resource management (ERM), improving business process efficiency, document management, and human resources (HR) processes. Less commonly, employers are engaged in projects on business analytics, sales planning, and procurement management.

The results of the study indicate that when answering the question of why the company needs digitalization, the opinions of employees and employers differ (Fig. 2). Henceforward, the sum of the answers is more than 100%, since respondents could choose several answers.

Along with understanding the importance of improving business efficiency and saving resources, employees underestimate the importance of the speed of decision-making in modern business and reducing errors related to the human factor. According to the focus group, the reasons for this situation are not only related to the presence of communication problems. The prevalence of the answer "to keep up

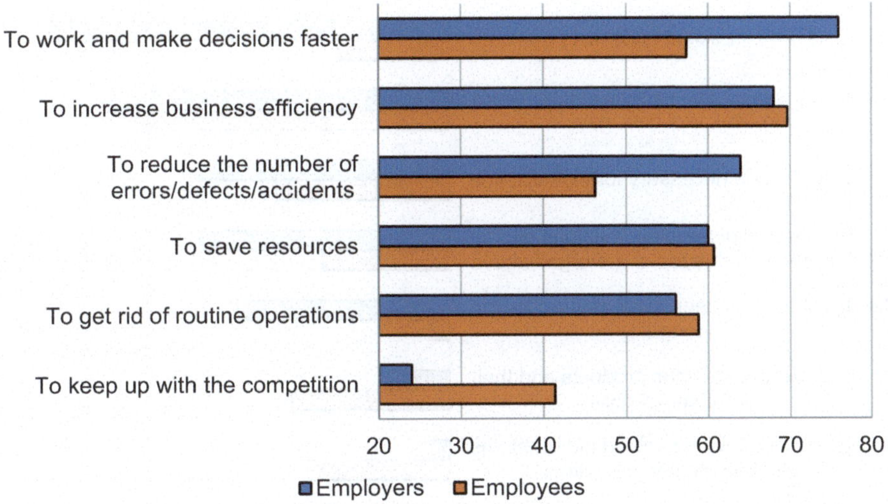


**Fig. 2** Distribution of the answers of employers and employees to the question "What is the purpose of digitalization in your organization?", % of respondents

with the competition" may indicate that digitalization is understood as a general trend, loosely related to solving specific tasks ("everyone does that").

The priority directions of digitalization, noted by the heads of manufacturing enterprises (distribution of employers' responses to the question "What areas of digitalization are used in your organization?", % of respondents):

- Digitalization of individual business processes—82.6%;
- Devices for automatic data collection, transmission, and visualization—65.2%;
- Integrated digitalization of business processes—60.9%;
- Control and measuring devices connected to digital infrastructure—58.7%;
- Tools for analytics and automatic interpretation of the received information—34.8%.

According to the majority of the focus group participants, the installation of computers at the workplaces is explained not by their absence, but the need to replace them with more productive ones. In addition, this work is not a one-time job and may take several years.

The next most frequent direction of digitalization is the digitalization of individual business processes. The choice of this answer in a third of cases indicates that the financing of digitalization is carried out on a residual basis. On the contrary, with the integrated digitalization of business processes, only 8% of managers believe that financing digitalization is not a priority.

Let us consider the results of the analysis of digitalization barriers (Fig. 3).

Here we again record the discrepancy in responses between employees and employers, and these differences are much more significant. It is more likely that specialists, rather than managers, will address issues associated with unresolved

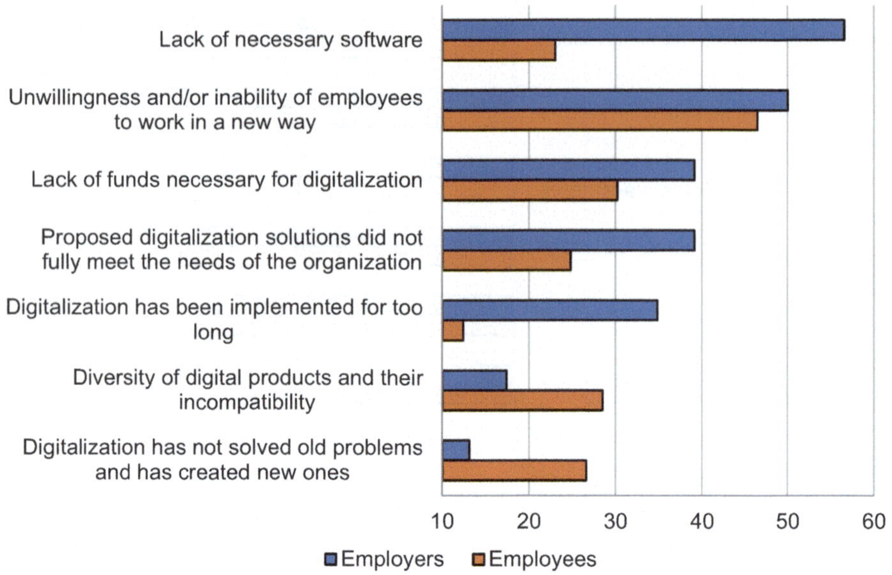


**Fig. 3** Distribution of the answers to the question "What problems did your organization face during digitalization?", % of respondents

business processes (i.e., "digitalization has not resolved old issues and has created new ones") and "piecemeal automation", where decisions on digitalizing individual business processes are made independently of each other.

It is interesting that managers for whom the speed of work and decision-making is an important goal of digitalization of business processes (see Fig. 2), note long terms of new technologies introduction, and employees who are much less likely to fix such a task as a priority, respectively, rarely note this problem.

Both from the point of view of the management and employees, an important barrier to digitalization is the quality of the workforce. Table 1 presents the results of employees' assessment of the required and actual level of formation of their own competencies.

At first glance, employees rate the level of digital competence formation quite highly, although in most cases at a lower level than required. However, this is due to the fact that low scores are rarely used in the assessment. Given this, the lack of competencies should be recognized as more significant.

The largest gap between the required and actual level is recorded for such competencies as to be able to:

- develop a sequence of understandable instructions for a computer system—0.95 points;
- identify technical problems when operating devices and using digital environments, as well as solve them (from troubleshooting to solving more complex problems)—0.91 points;

**Table 1** Assessment of the actual and required level of employees' digital competencies (1—"I don't know how to do it at all", 5—"I do it perfectly")

| Competencies | Level of development (standard deviation) | |
|---|---|---|
| | required | actual |
| To organize, store and extract digital data, information from the digital environment | 4.34 (0.87) | 4.00 (0.78) |
| To understand where your own digital competence needs to be improved or updated. To look for opportunities for self-development of digital competencies, to be aware of digital evolution | 4.34 (0.85) | 4.09 (0.74) |
| To formulate information needs, search for data, information and content in a digital environment | 4.31 (0.82) | 4.13 (0.66) |
| To analyze, compare data, conduct a critical assessment of the reliability of data and information sources | 4.2 (0.83) | 4.09 (0.77) |
| To be able to communicate in a digital environment | 4.18 (0.85) | 4.22 (0.92) |

- use one or more digital identifiers to be able to protect one's own reputation—0.75 points;
- use protective devices to protect information, as well as understand the risks and threats in the digital environment. To know about security measures and information protection and take into account reliability and confidentiality—0.72 points;
- change, refine, improve and integrate information and content into the existing body of knowledge to create new, original and relevant content and knowledge—0.68 points.

It should be noted that older workers (50+) estimate the level of development of their digital competencies by an average of 0.48 points lower than workers under 40. At the same time, older employees also rate the requirements for digital competencies lower, so the absolute indicators of the gap between the required and actual level of competence development in both groups turn out to be similar.

According to the survey results, employers are implementing various digitalization projects. The most commonly mentioned projects were those in the area of enterprise resource management, aimed at improving the efficiency of business processes and document management, as well as those related to human resources processes. Less frequently, projects were mentioned that related to business analytics, sales planning, and procurement management.

In general, employers are quite positive about the results of project implementation and note, first of all, an increase in the speed of work and decision-making, the quality of work and the volume of output (Fig. 4).

A significant part of the respondents noted a decrease in personnel labor input, however, the number of employees of most functional groups practically does not change, with the exception of employees of financial and economic services (every sixth employer declares a reduction in the number) and IT specialists (about 60% of respondents declare an increase in the number of personnel of this group).

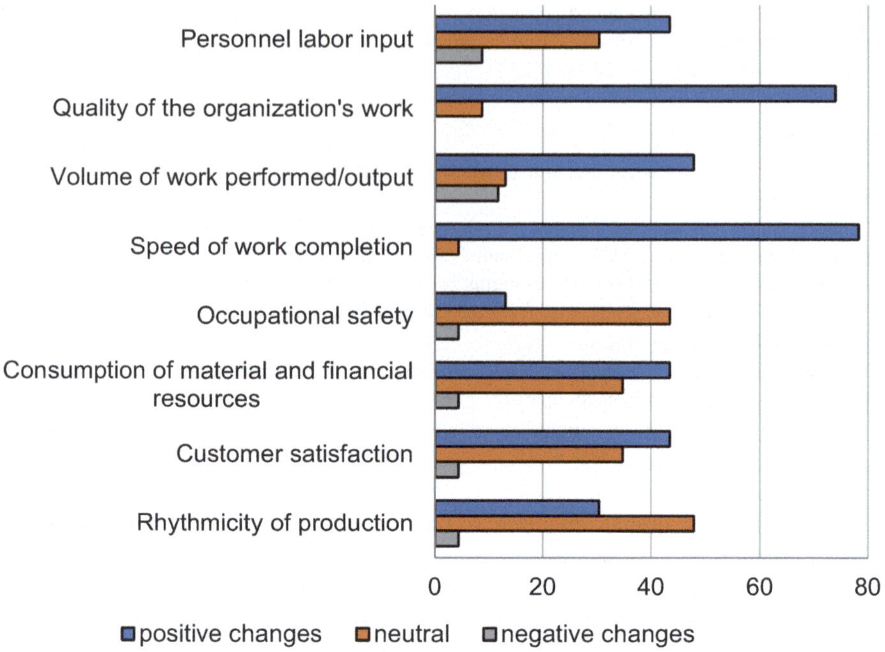


**Fig. 4** Results of digitalization projects (in % of managers surveyed)

## 5 Discussion

The conclusions of the study do not contradict the available data on the digitalization of manufacturing enterprises in terms of the goals and priorities of digitalization, competencies, barriers and its results. At the same time, they allow us to note several features.

Thus, the analysis shows not only the attention of manufacturing enterprises to digital technologies and the variety of projects they use, but also the existence of certain imbalances and barriers in this area.

Firstly, there is a lack of understanding by employees of digitalization goals, on the one hand, and the results of digitalization, on the other hand. Thus, employees do not always correctly understand digitalization tasks facing the organization, and employers, in turn, underestimate the problems that arise in the process of digitalization in the workplace. Achieving sustainable results in digitalization requires a set of organizational changes that involve explaining the goals and objectives of digital transformation, staff engagement, leadership, and the active participation of line managers. This includes developing feedback mechanisms and implementing changes to organizational culture [32]. We believe that an analysis of the relationship between digitalization success and organizational changes, based on empirical evidence, could be a promising area for future research.

Secondly, both employees and employers note the problem associated with the insufficient level of digital competencies of staff. At the same time, the majority of employees note that they acquire digital competencies mainly on their own, only 15.8% of respondents declare training provided by the employer. Since in modern conditions many digital competencies represent general human capital, the employer has quite serious risks associated with investing in the development of such competencies.

In a labor-shortage labor market, this issue does not have a straightforward solution. Nevertheless, the focus should be on integrating work on the employer's brand, retaining staff, and a range of tools for enhancing digital skills, including for older employees. It is essential to note that we assessed the development of these digital skills through survey methods and self-assessments. It would be also interesting to compare the findings from self-assessments with an objective evaluation of the acquisition of digital skills based on testing. Additionally, in relation to enhancing the digital skills of older employees, it is crucial to evaluate the effectiveness of the available tools and training techniques in addressing this challenge.

The results of the research can be applied in the HR management of organizations, particularly in cases where digitalization projects are implemented. Therefore, company management should pay attention to conveying the goals of digital transformation to employees, explaining the benefits of digitalization for their staff, as the study has revealed some lack of clarity regarding digitalization processes. In addition, it is essential to develop digital skills among staff at the company's expense or in a 50/50 partnership. Employers are in demand for these skills, but the availability of such skills among employees is still limited. Therefore, to effectively implement digitalization projects, it is crucial to enhance the development of these skills, despite the potential risks associated with retaining trained employees due to the overall human capital and employer.

## 6 Conclusion

The rapid development of digital technologies requires not only investments in infrastructure and software, but also the development of complementary practices. Overcoming the identified barriers may be associated with improving communication with employees, reviewing performance evaluation indicators, implementing programs to increase engagement and establish feedback.

Probably, given the importance of the industry and its digitalization, we can talk about creating special programs for the development of digital competencies available to the working population.

The results of digitalization are likely to have some positive impact on productivity growth. Employers note an increase in the output and a reduction in personnel labor input as a result of digitalization, but at the same time the number of most groups of employees does not change significantly. This is probably due to the fact that as a result of digitalization, employees have additional tools and functions that can lead to an increase in results, but at this stage it is not possible to assess their contribution to labor productivity growth.

**Acknowledgments** The article was prepared at the expense of the grant of the Russian Science Foundation No. 22-28-20336, https://rscf.ru/project/22-28-20336/

## References

1. Digital transformation of industries: starting conditions and priorities. (2021). https://conf.hse.ru/mirror/pubs/share/463148459.pdf.
2. Matt, D. T., Pedrini, D., Bonfanti, A., & Orzes, G. (2023). Industrial digitalization. A systematic literature review and research agenda. *European Management Journal, 41*(4), 47–78. https://doi.org/10.1016/j.emj.2022.01.001
3. Simachev, Y., Fedyunina, A., & Kuzyk, M. (2022). New contours of industrial policy. In *Review of new contours of industrial policy* (pp. 1–73). HSE Publishing House.
4. Measuring the Digital Transformation: A Roadmap for the Future. (2019). https://www.oecd-ilibrary.org/sites/9789264311992-en/index.html?itemId=/content/publication/9789264311992-en/. https://doi.org/10.1787/9789264311992-en/.
5. Cette, G., Fernald, J. G., & Mojon, B. (2016). The pre-great recession slowdown in productivity. *European Economic Review, 88*, 3–20. https://www.frbsf.org/wp-content/uploads/sites/4/wp2016-08.pdf
6. *Science, innovation and technology*. (2023). [Review of Science, innovation and technology]. Rosstat.gov.ru. https://rosstat.gov.ru/statistics/science#
7. *Labor force*. (2022). Rosstat.gov.ru. https://rosstat.gov.ru/labour_force
8. *Russia Longitudinal Monitoring Survey of HSE*. (n.d.). Rlms-Hse.cpc.unc.edu. https://rlms-hse.cpc.unc.edu
9. Attewell, P. (2001). The first and second digital divides. *Sociology of Education, 74*(3), 252–259. https://doi.org/10.2307/2673277
10. Norris, P. (2001). The digital divide: Civic engagement, information poverty, and the Internet worldwide. Cambridge https://doi.org/10.1017/CBO9781139164887
11. Vassilakopoulou, P., & Hustad, E. (2023). Bridging digital divides: A literature review and research agenda for information systems research. *Information Systems Frontiers, 25*, 955–969. https://doi.org/10.1007/s10796-020-10096-3
12. Van Deursen, A., & van Dijk, J. (2018). The first-level digital divide shifts from inequalities in physical access to inequalities in material access. *New Media and Society, 21*(2), 354–375. https://doi.org/10.1177/1461444818797082
13. Bucea, A. E., Cruz-Jesus, F., Oliveira, T., & Coelho, P. S. (2020). Assessing the role of age, education, gender and income on the digital divide: Evidence for the European Union. *Information Systems Frontiers, 23*, 1007–1021. https://doi.org/10.1007/s10796-020-10012-9
14. Büchi, M., Just, N., & Latzer, M. (2016). Modeling the second-level digital divide: A five-country study of social differences in internet use. *New Media & Society, 18*(11), 2703–2722. https://doi.org/10.1177/1461444815604154
15. Karikova, A. S. (2023). Overcoming the barriers to the digital transformation of industrial enterprises through the business model selection mechanism. *Strategic Decisions and Risk Management, 14*(1), 74–85. https://doi.org/10.17747/2618-947X-2023-1-74-85
16. Scheerder, A., Van Deursen, A., & Van Dijk, J. (2017). Determinants of internet skills, uses and outcomes. A systematic review of the second-and third-level digital divide. *Telematics and Informatics, 34*(8), 1607–1624. https://doi.org/10.1016/j.tele.2017.07.007
17. Ferreira, D., Vale, M., Carmo, R. M., Encalada-Abarca, L., & Marcolin, C. (2021). The three levels of the urban digital divide: Bridging issues of coverage, usage and its outcomes in VGI platforms. *Geoforum, 124*, 195–206.

18. Wang, L., & Liu, C. (2021). The role of motivation in the digital divide: The moderating effect of device access. *Mobile Media & Communication, 10*(3), 406–420. https://doi.org/10.1177/20501579211060621
19. Pihlainen, K., Ehlers, A., Rohner, R., Cerna, K., Kärnä, E., Hess, M., Hengl, L., Aavikko, L., Frewer-Graumann, S., Gallistl, V., & Mülle, C. (2023). Older adults' reasons to participate in digital skills learning: An interdisciplinary, multiple case study from Austria, Finland, and Germany. *Studies in the Education of Adults, 55*(1), 101–119. https://doi.org/10.1080/02660830.2022.2133268
20. Niu, Y., Wen, W., Wang, S., & Li, S. (2023). Breaking barriers to innovation: The power of digital transformation. *Finance Research Letters, 51*, 103457. https://doi.org/10.1016/j.frl.2022.103457
21. Horváth, D., & Szabó, R. Z. (2019). Driving forces and barriers of industry 4.0: Do multinational and small and medium-sized companies have equal opportunities? *Technological Forecasting and Social Change, 146*, 119–132. https://doi.org/10.1016/j.techfore.2019.05.021
22. Nadkarni, S., & Prügl, R. (2021). Digital transformation: A review, synthesis and opportunities for future research. *Management Review Quarterly, 71*, 233–341. https://doi.org/10.1007/s11301-020-00185-7
23. Brynjolfsson, E., & Hitt, L. (1996). Paradox lost? Firm-level evidence of the returns to information systems spending. *Management Science, 42*(4), 541–558. https://repository.upenn.edu/cgi/viewcontent.cgi?article=1108&context=oid_papers
24. Jorgenson, D., Mun, S., Ho, M., & Stiroh, K. (2003). Lessons from the U. S. Growth resurgence. *Journal of Policy Modeling, 25*(5), 453–470. https://doi.org/10.1016/S0161-8938(03)00040-1
25. Brynjolfsson, E., Rock, D., & Syverson, C. (2017). *Artificial intelligence and the modern productivity paradox: A clash of expectations and statistics.* https://www.nber.org/system/files/working_papers/w24001/w24001.pdf
26. Digital Factories. 2020. Shaping the Future of Manufacturing. https://www.pwc.de/de/digitale-transformation/digital-factories-2020-shaping-the-future-of-manufacturing.pdf. https://doi.org/10.1016/j.geoforum.2021.05.002.
27. Elhusseiny, H. M., & Crispim, J. (2022). SMEs, barriers and opportunities on adopting industry 4.0: A review. *Procedia Computer Science, 196*, 864–871. https://doi.org/10.1016/j.procs.2021.12.086
28. Bag, S., Sahu, A. K., Kilbourn, P., Pisa, N., Dhamija, P., & Sahu, A. K. (2022). Modeling barriers of digital manufacturing in a circular economy for enhancing sustainability. *International Journal of Productivity and Performance Management, 71*(3), 833–869. https://doi.org/10.1108/IJPPM-12-2020-0637
29. Favoretto, C., Mendes, G. H. D. S., Filho, M. G., Gouvea de Oliveira, M., & Ganga, G. M. D. (2022). Digital transformation of business model in manufacturing companies: Challenges and research agenda. *Journal of Business & Industrial Marketing, 37*(4), 748–767. https://doi.org/10.1108/JBIM-10-2020-0477
30. *Regions of Russia. Socio-economic indicators'.* (2022). Moscow: Russian State Statistics Service. https://rosstat.gov.ru/storage/mediabank/Region_Pokaz_2022.pdf
31. Vuorikari, R., Punie, Y., Carretero, S., & Van den Brande, L. (2016). DigComp 2.0: The Digital Competence Framework for Citizens. Update Phase 1: The Conceptual Reference Model. https://publications.jrc.ec.europa.eu/repository/handle/JRC101254
32. Melinda Pacolli, M. (2022). Importance of change Management in Digital Transformation Sustainability. *IFAC-PapersOnLine, 55*(39), 276–280. https://doi.org/10.1016/j.ifacol.2022.12.034

# Congruence of Skills and Technologies in the Conditions of Digitalization of Industry

**Ekaterina Votinova and Elena Kalabina**

**Abstract** Digitalization of industry is a challenge that is currently faced not only by manufacturing enterprises, but also the entire labor market. Digitalization can replace some professions; however, it is not always destructive. For engineering and technical specializations, digitalization will change the content of many professions and, as a result, the requirements for employee skills. The article analyzes the correspondence between the competencies of young specialists and the requests of enterprises. As shown, there is some incongruence between the skills available to university graduates and the requests of enterprises. The reasons for that are the following. Firstly, it is a various level of implementation of digital technologies at the enterprise. Secondly, there is a delay in the formation of the necessary skills. The response time to the company's requests can take up to 1 year. In addition, the training time of a specialist ranges from 4 to 6 years. Thirdly, enterprises expect specialists to have not only good soft skills, but also sufficient hard skills, which are necessary to be combined with the digital skills. And the last cause lies in the financial interest of the parties.

**Keywords** Digitalization of industry · Training of personnel · Competencies · Human resource management

## 1 Introduction

Digitalization of industry is a challenge that is currently faced not only by manufacturing enterprises, but also the labor market. There is a growing demand for competencies inaccessible to machines and skills in using digital technologies. At the same time, professions that require competencies which can be replaced by

---

E. Votinova (✉) · E. Kalabina
Ural Federal University named after the first President of Russia B.N. Yeltsin, Ekaterinburg, Russian Federation

Ural State University of Economics, Ekaterinburg, Russian Federation
e-mail: votinova.ekaterina@urfu.ru



A. Appolloni et al. (eds.), *The Future of Industry*, Lecture Notes in Information Systems and Organisation 70, https://doi.org/10.1007/978-3-031-66801-2_22

technology are becoming obsolete [1]. Anticipating this situation, educational institutions have focused on developing soft skills among students, which is undoubtedly necessary for future specialists, but cannot guarantee success in profession.

According to estimates [2–5], digitalization can replace some professions; however, it is not always destructive. In particular, all professions are divided into four broad groups depending on the availability of skills in them, which can be considered bottlenecks to computerization. The "rising star" is a broad group with low destructive and high transformative effects of digitalization. In contrast, "collapsing" occupations face a high risk of destructive effects. «Human area» occupations have low risks of both destructive and transformative digitalization, whereas «machine area» occupations are affected by both types [1]. The results of studies help identify which capabilities will be in demand and to what degree workers with different abilities can expect their occupations to be transformed in the digital era. Engineering and technical specialties belong to the "rising stars" group, digitalization will change the content of these professions and, as a result, the requirements for the employee skills will be significantly transformed.

Moreover, when forming requirements for a generalized group of specialties, it is necessary to evaluate not only the competencies of future specialists, but also the technical level of enterprises. The analysis carried out in [6–9] showed that the pace of technical re-equipment and modernization of fixed-capital assets today is unsatisfactory from the perspective of increasing labor productivity, optimizing the use of the existing capacities.

So, it is worth noting the differences between the speed of changes at industrial enterprises, changes in the content and skills of a particular profession and those skills formed in a future graduate. Accordingly, it is necessary to establish the difference between the personnel needs of industrial enterprises and the competencies offered by the staff, as well as to identify the causes of its occurrence.

To achieve this purpose, the following objectives were set: to estimate what skills of the staff are most in demand in the context of industrial digitalization; who should ensure that the personnel meet the enterprise's requirements; how we can assess the difference in production needs and labor market offers.

## 2 Digitalization As the Future of Industry

Digitalization of industry is the process of introducing digital technologies and innovations into the industrial sphere in order to optimize production processes and increase the efficiency and competitiveness of enterprises.

This process is new, dynamic and promises (in the future) high quality products at adequate costs. Scientific and practical interest in digitalization in production is primarily due to the great significance and economic rationality of digital technology integration activities [10].

However, the process of digitalization faces some problems, in particular:

- the problem of processing huge amounts of data. The process preceding digitalization—automation and robotization—involved receiving and processing data from several pieces of equipment (welding machine/robot, rotator, welding source or other power supply) and they were the only ones to be coordinated. In contrast, digitalization involves not only receiving data from a variety of processing equipment, but also receiving and transmitting data to other divisions of the enterprise;
- faster speed of decision-making;
- increasing variability of processes;
- the presence of a digital platform is the corresponding ecosystem of a digital enterprise, including suppliers of resources and components, consumers, as well as service and operational services;
- reduction in the number of employees involved in production;
- a different approach to recruitment (changes in employee competences).

Thus, all the risks considered, we can be conclude that the digitalization of industry should proceed in the following directions: accelerating the introduction of new products to the market; increasing the reliability and safety of production; improving the flexibility of production; an overall rise in production efficiency and personnel training of an industrial enterprise [11, 12].

## 3 Requests of Enterprise

What is the training of personnel for digital production? What is the difference between the requirements for personnel in traditional and digital production?

Until recently, there has been two types of staff skills in the professional environment:

- hard skills—professional and technical skills that can be clearly demonstrated. For example, the skill of blind printing, driving a car, knowledge of a programming language, etc.;
- soft skills—those that are difficult to track, check and demonstrate clearly. This group includes communication and management skills.

According to the results of research by Harvard University and Stanford Research Institute in the twenty-first century, the contribution of hard skills to the professional success of an employee is only 15%, while soft skills determine the remaining 85%. This is true if success depends more on the employee's involvement in the company's business processes [13].

According to [14, 15], there is a shortage of specialists with competencies in artificial intelligence: technical analysts, mathematical problem-setters, specialists in the field of computer vision.

The requirements of industrial enterprises follow from the problems/features that have been highlighted in digital production. Obviously, the processing of a huge amount of data is based on computer technology and software, but the decision is up to the person. Thus, there is the ability to analyze, make decisions, track changes in the data flow. An increase in the variability of processes implies the presence of such skills as the ability to quickly adapt, adjust, and switch between tasks. A digital platform is a kind of software that has its own interface. Accordingly, rapid learning and readiness to respond to changes are necessary. Perhaps, the most socially significant is the last point, namely the reduction in the number of employees. Most workers, whose duties are not intellectually loaded and consist in performing simple, repetitive actions, can and will be replaced by machines. Analyzing the requirements imposed by digital production, it can be concluded that there is another group of skills that may be decisive in the nearest future. These are digital skills.

Digital skills are currently in demand and in short supply:

- skills that determine the free use of technology and digital devices, as well as confident work in various programs;
- analytical skills that determine the ability to receive information, process it, draw the right conclusions and convey the results and solutions to the target audience;
- communication skills that allow one to communicate freely and organize work using digital channels;
- skills aimed at identifying problems and finding ways to solve them;
- personal characteristics that allow a person to easily adapt to a changing digital environment [16–19].

On the one hand, representatives of some companies also point to the absence of applied specialists who are not only professionals in their subject area, but are able or at least understand how to solve their problems through artificial intelligence technologies (in this context, e.g., metalworking technologists were mentioned) [15]. On the other hand, technology does not bypass the educational process. The widespread introduction of teamwork, result orientation, adaptability are developing soft skills in the future specialist.

The personnel requirements put forward by the enterprise are determined by the level of implementation of digital technologies. The higher it is, the more qualified employees are needed. We must admit that at the moment not all enterprises are ready to digitalize production. Accordingly, the requirements for personnel will be determined by the readiness of the enterprise for digitalization. And the university should be focused on training personnel for any of the listed types of enterprises.

It can be noted that an enterprise in the process of transition to digital production needs specialists with all types of competencies (Fig. 1).

In this context, congruence is the consistency, adequacy, mutual correspondence of knowledge, skills and abilities of a specialist and the requirements for personnel imposed by employers. It is worth asking the question: to what extent the skills acquired by future specialists are congruent with the requirements of the industry?

**Fig. 1** The need for young professionals' competencies

## 4 Methodology

The research used general scientific and special methods of scientific cognition, as well as content analysis and terminological analysis.

The authors reviewed the curricula and work programs of the disciplines of the specialty "Equipment and technology of welding production" (later the direction "Mechanical Engineering" trajectory "Equipment and technology of welding production", currently the specialty "Design of technological machines and complexes") since 2000. It is possible to trace changes in the formation of various types of competence within the framework of training specialists in welding production (Fig. 2).

Data analysis shows that the educational environment is gradually adapting to the requirements of industry, albeit with some delay.

## 5 Development of Required Competencies Among Students

Today, universities train specialists based on the experience of the past decades, when the main advantage of a person was his/her knowledge. Young specialists graduated from the university with a set of ready-made solutions (knowledge), basic professional skills and abilities. They were hired by enterprises where they could apply them. Thus, the system of personnel training existing in the twentieth century in Russia was focused on hard skills.

In the 2010s, there was a tendency to develop soft skills, while hard skills became secondary. This can be explained by various aspects. Firstly, the accelerated development of technology created the illusion that there is no point to obtain professional knowledge as technology is changing very quickly. Secondly, the availability of information. A future specialist believed that all the necessary information could be quickly obtained via the Internet and knowledge was not needed. Thirdly, the development of artificial intelligence and the saturation of technological equipment

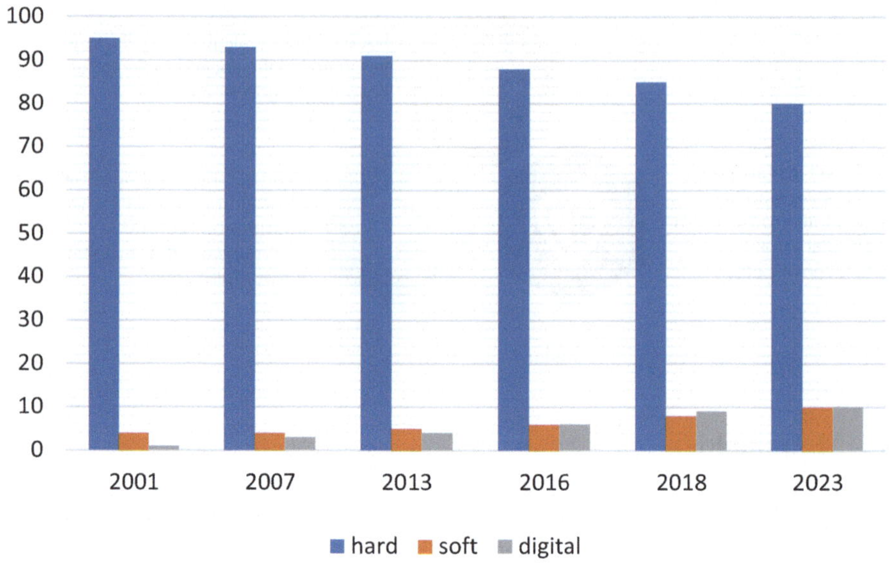


**Fig. 2** Distribution of competencies among students of the specialty "Equipment and technology of welding production"

with intelligent systems also created prerequisites for reducing the requirements for basic skills of engineer. As a result, enterprises faced the problem of personnel shortage.

Enterprises want to get a ready-made specialist with the competencies that each of them needs individually. The requirements for the enterprise personnel can be formed by participating in the development of professional standards. However, the process of discussion, adoption and approval of the professional standard is quite long. In addition, even when updating curricula with newly introduced professional standards taken into account, specialist training takes at least 4 years. So, the gap between the employer's request and the preparation of a ready-made specialist is at least 5 years (Fig. 3).

Another important point in personnel training is financial. Who is expected to pay for the compliance of personnel with the requested level? According to the Labor Code of the Russian Federation, this is the employer's responsibility that is in no hurry to invest in human capital [20–22]. Employees do not also strive for improving their skills, because they believe that education is free and everything should be taught to them. That is, there is another gap, i.e., the desire to pay for the compliance of the employee's qualifications with the requirements of the employer.

**Fig. 3** The process of responding to an enterprise's request for personnel training

## 6 Conclusion

In conclusion, it is noteworthy that digitalization of production is a dynamic process associated not only with changes in technological equipment, but also with changes in personnel requirements. Moreover, as a result of digitalization, there will be not so much a decrease in the employed able-bodied population as a restructuring of specializations and competencies. The need for the requested competencies will again shift towards hard skills, while soft and digital skills will remain an advantage for staff. The training of specialists should be designed for enterprises with any level of technical equipment [23]. In general, what employers want and what university graduates can offer are weakly congruent. The question remains open as to how to assess the difference in production demands and labor market supply. Perhaps, using some quantitative assessment of congruence, it would be easier to approximate the implementation of employers' requests in terms of graduates having the necessary skills [24]. Therefore, it is necessary to transform both the education system and the ways in which enterprises and educational institutions interact. At the same time, the regulatory function of the state as a guarantor of the quality of education remains necessary.

## References

1. Fossen, F., & Sorgner, A. (2019). Mapping the future of occupations: Transformative and destructive effects of new digital technologies on jobs. *Foresight and STI Governance, 13*(2), 10–18. https://doi.org/10.17323/2500-2597.2019.2.10.18
2. Fossen, F. M., & Sorgner, A. (2019). New digital technologies and heterogeneous employment and wage dynamics in the United States: Evidence from individual-level data. In *IZA discussion paper 12242*. Institute of Labor Economics.
3. Gontar, E. A. (2022). Labor market trends in the context of digitalization of the economy. In *The 35th international Plekhanov readings: Anniversary collection of articles by graduate students and young scientists in English* (pp. 47–51). Plekhanov Russian University of Economics.

4. Sorgner, A. (2017). The automation of jobs: A threat for employment or a source of new entrepreneurial opportunities? *Foresight and STI Governance, 11*(3), 37–48. https://doi.org/10.17323/25002597.2017.3.37.48
5. Sorgner, A. (2019). Technological development, changes on labor markets, and demand for skills. *Foresight and STI Governance, 13*(2), 6–8.
6. Drivolskaya, N. A., & Molozhavenko, O. A. (2021). Digitalization of industry as a factor of sustainable development of production. *Journal of Economy and Business, 9-1*(79), 74–77. https://doi.org/10.24412/2411-0450-2021-9-1-74-77
7. Goridko, N. P., & Nizhegorodtsev, R. M. (2012). A technological trap or a course towards new industrialization: A choice for Russia. In *Russian economic model: Contents and structure* (pp. 186–200).
8. Krasina, E. N., & Goridko, N. P. (2021). Technical re-equipment as a key factor of the production potential enhancement for separate branches of economy. *Bulletin of the South-Russian State Technical University (NPI). Series: Socio-Economic Sciences, 14*(3), 191–201. https://doi.org/10.17213/2075-2067-2021-3-191-201
9. Piskunov, A. I. (2019). Technical re-equipment as a basis of innovative development of industrial enterprises in Russia. *Russian Journal of Innovation Economics, 9*(1), 137–150. https://doi.org/10.18334/vinec.9.1.40079
10. Ugolnicova, O. D., Vorotkov, P. A., & Rizov, A. D. (2021). Digitalization of the Russian industry (the case of Ural region). *Technical and Technological Problems of the Service, 3*(57), 56–62.
11. Bakrunov, Y. O., Oleinik, A. V., Andreev, V. N., Ushakova, N. A., & Vivchar, G. A. (2022). Digitalization in the industry: The main trends and challenges of ensuring competitiveness. *Moscow Economic Journal, 7*(9). https://doi.org/10.55186/2413046X_2022_7_9_550
12. Innoprom. (2019). Digitalization for industry. *Standards and Quality, 8*, 86–89.
13. Belyak, O., Revina, A., & Kalabina, E. (2022). Do employee soft skills influence their engagement in organizations? In *Insights from industry and academia international research conference "GSOM emerging markets Conference-2022"* (pp. 53–59). St. Petersburg State University Graduate School of Management.
14. Osadchuk, E. V. (2022). Digitization of industry: Barriers to the creation of artificial intelligence and proposals for overcoming them. *Science Management: Theory and Practice, 4*(2), 201–209. https://doi.org/10.19181/smtp.2022.4.2.17
15. Shirinkina, E. (2019). Digitalization of business processes of industries as a factor in increasing the return of human capital. *Scientific Researches and Development. Economics, 7*(1), 53–57. https://doi.org/10.12737/article_5c598be6534ab0.00845034
16. Karpovich, V. F. (2023). Digitalization of the system of higher engineering and economic education as a basis for innovative development and increasing the competitiveness of industry. *Innovative Science, 3-1*, 57–62.
17. Korableva, O. N. (2023). Modern approaches to the formation of digital competencies for the knowledge-intensive economy. In *Intelligent engineering economics and industry 5.0 (ECOPROM): Proceedings of the international scientific and practical conference* (pp. 48–51). https://doi.org/10.18720/IEP/2023.4/9
18. Sarapultseva, A. V. (2023). Digitalization of science and education: direction and prospects. In *Improving humanitarian technologies in the educational space of the university: Factors, problems, prospects: Proceedings of the All-Russian (with international participation) scientific and methodological conference* (pp. 105–110). March 15–17, 2023. Ekaterinburg.
19. Vasilenkova, N. V. (2022). Digitalization of the industry: Direction and prospects. *Scientific Almanac of the Central Chernozem Region, 2-1*, 136–142.
20. Akmaeva, R. I. (2023). Strengthening the importance of training engineering personnel at all levels is a prerequisite for the successful implementation of the concept of technological development of the country. In *Intelligent Engineering Economics and Industry 5.0 (ECOPROM): Proceedings of the International Scientific and Practical Conference* (pp. 85–88). November 17–18, 2023. Saint-Petersburg. https://doi.org/10.18720/IEP/2023.4/9

21. Apina, A. M. (2014). Increasing the efficiency of personnel labor on the basis of optimizing investments in human capital. *Bulletin of the Saratov State Socio-Economic University, 1*(50), 9–12.
22. Borodin, V. A., & Shunina, O. A. (2018). Regional market of education services: Development problems. *Bulletin of Plekhanov Russian University of Economics, 4*(100), 173–183.
23. Sivolap, L. A. (2023). Features of digital transformation of the education system in the Russian federation. In *Professional education and mentoring in the period of educational transformations of the 21st century. The 9th Makhmut readings: Proceedings of the International Scientific and Practical Conference* (pp. 253–256). September 26–27, 2023. Elabuga.
24. Molotkov, Y. I. (2023). Managing students and specialists' soft skills and hard skills formation. In *In Technologies in education—2023: Proceedings of the international scientific and methodological conference* (pp. 152–167).

# The Role of Demographic Processes in the Digital Transformation of Industrial Regions

**Kursat Demiryurek, Ludmila Glezman, and Irina Tsarenko**

**Abstract** The article identifies the current problems of the modern Russian labor market. To study them more closely and provide solutions, the paper proposes a methodological toolkit for assessing the use and impact of labor resources on the development of an industrial region in the conditions of digital transformation. The testing was carried out in the regions of the Volga Federal District of the Russian Federation (hereinafter the Volga Federal District), where a quarter of the country's industrial production is concentrated. According to the testing results, the demographic factor was recognized as the most significant for the development and effective functioning of the labor market among numerous factors affecting the regional labor market amid digital transformation of industry. The analysis revealed the problems in the structure of available labor resources in the Volga Federal District, including the growing deficit of labor resources associated with the decline in the number of people below working age and the decline in the output of middle-level specialists (technical specialties). The results of the study confirm that the implemented set of state support measures is not fully efficient, so it is necessary to develop and introduce new tools and mechanisms that regulate the sustainable development of labor potential and meet the conditions of the transformational economy in the country's industrial regions.

**Keywords** Labour market · Labour resources · Demography · Digital transformation · Able-bodied population · Population reproduction · Workforce · Professional orientation

K. Demiryurek
Bafta Business School, Ondokus Mayis University, Sumsun, Turkey
e-mail: kuratd@omu.edu.tr

L. Glezman · I. Tsarenko (✉)
Institute of Economics of the Ural Branch of the Russian Academy of Sciences, Perm, Russian Federation
e-mail: glezman.lv@uiec.ru; tsarenko.iv@uiec.ru



A. Appolloni et al. (eds.), *The Future of Industry*, Lecture Notes in Information Systems and Organisation 70, https://doi.org/10.1007/978-3-031-66801-2_23

# 1 Introduction

The global digital agenda actualized by the Covid and post-Covid period, severe sanctions imposed by unfriendly countries amid high import dependence, the breakdown of major logistics chains due to geopolitical tensions and other global challenges have put the Russian Federation on the brink of global transformation of all socio-economic spheres.

Labor resources also require transformation. Thus, the federal project "Personnel for the Digital Economy" (https://digital.gov.ru/ru/activity/directions/866/) envisages the reproduction and preservation of labor resources, the main feature of which will be the availability of the necessary competencies, knowledge and skills required to accept and implement the challenges of the digital economy. The requirements of industrial enterprises to the qualifications, competences and skills of potential employees are increasing due to digital transformations that complicate business processes and production technologies in the new socio-economic conditions of production.

In industrialized regions, where the processes of digital transformation are more rapid, there is a growing deficit of qualified personnel. This is due to the system of higher and special education lagging behind the labor market requirements in terms of proactive training of specialists in demand at the new stage of economic development. In these conditions, the applicants possessing demanded qualifications and competences are able to choose, and in some cases make requirements to the potential employer concerning decent and comfortable labor conditions under low competition on the labor market in their niche.

In fact, there is a situation, where employers fight for the employee, and not vice versa to realize his/her knowledge, skills and abilities. This situation is aggravated not only by the shortage of highly qualified specialists, but also by the existing deficit of personnel in the labour market caused by the difficult demographic situation in the country.

Thus, in the light of the ongoing processes of digital transformation of industry for industrially developed regions, it is an urgent and practically significant task to determine and assess the impact of labor resources on the development of the industrial region in the conditions of digital transformation, which is due to the increase in industrial production in the context of the implementation of the state policy of import substitution and the national agenda for achieving technological sovereignty.

To solve these problems, we set and solved the problem of developing a methodological toolkit for assessing the demographic situation in the region from the perspective of reproduction of labor resources and their impact on the development of an industrial region in the conditions of digital transformation, based on multifactorial modelling, in order to identify the most important factors and effective tools for effective reproduction of labor resources for sustainable development of industrial regions in the digital economy.

## 2 Literature Review

The impact of demography on the reproduction of labor resources in the regions is of scientific interest to many researchers, who study this issue from different points of view, including the comparison with possible negative causes, the presentation of strategic developments with several scenarios, and so on.

Demographic processes are the most important tool for influencing macroeconomic indicators, which is directly related to the reproduction of labor resources [1]. But due to the endogenous model of interaction between fertility and labor productivity growth, this factor is relegated to the background, giving way to innovative forms of labor resources replacement. Thus, demographic processes are assigned the role of identification of labor income increment using the national state [2, 3]. Micek [4, 5] points out that "the reasons for the stagnation of aggregate productivity were the development of such trends as the decline in demand for public investment, the decline in import prices, the restraint of population growth and mobility", which indicates the need for stabilization and further population growth in the country to reproduce the economically active population.

For example, in Turkey and India, the pandemic period has sufficiently affected the labor market, but this is seen differently in various demographic groups. Researchers have found that the tendency for the labor force to decline is more pronounced in the female labor market than in the male labor market, and the population with a higher level of education was less affected by Covid-19 [6, 7]. Guclu [8, 9] proved that as the Turkish economy grows, it becomes more sensitive to workers mobility in the labour market, namely the age of potential candidates and gender, usually male. In addition, many studies of the world labor market have determined that gender change in the population composition is a determining factor in the level of unemployment. Understanding the trends of gender changes is necessary to choose an effective direction for influencing the labor market, that a significant gender gap in the analysis of the unemployment rate is possible taking into account the differences in the human capital of men and women [10–12].

When considering long-term trends in the development of the regional labor market from the perspective of demography, a number of researchers are of the opinion that when constructing scenario events, it is necessary to take into account a population category such as younger than working age, which will sufficiently influence the development of the labor market in the future [13]. Also, Stijn Baert [14] refers to the fact that in addition to the direct reproduction of labor resources, the indicator of the state of the labor market is "an economical analytical approach that uses the ratio of unemployment to the population and inactivity to the population as two very suitable and complementary indicators", which should also be taken into account when drawing up methods for assessing the state of the labor market, a certain territory and further selection of an effective mechanism. In addition, when studying the flexibility of the labor market and its dependence on external factors, it is necessary to carefully study the impact of various indicators in the long and short term. In the issues of studying the quality and quantity of the population, "high flexibility of the labor market in the long term correlates with an increase in the number of workers living in poverty, both in relative and absolute terms", which can lead not only to stagnation of the labor market, but also to the general standard of living of the population [15, 16].

Accelerating technological transformation also has a significant impact on the labor market, for a timely response it is necessary to establish cause-and-effect relationships, to choose further actions and determine the benefits of technological transformation, directly affecting the innovation progress in the labor market [17, 18].

In modern conditions, it is necessary to take into account the pace of digitalization, which directly affects the creation of potential jobs, labor productivity, the release of workers and the possibility of erasing the deficit of labor resources [19, 20].

Thus, the analysis of the scientific literature revealing the problems and prospects of reproduction of labor resources in industrial regions indicates the need to determine the directions of progressive development of regional economies related to the need for comprehensive consideration and development of effective measures, taking into account the existing advantages and opportunities in the regional space in the conditions of digital transformation.

## 3 Materials and Methods

The method of multifactorial modelling has been used to solve the problems of demography analysis as the most important factor of labor resources reproduction in the regions with industrial specialization of the production complex in terms of choosing the method and determining its impact on the development of labor resources in the industrial region. It is assumed that the multifactorial model is an optimal option for determining effective tools of labor resources reproduction for sustainable development of industrial region in the conditions of digital transformation, as it provides the opportunity to:

- determine the multicollinearity and directionality of the selected indicators;
- make calculations with additional indicators, depending on the advantages and needs of the industrial region under consideration in the context of digital transformation;
- analyze development trends in the short- and long-term perspective;
- determine the development directions depending on the obtained results, highlighting their regional advantages.

To assess the use of labor resources in the region, it is proposed to utilize the author's methodological tools presented in Fig. 1.

Next, let us consider each stage of the proposed methodology in more detail.

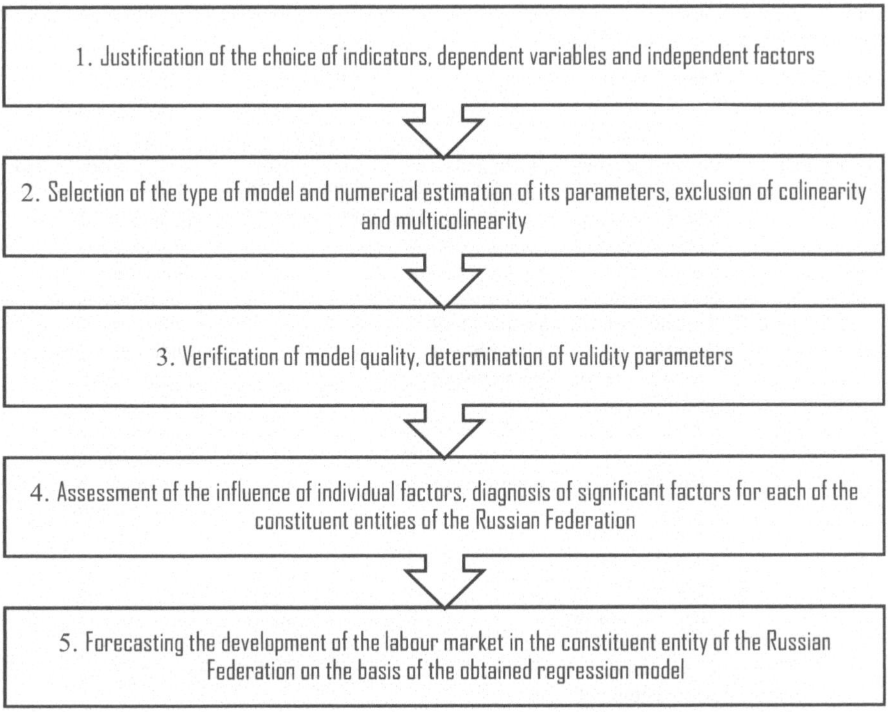


**Fig. 1** Algorithm for selecting indicators, models and determining the influence of factors on the development of labor resources

*Stage 1*. In order to conduct further research, it is necessary to determine the order of selection of the main indicators that reveal qualitative and quantitative characteristics of the labor market of the industrial region, based on which spatial series for the period of 2012–2022 were used for further simulation modeling, which allow us to trace the individual dynamics of the variable, determine the closeness of connection and accuracy of multifactorial modeling (Table 1).

The precise choice of the necessary indicators, which characterize the labor market both qualitatively and quantitatively, reflects the uniformity of the choice, which allows us to properly identify the problems and development trends of the industrial region for its long-term sustainable development in the context of digital transformation. Further, to test the author's methodology, we select the method of reproduction of labor resources and determine its impact on the development of the industrial region for calculations with the possibility of including additional indicators and trend analysis in the development of the region in the short and long term.

The choice of the time period of the study is conditioned by the fact that the data in it are continuous, without gaps in observation, which makes it possible to provide forecasts not only for the long-term or short-term period, but also for the medium term.

**Table 1** Information base of regression analysis of the labor resources, including indicators of dependent variables and independent factors

| Natural transformation | Migration transformation | Social transformation | Economic transformation | Labour transformation |
|---|---|---|---|---|
| • Number of labor force, thousand people (X1)<br>• Population numbers below working age per 1000 people, people (X2)<br>• Natural increase (+)/decrease (−) of population, % (X3) | • Distribution of the arrival numbers within the region, % (X4)<br>• Distribution of the arrival numbers from other Russian regions, % (X5)<br>• Distribution of arrivals from outside Russia, % (X6)<br>• Distribution of the departure numbers within the region, % (X7)<br>• Distribution of the number of departures to other regions of Russia, % (X8)<br>• Distribution of the number of departures outside Russia, % (X9)<br>• Migration growth/population loss per 10,000 people, people (X10) | • Employed total (technical activities and related specialties), thousand people (X11)<br>• Unemployed total, thousand people (X12)<br>• Number of unemployed registered in the employment service, thousand people (X13) | • GRP, in current prices: Total, RUR mln (Y) | • Graduation of skilled workers and clerks, thousand people (X14)<br>• Graduation of specialists with vocational education (technical specialities), thousand people (X15)<br>• Graduation of specialists with higher education (technical specialities), thousand people (X16) |

*Source*: compiled by the authors

By carrying out an informative economic evaluation of the selected indicators, the significant factor that affects these indicators to a greater extent is determined.

In order not to determine additional integral coefficients, it is proposed to choose GRP as a regression variable, as it comprehensively and qualitatively expresses the selected indicators by the main development groups. In case of choosing another indicator, it is possible to obtain biased results in the models, which will not allow determining qualitative and effective measures at the stage of selecting development directions.

Factors (X1-X16) were selected by matching certain groups of indicators of qualitative and quantitative characteristics of the labor market by directions of movement: natural transformation, migration transformation, social transformation, economic transformation and labor transformation.

*Stage 2.* A multifactorial model is built to determine the mutual relationship of each factor with another factor and their influence on each other. To determine the strong interdependence, we exclude from the matrix of pair correlations the indicators that do not correlate with the GRP indicator and have a value of more than 0.84.

To avoid the dispersion of errors, we will sequentially calculate the results of multiple dependence for each factor separately in interaction with other factors.

*Stage 3.* The reliability of the obtained results is determined by calculating the multiple correlation coefficients, determination, adjusted R-square and metrics to assess the accuracy of calculations.

*Stage 4.* Based on the identified relationships between the selected factors and the regression variable, the results obtained are subjected to interpretation.

*Stage 5.* Intermediate stages on the basis of the obtained results of the multifactorial model allow making short-, medium- and long-term forecasts.

Thus, the proposed multifactorial model for choosing the method of labour resources reproduction and determining its impact on the development of the industrial region in the conditions of digital transformation allows:

- involving the necessary number of indicators and considering their change over time in dynamics;
- adding or reducing factors depending on the research objective, adjusting the observation and forecasting periods;
- recognizing key factors in labor resources reproduction in the industrial region.

## 4 Results

The author's methodology was tested using the case of the Volga Federal District, where the regions of industrial specialization are predominant.

A sample of indicators in dynamics for 2012–2022 was carried out.

To determine the direct and inverse dependence, a correlation matrix was constructed in order to exclude insignificant and irrelevant factors (Table 2).

Next, we select factors from the correlation matrix using the Cheddock scale to determine the degree of relationship with the dependent variable (Y): strong, medium or weak. For this purpose, we establish the minimum acceptable boundary of 0.84, which corresponds to a high and very high degree of closeness of connection between mutually influencing factors. The analysis of the factors that have an indicator within these boundaries is carried out on the data with both direct and inverse dependence. In the process of analysis, it is revealed that factors X11, X14 and X16 will be insignificant and logically difficult to explain, in view of which they are excluded from further analysis.

As a result, it was revealed that the most significant and logically explanatory factors for the regions of the Volga Federal District are X2 "Population below

**Table 2** Correlation matrix based on data from the Volga Federal District

| | Y | X1 | X2 | X3 | X4 | X5 | X6 | X7 | X8 | X9 | X10 | X11 | X12 | X13 | X14 | X15 | X16 |
|---|---|---|---|---|---|---|---|---|---|---|---|---|---|---|---|---|---|
| Y | 1.00 | | | | | | | | | | | | | | | | |
| X1 | −0.73 | 1.00 | | | | | | | | | | | | | | | |
| X2 | 0.96 | −0.60 | 1.00 | | | | | | | | | | | | | | |
| X3 | −0.59 | 0.53 | −0.65 | 1.00 | | | | | | | | | | | | | |
| X4 | −0.90 | 0.61 | −0.82 | 0.28 | 1.00 | | | | | | | | | | | | |
| X5 | 0.81 | −0.54 | 0.87 | −0.50 | −0.71 | 1.00 | | | | | | | | | | | |
| X6 | 0.67 | −0.46 | 0.52 | −0.05 | −0.88 | 0.28 | 1.00 | | | | | | | | | | |
| X7 | −0.78 | 0.48 | −0.75 | 0.43 | 0.80 | −0.79 | −0.54 | 1.00 | | | | | | | | | |
| X8 | −0.19 | 0.41 | 0.01 | −0.39 | 0.48 | 0.02 | −0.67 | 0.19 | 1.00 | | | | | | | | |
| X9 | 0.75 | −0.56 | 0.67 | −0.26 | −0.86 | 0.70 | 0.70 | −0.95 | −0.49 | 1.00 | | | | | | | |
| X10 | −0.08 | −0.03 | −0.17 | 0.36 | −0.03 | −0.36 | 0.29 | 0.58 | −0.38 | −0.39 | 1.00 | | | | | | |
| X11 | −0.85 | 0.92 | −0.76 | 0.50 | 0.79 | −0.75 | −0.56 | 0.61 | 0.40 | −0.67 | −0.05 | 1.00 | | | | | |
| X12 | −0.75 | 0.62 | −0.60 | 0.36 | 0.78 | −0.32 | −0.83 | 0.60 | 0.45 | −0.68 | −0.04 | 0.58 | 1.00 | | | | |
| X13 | 0.03 | −0.22 | 0.05 | 0.19 | −0.12 | 0.40 | −0.12 | −0.12 | −0.27 | 0.20 | −0.01 | −0.39 | 0.42 | 1.00 | | | |
| X14 | −0.97 | 0.69 | −0.96 | 0.56 | 0.85 | −0.89 | −0.55 | 0.75 | 0.15 | −0.71 | 0.09 | 0.85 | 0.63 | −0.13 | 1.00 | | |
| X15 | 0.84 | −0.89 | 0.68 | −0.46 | −0.78 | 0.60 | 0.65 | −0.66 | −0.41 | 0.72 | −0.04 | −0.87 | −0.82 | 0.01 | −0.80 | 1.00 | |
| X16 | −0.93 | 0.83 | −0.83 | 0.55 | 0.85 | −0.77 | −0.62 | 0.69 | 0.28 | −0.70 | 0.01 | 0.93 | 0.73 | −0.11 | 0.92 | −0.94 | 1.00 |

*Source*: compiled by the authors

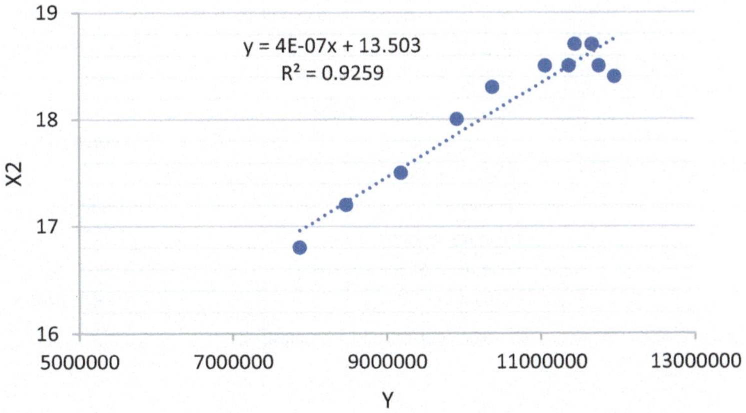


**Fig. 2** Linear regression analysis model for factor X2 "Population below working age". *Source*: compiled by the authors

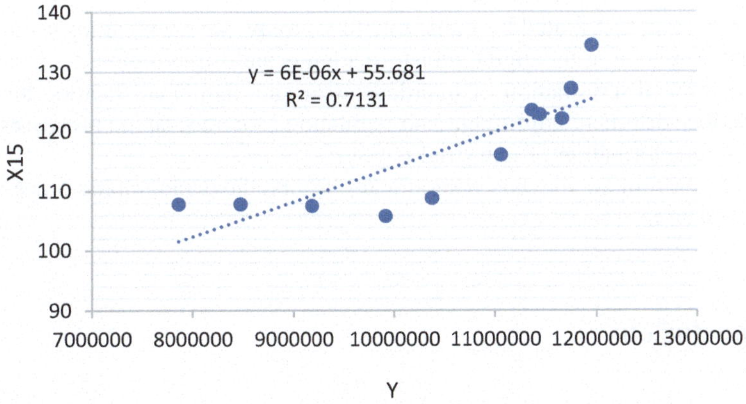


**Fig. 3** Linear regression analysis model for factor X15 "Graduation of specialists with vocational education (technical specialities)". *Source*: compiled by the authors

working age" and X15 "Graduation of specialists with vocational education (technical specialties)".

Factors X2 and X15 are closely related, there is multicollinearity between them. For better visualization, we provide linear regression plots for these significant factors (Figs. 2 and 3).

In our case, R-regression shows how much the GRP indicator (Y) will change if the factor "Population below working age" (X2) or the factor "Graduation of specialists with vocational education (technical specialties)" increases by one (Table 3).

Hence, the indicator that should be paid attention to when developing effective support measures aimed at stabilizing the situation in the labor market of industrial

**Table 3** Multifactorial model for choosing the method of labor resources reproduction and determining its impact on the development of industrial regions in the conditions of digital transformation

| Y = −24101042.5 + 1582858.9*X2 + 50661.7*X15 | |
|---|---|
| Multiple R | 0.995544022 |
| R-squared | 0.9911079 |
| Normalised R-squared | 0.988884874 |
| Standard error | 149610.413 |
| Observations | 11 |
| P-value | 0.0009 |
| Y-intersection | −24101042.48 |
| Variable X 1 | 1582858.894 |
| Variable X 2 | 50661.74403 |

*Source*: compiled by the authors

regions in the conditions of digital transformation of industry is "Population below working age" and "Graduation of middle-level specialists (technical specialties)". In addition, the conducted correlation analysis allows us to draw a number of conclusions:

- the indicators distributed by transformation groups have a significant impact on the labor market in the digital transformation of industrial regions;
- through the determination of interdependent and significant factors, there is a possibility of timely adjustment and regulation of demographic processes in the digital transformation of industrial regions;
- as follows from the diagnosed significant factors, the demographic processes are predominant.

## 5 Conclusion

Having analyzed the problems in the sustainable development of the industrial region's labor market, as well as in determining its development trends, we can state that demographic processes are the most important factor in the reproduction of labor resources for the regional labor market in the actively developing digital economy.

We have identified certain age groups actively involved in the labor market and demonstrated positive trends in related age groups, which are the potential labor force to attract to the labor market to maximize positive effect from their use in the digital transformation of industrial regions. The analysis revealed the problems in the structure of available labor resources in the subjects of the Volga Federal District due to the stagnation of population numbers, the mismatch in the professional and qualification profile, low level of income, etc. The results of the analysis make it possible to forecast the available labor resources in the Volga Federal District. According to the results obtained, it is possible to present forecast data of these processes, which will allow us to develop an effective organizational and management mechanism to regulate labor resources reproduction in the context of deepening digital transformation of regional industry.

The choice of ways and methods of demographic policy regulation should be considered and supported at all levels of government with the involvement of interested structures to determine the optimal areas of regulation leading to progressive socio-economic development of industrial regions in the conditions of digital development.

**Acknowledgments** The study was carried out in accordance with the Research Plan of the Institute of Economics of the Ural Branch of the Russian Academy of Sciences.

## References


1. Salvati, L., & Serra, P. (2019). One thing leads to another: Economic polarizations and social disparities in a pre-crisis Mediterranean city. *International Review of Applied Economics, 33*(3), 353–383. https://doi.org/10.1080/02692171.2018.1495696
2. Brunnschweiler, C. N., Peretto, P. F., & Valente, S. (2021). Wealth creation, wealth dilution and demography. *Journal of Monetary Economics*, 441–459. https://doi.org/10.1016/j.jmoneco.2020.02.002
3. Ran, R., Wang, X., Wang, T., & Hua, L. (2023). The impact of the digital economy on the servitization of industrial structures: The moderating effect of human capital. *Data Science and Management, 6*(3), 174–182. https://doi.org/10.1016/j.dsm.2023.06.003
4. Lopez, A., Ros-Garrido, A., & Marhuenda, F. (2018). Professionals supporting employment: Training and accompaniment in work integration enterprises. *Ciriec-espana revista de economia publica social y cooperative, 94*, 155–183. https://doi.org/10.7203/CIRIEC-E.94.12698
5. Micek, S. A. (2021). Macroeconomic dynamics of the Total factor productivity of the Russian economy. *Economy of Region, 17*(3), 799–813. https://doi.org/10.17059/ekon.reg.2021-3-6
6. Aldan, A., Çıraklı, M. E., & Torun, H. (2021). Covid-19 and the Turkish labor market: Heterogeneous effects across demographic groups. *Central Bank Review, 21*(4), 155–163. https://doi.org/10.1016/j.cbrev.2021.12.003
7. Goswami, D., & Kujur, S. K. (2023). Risk-reducing strategies and labour vulnerability during the pandemic in India. *International Journal of Disaster Risk Reduction, 93*, 103763. https://doi.org/10.1016/j.ijdrr.2023.103763
8. Egeraat, V., Morgenroth, E., & Rutger, K. (2018). A measure for identifying substantial geographic concentrations. *Papers in Regional Science, 97*(2), 281. https://doi.org/10.1111/pirs.12241
9. Guclu, M. (2018). The effect of unemployment by age cohorts and gender on economic growth in Turkey. *Ege Academic Review, 18*(3), 399–407.
10. Addabbo, T., Rodríguez-Modroño, P., & Muñoz, L. G. (2015). Gender differences in labor force participation rates in Spain and Italy under the great recession. *Revista de Economía Mundial, 41*, 21–42. https://doi.org/10.33776/rem.v0i41.3936
11. Coşar, E. E., & Yavuz, A. A. (2021). Okun's law under the demographic dynamics of the Turkish labor market. *Central Bank Review*, 59–69. https://doi.org/10.1016/j.cbrev.2021.03.002
12. Ivandić, R., & Lassen, A. S. (2023). Gender gaps from labor market shocks. *Labour Economics, 83*, 102394. https://doi.org/10.1016/j.labeco.2023.102394

13. Shahateet, M. I. (2022). Does child labour increase unemployment and reduce labour force participation? Empirical evidence from Jordan. *Children and Youth Services Review, 137*, 106444. https://doi.org/10.1016/j.childyouth.2022.106444
14. Baert, S. (2021). The iceberg decomposition: A parsimonious way to map the health of labour markets. *Economic Analysis and Policy*, 350–365. https://doi.org/10.1016/j.eap.2020.12.012
15. Canale, R. R., Liotti, G., & Musella, M. (2022). Labour market flexibility and workers' living conditions in Europe. *Structural Change and Economic Dynamics, 62*, 441–450. https://doi.org/10.1016/j.strueco.2022.06.003
16. Chris, V. E., Morgenroth, E., & Rutger, K. (2018). A measure for identifying substantial geographic concentrations. *Papers in Regional Science, 97*(2), 281. https://doi.org/10.1111/pirs.12241
17. Chi-Wie, S., Yuan, X., Umar, M., & Lobonţ, O. (2022). Does technological innovation bring destruction or creation to the labor market? *Technology in Society, 68*, 101905. https://doi.org/10.1016/j.techsoc.2022.101905
18. Lim, J., & Keun, L. (2019). Employment effect of innovation under different market structures: Findings from Korean manufacturing firms. *Technological Forecasting and Social Change, 146*, 606–615. https://doi.org/10.1016/j.techfore.2018.04.022
19. Bresciani, S., Ferraris, A., Romano, M., & Santoro, G. (2021). Human resource management and digitalisation. In *Digital transformation management for agile organizations: A compass to sail the digital world* (pp. 117–138). Emerald Publishing Limited.
20. Ključnikov, A., Popkova, E. G., & Sergi, B. S. (2023). Global labour markets and workplaces in the age of intelligent machines. *Journal of 0Innovation & Knowledge, 8*(4), 100407. https://doi.org/10.1016/j.jik.2023.100407

# Problem-Based Modular Learning in Instrument Engineering Within Education 5.0

**Aleksei Demin, Andrey Vlasov, Natalya Kuzmina, Igor Savenkov, Vladimir Zemlyakov, and Svetlana Kuzmina**

**Abstract** The paper examines the methods and tools of electronic learning systems for the implementation of problem-based modular learning. It analyzes the types of educational material and its characteristics, as well as digital tools of e-learning systems. We propose a concept of digital problem-based modular learning and scrutinize the benefits from its integration into the digital socio-educational environment. The article gives recommendations on effective digitalization of engineering education according to Education 5.0 requirements. The authors formulate the key needs of modern society that entail the transformation of traditional forms of learning and identify the factors affecting the development of a new-generation information system within the framework of the Education 5.0 paradigm. The research findings were utilized to create an online network learning system that improves the traditional forms of training, enhances performance of students and stimulates their interest. The proposed concept was tested using the case of the Instrument Engineering digital training course. In conclusion, a methodology for integrating adapted educational material into the digital learning environment is provided.

**Keywords** Electronic learning system · Problem-based modular learning · Education 4.0 · Education 5.0 · Industry 4.0 · Industry 5.0

## 1 Introduction

Due to the Fourth Industrial Revolution and the Education 4.0 strategy widely practiced within it, it is becoming increasingly relevant to develop and introduce e-learning methods and tools [1, 2]. The needs of modern society for improved forms

A. Demin (✉)
Shenzhen MSU-BIT University, Shenzhen, China

A. Vlasov · N. Kuzmina · I. Savenkov · V. Zemlyakov · S. Kuzmina
Bauman Moscow State Technical University, Moscow, Russian Federation
e-mail: vlasov@iu4.ru; kuzminanv@student.bmstu.ru; sii18u471@student.bmstu.ru; zemlyakov@bmstu.ru; kuzminasv@student.bmstu.ru

 
A. Appolloni et al. (eds.), *The Future of Industry*, Lecture Notes in Information Systems and Organisation 70, https://doi.org/10.1007/978-3-031-66801-2_24

of education give rise to trends in customization, introduction of artificial intelligence, flexibility and mobility of the learning process. The Fifth Industrial Revolution (Industry 5.0) imposes additional requirements for staff qualifications and combines human intelligence and creativity with the capabilities of digital devices to improve overall production efficiency. All this results in the emergence of the Education 5.0 model, which complies with today's trends in digitalization of the social and production sphere.

For the learning model to develop, educational approaches need to be revised and improved. The problem of introducing and implementing problem-based modular learning, which is described in this article, is gaining in relevance due to the need to enhance the effectiveness of the learning process and its intellectualization [3, 4]. Electronic learning systems (ELSs), as one of the tools for implementing such a model, have become widespread recently [5–8]. They are especially advantageous as they give the student an opportunity to learn at any place and at any time and choose independently when to start the training.

The transition from Education 4.0 to Education 5.0 is inevitably coupled with the intensification of people–digital tools relationships. In our article, we analyze the Blackboard and Moodle learning management systems [9] as ones of the key tools for digitalization in education. In contrast to the traditional education system, e-learning has a number of advantages, such as a greater number of students serviced in a relatively short time, the optimal combination of mass and individual approaches to the learning process, effective organization of open learning, and students' growing motivation for learning [10–19]. Although these advantages are pertinent for almost any discipline, they are especially evident in engineering disciplines and computer technology [20–25].

The *purpose* of the study is to propose a methodology for integrating ELSs methods and tools in the field "Instrument Engineering" that will make the learning process and its organization more effective, add to the traditional education system, and strengthen students' motivation for study.

We have come up with a paradigm of the learning environment that implements the concept of problem-based modular learning in the field of Instrument Engineering. The introduction of e-learning tools opens up the way to customization (students are free to choose the time and place for study), and problem-based modular learning increases students' interest in studying. In addition to e-learning courses, the e-learning environment embraces online library, which makes studying the theoretical basis significantly more effective. The knowledge control system makes it possible to perform its adaptive assessment providing comfortable conditions for the student and reducing the time spent by the teacher on student performance evaluation.

## 2 Literature Review

Let us analyze the key historical phases of the development of ELSs.

The decades of the 1950s–1960s are the first phase of the ELS development. In 1954, Professor Burrhus Skinner put forward the idea of programmed learning [8], which actually means the introduction of automation into learning practice [9–11]. In the 1960s–1970s, the concept of artificial intelligence came into existence. There were developed fundamental knowledge representation models and the first AI-based systems. Thus, developers of learning systems formulated the following goal: to devise such a learning system that could completely imitate a teacher. As a result of research studies, the structure of learning systems was developed and some methods for attaining the goal were proposed. However, at that time, digital learning systems were selective type systems, in which it was the teacher who decided on teaching methods and teaching influences, while their implementation and results evaluation were carried out by ELSs. Among possible examples are Licklider's system for analytic geometry training [12] and Buiten and Lane's pronunciation training system for language students [13].

The next phase in the development of the automated learning is the period between the early 1970s and the mid-1980s. The emerging ideas of artificial intelligence were incapable of solving the learning management problem. The main results were attained in terms of interface implementation of dialog interaction subsystems.

The third phase is the second half of the 1980s and the 1990s. This period is characterized by the widespread use of personal computers and the development of computer networks; one of the main directions in the development of learning systems was the use of new digital technologies.

With the development of computer networks and, in particular, the Internet, learning systems reached a new level. In the late 1990s and the early 2000s, online network learning systems came on the scene. Telecommunications allow significantly expanding the circle of system users; the teacher gets the opportunity to constantly monitor the learning process, and the student has access to online consultations [14–17].

The fifth phase is between the end of 2000 and early 2010. This period saw the rapid development of the Internet and the emergence e-Learning and Web 2.0 technologies. By the beginning of 2014, a huge number of online and information-educational resources had been created [18–26].

Contemporary education is subject to constant transformations and changes. Within Industry 4.0, the Education 4.0 model has occupied a special place [1, 2]. The traditional education system founded on passive forms of learning is unable to activate the full creative potential of the educational process. This fact makes the assimilation of information from training courses more complicated. Providing for these downsides, the problem-based modular learning has been developed, which allows boosting the effectiveness of the learning process [3].

The problem-based modular learning is an approach allowing students to learn from problem solving experience. The teacher creates a problem situation and encourages students to be active and independent in finding optimal solutions to it. As a result, students gain knowledge and master new skills in a creative manner [4].

Among the key elements of the modular learning is a system for monitoring and evaluating student performance, and particularly one of its forms, i.e., the individual communication index (rating). The index prescribes a student to obtain the maximum number of points when studying a module. The points are distributed by types of control. Such a system stimulates students to study on a daily basis, significantly increases competition in studies, and eliminates accidents at exams [5].

The central advantages of the problem-based modular learning are: Focus on developing knowledge mobility, methodology flexibility and students' critical thinking, which underlies the creative approach to problem solving; Variability in the structure of the problem module, which helps adapt the learning process to changes in the direction and training outcome due to the ability to variably combine one module with others; Differentiation of the content of educational material that allows promoting the effectiveness of assimilation of the training program by students; Personalization of educational activities, which increases the learning effectiveness due to an individual approach to each student; A variety of forms and methods of learning, which provides the opportunity to personalize educational activities, strengthen students' motivation for study, and enhances the effectiveness of mastering the course content; A shorter period of study that, however, does not compromise the depth and completeness of students' knowledge; An effective system of rating and performance evaluation that helps students systematize their study, improve their motivation for learning, get the maximum score, and most accurately evaluate the training outcome.

Among the disadvantages of the problem-based modular learning are the following [6]: Fragmented learning that implies a significant share of students' independent work; Ignoring the integrity and logic of the training course; Limiting the course to a series of discrete and incoherent problems or assignments (an increase in the role of mentor when formulating the relevant problems to be solved); Labor intensity of the problem modules creation.

The concept of Education 4.0 concentrated on automating the sequence in which the studied material was presented, as well as on various forms of its presentation. With the development of Education 5.0, the idea of "bringing the work of learning programs closer to the work of a teacher" is being revived again, and at a higher intellectual level than before.

## 3 Digitalization in Education

### *3.1 Education 5.0: The Concept of Digitalization in Education*

The Fourth Industrial Revolution (Industry 4.0) based on robotics, artificial intelligence and the Internet of Things has led to the rapid development of new technologies that form new requirements for personnel training. Digital transformation resulted in the emergence of the Education 4.0 model, which has been gradually transformed into Education 5.0. Within the latter, the sphere of education is integrated into the digital society (Society 5.0). In such a society, the development of human resources involves self-actualization, self-fulfillment and self-expression.

Digital tools in education can be categorized into four main groups (Fig. 1): pedagogical programs, educational web-resources, modeling programs, and databases and knowledge bases.

E-learning environment refers to a software complex for training specialists used to provide them with necessary knowledge and help them master the required skills. E-learning system is comprised of modern multimedia technologies, which implies using various communication tools and technologies. Relying on the emotional sphere and all sensory channels—auditive, visual, and kinesthetic—this combination affects participants' perception and assimilation of information in the learning process [4]. This makes the studied material as visual as possible, and therefore understandable and memorable. Another important advantage of the system is interactivity that allows the participants to maintain dialogue at all stages of the learning process.

Currently, network-based learning is one of the promising ways to enhance the effectiveness of education [5]. The following tasks can be accomplished within network-based learning systems:

- Registration and statistical analysis of learning performance indicators: determining the time needed for solving problems and the total number of errors, managing educational activities, etc.;
- Testing students' knowledge, skills and abilities before and after the training, their individual talents and motivations;
- ELS tasks related to the preparation and presentation of learning material, difficulty in adapting material to complexity levels, preparation of dynamic illustrations, tests, laboratory classes, independent student work;
- System administration, learning material delivery to workstations and student feedback.

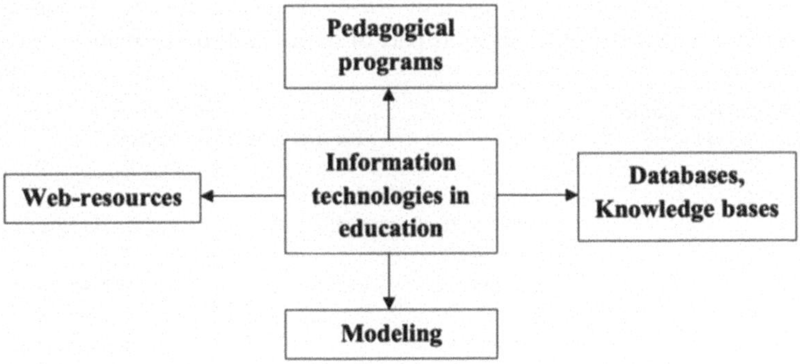


**Fig. 1** Classification of digital tools in education

The advantages of ELSs are their mobility, accessibility, and adequacy (operational adaptation) to the development level of modern scientific knowledge. In addition, ELSs are instrumental in constant updating of learning material.

Among the shortcomings of ELSs are tool dependence and more complex planning. Another problem is self-directed learning, since some students are unable to study independently, without direct interaction. In such cases, an e-learning program may make the material more difficult to learn or lengthen the training time. However, some student can be quite successful in self-study while concentrating on new material only and brushing up on information they already know. One more difficulty is that some students need external guidance and supervision to succeed.

### 3.2 Classification of ELSs

Each ELS is structured as a set of modules. Based on the structure of interaction between the learning system and student, ELSs are divided into open (without feedback) and closed (with feedback) systems that follow principally different approaches to the learning process [6]. Classification of ELSs by structural attributes is presented in Fig. 2.

In open ELSs, students are provided with the learning material irrespective of how successful they are in mastering it. In this case, the educational process comes down to presenting the material and review questions in the order predetermined by the software. It is worth noting that presentation-based systems are the simplest type of open ELSs.

Closed ELSs focus on establishing students' knowledge level at a certain point of the learning process. Using various methodologies, such systems test learners by asking them open or closed-ended (providing a limited number of options) questions. The student is expected to give an answer (feedback) to the question posed. The answer is recorded in the control unit. Based on test results, the student receives a certain score which is further used as part of the overall performance assessment.

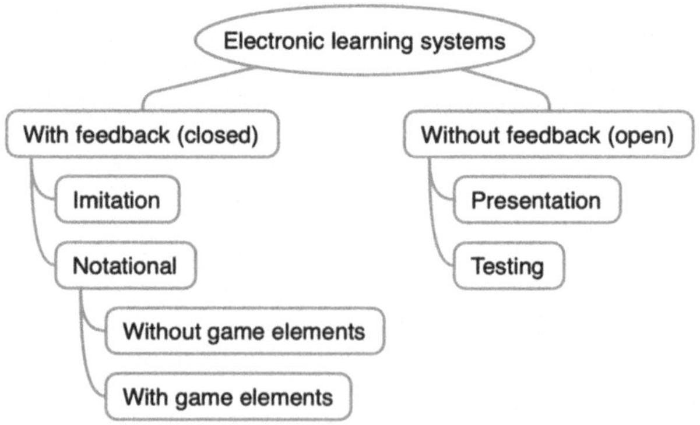


**Fig. 2** ELSs classification by structural attributes

ELSs with the adaptive feedback between students and the learning system, i.e., where the student is offered to undergo the training course again if the score is below the certain threshold, possess the maximum functionality and the highest efficiency in the learning process. Adaptive ELSs use a complex approach. The system performs both teaching and knowledge evaluation functions. An important factor here is the student's feedback on the material provided, which helps the system to rearrange the learning process accordingly.

Imitation learning system is a rather widespread type of closed ELSs. In the systems of this type, the core element is the model of the real situation in a specific subject field. Such ELSs can be exemplified by all kinds of gaming simulators, simulation systems, etc.

Hence, this is apparent that closed ELSs providing maximum flexibility in communication with the user have the widest capabilities in the context of today's requirements for electronic learning systems.

A crucial component of e-learning is the constant monitoring of the user's actions and knowledge progression. The most adequate way to do so is adaptive testing methods: the complexity of each assignment is assessed by processing data on previous test results, which eliminates the subjectivity of the overall performance assessment and automatically creates an individual learning route.

## 4 ELSs Development Concept Based on the Moodle Learning Management System

### *4.1 Comparative Analysis of the Learning Management Systems Blackboard and Moodle*

Contemporary electronic learning systems can be implemented through a number of solutions. Compare the functionality of two widely used learning management systems (LMSs) Blackboard and Moodle.

On Blackboard, teachers can publish course description, learning materials, reading and test materials; the system serves as a platform for student-teacher communication providing various tools for collaboration.

Moodle is a modular object-oriented dynamic learning environment (an open-source learning management system). It provides both cloud hosting and dedicated hosting for ELSs. The cloud platform Moodle Cloudis easily configured, scalable and has many library functions. Logan and Neumann [9] have studied the usability of the LMSs Blackboard (BB) and Moodle and found that the latter provided a wider range of services. This conclusion was based on a statistical analysis of the following LMS components:

- Course format of both LMSs;
- BB announcements and Moodle news forum;
- BB course documents and Moodle modules;

- Collaboration tools for both LMSs;
- Control module in both LMSs.

The course design on BB differs drastically from that on Moodle. BB provides a teacher template with sections for each course management tool, users and course content. Moodle offers the teacher to choose one of three course formats: weekly, one topic, and social. In the weekly course format, course material sare organized by week, with fixed start and end dates. Moodle creates a section for each learning week of the course. The teacher can add content, forums, assignments, and other course elements for each week of study. The one topic format is similar to the weekly one. It consists of a topic, a course format, and a menu module that allows blocks and modules to be shuffled in a 3-column format. Using tabs, this format navigates through the course content, line display of resources and forums, etc. The social format is essentially a forum. In this format, all learning activities are centered around one key forum located on the main page. This format is suitable for independent (informal) learning and may not even be a course; for example, this format can be used for announcements, consultations, etc.

On Blackboard, the announcements section is in the section for creating and viewing private messages. On Moodle, the news forum is used for general announcements and can be found in the central section. On BB, there is a course documents module for presenting the course materials in text, image or video formats. On Moodle, for this purpose the lesson module is utilized, which presents a series of HTML pages to the student. Both BB and Moodle provideroughly the same elements for the teacher to create groups for sharing documents, e-mails, etc.

The control module allows teachers to publish, edit or delete students' grades. The student can view his/her grades using this module. BB and Moodle have similar grading module features providing monitoring and statistical reporting.

## *4.2 Comparative Analysis of Blackboard and Moodle Architectural Models*

Blackboard application consists of three main components [9]:

- Software modules referred to as Knowledge Space (KS) (contains specific material);
- Navigation module that includes the assignment repository, partial solutions, suggestions and information; they can be regarded as a dynamic 'library' of sub-assignments of the current assignment that have recently been published by other KSs;
- The control shell administers the flow of actions to solve tasks in the system; a mechanism is created for KSs to organize their use in the most efficient and consistent manner. On Blackboard, this is performed by the control shell.

Table 1 compares Blackboard and Moodle.

**Table 1** Comparison of Blackboard and Moodle

| Criteria | Moodle | Blackboard |
|---|---|---|
| Course format | Three course formats (weekly, onetopic, and social) | Single format |
| Location of operational information (news/announcements) | Front section of the student interface which makes it easier to access operational information | Personal messages section |
| Organization of the course material | Course can be split into separate lessons | No course splitting |
| Grade module | Identical | Identical |
| Open source | Yes | No |

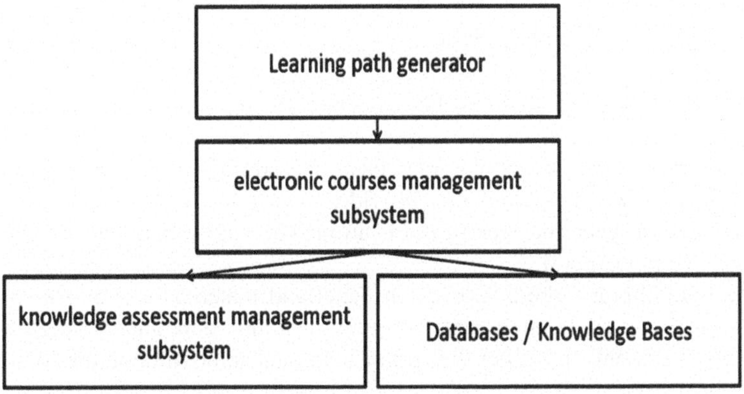


**Fig. 3** Standard structure of a problem-based modular ELS

From Table 1, we can conclude that it is expedient to use Moodle forimplementing an online network-based learning system as this LMS allows creating an environment for courses in various disciplines, splitting the course into lessons while monitoring student performance, and gives an opportunity to choose the format of the course and customize it.

## *4.3 A Moodle-Based ELS: The Implementation Concept*

E-learning environment should provide access to course materials in various formats (video lectures, textbooks, and manuals) and include a student performance assessment system. Having analyzed the most widespread LMSs, the Moodle platform was selected to implement the training course in the field of Instrument Engineering. Figure 3 presents the structure of the network problem-based modular ELS that

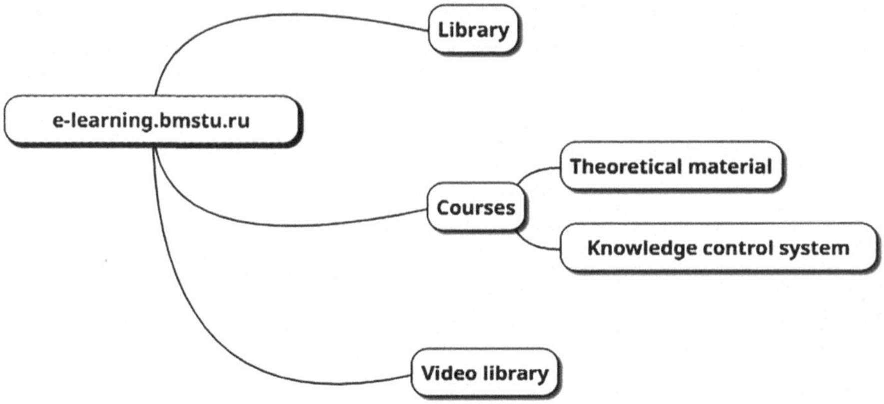


**Fig. 4** Structure of the ELS e-learning.bmstu.ru

consists of the following modules: library, video library, courses, management, and control.

The library includes textbooks, manuals, methodological and didactic aids and has an effective search system that provides access to the learning materials by discipline, author, year and type of publication. The course materials can be sorted out by year of publication.

In the video library, there is a search panel and materials can be sorted out by discipline and author. Lectures are presented in multimedia and/or video formats, which allows students to master the course materials at any time in the format most suitable for them.

Disciplines are grouped educational materials arranged in a particular order for students to study and master the course using an adaptive knowledge control system, which consists of online testing on the topic completed (or part of it). The structure of the e-learning system is given in Fig. 4. The block of courses is arranged in a hierarchical order and decomposes the educational materials into different disciplines and modules.

The generalized hierarchical structure of the *Courses* block is presented in Fig. 5. It provides students with a well-arranged framework for mastering the material and makes learning more effective. A discipline is studied by modules containing the material on a specific topic. The modules are divided into submodules by topic, thus ensuring consistent mastery of the material.

The proposed structure contributes to improving student performance and builds individual learning paths. Figure 6 shows the sequence of actions when working with the ELS e-learning.bmstu.ru.

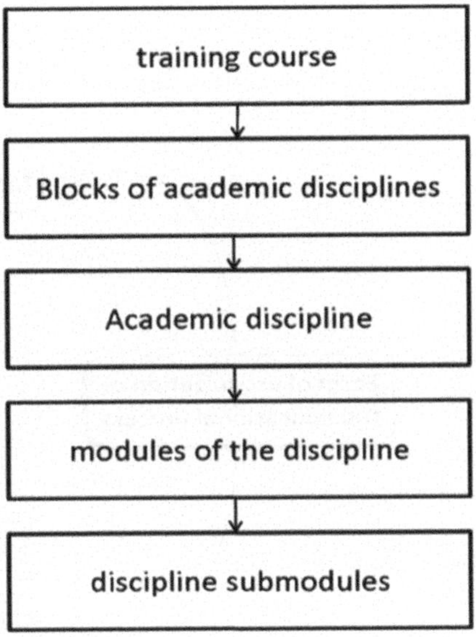


**Fig. 5** Hierarchy of educational materials in the Courses block in the ELS e-learning.bmstu.ru

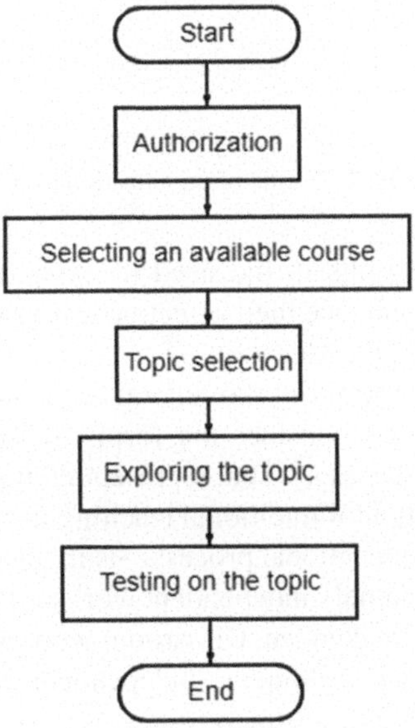


**Fig. 6** Sequence of actions when working with the ELS e-learning.bmstu.ru

## 5 Results

Evidently, the standard teaching methods and forms of organizing the educational process cannot always meet the requirements for the novelty of the knowledge acquired. Over time, the amount of material to be studied increases, no extra time is allocated on learning the course, and the intensity of training increases; all this

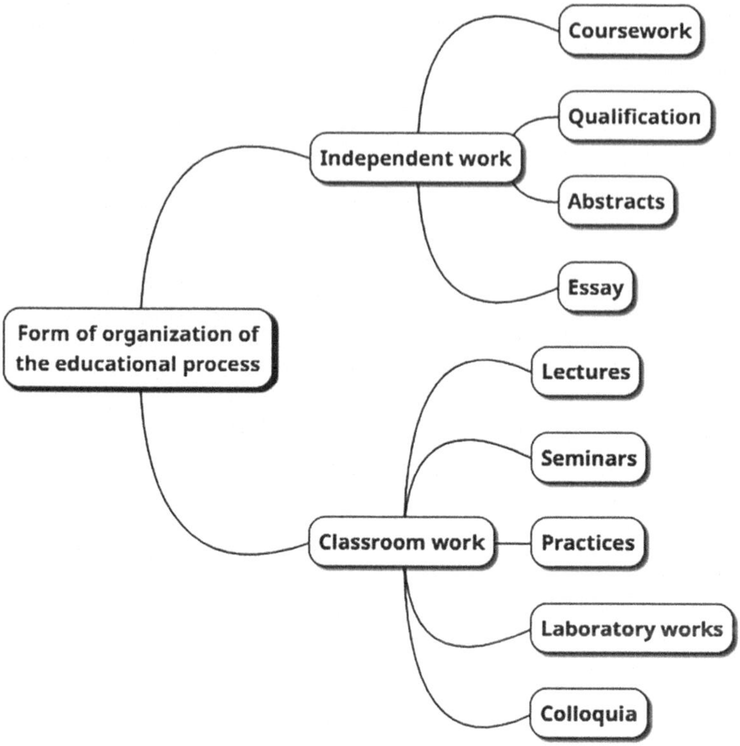


**Fig. 7** Forms of organization of the educational process

results in the need to expand and supplement traditional methods, as well as to enhance their effectiveness [21]. To that end, it is reasonable to use the resources of open education.

Prior to moving on to the analysis of various types of learning materials, we will first consider the forms of the entire educational process organization. Figure 7 shows a visual representation of the key forms of the educational process organization of traditional teaching methods. The main object—Forms of organization of the educational process—is in the center of the model. It has two dependent sub-groups, namely independent work and classroom work. Next, the key forms of organizations are detailed. Classroom work includes lectures, seminars, practices, laboratory work, and colloquia. Independent work embraces lectures, course work, qualification work, abstracts, essays, etc.

Among the ways of representing educational material (Fig. 8) are verbal communication, drawings (visuals), tables, schemes, presentations, mental maps, multimedia, formulas, etc.

When integrating educational materials on Instrument Engineering into the ELS e-learning.bmstu.ru, a library of textbooks, teaching aids and guidelines was formed.

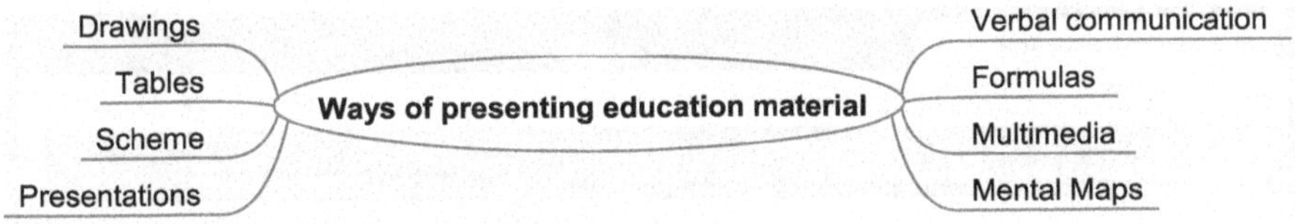


**Fig. 8** Ways of representing educational material

Unfettered access to learning materials provides students with the opportunity to develop a personalized approach to learning which results in better performance as each student can study with his/her own pace. This allows customizing the educational process. Figure 9 illustrates the library interface in the ELS e-learning.bmstu.ru.

To make the library navigation more convenient, a search module is built in that sorts out educational materials by title, discipline, year of publication, and the author's last name, first name or patronymic.

Video library contains all the necessary lectures in the video format, which provides students with a significant amount of information in a short time, increases their interest in and facilitates their perception of the educational material.

Students' knowledge is assessed using the control system (online tests). This approach creates comfortable conditions for students, improves the accuracy of knowledge evaluation, and reduces anxiety while taking tests. Knowledge is assessed on a constant basis once a certain part of the course is mastered. The knowledge control system helps solidify knowledge and, if needed, retake the part of the course. The interface of the knowledge control system in the ELS e-learning.bmstu.ru is presented in Fig. 10.

In our study, we have introduced the concept of the ELS of open engineering education, which includes an online library (textbooks, methodological and didactic aids), video library (video lectures on Instrument Engineering), and the *Disciplines* section that contains theoretical materialsordered by disciplineand the knowledge control system. The proposed ELS aims to boost the effectiveness of the teaching and learning processes. The primary benefits of this approach are personalized learning, lower time costs, and greater comfort of the educational process since it is the student who chooses the time, place and speed of learning according to their strengths and interests.

The trial operation of the ELS showed that there is the need to introduce a module for interactive work with students, expand the *Disciplines* section, and develop and introduce a block of teacher-student interaction via social digital environment.

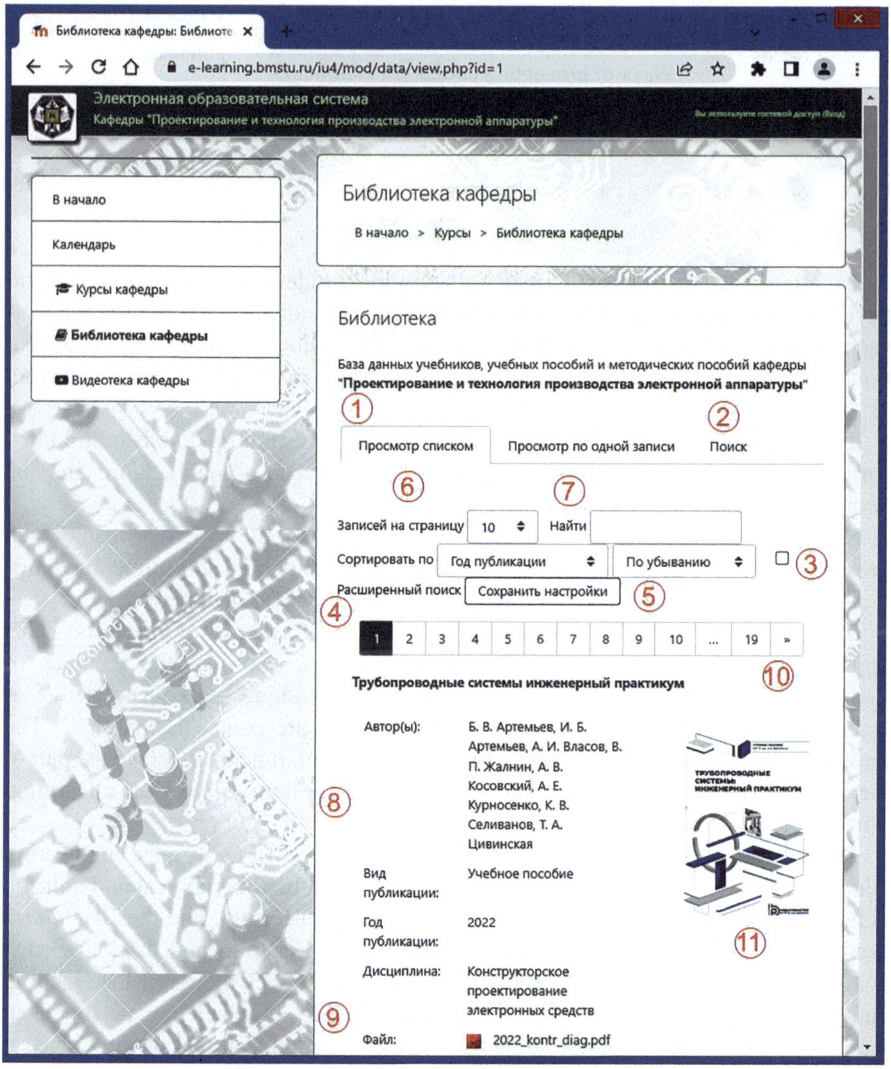


**Fig. 9** Interface of the library of Instrument Engineering educational materials in the ELS e-learning.bmstu.ru: 1—display options; 2—go to the library search module; 3—sortation options; 4—advanced search; 5—save search and display settings; 6—number of items displayed; 7—library search bar; 8—textbook/manual info; 9—pdf file of the textbook/manual; 10—page navigation; 11—textbook/manual cover

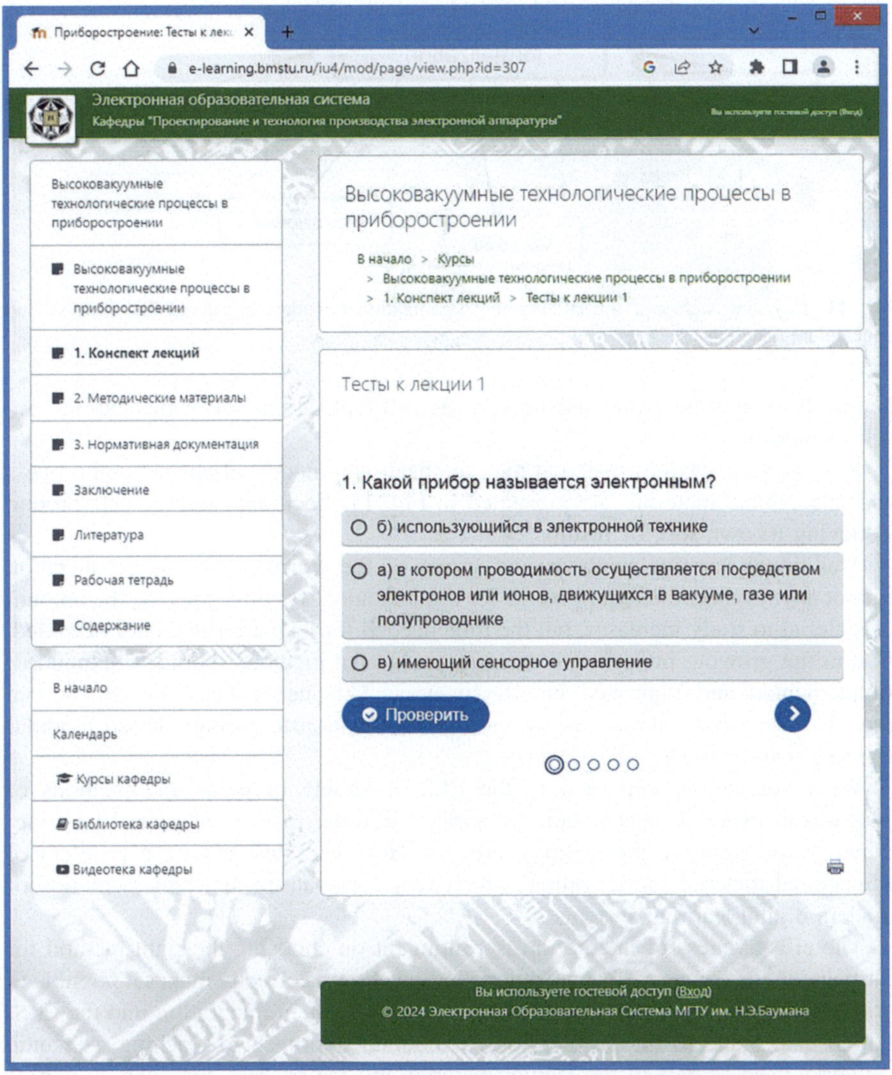


**Fig. 10** Interface of the knowledge control system in the ELS e-learning.bmstu.ru

## 6 Discussion

Education 4.0 involves personalized learning coupled with individual learning routes, availability of learning, project-based modular learning, simple and accurate assessment, deep analytics, in-field practices, and adaptive mentoring. Implementation of Education 5.0 adds deep digitalization and intellectualization, which frees

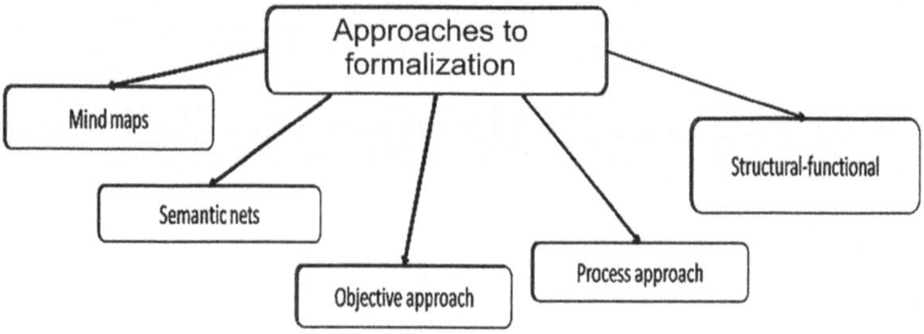


**Fig. 11** Key approaches to formalizing the organizational models of educational process and educational materials

people from routine work and maximizes self-realization, self-actualization, and self-expression.

Key approaches to formalizing the organizational models of educational process and educational materials are presented in Fig. 11. Each approach centers around achieving its own specific results.

Traditional learning methods and forms of the learning process organization cannot always meet the requirements for digitalization. As time goes by, the amount of material to study increases, but the time needed for its mastering is not extended. Due to the growing intensity of learning, traditional methods should be expanded, supplemented and improved in effectiveness. This necessitates the educational process to be digitized and, in particular, the transition to problem-based modular learning is to be made.

When integrating courses into the ELS, a variety of types and methods of educational material presentation are applied in order to maximize the ELS functionality and improve the learning process. However, this raises the problem of educational material formalization, which keeps relevant in the implementation of modern digital learning systems.

The effectiveness of integration is contingent on choosing the right method for formalizing the course. A formalization method chosen correctly makes it possible to properly decompose the training course for its subsequent integration into the ELS. For instance, due to the problem-based modular approach to teaching, semantic networks used as part of the lecture material and the process approach as part of seminars are best able to enhance the effectiveness and quality of teaching. Semantic-networks-based solutions allows one to structure the learning material and increase the effectiveness with which it is perceived by students due to its compact presentation, the absence of repetitions and loops, consistency, and interrelated topics. This makes it possible to build modern educational courses with a growing scope of knowledge to be processed on the principle of cognitive economy. The whole variety of ways to adapt learning materials allows maximizing the functionality of problem-based modular learning and improve the educational process.

The concept of problem-based modular learning implies simulation of real situations in various subject areas. Owing to such tools, it is possible to actively use various business games and project methods in distributed learning. This implements a comprehensive, interactive approach to learning. The proposed approach fully adopts the multidisciplinary STEAM (science, technology, engineering, arts, mathematics) education and promotes sustainable development when considering the social and production environment in the VUCA (volatility uncertainty, complexity, ambiguity) strategy.

## 7 Conclusion

In our research, we have analyzed the approaches to the formalization of educational materials, their characteristics, as well as the key tools of e-learning systems. The proposed concept was tested using the case of the Instrument Engineering training course. The educational material is integrated in the ELS and distributed between such modules as libraries, video libraries (video lectures), and the knowledge control designed to test and solidify students' knowledge. The proposed approach ensures self-actualization, self-fulfillment and self-expression of both the student and the teacher and contributes to the transition to Education 5.0, where the educational sphere is integrated into the digital society (Society 5.0).

**Acknowledgments** The results were partially obtained within the project «U2U» under the Development Program of Bauman Moscow State Technical University as part of the Priority-2030 federal academic leadership program.

## References

1. Chaka, C. (2022). Is education 4.0 a sufficient innovative, and disruptive educational trend to promote sustainable open education for higher education institutions? A review of literature trends. *Frontiers in Education, 7*, 824976. https://doi.org/10.3389/feduc.2022.824976
2. Kurnosenko, A.E., Juravleva, L.V., Lysenko, O.A., & Vlasov, A.I. (2021). Trend analysis in the development of factories of the future, taking into account digital transformation of active systems. *ACM International Conference Proceeding Series. 4. DEFIN 2021*. No. 3490881. https://doi.org/10.1145/3487757.3490881
3. Shaknov, V. A., Vlasov, A. I., & Juravleva, L. V. (2019). Concept of automated support to problem: Modular vocational training. *Handbook of Research on Engineering Education in a Global Context* (pp. 101–114). Hershey. https://doi.org/10.4018/978-1-5225-3395-5.ch010
4. Choshanov, M. A. (1996). *Flexible technology of problem-based modular learning*. Narodnoeobrazovanie.
5. Aksyukhin, A. A., Vintsen, A. A., & Mesheneva, Z. V. (2009). Information technologies in education and science. *Modern High Technologies, 11*, 50–52.
6. Melnikov, A. V., & Tsytovich, P. L. (2001). Principles of constructing training systems and their classification. *Pedagogical and Information Technologies in Education, 4*. http://journals.susu.ru/pit-edu/article/view/316

7. Maslov, S. I. (2012). Informatization as an integral component of modern engineering education. In *Proc. of Int. sci.-method. conf. Informatization of engineering education—INFORINO-2012 (Moscow, April 10–11, 2012)* (pp. 79–82). MPEI Publishing House.
8. Skinner, B. F. (1954). The science of learning and art of teaching. *Harvard Education Review, 24*, 86–97.
9. Logan, K., & Neumann, T. (2010, August). *Comparison of blackboard 9.1 and Moodle 2.0*. University of London.
10. Talyzina, N. F. (1969). *Theoretical problems of programmed learning*. MSU Publisher.
11. Berg, A. I. (Ed.). (1970). *Cybernetics and learning problems*. Progress.
12. Licklider, J. (1962). Preliminary experiments in computer-aided teaching. In *Programmed learning and computer based instruction* (pp. 217–239). Wiley.
13. Buiten, R., & Lane, H. S. (1965). *Experimental system gives language student instant error feedback*. Digital Equipment Corporation Computer Application Note.
14. Mkrttchian, V., & Brandt, D. (2005). Open distance education: A technological approach within social perspective. *IFAC Proceedings Volumes (IFAC-PapersOnline), IFAC 2005* (pp. 178–181).
15. Yudin, A., Vlasov, A., Salmina, M., & Sukhotskiy, V. (2022). Educational Robotics: Methodological Considerations and Practice of Mechatronics (pp. 63–77). *Lecture Notes in Networks and Systems. 515 LNNS*.
16. Juravleva, L. V., Shaknov, V. A., & Vlasov, A. I. (2019). Concept of automated support to problem: Modular vocational training. *Handbook of Research on Engineering Education in a Global Context* (pp. 101–114).
17. Yudin, A., Zatekin, D., Lapshinov, S., & Vlasov, A. (2021). Educational robotics: School to university, examples of interconnected longitudinal individual student routes. *Studies in Computational Intelligence, 982*, 202–215. https://doi.org/10.1007/978-3-030-77022-8_18
18. Rastrigin, L. A., & Erenshtein, M. K. (1988). *Adaptive learning with learner model*. Zinatne.
19. Unal, Z., & Unal, A. (2011). Evaluating and comparing the usability of web based course management systems. *Journal of Information Technology Education, 10*, 19–38.
20. Aleksandrov, A. A., Fang, K., Proletarsky, A. V., & Neusypin, K. A. (2012). Conception of complex continuous education with innovative information technologies. *Proceedings of the 2$^{nd}$Int.conf. on Education and Education Management* (pp. 374–378).
21. Krasilnikova, V. A. (2012). *Use of information and communication technologies in education*. OSU Publisher.
22. Grizzle, A., & Wilson, C. (2012). *Media and information literacy curriculum for teachers*. UNESCO IITE.
23. Buryi, A. S., Loban, A. V., & Lovtsov, D. A. (1998). Compression models for arrays of measurement data in an automatic control system. *Automation and Remote Control, 59*(5–2), 613–631.
24. Aleksandrov, A. A., Neusipin, K. A., Proletarsky, A. V., & Fang, K. (2012). Innovation development trends of modern management systems of educational organizations. *Proc. of 2012 Int.conf. on Information Management, Innovation Management and Industrial Engineering* (pp. 187–189). 25 October 2012.Sanya. China.
25. Yudin, A., Vlasov, A., Shalashova, M., & Salmina, M. (2020). Evolution of educational robotics in supplementary education of children, *1023*, 336–343. https://doi.org/10.1007/978-3-030-26945-6_30
26. Shelkunov, M. D., & Karimov, A. P. (2019). Society 5.0 in technological, social and anthropological dimensions. *The Review of Economy, the Law and Sociology, 3*, 158–164.

# Big and Small Data in Corporate Human Resource Management

**Ainura Kocherbaeva, Ainur Osmonova, Guzalbegim Rakhimova, and Evgeny Kuzmin**

**Abstract** The authors explore the influence of Big Data and Small Data concepts on human resource management. They emphasize that, despite a widespread use of Big Data in the context of digitalization, Small Data have significant potential as they make it possible to do a more detailed analysis and achieve goals in time. The main objective of the research is to clarify how Big and Small Data integration might be applied to achieve more efficient human resource management, what opportunities they provide and what risks may accompany this process. The authors reviewed the cases reported by leading companies that have successfully integrated data analytics into their HR management strategies and demonstrated extensive prospects in human capital development. The paper includes details on main characteristics and applications of Big and Small Data in human resource management. It also includes a comparison of these concepts by a number of parameters to understand their application specifics. The research is aimed at a deeper theoretical and practical understanding of data applications in human resource management. It highlights strategic importance of Big Data and operational importance of Small Data in this field. The authors show how integration of Big Data and Small Data can contribute to the development of more efficient strategies in human capital management and how this helps enterprises adjust to ever-changing requirements in the labour market, contributing to better sustainability of enterprises.

A. Kocherbaeva (✉)
Department of Management, Kyrgyz Russian Slavic University named after First President of Russia B.N. Yeltsin, Bishkek, Kyrgyzstan

A. Osmonova
Department of Accounting, Analysis and Audit, Scientific Research University Kyrgyz Economic University named after Musa Ryskulbekov (SRU KEU), Bishkek, Kyrgyzstan

G. Rakhimova
National Research University "Tashkent Institute of Irrigation and Agricultural Mechanization Engineers" (TIIAME National Research University), Tashkent, Uzbekistan

E. Kuzmin
Institute of Economics of the Ural Branch of the Russian Academy of Sciences, Ekaterinburg, Russian Federation
e-mail: kuzmin.ea@uiec.ru

 
A. Appolloni et al. (eds.), *The Future of Industry*, Lecture Notes in Information Systems and Organisation 70, https://doi.org/10.1007/978-3-031-66801-2_25

**Keywords** Big data · Small data · Human resource management

## 1 Introduction

In recent decades, researchers have paid significant attention to data analysis [1–5]. Big Data and Small Data concepts opened up new opportunities for more efficient human resource management [6–9]. Data have become an integral element in managerial decision making. This is especially important in the context of growing competition and necessary improvements to all aspects of organizational activities [10, 11].

In human resource management, Big Data allow identifying hidden influencing factors, predicting trends, and improving processes based on an analysis of large amounts of unstructured information. Updated with a high speed and being in various formats, these data might include information on employee interactions, their performance, as well as various external data on the labour market [12].

At the same time, Small Data play a crucial role in specific aspects of HR management. These data, often more structured and available for a quick analysis, might be applied for direct solutions to operational tasks [13], such as employee performance assessment, recruitment planning, improving working conditions, and personalizing approaches to personnel training and development, etc. Small Data, with a focus on specific information, are valuable in the context of certain aspects of control over employees' activities.

Therefore, the research purpose is to clarify how Big and Small Data integration might be applied to improve performance in HR management, what opportunities they provide and what risks might accompany this process. We are exploring various aspects in applications of these data in the HR sector, discussing approaches to the data analysis, identifying shared tools to deal with Big and Small Data, and discussing cases from practice of the companies that have successfully integrated data into their HR strategies.

## 2 Big Data in Human Resource Management: Definition, Characteristics, and Applications

The concept of Big Data appeared from the need for an analysis of a large amount of information that is too complex to be effectively processed with classical tools and in the environment of conventional information systems [14–17]. Big Data are often described with three parameters: volume, speed, and variety [18–20]: data are generated on a colossal scale. They are accumulated from many sources. The speed at which information is produced and must be processed requires involvement of those technologies with which we can in a quick manner collect, analyse, and present data in real time; and this information is presented in various formats.

Let us explore main types of information in HR management, which might be referred to as Big Data. *First*, these data are on employee interactions and communications. This might include an automated analysis of e-mails, corporate chat messages, calls, and video conferences, activities, and messages on corporate social networks and systems [21, 22]. The volume of these data might be overwhelming, especially in large companies. The data might be analysed to explore communication patterns and identify key persons in an organization. *Second*, they are aggregated data on employee performance. They include software logs, Internet traffic data and information from other corporate systems, such as ERP and CRM [23, 24]. These data might be useful to control the following: working time, execution of production tasks, analysis of periods when employees actively work and their performance tracking, prospective areas where business processes can be improved. *Third*, these data also include details on occupational health and safety. Tracker devices (for monitoring of health, activity, and movements) are used for a control over a psychophysiological state of employees, their health and well-being management, as well as for workspace improvements [25, 26]. *Fourth*, these data come from social networks and professional platforms [27, 28]. This includes data on employees' professional activities, their interactions and ties with others in social and professional networks. Such data might help understand the depth and scale level of professional networks and a potential influence of employees on talent recruitment and their commitment to a company.

Other types of information related to Big Data can be also effectively involved in HR management. Table 1 shows examples of data, their sources and significance of each type of data in HR management.

These basic types of data provide insight into structural dynamics within a company. They will be also useful for more efficient managerial decision making. Big Data are transforming into a powerful tool. The tool allows HR practitioners and managers not only to respond to ongoing challenges, but also to predict future trends and adjust strategies to achieve the best HR results [29, 30].

The use of machine learning algorithms in CV processing, social media profiles, and assessment results facilitate quick and efficient recruitment of the applicants that are most suitable for vacant positions [31–33]. This reduces recruiting time and costs. The analysis of Big Data on job openings in the labour market and applicant qualifications allows predicting changes in the labour market. This is important for recruitment strategic planning and development of training and career development programs. Collecting real-time data on employee performance allows improving work processes and overall organizational efficiency [34, 35]. This helps identify bottlenecks in work and the most suitable tools to improve employee performance. Moreover, Big Data allow collecting and analysing information on ongoing and future trends in the labour market [36, 37]. This helps HR managers make informed decisions on the development of motivation programs, control personnel turnover (including identifying reasons for leaving), help develop strategies to retain talents and reduce costs associated with frequent staff rotation. Internally, Big Data help

**Table 1** Examples of Big Data information types in corporate HR management

| Data type | Data source | Relevance in HR management |
|---|---|---|
| Data on employees' interactions and communications | E-mail, corporate chats, calls and video conferences, actions and messages on corporate social networks, etc. | Help analyse communication, cooperation, and social structure in a company |
| Data on employee performance | Software logs, internet traffic data (network activity), information from corporate systems (such as ERP and CRM, project management systems, time trackers), etc. | Used to analyse the application of corporate systems and for process improvements. They allow evaluating employee performance and improving work processes. The analysis of network activity might help identify those employees' behaviours that are unusual or undesirable for an organization |
| Biometric and tracking data | Health monitoring devices, activity trackers, geospatial data (GPS trackers, mobile applications) | Devices and sensors (to monitor employee attendance or physiological state) are used to manage employees' health and well-being. These data might be also used to improve workplaces, office space, and business processes |
| Data from social networks and professional platforms | Cross-functional public social networks and special-purpose professional platforms | Used to explore a social structure and communication patterns among employees. Data are important for understanding of employees' professional networks and their ability to attract talents from the outside and understand their commitment to a company |
| Data on interaction with digital media | Social networks, web analytics | Allow analysing how employees represent a company online, what their personal consumer preferences look like, what their commitment to company's brand promotion looks like |
| Data on cross-functional work | Project and task management systems, corporate portals | Evaluating collaboration between various departments and its impact on performance and innovations |
| Integrated data on customer service | CRM systems, call centres, customer feedback | Information is used to evaluate an impact of a service level on customer loyalty and employee performance |

identify and manage risks [38, 39] associated with unacceptable employee behaviours, misuse of corporate operating resources, and compliance with occupational safety and health regulations. The analysis of data on all aspects of personnel work gives management a comprehensive idea of efficiency of established organizational structures, staff performance, and a potential for better performance.

## 3 Small Data in Human Resource Management: Definition, Characteristics, and Applications

Today, in time of active digitalization with a focus on large-scale solutions in the field of Big Data, the importance of Small Data is often underestimated. However, in the context of HR management, Small Data are a valuable resource [40]. They can provide a more detailed understanding of employee behaviours, preferences, and needs. This section of the research focuses on a role of Small Data in HRM, exploring main characteristics, as well as applications of Small Data by HR practitioners.

Small Data, unlike Big Data, are usually limited in volume, but easily available. This makes them indispensable in a search for quick solutions to current problems and decision-making support [41–43]. Also, Small Data usually focus on meeting local needs and might be easily processed with conventional tools and techniques without a need for the complex IT infrastructure [44]. The data are structured and accessible for quick and easy interpretation. They can be easily aggregated and analysed by an individual, as well as by small working groups or teams. Thus, it can be stated that Small Data are described with clarity. It makes them the most suitable for a direct application in business processes [45]. These data are usually accessible with core business systems and applications without a need for advanced technologies to collect and analyse the data. Small Data reflect the relevant approach as they are directly related to certain objectives and goals [46]. Volumes of data are relatively small and do not require additional processing capacities. Small Data are often used to obtain operational information. Small Data are applied in various fields: performance monitoring, customer analytics, financial planning, inventory management, etc. Small Data help companies remain flexible and respond to changes in a quick and efficient way to achieve high resilience.

In the development of the company's human capital, Small Data provide extensive opportunities to improve many aspects of HR functions. Here are a few ways to use Small Data in HR management. *First*, there are recruitment tasks like applicant profiling and making recruitment much more accurate. Small Data, as well as Big Data, are used in CV processing. This helps HR practitioners identify applicants with the most suitable skills and work experience for certain job openings. *Second*, to address the issues of employee performance assessment and monitoring, Small Data allow collecting information on specific performance indicators of each employee. This might include information on a number of assignments completed, work quality, meeting deadlines, and other criteria that directly influence work performance. Regular collection and analysis of data on performance of each employee allow identifying strengths and weaknesses, as well as a need for additional training or continuing professional development. *Third*, using questionnaires, surveys, and interviews, HR departments can collect Small Data on employee opinions regarding an organizational environment, corporate culture, and management style. This information is crucial to assess employee satisfaction and commitment. *Fourth*, Small Data can be used to evaluate efficiency of educational programs and trainings.

The analysis of data on employees' current skills and market demands allows developing targeted training programs to close competency gaps. By collecting data on employee attendance, performance, and feedback from training events, companies might tailor their training programs to better meet employee needs and company's strategic development goals. *Fifth*, by analysing Small Data on employee career achievements, skills, and interests, HR managers might better plan career paths and offer employees suitable professional development opportunities. Small Data here help predict potential career trajectories of employees based on an analysis of their performance, competencies, and interests. *Sixth*, Small Data help analyse trends in employee turnover and define when and where there are recruitment needs. This includes analysing data on employees' average length of previous employment compared to valid employment, changes in volumes of work tasks, etc. Using data on reasons for leaving, a company can develop strategies to retain key talents. *Seventh*, information on work incidents and other problematic situations helps identify potential occupational health and safety risks. These data can be used to prevent threats and improve working conditions.

Thus, Small Data in HR management provide extensive opportunities for a more person-centric approach to HR. This contributes to the creation of stronger, more motivated, and efficient employees. See examples of key applications of Small Data in Table 2 below.

The table covers a wide range of information types related to Small Data and shows their role in various HR management tasks. Small Data allow companies to focus on specific, targeted HRM aspects, providing more accurate and efficient solutions to emerging problems. The companies that integrate Small Data analytics into their human resource management strategies are able to understand better the needs of their employees, respond appropriately to changes in the working environment, and make informed decisions that support employee career growth and professional development. Owing to such data analysis, companies can not only improve internal processes, but also create a healthier and more efficient working environment. This, in turn, does not only make management decisions more efficient, but also contributes to a deeper understanding of relationships in a company.

## 4 Cases of Big and Small Data Application

Many companies are actively implementing data analytics technologies to improve processes in human resource management [47–49]. Despite different scales and structures, both types of data (Big & Small Data) provide an information and analytical basis for decision making in HR. We refer to cases of how the world's leading companies apply Big & Small Data to explore their approaches, methodologies, and results in terms of an impact on human capital. The focus is on how companies apply data to improve recruitment strategies, learning and development, performance management, employee satisfaction and commitment. Let us explore their experience and the areas in which they apply these technologies (Table 3).

**Table 2** Examples of Small Data information types in corporate human resource management

| Data type | Data source | Relevance in HRM |
|---|---|---|
| Data on staff turnover | HR reports, exit interviews, feedback systems | Provide information on workforce dynamics, turnover reasons, and recruiting efficiency. Help analyse reasons for leaving and develop employee retention strategies |
| Employee feedback | Questionnaires, feedback systems, periodic or regular evaluation procedures | Information is used to improve corporate and organizational culture, workplace conditions.<br>Colleague feedback is important to evaluate and develop management skills and develop leadership qualities. Data on conflicts and complaints help solve internal corporate conflicts and improve the working environment. Assessment procedures help understand employee personal qualities, motivation, and potential to perform certain roles |
| Results of corporate training and professional development | Learning management systems (LMS), HR reports | Helps evaluate whether training programs are efficient and evaluate their impact on employee performance. They are important for monitoring and analysis of employee training and career development processes |
| Customer feedback on employees | CRM systems, customer feedback | They are used to evaluate external interaction and quality of service provided by employees |
| Data on internal movement of employees and business trips | HR reports | Analyse career development and internal movements. This helps improve career paths and retain talents. Provides information on business trip intensity |
| Data on attendance and good sense of time | ERP systems, access control systems, time cards | Make it possible to monitor employee attendance, analyse their sense of time and general discipline |
| Data on project activities | Project management systems, project reports | Provide analysis of project implementation, team involvement and efficiency of labour resource allocation |
| Data on job satisfaction | Questionnaires, feedback systems, periodic or regular appraisals | Help measure and improve job satisfaction, which directly impacts performance |
| Information on employee health | Medical records, health questionnaires | Important to manage corporate health programs and prevent occupational diseases |
| Payroll data | Accounting systems, payroll accounting systems | Provide information to analyse a structure of personnel costs, help |

(continued)

**Table 2** (continued)

| Data type | Data source | Relevance in HRM |
|---|---|---|
| | | redistribute a wage budget to improve employee motivation |
| Information on corporate culture events | Reviews of corporate events | Assessment of employee participation and involvement in the corporate life that helps strengthen the team spirit |

**Table 3** Cases of Big and Small Data application in human resource management

| Company | Usage description |
|---|---|
| *Google* | Identifying key traits of effectivemanagers |
| *Xerox* | Reducing staff turnover |
| *Walmart* | Creating an engaged working environment |
| *Coca-Cola* | Recruitment improvements |
| *IBM* | Monitoring and analysis of employee satisfaction |
| *Tesco* | Forecasting recruitment needs |
| *Credit Suisse* | Analysis of employee commitment and turnover |
| *AT&T* | Forecasting career success of employees |
| *Cisco* | Making position profiles and recruitment assessment |
| *Procter & gamble* | Talent management and decision making |
| *Amazon* | Employee performance analysis |
| *HSBC* | Identifying employee skills to establish sustainable interactions with customers |
| *Netflix* | Improving team/project structures |
| *Toyota* | Monitoring of a physical condition of personnel and occupational safety support |
| *Adobe* | Improving internal communications and developing collaboration between teams |

***Google [50]*** *Google* launched *Oxygen Project*, which uses various data to determine key qualities of efficient managers. Having analysed data on performance, employee feedback, and other metrics, *Google* identified eight behavioural traits that distinguish the best managers. These traits include a capacity for efficient coaching, empathy for needs of a team, involvement of employees in decision making, and a capacity for strategic thinking. Based on the findings, *Google* also developed training and development programs for managers to strengthen and develop precisely those skills that had been identified earlier as the most valuable. This does not only improve overall management efficiency, but also allow to improve employee motivation and satisfaction.

***Xerox [51]*** *Xerox* used Big Data to analyse the factors that influence personnel turnover in its call centres. The company analysed data from recruitment questionnaires and data on performance to identify the factors that correlate with employee long-term success and leaving likelihood. The findings helped *Xerox* identify leaving reasons, as well as develop prevention measures. As a result, based on the data obtained, the company launched targeted adaptation and training programs aimed at skill consolidation and working conditions improvements. This significantly reduced staff turnover and increased overall employees' satisfaction.

***Walmart [52, 53]*** *Walmart* actively uses Big Data analytics to process employee feedback received through social media. This allows the company to understand in a better way the needs, expectations, and moods of employees, to respond to them more effectively, improving corporate culture and internal communications. Besides, these data help *Walmart* implement strategic changes and innovations to improve operational efficiency and achieve higher commitment level in its working environment.

***Coca-Cola [54]*** *Coca-Cola* used Big Data to improve its recruitment processes by analysing data from various sources, including social media and CV databases. This allowed the company to speed up the recruitment process, as well as to improve the recruitment quality owing to a more accurate comparison of applicants' qualifications with company's requirements. The usage of data has allowed *Coca-Cola* to adjust its talent acquisition strategies to changing trends in the labour market and improve interaction with potential employees, increasing their interest in working for the company.

***IBM [55]*** *IBM* uses analytics tools to monitor and analyse employee satisfaction. The company systematically collects data from surveys and regular feedback. This allows it to identify key areas for improvement in the working environment and corporate culture. These data help *IBM* respond quickly to emerging problems and contribute to ongoing improvement of the corporate climate. Thanks to this approach, the company does not only increase employee satisfaction, but also contributes to their better performance and commitment. Moreover, regular data analysis allows *IBM* to adjust to changes in recruitment needs and make timely adjustments to strategies of HR management.

***Tesco [56]*** *Tesco* chain of stores actively uses Big Data technologies to analyse consumer behaviours and define recruitment needs, taking into account seasonality factors, holiday periods, and even weather changes. Based on data on sales and store footfall, *Tesco* can determine when and where it will need more employees. This does not only allow the company to improve operational efficiency, but also significantly improve customer satisfaction through better service. Additionally, *Tesco* uses this information to improve inventory management and logistics, ensuring that needed items are available at peak times. This helps increase sales and overall business profitability.

***Credit Suisse [57]*** *Credit Suisse* analyses employee reviews, career progression, and compensation history to identify those employees who are likely to leave. Next, the company takes proactive steps to offer these employees new career opportunities to encourage retention. *Credit Suisse* processes vast amounts of data to identify patterns that might explain low employee retention rates. These data are also used to improve employee recruiting, onboarding, and development strategies to create a more stable and committed working environment, which ultimately improves overall performance and reduces recruiting costs.

***AT&T [58–60]*** *AT&T* uses Big Data analytics to identify the factors that can help predict employee success. Using data on previous career achievements, education, community commitment, etc., the company might have more accurate recruitment and develop individual career development paths. *AT&T*'s core vision here is to help every employee achieve maximum success in his or her career by providing resources and opportunities for ongoing professional growth. To do this, the company does not only identify key skills and potential of employees, but also creates an environment where everyone can become the "CEO" of his or her career, implementing his or her professional potential at the most.

***Cisco [61]*** *Cisco* uses Big Data to analyse workloads, improve task allocation between employees, analyse if position profiles meet talented candidate skills, etc. *Cisco* uses data from various sources, including *Burning Glass Technologies* (information provider on job openings) and job openings posted by others companies to define required skills. These data, combined with internal information and interviews with managers, are used to develop the unified taxonomy of positions. The taxonomy, approved by managers, provides a single framework to identify key skills that *Cisco* needs to be successful. Roles and skills are mapped to business priorities to identify possible gaps and development opportunities within the company. This allows *Cisco* to develop adaptive learning and development programs, identify crucial skills, and ensure a reserve of talents. Besides, the company evaluates whether it is possible to share these roles and skills for training purposes.

***Procter & Gamble [62, 63]*** *Procter & Gamble* uses Big & Small Data to manage talents by analysing data on performance, satisfaction, and career development of employees around the world. This allows the company to make more efficient plans for recruitment, development, and rotation of personnel internationally. *Procter & Gamble* has introduced data visualization as a central management tool. *P&G* now gives employees an access to the *Decision-Making Dashboard*, which displays key information in a visual form.

***Amazon [64–66]*** *Amazon* integrates machine learning and Big Data to analyse performance. *Amazon* developed software to track employee movements at its fulfilment centres. The company says that the use of algorithms in performance reviews ensures that limits of human performance are respected. This prevents from setting unattainable goals for employees. With data on performance and feedback, *Amazon* develops customized training programs to improve employee skills and job satisfaction.

***HSBC [67]*** *HSBC* completed deep data analysis-driven transformation of its service to understand customer needs and desires. This initiative encouraged strategic interaction with customers, driven by new data and insights and improved collaboration between conventional business units. The main goal of this transformation is to create better customer service teams and develop approaches to service that are based on thoroughly explored customers' strategies and needs. *HSBC* uses Big Data to analyse employee-customer interactions to enhance the service quality. By analysing data from various customer-company touchpoints and customer feedback, the bank defines what employee skills are most effective to build efficient and sustainable interactions.

***Netflix [68, 69]*** *Netflix* actively uses data in HR decision making, including recruitment, evaluation of new employee performance and identifying opportunities for improvements. The company uses analytics to identify the skills and qualifications that are most in demand under ongoing and future projects. This allows it to improve recruitment. In addition, *Netflix* analyses employee performance indicators to make specific recommendations for their professional development and promotion. It thereby does not only ensure better individual performance, but also overall team performance. *Netflix* uses analytics to analyse employee interactions and efficiency of project teams. This allows the company to strengthen team structures, ensuring high performance and a quick launch of new projects.

***Toyota [70]*** *Toyota* uses Big Data to analyse and prevent industrial accidents and improve occupational safety. By collecting and analysing these data, the company develops strategies to reduce injury risks and prevent accidents. *Toyota Motors Europe* actively uses data analytics in its ergonomic analysis systems to monitor and evaluate body positions of employees while working. Introduction of the motion capture technology makes it possible for the company to monitor a personnel physical condition and maintain occupational safety. The collected data provide detailed insight into employee postures when they make assembly operations. This information is then used to train employees to have proper body positions at work to minimize the risk of injury. It is also used to make changes to production processes. This improves overall working conditions and performance. In addition, data analysis facilitates development of new ergonomic tools and equipment, further improving the working environment and reducing volumes of manual labour.

***Adobe [71, 72]*** *Adobe* uses data analytics to promote internal communications and collaboration between teams. Using data on interactions and the information exchange between employees, the company improves tools and processes. This contributes to higher performance and more efficient project management. As part of these efforts, *Adobe* introduced Adobe Analytics, the tool that facilitates data-driven decision making. Adobe Analytics makes it easy to communicate and share data across an organization and between teams to make them accessible to all the stakeholders. This transforms decision making. The platform encourages active collaboration and knowledge sharing between employees. This increases the level of everyone's competencies and facilitates the exchange of best practices and ideas. Such "extended" teams of employees refocus their operations with the strategic approach. This creates new opportunities for career and professional development. This change enhances their ability to make significant contributions to corporate goal achievement and develops the skills that are necessary in complex project management. This approach makes it possible for employees to actively participate in strategy development and decision making. This improves their competencies and prepares them for future career development. Introduction of Adobe Analytics helps implement the value of technology investments as it maximizes their potential across the organization. Thus, *Adobe* stimulates its internal processes and creates the environment where every employee has an opportunity to develop, contribute to overall success and implement his or her maximum potential.

These cases show an extensive potential of Big & Small Data in various aspects of HR management: from an increase in employee satisfaction and commitment to improvements of workflow and strategic planning. Data application is becoming one of the key factors to achieve competitive advantages. Cases clearly show how Big & Small Data help enhance training and development programs, safety and well-being of employees, improve a company's project structure, quality of customer service, help develop corporate culture and reduce staff turnover. All this highlights deep integration of data analytics into strategic and operational aspects of the world's leading companies. The application of Big & Small Data analytics makes it possible for companies not only to adjust to current labour market conditions and internal demands for labour resources, but also to predict future changes in recruitment needs, actively responding to them to achieve sustainable development goals.

## 5 Discussion

Both Big Data and Small Data have key positions in today's business strategies. The comparative analysis of these two approaches to data reveals their main differences (Table 4) [13, 44, 72–74]. This table highlights how each type of data might be used to improve different aspects of work, from strategic planning to operational management and tactical problem solving.

The comparison of Big Data and Small Data highlights that each of these approaches has its own unique advantages and applications. Big Data provide large-scale capabilities for analytics to identify complex trends. This is especially valuable for corporate strategic planning and decision making. At the same time, Small Data play a vital role in operational management as they offer higher specificity. This makes them ideal for quick decision making and improvements to day-to-day workflow aspects. The application of these data together might significantly enhance HRM efficiency as it provides both an in-depth strategic analysis, and higher operational efficiency and more intensive collaboration at all levels. The companies that effectively integrate both approaches might gain significant competitive advantages as they adjust to rapidly changing labour market demands and maximize the potential of their human capital. As a result, Big Data and Small Data should not be considered alternatives. They supplement each other, each of them brings its own unique value to an HR strategy.

**Table 4** Comparison of big and small data

| Criterion | Big data | Small data |
|---|---|---|
| Data volume | Huge data amounts | Relatively small data amounts, easily managed by an individual or small group |
| Data sources | Diverse sources, including social networks, sensors, mobile data, etc | Most often, structured data from internal corporate systems, such as ERP, CRM, HRM, as well as surveys, and evaluation procedures |
| Processing speed | High, requires powerful computing resources | Relatively low, it does not require an elaborated IT infrastructure |
| Type of analysis | Complex analysis, machine learning, predictive analytics | Descriptive analysis, descriptive statistics, simple forecasting |
| Decision making | Support to high-level strategic decision making | Support to operational decision making and decision making by certain departments or employees |
| Personalization | Aggregated, most often anonymized data. Less focused on individual needs | High personalization, targeted solutions to specific challenges |
| Usage purposes | Research of complex correlations, process improvements at the macro level | Solutions to specific, often day-to-day HR challenges, such as performance evaluation and career development planning |
| Efficiency | Ideal for trend spotting | Better suit as an immediate response to emerging local challenges and requests |
| Analytical tools | Require special-purpose analysis tools, such as Hadoop, Spark | Might be analysed using standard office tools, such as Excel |
| Data visualization | Sophisticated visualizations to process and present large data amounts | Simple and clear visualizations that are easily interpreted at any level of an organization |
| Privacy and security | Management of large data volumes places high-level demands on security and privacy | Less data amounts make it easier to manage privacy and comply with security policies |
| Change implementation speed | It often takes longer to analyse and implement data-driven changes | They make it possible to respond quickly to challenges and implement changes in a short time |
| Strategic planning | They make it possible to have large-scale strategic planning based on extensive data and forecasts | They are more suitable for tactical planning and a search for solutions to current operational challenges |
| Integration with other systems | They require complex integration with numerous other systems and data platforms | They are more suitable for easier integration with existing management systems and databases |
| Decision making | They support corporate decision making, often involving complex multivariate analyses | They promote quick and accurate decision making by certain departments or employees |
| Replication capability | Research projects based on big data might be difficult or not always necessary | Entire project, including data collection phases, should be organised in such a way as to be replicable |

## 6 Conclusion

Human resource management in today's conditions is actively transformed under an influence of digitalization and a growing role of data in managerial decision making. Human resource management as a field is now more and more using data as a strategic resource. In the context of this transformation, Big Data and Small Data are especially significant as they independently create unique opportunities for HR management. Big Data make it possible for companies to analyse extensive arrays of information on employee interactions, performance and behaviours, while Small Data promote deeper understanding of individual aspects of work and provide a detailed picture of an impact of local factors on corporate success.

The integrated application of Big and Small Data is revolutionizing approaches to human resource management. These technologies do not only enlarge the HR analytics and forecasting toolkit, but also significantly improve accuracy of decision making in such fields as from recruitment and training to performance assessment and employee career development planning. The combination of these approaches makes it possible for companies not only to respond to current challenges in an efficient way, but also to adapt quickly to changes in the labour market, contributing to sustainable development and competitiveness maintenance. Thus, Big Data and Small Data are not only becoming tools, but the strategic assets that help companies develop human capital.

**Acknowledgments** The research was supported by grant No. 23-28-01768 provided by the Russian Science Foundation, https://rscf.ru/project/23-28-01768/.

## References

1. Bose, I., & Mahapatra, R. K. (2001). Business data mining — A machine learning perspective. *Information & Management, 39*(3), 211–225. https://doi.org/10.1016/S0378-7206(01)00091-X
2. Xia, B. S., & Gong, P. (2014). Review of business intelligence through data analysis. *Benchmarking: An International Journal, 21*(2), 300–311. https://doi.org/10.1108/BIJ-08-2012-0050
3. Provost, F., & Fawcett, T. (2013). *Data science for business: What you need to know about data mining and data-analytic thinking*. O'Reilly Media.
4. Mikalef, P., Pappas, I. O., Krogstie, J., & Pavlou, P. A. (2020). Big data and business analytics: A research agenda for realizing business value. *Information & Management, 57*(1), 103237. https://doi.org/10.1016/j.im.2019.103237
5. Giudici, P. (2005). *Applied data mining: Statistical methods for business and industry*. John Wiley & Sons.
6. Shet, S. V., Poddar, T., Samuel, F. W., & Dwivedi, Y. K. (2021). Examining the determinants of successful adoption of data analytics in human resource management—A framework for implications. *Journal of Business Research, 131*, 311–326. https://doi.org/10.1016/j.jbusres.2021.03.054

7. Caputo, F., Cillo, V., Candelo, E., & Liu, Y. (2019). Innovating through digital revolution: The role of soft skills and big data in increasing firm performance. *Management Decision, 57*(8), 2032–2051. https://doi.org/10.1108/MD-07-2018-0833
8. Verma, S., Singh, V., & Bhattacharyya, S. S. (2021). Do big data-driven HR practices improve HR service quality and innovation competency of SMEs. *International Journal of Organizational Analysis, 29*(4), 950–973. https://doi.org/10.1108/IJOA-04-2020-2128
9. Isson, J. P., & Harriott, J. S. (2016). *People analytics in the era of big data: Changing the way you attract, acquire, develop, and retain talent*. John Wiley & Sons. https://doi.org/10.1002/9781119083856
10. Lavrinenko, S. (2023). Top 20 highly effective use cases of big data analytics for businesses in 2024. *DataForest*. https://dataforest.ai/blog/big-data-analytics-use-cases
11. Mazzei, M. J., & Noble, D. (2017). Big data dreams: A framework for corporate strategy. *Business Horizons, 60*(3), 405–414. https://doi.org/10.1016/j.bushor.2017.01.010
12. Zhang, Y., Xu, S., Zhang, L., & Yang, M. (2021). Big data and human resource management research: An integrative review and new directions for future research. *Journal of Business Research, 133*, 34–50. https://doi.org/10.1016/j.jbusres.2021.04.019
13. Chen, E. E., & Wojcik, S. P. (2016). A practical guide to big data research in psychology. *Psychological Methods, 21*(4), 458–474. https://doi.org/10.1037/met0000111
14. Cheung, M. W. L., & Jak, S. (2016). Analysing big data in psychology: A split/analyze/meta-analyze approach. *Frontiers in Psychology, 7*, 182798. https://doi.org/10.3389/fpsyg.2016.00738
15. Naeem, M., Jamal, T., Diaz-Martinez, J., Butt, S. A., Montesano, N., Tariq, M. I., & De-La-Hoz-Valdiris, E. (2022). Trends and future perspective challenges in big data. In *Advances in intelligent data analysis and applications: Proceeding of the sixth euro-China conference on intelligent data analysis and applications, 15–18 October 2019, Arad, Romania* (pp. 309–325). Springer. https://doi.org/10.1007/978-981-16-5036-9_30
16. Simon, P. (2013). *Too big to ignore: The business case for big data* (Vol. 72). John Wiley & Sons. https://doi.org/10.1002/9781119204039
17. Katal, A., Wazid, M., & Goudar, R. H. (2013). Big data: Issues, challenges, tools and good practices. In *2013 Sixth international conference on contemporary computing (IC3)* (pp. 404–409). IEEE. https://doi.org/10.24840/2183-0606_004.001_0006
18. Ylijoki, O., & Porras, J. (2016). Perspectives to definition of big data: A mapping study and discussion. *Journal of innovation management, 4*(1), 69–91. https://doi.org/10.24840/2183-0606_004.001_0006
19. Russom, P. (2011). Big Data analytics. *TDWI Best Practices Report, Fourth Quarter, 19*(4), 1–34.
20. Dmitriev, A. S. (2015). Big Data, 4v: Volume, velocity, variety, value. *Monitoring of Public Opinion: Economic and Social Changes, 3*(127), 156–159.
21. Guilfoyle, S., Bergman, S. M., Hartwell, C., & Powers, J. (2016). Social media, big data, and employment decisions: Mo'data, mo'problems? In R. Landers & G. Schmidt (Eds.), *Social Media in Employee Selection and Recruitment: Theory, practice, and current challenges* (pp. 127–155). Springer. https://doi.org/10.1007/978-3-319-29989-1_7
22. Tonidandel, S., King, E. B., & Cortina, J. M. (2018). Big data methods: Leveraging modern data analytic techniques to build organizational science. *Organizational Research Methods, 21*(3), 525–547. https://doi.org/10.1177/1094428116677299
23. Pajević, F., & Shearmur, R. G. (2017). Catch me if you can: Workplace mobility and big data. *Journal of Urban Technology, 24*(3), 99–115. https://doi.org/10.1080/10630732.2017.1334855
24. Bandari, V. (2023). Enterprise data security measures: A comparative review of effectiveness and risks across different industries and organization types. *International Journal of Business Intelligence and Big Data Analytics, 6*(1), 1–11.
25. Dimitrov, D. V. (2016). Medical internet of things and big data in healthcare. *Healthcare Informatics Research, 22*(3), 156. https://doi.org/10.4258/hir.2016.22.3.156

26. Vijayan, V., Connolly, J. P., Condell, J., McKelvey, N., & Gardiner, P. (2021). Review of wearable devices and data collection considerations for connected health. *Sensors, 21*(16), 5589. https://doi.org/10.3390/s21165589
27. Chang, V. (2018). A proposed social network analysis platform for big data analytics. *Technological Forecasting and Social Change, 130*, 57–68. https://doi.org/10.1016/j.techfore.2017.11.002
28. Ryan, J., & Herleman, H. (2015). A big data platform for workforce analytics. In *Big Data at Work* (pp. 19–42). Routledge.
29. Angrave, D., Charlwood, A., Kirkpatrick, I., Lawrence, M., & Stuart, M. (2016). HR and analytics: Why HR is set to fail the big data challenge. *Human Resource Management Journal, 26*(1), 1–11. https://doi.org/10.1111/1748-8583.12090
30. Kosinski, M., Wang, Y., Lakkaraju, H., & Leskovec, J. (2016). Mining big data to extract patterns and predict real-life outcomes. *Psychological Methods, 21*(4), 493. https://doi.org/10.1037/met0000105
31. Mrsic, L., Jerkovic, H., & Balkovic, M. (2020). Interactive skill-based labour market mechanics and dynamics analysis system using machine learning and big data. In *Asian conference on intelligent information and database systems* (pp. 505–516). Springer. https://doi.org/10.1007/978-981-15-3380-8_44
32. Pal, R., Shaikh, S., Satpute, S., & Bhagwat, S. (2022). Resume classification using various machine learning algorithms. In *ITM web of conferences* (Vol. 44, p. 03011). EDP Sciences. https://doi.org/10.1051/itmconf/20224403011
33. Roy, P. K., Chowdhary, S. S., & Bhatia, R. (2020). A machine learning approach for automation of resume recommendation system. *Procedia Computer Science, 167*, 2318–2327. https://doi.org/10.1016/j.procs.2020.03.284
34. Bharadwaj, A., El Sawy, O. A., Pavlou, P. A., & Venkatraman, N. V. (2013). Digital business strategy: Toward a next generation of insights. *MIS Quarterly*, 471–482. https://doi.org/10.25300/MISQ/2013/37:2.3
35. Sánchez-Monedero, J., & Dencik, L. (2019). *The datafication of the workplace. Working Paper.* https://orca.cardiff.ac.uk/id/eprint/125552/1/Report-The-datafication-of-the-workplace.pdf
36. Alibasic, A., Upadhyay, H., Simsekler, M. C. E., Kurfess, T., Woon, W. L., & Omar, M. A. (2022). Evaluation of the trends in jobs and skill-sets using data analytics: A case study. *Journal of Big Data, 9*(1), 32. https://doi.org/10.1186/s40537-022-00576-5
37. Ramasubbareddy, S., Walia, A. S., Luhach, A. K., Kannayaram, G., & Evakattu, S. (2021). Big data analysis on job trends using R. *Recent Advances in Computer Science and Communications, 14*(1), 100–108. https://doi.org/10.2174/2213275912666190801113359
38. Zaki, T., Uddin, M. S., Hasan, M. M., & Islam, M. N. (2017). Security threats for big data: A study on Enron e-mail dataset. In *2017 international conference on research and innovation in information systems (ICRIIS)* (pp. 1–6). IEEE. https://doi.org/10.1109/ICRIIS.2017.8002481
39. Mahmood, T., & Afzal, U. (2013). Security analytics: Big data analytics for cybersecurity: A review of trends, techniques and tools. In *2013 2nd national conference on information assurance (NCIA)* (pp. 129–134). IEEE. https://doi.org/10.1109/NCIA.2013.6725337
40. George, G., Haas, M. R., & Pentland, A. (2014). Big data and management. *Academy of Management Journal, 57*(2), 321–326. https://doi.org/10.5465/amj.2014.4002
41. Kitchin, R., & Lauriault, T. P. (2015). Small data in the era of big data. *GeoJournal, 80*, 463–475. https://doi.org/10.1007/s10708-014-9601-7
42. Borgman, C. L. (2017). *Big data, little data, no data: Scholarship in the networked world.* MIT Press.
43. Faraway, J. J., & Augustin, N. H. (2018). When Small Data beats Big Data. *Statistics & Probability Letters, 136*, 142–145. https://doi.org/10.1016/j.spl.2018.02.031
44. George, G., Osinga, E. C., Lavie, D., & Scott, B. A. (2016). Big data and data science methods for management research. *Academy of Management Journal, 59*(5), 1493–1507. https://doi.org/10.5465/amj.2016.4005

45. Constantiou, I. D., & Kallinikos, J. (2015). New games, new rules: Big data and the changing context of strategy. *Journal of Information Technology, 30*, 44–57. https://doi.org/10.1057/jit.2014.17
46. Van Beurden, J., Van de Voorde, K., & Van Veldhoven, M. (2021). The employee perspective on HR practices: A systematic literature review, integration and outlook. *The International Journal of Human Resource Management, 32*(2), 359–393. https://doi.org/10.1080/09585192.2020.1759671
47. Zeeshan, M. (2024, March 1). *9 key applications of Big Data analytics in the telecom industry*. AppVerticals. https://www.appverticals.com/blog/big-data-analytics-in-the-telecom-industry/
48. Yahia, N. B., Hlel, J., & Colomo-Palacios, R. (2021). From big data to deep data to support people analytics for employee attrition prediction. *IEEE Access, 9*, 60447–60458. https://doi.org/10.1109/ACCESS.2021.3074559
49. Marr, B. (2016). *Big data in practice: How 45 successful companies used big data analytics to deliver extraordinary results*. John Wiley & Sons. https://doi.org/10.1002/9781119278825
50. Garvin, D. A. (2013). *How Google sold its engineers on management*. Harvard Business Publishing. https://hbr.org/2013/12/how-google-sold-its-engineers-on-management
51. Walker, J. (2012, September 20). *Meet the new boss: Big Data*. The Wall Street Journal. https://www.wsj.com/articles/SB10000872396390443890304578006252019616768
52. Rae, H. (2016, November 22). What Wal-Mart's battle with workers over a Chat App Means for Big-Box Retailers. Forbes. https://www.forbes.com/sites/haniyarae/2016/11/22/walmarts-app-retailers/?sh=2b7cd06377f7
53. Marr, B. (2021). *Walmart: Big data analytics at the world's biggest retailer*. Bernard Marr &. https://bernardmarr.com/walmart-big-data-analytics-at-the-worlds-biggest-retailer/
54. Liu, J., & Li, X. (2016). Innovation business model of big data-taking Coca-Cola as an example. In *2016 3rd international conference on management, education technology and sports science (METSS 2016)* (pp. 102–110). Atlantis Press. https://doi.org/10.2991/metss-16.2016.24
55. User, G. (2020, September 18). *How does IBM use AI and analytics to measure employee skillsets?* https://www.myhrfuture.com/blog/2020/9/17/how-does-ibm-use-ai-and-analytics-to-measure-employee-skillsets#ibm-skills-demand-in-marketplace
56. Tesco: Using data analysis to make better business decisions. Station10. https://station10.co.uk/case-studies/tesco-using-data-analysis-to-make-better-business-decisions/.
57. Boudreau, J. (2014). *Predict what employees will do without freaking them out*. Harvard Business Publishing. https://hbr.org/2014/09/predict-what-employees-will-do-without-freaking-them-out
58. Donovan, J., & Benko, C. (2016). *AT&T's talent overhaul. Can the firm really retrain hundreds of thousands of employees?* Harvard Business Publishing. https://hbr.org/2016/10/atts-talent-overhaul
59. Abril, D. (2015). AT&T: How we leverage big data to improve internal, external operations. *Dallas Business Journal*. https://www.bizjournals.com/dallas/blog/techflash/2015/10/at-t-how-we-leverage-big-data-to-improve-internal.html
60. Markus, A. (2022). Harnessing data and AI for business value. *AT&T*. https://about.att.com/innovationblog/2022/data-ai-part-1.html
61. Martin, K. (2020). *How Cisco uses a data-driven approach to strategic workforce planning*. i4cp. https://www.i4cp.com/interviews/how-cisco-uses-a-data-driven-approach-to-strategic-workforce-planning
62. Englert, H. (2021). How gamification is helping Procter & Gamble boost employee learning. *Salesforce*. https://www.salesforce.com/blog/procter-gamble-gamification-employee-learning/
63. Davenport, T. H. (2013). *How P&G presents data to decision-makers*. Harvard Business Publishing. https://hbr.org/2013/04/how-p-and-g-presents-data
64. Biswas, D. (2021). *Amazon's use of algorithms to increase employees' productivity: Fair or not?* Analytics India Magazine. https://analyticsindiamag.com/amazons-use-of-algorithms-to-increase-employees-productivity-fair-or-not/

65. Bhateja, S., & Goswami, N. (2017). *Amazon employee data analysis*. GitHub. https://goswamin20.github.io/Amazon%20Employee%20Data%20Analysis.html
66. Murambinda, B. (2023). *Amazon human resources management: What you need to know*. Human Capital Hub. https://www.thehumancapitalhub.com/articles/amazon-human-resources-management-what-you-need-to-know
67. Bickerton, J., & Moon, J. (2022). *How data and analytics are transforming the wholesale bank at HSBC*. McKinsey. https://www.mckinsey.com/industries/financial-services/our-insights/how-data-and-analytics-are-transforming-the-wholesale-bank-at-hsbc
68. Mixson, E. (2021). *Data science at Netflix: How advanced data & analytics helps Netflix generate billions*. AI, Data & Analytics Network. https://www.aidataanalytics.network/data-science-ai/articles/data-science-at-netflix-how-advanced-data-analytics-helped-netflix-generate-billions#:~:text=Netflix%20uses%20analytics%20to%20optimize,reducing%20bottlenecks%20and%20streamlining%20workflows
69. Şentürk, B. (2022). *What human resources professionals can learn from Netflix*. Enstitü Oü. https://www.iienstitu.com/en/blog/what-human-resources-professionals-can-learn-from-netflix
70. Henderson, N. V. (2023). *Movella enhances employee safety measures at Toyota*. Movella. https://investors.movella.com/news-releases/news-release-details/movella-enhances-employee-safety-measures-toyota
71. Reines, M. (2023). *Adobe unveils new collaboration tool for marketing teams*. TechTarget. https://www.techtarget.com/searchcustomerexperience/news/365533656/Adobe-unveils-new-collaboration-tool-for-marketing-teams
72. Adobe. (2021). *Adobe delivers award-winning intranet experience*. Adobe. https://business.adobe.com/customer-success-stories/adobe-on-adobe-intranet-case-study.html
73. Berman, J. J. (2013). *Principles of big data: Preparing, sharing, and analyzing complex information*. Newnes.
74. Kaufman, B. E. (2010). SHRM theory in the post-Huselid era: Why it is fundamentally misspecified. *Industrial Relations: A Journal of Economy and Society, 49*(2), 286–313. https://doi.org/10.1111/j.1468-232X.2009.00600.x

# Strategic Integration of Industry 5.0 Assistive Technologies for Cognition in Business for Human Capital Development

**Jun Li, Ilia Chernenko, and Irina Semenova**

**Abstract** The study sheds light on the implementation of a specialized yet promising category of technology solutions into business models, aiming to support human cognitive functions, fostering both inclusivity and optimal mental performance for neurotypical individuals. The purpose of the article is to study the latest trends in Industry 5.0-related digital assistive technologies for cognition (ATC) and develop a strategic integration roadmap that combines several models. The roadmap includes a range of options, from incremental improvements in product, service or business process functionality to comprehensive lifecycle management to improve customer value. Methods include a systematic literature review and analysis of patent activity in the field of cognition assistance based on PATENTSCOPE data from the World Intellectual Property Organization (WIPO). Through keyword analysis, the study identified over 43,000 patents worldwide registered between 2013 and 2022. The patents were analyzed, highlighting key technologies of significant commercial relevance. Subsequently, the authors propose a framework for strategic integration of digital cognition assistance across diverse models. It is shown that cognition assistance is a growing technological and investment trend; the share of related patents in the portfolios of leading manufacturers increased from 0.19% to 2.44% over the period under review.

**Keywords** Industry 5.0 · Digitalization · Assistive technologies for cognition · Human capital · Business models

J. Li
University of Science and Technology Liaoning, Anshan, Liaoning, China

I. Chernenko (✉) · I. Semenova
Ural Federal University, Ekaterinburg, Russian Federation
e-mail: i.m.chernenko@urfu.ru; i.i.semenova@urfu.ru

 
A. Appolloni et al. (eds.), *The Future of Industry*, Lecture Notes in Information Systems and Organisation 70, https://doi.org/10.1007/978-3-031-66801-2_26

## 1 Introduction

Recent challenges faced by developed countries, such as demographic crises, shifts in labor market behavior due to the pandemic, increasing social tensions, and inequality in a fragmented global economy, have prompted both the academic community and policymakers to think about the role of advanced technologies in the evolution of society [1]. Priority is being assigned to support and assistive functions to enhance the quality of life and subjective well-being for a diverse population. These functions also directly impact learning strategies and the efficacy of knowledge application, reducing the risks associated with the digital divide. The concept of Industry 4.0, actively promoted in public policy in both developed and developing nations since the 2010s, has attracted substantial attention in recent literature. Industry 4.0's influence has become evident in the digital transformation of companies, improving data management, streamlining production and service processes, enhancing the customer experience, and facilitating valuable feedback [2, 3]. The development of cyber-physical systems supports the connectivity of the value creation environment, enabling stakeholders to plan and coordinate the operations of fully interconnected corporate ecosystems that respond to external signals through intelligent automation [4]. Consequently, genuine smart manufacturing has emerged in recent decades, facilitating the rapid, large-scale production of innovative products. As part of this new industrial revolution, intelligence is embodied in non-linear, neural network algorithms for processing incoming data. These algorithms effectively substitute human capabilities in routine analysis and data processing and provide deeper insights for optimal decision-making. Industry 4.0 has caused significant concern in the professional community due to the lack of standardized principles and strategies for replacing human functions in manufacturing. This concern arises from the potential for structural unemployment and the devaluation of human capital.

The emerging paradigm of Society 5.0 underscores the need to seek the roots of economic growth in the social realm, emphasizing the dynamic processes of knowledge generation and accumulation, as well as human-centered approaches to value creation. This shift encourages society to avoid overemphasizing technologies that are not linked to human activity and structural capital [5, 6]. It seems most appropriate to view Society 5.0 and its subsequent evolution into Industry 5.0 as a conceptual extension of the knowledge-based society and cyber-physical systems. Industry 4.0 solutions are transformed under the influence of general-purpose technologies into cyber-social systems [7]. From one perspective, knowledge theory highlights the significance of artificial intellectual capital and the processes of knowledge generation and utilization in achieving new dimensions of production efficiency. Artificial intelligence (AI) enables flexibility, customization, substitution, and efficient augmentation of a highly skilled workforce. On the other hand, Industry 5.0 pays attention to the strengthening convergence between humans and machines [8]. Currently, this convergence mainly takes place on a non-invasive basis, without direct interaction with the human body and its tissues. In this context, cooperation assumes the form of assistance, where human abilities take precedence and ensure the coordination of production or service processes, including goal setting and strategic control.

Assistive technologies for cognition (ATC) are non-invasive solutions that complement human abilities, relying on abstract thinking, the capacity to learn, timely recognition of external elements and signals, critical thinking based on available data, and the ability to generate complex responses, adaptation solutions, and feedback mechanisms [9, 10]. Assistive technologies offer support to a diverse range of stakeholders, including individuals with congenital or acquired cognitive disorders, those facing challenges related to memory and cognitive function, physical capabilities, and neurotypical individuals with typical cognitive abilities. Even neurotypical individuals with normal cognitive function use these support functions for decision-making, critical analysis, and automating daily tasks [11]. For all these stakeholders, digital cognitive assistance plays a significant role in enhancing the quality of life and expanding opportunities for work and communication. These technologies are closely associated with dynamic processes that take advantage of network capabilities. Cognitive assistance underpins the central function of Industry 5.0, which is the collaboration between stakeholders and cyber-physical systems.

The purpose of this article is to investigate the most recent developments in digital assistive technologies for cognition and propose a strategic integration roadmap. The roadmap encompasses a variety of models, from partial support of product or service features to full implementation of market solutions that add value to customers. In the existing literature, there is an abstract conception of Industry 5.0 as a set of numerous general-purpose technologies that can be combined in various ways, yielding diverse outcomes. While best practices, implementation roadmaps [2, 12], and maturity assessment methods were previously established for Industry 4.0, the principles of development and prevailing technological trends for this new wave of socially-oriented digitalization remain implicit. In our perspective, the most promising direction for merging human and machine capabilities is in the realm of assistance, involving enhancing and extending human abilities at the intersection of contemporary environmental, geopolitical, demographic, and socio-economic challenges.

## 2 Literature Review

### *2.1 Industry 5.0 in the Light of Global and National Problems of Human Capital Development*

Society's expectations regarding the use of digital technologies in the modern world are increasingly centered on promoting well-being across various age groups, addressing specialized needs, and adapting to different contexts. A substantial portion of the potential of human-centric digitalization is dedicated to addressing

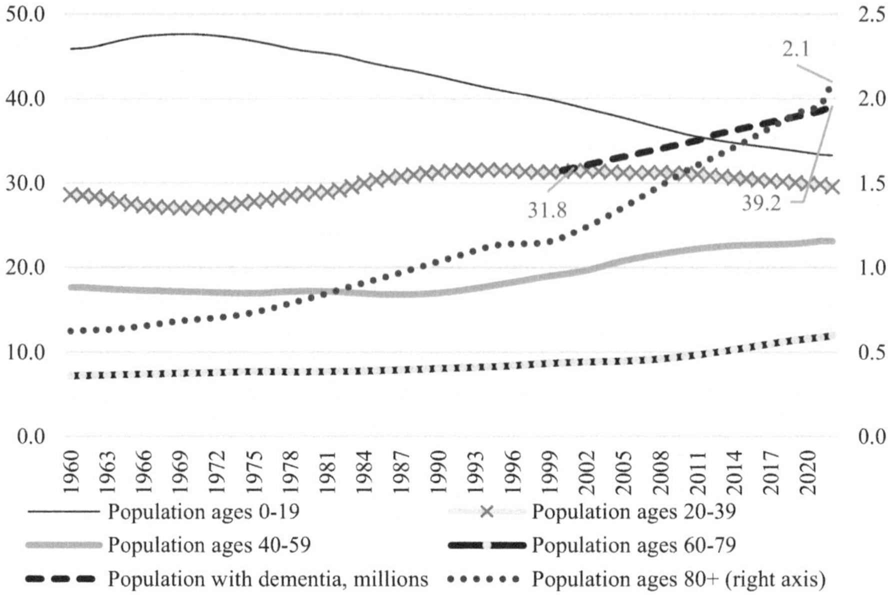


**Fig. 1** Dynamics of world population structure by age and number of people with dementia from 1960 to 2021 and related disorders from 2000 to 2021. Source: Obtained by the authors using World Bank database

the challenges posed by an aging population and enhancing the social inclusion of older generations. These older cohorts are accumulating both tangible wealth and human capital. Over the past six decades, trends in population aging have resulted in a notable increase in the proportion of individuals over 80 years, rising from 0.6 to 2.1% in the population structure (Fig. 1). Currently, the percentage of people over 60 years who are still employed continues to rise, while birth rates decline in both developed and developing countries. In the context of Russia, older generations are accumulating a significant stock of human capital and actively engaging in social participation. They not only remain in the workforce but also contribute to family well-being, parenting, volunteer work, and lifelong learning [13]. These active and engaged older generations face unique challenges associated with the natural decline in cognitive abilities. Notably, computer literacy among these older cohorts remains significantly low, including both general and specialized digital skills. The largest gap is observed within the group aged 55 and above, with more than half of this population having limited or no digital skills at all [14]. Intelligent human-centric digitalization aims to facilitate seamless collaboration and adaptation for these segments of the population within the digital environment, enhancing safety and overall quality of life.

Within the global development environment, pressing issues such as the climate agenda, labor market disparities, and geopolitical fragmentation reveal the vulnerabilities of development strategies that solely emphasize technological progress [15–

17]. The emerging wave of digitalization seeks to address the limitations of previous automation, which has often been linked to structural unemployment, precarious working conditions, and uncertainty arising from the absence of transparent retraining strategies in the face of rapid digital expansion [16]. In this evolving digital environment, there is also a shift in the way society views issues related to mental stress and the resilience of organizational employees. The emotional and informational demands of work are on the rise. Therefore, managing the human-centric digital transformation of everyday life becomes a critical factor for personal and family well-being. Two key trajectories in the development of digital technologies that support human capital are: (1) reducing the levels of psychological and physical stress on older workers, and (2) cultivating degrowth strategic values that underpin informed and intelligent decision-making for resource conservation and business process optimization.

The new phase in the evolution of cyber-social systems emphasizes the increasing efficiency in utilizing human capital, as well as the collaborative impact of participants in the value creation process and the distribution of executive and leadership functions between humans and artificial intelligence [3, 18]. It is important to recognize that human capital is inherently subjective. Each individual possesses unique sensory-emotional abilities, emotional intelligence, empathy, and flexible thinking [7]. Therefore, each person is not just an abstract adaptive neural network but a distinct entity shaped by a multitude of factors and intentions [19]. Consequently, in cyber-social systems, human capabilities are not replaced; they are supplemented to enhance socio-economic outcomes and various performance indicators of social systems in the broadest sense [20]. The digitalization of organizations and digital education as characteristic of Industry 5.0 must, therefore, adhere to the principles of humanization and the acknowledgment of the valuable human abilities. This principle also extends to the process of creating and commercializing service products. Participatory design involves engaging the community in the development of cyber-social systems and applying general principles for their operation. To sum up the literature review on digital technology development, Table 1 highlights the key distinctions between Industry 4.0 and Industry 5.0 in terms of crucial issues, technological development trajectories, and value creation strategies.

## 2.2 *Industry 5.0 for Cognition Assistance: Features and Development Prospects in Business*

The context of Industry 5.0 technology solutions remains unclear, given that many of them are of a general-purpose nature, making it challenging to prioritize and invest in specific solutions. A significant portion of the literature on cognition assistance is centered around fields such as medicine, neurophysiology, and the restoration of impaired brain functions with the aim of enhancing the overall quality

**Table 1** Dimensions of transition from Industry 4.0 towards Industry 5.0

| Dimension | Industry 4.0 | Industry 5.0 |
|---|---|---|
| Key problem that the concept aims to solve | Low performance of production and service systems due to low connectivity and inefficient processing of large amounts of unstructured and semi-structured data. Moderate integration into supply chains and limited opportunities for customization of products and services | Problems of reproduction of high-quality labor in conditions of the global demographic crisis and climate uncertainty, rising costs of human capital reproduction in developed countries, manifestation of green skepticism. Limited possibilities for individualization of platforms and teaching methods, decision support |
| Technological vector of development | Cyber-physical systems, digital twins, internet of things and data mining for decision making, elimination of human-dependent operations | Cyber-social systems, internet of people, cognitive assistance and support of human abilities, development of a society ready for the use of high-performance AI, involvement of human capital in operations |
| Robotization principles | Fenced and coexisted robots with limited cooperative abilities, sequential movements of robot and human are dominating the manufacturing or service processes | Robots have ability to cooperate and respond to human actions and behavioral patterns, feedback is given in a real-time manner, operations are often conducted simultaneously |
| Intellectual capital and knowledge management | Preference is given to structural capital—Formalized results of intellectual activity, accumulated data and information | The potential of human capital, dynamic processes of knowledge sharing supported by digital technologies is considered |
| Value creation strategies | Digital automation based on smart machines, factories and applications supporting data mining | Information and communication technologies to support human capabilities, participative design for digital environment, customization and individualization |
| Ways to achieve competitive advantage | Automation of data collection, data mining and application of machine learning for a predictive approach throughout the entire life cycle of products and services | Supporting cognitive and other functions for decision making, facilitating access to information, finding solutions for job development based on the harmonious and responsible implementation of AI |
| Development strategies | Sustainable development strategies that support high environmental standards and investments in green technologies. Investments in infrastructure and equipment | Limited growth and degrowth strategies that prioritize environmental performance. Promoting the values of democratization, equality and inclusion that enhance human potential. Investments in human capital are a priority |

*Source*: Compiled by the authors based on literature analysis

of life. ATC includes a broad array of both digital and analog solutions that have been developed over the past five decades to compensate for lost memory or cognitive functions, as well as to support sensory abilities [21, 22]. ATC utilizes computer technology and is specifically designed for rehabilitation purposes, addressing the daily needs and unique functions of individuals [21]. Digital assistance extends across various domains, including the restoration of lost auditory, visual, and communication functions [10]. A significant portion of the population afflicted with brain disorders and dysfunctions also requires support in areas like complex attention, decision-making and justification, memory functions, adaptation, and the initiation of actions. Given the increasing proportion of older generations in the population, the likelihood and scope of current health issues are expected to rise. Research conducted by the World Intellectual Property Organization (WIPO) reveals that a substantial share of such technologies belongs to the medical devices and mechanisms market, particularly in the realm of medication management. Notably, more than half of all inventions developed between 1998 and 2019 are aimed at supporting memory, time management, and calculation abilities [9]. Sohn et al. [22] highlight that digitalization plays a crucial role in supporting the cognitive functioning of individuals with dementia. However, the presence of individual differences and the wide array of technological solutions make it challenging to conduct research in this field and establish consistent best practices. Potential applications for these technologies span both the external environment of organizations, such as the digital technology market for individuals with cognitive disabilities or older generations, and the internal environment of organizations, with the aim of enhancing employee engagement and productivity.

It is also important to distinguish another category—neurotypical stakeholders who exhibit typical neurological patterns and are considered normal based on current medical knowledge [11]. While for individuals with neurological and cognitive disabilities, digitalization is primarily associated with compensating for lost functions, for neurotypical individuals, the focus often lies in expanding cognitive capabilities to increase productivity. The previous wave of Industry 4.0 brought forth numerous innovations in intelligent support for human cognitive functions. Principles and methods for decision-making, data processing, and the automation of routine tasks, as well as advancements in education through virtualization, remote communication, enhanced content accessibility, and customization, are widely recognized [23, 24]. However, automation has presented certain challenges to human capital, particularly concerning the displacement of low-skilled labor tasks. Conversely, the intellectual evolution of Industry 5.0 is linked to creative and emotional components, along with the potential for direct collaboration with humans in creating consumer value. This aspect needs to be considered when developing models for the strategic integration of cyber-social systems into a company's business models. Digitalization enables the structuring of the individual space for neurotypical stakeholders, supporting functions like self-regulation, transparent algorithmization, transitioning between complex tasks, and long-term planning.

A review of the literature shows that cognition assistance offers a significant value proposition for a diverse range of stakeholders and, therefore, can be strategically integrated into business models. Firstly, cyber-social systems not only facilitate individualized functions but are also context-sensitive, amplifying their significance for human capital development. Each person possesses unique cognitive attributes, emotional strengths and weaknesses, intelligence, creativity, and distinct attitudes towards various aspects and values [22]. Cyber-social systems have the capacity to adapt optimal modes of interaction with the environment based on the recognition of an individual's cognitive state and regular feedback. Industry 5.0 advances and enhances technologies for smart homes and offices, digital assistants and pets, telemedicine, and the monitoring of individuals' conditions to diagnose early signs of psychological stress and cognitive decline while formulating preventive measures. Preventive strategies are particularly crucial for occupations that involve stress, burnout, and challenging physical demands. However, the accuracy of cognitive function diagnostics remains a significant barrier in the implementation of assistance technologies due to the extensive use of unstructured data and complex medical information for recognition [25].

Secondly, the assistive technologies of Industry 5.0 have a direct impact on employment and the nature of work, paradoxically emphasizing the significance of human presence within the production system. Human-centric technological shift revisits the advancements of Industry 4.0 in terms of organizing remote work [26]. For the majority of contemporary professions, the possibility of remote work is often unfeasible, underscoring the increasing importance of integrating human capital into the digital production environment. Furthermore, cyber-physical digitalization has exacerbated labor market polarization creating more favorable conditions for skilled and well-compensated employees [17]. The predominant use of Industry 4.0 to optimize internal processes has created an ideal environment for labor substitution, which, in turn, reduces the motivation for retraining. In contrast, Industry 5.0 presents greater potential for human capital within businesses, placing an increased emphasis on creativity, introducing gamification into individual processes, enhancing employee resilience to stress, tolerance for complex working conditions, and adaptability in high uncertainty. Consequently, most employers should adopt personalized training using cognitive assistance technologies to nurture talent and cultivate process champions [17]. These assistive technologies are poised to significantly boost worker autonomy, foster creative specialization, and encourage the acquisition of new competencies. This, in turn, promotes the sharing of tacit knowledge and transcending the confines of traditional corporate relationships and organizational structures.

Thirdly, specific assistive technology platforms and solutions, such as collaborative robots (cobots), offer a promising avenue for reinforcing trust in the digital environment. They can help address the challenges of structural unemployment, enhance the precision and operational efficiency of innovation processes, and compensate for the shortage of qualified assistants in high-tech industries. Industry 4.0 scenarios tend to emphasize deskilling and labor replacement, whereas Industry 5.0 places a greater emphasis on skill augmentation, reskilling, and training for the integration of new technologies [18]. The shift involves a transformation from coexistence and external control to collaboration and signal exchange to achieve shared objectives. Users of equipment and infrastructure work in parallel with robots within a shared space. Cobots are actively being deployed in synchronous assembly operations, load handling, labeling, equipment maintenance, process control, and product design. Nevertheless, in most cases, companies strive to establish a basic coexistence of human workers and robots, resulting in the gradual displacement and substitution of human labor. Instances of cooperation and collaboration between humans and robots remain relatively unique [18].

Fourthly, applications based on AI integrated into cyber-social systems can serve to learn and generate new content while facilitating regulated interactions with other community members within clusters or groups. One of the significant potentials of Industry 5.0 lies in predictive functions derived from intelligent analysis of big data. AI enables the detection of subtle changes in the cyber-social system by analyzing fluctuations in parameters gathered from sensors capable of recognizing images, temperature, vibrations, voices, sounds, and more [26]. AI models for cognitive assistance should provide transparent justifications for decisions, especially in critical or sensitive areas of a company's operations, ensuring responsibility and trust among stakeholders [20]. In their research, Rožanec et al. [20] identify the enabling technologies necessary to impart such qualities to AI in cyber-social systems. These technologies include active learning, explainable "white-box" decision-making models, as well as simulated reality and the ability to recognize stakeholder intentions. Caiazzo et al. [27] argue that AI in Industry 5.0 predominantly harnesses the creativity of human experts, involving various mathematical models based on cause-and-effect relationships. However, a substantial barrier to the implementation of assistive AI lies in the availability of vast datasets for deep learning, challenges related to adaptability, and the incorporation of fuzzy logic into the analysis and diagnosis process.

In light of the findings from the literature review, we formulate the following research questions:

1. What are the inherent characteristics, attributes, and domains of value creation associated with both established and emerging Industry 5.0 technologies that facilitate cognitive assistance?
2. How can these technologies be effectively integrated into a unified roadmap to cultivate customer value and sustain human capital among stakeholders?

## 3 Data and Methods

To address the first research question, the authors conducted a study of technological trends within Industry 5.0 by employing content analysis of the titles and abstracts of existing patents. Analyzing patent activity is a valuable method for discerning pertinent technological trends as it provides insights into the dynamics of the number of inventions and the level of activity associated with specific emerging technologies. The study utilized the PATENTSCOPE database [28] spanning the years

2013 to 2022. The PATENTSCOPE includes patent application numbers, full document titles and abstracts, invention categories, applicant information, filing dates, and the names of inventors. The research aimed at identifying relevant patents using keywords such as "digital", "cognitive", "assistance", or "support". The focus of the search was on a narrow set of digital technologies that offer supportive and assistive functions for human cognitive processes. Notably, the search was specifically concentrated on digital solutions associated with computer technology, information technology, and digital process automation. Solutions pertaining to chemistry or biochemistry were excluded from the analyzed patent database. The total number of applications reviewed during the specified timeframe amounted to 43,430, with duplicate applications consolidated within a single patent family.

To address the second research question, the authors drew from a prior literature review and an examination of technology solutions. Key areas of analysis include external environmental signals that shape individual technological trends, guiding principles, implementation strategies, and a comprehensive model of implementation that considers the depth of transformation within companies. Additionally, to propose the integration model, data from technological solutions disclosed in patents obtained from leading companies in the development of cognitive assistance technologies were incorporated.

## 4 Results and Discussion

The analysis reveals that over 75% of the examined solutions fall within three primary technology categories, such as computer computing, medical inventions, and electrical communication techniques. In contrast, only 3.6% of all patents pertain to educational technologies. Most of the companies under examination are prominent players in the market for high-tech products and smart applications. The analysis also suggests an examination of the top ten leading companies, which collectively submitted the majority of the applications. Figure 2 presents the percentage of patents that incorporate digital ATC in the overall volume of applications by these companies, along with an estimation of the total number of applications integrating digital cognitive assistance. For some of these companies, digital ATC serves as a supporting component within their broader intellectual property portfolios. However, companies such as IBM and Facebook have notably increased the share of solutions related to AI assistants, personalized smart analytics, and support for the unique cognitive needs of older age cohorts. Nvidia, Pure Storage, and Commvault Systems incorporate these technologies extensively into their patent portfolios, largely in conjunction with the widespread implementation of AI for tasks like gameplay, situation modeling, big data processing, and collaborative AI structures. Several of the studied technologies include various forms of assistance to compensate for cognitive functions, motor skills, auditory capacities, or other sensory functions during operation. A noteworthy emerging trend is the Brain-Computer Interface (BCI), which comprises recording devices, software, and output

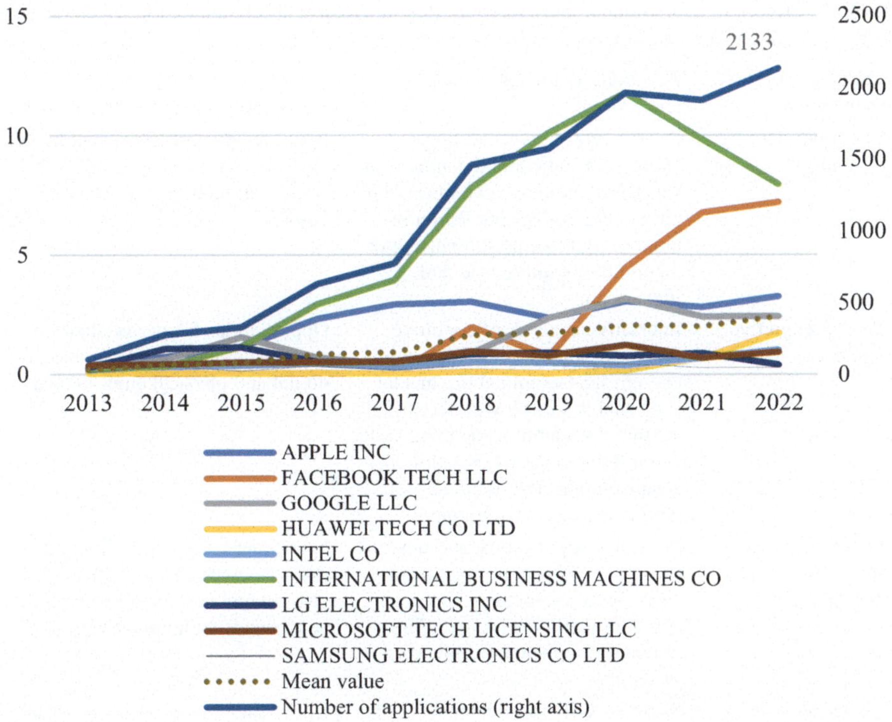


**Fig. 2** Share of patent applications involving cognitive assistance digital technologies in the total number of company filings and total number of related patent applications during the year. *Source*: Obtained by authors using PATENTSCOPE [28]

devices that facilitate the display of results on a screen or even the activation of mechanisms, movements, or procedures. In total, the ten leaders in patent activity within this field successfully filed more than 2000 patent applications in 2022.

Based on the outcomes of the analysis, the technologies were categorized into seven principal groups, as shown in Table 2. These groupings highlight the varied business potential of Industry 5.0 concerning the content of patentable solutions. The functions and applications of these technologies are outlined, and the value propositions for stakeholders are delineated. The analysis indicates that digital ATC facilitates users in recognizing cognitive states through means such as facial expressions, posture, or voice intonation. Technologies also enable intelligent diagnostics to assess the cognitive abilities of individuals with brain disorders as well as neurotypical individuals. The potential of this field is associated with non-invasive technologies that employ electroencephalography in connection with visual recognition in video or photographic materials. Technologies focused on memory support and time management provide opportunities to improve the quality of life of stakeholders by intelligently prioritizing tasks. Previous research has underscored that this domain is a key trend for all assistive technologies, considering both digital

**Table 2** Overview of traditional and emerging digital assistive technologies for cognition and value propositions for stakeholders identified based on patent analysis

| Cognition assistive technology | Functions and technological applications | Value proposition for stakeholders |
|---|---|---|
| Cognitive state recognition | Passive, non-interactive facial expression static and dynamic analysis based on image classifiers, 24/7 online monitoring, prediction of human cognitive performance, prediction of cognitive load and impairment | Real time control and dynamic analysis of processes/results, personal cognition-related data and knowledge |
| Testing cognitive functions | Interactive analysis of cognitive functions, including questionnaires and physical examination, mental state analysis using web services. Testing for adaptive cognitive skills and training results evaluation, personalization of training feedback, optimizing cognitive training | Opportunities for personalization, customization, individualization of digital and physical environment |
| Memory support and time-management | Software, applications, and devices to provide support in organizing tasks, setting reminders, and managing time efficiently, including calendars, applications and voice assistance | Sustaining focus on Well-being and value creation, prioritization of tasks in real-time manner, independence from human assistance |
| Digital security assistance | Smart security management for data creation, sharing and access according to user preferences. Cognition assistance for decision-making when transferring data and information, automation. Restriction and controlling access to personal and other sensitive information | Knowledge management in uncertain environment involving plenty of automated transactions, digital security risk management |
| Cognitive management | Transmitting neural stimulus response to digital environment using sensors, cognitive patterns recognition for tracking changes and results in management systems, assistance for human sensory systems. Enhancing brain functions through graphical and visual control, adaptive communication, speech and gesture recognition | Support of analytical decision-making and interactions, tools and knowledge providing insights into accumulated data and information |
| Cognitive bias correction and critical thinking support | AI-powered detection and correction of cognitive biases in reports; intelligent recommendations, virtual assistants and media analyzers, triggers for critical thinking | Support of expert-based prediction processes, decision implementation through critical thinking |
| Cognitive rehabilitation and recreation | Assistance in treating neurodegenerative disease, recovery, daily cognitive recreation from job and environmental stress | Physical and neurological, psychological recreation and cognitive function restoration |

and traditional solutions based on analog or mechanical systems. Digital ATC designed to improve individuals' analytical thinking, aiding in the formulation of operational or strategically significant decisions, exhibit substantial business potential. This category includes robotic companions and digital assistants that respond to human gestures, analyze behavioral aspects through sensors, as well as various software and applications for interactive decision support rooted in artificial intelligence. ATC leverages interaction with users, enabling neural network models to learn and provide relevant answers to tasks. The implementation of these elements gives rise to machine vision, sensor systems, and technological units responsible for intelligent decision-making, data analysis, and systematization to yield knowledge. Technologies are usually integrated into machinery, equipment, smart devices like smartphones, or other personal devices.

Several devices and applications within this domain have a particular focus on enhancing digital security. The inventors highlight that the proliferation of smart devices in people's lives has led to a significant increase in daily interactions with third-party applications that collect sensitive information. Cyber-social security digital assistants play a crucial role in this context, as they engage with stakeholders to define security configurations, filter content of interest, and securely store personal data and other sensitive information. Digital management and cybersecurity assistance have a broad spectrum of applications, both in the business environment (such as robotic cooperation in production settings) and within domestic environments, where they manage personal affairs and smart homes. Another noteworthy aspect of digital solutions within Industry 5.0 is related to assisting in correcting cognitive distortions, behavioral patterns, and decision-making methods to mitigate the risk of errors. This application area aims to enhance cognitive functioning, thereby improving the decision-making process. Lastly, within the realm of the considered technologies, attention is directed toward the recreation and rehabilitation of stakeholders, including recovery from illness, adaptation, or the restoration of normal cognitive functions for neurotypical individuals. The process of recreation entails AI-guided or AI-supported activities that facilitate the restoration of regular brain activity and include providing recommendations, exercises, and tasks for users to engage in, therefore digital ATC seeks to enhance well-being and cognitive capabilities.

As a result of the analysis of patents, we identified nine main groups of stakeholders, for each of which the level of influence of technology in the next 5–10 years was assessed. We assume limited or no influence (S), moderate influence (M) and significant influence (L) for each stakeholder group. In the company's environment we identified managers (ME), neurotypical employees (NE), employees with special needs (ES), business partners in the supply chain (BS), company customers (CL), company customers with special needs (CS), educational and research organizations (ER), government (GV) and the surrounding community (LS). The estimates are given by the authors conditionally, based on an understanding of the nature and prospects of technologies based on the studied patents and literature. Estimates may require expert clarification in further studies.

Technologies were identified using patent applications. Based on the keywords corresponding to the technologies, the frequency (FQ) of their occurrence in the

**Table 3** Analysis of the prevalence (FQ) of technologies in patents and assessment of their potential impact on stakeholders in the next decade

| Industry 5.0 ATC value proposition | FQ | MA | NE | ES | BP | CL | CS | ER | GV | LS |
|---|---|---|---|---|---|---|---|---|---|---|
| *Health capital:* Medication management (digital, e.g. predicting hypoglycemia) | F | S | S | L | S | S | L | S | M | M |
| AI-based stress management (e.g. detecting stress level) | C | M | M | M | S | M | M | S | S | S |
| AI-based general Well-being management | C | M | M | L | S | L | L | M | M | M |
| *Knowledge and skills:* AI-based smart feedback in education and training | C | M | M | L | M | L | L | L | M | M |
| Personalized assistance in learning (digital) | C | L | L | L | M | L | M | L | S | M |
| VR-based imaging and augmentation (e.g. augmented reality glasses) | C | L | L | L | M | L | L | L | M | L |
| Memory management (e.g. smart scheduling devices and apps) | F | M | M | M | M | M | L | M | S | S |
| *Social capital and smart communication:* AI-based cybersecurity | R | L | L | L | L | L | L | L | L | L |
| AI-based networking and structured knowledge sharing with people and other devices | F | L | L | L | L | L | L | L | M | M |
| Virtual kinematic intelligence | R | S | S | L | S | S | L | S | S | M |
| Nature language processing | C | M | M | L | M | M | L | M | S | M |
| Eye movement recognition | C | M | M | L | S | M | L | M | S | S |
| Complex smart collaboration (e.g. office and manufacturing cobots) | R | M | L | L | M | L | L | L | M | M |

reviewed patents was determined: rare (R, less than 1%), common (C, from 1 to 5%), frequent (F, more than 5%). Each of the technologies supports human capital in three areas: health capital, knowledge and skills, social capital and smart communication in the digital environment. The results of the analysis are presented in Table 3. The rarest are smart kinematic systems that support interaction with users, as well as complex collaboration systems or collaborative robots. Among the emerging technologies of Industry 5.0, we can highlight solutions in the field of motion processing and complex behavior recognition, which remain quite rare, although they are being developed, for example, by manufacturers of self-driving cars and smart devices. This type of technology also includes kinematic intelligence technologies, which adjust the movements of robotic and cobotic manipulators to human movements. In our opinion, the greatest impact on cognitive assistance in the coming years will come from cybersecurity assistance and augmented reality technologies, as well as devices for smart knowledge sharing based on natural language processing. It is likely that technologies for managing general well-being and stress management will also remain promising niche markets.

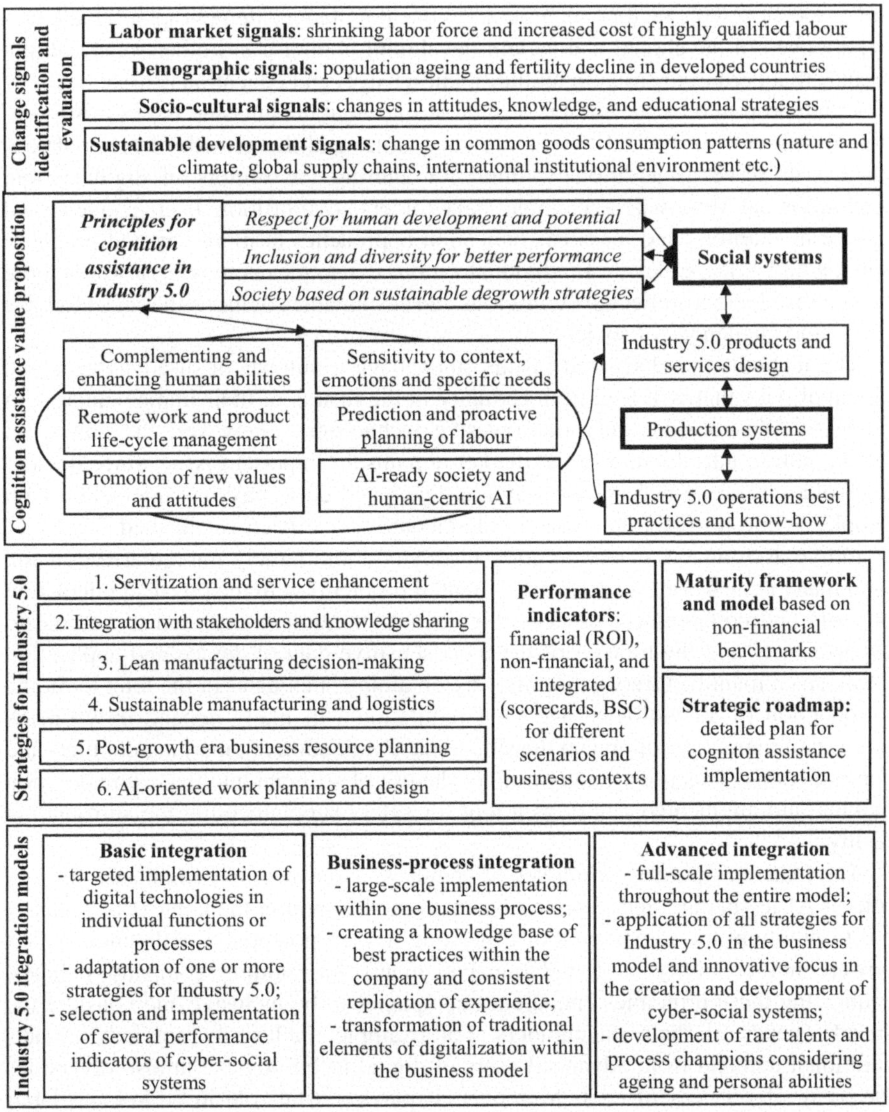


**Fig. 3** The roadmap of strategic integration of Industry 5.0 into business model

Based on a comprehensive review of both literature and patents, the authors have proposed a strategic integration roadmap that includes critical areas of environmental analysis, the selection of guiding principles, strategies, and an integration model operating at the level of individual functions, processes, or even an entire business model within a company (Fig. 3). In this context, external environmental signals are regarded as informational sources that compel stakeholders to reassess their strategies for market behavior. In the context of digital cognitive assistance, weak signals are associated with factors such as an aging population, demographic challenges experienced in developed and certain developing nations, and other socio-cultural signals that pertain to shifts in attitudes, knowledge, and educational strategies. The roadmap proposed by the authors also underlines that the pressing issues of sustainable development, marked by climate uncertainty and the growth of green skepticism, will serve as additional stimuli for altering the vectors of digitalization. Technological shift will encourage stakeholders to transition from conventional industrial solutions and mass customization approaches to more targeted problem-solving and a deeper level of individualization. It also means moving towards more personalized, environmentally conscious and sustainable solutions that meet today's needs and challenges of society.

The technologies discussed in this study have a number of disadvantages and potential risks that will lead to uncertainty in the results of their implementation in business. We consider only non-invasive technologies, however, the quality of testing before introduction to the market remains an important issue, since devices and solutions are aimed at everyday assistance and close physical interaction with people. While testing frameworks and standards have been established for drugs, cognitive assistance remains a poorly understood and largely unregulated domain, with many ethical controversies and potential problems with the physical interaction of users and collaborative devices. Significant attention is expected to be paid to cybersecurity and the transfer of the most sensitive data of device and application users, since manufacturers gain power by obtaining such data. In the long term, the introduction of technologies and their regulation will likely depend only on the practice of their application and the situational elimination of emerging conflicts and contradictions. This is especially true for the use of artificial intelligence in decision making and augmented reality as a tool for safely supplementing the surrounding reality.

The map incorporates principles of cognitive assistance that emphasize the key role of AI in shaping and evolving business models within the context of Industry 5.0 to highlight the importance of respecting human potential, intelligence, expert power, and creativity as foundational elements for guiding company policies. Embracing these principles encourages companies to be inclusive and consider the specific needs of their stakeholders. For example, inclusivity not only attracts additional demand from advanced users of digital technologies but also diversifies the array of services offered. Moreover, it plays a vital role in addressing labor shortages that might arise in the face of diminishing opportunities in the labor market. In support of sustainable development, the strategic integration of cognitive assistance technologies must also highlight the role of degrowth strategies. By doing so, companies can secure a competitive advantage in an era marked by geopolitical and geo-economic fragmentation. Following these principles is believed to not only complement and enhance human abilities or compensate for lost functions but also do so with a high degree of sensitivity to context. Furthermore, cognitive assistance plays an essential role in achieving operational efficiency as well as in predictive workforce planning. This capability forms the bedrock of a society that is prepared to improve the potential of AI in a responsible and sustainable manner. Integration strategies are also an inevitable component of the proposed roadmap, they are designed to expand service capabilities, facilitate reliable knowledge sharing with stakeholders, ensure effective resource planning, and foster a profound understanding of the full potential of AI across all key business processes within a company. By including these principles and implementing effective integration strategies, businesses can position themselves to thrive within the evolving context of Industry 5.0.

The roadmap examines three integration models related to the maturity level of companies. First, there is basic integration, which involves single or targeted implementation of digital technologies that support cyber security, decision support or recognition of the cognitive state of stakeholders. Second, an integration model is considered within one or more key business processes, which are likely to involve, for example, manufacturing enterprises, the use and development of cobots in systems for maintenance, assembly operations or product design and prototyping. Third, it is assumed that some of the market leaders will implement Industry 5.0 as part of their entire business model in the coming years. Full-scale implementation throughout the entire value chain is based on understanding not only the needs within the company, but also the priority use of cognitive assistance in the company's relevant products or services. At the design stage, companies can select relevant technology solutions to differentiate products or create new solutions to expand or create a fundamentally new value proposition. Deep adoption of digital cognitive assistance also involves understanding the market potential for healthcare products and services and ensuring adequate levels of testing to support context-specific personalization.

## 5 Conclusion

The purpose of this study is to gain insight into the role of digital technologies for cognition assistance (ATC) in developing sustainable human capital and to propose a roadmap illustrating their integration into companies' business models. Drawing from an analysis of both the literature and patent activity, the study has identified key technology clusters and established a value proposition designed to support stakeholders and guide the evolution of business models within both manufacturing and service-oriented companies. Digital cognitive assistance, at its core, represents an augmentation of human cognitive capacities using general-purpose technologies. It empowers individuals to complement and extend their existing intellectual capabilities, enhancing skills in planning, critical analysis, and decision-making while also countering cognitive distortions. This can lead to a notable improvement in the quality and speed of decision-making processes. Understanding the essence and value of digital cognitive assistance is instrumental in enabling companies to maintain their competitive edge in the face of diminishing available resources and shifting structural dynamics in markets for goods, services, and labor, whether in developed or developing nations. The principles underpinning the implementation of human-centric cyber-physical systems center around the recognition of human cognitive abilities and the expert creativity that humans bring to the value creation process. Additionally, there is a strong emphasis on the responsible use of AI to improve decision-making processes. The primary beneficiaries of digital cognitive assistance include two major stakeholder groups: individuals dealing with acquired or congenital cognitive disabilities and neurotypical individuals who are striving to enhance their cognitive capabilities and optimize their decision-making processes. Integrating these technologies into business models promises to open up new opportunities for personal and professional growth, increase sustainability, and help create a more inclusive and adaptive economic landscape.

The study found that in the existing literature, Industry 5.0 case reports are fragmented and isolated, making it difficult to understand their business implications and the creation of commercially viable value for customers. In Russia, enterprises are currently more focused on the implementation of Industry 4.0, obtaining the benefits of increased transparency within their production environments and enhanced operational efficiency. For this reason, the study focused on technological solutions documented in the organized patent data available in the PATENTSCOPE database. Digital ATC under examination include methodologies for identifying the cognitive states of stakeholders and assessing their cognitive functions. These technologies enable real-time recommendations for the management of human capital and individual performance. In the quest for a holistic vision of smart work environments, cognitive assistance technologies play a key role in overcoming the barriers associated with the fourth industrial revolution, especially those associated with deskilling and workforce replacement.

The study has a number of limitations. First, the sample of patents examined is based on a few keywords relevant to Industry 5.0, while some applications may contain complex solutions that have alternative business applications. However, technology analysis is always complex and requires the involvement of experts. It is likely that AI systems in the future will allow natural language processing to analyze technology trends more efficiently. Second, we have highlighted only digital technologies, without paying close attention to complex and interdisciplinary solutions that are embodied directly in complex and holistic devices, for example, cobots or cars. Third, we took a limited time range for our study, therefore analysis of new patents will be important for understanding current trends in the development of ATC. Further research should focus on identifying trends in the effectiveness of commercialization of cognitive assistance technologies. It will be important to identify the promising areas for human capital creation using next generation digital technologies.

**Acknowledgments** The study was supported by the Russian Science Foundation grant No. 23-78-10165, https://rscf.ru/project/23-78-10165/.

## References


1. Onday, O. (2019). Japan's society 5.0: Going beyond industry 4.0. *Business and Economics Journal, 10*(2), 161–170. https://doi.org/10.4172/2151-6219.1000389
2. Ghobakhloo, M., Iranmanesh, M., Grybauskas, A., Vilkas, M., & Petraitė, M. (2021). Industry 4.0, innovation, and sustainable development: A systematic review and a roadmap to sustainable innovation. *Business Strategy and the Environment, 1*(6), 1–21. https://doi.org/10.1002/bse.2867
3. Chiarini, A. (2021). Industry 4.0 technologies in the manufacturing sector: Are we sure they are all relevant for environmental performance? *Business Strategy and the Environment, 30*(7), 3194–3207. https://doi.org/10.1002/bse.2797
4. Erro-Garcés, A., & Aramendia-Muneta, M. E. (2023). The role of human resource management practices on the results of digitalisation. From industry 4.0 to industry 5.0. *Journal of Organizational Change Management, 36*(4), 585–602. https://doi.org/10.1108/JOCM-11-2021-0354
5. Mihardjo, L. W. W., Sasmoko, Alamsyah, F., & Elidjen. (2019). Boosting the firm transformation in industry 5.0: Experience-agility innovation model. *International Journal of Recent Technology and Engineering, 8*(2 Special Issue 9), 735–742. https://doi.org/10.35940/ijrte.B1154.0982S919
6. Ivanov, D. (2023). The industry 5.0 framework: Viability-based integration of the resilience, sustainability, and human-centricity perspectives. *International Journal of Production Research, 61*(5), 1683–1695. https://doi.org/10.1080/00207543.2022.2118892
7. Magni, D., Del Gaudio, G., Papa, A., & Della Corte, V. (2023). Digital humanism and artificial intelligence: The role of emotions beyond the human–machine interaction in society 5.0. *Journal of Management History*. https://doi.org/10.1108/JMH-12-2022-0084
8. Javaid, M., Haleem, A., Singh, R. P., Ul Haq, M. I., Raina, A., & Suman, R. (2020). Industry 5.0: Potential applications in covid-19. *Journal of Industrial Integration and Management, 5*(4), 507–530. https://doi.org/10.1142/S2424862220500220
9. WIPO. (2021). *WIPO technology trends 2021: Assistive technology*. World Intellectual Property Organization. https://doi.org/10.34667/tind.42582
10. Brandt, Å., Jensen, M. P., Søberg, M. S., Andersen, S. D., & Sund, T. (2020). Information and communication technology-based assistive technology to compensate for impaired cognition in everyday life: A systematic review. *Disability and Rehabilitation: Assistive Technology, 15*(7), 810–824. https://doi.org/10.1080/17483107.2020.1765032
11. Shahid, N. M. I., Law, E. L.-C., & Verdezoto, N. (2022). Technology-enhanced support for children with down syndrome: A systematic literature review. *International Journal of Child-Computer Interaction, 31*, 100340. https://doi.org/10.1016/j.ijcci.2021.100340
12. Ghobakhloo, M., Iranmanesh, M., Foroughi, B., Babaee Tirkolaee, E., Asadi, S., & Amran, A. (2023). Industry 5.0 implications for inclusive sustainable manufacturing: An evidence-knowledge-based strategic roadmap. *Journal of Cleaner Production, 417*(June), 138023. https://doi.org/10.1016/j.jclepro.2023.138023
13. Varlamova, M., & Sinyavskaya, O. (2021). Active ageing index in Russia - identifying determinants for inequality. *Journal of Population Ageing, 14*(1), 69–90. https://doi.org/10.1007/s12062-020-09277-4
14. Abdrakhmanova, G., Vasilkovsky, S., Vishnevskiy, K., & Gokhberg, L. (2023). *Digital economy indicators in The Russian Federation: 2022 : Data book*. National Research University Higher School of Economics. https://doi.org/10.17323/978-5-7598-2697-2
15. Grybauskas, A., Stefanini, A., & Ghobakhloo, M. (2022). Social sustainability in the age of digitalization: A systematic literature review on the social implications of industry 4.0. *Technology in Society, 70*(May), 101997. https://doi.org/10.1016/j.techsoc.2022.101997
16. Frey, C. B., & Osborne, M. A. (2017). The future of employment: How susceptible are jobs to computerisation? *Technological Forecasting and Social Change, 114*(1), 254–280. https://doi.org/10.1016/j.techfore.2016.08.019

17. Kolade, O., & Owoseni, A. (2022). Employment 5.0: The work of the future and the future of work. *Technology in Society, 71*(March), 102086. https://doi.org/10.1016/j.techsoc.2022.102086
18. de Dornelles, J. A., Ayala, N. F., & Frank, A. G. (2023). Collaborative or substitutive robots? Effects on workers' skills in manufacturing activities. *International Journal of Production Research, 61*(22), 7922–7955. https://doi.org/10.1080/00207543.2023.2240912
19. Sá, M. J., Santos, A. I., Serpa, S., & Ferreira, C. M. (2021). Digital literacy in digital society 5.0: Some challenges. *Academic Journal of Interdisciplinary Studies, 10*(2), 1–9. https://doi.org/10.36941/ajis-2021-0033
20. Rožanec, J. M., Novalija, I., Zajec, P., Kenda, K., Tavakoli Ghinani, H., Suh, S., Veliou, E., Papamartzivanos, D., Giannetsos, T., Menesidou, S. A., Alonso, R., Cauli, N., Meloni, A., Recupero, D. R., Kyriazis, D., Sofianidis, G., Theodoropoulos, S., Fortuna, B., Mladenić, D., & Soldatos, J. (2023). Human-centric artificial intelligence architecture for industry 5.0 applications. *International Journal of Production Research, 61*(20), 6847–6872. https://doi.org/10.1080/00207543.2022.2138611
21. LoPresti, E. F., Mihailidis, A., & Kirsch, N. (2004). Assistive technology for cognitive rehabilitation: State of the art. *Neuropsychological Rehabilitation, 14*(1–2 spec iss), 5–39. https://doi.org/10.1080/09602010343000101
22. Sohn, M., Yang, J. Y., Sohn, J., & Lee, J. H. (2023). Digital healthcare for dementia and cognitive impairment: A scoping review. *International Journal of Nursing Studies, 140*, 104413. https://doi.org/10.1016/j.ijnurstu.2022.104413
23. Gashenko, I. V., Khakhonova, N. N., Orobinskaya, I. V., & Zima, Y. S. (2020). Competition between human and artificial intellectual capital in production and distribution in industry 4.0. *Journal of Intellectual Capital, 21*(4), 531–547. https://doi.org/10.1108/JIC-11-2019-0275
24. Nayernia, H., Bahemia, H., & Papagiannidis, S. (2021). A systematic review of the implementation of industry 4.0 from the organisational perspective. *International Journal of Production Research, 1*(1), 1–32. https://doi.org/10.1080/00207543.2021.2002964
25. Gillespie, A., Best, C., & O'Neill, B. (2012). Cognitive function and assistive technology for cognition: A systematic review. *Journal of the International Neuropsychological Society, 18*(1), 1–19. https://doi.org/10.1017/S1355617711001548
26. Kraus, K., Kraus, N., Manzhura, O., Ishchenko, I., & Radzikhovska, Y. (2023). Digital transformation of business processes of enterprises on the way to becoming industry 5.0 in the gig economy. *WSEAS Transactions on Business and Economics, 20*, 1008–1029. https://doi.org/10.37394/23207.2023.20.93
27. Caiazzo, B., Murino, T., Petrillo, A., Piccirillo, G., & Santini, S. (2023). An IoT-based and cloud-assisted AI-driven monitoring platform for smart manufacturing: Design architecture and experimental validation. *Journal of Manufacturing Technology Management, 34*(4), 507–534. https://doi.org/10.1108/JMTM-02-2022-0092
28. Patentscope. (2023). *The PATENTSCOPE database*. https://www.wipo.int/patentscope/en/

# The Impact of the Digital Economy on the Development of Human Capital in the Oil and Gas Industry

**Maxim Vlasov and Alexey Safonov**

**Abstract** The article examines the impact of digitalization on the development of human capital in the oil and gas industry, which is a relevant topic given the growing role of digital technologies in the modern economy. The purpose of this study is to analyze the impact of digitalization on the development of human capital in the oil and gas industry. The main method used to examine the problem is meta-analysis. A close connection has been revealed between digitalization and the development of human capital in the oil and gas industry. It has been established that digitalization of companies has a positive effect on the development of human capital, encourages personnel to master the necessary digital skills reducing the likelihood of accidents and injuries to personnel, and contributes to the formation of a knowledge economy. Oil companies need to simultaneously intensify digitalization processes and measures for developing human capital.

**Keywords** Digital transformation · Human capital · Digitalization · Oil and gas industry

## 1 Introduction

In today's conditions, the development of the oil and gas industry is closely connected with the processes of digitalization and digital transformation, and as a consequence their influence on human capital, which is also a component of the economic development of companies and the state.

The oil and gas industry in Russia is an important component of the economy, namely: more than a quarter of the industrial production volume, more than a third of tax payments and more than half of state revenues from exports go to the budget system [1]. It is worth emphasizing that the importance of the oil and gas industry for the Russian economy has become especially relevant in recent years, due to the new

M. Vlasov (✉) · A. Safonov
Institute of Economics of the Ural Branch of the Russian Academy of Sciences, Ekaterinburg, Russian Federation



A. Appolloni et al. (eds.), *The Future of Industry*, Lecture Notes in Information Systems and Organisation 70, https://doi.org/10.1007/978-3-031-66801-2_27

emerging foreign policy conditions, as well as its rapid development, taking into account the growing role of digital technologies in the modern economy. Digitalization and the digital economy are rapidly gaining momentum both in Russia and the world. These processes have not spared the oil and gas industry in Russia.

It is known that human capital is the totality of a person's professional knowledge, their skills, and abilities that help achieve a certain labor productivity, ensure a stable income and growth. The development of human capital involves the process of investing in it to increase returns. Companies realize that investments in human capital are necessary and effective, since they bring income to the business itself, in the form of increased productivity and product quality, and as a result of increased profits, to employees in the form of an increase in their competence, income and job satisfaction. In this regard, the problem of the influence of digitalization on the development of human capital in the oil and gas industry is relevant and not fully studied. There is an assumption that digitalization of companies in the oil and gas industry has a beneficial effect on the formation and development of human capital within the companies under consideration, creates a knowledge economy, and increases labor protection and industrial safety. The purpose of this study is to analyze the impact of digitalization on the development of human capital in the oil and gas industry. In this regard, the following objectives were set: to assess the impact of digitalization and digital transformation on the development of the oil and gas industry, to assess the state of human capital development in the oil and gas industry; identify the relationship between digitalization and human capital development in the oil and gas industry.

The results of the study highlight the positive impact of digitalization on the development of human capital in the oil and gas industry, including the formation and development of the necessary professional skills in the field of digital technologies. These findings expand understanding of the role of digitalization in optimizing human capital and improving industrial safety. The article is of interest to the scientific community, experts in the field of economics and human resource management, as well as for decision-makers in the oil and gas industry.

## 2 Literature Review

### *2.1 The Impact of Digitalization and Digital Transformation on the Development of the Oil and Gas Industry*

In the process of studying the influence of digitalization and digital transformation on the development of human capital in the oil and gas industry, logical analysis and meta-analysis were used. The object of the study is companies in the oil and gas industry in Russia. The subjects of the study are the directions of digitalization in the oil and gas industry, the directions of development of human capital in the oil and gas industry, taking into account digitalization processes. The information base consisted of articles on digitalization and the effects of its implementation, as well as the development of human capital at Russian oil and gas enterprises.

Let us consider the impact of digitalization and digital transformation on the development of the oil and gas industry based on the following researchers.

Digital and robotic innovations are gradually being introduced into the oil and gas industry, especially in such sectors as upstream and downstream, which increase the quantity and quality of products and services produced. Currently, the digitalization of the industry is carried out in the following areas: the introduction of a digital management system, automation of production processes, optimization of business processes, digitalization of personnel management tools, the industrial Internet of Things, the use of big data technology (Big Data), ensuring cybersecurity, the use of digital twins, robotization jobs and processes, the use of artificial intelligence.

Such main areas as digital management, automation of production processes, optimization of business processes, and digitalization of personnel management tools are discussed in [2–5]. The need for digital management will allow one to plan and manage business processes including management accounting, production process management, procurement and logistics, marketing, and human resource management. The ultimate goal of information management is to increase the efficiency of digital technologies used for making management decisions.

Key areas of digitalization such as robotization of jobs and processes, the use of artificial intelligence, the industrial Internet of Things and the use of Big Data, ensuring cybersecurity, the use of digital twins, are found mainly in [2, 5–9].

When introducing these areas of digitalization in the oil and gas industry, the effects such as increasing oil and gas production, optimizing business processes, reducing costs, accelerating transportation, and improving product quality are observed. These key effects are highlighted in [3, 10–13].

Thus, digitalization and digital transformation increase the efficiency of field operation and the share of recoverable hydrocarbon reserves, as well as reduce operating costs. It is known that the global average value of the oil recovery coefficient is 30%, and with the introduction of digital technologies, this indicator has increased to 50% [14].

When introducing information technologies to the oil and gas industry as a whole, there is a significant economic effect. In the new conditions, some difficulties arise such as a rather high cost of introducing digital technologies in production and a shortage of specialists; however, based on existing experience, for the successful development of this sector of the economy, it is necessary to further introduce digital technologies [15].

Successful experience in the introduction of digital technologies shows that it is possible to increase labor productivity, reduce time and material costs; accelerate the transportation of raw materials and finished products, increase the speed of decision-making and operational management, as well as improve product quality.

## 2.2 Development of Human Capital in the Oil and Gas Industry

Let us consider the current state and development of human capital in the oil and gas industry in Russia.

Currently, oil and gas companies are experiencing the following difficulties: the aging of experienced and highly qualified workers, the lack of specialists and skilled staff in the field of digital technologies.

The cumulative impact of major human capital trends in the oil and gas industry requires companies to create and develop social enterprise, develop personalized and flexible reward programs, prepare for the longevity dividend due to an aging workforce, and expand training, upskilling and reskilling programs to build digital competencies, creating teams of talents. Business leaders and HR managers must refine their human resource strategies and continually align them with business goals and objectives.

It is important to note that company pay special attention to the development of infrastructure in the regions, where the main oil and gas production and production facilities are located.

Currently, to develop human capital in the oil and gas industry, companies use the following measures: investments in education and healthcare, development of regional infrastructure, development of social infrastructure, social payments, bonus system, corporate training [16, 17].

As a result, we can say that the social responsibility of oil companies can significantly develop the infrastructure of the regions.

It is worth noting that healthcare and sports are priority areas of support. But science and education are aimed at pursuing the company's own interests. Companies organize specialized classes where students focus on special fields. School graduates study at target universities and training programs corresponding to the company's areas. University graduates are distributed between job positions, where they are assigned to mentors to gain experience.

Leading domestic companies strive to support the development and training of their employees. Currently, manufacturing in the oil and gas industry is a weak link. The main problem is the insufficient technological equipment of manufacturing enterprises—the use of outdated technologies implies the involvement of additional labor and an increase in product costs caused by an increase in labor costs, resource losses, etc. To eliminate this problem, it is necessary to review the directions of investment policy development and boost investment in human capital. Under the current state of affairs, increasing the volume of exports of petroleum products turns out to be a priori an inefficient solution—expansion of production is possible only due to extensive factors, which will lead to a sharp increase in the product price and a decrease in its competitiveness in the world market. In this regard, one of the main tasks facing the state and the subjects of the oil and gas industry is the use of intensive growth factors, the improvement of the technological potential of enterprises and the development of human potential and capital, which assumes the role of an instrument for the formation of innovative ideas that can lead to the optimization of the production process. Investing in human capital plays a huge role in employees' high performance. The larger the state, including enterprises that will support the activities of employees and their desire to improve their abilities, the more effective the developments will be to increase the production of the final product of the oil and gas industry.

## 3 Methodology: Identification of the Relationship Between Digitalization and Human Capital Development

In the study, meta-analysis was used as the main research method. The basis for this method was studies of the last 5 years [2–23], which examined the impact of various areas of digitalization on the development of Russian oil and gas companies and human capital. The main assumptions and limitations were the search for scientific papers on "the impact of digitalization on the oil and gas industry in Russia," as well as "the development of human capital in the oil and gas industry." The methodology was to identify the relationship between digitalization and human capital development (in the oil and gas industry). To do this, it is necessary to formulate the main directions of digitalization of the oil and gas industry in Russia, as well as the effects of their implementation, taking into account their position in the text as part of the literature review. Then it is necessary to formulate measures to support and develop human capital in the oil and gas industry. Next, the main directions for the development of human capital are determined, taking into account digitalization processes in the oil and gas industry. Also, for all the generated directions, it is necessary to determine the proportion of their mention in the studies under consideration (weighting coefficient), in order to establish the direction that has a greater or lesser degree of influence on this or that direction of human capital development.

The weighting coefficient is calculated using the formula:

$$\mathrm{K}i = \frac{\text{Number of mentions of the i} - \text{th direction}}{\text{Total number of mentions of the areas under consideration}} \tag{1}$$

This formula for determining the weighting coefficient is also applicable to determining the weighting coefficients of the effects of digitalization, measures to support and develop human capital, and directions for the development of human capital taking into account digitalization processes.

## 4 Results and Discussion

Based on the review of researchers, it is possible to identify the main directions of digitalization of the oil and gas industry in Russia, as well as the effects of their implementation, which are presented in Table 1.

**Table 1** The main directions of digitalization in the Russian oil and gas industry and the effects of their implementation

| | Authors | Number of mentions | Weight factor |
|---|---|---|---|
| Directions of digitalization | | | |
| Implementation of a digital control system | [2–5, 13, 21] | 6 | 0.19 |
| Automation of production processes | [2, 5, 23] | 3 | 0.09 |
| Business process optimization | [3, 10] | 2 | 0.06 |
| Digitalization of HR tools | [2, 4, 18] | 3 | 0.09 |
| Industrial internet of things | [5, 7, 8] | 3 | 0.09 |
| Using big data technology | [7–9] | 3 | 0.09 |
| Ensuring cybersecurity | [2, 9] | 2 | 0.06 |
| Using digital twins | [2, 7] | 2 | 0.06 |
| Robotization of workplaces and processes | [2, 5–8] | 5 | 0.15 |
| Using artificial intelligence | [5, 6, 8, 11] | 4 | 0.12 |
| Total | | 33 | 1 |
| Effects of the above areas of digitalization | | | |
| Increase in oil and gas production | [7, 11, 13, 14] | 4 | 0.23 |
| Optimization of business processes | [3, 10–12] | 4 | 0.23 |
| Cost reduction | [3, 6, 10, 13] | 4 | 0.23 |
| Speeding up transportation | [6, 12, 13] | 3 | 0.18 |
| Improving product quality | [2, 13] | 2 | 0.12 |
| Total | | 17 | 1 |

It is important to note that the main directions of digitalization in the oil and gas industry are: the introduction of a digital management system, the robotization of workplaces and processes, to a lesser extent: automation of production processes, digitalization of personnel management tools, the industrial Internet of Things, the use of big data technology. The greatest effects of digitalization are an increase in oil and gas production, optimization of business processes, and cost reduction, which indicates their greatest application in the upstream sector.

It is important to emphasize that the processes of digitalization in the oil and gas industry are very dependent on the level of human capital development.

In this regard, companies are trying to develop human capital. Table 2 shows the main measures to support and develop human capital.

Based on the results obtained, it can be seen that the main measures to support and develop capital are the development of regional infrastructure, the development of social infrastructure, as well as social payments. However, these measures are not enough to improve the quality and efficiency of the use of human capital. It is important to analyze how digitalization affects human capital, as well as its development. Table 3 shows the areas of human capital development affected by digitalization in the oil and gas industry.

**Table 2** Measures to support and develop human capital in the Russian oil and gas industry

| Measures to support and develop human capital by companies | Authors | Number of mentions | Weight factor |
|---|---|---|---|
| Investments in education and health | [16] | 1 | 0.11 |
| Development of regional infrastructure | [16, 17] | 2 | 0.22 |
| Development of social infrastructure | [16, 17] | 2 | 0.22 |
| Social payments | [16, 17] | 2 | 0.22 |
| Bonus system | [16] | 1 | 0.11 |
| Corporate training | [16] | 1 | 0.11 |
| Total | | 9 | 1 |

**Table 3** The main directions of human capital development, taking into account the processes of digitalization in the oil and gas industry

| Development of human capital through | Authors | Number of mentions | Weight factor |
|---|---|---|---|
| Formation and development of personnel with the necessary professional IT skills | [4] | 1 | 0.25 |
| Advanced training and retraining to develop digital competencies | [22] | 1 | 0.25 |
| Formation of the knowledge economy | [23] | 1 | 0.25 |
| Reducing the risk of personnel injuries and the likelihood of accidents | [2] | 1 | 0.25 |
| Total | | 4 | 1 |

In our opinion, digitalization processes in the oil and gas industry have an equally positive effect on the formation and development of personnel with the necessary professional IT skills, as well as on advanced training and retraining for the formation of digital competencies, contribute to the formation of a knowledge economy and reduce the risk of personnel injury and the likelihood of accidents.

Based on the analyzed material, we have formed a relationship between the main directions of digitalization and the key avenues of human capital development in the oil and gas industry (Table 4).

Depending on the direction of human capital development to be influenced, companies can use certain main directions of digitalization.

Based on the analysis, it can be concluded that digitalization processes, in addition to reducing logistics costs; decreasing the volume of document flow, optimizing production processes, also contribute to improving industrial safety and labor protection, creating new jobs in the field of digital technologies, attracting and forming IT specialists, as well as retraining engineering and technical personnel, using new digital technologies. It is also worth noting that for the development of Industry 4.0 and the transition to Industry 5.0 in the oil and gas industry, companies need to allocate funds for the formation of human capital. In the new conditions, Russian oil companies and the government need to focus on the intensification of digitalization processes and the formation of human capital in the field of digital technologies.

**Table 4** The impact of digitalization trends on human capital and its development in the oil and gas industry

| Directions of digitalization | Directions for human capital development |
|---|---|
| Implementation of a digital control system | Formation and development of personnel with the necessary professional IT skills |
| Digitalization of HR tools | |
| Industrial internet of things | |
| Using digital twins | |
| Implementation of a digital management system (digital management) | Advanced training and retraining to develop digital competencies |
| Automation of production processes | |
| Business process optimization | |
| Digitalization of HR tools | |
| Industrial internet of things | |
| Ensuring cybersecurity | |
| Using digital twins | |
| Industrial internet of things | Formation of the knowledge economy |
| Using big data technology | |
| Robotization of jobs and processes | |
| Using artificial intelligence | |
| Automation of production processes | Reducing the risk of personnel injuries and the likelihood of accidents |
| Industrial internet of things | |
| Using artificial intelligence | |
| Robotization of jobs and processes | |

It is necessary to develop and formulate programs and measures aimed at creating places for IT programs in universities, for the oil and gas industry, the formation of close cooperation between universities and companies in this industry, between domestic IT companies that are able at this stage to fully carry out the scope of work on digitalization. The intensification of the digitalization processes of companies in the oil and gas industry will allow one to sufficiently promote the human capital of the industry, develop the upstream and further downstream sectors, which will further facilitate the transition from Industry 4.0 to Industry 5.0, and will also allow competing with global companies in this industry under consideration.

## 5 Conclusion

Digitalization of the oil and gas sector will allow the Russian economy to maintain competitive advantages, as well as develop human capital in the industry and cooperation between companies within the country and with foreign partners.

In the paper, a review of research on digitalization and human capital and its development in the Russian and foreign oil and gas industry was conducted. We have analyzed the main directions of digitalization, the effects of their implementation, and measures to support and develop human capital.

Digitalization of oil and gas companies was found to have a positive impact on the formation of human capital and its development. To ensure economic growth and well-being, companies need to develop measures to intensify the digitalization of the oil and gas sector and the development of human capital. It is necessary to promote the formation of close ties between companies in the oil and gas industry, universities, IT companies, and create their own IT departments within companies.

The theoretical significance of the study is to identify the interrelationships between the processes of digitalization and the development of human capital in the oil and gas industry, and reveal the impact of digitalization on the development of human capital. Further research in this area will allow us to determine the effectiveness of the impact of certain areas of digitalization on human capital, its development, as well as to study the conditions and potential for the transition from Industry 4.0 to Industry 5.0, to the knowledge economy, digital economy, sustainable socio-economic development.

***Practical Significance*** The results of this study can be used by federal and regional government agencies, as well as companies in the oil and gas industry to develop policies and develop measures to intensify the processes of digitalization and human capital development.

## References

1. Ovinnikova, K. N. (2013). The current state of the Russian oil and gas complex and its problems. *News of Tomsk Polytechnic University, 322*(6), 47–51. http://earchive.tpu.ru/handle/11683/4850
2. Tukaev, K. R. (2022). Trends in digital transformation in the oil industry. *Bulletin of Economics and Management, 5*, 66–68. http://vem.rusoil.net/files/slider/2_2022.pdf
3. Deberdieva, E. M., Vechkasova, M. V., Petrova, A. A., Garanin, E. O., Kostikov, P. A., & Bugrov, K. E. (2018). The influence of digital transformation on business processes of enterprises in the petrochemical industry. *Bulletin of the Altai Academy of Economics and Law, 5*, 114–119. https://vaael.ru/ru/article/view?id=94
4. Tasueva, T. S., Idigova, L. M., & Rakhimova, B. Kh. (2020). Digital technologies as the basis for the efficiency of development of oil and gas enterprises. In *Spatial development of territories in the conditions of digitalization: socio-ecological-economic systems: materials All-Russian scientific and practical conference with international participation*, December 08–09, 2020. (pp. 148–153). https://doi.org/10.34708/GSTOU.CONF.2021.90.93.023.
5. Azieva, R. K., & Taimashanov, K. E. (2020). The need and possibilities of using digital technologies in the oil and gas industry in the context of digital transformation of the economy. *News of the St. Petersburg State University of Economics, 5*, 178–185. https://elibrary.ru/item.asp?id=44031004
6. Kazanin, A. G. (2020). Trends and prospects of development of the oil and gas sector in the context of digitalization. *Economics and Management, 26*(1), 35–45. https://doi.org/10.35854/1998-1627-2020-1-35-45
7. Balashova, A. D., & Bolshakova, O. I. (2019). The impact of business digitalization on oil recovery rates and increasing the efficiency of oil and gas companies. *University Bulletin, 5*, 73–79. https://doi.org/10.26425/1816-4277-2019-5-73-79

8. Linnik, Y., & Kiryukhin, M. (2019). Digital technologies in the oil and gas industry. *Vestnik Universiteta, 1*(7), 37–40. https://doi.org/10.26425/1816-4277-2019-7-37-40
9. Malykh, O. E., & Khodkovskaya, Y. V. (2020). The influence of digital technologies on the capitalization of oil and gas business. *Bulletin of USPTU. Science, education, economics. Series: Economics, 4*, 66–71. https://elibrary.ru/item.asp?id=44514408
10. Tasueva, T. S., & Elibaeva, P. T. (2020). Formation of resource-saving logistics potential at oil and gas enterprises. *Bulletin of GGNTU. Humanities and socio-economic sciences, 16*(2), 30–34. https://doi.org/10.34708/GSTOU.2020.75.52.005
11. Raunholt, L., Servodio, R., Maliardi, A., & Torvund, S. (2017). First Implementation of Robot Technology for the Drill Floor. *Offshore Mediterranean Conference*, 2017 (pp. 29–31). https://www.onepetro.org/conference-paper/OMC-2017-596
12. Bortolotti, T., & Romano, P. (2012). 'Lean first, then automate': A framework for process improvement in pure service companies. A case study. *Production Planning & Control, 23*(7), 513–522. https://doi.org/10.1080/09537287.2011.640040
13. Drogovoz, P. A., & Kharin, N. I. (2021). The economic benefits of digitalization in the oil and gas industry. *Finance and Credit, 27*(3), 672–692. https://doi.org/10.24891/fc.27.3.672
14. Eremin, N. A., Dmitrievsky, A. N., & Tikhomirov, L. I. (2015). The present and future of intellectual deposits. *Oil Gas Innovations, 12*, 44–49. https://istina.msu.ru/publications/article/19850959/
15. Kozlova, M. A., Fedosov, P. V., & Izmailov, I. Y. (2019). Economic effect from the introduction of digital technologies in the oil and gas industry. *Russian Economic Bulletin, 2*(5), 226–230. https://dgpu-journals.ru/wp-content/uploads/2019/12/kozlova.pdf
16. Druzhinin, G. V., Pruzhinin, A. N., & Mamurkov, E. V. (2019). Strategies for developing human capital of oil companies. *Sociology, 1*, 114–123.
17. Knippel, A. S., & Chekhovskaya, I. A. (2020). The role of investments for the development of human capital in the oil and gas industry of Russia. *Bulletin of Scientific Thought, 3*, 126–135. https://doi.org/10.34983/DTIPB.2020.51.52.001
18. Anisimova, Y. A., & Plotnikov, V. A. (2022). Prospects for digital transformation in oil industry. *News of the South-Western State University. Series: Economics. Sociology. Management, 12*(5), 106–119. https://doi.org/10.21869/2223-1552-2022-12-5-106-119
19. Bryant, K., & Wells, A. (1998). A new economic paradigm? Innovation-based evolutionary systems. *Prometheus, 17*(3), 338–340. https://www.scienceopen.com/hosted-document?doi=10.1080/08109029908632137
20. Kitova, O. V., & Bruskin, S. N. (2018). Digital transformation of business. *Digital Economy, 1*, 20–25. https://elibrary.ru/item.asp?id=36479539
21. Matveeva, E. P. (2022). Changing the management system of an oil and gas company in a digital economy. *Economic Sciences, 9*(214), 101–106. https://doi.org/10.14451/1.214.101. https://ecsn.ru/wp-content/uploads/202209_101.pdf
22. Yakhvarova, E. V., Chumakov, D. V. & Isakova, V. D. (2021). Investments in human capital in oil and gas companies in the context of digitalization. *Priorities for economic development in the conditions of digitalization: Proceedings of the International Scientific and Practical Conference, Saratov, November, 30* (pp. 468–472). https://elibrary.ru/item.asp?id=48296627
23. Miller, A. E., & Davidenko, L. M. (2021). Development of a concept for managing scientific, technological and financial risks of technological integration of russian enterprises in the oil refining and petrochemical industry. *Herald of Omsk University. Series "Economics", 19*(2), 12–22. https://doi.org/10.24147/1812-3988.2021.19(2).12-22

# Digitizing Human Capital Management at Industrial Enterprises: A Case of Business Process Modeling in the Fuel and Energy Sector

**Evgeny Kuzmin, Begimai Sydygalieva, Ainura Kocherbaeva, and Chingiz Koshoev**

**Abstract** The study scrutinizes the need for reconsidering traditional approaches to human resources management amid the unfolding digital transformation, which is a response to changes in the socio-economic environment. The research rests on the soft systems methodology used to deeply comprehend and model the complex relationships between the existing production processes, technologies and human resources of an enterprise. A conceptual model of human capital management using the case of the fuel and energy sector (FES) is developed allowing for the interaction of formal and informal aspects. The model describes the perfect construct for managing human capital development through a set of intertwined business processes—from establishing staff members' needs to their displacement. Business process modeling helps not only visualize and optimize the interface between employees and processes, but also predict their progress. Due to the special aspects of human resources policy in the FES, the model has certain limitations and rigidity boundaries. The paper also clarifies a number of regional factors that may be included in the study. The model emphasizes the importance of a dynamic approach in business process modeling to ensure their flexibility and adaptability. The study is intended to contribute to the formation, discussion and improvement of strategies for effective human capital management. The research results can be utilized to complement theoretical models and improve human capital management practices, which is relevant for various industries.

E. Kuzmin (✉)
Institute of Economics of the Ural Branch of the Russian Academy of Sciences, Ekaterinburg, Russian Federation
e-mail: kuzmin.ea@uiec.ru

B. Sydygalieva · A. Kocherbaeva
Department of Management, Kyrgyz Russian Slavic University named after First President of Russia B.N. Yeltsin, Bishkek, Kyrgyzstan

C. Koshoev
Institute of Modern Information Technologies in Education, Bishkek, Kyrgyzstan



A. Appolloni et al. (eds.), *The Future of Industry*, Lecture Notes in Information Systems and Organisation 70, https://doi.org/10.1007/978-3-031-66801-2_28

**Keywords** Human capital · Digitalization · Business process modelling · Fuel and energy sector · Soft systems methodology

## 1 Introduction

Amid the rapid development of digital technologies and their increasingly deep integration into socio-economic processes, the issues of human capital management (HCM) are gaining in relevance. In a modern economy, human capital is one of the key assets of a company that underlies its competitiveness and innovation potential, and must be developed and maintained [1–5]. Effective HCM is critical for enterprises' successful adaptation to changing market conditions and technological progress. The fuel and energy sector (FES), as one of the most significant and technology-intensive industries, is receptive to changes in the external environment and requires its staff to be highly qualified. In the context of digital transformation of the economy, there is a growing need for innovative approaches to human capital management, which implies not only the introduction of new technologies, but also a revision of established business processes and HR practices. This is where the soft systems methodology (SSM) can highlight prospects for improvements in line with the demands of a dynamic environment. The SSM in human capital management within the FES allows one to better understand and effectively model complex relationships between employees, processes and technologies as well as to adapt management practices to the rapid changes in the digital economy. In this context, dynamic modeling of business processes acts as a valuable tool for assessing the interaction of employees, the organizational environment and business processes, as well as forecasting their development within the digital ecosystem of the enterprise.

Digital transformation of human capital management involves not solely automation of the existing processes, but the formation of a new interaction environment, where digital tools and platforms are an integral part of corporate management. Digital innovations in HCM are diverse, they include big data analytics, artificial intelligence, digital twins (digital twins of social systems [6]), digital modeling and simulation, collaborative platforms [7, 8], etc. In this new interaction environment, a key role is attributed to business process modeling that allows one to get a deeper understanding of internal relationships, analyze potential changes and make informed managerial decisions. It is modeling and simulation that can be used to visualize and analyze business processes, which makes it possible to project the consequences of changes in the organizational structure and HR management. The SSM used in the context of these digital innovations allows systematizing approaches through their integration. As a result, specific models will emerge that allow for both soft and hard variables and able to adapt to the dynamic business environment. Thus, the present study aims to develop a conceptual model of HCM business processes at fuel and energy enterprises, capable of providing flexibility, adaptability and increased efficiency of HR policies amid digitalization.

The backbone of the study is an analytical overview of the current approaches and practices, as well as the original research results. The paper is structured to cover theoretical, methodological and practical aspects. In introduction, we substantiate the relevance of the topic and formulate the purpose and objectives. The theoretical foundations of the study reside in the soft systems methodology as a tool for flexible HCM in addition to analytical and modeling methods. The practical part of the study consists in designing a conceptual model of HCM business processes in the fuel and energy sector. We identify the components of the model and analyze the interface of employees, the organizational environment and business processes within the enterprise's digital ecosystem. In conclusion, the research findings are summed up and directions for further research are discussed. Such a research structure has allowed us to comprehensively review the problems of human capital management at enterprises and propose an effective dynamic model.

## 2 The Concept and Research Methods

### *2.1 Research Design*

The research approach is based on a comprehensive analysis of the human capital of industrial enterprises considering the peculiarities of the fuel and energy sector. The study answers the question of how the use of the SSM and dynamic business process modeling can contribute to human capital management. The emphasis is on analyzing the interaction of formal and informal aspects of HR management, their integration and impact on the efficiency and competitiveness of companies.

Due to the SSM, it is possible to create more flexible and adaptive systems [9]. In human capital management, the SSM enables organizations to get a holistic view of the environment and activities, while taking into account the interests of various stakeholders [10, 11]. The methodology also involves a solid understanding of not only the structural formal aspects of the company, but also informal ones, such as corporate and organizational culture, social connections and contacts, attitudes to change, leadership positions, motivational recognition, social responsibility, moral and ethical guidelines, etc. Managing these informal aspects requires comprehending human relationships and dynamics within the organization. Both formal and informal aspects can be harmoniously integrated within the soft systems approach. This allows considering not only structured and clearly defined processes and hierarchies, but also less obvious, but equally important elements. Through the lens of the SSM, human capital management is reimagined as a holistic system, where each element affects the others and enhances the overall performance of the organization.

The interdependence of formal and informal interactions indicates the need for a dynamic model for managing human capital development. Dynamic modeling serves as a tool for exploring complex interactions between employees, the organizational environment and business processes [12–16]. It is of special importance here to analyze how various business processes affect employees and their movement within the organization, how they influence the efficiency and performance of the company.

The role of dynamic modeling is fully revealed within strategic decision-making [17–19]. This implies not only responding to current challenges, but also anticipating future demands for human capital, which may include career planning, advanced training programs, and employing new approaches to motivating and retaining talents. *Modeling employees' movement in a company, therefore, can be regarded as a series of interconnected business processes that describe a perfect construct for managing human capital development.* Such a conceptual model is consistent with the soft systems methodology. The key idea is to find out how movement of employees within business processes affects the formation, development and effectiveness of human capital in the organization. We are talking about not internal mobility (which is, however, part of the model), but how employees go through various stages of vocational training and job involvement, steps in career development, etc. It is important to ascertain how different business processes and HR practices affect this journey and how to optimize them to enhance employee potential and ultimately boost productivity. Modeling thus allows organizations to manage employees' movement while focusing on an ever-changing environment, making it more targeted and concentrated on the interests of both the employee and the company.

It is crucially important to monitor changes in the business environment. Constructing a dynamic model of human capital development makes it necessary to analyze the specific features of the industry and the region [20–23]. Additionally, there is a plethora of other requirements and factors to pay attention to. These are demographic trends, cultural patterns, macroeconomic and institutional frameworks, labor market condition and other aspects, which are critical to ensure the relevance of the model. Business processes in human capital development should follow the principles of interoperability, scalability and upgradability. Therefore, HR management systems should be integrated with other corporate systems and processes, thus ensuring their smooth interaction. All these aspects taken together form a flexible and adaptable dynamic model.

## 2.2 Region-Specific Features

Regional peculiarities can be investigated from several perspectives.

First, the company accounts for local cultural patterns and traditions specific for each territory of presence. The mentality of the region's residents can influence the company's approaches to training, building communication, creating corporate and organizational culture, and implementing employee motivation and retention programs. Another aspect here is overcoming language barriers that may emerge in multicultural corporations.

Second, the region's economic environment and the level of infrastructure directly affect the resources and technologies available for employee training and development. Budget and infrastructure constraints in the region largely predetermine the situation in the healthcare industry, vocational education, etc., while market trends and consumer activity have a significant impact on the conditional characteristics of the quality of human resources (mainly as part of the accumulated set of human capital elements related to the superstructure).

Third, regional institutions and statutory requirements create a regulatory framework for both the functioning of the company and internal business processes. What is meant here is local legislative and regulatory requirements to safety, work/rest regimens, special support measures for workers (additional leave, regional coefficients and bonuses, etc.), such as those adopted in the regions of the Far North and equated localities and other areas with special climatic conditions.

Fourth, the distinctive features of the regional labor market, including workforce characteristics and competition for talent, underlie the approaches to recruiting and retaining employees. The emphasis here is on the availability and quality of the workforce. The territories with a developed educational system usually have more qualified human resources. The skills and professions prevailing in the labor market are often determined by the region's specialization, while the salary level affecting the expectations and satisfaction of employees is dependent on the economic situation in the region. Economically, dynamic territories offer more career opportunities. The demographics of the workforce set strategic recruitment priorities and are simultaneously reflected in differential retention of workers of different age groups.

Fifth, regional social values and expectations can influence corporate culture and HR policies. It is worth noting that it does not apply to cultural norms and traditions. In this context, social expectations and values address the issues of "life rhythm", expectations regarding working conditions, including clear job responsibilities, decent salary, suitable career opportunities, and an overall inclusive work environment.

Thus, the above aspects allow revealing local conditions in which the organization operates in order to effectively implement and optimize business processes in human capital development.

## 2.3 Industry-Specific Features

Industry-specific features of HCM dynamic modeling are similar to regional ones and can be detailed as follows.

First, these are special requirements for employees' skills and competencies varying by the type of activity. They also include requirements for accreditation, recognition of professional qualifications, etc. This affects not only approaches to employee training and development, but also imposes requirements for the recruitment and selection processes. As a result, high professional standards make it difficult to attract personnel.

Second, modeling should take into account industry-specific technology trends, which may require continuous or occasional retraining and adaptation of learning programs. Dramatic technological shifts in the industry draw increasing attention to more flexible approaches to developing employee skills. For example, in some industries, progress in digitalization and automation makes it especially important for employees to possess the appropriate skills. Organizations have to stay abreast of the latest innovations in the industry and incorporate them into learning programs to keep staff competencies up-to-date. This is also true for the industry-specific market in terms of knowledge and practical experience.

Third, some attention should be paid to industry standards and regulations. Licensing and certification of workplaces should be built into the company's HR-related business processes. Based on the industry, this may imply introducing specific quality management systems, complying with particular health and safety regulations or implementing workplace health and safety standards.

Fourth, the sectoral dynamics of the labor market has to be monitored, including the level of competition for talent and special aspects of labor demand. The structure of the latter in the industry can vary from high-tech skills to specialized manual labor. Just like in the case of regional peculiarities, this affects employee recruitment, motivation and retainment strategies. Industry cycles are equally important. During economic downturn and recovery, it is of high importance to keep a balance between workforce optimization and retention of key employees. Industry cycle analysis helps anticipate future changes and adapt HCM strategies by planning for staffing needs, developing flexible training programs that can quickly adapt to industry changes, etc. This allows organizations to effectively manage available human resources with the focus on both current and future workforce needs.

Fifth, industries differ in the levels of environmental and social responsibility, which is reflected in the state of human capital. ESG principles (environmental responsibility, strong social responsibility and high-quality corporate governance) are of great importance in deciding on corporate strategy [24–26] and human capital policies. Companies that actively integrate ESG practices often concentrate on creating a safe, healthy and engaging work environment. These principles have implications for attracting and retaining talents, especially young professionals who increasingly value employers' environmental and social responsibility. Moreover, investors and consumers are often more interested in ESG-focused companies [27–29], which creates additional incentives for human capital development and innovation. This results in the emergence of more sustainable business models and increased competitiveness in the market.

In general, the specific features of the company activities allow mapping out more targeted and effective human capital management strategies. Thus, HCM is based on a multi-level model covering both regional and sectoral characteristics.

# 3 Results

## 3.1 Peculiarities of the FES

Let us consider the fuel and energy sector and clarify its specific features in the context of human capital management.

There are a number of distinctive characteristics displayed by FES companies. They represent a combination of business facets, such as high technical complexity, strict safety standards, a significant impact on the environment, the need to comply with international standards, etc. This implies equally stringent requirements for their staff in terms of qualifications, expertise, professionalism and willingness to engage in continuous learning. We have identified a number of aspects revealing the specific requirements for human resources in the FES (Table 1).

Table 1 lacks certain features of the FES that have an indirect effect on personnel, but they are worth being mentioned. The fuel and energy sector is rather extensive and includes the gas, oil and coal industries, electric power industry [30], i.e., those engaged in the extraction, processing, transportation of energy resources, as well as the production, transmission and distribution of electrical energy. Such markets are

**Table 1** Specific requirements for human resources in the FES

| Aspects | Requirements (need for skills and competencies) |
|---|---|
| Technology | High level of special technical and engineering skills, including operation and maintenance of sophisticated equipment, competence in specialized information systems and technologies. Ability to innovate and quickly adapt to new technologies |
| Safety | Strict safety and compliance requirements, including workplace safety, environmental standards and general industry safety rules. Risk assessment and risk management skills in constructing and operating fuel and energy facilities. Awareness of and commitment to ESG principles |
| Health | Increased demands for physical fitness due to hazardous working conditions (for example, on oil rigs, in the far north, etc.) |
| Education and development | Mandatory continuous and advanced training due to the complexity of fuel and energy technologies and their rapid development |
| Labor discipline | Strict requirements for discipline, responsibility and reliability of employees due to the risk of accidents and disasters |
| Social skills | Communication and teamwork skills, especially those relevant for new large projects implemented in remote areas, inclement weather, on a rotating scheme, etc. high stress tolerance to work in risky and critical situations. Strong conflict resolution and effective communication skills |
| Management | Project management skills, including planning, coordinating and monitoring multiple tasks. Possessing a wide range of skills (cross-functionality) allowing employees to effectively interact with various departments and specialists within the company. Effective work planning, time and resource management, especially when working on complex projects |
| International standards | Knowledge and application of international standards and practices, especially in companies with international presence |

heterogeneous, which creates certain risks. Fluctuating energy prices can affect the economic stability of companies and, as a result, the behavior and morale of employees. At the same time, employee attitude to market factors is indirectly projected into their motivation, commitment and productivity. Employee perception of external economic conditions, trends and changes in the industry directly affects the company's ability to respond to market challenges and stay competitive. Another peculiarity of the FES in Russia is the intense involvement of the state, which also has an impact on ongoing business processes. The specific organizational culture and the complex hierarchical structure distinguishing this sector from others influence the method and the speed of decision-making as well as employees' organizational behavior.

The above requirements for the skills and competencies of FES companies' employees are prescribed by both formal occupational standards (see the list for Russia's FES [31–33]) and informal working conditions. Occupational standards, which describe labor functions, labor actions, required skills and knowledge, are a key factor in human capital development. They structure worker roles and tasks, which directly affects the formation and optimization of business processes. Moreover, occupational standards ensure that the scope of work are aligned with industry requirements, including safety, organizational efficiency and environmentally sound production processes. They also facilitate the processes of hiring, training and evaluating staff through clear criteria and requirements.

In addition to formal standards, informal requirements—those special skills that are not always documented, but are critical for work to be productive—are also of high importance in the fuel and energy sector. They include good adaptability to the changing environment, strong teamwork qualities, skills in communicating with coworkers, managing conflicts and building healthy work relationships. It is also important to develop certain personal qualities, such as stress resistance, responsibility and self-discipline. These skills help employees successfully cope with the industry's high demands. Informal requirements imply the development of a safety culture and responsible environmental attitudes at all organizational levels, which contributes not only to compliance with environmental standards, but to the formation of an industry-wide sustainable development culture.

The aforementioned peculiarities of HR policy in the FES are reflected in business processes of human capital development, indicating that recruitment, training, motivation and retention strategies should be carefully planned and implemented in accordance with the industry's unique requirements and conditions. Human capital development programs should include specific modules aimed at increasing technical competence and understanding environmental and safety standards. All this is fundamental for aligning employee qualifications with the dynamic and technologically advanced environment of the fuel and energy sector.

## 3.2 *Business Process Modeling*

As noted above, the SSM-based model of employees' movement in the company can take the form of a set of interrelated business processes that describe in detail the optimal structure for managing human capital development. These business processes are typical of the unidirectional path of personnel in the company, from onboarding to displacement. At the same time, each employee follows a unique path differing in complexity, scope and combinations of quality characteristics, which results in a multitude of individual career trajectories. Each step in this journey, be it advanced training, rotation or promotion, should be designed so that to ensure maximum synergy between employees' personal development and the company's strategic goals.

Look at the structure of business processes of human capital development:

1. Identifying recruitment needs and staff requirements;
2. Employee onboarding to production process;
3. Staff training and professional development;
4. Ensuring staff efficiency;
5. Staff displacement.

The system of the above business processes forms the concept of a human capital management model. Each of these processes contributes to achieving the company's goals and enhances employee efficiency. Figure 1 presents the business processes as a single construct.

**Identifying Recruitment Needs and Staff Requirements**

This is an initial HR-related business process in the company. It aims to analyze and assess the current staff both quantitatively (staffing) and qualitatively (job certification, employee requirements). Based on data about the established production program, the company calculates the planned need for appropriately qualified personnel with certain skills, abilities, experience and competencies that are necessary to perform certain production functions and achieve the enterprise's strategic goals. The business process consists of the following steps: assessing the current workforce; analyzing its performance and competencies; workplace certification; determining changes in the workforce and competencies needed to attain the company's goals (production plan, production program); and coordinating labor resource needs with department heads. This will allow one to proceed to hiring staff. Schematically, the process is shown in Fig. 2, Appendix.

**Employee Onboarding to Production Process**

This is a series of organized steps aimed at attracting new employees and introducing them to the company's work processes. The business process includes hiring staff, familiarizing employees with job responsibilities, work activities and procedures, including introduction to the team. Staff hiring is based on current labor needs. The adequate solution here is either to attract personnel from the labor market or to fill vacant positions with internal human resources. The process is initiated with a request for additional staff or a request for movement (horizontal or vertical). To attract personnel from the labor market, a hiring strategy and measures are developed, candidates are short-listed and interviewed. After that, admission to work is granted and candidates acquire the status of employees on a probationary period. There are several employee exit statuses possible, depending on the set of skills/competencies and successful completion of the probationary period: first, employees who have successfully completed the probationary period, hired and fully integrated into the production process; second, employees who need additional training or skills improvement; third, employees failing to meet the company's requirements and subject to displacement. Figure 3, Appendix shows a schematical representation of the business process.

### Staff Training and Professional Development

At this stage, the employee skills are upgraded in accordance with the company's needs. The business process covers planning, conducting and evaluating the effectiveness of staff training activities. The increased demand for advanced training may be due to a number of reasons. First, this is a discrepancy with strategic guidelines or their adjustments. In one case, it is referred to the existing lack of competencies, in the other—to the projected one. The company growth, the transition to a new development stage, and an increase in the market share require employees to have appropriate skills and experience. Refocusing on new products and services or entering new markets create a need to acquire new knowledge and competences. Second, new skills may be gained due to technological changes. The introduction of any technical innovations implies that employees are competent in both using new technologies and adapting work methods. It is noteworthy that technological innovations can change the nature of work and demand for certain jobs, which entails a partial retraining or, in case of radical changes, complete staff reskilling. Vocational education in the context of technological innovation helps minimize organizational resistance and increases employee involvement during the company's modernization maneuvers. Third, staff training may be due to the company's own needs. The request "from the top" is associated with performance evaluation and identification of defects in work (quality indicators) that can be eliminated through training. The request "from the bottom" is manifested in employee suggestions about the need for training to improve their efficiency or career growth (excluding the reasons for introducing technological or other innovations, when all other job requirements are met, which can be regarded as a management problem). Other reasons behind the high demand for vocational training are legal regulations or industry standards, the desire to maintain and improve the company's competitiveness in response to market changes.

The business process consists of several procedures: analyzing the company's current and future needs for qualified personnel; making proposals to improve employee skills; managers or employees drawing up applications for training; developing programs and plans for personnel training; summarizing data from the previous round of training (if available) to expand current programs; providing individual or group training; assessing the effectiveness of training, including employees' developed skills, abilities, knowledge and competencies. The final stage is to further improve training programs and activities based on analysis of the results. This business process plays a key part in continuous development of the company's employees. It not only strengthens their professional skills and knowledge, but also helps them adapt to changes in industry, technology and the market. Such an approach supports innovation, increases motivation and job satisfaction among employees, and fosters the corporate culture of continuous learning. The stages of the business process are illustrated in Fig. 4, Appendix.

## Ensuring Staff Efficiency

The process is a set of measures aimed at maintaining and enhancing labor efficiency of employees. It incorporates a number of activities that contribute to favorable working conditions, motivation, social guarantees and benefits, and promote key and auxiliary competences of the staff. To that end, the company implements a range of initiatives.

In terms of creating favorable working conditions, workplaces are audited to ensure employees' comfort and safety. The company conducts sanitary and epidemiological surveillance, ensures labor protection standards and provides personal protective equipment.

When it comes to developing professional competencies, the company can implement mentoring programs (p2p-based learning, peer-to-peer or professional-to-professional principle) and internal coaching to sharpen leadership and management skills, which together can be treated as optional. Mentoring is especially effective in areas that require deep specialized knowledge and great professional competence. While teaching less experienced colleagues the subtleties and nuances of the profession, a mentor conveys unique knowledge and skills and shows how to apply them in practice. This fits technically complex industries, such as the fuel and energy sector. In addition, professional competencies are strengthened by participating in industry events to exchange experience and knowledge (conferences and seminars). This aspect does not include vocational courses, seminars and advanced training, which are implemented as part of the business process "Training and professional development of personnel" and are mandatory.

Auxiliary skills, often referred to as soft skills, are a wide range of personality traits, social and communication skills that help employees interact effectively and adapt to the work environment. They include critical thinking, emotional intelligence, communication and organizational skills, social capital (social contacts and ties), adaptability, teamwork skills, etc. These skills are boosted through self-development, participation in group projects, mentoring and coaching programs, problem-oriented simulation (practical exercises reproducing real situations), feedback and other practices crucial for personal growth and professional development.

Social benefits are a significant part of an extensive motivation program, since they directly affect employee satisfaction and loyalty to the company. They embrace medical insurance and healthcare activities (sports, preventive treatment), pension plans (while working and after the end of the employment contract), housing benefits, concessional loans and financial assistance in difficult life situations. All this facilitates creating a favorable psychological climate in the team, strengthens motivation and productivity, and also allows attracting and retaining highly qualified personnel.

The motivation program covers many aspects. In addition to the above-mentioned social benefits, the business process "Ensuring staff efficiency" also contains the elements of a system of rewards and incentives, career growth and succession planning (development of succession plans for key and linear positions in the company, for example, personnel reserve creation), talent management and onboarding programs. The reward and incentive system should be aimed at motivating employees, recognizing their contribution to the company's performance and stimulating high productivity. These can be financial incentives, e.g., volume-based compensation, bonuses and premiums, equity participation (stocks and options), or non-financial intangible incentives, i.e., awards, honorary titles and positions, various forms of merit recognition and work achievements, extra opportunities for career growth, flextime or remote work, participation in corporate events, etc.

Talent management is an important component of the incentive program. It includes activities aimed at attracting, developing, engaging and retaining highly qualified and talented specialists. As part of this subprocess, the company identifies key talents, provides a favorable work environment and optimal conditions for their professional growth and devises strategies for long-term cooperation. Talent management places special emphasis on personalized career paths. This not only enhances the potential of each employee, but also creates a strong team capable of making a significant contribution to the company's performance.

Another aspect of the company's motivational activity is to develop and implement the processes aimed at strengthening employee commitment, which is characterized by emotional attachment, enthusiasm, loyalty and dedication of staff members to their job and employer. This requires fostering a positive and inspiring work environment, building a corporate culture based on mutual respect and recognition, and implementing feedback and communication systems that make workers feel valued and important to the company. Similar to talent management, commitment management focuses on encouraging sustainable employee engagement with the organization, cultivating their desire to grow with it and promote long-term cooperation. Dedicated personnel are satisfied with their work and actively participate in the firm's life, show initiative and creativity, strive to work more productively and are less inclined to leave the company, which creates a favorable climate in the team. All these elements strengthen the organization's human capital.

One more important component of motivational initiatives is adaptation processes. Adaptation is designed to make it easier for new employees to blend into the team and work environment (which is also relevant for employees in the process of horizontal and vertical movement). These processes combine various orientation programs and are coupled with other tools such as mentoring, training and induction into the corporate culture, which helps new employees quickly adapt, feel part of the team, establish professional connections and effectively integrate into the work process. Properly organized staff integration programs help reduce the productivity gap between newly hired workers (including those moved to other positions) and long-term employees.

The final and at the same time initial steps in the business process "Ensuring staff efficiency" are periodic non-qualification certification and evaluation of employee competencies. Feedback is provided to the staff, which implies summarizing opinions on working conditions, measuring satisfaction with them and collecting proposals for their improvement. As a result, an individual development plan is drawn up for each employee considering their unique needs and career goals.

The business process "Ensuring staff efficiency" is based on a set of incoming data and resources: information about organizational/production working conditions and workplace compliance with safety and comfort standards; information about the current competency profile and staff needs; wishes and requirements of employees regarding working conditions and social benefits; details on corporate policy and strategy in the field of HR management; the degree of job satisfaction. These data are used to formulate strategic plans and measures to improve working conditions, motivate and retain personnel. Additional initiatives are also being introduced to enhance employee commitment and satisfaction.

The business process "Ensuring staff efficiency" plays a critical role in maintaining high productivity, ensuring employee well-being and strengthening the company's competitive position in the market. Schematically, the process is shown in Fig. 5, Appendix. It can be divided into subprocesses related to: (a) providing adequate working conditions; (b) collective bargaining; (c) periodic employee certification; (d) development of professional and auxiliary competencies; (e) implementation of social program; (f) implementation of a motivational program; (g) non-qualification certification and competency assessment. These subprocesses are beyond the scope of the present study.

## Staff Displacement

Staff displacement management is a process associated with reducing the number of employees, including an analysis of the reasons for leaving (Fig. 6). This process may involve suspension, dismissal or extended leave. The reasons for staff displacement can vary, and, when dealing with this process, organizations should consider legal requirements, corporate policy and social responsibility. Internal reasons for staff displacement can be rooted in organizational changes (restructuring, merger, acquisition or closure of certain divisions of the company, a reduction in staff numbers due to business process optimization), shifts in strategic goals (reorientation to new types of activities that require a different quantitative and qualitative structure of human resources with a different set of competencies), changes in employee behavior (low productivity, unprofessional behavior or labor discipline violation), natural (retirement age, death, maternity leave) and other reasons, including the employee's personal decision to end their career in the company. External reasons are mostly associated with economic fluctuations and regulatory changes. An economic downturn, decreasing demand for the company's products/services, or changes in industry trends force the firm to revise its business strategy, which usually results in workforce reduction. In any case, efforts should be taken to minimize the negative impact. If a reduction in staff numbers is inevitable, the organization can assist in finding employment, offer options for vocational retraining, etc. Displacing personnel in a respectful manner preserves the company's reputation and maintains the morale of the rest of the employees. In this context, companies should plan ahead for displacement scenarios while ensuring adequate support and compensation.

Following staff displacement, the company should take measures to retain available human capital. Internally focused activities aim to upgrade trainings and skills development programs, advance communication and change management, and strengthen staff motivation and commitment. It is also important to re-evaluate and optimize work processes to ensure efficient distribution of tasks and resources when reducing staff. Moreover, upholding the values of the corporate culture is also of high importance, which can be implemented through team sessions, feedback and working conditions optimization. Such measures maintain key competencies within the company, help staff adapt to new working conditions, keep overall productivity and stimulate business progress.

At the same time, there are extraordinary human capital activities targeted at the external environment of the organization. The most notable example is Alumni programs, i.e., initiatives aimed at maintaining connections with former employees. Alumni programs are networking platforms that allow participants to keep professional and social contacts, share experience and knowledge, and derive other benefits. Corporate Alumni programs may include meetings, conferences and other events where former employees can communicate and share experience with the company's current workers; access to learning materials, experience books and seminars on professional topics created or organized by the company; limited or full access for former employees to specific corporate resources (specialized tools); notification about company news, achievements and vacancies; offering former employees counseling assistance; providing them with discounts on company products or services, if applicable. Alumni programs are beneficial to companies since they help maintain long-term relationships with qualified professionals, which can be used to develop the company's networking opportunities (former employees as valuable partners and clients), re-hire talents and create a loyal community. External activities may also include initiatives to participate in educational and social projects, as well as partnerships with educational institutions to establish internship programs. All this contributes to the company's human capital accumulation despite the ongoing staff displacement processes.

The business process "Staff displacement" requires strict compliance with labor laws and corporate rules. The data it is based on are labor demand, reduction or employee movement strategies and procedures, information on furloughed and suspended personnel, and employees scheduled for termination. The outcome of the business process is a change in the staff numbers and the actual job displacement.

## 4 Discussion

The study focuses on using the soft systems methodology. This approach is not new to the learned society, but its specificity in the context of human capital management is of interest. The SSM is often viewed as an effective tool for solving complex organizational problems, especially where there is a high uncertainty and an in-depth analysis of the interaction of the system elements is needed [9, 34–37]. Through the prism of the SSM, an organization within HCM is perceived as a complex system, where human capital interacts with other elements of the system (technology, processes, organizational culture). This promotes a deeper understanding of the relationships and interdependencies within the organization. The SSM emphasizes the importance of informal aspects of management, such as organizational culture, values and behavioral norms, influencing HCM effectiveness. The SSM makes it easier to analyze employee needs, expectations and motivations, which is important for formulating successful management strategies aimed at increasing productivity. In the context of digital transformation, the SSM provides flexibility in managerial decisions, allowing one to adapt to new challenges and trends, which is critical for the sustainable development of the organization. Moreover, the SSM integrates new technologies and innovative practices into HCM processes and, thus, builds an innovative culture within the enterprise. Hence, the soft systems methodology in human capital management opens up new prospects for enhancing the efficiency of organizational processes, adapting to a changing environment and promoting sustainable development of the company.

Dynamic modeling coupled with the soft systems methodology in human capital management provide unique opportunities for analyzing and forecasting changes in HR processes. This allows one to more accurately predict the effects of human capital management based on established relationships between the organization's elements. When the dynamic model is analyzed, bottlenecks in organizational processes are identified and measures to optimize them are proposed. Dynamic modeling itself makes it possible to evaluate the long-term consequences of these transformations and devise HCM strategies aligned with the company's overall strategic goals.

We have found that the key idea of the dynamic model for managing the human capital development in a company is to create a cyclical approach that starts with attracting talents and continues through their development and retention, moving on to constant renewal. By integrating into the general strategy, the conceptual dynamic model allows one to balance the production transformation function of the enterprise. These actions aim to promote human potential of employees and boost their productivity, which ultimately increases overall efficiency and strengthens the company's competitive advantage.

There are a number of avenues in which the proposed model of human capital management at industrial enterprises can be used. It can serve as a basis for designing and implementing HCM strategies at enterprises of the fuel and energy sector, as well as in other industries. This implies adapting management practices to the existing needs of the organization and integrating digital technologies into the processes of hiring, training, motivating and retaining employees. The research results can be used to create training programs and advanced courses aimed at polishing the employee skills demanded by the company. The model can also be used to optimize the current HR management processes, allowing organizations to become more adaptable to changing market conditions and technological progress. The use of the soft systems methodology for analyzing and modeling HCM business processes can underlie subsequent research as it demonstrates the value and effectiveness of this approach in complex and dynamically changing conditions. One of the primary avenues for further research is experimental testing and adaptation of the model to particular enterprises, as well as producing recommendations for the introduction of digital technologies in human capital management. The results can underlie corporate policies and standards in the field of HCM.

Thus, the research findings are of both practical and theoretical interest and contribute to the development of HCM approaches.

## 5 Conclusion

In the context of globalization and intense technological competition, the effectiveness of human capital management has become a key factor in sustainable development and competitiveness of enterprises. This has increased the importance of digital technologies in HR management at industrial enterprises, especially in such strategically important industries as the fuel and energy sector. However, despite significant investments in digital transformation, many enterprises face numerous challenges—from the lack of qualified personnel capable of working with new systems to the difficulties with integrating digital solutions into current processes. Digital modeling and simulation technologies offer promising opportunities in this area.

The study is devoted to modeling HCM processes at fuel and energy enterprises. While integrating formal and informal aspects of management, the proposed conceptual model emphasizes the need for an adaptive approach to building business processes within the enterprise's digital ecosystem. The model brings flexibility to management decisions, which is extremely important for keeping the organization competitive and efficient amid uncertainty. The soft systems methodology used in the study demonstrates the importance of a consistent and system approach to managing human capital development, from employee needs identification to staff displacement. This provides a holistic view of business processes and facilitates informed decision-making. The research results highlight the importance of regional and industry specificity, which are crucial for formulating effective recruiting, training, motivating and retaining strategies with reference to the cultural, socio-economic and technological context. Dynamic modeling of business processes acts here not only as an optimization tool for increasing efficiency, but also as a means of creating a corporate and organizational environment based on innovation, flexibility and continuous learning.

The research findings confirm the significance of digital tools for optimizing business processes and improving human capital management in industrial enterprises. This opens up new prospects for adopting modern HR management approaches. Further research will focus on the methods for assessing the effectiveness of digital innovations in human capital management, as well as studying specific business processes and their impact on labor productivity in a company.

**Acknowledgments** This research was supported by the Russian Science Foundation grant No. 23-28-01768, https://rscf.ru/project/23-28-01768/.

**Author Contributions** EK: investigation, conceptualization, data curation, formal analysis, methodology, project administration, visualization, writing–original draft, and writing–review and editing. BS, AK, CK: investigation, writing–original draft (Sects. 2.2, 2.3, 4, 5).

# Appendix

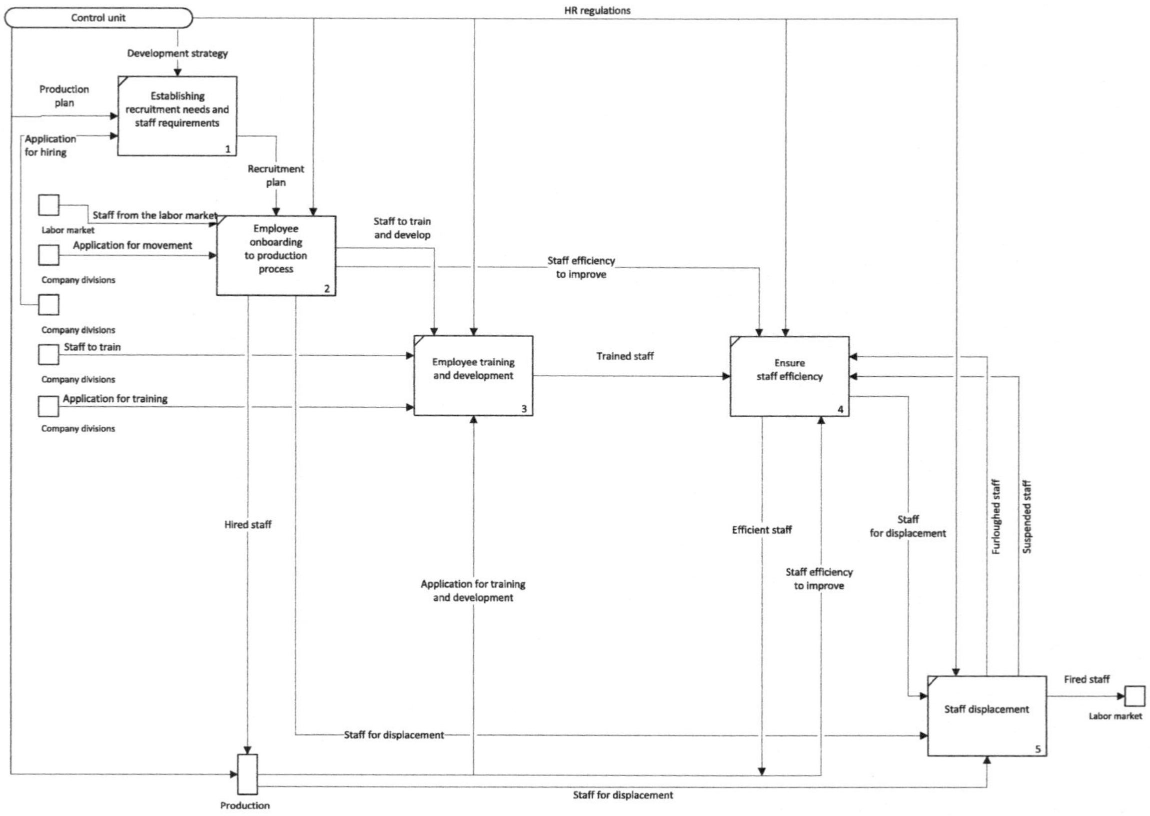


**Fig. 1** Human capital management in a company (a system of business processes)

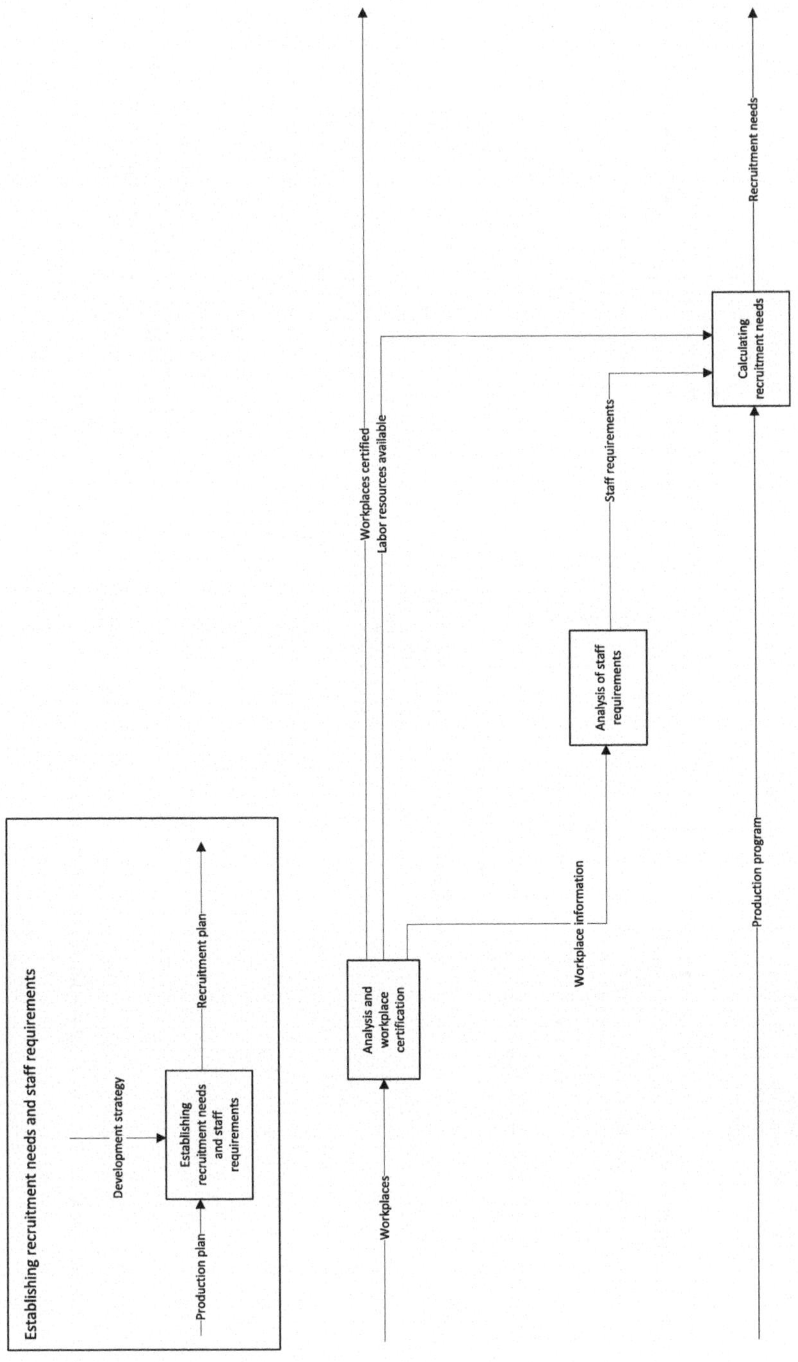


**Fig. 2** Business process: Identifying recruitment needs and staff requirements

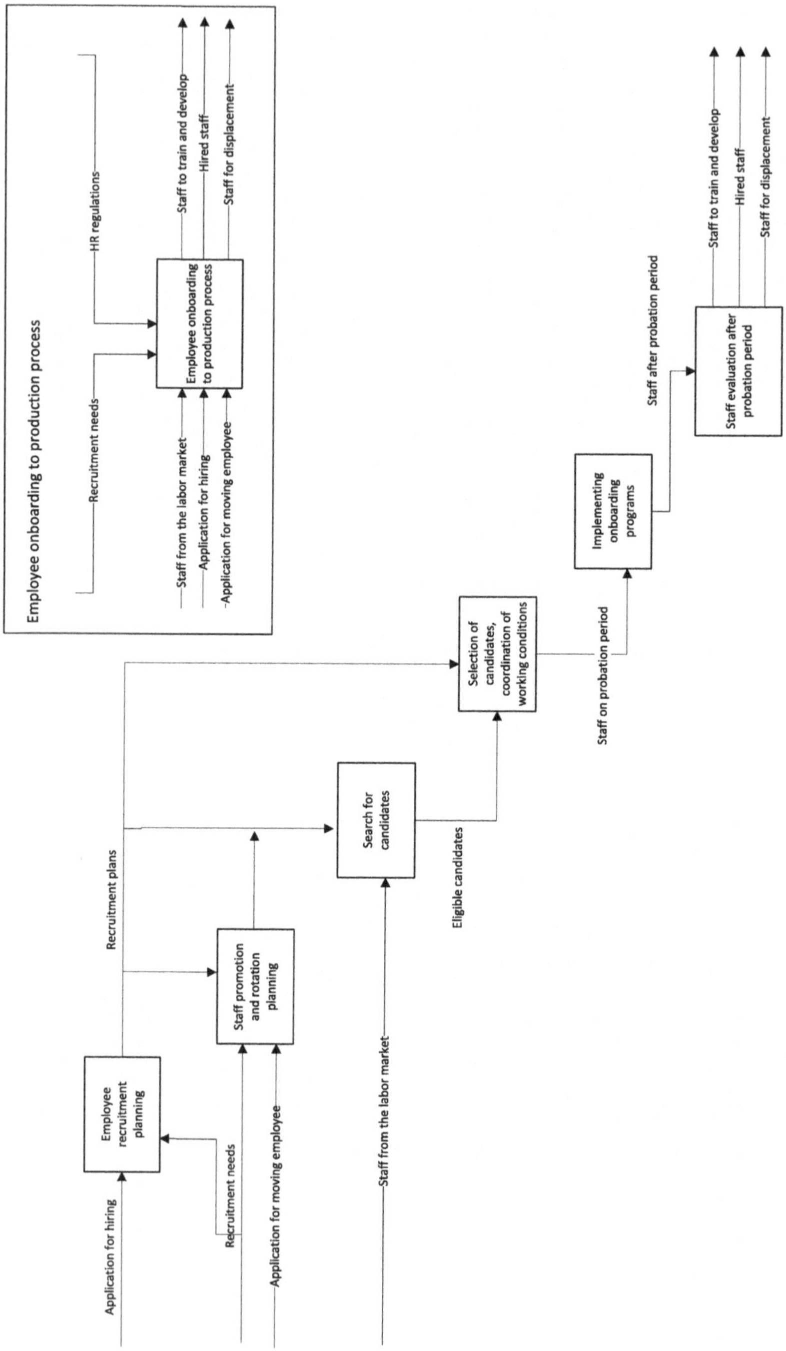


**Fig. 3** Business process: Employee onboarding to production process

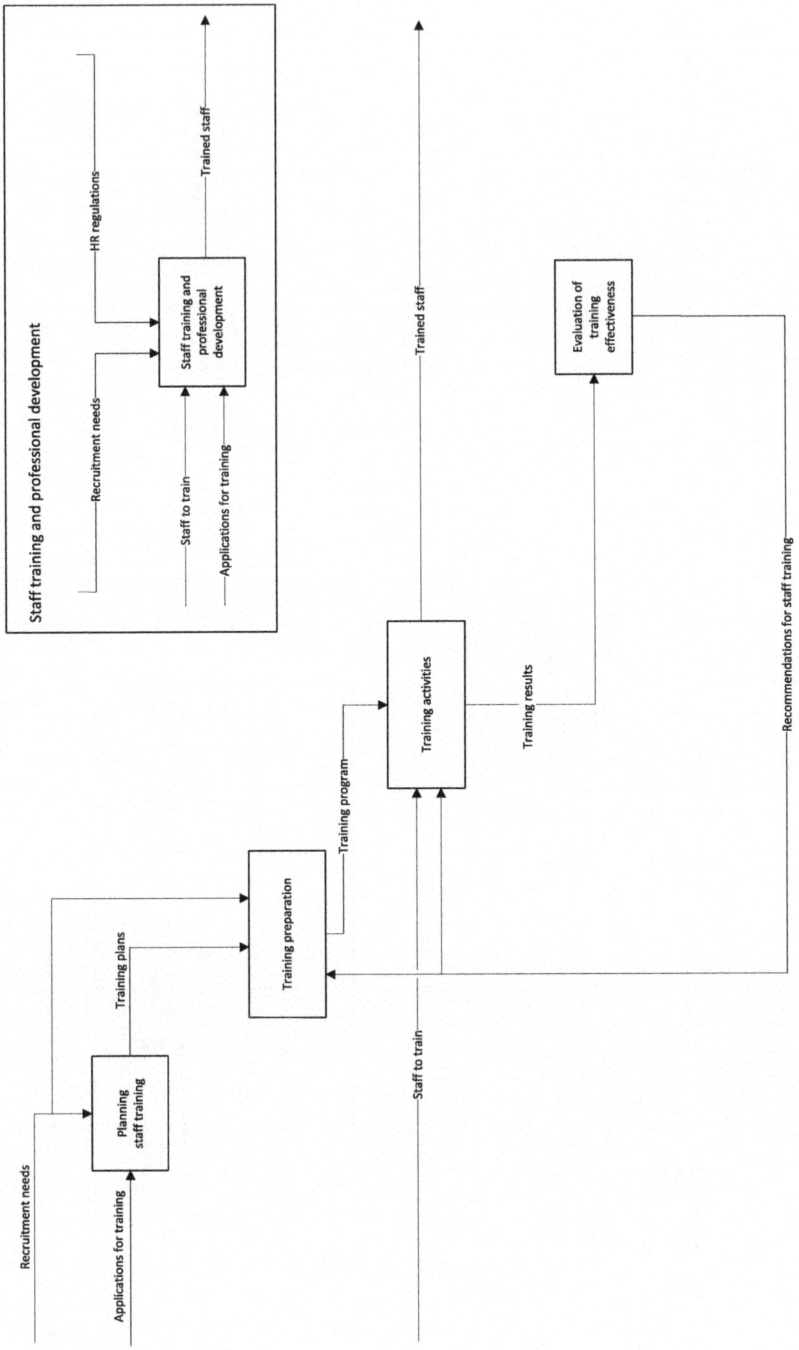


**Fig. 4** Business process: Staff training and professional development

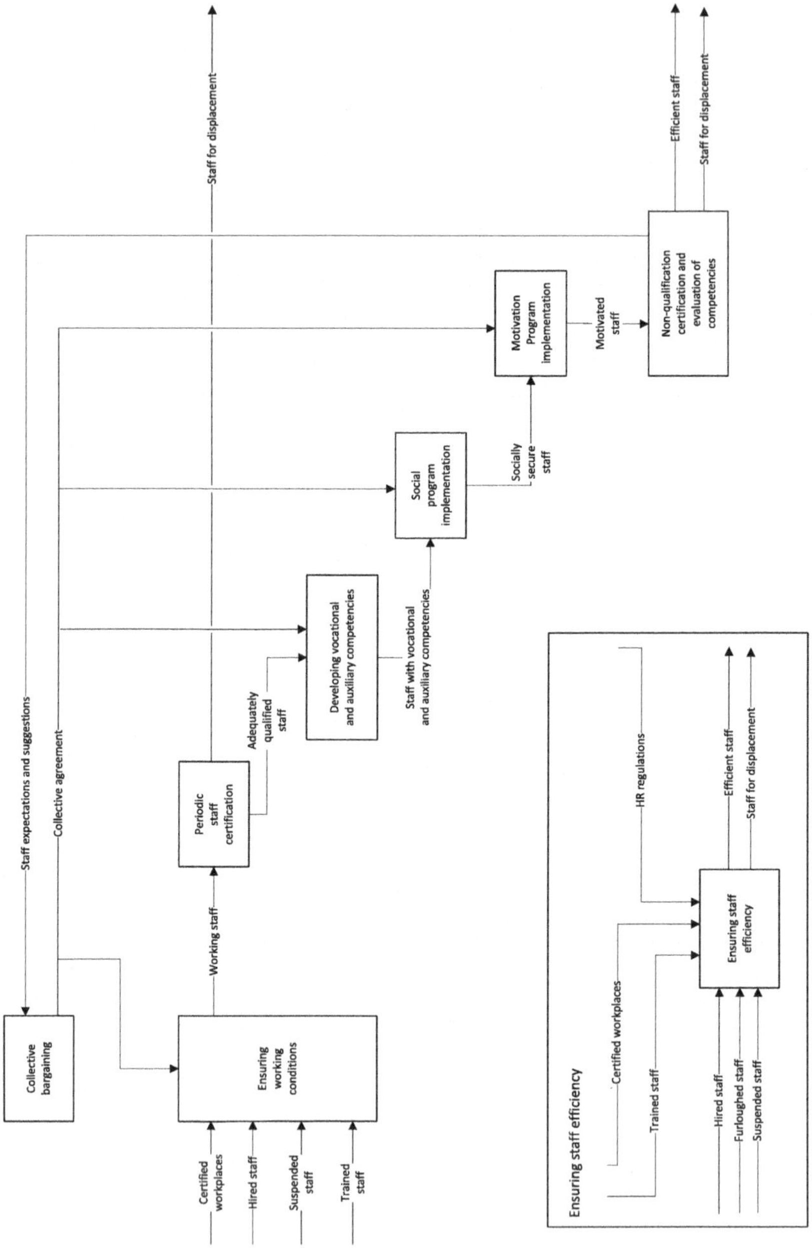


**Fig. 5** Business process: Ensuring staff efficiency

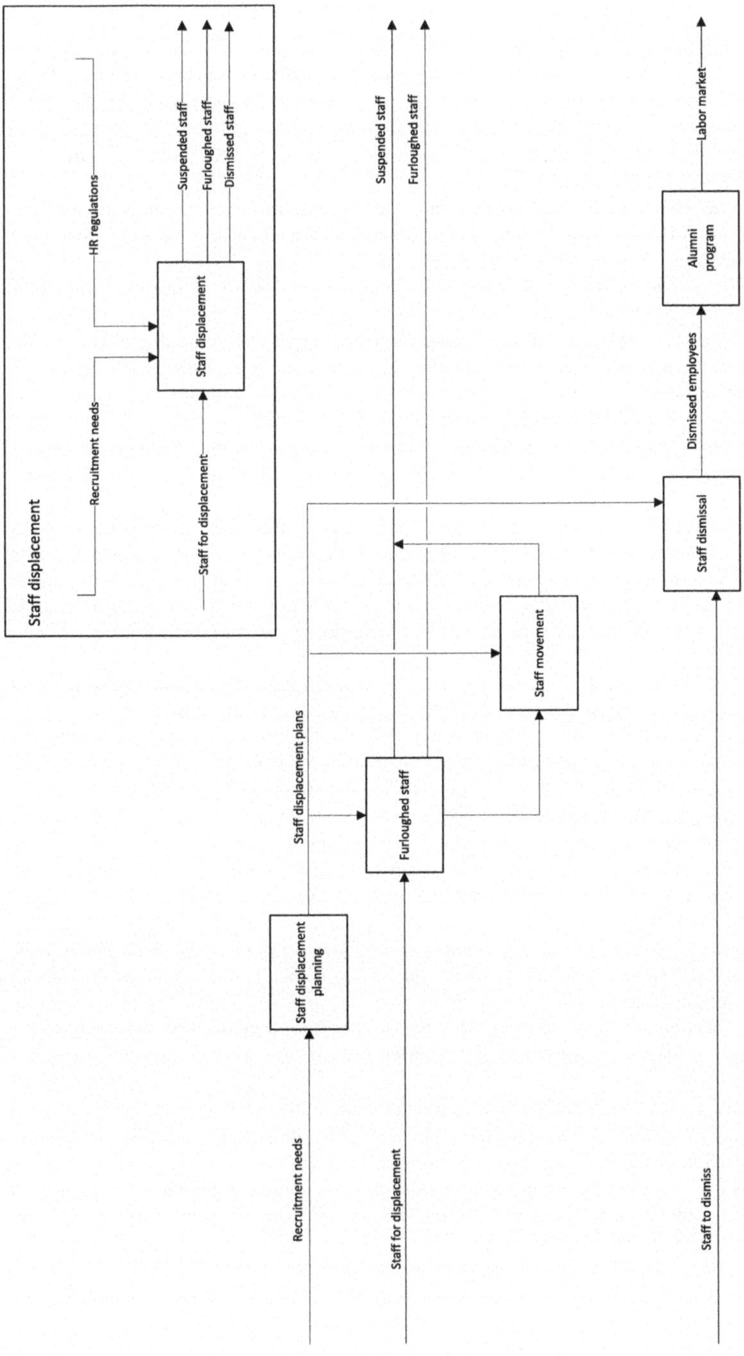


**Fig. 6** Business process: Staff displacement

## References


1. Bassi, L., & McMurrer, D. (2005). What to do when people are your most important asset. *Handbook of Business Strategy, 6*(1), 219–224. https://doi.org/10.1108/08944310510557503
2. Benowitz, S. (2008). Human capital-the most critical asset. *Public Manager, 37*(1), 29–32.
3. Dupret, K., & Pultz, S. (2020). People as our most important asset: A critical exploration of agility and employee commitment. *Project Management Journal, 53*(3), 219–235. https://doi.org/10.1177/87569728221077013
4. Fulmer, I. S., & Ployhart, R. E. (2014). "Our Most important asset" a multidisciplinary/multilevel review of human capital valuation for research and practice. *Journal of Management, 40*(1), 161–192. https://doi.org/10.1177/0149206313511271
5. Greene, R. (2017). *The most important asset: Valuing human capital.* Routledge. https://doi.org/10.4324/9781315141787
6. Samosudov, M. (2023). Specifics of accounting for agent activeness in the digital twin of the social system. In V. Kumar, G. L. Kyriakopoulos, V. Akberdina, & E. Kuzmin (Eds.), *Digital transformation in industry. DTI 2022. Lecture notes in information systems and organisation* (Vol. 61). Springer. https://doi.org/10.1007/978-3-031-30351-7_35
7. Ansell, C., & Gash, A. (2018). Collaborative platforms as a governance strategy. *Journal of Public Administration Research and Theory, 28*(1), 16–32. https://doi.org/10.1093/jopart/mux030
8. Wagner, N., & Strulak-Wójcikiewicz, R. (2020). Concerns about the technology used by collaborative platforms-a challenge for managers. *Procedia Computer Science, 176*, 2536–2545. https://doi.org/10.1016/j.procs.2020.09.319
9. Checkland, P., & Poulter, J. (2020). Soft systems methodology. In *Systems approaches to making change: A practical guide* (pp. 201–253). https://doi.org/10.1007/978-1-4471-7472-1_5.
10. Hildbrand, S., & Bodhanya, S. (2014). Applying SSM to explore the complexity in a multi-stakeholder setting. *Journal of Contemporary Management, 11*(1), 406–430.
11. Wang, W., Liu, W., & Mingers, J. (2015). A systemic method for organisational stakeholder identification and analysis using soft systems methodology (SSM). *European Journal of Operational Research, 246*(2), 562–574. https://doi.org/10.1016/j.ejor.2015.05.014
12. Alefari, M., Almanei, M., & Salonitis, K. (2020). A system dynamics model of employees' performance. *Sustainability, 12*(16). https://doi.org/10.3390/su12166511
13. Jiang, G., Hu, B., & Wang, Y. (2011). Agent-based simulation approach to understanding the interaction between employee behavior and dynamic tasks. *Simulation, 87*(5), 407–422. https://doi.org/10.1177/0037549710385745
14. Lainema, T. (2003). *Enhancing organizational business process perception: Experiences from constructing and applying a dynamic business simulation game.* Turku School of Economics and Business Administration.
15. Rosenberg, Z., Riasanow, T., & Krcmar, H. (2015). A system dynamics model for business process change projects. In *International Conference of the System Dynamics Society* (pp. 1–27).
16. Wang, M., Zhou, L., & Zhang, Z. (2016). Dynamic modeling. *Annual Review of Organizational Psychology and Organizational Behavior, 3*, 241–266. https://doi.org/10.1146/annurev-orgpsych-041015-062553
17. Groesser, S. N., & Jovy, N. (2016). Business model analysis using computational modeling: A strategy tool for exploration and decision-making. *Journal of Management Control, 27*, 61–88. https://doi.org/10.1007/s00187-015-0222-1
18. Vennix, J. A. (1995). Building consensus in strategic decision making: System dynamics as a group support system. *Group Decision and Negotiation, 4*, 335–355. https://doi.org/10.1007/bf01409778

19. Yim, N. H., Kim, S. H., Kim, H. W., & Kwahk, K. Y. (2004). Knowledge based decision making on higher level strategic concerns: System dynamics approach. *Expert Systems with Applications, 27*(1), 143–158. https://doi.org/10.1016/j.eswa.2003.12.019
20. Florida, R., Mellander, C., & Stolarick, K. (2008). Inside the black box of regional development—Human capital, the creative class and tolerance. *Journal of Economic Geography, 8*(5), 615–649. https://doi.org/10.1093/jeg/lbn023
21. Gennaioli, N., La Porta, R., Lopez-de-Silanes, F., & Shleifer, A. (2013). Human capital and regional development. *The Quarterly Journal of Economics, 128*(1), 105–164. https://doi.org/10.1093/qje/qjs050
22. Sanso-Navarro, M., Vera-Cabello, M., & Ximénez-De-Embún, D. P. (2017). Human capital spillovers and regional development. *Journal of Applied Econometrics, 32*(4), 923–930. https://doi.org/10.1002/jae.2541
23. Unger, J. M., Rauch, A., Frese, M., & Rosenbusch, N. (2011). Human capital and entrepreneurial success: A meta-analytical review. *Journal of Business Venturing, 26*(3), 341–358. https://doi.org/10.1016/j.jbusvent.2009.09.004
24. Afanasyev, M. P., & Shash, N. N. (2022). ESG transformation in the corporate sector: Systematizing the global approach. *Studies on Russian Economic Development, 33*(6), 707–715. https://doi.org/10.1134/s1075700722060028
25. Chevrollier, N., Zhang, J., van Leeuwen, T., & Nijhof, A. (2022). The predictive value of strategic orientation for ESG performance over time. *Corporate Governance, 20*(1), 123–142. https://doi.org/10.1108/CG-03-2019-0105
26. Pérez, L., Hunt, V., Samandari, H., Nuttall, R., & Bellone, D. (2022). How to make ESG real. *The McKinsey Quarterly*.
27. Khalil, M. K., & Khalil, R. (2022). Leveraging buyers' interest in ESG investments through sustainability awareness. *Sustainability, 14*(21), 14278. https://doi.org/10.3390/su142114278
28. Kotsantonis, S., Pinney, C., & Serafeim, G. (2016). ESG integration in investment management: Myths and realities. *Journal of Applied Corporate Finance, 28*(2), 10–16. https://doi.org/10.1111/jacf.12169
29. Lee, H. J., & Rhee, T. H. (2023). How does corporate ESG management affect consumers' brand choice? *Sustainability, 15*(8). https://doi.org/10.3390/su15086795
30. Sinelnikov, A. M. (2014). The fuel and energy sector in The Russian Federation: Structure and problems of functioning. *New University. Series: Economics and Law [Novyy universitet. Seriya «Ekonomika i pravo»], 10*(44), 35–39.
31. The list of occupational standards assigned to the Council for Vocational Qualifications in the Oil and Gas Sector. The National Council under the RF President for Vocational Qualifications. https://www.spkngk.ru/about/activity/standards/list/.
32. The list of occupational standards assigned to the Council for Vocational Qualifications in Power Industry. The National Council under the RF President for Vocational Qualifications. https://espkrf.ru/ps/.
33. The list of occupational standards assigned to the Union of Employers of the Nuclear Industry, Energy and Science of Russia. The National Council under the RF President for Vocational Qualifications. http://srrosatom.ru/node/1281.
34. Checkland, P. (2000). Soft systems methodology: A thirty year retrospective. *Systems Research and Behavioral Science, 17*(S1), S11–S58. https://doi.org/10.1002/1099-1743(200011)17:1+<::aid-sres374>3.0.co;2-o
35. Cundill, G., Cumming, G. S., Biggs, D., & Fabricius, C. (2012). Soft systems thinking and social learning for adaptive management. *Conservation Biology, 26*(1), 13–20. https://doi.org/10.1111/j.1523-1739.2011.01755.x
36. Patel, D., & Patel, S. (2003). The cognitive process of problem solving: A soft systems approach. *Brain and Mind, 4*, 283–295. https://doi.org/10.1023/A:1025470015275
37. Rodriguez-Ulloa, R., & Paucar-Caceres, A. (2005). Soft system dynamics methodology (SSDM): Combining soft systems methodology (SSM) and system dynamics (SD). *Systemic Practice and Action Research, 18*, 303–334. https://doi.org/10.1007/s11213-005-4816-7

# The Impact of Industry 5.0 Human Capital on Production System Performance: Evidence from Russian Metallurgy

**Ilia Chernenko**

**Abstract** Socially oriented digital transformation of the new wave is closely related to dynamic knowledge processes. Despite the conservatism towards innovation and technological progress in the Russian industrial sector, digital human capital associated with cyber-social systems will play an integral role in shaping the competitive advantages of companies due to the challenges of achieving employee well-being and shortages of skilled labor. The article aims to investigate the impact of organizational learning, employee Industry 5.0 knowledge, and basic digital competencies on manufacturing system performance in conventional industries using the case of metallurgy. Partial least squares structural equation modeling (PLS-SEM) is used to estimate path coefficients in models. The empirical base consists of the results of a survey of 2156 employees of eight Russia's metallurgical enterprises undergoing digital transformation. The results confirm that Industry 5.0 competencies have a weak but significant effect on manufacturing system performance, while core competencies have no direct effect. Industry 5.0 knowledge predominantly derives from basic digital skills and advanced training initiatives. Consequently, conventional production systems of Russian enterprises are in the initial stage of transition to Industry 5.0, moderately adapting to practice the general knowledge and competencies of employees in the field of cyber-social systems, smart robots, and human-centric artificial intelligence.

**Keywords** Industry 5.0 · Digitalization · Human capital · Knowledge · Production system

I. Chernenko (✉)
Ural Federal University, Ekaterinburg, Russian Federation
e-mail: i.m.chernenko@urfu.ru



A. Appolloni et al. (eds.), *The Future of Industry*, Lecture Notes in Information Systems and Organisation 70, https://doi.org/10.1007/978-3-031-66801-2_29

## 1 Introduction

Despite skepticism regarding the possibility of clearly distinguishing modern stages of technological development, in recent years the idea of the emergence of a new type of society in which anthropocentric technologies fully support people's cognitive and physical abilities to create value has been actively promoted. Notably, a consensus among most scholars is evident, with regard to pivotal role played by declaration of the transition to "Society 5.0" by the Japanese Council for Science, Technology, and Innovation in 2016, as a significant catalyst for cyber-social systems conceptualization and design [1–4]. It is widely acknowledged that this new phase in understanding of technological evolution is associated with society, rather than confined solely with industry. The new society aims to create information technologies that meet various needs of people, regardless of contexts, health status, gender and age differences. The concept of Industry 5.0 was proposed in the work of subcommittees of the European Commission and concerned the prospects for harmonious, sustainable, and personalized interaction between humans and machines in the era of mass digitalization [5]. The motivation for developing the concept of Society or Industry 5.0 is not difficult to understand in an increasingly complex world: developed and some developing countries are facing labor shortages due to an aging population, a significant decline in the birth rate and the long-term effects of the pandemic [6, 7]. In addition, geopolitical fragmentation has also contributed to the rise of green skepticism, offering alternative theories of growth based on a primary focus on the social consequences of business operations, promoting ideas of social transformation to preserve the environment [8]. Existing digital technologies, which have a wide range of potential applications for supporting human abilities such as intelligence, innate talents, health capital, and physical strength, can serve as the foundation for this new social transformation.

Undoubtedly, for the vast majority of contemporary manufacturing enterprises, the Industry 5.0 concept may appear distant from the conventional financially-oriented models of value creation and the strategic priorities typically favored by management. However, it is crucial to recognize that promotion of the Industry 5.0 principles has pivotal role in the establishment of intellectually-driven businesses ready to thrive in the forthcoming decades. Conventional production systems are characterized by a high level of process standardization, structural certainty, moderate innovative activity, and widespread implementation of lean manufacturing. Therefore, while elements of Industry 4.0 are already being implemented in production systems, most companies are just preparing for Industry 5.0 [9]. However, comprehensive understanding, rigorous critical analysis, and proactive strategic planning concerning the transition to the new digitalization paradigm are imperative for the mining and manufacturing sectors in the observable future for a number of reasons. First, there is the uncertainty for human capital that arises from the potential job displacement caused by the mass adoption of artificial intelligence (AI) in production systems. Second, the significance of human capital escalates further due to the substantial rise in the cost associated with cultivating and retaining skilled labor in developed nations, a trajectory being increasingly followed by many developing countries. Indeed, most manufacturing enterprises are already confronting the acute challenge of securing a competent workforce owing to the evolving dynamics of the labor market [10]. Third, it appears that digital technological expansion and the accompanying optimism of limitless growth are playing a decisive role in critically exacerbating the risks of not achieving sustainable development goals until 2030, which jeopardizes the well-being of future generations.

Transformation towards a model of socially oriented degrowth in a sustainable paradigm is most difficult for traditional industries with low added value in developing countries, such as Russia and China, which actively exploit natural resources. Over the past decade and a half Russian companies in the mining, metallurgical, engineering, and chemical sectors have undergone significant digital transformation [11, 12]. The introduction of digital twins, the Internet of Things (IoT), and data mining has yielded tangible benefits, including enhanced process accuracy and transparency, increased equipment productivity, and an overall boost in the competitiveness and innovative capabilities of manufacturing enterprises [13–15]. However, the literature on industrial digitalization from the perspective of human capital accumulation and use is scarce [16–18]. In recent years, the Russian economy has occupied a moderate 40th place in the Global digital competitiveness ranking, with a decline in positions over the past 10 years attributed to a deterioration in population knowledge and technology development conditions [19]. Companies are employing contingent learning strategies, developing specific knowledge in the field of the digital industrial revolution, and shifting their focus to survival in the face of supply chain disruptions and technological regression caused by Russia's international isolation. Consequently, the recent literature primarily focuses on short-term operational efficiency of digitalization and highlights the technocratic nature of the fourth industrial revolution, leaving gaps in addressing the question of the social implications of smart technologies.

The purpose of the article is to the impact of organizational learning, employee Industry 5.0 knowledge, and basic digital competencies on manufacturing system performance in industries with low added value using the example of metallurgy. In this study, the author aims to close the gap in understanding of the knowledge component of digital technological transformation towards human-centric production models, using novel approach to investigate the processes of knowledge accumulation from dynamic (organization learning) and static (accumulated knowledge) perspectives. The originality of the study, therefore, lies in the development of a structural model that combines factors of the organizational learning environment, such as qualified coaches and mentors, the subjective efficiency of learning, and the measurement of accumulated digital human capital. The model implies that cyber-social systems are expected to become a new source of productivity growth in the future by improving the quality of training, engagement and human capital of manufacturing company personnel.

## 2 Transition Towards Industry 5.0: Knowledge-Related Implications for the Manufacturing Industry

### *2.1 The Impact of Industry 5.0 on the Competitiveness of a Manufacturing Company*

Many authors agree that Industry 5.0 is an evolutionary progression of the Fourth Industrial Revolution, which introduced cyber-physical systems and industrial-scale data mining technologies [2, 20]. The latest wave of information and computer technology (ICT) places a strong emphasis on the social implications for general-purpose technologies application within a wide range of solutions to improve human interaction with cyber-physical systems [21]. In certain high-tech sectors, such as medicine, key areas of improvement to achieve high performance include personalized experiences and the creation of data and knowledge-sharing networks to address staffing shortages and workload surges [22]. Manufacturing is still a labor-intensive industry, even though technological advancements have reduced the reliance on physical labor. However, digitalization has led to more complex automation frameworks, which have in turn created new monotonous manual tasks that increase intellectual and psycho-emotional strain and reduce endurance levels [23]. Apparently, labor shortages could impact manufacturing sector productivity in the coming years, affecting both developed and developing countries. This phenomenon is driven by demographic decline and shifting workforce values, as the social status of work in production has changed post-pandemic [10]. Employee well-being and creating an attractive job in terms of social welfare, self-realization are becoming important priorities in digital business transformation [24].

Industry 5.0 draws attention to two key areas of interaction with a company's internal and external stakeholders, ensuring an increase in its competitiveness. On the one hand, this is a transformation of customer experience by increasing the quality of feedback and the possibility of individualization, reducing the labor intensity of routine interaction and supporting customers and other stakeholders. Cyber-social systems support virtual interaction between the customer and the manufacturer, creating an ecosystem of knowledge sharing, for example, in the implementation of a servitization strategy [25]. On the other hand, important social effects arise in the field of human resources, the performance of complex functions that require intellectual support, and high speed of decision-making [18]. General purpose technologies are often thought of as an add-on to existing equipment in a production system, helping operators make decisions and transforming the accumulated data into information for strategic decision makers. Collaborative robots can also assist people in specific areas of the production chain, and they can close specialization gaps within an organization, ensuring precision operations, meeting stringent safety conditions, and maintaining flexibility in the deployment of different environmental scenarios [26].

While digital automation has long been viewed as a competing labor substitute in manufacturing [27], the emphasis in the design and delivery of digital transformation is shifting to collaboration and complementarity between machine and human capabilities. Setting up and supporting cyber-social systems allows companies to optimize the time spent by highly qualified personnel on routine tasks, freeing up time for creative functions. Smart specialization and high creativity enable the creation of more attractive manufacturing jobs [21], but digital optimism in practice is often met with a lack of basic and specialized competencies of line personnel that are necessary for the successful integration of Industry 4.0 or 5.0 into the production system. This is why human capital is the key to the transition between digital automation and the development of cyber-social systems in production value chains.

### *2.2 General or Basic Digital Competencies*

Manufacturing companies need to have a workforce with adequate general or basic competencies in information and computer systems to implement new digital technologies. General or basic competencies allow employees to search for new sources of information, critically reflect on them, and create content that is relevant to their production tasks [17]. Digital literacy of personnel helps companies to introduce new technologies into production systems more quickly and efficiently, and to develop the design, development, and research skills of their workforce in an integrated information environment, which is especially important for medium- and high-tech industries [28]. Basic competencies are developed in workers throughout the life cycle of a production system, but they are at risk due to the attractiveness of outsourcing [29]. Basic competencies include a general understanding of the company's IT infrastructure and digital capabilities, as well as skills in working productively with computers, networks, and specialized applications. Advanced skills may also include programming, connecting devices, and working with hardware in cyber-physical systems [30]. General competencies can be supported through lifelong learning, interdisciplinary educational programs, and project-based education that emphasizes creative skills [31].

Addressing gaps in core digital competencies that contribute to manufacturing company competitiveness is an important area of research. Rikala et al. [32] show that companies use surveys, interviews, focus groups and other community-based tools to identify and measure gaps in basic and advanced workforce skills. Less common measures of relevant components of digital human capital involve analyzing the content of educational materials, textbooks, and educational frameworks. The primary skill holders are organizational professionals, such as workers and engineers, but conceptualizing engineering education in the Industry 5.0 era is largely an emerging area of research [33]. Retrospective analysis shows that interdisciplinary education must be complemented by the principles of resilience, sustainability and human-centered design [34].

A significant body of literature on smart digitalization associates changes with the introduction of specific technical elements and financial capital [35, 36], while the processes of developing digital competencies, knowledge and their impact on the production system remain poorly understood. Meng and Wang [37] show that the knowledge embodied in the digital work of ICT professionals plays an important role in the value chain, being a prerequisite for the effective implementation of system solutions in manufacturing. General digital competencies can support the implementation of technologies that increase the operational efficiency of conventional production systems through lean manufacturing practices [35]. In the case of conventional production systems, performance is the degree to which the company achieves its planned goals, including product-service indicators, operational indicators, and indicators related to process duration, resource quality, and impacts on various stakeholders [29, 38]. Throughout investment cycles, digital competencies build up and are facilitated by digital technologies, leading to a mutual synergy that enables companies to manage and enhance resource utilization, equipment uptime, waste reduction, and other related indicators of production system performance [39]. Digital skills are enablers for the information and computer platforms in companies, which has a positive impact on organizational performance [40]. The introduction of digital technologies in the form of cyber-physical systems to support production and management processes increases the digital capabilities of the company and also has a positive effect on innovative performance [41].

The core competencies of Industry 4.0 for most industrial personnel in an environment of intense digitalization are influenced by on-the-job learning [42]. The quality of internal employee training can play a significant role in developing these competencies, and it is essential for the successful digital transformation of production systems. High-quality training requires qualified teachers, innovative teaching methods, and a high level of employee engagement [43]. Additionally, digital technologies require a corresponding evolution in competencies, such as problem-solving skills, critical thinking, analytical abilities, high levels of responsibility, and teamwork [44]. Unlike previous eras of automation, digital core competences are based on the skills of system integration, collective learning, and coordination of efforts of multiple parties in a complex environment [38]. Developed core digital competencies can further enable technological innovation, knowledge management, and accelerate the training of new employees. As a result of analyzing the nature of general and advanced digital competencies, the author puts forward the following hypotheses concerning the impact of basic skills and human capital:

**H1.1** The organizational learning environment has a positive impact on the basic digital competencies of employees of a manufacturing company.

**H1.2** The organizational learning environment has a positive impact on the performance of the company's production system.

**H1.3** The basic digital competencies of employees have a positive impact on the performance of the company's production system.

## 2.3 Digital Human Capital of Industry 5.0

While digital automation is displacing some workers, the complex processes of generating and using knowledge in a networked environment are a natural barrier to the further expansion of traditional Industry 4.0 [29]. As practice has shown, digital transformation in industry has not replaced knowledge work. Instead, it has changed the way workers interact within the production system to create value, exacerbating new social problems. Aimed at overcoming social barriers, Industry 5.0 knowledge and competencies build the path to human-centric production, forming the basis of intellectual capital and providing a competitive advantage to the company as a supplier of goods and services, and as an employer [5]. Melnyk et al. [16] note, a new model of education in the digital economy should be based on the principles of humanism, cognitivism, and understanding behavioral patterns when working with technologies in a way that correlates with student motivation. General digital competencies support the use of solutions that replace routine, monotonous, dangerous, and time-consuming functions, while Industry 5.0 specific knowledge supports the cognitive and communication abilities to solve creative problems.

Industry 5.0 human capital represents the specific complementary skills that support design, planning, organization and control of cyber-social systems. On the one hand, these skills enable workers to support the sustainable production system functions inherent to Industry 4.0, such as achieving sustainable goals, increasing product life cycles, using alternative materials, and introducing digital lean technologies for zero defects, enhanced by data mining [45]. On the other hand, Industry 5.0 human capital includes the skills to use digital technologies to monitor the condition of workers in real time, measure the level of physical stress, task completion time, and spatial and dynamic ergonomic risks [23]. Taken together, this approach allows for a meaningful workforce diversification strategy and optimized rotation and outstaffing plan. It also helps to identify the need for training or workplace redesign to better engage older workers with special needs. Based on a literature review, the human capital of Industry 5.0 includes knowledge in the field of big data, digital twins and the Internet of things, smart robotics [21].

Previous research suggests that companies need to distinguish between formal and tacit knowledge flows when managing Industry 4.0 technological transformation [46]. Cyber-physical systems require the successful integration of equipment into a cohesive production ecosystem, while cyber-social systems are sensitive to the social context, understanding the role of humans and living intellectual resources in achieving efficiency and resource conservation. Thus, the human capital of Industry 5.0 is essential for Industry 5.0, not only for learning processes but also for the overall performance of the production system. Competencies in the field of cyber-social systems form the basis of companies' long-term technological advantage, allowing them to implement new technologies faster than competitors. In traditional production systems, the emphasis lies not only in conserving resources but also in fostering innovation, which requires employees to be able to skillfully integrate diverse general-purpose technologies while maintaining social sustainability [38]. Thus, performance extends beyond the direct effects of automation, emphasizing the role of individual abilities that are unique to human intelligence and thinking, as well as harmonious well-being, which radically reduces the risks of technological unemployment. By studying the impact of human capital specific to Industry 5.0 on production systems, the following hypotheses can be put forward:

**H2.1** Basic digital competencies have a positive impact on the knowledge and human capital relevant to Industry 5.0.

**H2.2** The organizational learning environment has a positive impact on the knowledge and human capital relevant to Industry 5.0.

**H2.3** The knowledge and human capital relevant to Industry 5.0 has a positive impact on the performance of the company's production system.

# 3 Methods and Materials

## *3.1 Methods*

This study examines complex social processes that involve implicit theoretical constructs, such as Industry 5.0 knowledge, learning, general digital competencies, and production system performance. Therefore, the author choses structural equation modeling (SEM) to analyze data and determine the significance of cause-and-effect relationships based on path coefficients. The choice of SEM methodology in analysis is influenced by the non-normal distribution of the data, leading to use partial least squares SEM (PLS-SEM) over covariance-based SEM (CB-SEM). In addition, the literature analysis shows a weak theory showing the relationship between digital competencies and tools for measuring the performance of production systems, which also provides arguments in favor of PLS-SEM. PLS-SEM has become popular in recent years, but it is not used to confirm theory as much as to predict possible outcomes based on the data.

As a rule, PLS-SEM is applied in several stages. First, the measurement model is estimated. Once convergent and discriminant validity are confirmed, the path coefficients in the structural model are estimated. The significance of the path coefficients is determined based on the calculated *t*-statistics, which are bootstrapped for 5000 subsamples. Convergent validity is the extent to which the explicit variables in a questionnaire are related to the implicit theoretical constructs, while discriminant validity is the lack of correlations between the directly observable variables and the various competing implicit constructs in the model [47]. For each implicit construct, the proportion of explained variance is also estimated. This indicates the explanatory power of the variables included in the model. The dependent variable in the model is the performance of the metallurgical company's production system.

To measure the indicators, a structured questionnaire was developed; it included several sets of statements that reflectively showed various aspects of the phenomena being studied. The questionnaire was developed by the author based on an analysis of the literature, the full formulations of the items used for modeling are given below in Table 2. The questionnaire included control questions, questions for assessing the effectiveness of the production system based on lean manufacturing indicators [48, 49], as well as questions for assessing general and special Industry 5.0 skills that we compiled according to the understanding of cyber-social technologies in the literature, including digital twins and smart collaborative robots [3, 26]. Respondents were asked to rate each statement on a 5-point Likert scale, with the answers worded differently for the range of the scale. Questions about the level of knowledge of Industry 5.0 and basic digital competencies assessed the level of skills on a scale from 1 to 5, with "1" being a complete lack of understanding and "5" being the presence of confident skills in using these digital technologies. Statements about the performance of the production system were included in the questionnaire, and respondents were asked to express their degree of agreement on a 5-point scale. Inverted scales were not used for any items.

### 3.2 *Materials*

The sample size was determined using the rule of thumb and inverse square root method [50]. In the first case, the sample size was 180 observations (the number of arrows between implicit and explicit variables multiplied by 10). In the second case, the sample size was 618 observations (calculated using the inverse square root method with a 5% significance level and a minimum path coefficient of 0.1: $(2486/0.1)^2 = 618$ observations). The maximum sample size chosen was 618. The survey was conducted in the fall of 2022 at eight Russian metallurgical enterprises. The companies were chosen because they are actively transforming their production systems through the introduction of Industry 5.0 technologies, such as digital twins for metallurgical processes, robots in production, and data mining systems that support operators in real time.

Data on digital transformation was clarified by interviewing managers and reviewing open sources of information, such as company reports and websites. In addition to investing in technology, companies also actively supported digital human capital through annual employee training, an exchange of ideas for digital operational improvements, and process champions in departments. The questionnaire was distributed to managers and production personnel through the company's corporate system of personal accounts. A total of 3708 respondents participated, which represents about 7% of the total number of employees at the companies. The survey results were downloaded from the system and transferred to the author in anonymized form for research purposes. Because the survey was mandatory, a significant number of questionnaires were excluded due to suspicious response patterns (e.g., monotonic responses or responses with large variance within one or

**Table 1** Structure of respondents by job specialization and position in the company, as a percentage of the total number of respondents

| Job specialization/position | Workers | Specialists | Managers |
|---|---|---|---|
| Production | 59.1 | 0.7 | 5.6 |
| Quality control | 0.0 | 14.8 | 0.0 |
| Maintenance and repair | 10.5 | 1.0 | 0.0 |
| Energy | 2.7 | 0.0 | 0.9 |
| Logistics | 0.0 | 2.8 | 0.0 |
| Other production services | 0.0 | 1.1 | 0.0 |
| Design | 0.0 | 0.5 | 0.0 |
| IT | 0.0 | 0.1 | 0.2 |

more questions). After excluding low-quality responses, 2156 questionnaires remained (a 58.1% response rate). The characteristics of the respondents are shown below in Table 1. More than 70% of the respondents are production and service workers, while managers and specialists represent less than a quarter of respondents, which corresponds to the structure of job distribution in the company.

## 4 Results and Discussion

SmartPLS version 4 was used to analyze the data, which involves two main stages: testing the measurement model and testing the structural model. The Kolmogorov-Smirnov test showed that the distribution of valid variables was not normal, so PLS-SEM was used. Questionnaire items with loadings above 0.65 were selected, which resulted in the exclusion of some questions. The remaining variables are presented in Table 2. All *t*-statistics are above the threshold value, indicating that all loadings are statistically significant at the level less than 1%. Basic digital competencies include the use of standard office equipment, standard resource management systems, and database skills. Specific competencies include knowledge and operational application of digital twins, AI technologies, and smart robots in manufacturing. As expected, the average values of specific competencies are lower than those of general digital competencies. The effectiveness of training was assessed using indicators of sufficiency, usefulness, and the ability to convert acquired skills into specific production results. Respondents were also asked to evaluate the quality of mentors in on-the-job training programs. The assessment of the effectiveness of the production system also showed high results, above the neutral value of three points. Reducing production system downtime and organizing work to reduce losses are priorities for manufacturing companies. Over the past years, production systems have accumulated the best experience in implementing lean manufacturing, which has become the main way to achieve efficiency and competitive advantage in the face of the need for comprehensive cost reduction.

**Table 2** Descriptive statistics and loadings, *t*-statistics for selected variables

| Construct | Questionnaire items (measures) | Mean | SD | L | *t* |
|---|---|---|---|---|---|
| DIG_HC digital human capital (basic competences) | DIGICOM_1 working with spreadsheets in MS excel | 3.07 | 1.33 | 0.848 | 111.6 |
| | DIGICOM_3 creation of electronic presentations | 2.60 | 1.39 | 0.878 | 140.4 |
| | DIGICOM_4 working in a enterprise resource planning system (SAP, 1C, etc.) | 2.31 | 1.35 | 0.875 | 156.5 |
| | DIGICOM_5 working with databases (for example, reference databases) | 2.94 | 1.42 | 0.869 | 133.1 |
| INDUSTRY5_0 knowledge of INDUSTRY 5.0 | IND50_1 digital twins | 2.23 | 1.22 | 0.913 | 187.7 |
| | IND50_3 AI-powered smart technologies (e.g., video and image recognition systems) | 2.54 | 1.31 | 0.935 | 267.5 |
| | IND50_4 smart robots in production | 2.51 | 1.34 | 0.923 | 196.6 |
| LEARN learning performance | LEARN_2 the amount of training provided is sufficient for successful work | 3.95 | 1.03 | 0.852 | 90.4 |
| | LEARN_3 on-the-job formal training is practice-oriented | 3.94 | 1.04 | 0.858 | 102.4 |
| | LEARN_4 the presentation of material during training is always interesting | 3.80 | 1.05 | 0.861 | 110.3 |
| | LEARN_5 teachers are highly qualified in their field | 4.19 | 0.98 | 0.835 | 79.0 |
| PS_PERF production system performance | LEAN_1 work is organized in such a way as to minimize losses at all stages of production | 3.81 | 1.01 | 0.808 | 83.6 |
| | LEAN_2 we are successfully reducing the level of bureaucratic burden on departments | 3.27 | 1.17 | 0.737 | 57.3 |
| | LEAN_3 equipment repairs and maintenance system are very effective | 3.27 | 1.19 | 0.733 | 54.7 |
| | LEAN_4 we successfully reduce unnecessary inventory to save resources | 3.61 | 1.06 | 0.780 | 58.2 |
| | LEAN_5 we reduce production system downtime in every possible way | 4.17 | 0.96 | 0.672 | 40.3 |
| | LEAN_6 we successfully reduce the number of unnecessary movements of goods within the department (in the workshop) | 3.75 | 1.08 | 0.784 | 64.6 |
| | LEAN_8 the production monitoring system gives us the necessary information for decision-making | 3.83 | 1.01 | 0.802 | 83.3 |

Note: *SD* standard deviations, *L* loadings, *t* *t*-statistics
*Source*: Obtained by the author using SmartPLS

**Table 3** Indicators of composite validity and adjusted R-squares

| Construct | Cronbach's alpha | Composite reliability (rho_a) | Composite reliability (rho_c) | Average variance extracted (AVE) | R-square adjusted |
|---|---|---|---|---|---|
| DIG_HC | 0.891 | 0.893 | 0.924 | 0.753 | 0.089 |
| INDUSTRY5_0 | 0.914 | 0.915 | 0.946 | 0.853 | 0.553 |
| LEARN | 0.874 | 0.876 | 0.913 | 0.725 | n.a. |
| PS_PERF | 0.878 | 0.884 | 0.905 | 0.579 | 0.411 |

*Source*: Obtained by the author using SmartPLS

**Table 4** Discriminant Validity Indicators (HTMT)

| | DIG_HC | INDUSTRY5_0 | LEARN |
|---|---|---|---|
| INDUSTRY5_0 | 0.819 | | |
| LEARN | 0.327 | 0.337 | |
| PS_PERF | 0.346 | 0.392 | 0.698 |

*Source*: Obtained by the author using SmartPLS

Composite validity indicators in Table 3 demonstrate a high level of consistency (Cronbach's alpha is above the threshold value of 0.7 for all theoretical constructs), and all indicators have an average variance extracted above 50%, indicating that the resulting constructs also have a high proportion of explained variance. The specific competencies of Industry 5.0 required for the transition to human-centric production systems had the highest level of consistency. The coefficient of determination for models in which theoretical constructs are dependent variables is above 30%, except for indicator of the basic competences, which has a coefficient of determination of only 8.9%. This is likely due to the presence of additional factors influencing general digital competencies that were not considered in the study, such as personal experience, level of qualifications, and area of specialization.

The assessment of discriminant validity in Table 4 reveals that each construct exhibits its strongest relationships with the variables that were included in the analysis. This indicates that the chosen variables are indeed reflecting the constructs effectively. Additionally, the Heterotrait-Monotrait ratio of correlations (HTMT) along the diagonal of the table exceeds the threshold values, further confirming that the constructs are distinct from each other and not strongly correlated. This finding supports the discriminant validity of the constructs. Furthermore, the Variance Inflation Factor (VIF) for each explicit variable surpasses the threshold of 5. This outcome suggests that multicollinearity, which can inflate standard errors and hinder the interpretability of path coefficients, is not a significant concern in the analysis.

The main hypotheses were tested using bootstrapping for 5000 iterations, and the results are presented in Table 5 [47]. Basic digital competencies have a strong direct effect on the accumulation of knowledge about Industry 5.0. This finding emphasizes the importance of transforming cyber-physical systems for the transition to cyber-social technologies in production. Employees with the highest level of general competencies are more likely to be knowledgeable about and directly involved in

**Table 5** Path coefficients for direct and indirect effects, results of hypothesis testing and effect size evaluations (5000 bootstrap samples)

| | OS | M | SD | T | p | Hypothesis testing (Effect size) |
|---|---|---|---|---|---|---|
| Direct effects: DIG_HC -> INDUSTRY5_0 | 0.717 | 0.717 | 0.012 | 59.88 | 0.000 | H2.1 accepted (Large) |
| DIG_HC -> PS_PERF | 0.007 | 0.007 | 0.027 | 0.25 | 0.802 | H1.3 rejected (No effect) |
| INDUSTRY5_0 -> PS_PERF | 0.184 | 0.184 | 0.026 | 6.98 | 0.000 | H2.3 accepted (Weak) |
| LEARN -> DIG_HC | 0.299 | 0.299 | 0.018 | 16.43 | 0.000 | H1.1 accepted (Medium) |
| LEARN -> INDUSTRY5_0 | 0.079 | 0.079 | 0.015 | 5.37 | 0.000 | H2.2 accepted (Weak) |
| LEARN -> PS_PERF | 0.560 | 0.561 | 0.018 | 30.79 | 0.000 | H1.2 accepted (Large) |
| Specific indirect effects: DIG_HC -> INDUSTRY5_0 -> PS_PERF | 0.132 | 0.132 | 0.019 | 6.84 | 0.000 | n.a. |
| LEARN -> DIG_HC -> INDUSTRY5_0 | 0.214 | 0.214 | 0.014 | 15.60 | 0.000 | n.a. |
| LEARN -> DIG_HC -> INDUSTRY5_0 -> PS_PERF | 0.039 | 0.039 | 0.006 | 6.23 | 0.000 | n.a. |
| LEARN -> DIG_HC -> PS_PERF | 0.002 | 0.002 | 0.008 | 0.25 | 0.802 | n.a. |
| LEARN -> INDUSTRY5_0 -> PS_PERF | 0.015 | 0.015 | 0.003 | 4.29 | 0.000 | n.a. |

Note: *OS* original sample, *M* sample mean, *SD* standard deviation, *T* *t*-statistics, *p*-values
*Source*: Obtained by the author using SmartPLS

projects related to the implementation of general-purpose technologies. Basic competencies have a weak direct relationship with production system performance because technological factors have a decisive influence on final productivity and resource efficiency. Human capital specific to Industry 5.0 has a weak but statistically significant impact on production system performance. Effective training plays a significant role, not only in digitalization but also in developing the general technical skills needed to implement specific solutions in production. As expected according to proposed hypotheses, training has a positive impact on the basic and special digital skills of production personnel.

To enhance comprehension of the indirect effects, a graphical representation of the results is provided in Fig. 1. Within this visual representation, it becomes evident that basic digital competencies play a pivotal role as a moderator in determining the efficacy of training in fostering human capital specific to Industry 5.0. These competencies serve as a crucial determinant of the effectiveness of converting skills into valuable knowledge resources for the production system, enabling the integration of lean manufacturing technologies and the perpetuation of competitiveness within conventional production systems.

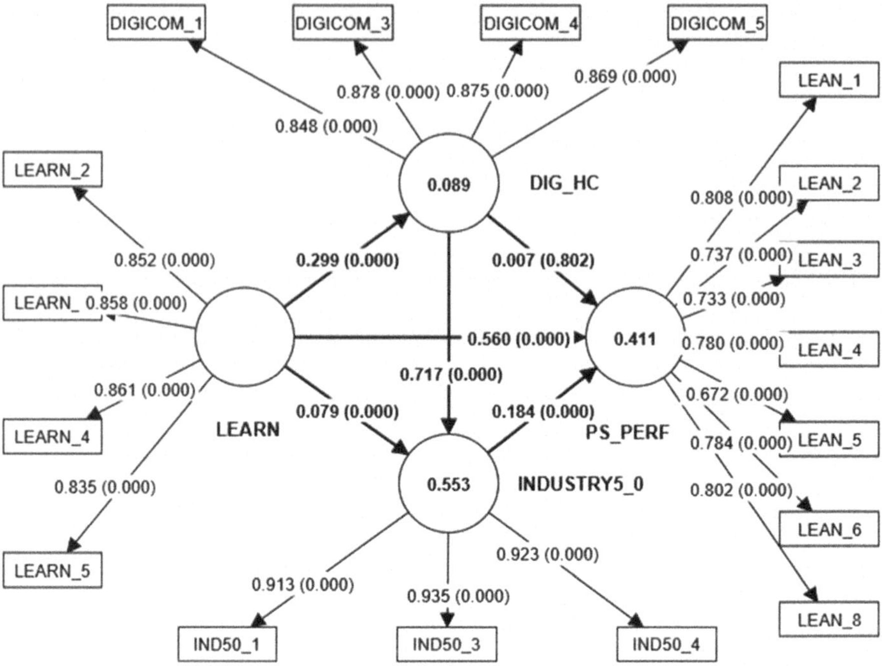


**Fig. 1** Output for of PLS SEM analysis. *Source*: Obtained by the author using SmartPLS

To test for robustness, the author assessed the presence of unobserved heterogeneity and the presence of anomalous deviations from normality that could bias the data [51, 52]. In the first case, a comparison of path coefficients between different groups of respondents, in particular, managers, workers and specialists, did not show significant differences, and therefore the data obtained are characterized by homogeneity. In the second case, the test of skewness and kurtosis measures ranged from −1.37 to 1.95, which imply non-normality of the data, but without significant deviations within the recommended values [51].

Notably, in the current stage of production system transformation, knowledge concerning cyber-social systems assumes a relatively limited role, with the path coefficient for the specific indirect effect of Industry 5.0 on performance measuring less than 0.1. The result is consistent with previous studies assessing knowledge about Industry 4.0 in Russian regions as a precursor to cyber-social systems development stage [43]. However, when considering the influence of general digital competencies, this effect surpasses 0.1 threshold. Observed discrepancy can likely be attributed to the fact that individuals proficient in human-centric digital technologies make up a relatively small segment of the overall manufacturing workforce. Employees' efforts tend to be channeled exclusively toward cutting-edge projects, which, although impactful, exert only a limited influence on the overall performance of manufacturing operations. The findings also generally demonstrate a positive impact of advanced digital skills on firm performance, which is consistent with previous studies of digitalization using structural equation modeling [40, 41].

The surveyed enterprises have been actively implementing technologies in recent years to support operator decision-making, leveraging digital twins and artificial intelligence. These innovations have yielded notable benefits, including optimization of scrap processing, smelting processes, manufacturing of metal products, and quality control before sale. Furthermore, Industry 4.0, by reducing the labor intensity of routine tasks, has created a transitional environment conducive to the integration of cyber-physical systems. However, digitalization has significantly increased the complexity of the internal operational landscape of these enterprises, consequently escalating the demand for highly skilled labor and necessitating the retraining of existing employees. The obtained results confirm the main hypotheses of the study, namely that transition to a new wave of digitalization will improve production efficiency and significantly influence the human capital of companies. Transformation is likely to be even more difficult for companies due to the technological regression of the industry, which is intensifying as a result of the latest sanctions. The competitiveness of conventional industries in the international arena also depends on the technological capabilities of the companies, which lead to more efficient use of resources. It is especially typical for the resource-intensive metallurgy industry. Smart and human-centric digitalization is particularly pertinent to the resource-intensive metallurgy industry that serves as the focus of this study.

## 5 Conclusion

In the past decade, digital transformation has emerged as a central trend in the technological advancement of conventional manufacturing companies. Digital transformation has empowered these companies to enhance environmental transparency, quality of decision-making processes, and to optimize labor costs. While literature continues to deliberate the new wave of digitalization associated with the implementation of cyber-physical systems, companies are now taking their initial practical steps towards realizing the potential of Industry 5.0 on an industrial scale. The primary objective of this article is to investigate the influence of formal on-the-job training effectiveness, the basic and specific digital competencies of personnel on the efficiency of conventional production systems. Illustrated through the context of metallurgy, the study reveals that, although basic digital competencies do not have a direct impact on the performance of the production system, competencies specific to Industry 5.0 establish a robust foundation for lean manufacturing and overall system efficiency. These competencies, in turn, contribute significantly to reinforce the competitiveness of companies. Crucially, the acquisition of knowledge and skills required for working with cyber-social systems is underpinned by the basic digital skills of employees, which encompass proficiency in working with resource management systems, documents, analytical applications, and databases. Such skills serve as the primary driving force behind advanced digitalization, which encompasses artificial intelligence, smart robots, and digital twins.

The theoretical contribution of this study is rooted in its exploration of issues concerning the management of human capital and knowledge in the context of a new technological revolution. The creation of human-centric production systems in conditions of limited labor force associated with the demographic situation, changing preferences of the employed population in the labor market. Migration crisis and sanctions pressure in Russian conditions further sharpen attention to the retention of human capital. Digitalization creates attractive jobs, however in order to implement new technological solutions, companies must first strengthen basic ICT competencies, which will then provide a solid basis for developing more advanced skills. The study also shows the critical role of corporate education quality as a dynamic characteristic of knowledge accumulation that enhances performance of the value chain management. Companies need to attract talent and process champions to build the education and manufacturing digital infrastructure that provides attractive workplaces to retain key, high-skilled talent. The findings of this study emphasize the substantial role played by both the dynamic and static components of knowledge management processes within the context of this new wave of digital transformation.

Cyber-social systems knowledge and skills play a critical role in the future change in the image of conventional industry as an inefficient employer, predominantly exploiting regional resource advantages and physical capital. Social transformation of enterprises must be in accordance with relevant technological trends that determine the role and place of human intelligence in the development of production systems, resource conservation and the implementation of limited growth strategies in the context of global problems of achieving sustainable development goals. The degree of negative impact of the structural restructuring of the labor market caused by the massive introduction of AI will depend on the success of companies in this area. In this regard, this study can confirm the suggestions of the authors, expressed in the previous literature, that Industry 5.0 will be an important historical turn in understanding the harmonious transformation of social and technical systems in the era of intelligent digital automation and collaboration [53, 54].

The practical significance of these findings lies in the recommendations offered to companies for developing strategies aimed at cultivating a workforce that aligns with the requirements of cyber-social systems. Enterprises are currently in the initial stages of restructuring, and they must now consider the convergence of both the social and technical dimensions of development to ensure the performance of their conventional production systems. Measurable goals in a digitalization strategy should pay attention to social aspects, such as quantitative and qualitative characteristics of jobs eliminated and newly created, percentage of staff that will require retraining to integrate virtual and social spaces, and level of return on investment in human capital. Internal standards also need to clarify and separate the competencies characteristic of Industry 4.0 and 5.0 to ensure a clear vector of training and assessment of the technological advantage of an individual company. A more detailed analysis of the risks associated with a new wave of digitalization under the influence of technological sovereignty strategies and sanctions pressure should also be carried out. It is obvious that the competencies created by enterprises will have universal significance for the entire industry on a global scale, increasing competition among employers for human capital.

The concept of human capital within the context of Industry 5.0 is still in its early stages of development, offering ample opportunities for further research and a deeper understanding of the social implications of digital technologies. Numerous authors stress the necessity for both qualitative and quantitative empirical research on the social consequences of technological transformation [54]. Continued exploration in this field is crucial to ensure the alignment of interests among companies, society, and governmental entities in the creation of intelligent production systems, which are designed to harness the creative capabilities and potential of individuals while also leveraging and transforming the existing human capital to facilitate professional and career development.

The study has several limitations. First, an example of the single industry is used for which Industry 5.0 technologies provide only a supporting function and are not at the core of value creation processes. However, understanding the impact of Industry 5.0 knowledge on the performance of low value-added industries is necessary to develop appropriate recommendations and policies for the companies. Second, the use of the PLS-SEM method assumes only linear relationships, but in reality, there is a possibility of diminishing returns from accumulated Industry 5.0 skills in core industries. Third, the study examined a very narrow set of Industry 5.0 digital skills, and soft skills were not included in the model. Future research should examine the presence of nonlinear relationships between competencies and performance in manufacturing systems, but such research will inevitably encounter problems in interpreting coefficients in nonlinear equations. In addition, future research needs to explore the complex impact of Industry 5.0 soft skills on manufacturing performance through the effectiveness of teamwork, communication and internal knowledge sharing.

**Acknowledgments** The study was supported by the Russian Science Foundation grant No. 23-78-10165, https://rscf.ru/project/23-78-10165/.

## References

1. Fukuyama, M. (2018). Society 5.0: Aiming for a new human-centered society. Japan SPOTLIGHT, August, 8–13.
2. Onday, O. (2019). Japan's society 5.0: Going beyond industry 4.0. *Business and Economics Journal, 10*(2), 161–170. https://doi.org/10.4172/2151-6219.1000389
3. Ghobakhloo, M., Iranmanesh, M., Morales, M. E., Nilashi, M., & Amran, A. (2023). Actions and approaches for enabling industry 5.0-driven sustainable industrial transformation: A strategy roadmap. *Corporate Social Responsibility and Environmental Management, 30*(3), 1473–1494. https://doi.org/10.1002/csr.2431
4. Holroyd, C. (2022). Technological innovation and building a 'super smart' society: Japan's vision of society 5.0. *Journal of Asian Public Policy, 15*(1), 18–31. https://doi.org/10.1080/17516234.2020.1749340

5. Saniuk, S., Grabowska, S., & Fahlevi, M. (2023). Personalization of products and sustainable production and consumption in the context of industry 5.0. In C. F. Machado & J. P. Davim (Eds.), *Industry 5.0* (pp. 55–70). Springer International Publishing. https://doi.org/10.1007/978-3-031-26232-6_3
6. Acemoglu, D., & Restrepo, P. (2022). Demographics and automation. *Review of Economic Studies, 89*(1), 1–44. https://doi.org/10.1093/restud/rdab031
7. Iivari, N., Sharma, S., & Ventä-Olkkonen, L. (2020). Digital transformation of everyday life—How COVID-19 pandemic transformed the basic education of the young generation and why information management research should care? *International Journal of Information Management, 55*(June), 102183. https://doi.org/10.1016/j.ijinfomgt.2020.102183
8. Smith, T. S. J., Baranowski, M., & Schmid, B. (2021). Intentional degrowth and its unintended consequences: Uneven journeys towards post-growth transformations. *Ecological Economics, 190*(December 2020), 107215. https://doi.org/10.1016/j.ecolecon.2021.107215
9. Lachvajderová, L., & Kádárová, J. (2022). Industry 4.0 implementation and industry 5.0 readiness in industrial enterprises. *Management and Production Engineering Review, 13*(3), 102–109. https://doi.org/10.24425/mper.2022.142387
10. Kapeliushnikov, R. I. (2023). The Russian labor market: A statistical portrait on the crises background. *Voprosy Ekonomiki, 8*, 5–37. https://doi.org/10.32609/0042-8736-2023-8-5-37
11. Chernenko, I. M., Kelchevskaya, N. R., & Pelymskaya, I. S. (2021). Industry 4.0-specific intellectual capital and its impact on human capital and value added: Evidence from Russian regions. *Lecture Notes in Information Systems and Organisation, 44*. https://doi.org/10.1007/978-3-030-73261-5_16
12. Akberdina, V., Naumov, I., & Krasnykh, S. (2023). Regional digital space and digitalisation of industry: Spatial econometric analysis. In *Lecture Notes in Information Systems and Organisation* (pp. 7–19). https://doi.org/10.1007/978-3-031-30351-7_2.
13. Turovets, Y., & Vishnevskiy, K. (2019). Patterns of digitalisation in machinery-building industries: Evidence from Russia. *Engineering Management in Production and Services, 11*(4), 7–22. https://doi.org/10.2478/emj-2019-0029
14. Akberdina, V., Kalinina, A., & Vlasov, A. (2018). Transformation stages of the Russian industrial complex in the context of economy digitization. *Problems and Perspectives in Management, 16*(4), 201–211. https://doi.org/10.21511/ppm.l6(4).2018.17
15. Sharma, M., Sehrawat, R., Luthra, S., Daim, T., & Bakry, D. (2022). Moving towards industry 5.0 in the pharmaceutical manufacturing sector: Challenges and solutions for Germany. *IEEE Transactions on Engineering Management*, 1–18. https://doi.org/10.1109/TEM.2022.3143466
16. Melnyk, L., Kubatko, O., Matsenko, O., Balatskyi, Y., & Serdyukov, K. (2021). Transformation of the human capital reproduction in line with industries 4.0 and 5.0. *Problems and Perspectives in Management, 19*(2), 480–494. https://doi.org/10.21511/ppm.19(2).2021.38
17. Sá, M. J., Santos, A. I., Serpa, S., & Ferreira, C. M. (2021). Digital literacy in digital society 5.0: Some challenges. Academic. *Journal of Interdisciplinary Studies, 10*(2), 1–9. https://doi.org/10.36941/ajis-2021-0033
18. Suan Chin, S. T. (2021). Influence of emotional intelligence on the workforce for industry 5.0. *Journal of Human Resources Management Research, 2021*, 1–7. https://doi.org/10.5171/2021.882278
19. Abdrakhmanova, G., Vasilkovsky, S., Vishnevskiy, K., & Gokhberg, L. (2023). *Digital economy indicators in The Russian Federation: 2022 : Data book*. National Research University Higher School of Economics. https://doi.org/10.17323/978-5-7598-2697-2
20. Ghobakhloo, M. (2018). The future of manufacturing industry: A strategic roadmap toward industry 4.0. *Journal of Manufacturing Technology Management, 29*(6), 910–936. https://doi.org/10.1108/JMTM-02-2018-0057
21. Javaid, M., & Haleem, A. (2020). Critical components of industry 5.0 towards a successful adoption in the field of manufacturing. *Journal of Industrial Integration and Management, 5*(3), 327–348. https://doi.org/10.1142/S2424862220500141

22. Javaid, M., Haleem, A., Singh, R. P., Ul Haq, M. I., Raina, A., & Suman, R. (2020). Industry 5.0: Potential applications in covid-19. *Journal of Industrial Integration and Management, 5*(4), 507–530. https://doi.org/10.1142/S2424862220500220
23. Battini, D., Berti, N., Finco, S., Zennaro, I., & Das, A. (2022). Towards industry 5.0: A multi-objective job rotation model for an inclusive workforce. *International Journal of Production Economics, 250*(August), 108619. https://doi.org/10.1016/j.ijpe.2022.108619
24. Elmassah, S., & Hassanein, E. A. (2022). Digitalization and subjective wellbeing in Europe. *Digital Policy, Regulation and Governance, 24*(1), 52–73. https://doi.org/10.1108/DPRG-05-2021-0060
25. Kolagar, M., Parida, V., & Sjödin, D. (2022). Ecosystem transformation for digital servitization: A systematic review, integrative framework, and future research agenda. *Journal of Business Research, 146*(May 2021), 176–200. https://doi.org/10.1016/j.jbusres.2022.03.067
26. de Dornelles, J. A., Ayala, N. F., & Frank, A. G. (2023). Collaborative or substitutive robots? Effects on workers' skills in manufacturing activities. *International Journal of Production Research, 61*(22), 7922–7955. https://doi.org/10.1080/00207543.2023.2240912
27. Frey, C. B., & Osborne, M. A. (2017). The future of employment: How susceptible are jobs to computerisation? *Technological Forecasting and Social Change, 114*(1), 254–280. https://doi.org/10.1016/j.techfore.2016.08.019
28. Taverner, C., Trojan, L., Simion, O., & Szkudlarek, E. (2021). Design culture in the era of industry 5.0: A review of skills and needs. *Cultural Management: Science and Education, 5*(1), 41–58. https://doi.org/10.30819/cmse.5-1.03
29. Kolade, O., & Owoseni, A. (2022). Employment 5.0: The work of the future and the future of work. *Technology in Society, 71*(March), 102086. https://doi.org/10.1016/j.techsoc.2022.102086
30. Maisiri, W., Darwish, H., & van Dyk, L. (2019). An investigation of industry 4.0 skills requirements. *South African Journal of Industrial Engineering, 30*(3), 90–105. https://doi.org/10.7166/30-3-2230
31. Olšanová, K., Křenková, E., Hnát, P., & Vilikus, O. (2022). Workforce readiness for industry 4.0 from the perspective of employers: Evidence from The Czech Republic. *Industry and Higher Education, 36*(6), 807–823. https://doi.org/10.1177/09504222221075552
32. Rikala, P., Braun, G., Järvinen, M., Stahre, J., & Hämäläinen, R. (2024). Understanding and measuring skill gaps in industry 4.0 — A review. *Technological Forecasting and Social Change, 201*(January), 123206. https://doi.org/10.1016/j.techfore.2024.123206
33. Quintero, W. R. (2022). Digital competences of the industrial engineer in industry 4.0 a systematic vision. *Production, 32*. https://doi.org/10.1590/0103-6513.20220028
34. Gürdür Broo, D., Kaynak, O., & Sait, S. M. (2022). Rethinking engineering education at the age of industry 5.0. *Journal of Industrial Information Integration, 25*(May 2021), 100311. https://doi.org/10.1016/j.jii.2021.100311
35. Abiodun, T. S., Rampersad, G., & Brinkworth, R. (2023). Driving smartness for organizational performance through industry 4.0: A systems perspective. *Journal of Manufacturing Technology Management, 34*(9), 40–63. https://doi.org/10.1108/JMTM-09-2022-0335
36. Bhandari, K. R., Zámborský, P., Ranta, M., & Salo, J. (2023). Digitalization, internationalization, and firm performance: A resource-orchestration perspective on new OLI advantages. *International Business Review, 32*(4). https://doi.org/10.1016/j.ibusrev.2023.102135
37. Meng, F., & Wang, W. (2023). The impact of digitalization on enterprise value creation: An empirical analysis of Chinese manufacturing enterprises. *Journal of Innovation and Knowledge, 8*(3), 100385. https://doi.org/10.1016/j.jik.2023.100385
38. Yuan, C., Liu, W., Zhou, G., Shi, X., Long, S., Chen, Z., & Yan, X. (2022). Supply chain innovation announcements and shareholder value under industries 4.0 and 5.0: Evidence from China. *Industrial Management and Data Systems, 122*(8), 1909–1937. https://doi.org/10.1108/IMDS-12-2021-0802
39. Rossini, M., Costa, F., Tortorella, G. L., Valvo, A., & Portioli-Staudacher, A. (2022). Lean production and industry 4.0 integration: How lean automation is emerging in manufacturing

industry. *International Journal of Production Research, 60*(21), 6430–6450. https://doi.org/10.1080/00207543.2021.1992031

40. Hautala-Kankaanpää, T. (2022). The impact of digitalization on firm performance: Examining the role of digital culture and the effect of supply chain capability. *Business Process Management Journal, 28*(8), 90–109. https://doi.org/10.1108/BPMJ-03-2022-0122
41. Kastelli, I., Dimas, P., Stamopoulos, D., & Tsakanikas, A. (2022). Linking Digital Capacity to Innovation Performance: the Mediating Role of Absorptive Capacity. Journal of the Knowledge Economy (Issue 0123456789). Springer US. https://doi.org/10.1007/s13132-022-01092-w.
42. Tortorella, G. L., Anzanello, M. J., Fogliatto, F. S., Antony, J., & Nascimento, D. (2022). Effect of industry 4.0 technologies adoption on the learning process of workers in a quality inspection operation. *International Journal of Production Research.* https://doi.org/10.1080/00207543.2022.2153943
43. Amiron, E., Latib, A. A., & Subari, K. (2019). Industry revolution 4.0 skills and enablers in technical and vocational education and training curriculum. *International Journal of Recent Technology and Engineering, 8*(1C2), 484–490.
44. Rossini, M., Cifone, F. D., Kassem, B., Costa, F., & Portioli-Staudacher, A. (2021). Being lean: How to shape digital transformation in the manufacturing sector. *Journal of Manufacturing Technology Management, 32*(9), 239–259. https://doi.org/10.1108/JMTM-12-2020-0467
45. Rožanec, J. M., Novalija, I., Zajec, P., Kenda, K., Tavakoli Ghinani, H., Suh, S., Veliou, E., Papamartzivanos, D., Giannetsos, T., Menesidou, S. A., Alonso, R., Cauli, N., Meloni, A., Recupero, D. R., Kyriazis, D., Sofianidis, G., Theodoropoulos, S., Fortuna, B., Mladenić, D., & Soldatos, J. (2023). Human-centric artificial intelligence architecture for industry 5.0 applications. *International Journal of Production Research, 61*(20), 6847–6872. https://doi.org/10.1080/00207543.2022.2138611
46. Kolyasnikov, M. S., & Kelchevskaya, N. R. (2020). Knowledge management strategies in companies: Trends and the impact of industry 4.0. *Upravlenets (The Manager), 11*(4), 82–96.
47. Hair, J. F., & Hult, G. T. M. (2022). *A primer on partial least squares structural equation modeling (PLS-SEM)* (3rd ed.). Sage Publications, Inc.
48. Terdpaopong, K., Puapradit, A., & Malisuwan, U. (2021). The effect of lean on the operational performance of medium-sized Thai manufacturing companies. *Uncertain Supply Chain Management, 9*(3), 647–658. https://doi.org/10.5267/j.uscm.2021.5.005
49. Valente, C. M., Sousa, P. S. A., & Moreira, M. R. A. (2020). Assessment of the lean effect on business performance: The case of manufacturing SMEs. *Journal of Manufacturing Technology Management, 31*(3), 501–523. https://doi.org/10.1108/JMTM-04-2019-0137
50. Kock, N., & Hadaya, P. (2018). Minimum sample size estimation in PLS-SEM: The inverse square root and gamma-exponential methods. *Information Systems Journal, 28*(1), 227–261. https://doi.org/10.1111/isj.12131
51. Vaithilingam, S., Ong, C. S., Moisescu, O. I., & Nair, M. S. (2024). Robustness checks in PLS-SEM: A review of recent practices and recommendations for future applications in business research. *Journal of Business Research, 173*(5), 114465. https://doi.org/10.1016/j.jbusres.2023.114465
52. Sarstedt, M., Ringle, C. M., Cheah, J. H., Ting, H., Moisescu, O. I., & Radomir, L. (2020). Structural model robustness checks in PLS-SEM. *Tourism Economics, 26*(4), 531–554. https://doi.org/10.1177/1354816618823921
53. Ghobakhloo, M., Iranmanesh, M., Foroughi, B., Babaee Tirkolaee, E., Asadi, S., & Amran, A. (2023). Industry 5.0 implications for inclusive sustainable manufacturing: An evidence-knowledge-based strategic roadmap. *Journal of Cleaner Production, 417*(June), 138023. https://doi.org/10.1016/j.jclepro.2023.138023
54. Grybauskas, A., Stefanini, A., & Ghobakhloo, M. (2022). Social sustainability in the age of digitalization: A systematic literature review on the social implications of industry 4.0. *Technology in Society, 70*(April), 101997. https://doi.org/10.1016/j.techsoc.2022.101997

# Part V
# Prospects for Digital Transformation Towards Industry 5.0

# The Impact of Digital Transformation on Labor Productivity of Chinese Small and Medium-Sized Enterprises (SMEs)

**Yongjing Shi**

**Abstract** As an important driving force and trend in world economic development, digital transformation is reshaping operations and competitiveness of enterprises globally. However, empirical evidence regarding its impact on labor productivity remains limited, especially for small and medium-sized enterprises (SMEs). The study aims to examine the impact of digital transformation on labor productivity of Chinese SMEs. By using panel data on 7762 Chinese SMEs from The 14th Survey of Private Enterprises in China conducted by ACFIC in 2020, the study presents a quantitative analysis of the direct and indirect impact of digitization level on labor productivity. The results revealed an initial negative impact of digitization followed by positive returns after reaching the threshold, demonstrating an overall U-shaped relationship between them. Technological progress, organizational change, and labor mobility are key impact mechanisms linking digital transformation and labor productivity. Moreover, the impact varied across regions and industries due to differences in contextual factors. Furthermore, the study also offers practical implications for Chinese SMEs to enhance labor productivity through digital transformation, such as aligning technical and social subsystems to maximize synergy, refreshing employee skills, and embracing labor mobility, developing digital strategies tailored to their industries and regions, etc.

**Keywords** Digital transformation · Labor productivity · SMEs

## 1 Introduction

In recent years, many enterprises have accelerated their pace of digitalization, which has become a key force guiding traditional businesses to transform into networking, intelligence, and automation [1]. Digital transformation has changed the production methods and business models of enterprises, and improved their operating efficiency

Y. Shi (✉)
Southern Federal University, Rostov-on-Don, Russian Federation
e-mail: yushi@sfedu.ru



A. Appolloni et al. (eds.), *The Future of Industry*, Lecture Notes in Information Systems and Organisation 70, https://doi.org/10.1007/978-3-031-66801-2_30

[2]. As a significant impetus for the advancement of the global economy, digital transformation has extensively influenced various sectors across the world [3]. According to forecasts by the of International Data Corporation (IDC) [4], global spending on digital transformation is expected to reach $3.4 trillion by 2026, accounting for more than 53% of global GDP. However, empirical evidence on whether digital transformation of enterprises improves labor productivity is still scarce, and its potential impact mechanism remains to be elucidated. This is the main gap in research.

China, being the largest developing country globally, also has the greatest concentration of small and medium-sized enterprises (SMEs) worldwide. By the end of 2022, China had over 52 million SMEs, representing 99.8% of all market entities. These SMEs contributed over 60% of China's GDP, 50% of tax revenues, and 80% of the employment, and drove China's economic growth [5]. However, Chinese SMEs are currently facing many difficulties and challenges, such as small scale, difficult financing, low labor productivity, etc.

The article aims to examine the impact of digital transformation on labor productivity of Chinese SMEs and provide some recommendations for improving their labor productivity through digital transformation. The study adopts empirical research methods and uses panel data on Chinese SMEs to comprehensively examine the impact of digitalization level on their labor productivity and the impact mechanisms. This could compensate for the disadvantages of existing research.

The study will examine the impact of digital transformation on labor productivity of Chinese SMEs in five steps. Part 1 presents a critical analysis of existing theories pertaining to digital transformation, labor productivity, and the impact of digital transformation on labor productivity. Part 2 justifies the research methodology, including the overall research design, samples, data collection methods, and data analysis methods of the study. Part 3 conducts quantitative analysis of the collected panel data and obtain corresponding results. Part 4 discusses the research results and makes comparative analysis of the similarities and differences between the results and existing research results. Part 5 draws the conclusion and makes recommendations for Chinese SMEs to improve their labor productivity through digital transformation.

## 2 Literature Review

Digital transformation has become an increasingly important topic in recent years as new digital technologies reshape the way in which enterprises operate and compete. Many researchers have examined how digital transformation affects various aspects of corporate performance, including labor productivity. To investigate the impact of digital transformation on labor productivity of Chinese SMEs, the study reviews the current research on digital transformation, labor productivity, and the impact of the former on the latter.

## 2.1 Digital Transformation

Digital transformation entails the integration and utilization of digital technologies across business operations, which fundamentally changes traditional ways of doing business [2, 6]. It is not just about adopting new technologies, but also digitally implementing all processes, functions, and models to improve operational efficiency and competitiveness [1, 7]. The core of digital transformation lies in data-driven decision making that leverages internal and external data sources [8]. Digital transformation aims to improve an organization by optimizing operational efficiency, reducing costs, and enhancing customer experience [3].

Several studies have attempted to measure the level of digital transformation across enterprises and industries. Parviainen et al. [9] proposed a Digital Transformation Scoreboard to assess the progress of digital transformation from three key dimensions, namely digital intensity, transformation capacity, and transformation management. Some other researchers (see, e.g., [10, 11]) evaluated digital maturity by using surveys on the adoption level of digital technologies. However, the research on systematically measuring the digitization level of SMEs remains limited.

Key technologies driving digital transformation include artificial intelligence, cloud computing, big data analytics, the Internet of Things (IoT), and mobile technologies [12]. These technologies enable virtual collaboration, data-based optimization, automation, and new digital business models. Enterprises implement digital transformation through initiatives in areas like digital marketing, digital production, digital supply chain, and digital decision-making [1].

In addition, digital transformation has several defining characteristics that differentiate it from isolated technology adoption. Firstly, it is multidimensional, involving strategy, leadership, culture, and technology across the organization [2]. Secondly, the scope and depth of digital transformation is significant, and affects most operations and processes. Thirdly, the integration between digital technologies creates synergistic value. Lastly, digital transformation could cause disruptive transformation rather than incremental improvement [6].

## 2.2 Labor Productivity

Labor productivity refers to the efficiency of labor in generating output, which is measured by output per labor hour and other indicators [13]. Labor productivity, as a vital catalyst for long-term economic expansion and competitiveness, is deemed one of the most crucial factors influencing a country's economic growth and competitiveness. Existing literature has examined labor productivity by using various indicators (such as GDP per hours, value-added per employee, sales per employee, etc.), mostly based on macroeconomic and industry-level data.

At the enterprise level, some researchers (see, e.g., [14, 15]) found that managerial practices, human capital, and information technology are positively associated with labor productivity, while labor regulations and volatility exhibit negative impacts on it. Recent research also investigated the link between Artificial Intelligence (AI) and labor productivity, and showed an inverted U-shaped relationship [16, 17]. However, there is limited enterprise-level empirical evidence on how emerging digital technologies affect labor productivity, especially for SMEs.

Several factors are proved to have influence labor productivity, including labor quality, corporate strategy, operational efficiency, technology adoption, and management capabilities [3, 13]. Investments in human capital, job training, and skills development are critical for improving labor quality [18]. Labor productivity also depends on how enterprises effectively use automation, streamline processes, and best practices [19].

According to Wang et al. [8], enterprises try to enhance labor productivity through various initiatives, such as optimizing industry structure, strengthening technology innovation, improving incentive systems, and increasing human capital investment. Government policies around areas like education, infrastructure, and the business environment also play an important role [19].

## 2.3 *Impact of Digital Transformation on Labor Productivity*

The emerging research has started examining the impact of digital technologies and transformation initiatives on labor productivity, though studies focused specifically on SMEs remain scarce.

Earlier studies concentrated more on the productivity paradox—the lack of productivity gains from IT investment [20], but recent empirical research has identified a positive correlation between technology adoption and labor productivity. Advanced manufacturing technologies and data-driven decision-making platforms could improve operational performance and labor productivity of manufacturing enterprises [21, 22].

Apart from specific technologies, a comprehensive digital transformation strategy can also boost labor productivity. Digital transformation enhances the labor productivity of European enterprises by improving information flow and access, increasing labor flexibility, and accelerating decision-making speed [23]. A study on manufacturing SMEs found that a higher level of digital transformation positively influences labor productivity [24].

However, the impact of digital transformation on labor productivity depends on how well digital technologies are integrated into work processes and routines [25]. Complementary organizational changes involving human resource practices, decentralized decision rights, and personnel training are often needed to realize productivity gains [14].

Moreover, differences in managerial capabilities and limited financial resources may constrain technology absorption in SMEs [26]. From a socio-technical perspective, Rai et al. [27] concluded that SMEs can achieve higher returns on digital technologies when the social and technical subsystems are aligned. Bounfour [28] suggested that digital technologies enable enterprises to conduct process innovations, reduce production costs, and improve labor productivity. Leveraging automation and data analytics can optimize operational efficiency and raise productivity of enterprises [29]. However, Acemoglu and Restrepo [30] argued that digital innovation may also displace labor and cause temporary productivity decline before reaching symbiotic integration between human beings and digitalization.

Although many studies indicate an overall positive impact of digital transformation on labor productivity, the relationship between them may be non-linear. Digital technologies could initially displace laborers performing routine tasks, and hurt productivity until processes are redesigned and laborers acquire new skills [30]. The influencing factors of labor productivity may vary across industries, regions, and enterprise sizes [25].

In particular, several empirical studies examined the impact of IT investment and usage on labor productivity at the enterprise and industry levels, and showed mixed results [31, 32]. Although IT capital was found to make a small contribution, its impact depends on complementary organizational investment and transformation [33].

### *2.4 Summary*

The existing literature provides preliminary evidence that digital transformation and adoption of emerging digital technologies could improve labor productivity, depending on complementary organizational change. However, conclusions remain tentative due to the focus on large enterprises. The mechanisms that digital transformation affects labor productivity include the role of technical and social alignment, which requires further investigation. Additionally, further research is needed on how digital transformation influences the labor productivity of SMEs across different industries and regions could provide valuable practical insights. This study could bridge this research gap by systematically investigating the impact of digital transformation on labor productivity of Chinese SMEs and the potential impact mechanisms. The results are expected to provide valuable theoretical and practical implications.

## 3 Research Methodology

### *3.1 Research Design*

The study adopted a quantitative research design. Specifically, it conducted empirical research on the impact of digital transformation on labor productivity of Chinese SMEs. Through quantitative research, this paper could collect quantitative data on the digital transformation, and labor productivity of Chinese SMEs, and identify the relationship between them through statistical analysis. By controlling some variables, this study could examine under what conditions digital transformation has a positive or negative impact on labor productivity. In addition, through quantitative research, we could collect large-scale data samples and make the research results more representative. Meanwhile, quantitative research allowed the study to empirically test whether the correlation between digital transformation and labor productivity is statistically significant, summarize the strength of this relationship, and make the research conclusions more explanatory. Furthermore, empirical results could also help validate or improve existing theories, and provide practical guidance for Chinese SMEs to better carry out digital transformation, so as to improve their labor productivity.

### *3.2 Sample*

The data utilized in the research was gathered from The 14th Survey of Private Enterprises in China conducted by All-China Federation of Industry and Commerce (ACFIC) [34]. With the stratified random sampling, this nationwide survey collected detailed data on more than 10,000 private enterprises across 31 provinces/municipalities in China. The original samples contained 8907 enterprises, of which over 95% were SMEs with less than 300 employees. After eliminating observations with missing values, the final samples included 7762 SMEs, which provided representative samples of Chinese SMEs suitable for this empirical research.

### *3.3 Data Collection*

The Survey of Private Enterprises in China is organized by ACFIC every 2 years. The survey collects comprehensive data regarding the operations, management, and growth of private enterprises in China. It provides rich firm-level data, such as financial performance, use of digital technologies, entrepreneur characteristics, management practices, institutional environment, etc. The 2016 Survey of Private Enterprises in China contained specific information on Chinese private enterprises' digital transformation and Internet usage, which allowed this study to construct measurements of their digitization level. The samples covered 31 provinces or municipalities in China, which enabled the analysis to well control regional heterogeneity.

## *3.4 Model Specification*

To examine the impact of Chinese SMEs' digital transformation on labor productivity, the study proposed the following model:

$$\text{Labor}_{ijp} = \beta_0 + \beta_1 \text{Digitize}_{ijp} + \beta_2 \text{Digitize}_{ijp}^2 + \beta_3 \text{Controls} + \varepsilon_{ijp} \qquad (1)$$

In the model, *i, j* and *p* represented respectively enterprise, industry, and province. Clustered standard errors at the enterprise level were used to address heteroskedasticity and autocorrelation. $\text{Labor}_{ijp}$ denotes Chinese SMEs' labor productivity; $\text{Digitize}_{ijp}$ denotes the level of Chinese SMEs' digitization; and $\text{Digitize}_{ijp}^2$ denotes its squared term. In addition, Controls denote the control variables; and $\varepsilon_{ijp}$ denotes the error term.

The setting of the model was mainly based on three considerations. Firstly, previous studies have shown that there may be a non-linear relationship between enterprise digital transformation and labor productivity [30]. Thus, the model incorporated both the linear and quadratic terms of enterprise digitalization level to examine the possible non-linear relationship between the two variables. Secondly, the level of enterprise digitalization is affected by some other factors (such as entrepreneurial characteristics, corporate characteristics, etc.), so the model introduced several control variables to distinguish the impact of these factors. Thirdly, since the samples involved SMEs from different industries and regions, the model adopted clustering robust standard error to solve intergroup heteroscedasticity, autocorrelation, and other econometric issues. Generally, the model involved the following three types of variables:

(1) *Dependent variable*

Labor productivity (Labor) was the dependent variable, which was measured by the natural logarithm of (tax revenue + post-tax profit + total salary) / number of employees, representing the added value created by per employee [35]. This indicator directly reflected the efficiency of enterprises in using human resources to create value, and can effectively measure the labor productivity level of enterprises. Previous studies on the impact of information technology on labor productivity have used this indicator [33] for comparison with existing literature.

*(2) Independent variable.*

Digitization level (Digitize) was the independent variable, which was constructed by using iterative principal component analysis based on the intensity of enterprises' usage of nine Internet applications, including e-commerce (i.e., establishing a corporate website, and opening an online shop), online marketing, social media adoption, talent recruitment, and others [3, 36]. These nine aspects could provide a comprehensive measurement of digitization level of Chinese SMEs from aspects of products, channels, processes, and business models. The principal component analysis could solve the problem of multicollinearity among indicators in various fields, and extract common factors as comprehensive measures, so this method is reasonable.

Among those nine aspects, the intensity of e-commerce usage was measured by the weighted average of whether an enterprise has established an official website or opened an online store, with weights assigned based on their importance in the e-commerce field. The intensity of online marketing was measured by the weighted average of whether an enterprise conducts online advertising and publicity. The operation intensity of social media was measured by the weighted average of whether an enterprise has established microblog, WeChat official account, and search auction ranking. The intensity of talent recruitment was measured by the frequency of an enterprise publishing recruitment information on the Internet. Moreover, the intensity of other Internet applications was measured by the sum of scores of enterprises in cooperation with Internet enterprises and customer communication services.

*(3) Control variables.*

Control variables mainly involved entrepreneurs' characteristics (such as entrepreneurs' age, gender, education level, etc.), SMEs' characteristics (such as SMEs' age, size, average wage, etc.), and the institutional development of the provinces where SMEs are located. Among them, entrepreneurs' characteristics could affect corporate strategy, which in turn affects digital transformation and labor productivity of their enterprises [3]. In addition, there are differences in resource endowments and factor costs among different enterprises and provinces, which could also affect two key variables [8].

Moreover, based on Solow's [37] research, our study also incorporated total factor productivity as a control variable into the model to distinguish between the direct effects of digital transformation on labor productivity and the indirect effects generated by influencing total factor productivity.

Generally, the model could systematically examine the nonlinear impact of digitalization level of Chinese SMEs on labor productivity based on previous research, while strictly distinguishing the impacts of other factors. The measurement of variables was direct and reasonable, and the required data could also be directly obtained or indirectly calculated from survey data. Thus, the model could effectively answer the core question of this study.

## 3.5 Data Analysis

In our research, the ordinary least squares (OLS) regression was first conducted to examine the baseline relationship between digital transformation on labor productivity of Chinese SMEs. To address endogeneity concerns, we adopted the instrumental variable approach by using the industry and province average digitization level as instrument.

In addition, the study analyzed the roles of three mediating variables (i.e., technological progress, organizational change, and labor mobility) between digital transformation on labor productivity of Chinese SMEs, so as to test the mechanisms through which digital transformation affects labor productivity.

Moreover, the paper also conducted heterogeneity analysis to investigate potential variations across regions and industries.

# 4 Results

With the panel data collected from The 14th Survey of Private Enterprises in China conducted by ACFIC [34], our study carried out the regression analysis to examine the direct impact of digital transformation on labor productivity of Chinese SMEs, analyzed the mediating role of three control variables between digital transformation and labor productivity, and made heterogeneity analysis to examine potential variations across regions and industries. The results are shown below.

## *4.1 Direct Impact of Enterprise Digitization on Labor Productivity*

The baseline regression results in Table 1 demonstrate a significant non-linear U-shaped relationship between digitization level and labor productivity of Chinese SMEs. The estimated correlation coefficient on the digitization item was negatively significant, while its squared item was positively significant. This suggests that at lower levels, increasing digitalization hampers labor productivity, but once digitization goes beyond a threshold, further digitalization could enhance labor productivity of Chinese SMEs.

One potential explanation is that initial automation and digital integration may displace some laborers and temporarily reduce productivity until processes are redesigned and laborers acquire new skills. However, at higher digitization levels, the benefits of improved information flows, flexibility, and management could outweigh the costs. Crossing the digitization threshold may lead to synergistic gains in labor productivity.

**Table 1** Baseline regression results

| Variables | Coefficient | Standard Error |
|---|---|---|
| Digitization | −0.6362*** | 0.1064 |
| $\text{Digitization}^2$ | 0.2393* | 0.1207 |
| Constant | 4.3853*** | 0.7399 |
| Observations | 6233 | |
| $R^2$ | 0.53 | |

Dependent variable: Labor productivity
* $p < 0.05$; ** $p < 0.01$; *** $p < 0.001$

**Table 2** Instrumental variable regression results

| Variables | Coefficient | Standard Error |
|---|---|---|
| Digitization | −1.3425* | 0.5702 |
| Digitization$^2$ | 0.8390* | 0.3862 |
| Constant | 4.1398*** | 0.7594 |
| Observations | 6233 | |
| $R^2$ | 0.527 | |

* $p < 0.05$; ** $p < 0.01$; *** $p < 0.001$

**Table 3** Mediation analysis—Technological progress

| Variables | Coefficient | Standard Error |
|---|---|---|
| Digitization | −0.6362*** | 0.1064 |
| Digitization$^2$ | 0.2393* | 0.1207 |
| Technology innovation | −0.3457*** | 0.0891 |
| Green R&D | −0.1489* | 0.0692 |
| Constant | 4.3853*** | 0.7399 |
| Observations | 6233 | |
| $R^2$ | 0.53 | |

* $p < 0.05$; ** $p < 0.01$; *** $p < 0.001$

Calculations using the regression estimates indicate that only 65 Chinese SMEs out of nearly 8000 sample enterprises have surpassed the digitization threshold and had a positive impact on their labor productivity. This highlights that most Chinese SMEs still have a lot of room to implement digital transformation and reap productivity gains.

In addition, the non-linear relationship was verified through an instrumental variable approach to address endogeneity concerns, as shown in Table 2. The instruments passed weak identification and overidentification tests, and confirmed their validity. The U-shaped pattern remains robust after instrumenting for potential reverse causality and omitted variable bias.

### 4.2 *Indirect Impact of Enterprise Digitization on Labor Productivity*

In addition to direct impact, this study also examined the indirect impact of digital transformation on labor productivity of Chinese SMEs through the following three mediating variables, so as to understand the impact mechanisms between two key variables.

(1) *Mediating role of technological progress*

The results in Table 3 indicated that promoting technological innovation and green R&D investment partially explains the negative impact of digitization on labor

**Table 4** Mediation analysis—Organizational change

| Variables | Coefficient | Standard Error |
|---|---|---|
| Digitization | −0.6362*** | 0.1064 |
| $Digitization^2$ | 0.2393* | 0.1207 |
| Organizational structure | −0.1959*** | 0.0141 |
| Constant | 4.3853*** | 0.7399 |
| Observations | 6233 | |
| $R^2$ | 0.53 | |

* $p < 0.05$; ** $p < 0.01$; *** $p < 0.001$

**Table 5** Mediation analysis—Labor mobility

| Variables | Coefficient | Standard Error |
|---|---|---|
| Digitization | −0.6362*** | 0.1064 |
| $Digitization^2$ | 0.2393* | 0.1207 |
| Employee turnover | 1.1373*** | 0.1418 |
| Constant | 4.3853*** | 0.7399 |
| Observations | 6233 | |
| $R^2$ | 0.53 | |

* $p < 0.05$; ** $p < 0.01$; *** $p < 0.001$

productivity of Chinese SMEs. The substitution of technology for labor contributes to the initially inhibitory impact. However, once digital integration reaches a mature level and complementary utilization of technology and labor is achieved, the net impact would become positive. The evidence confirmed the non-linear impact of digitization level on labor productivity through promoting technological progress.

(2) *Mediating role of organizational change*

Table 4 revealed that increased lateral coordination and flattening of organizational structure due to digitization negatively affects labor productivity of Chinese SMEs. This suggests that organizational change brought by SMEs' digital transformation has not effectively improved decision-making efficiency. Capturing the benefits of decentralization remains a challenge.

As digitization level deepens and decision autonomy gets guided through appropriate mechanisms, organizational change can contribute positively to labor productivity of Chinese SMEs. However, the current negative mediating effect explains the U-shaped relationship between digitization transformation and labor productivity.

(3) *Mediating role of labor mobility*

Results in Table 5 showed that digital transformation increases labor mobility in terms of employee turnover, which in turn improves labor productivity. This indicates that the use of digital technology and data-driven management enables Chinese SMEs to optimize employee composition and skill profiles more frequently through external employment. By refreshing skill sets and enhancing employee motivation, increased labor mobility is a positive mediator in the nonlinear productivity impact of digitalization. This complements the substitution effect arising from technological progress.

## 4.3 Heterogeneity Analysis

Further analysis revealed heterogeneity in the relationship between digitization and productivity across regions and industries of Chinese SMEs. As shown in Table 6, the U-shaped relationship between the two key variables in the Eastern region of China was the most obvious, while the relationship between them in the Central and Northern regions was relatively weaker. This highlights the moderating impact of economic and Internet maturity levels.

Examining industry variation in Table 7 suggests that the negative impact of digitization on labor productivity is relatively larger in non-industrial (such as service, agriculture, etc.) and labor-intensive industries than industrial and capital-intensive industries. Therefore, industry production modes and factor intensity are also main factors of heterogeneity.

In summary, the quantitative results provide robust evidence that enterprise digitization has a nonlinear, U-shaped impact on labor productivity of Chinese SMEs. Technological progress, organizational change, and labor mobility are key mechanisms explaining this relationship. Moreover, the impact of enterprise digitization on labor productivity varies considerably based on regional and industry contexts.

**Table 6** Regional heterogeneity

| Region | Digitization | $\text{Digitization}^2$ |
|---|---|---|
| Eastern | −0.7877*** | 0.4502** |
| Central | −0.3355 | −0.2980 |
| Northern | 0.0760 | −0.2920 |
| Western | −0.9353*** | 0.3393 |

* $p < 0.05$; ** $p < 0.01$; *** $p < 0.001$

**Table 7** Industry heterogeneity

| Industry | Digitization | $\text{Digitization}^2$ |
|---|---|---|
| Industrial | −0.4085* | 0.2524 |
| Non-industrial | −0.7669*** | 0.1982 |
| Labor-intensive | −0.7454*** | 0.2497 |
| Capital-intensive | −0.0224 | 0.0497 |

* $p < 0.05$; ** $p < 0.01$; *** $p < 0.001$

## 5 Discussion

The empirical results provide several interesting findings that add to the existing research on digital transformation and its relationship with labor productivity.

Firstly, the U-shaped relationship between enterprise digitization level and labor productivity of Chinese SMEs aligns with existing evidence of an initial substitution effect followed by complementary gains [30]. However, our study offers a more nuanced analysis by identifying the digitization threshold, which most Chinese SMEs are yet to exceed. The negative impact of digitization level on labor productivity before reaching adequate maturity corroborates Arvanitis' [31] research on the productivity paradox of IT investment. Nevertheless, potential synergistic productivity gains at higher digitization levels are consistent with more recent studies that demonstrate positive returns from advanced IT applications when combined with appropriate organizational change [14, 24].

Secondly, the analysis of mediating mechanisms provides empirical support for the socio-technical perspective emphasized by Rai et al. [27]. The negative impact of technological progress and organizational change align with the notion that realizing productivity benefits requires compatible social and technical subsystems. This explains the non-linear relationship better than a purely technical focus. In addition, increasing labor mobility reflects refreshing of employee skills, and offers new evidence on how digital technologies may positively transform the workforce.

Thirdly, identifying regional and industry variations enriches the research by underscoring the significance of contextual factors in digital technology adoption and impact [25]. The moderating effects of economic and Internet maturity levels as well as production modes and factor intensity across regions and industries are consistent with the key findings of Bloom et al. [14] and Mazzarol [26] on the role of complementary capabilities and constraints faced by SMEs.

Overall, the current study provides some of the first empirical evidence regarding the impact of comprehensive digital transformation on labor productivity specifically for SMEs in China and other emerging economies. The results deepen the understanding of the mechanisms through which enterprise digitization level affects labor productivity. The findings suggest that efforts to coordinate technical and social aspects as well as tailored strategies based on context are needed to realize the benefits of digital transformation. More research can further examine the development of complementary organizational capabilities in SMEs that shape the impact of digital technologies on labor productivity.

## 6 Conclusion

The present study conducted empirical research on the impact of digital transformation on labor productivity of Chinese SMEs and the specific impact mechanisms. By analyzing the panel data from The 14th Survey of Private Enterprises in China conducted by ACFIC, we obtained some key results.

The current research provided strong empirical evidence that digital transformation has a nonlinear impact on labor productivity of Chinese SMEs, demonstrating an initial negative impact followed by positive returns after reaching a threshold. However, most Chinese SMEs have not yet exceeded the digitization level required to improve labor productivity. In addition, technological progress, organizational change, and labor mobility were key impact mechanisms linking enterprise digitization level and labor productivity of Chinese SMEs. Moreover, the impact of enterprise digitization level on labor productivity varies significantly across regions and industries due to differences in contextual factors. These results make several implications for Chinese SMEs aiming to enhance labor productivity through digital transformation.

First of all, Chinese SMEs are recommended to take a phased approach by focusing on building complementary capabilities before scaling up technology adoption. Implementing basic automation and digital tools may backfire without process redesign and skill development.

Second, Chinese SMEs should align technical and social subsystems to maximize synergy. Flatter organization structures need decentralized decision rights and incentives to boost productivity.

Third, Chinese SMEs need to refresh employee skills and embrace labor mobility in the digital era, rather than resist employee turnover. Workforce training and external employment are vital to keep skills relevant.

Furthermore, SMEs must develop digital strategies tailored to their industries and regions, and consider local infrastructure, development stages, factor inputs, and other factors.

In addition to Chinese SMEs, the Chinese government could also provide funding for management training programs and technical consultants to help Chinese SMEs formulate effective digitization roadmaps, so as to promote them to improve their labor productivity.

## References

1. Berman, S. J. (2012). Digital transformation: Opportunities to create new business models. *Strategy & Leadership, 40*(2), 16–24. https://doi.org/10.1108/10878571211209314
2. Matt, C., Hess, T., & Benlian, A. (2015). Digital transformation strategies. *Business & Information Systems Engineering, 57*(5), 339–343. https://doi.org/10.1007/s12599-015-0401-5
3. Li, L., Su, F., Zhang, W., & Mao, J. Y. (2018). Digital transformation by SME entrepreneurs: A capability perspective. *Information Systems Journal, 28*(1), 1129–1157. https://doi.org/10.1111/isj.12153
4. IDC. (2022). *IDC Spending Guide Sees Worldwide Digital Transformation Investments Reaching $3.4 Trillion in 2026*. https://www.idc.com/getdoc.jsp?containerId=prUS49797222&src_trk=em65e6e06b552592.23458809523029415
5. EU SME Centre. (2023). *SMEs in China: 2023 Policy Environment Report*. https://www.eusmecentre.org.cn/publications/smes-in-china-2023-policy-environment-report/

6. Vial, G. (2019). Understanding digital transformation: A review and a research agenda. *The Journal of Strategic Information Systems, 28*(2), 118–144. https://doi.org/10.1016/j.jsis.2019.01.003
7. Hanelt, A., Bohnsack, R., Marz, D., & Marante, C. A. (2021). A systematic review of the literature on digital transformation: Insights and implications for strategy and organizational change. *Journal of Management Studies, 58*(5), 1159–1197. https://doi.org/10.1111/joms.12639
8. Wang, Y., Kung, L., & Byrd, T. A. (2018). Big data analytics: Understanding its capabilities and potential benefits for healthcare organizations. *Technological Forecasting and Social Change, 126*, 3–13. https://doi.org/10.1016/j.techfore.2015.12.019
9. Parviainen, P., Tihinen, M., Kääriäinen, J., & Teppola, S. (2017). Tackling the digitalization challenge: How to benefit from digitalization in practice. *International Journal of Information Systems and Project Management, 5*(51), 63–77. https://doi.org/10.12821/ijispm050104
10. Kirmizi, M., & Kocaoglu, B. (2023). Design features of digital transformation maturity models: A systematic literature analysis and future research directions. *Journal of Modelling in Management, 19*(2), 313–341. https://doi.org/10.1108/JM2-11-2022-0271
11. Schumacher, A., Erol, S., & Sihn, W. (2016). A maturity model for assessing industry 4.0 readiness and maturity of manufacturing enterprises. *Procedia CIRP, 52*, 161–166. https://doi.org/10.1016/j.procir.2016.07.040
12. Warner, K. S. R., & Wäger, M. (2019). Building dynamic capabilities for digital transformation: An ongoing process of strategic renewal. *Long Range Planning, 52*(3), 326–349. https://doi.org/10.1016/j.lrp.2018.12.001
13. Tang, H. L., Liu, J. M., & Wu, J. G. (2020). The impact of command-and-control environmental regulation on enterprise total factor productivity: A quasi-natural experiment based on China's "two control zone" policy. *Journal of Cleaner Production, 254*, 120011. https://doi.org/10.1016/j.jclepro.2020.120011
14. Bloom, N., Sadun, R., & Van Reenen, J. (2014). *Management as a technology. Working Paper 16-133*, 1–81. https://doi.org/10.2139/ssrn.2788794
15. Syverson, C. (2011). What determines productivity? *Journal of Economic Literature, 49*(2), 326–365. https://doi.org/10.1257/jel.49.2.326
16. Frey, C. B., & Osborne, M. A. (2017). The future of employment: How susceptible are jobs to computerisation? *Technological Forecasting and Social Change, 114*, 254–280. https://doi.org/10.1016/j.techfore.2016.08.019
17. Raj, M., & Seamans, R. (2019). Artificial intelligence, labor, productivity, and the need for firm-level data. In *The economics of artificial intelligence: An agenda* (pp. 553–556). University of Chicago Press. https://doi.org/10.7208/chicago/9780226613475.003.0022
18. Crook, T. R., Todd, S. Y., Combs, J. G., Woehr, D. J., & Ketchen, D. J., Jr. (2011). Does human capital matter? A meta-analysis of the relationship between human capital and firm performance. *Journal of Applied Psychology, 96*(3), 443–456. https://doi.org/10.1037/a0022147
19. Tortorella, G. L., Vergara, A. M. C., Garza-Reyes, J. A., & Sawhney, R. (2020). Organizational learning paths based upon industry 4.0 adoption: An empirical study with Brazilian manufacturers. *International Journal of Production Economics, 219*, 284–294. https://doi.org/10.1016/j.ijpe.2019.06.023
20. Brynjolfsson, E. (1993). The productivity paradox of information technology. *Communications of the ACM, 36*(12), 66–77. https://doi.org/10.1145/163298.163309
21. Dalenogare, L. S., Benitez, G. B., Ayala, N. F., & Frank, A. G. (2018). The expected contribution of industry 4.0 technologies for industrial performance. *International Journal of Production Economics, 204*, 383–394. https://doi.org/10.1016/j.ijpe.2018.08.019
22. Zhong, R. Y., Xu, X., Klotz, E., & Newman, S. T. (2017). Intelligent manufacturing in the context of industry 4.0: A review. *Engineering, 3*(5), 616–630. https://doi.org/10.1016/J.ENG.2017.05.015

23. Polder, M., Leeuwen, G. V., Mohnen, P., & Raymond, W. (2010). Product, process and organizational innovation: Drivers, complementarity and productivity effects. *SSRN Electronic Journal*, 1–45. https://doi.org/10.2139/ssrn.1626805
24. Müller, J. M., Buliga, O., & Voigt, K. I. (2018). Fortune favors the prepared: How SMEs approach business model innovations in industry 4.0. *Technological Forecasting and Social Change, 132*, 2–17. https://doi.org/10.1016/j.techfore.2017.12.019
25. Biagi, F. (2013). ICT and productivity: A review of the literature. *Institute for Prospective Technological Studies Digital Economy Working Paper 2013/09*, (2013/09), 1–78. https://doi.org/10.2788/32940
26. Mazzarol, T. (2015). SMEs engagement with e-commerce, e-business and e-marketing. *Small Enterprise Research, 22*(1), 79–90. https://doi.org/10.1080/13215906.2015.1018400
27. Rai, A., Patnayakuni, R., & Seth, N. (2006). Firm performance impacts of digitally enabled supply chain integration capabilities. *MIS Quarterly, 30*(2), 225–246. https://doi.org/10.2307/25148729
28. Bounfour, A. (2016). *Digital futures, digital transformation, progress: From lean production to Acceleuction*. Springer.
29. Brynjolfsson, E., & McAfee, A. (2014). *The second machine age: Work, progress, and prosperity in a time of brilliant technologies*. WW Norton & Company.
30. Acemoglu, D., & Restrepo, P. (2018). Artificial intelligence, automation and work. *NBER Working Paper, 24196*, 1–43. http://www.nber.org/papers/w24196
31. Arvanitis, S. (2005). Computerization, workplace organization, skilled labour and firm productivity: Evidence for the Swiss business sector. *Economics of Innovation and New Technology, 14*(4), 225–249. https://doi.org/10.1080/1043859042000226257
32. Draca, M., Sadun, R., & Van Reenen, J. (2007). Productivity and ICTs: A review of the evidence. In R. Mansell, C. Avgerou, D. Quah, & R. Silverstone (Eds.), *The Oxford handbook of information and communication technologies* (pp. 100–147). Oxford University Press.
33. Brynjolfsson, E., & Hitt, L. M. (2000). Beyond computation: Information technology, organizational transformation and business performance. *Journal of Economic Perspectives, 14*(4), 23–48. https://doi.org/10.1257/jep.14.4.23
34. ACFIC. (2020). *The 14th Survey of Private Enterprises in China*. https://dcwj.acfic.org.cn/survey/web
35. Lyu, Y., Wang, W., Wu, Y., & Zhang, J. (2023). How does digital economy affect green total factor productivity? Evidence from China. *Science of the Total Environment, 857*(Part 2), 159428. https://doi.org/10.1016/j.scitotenv.2022.159428
36. Verhoef, P. C., Broekhuizen, T., Bart, Y., Bhattacharya, A., Qi Dong, J., Fabian, N., & Haenlein, M. (2021). Digital transformation: A multidisciplinary reflection and research agenda. *Journal of Business Research, 122*(4), 889–901. https://doi.org/10.1016/j.jbusres.2019.09.022
37. Solow, R. M. (1957). Technical change and the aggregate production function. *The Review of Economics and Statistics, 39*(3), 312–320. https://doi.org/10.2307/1926047

# Defining Performance Indicators for a Multi-Stakeholder Manufacturing Digital Platform: An ECOGRAI Adaptation

**Walter Quadrini, Mohammadmahdi Mohammadianghovaghloo, Claudio Sassanelli, Sergio Terzi, and Luca Fumagalli**

**Abstract** Key Performance Indicators (KPIs) are nowadays a *de facto* standard for the majority of manufacturing companies using them to assess their production and business targets to drive their development. Recent digitalisation trends in the manufacturing sector enabled several business opportunities, in particular when it comes to data sharing among the stakeholders of the same supply chain. Several methodologies have been developed so far to properly design indicators from the perspective of business targets. Among these methodologies populating the literature, ECOGRAI is a consolidated approach to design KPIs starting from business objectives. In this work, an application of the methodology is proposed to define KPIs in the industrial marketplace domain meeting the business need of its stakeholders. This application required some adaptation with respect to the original methodology, and the further steps implemented (in particular, during the BOs evaluation) are documented in this manuscript, as well as are referenced the three application cases subject to the analysis, which brought to the identification of a total of 34 KPIs related to the different stakeholders involved with respect to their internal performance as well as with the platform demanded to the sharing of data among the different actors.

**Keywords** ECOGRAI · Key performance indicators · Manufacturing · KPI definition · Digitalisation

W. Quadrini (✉) · M. Mohammadianghovaghloo · S. Terzi · L. Fumagalli
Politecnico di Milano, Milan, Italy
e-mail: walter.quadrini@polimi.it; mohammadmahdi.mohammadianghovaghloo@polimi.it; sergio.terzi@polimi.it; luca1.fumagalli@polimi.it

C. Sassanelli
Politecnico di Bari, Bari, Italy
e-mail: claudio.sassanelli@poliba.it



A. Appolloni et al. (eds.), *The Future of Industry*, Lecture Notes in Information Systems and Organisation 70, https://doi.org/10.1007/978-3-031-66801-2_31

# 1 Introduction

## 1.1 Industrial Context

Industrial performance measurement is now one of the most important tools for production unit control [1] and in the last decades it has gained a priority role, not only in production, but also in phases like design and prototyping, which imply a "benchmarking" approach [2]. Organizations deal with many key performance indicators (KPIs) in different areas. In recent years, organizational learning, knowledge creation, and innovation capability have emerged as the dominant factors of competitive advantage [3, 4], pushed by the globalization phenomenon, always increasing competition [5] and a surge in terms of technology innovation [6] and progress [7]. Manufacturing businesses today must operate in a volatile environment of fierce competition, shrinking budgets, and intense price pressures. Complex systems [8, 9], embedded with digital technologies [10], continuously arise in the market, asking for the creation of dedicated marketplaces to foster their diffusion. Indeed, in this context, new manufacturing Product-Service Systems (PSS), developed to better satisfy customer expectations, foster sustainable/circular development, and improve the product lifecycle [11], are enabled and provided through different manufacturing marketplaces (e.g., DIVERSITY [12]; FENIX [13, 14]; HUBCAP [15]; DIH4CPS [16]).

## 1.2 Objectives of Research

So far, several methods, utilising either qualitative or quantitative measures [17], are available for developing specifications useful to select or develop Production Management Systems. However, once the system has been selected and implemented, the user needs to know how well it performs [18–20]. Among the most practical methods that have been widely used in recent years, ECOGRAI [2], Supply Chain Operations Reference Model (SCOR) [21, 22], and Specific, Measurable, Attainable, Realistic, and Time Sensitive (SMART) [23, 24], can be mentioned. ECOGRAI can be applied to all the production functions, with a global approach or more specifically on only one function. ECOGRAI method of performance evaluation can be applied for example in a maintenance or logistics process to implement a system performance indicator [25, 26]. In addition, it is also suitable to evaluate performance of skills production systems [27, 28]. Furthermore, it can be adapted to multi-stakeholders' scenarios, but other conventional methods have some drawbacks, for example the SCOR methodology considers actors as an input and output (simplifying their effectiveness as agents), and the SMART methodology only provides conceptual rating scales about KPI prioritisation, without explicitly addressing the actions to be taken in order to improve the system performances [24]. As a result, in this paper, due to the logical process of analysis/design, using a top-down approach, an adaption of the traditional ECOGRAI [2] method is introduced, allowing to decompose the different Business Objectives (BOs) to identify KPIs in multi stakeholders' scenarios project. The project's core goal is to address the development of a software platform and the evaluation of KPIs; this procedure has been applied to its various business scenarios.

The paper is organized as follows. In Sect. 2, we provide an overview of the research context, with a particular emphasis on the original ECOGRAI methodology. Section 3 delves into the research results, presenting the newly adapted ECOGRAI methodology in detail. This section outlines the various phases and actors involved, offering a comprehensive understanding of the methodology's evolution. Moving on to Sect. 4, we illustrate an example of the methodology's application within a multi-stakeholder scenario. This practical use case, within the context of the methodology's adaptation, offers a clearer perspective on its real-world implications. Finally, in Sect. 5, we bring the paper to a conclusion, summarizing the key findings and highlighting the significance of the adapted ECOGRAI methodology in the broader research landscape.

## 2 Research Background

The ECOGRAI approach [2] is a structured methodology comprising several subsequential steps. It begins with the identification of objectives assigned to decision-makers at different management levels. This involves a precise understanding about which objectives are associated with the actors involved in the decision-making process. Next, the method focuses on selecting the parameters or "drivers" that these decision-makers can influence to achieve their assigned objectives. This step is crucial in the ECOGRAI method, as it seeks to find the levers on which decision-makers can act to reach their goals. The Performance Indicators, which measure the efficiency of the activity in fulfilling the proposed objectives, are not only defined in isolation but are also consequence of this preliminary choice. They should hence be logically distributed to cover various functions and decision levels, including strategic, tactical, and operational aspects.

The ECOGRAI approach follows a structured approach with six distinct phases. Phase 0 involves analyzing the Production Management System and determining the Decision Centre (DC) where Performance Indicators will be defined. Phases 1 and 2 are dedicated to identifying the fundamental elements: objectives and drivers. Phase 3 focuses on the identification of Performance Indicators, while Phase 4 involves designing the information system for these indicators. Finally, Phase 5 is about implementing the system on the Production Management Information System.

To further this research work, the original ECOGRAI method has been simplified and applied in the context of a multi-stakeholder manufacturing marketplace. This adaptation involves the use of the ECOGRAI methodology in three distinct application scenarios: one in the "Metal domain," where equipment and services related to metal-based manufacturing are offered through the marketplace platform, another in the "Plastic domain," where services related to plastic manufacturing are provided, and a third scenario related to data exchange for the supply chain tracking of Original Equipment Manufacturers in the "High-Tech domain," where the infrastructure for data exchange is facilitated by the marketplace platform. This research work seeks to adapt and apply the ECOGRAI method effectively within these diverse manufacturing contexts.

The originality of the ECOGRAI method is not defining the Performance Indicators, but the search of drivers, on which decision-makers can act to reach their objectives. The Performance Indicator is a consequence of the preliminary choice, a coherent distribution of Performance Indicators covering the various functions and the various decision levels (strategic, tactical, and operational).

## 3 Results

The methodology proposed in this work is an adaption of the traditional ECOGRAI methodology [2], to tailor it to the multi-stakeholder scenario. This update is needed to drive the Key Performance Indicators (KPIs) of an industrial marketplace towards the business need of its stakeholders. In addition, it is required some integration with respect to the original methodology which is mentioned in different phases.

### *3.1 Phase 0*

This phase is introduced by providing a concise description of the scenario, including the presentation of a table that lists the various steps of the process, a BPMN (Business Process Model and Notation, [29]), which vividly illustrates the scenario, and another table highlighting the specific files and data transfers integral to the process.

The actual Phase 0 within the ECOGRAI methodology entails the translation of the production process into a structured table divided along two essential axes: a process axis and a management axis. The process axis meticulously catalogues all the functions involved in the process. Traditionally, this axis is subdivided into categories like "product management," "planning," and "resource management." However, in the context of this research, a simplified approach is taken, and the axis is divided based on the different participating companies in the process, reflecting the multi-company aspect of the use cases.

In contrast, the management axis meticulously enumerates the different levels of management that participate in the process. Typically, this axis is categorized into "operational," "tactical," and "strategic" levels. Nevertheless, in this research, a more straightforward approach is adopted, wherein the axis is divided based on

**Table 1** DC identification example

| | Funct. 1 | Funct. 2 | Funct. 3 | Funct. 4 | Funct. 5 | Funct. 6 |
|---|---|---|---|---|---|---|
| Agent 1 | DC1 | | | DC4 | | |
| Agent 2 | | DC2 | | | DC5 | |
| Agent 3 | | | DC3 | | | DC6 |

the various participating companies in the process, aligning with the multi-company nature of the use cases.

The primary goal of this phase is to identify the Decision Centers (DCs) within the system where the Key Performance Indicators (KPIs) will be defined. A Decision Center, in this context, is defined as a point of intersection between the process and management axes. It signifies that the agent or agents on the management axis, who significantly contribute to a specific process on the horizontal axis, are designated as DCs. Table 1 serves as a comprehensive representation of a generic Phase 0 table, encapsulating the critical elements of this initial phase.

## 3.2 *Phase 1*

Phase 1 has a fundamental objective, which is to determine the objectives for each Decision Center (DC) identified in the previous phase. Following a top-down perspective, this phase unfolds in two distinct steps. The initial step involves addressing the Business Objectives (BOs) pertinent to each function along the production axis. In the second step, the focus shifts towards identifying the "local" objectives specific to the DCs, where "local" implies objectives within each function. These objectives are aptly termed Function Objectives (FOs). The significance of these FOs lies in their role in contributing to the realization of the BOs that were defined in the first step. This connection is not only essential but also aligns with the conceptual hierarchy, whereby the FOs at the lower level are designed to support the BOs above them.

To provide a more visual representation of these logical contributions, a breakdown diagram is included. This diagram serves to highlight and acknowledge the contributions of each FO towards the achievement of the BOs. It offers a comprehensive view of how the various components within the DCs work together to fulfil the overarching goals set out in the Business Objectives. This phase plays a pivotal role in aligning the objectives of each DC with the broader business objectives, creating a structured framework for the subsequent stages of the ECOGRAI methodology.

To identify the BOs, the business models of all scenarios are analysed through a Business Model Navigator (BMN, [30]), which starts with the definition and analysis of four main factors in a business model as well as three subsequent possible enhancement areas, as represented in Fig. 1.

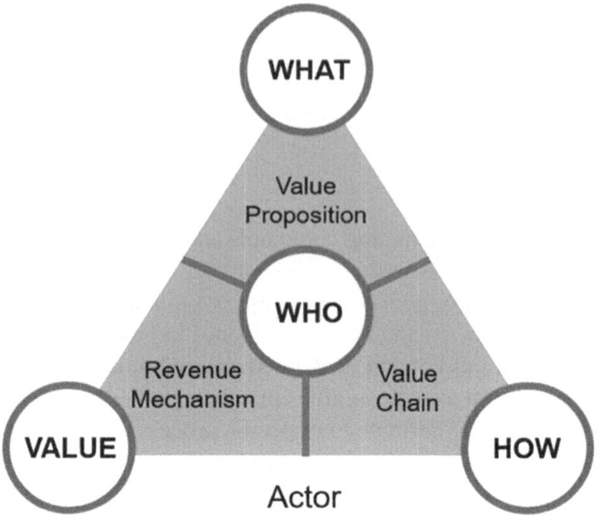


**Fig. 1** Business Model Navigator (BMN) example

All these actors are going to be analysed one by one based on BMN that is built on the analysis of four factors and following three possible enhancement areas.

The factors are:

- Who: who does the proposed business model change the actor/players in the business procedure?
- What: what does the proposed business model change the exchanged objects and services?
- How: how does the proposed business model change the way the various operations are done?
- Value: how does the proposed business model change the value of the outcoming business?

Eventually, the combination of the four factors above generates three main areas of business enhancement such as revenue mechanism, value chain, and value proposition.

FOs are, on the other hand, stated based upon the process objectives for every decisional centre.

## *3.3 Phase 2*

Building upon the previous phase, Phase 2 strategically proceeds with the development of a driver for each of the Function Objectives (FOs) that were identified. In the context of the ECOGRAI methodology, a driver can be defined as a variable that a Decision Center (DC) can actively manipulate or be influenced by in its quest to achieve the assigned FOs. This crucial step contributes significantly to the formalization of the triple set {objectives, drivers, key performance indicators}, a distinctive feature that sets ECOGRAI apart.

The establishment of this triple set encapsulates the essence of the ECOGRAI approach, enhancing the overall transparency of the process. The incorporation of drivers not only provides a structured framework but also facilitates a higher degree of control over the entire process. It renders the methodology more comprehensible and manageable, ultimately simplifying the task of ensuring coherence and consistency within the system. This stage marks a pivotal milestone in the ECOGRAI methodology, laying the foundation for a systematic and controlled approach to achieving the set objectives [2].

### *3.4 Phase 3*

While the aforementioned phases enable the identification of one or more objectives and drivers for every DC, Phase 3 is devoted to the precise addressing of KPIs. To achieve this target, every actor's expertise is involved, and each DC is supposed to develop a coherence analysis in order to validate the existence of each KPI.

### *3.5 Final Testing*

According to the ECOGRAI standard definition, Phase 3 is supposed to be followed by two other phases, whose aim is to design the company information system to gather the designed KPIs and to integrate the so-gathered indicators into the company high-level decisional tools (e.g., Enterprise Resource Planning software). However, because of lack of horizontal integration among the different stakeholders, it has not been possible to instruct the respective companies' software application to collect KPIs, so some performance tests in the "hazy good old way" have been performed and these two additional phases have been substituted by a unique one, where a detailed list of testing activities has been tabled.

## 4 Implementation Scenarios

The ECOGRAI methodology mentioned in Sect. 3, has been adapted and used to evaluate the performances of an industrial-devoted marketplace. In this digital marketplace, three application scenarios have been defined (Metal, Plastic, and High-Tech domains). For each of them, the phases mentioned in the previous section were implemented phase by phase. As a result of the research work done about this digital marketplace, a total of 34 KPIs were introduced, which the share of each

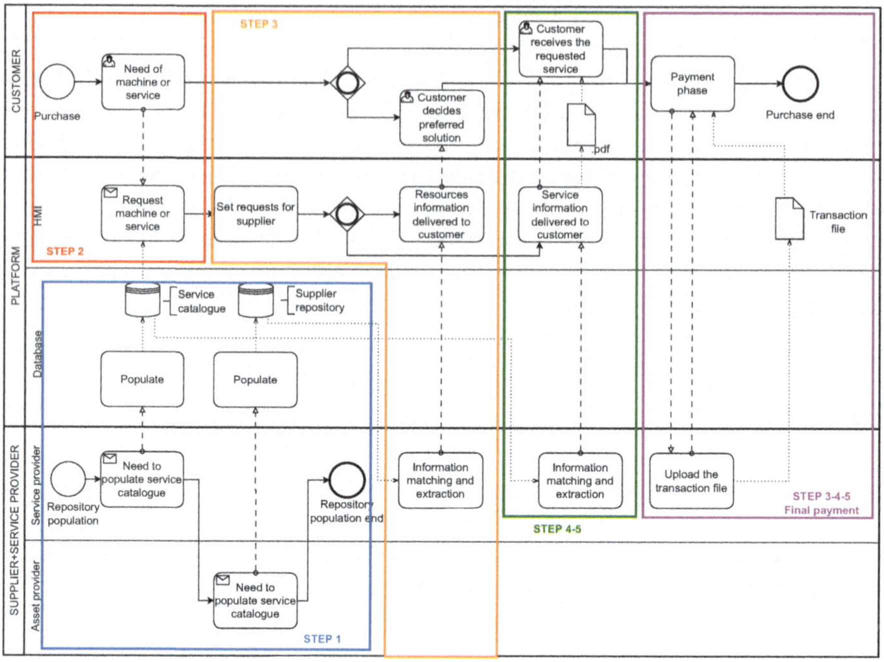


**Fig. 2** BPMN scenario

domain is (Metal domain: 11 KPIs, Plastic domains: 10 KPIs, and High-tech domain: 13 KPIs).

In this paper, to better display the phases of the methodology, and due to privacy and space constrain, we will go over the phase-by-phase implementation in a digital marketplace (Metal domain), that will serve to match machine suppliers' offers and customers' demands. (It should be noted, the steps and implementation of this method in other domains are the same as the metal domain which is mentioned below). In addition, third parties will be involved in providing services that can be used in the marketplace to enable more features than the mere matchmaking between supply and demand. The various actors are the customers and the suppliers (service and equipment providers).

The BPMN diagram of the metal domain is depicted in Fig. 2.

In addition, the overall scenario breakdown can be separated into the phases described in Table 2.

A clear explanation of the various data exchanged in the aforementioned phases is summarized in Table 3, to clarify inputs and outputs of each step of the procedure (notice that in Step 2 no data exchange is supposed to take place).

**Table 2** Steps of scenario

| Step | Action |
|---|---|
| 1 | All service providers upload their material (service description and URL), via the platform. All equipment providers upload their material in the supplier repository, via the platform |
| 2 | The purchasing process starts with a request by a customer for a peculiar machine and or service (access to portal) |
| 3 | The customer selects the service required, adds his/her specific inputs on the portal, and the portal provides the results to the customer for him/her to set his/her requirements |
| 4 | In the portal, the customer can select also additional services related to it |
| 5 | Services require specific files transferring (between customer and supplier) |

**Table 3** Data transfer scenario

| Step | From | To | Exchanged files |
|---|---|---|---|
| 1 | Service provider | Service catalogue | Information about services |
| | Equipment provider | Supplier repository | Information about machinery |
| 2 | – | – | – |
| 3 | Customer | Platform | Equipment requirements |
| | Supplier repository | Supplier | Information about equipment |
| | Supplier | Customer | Filtered information about equipment and transaction files |
| 4 | Customer | Platform | Service requirements |
| | Platform | Customer | Filtered information about services |
| | Supplier | Customer | Transaction files |
| 5 | Customer | Platform | Service requirements |
| | Service catalogue | Supplier | Service information |
| | Supplier | Customer | Filtered downloadable files about services and transaction files |

## *4.1 Phase 0: Decision Centres Identification*

In this phase, as is mentioned in Sect. 3.1, "ECOGRAI methodology consists of the translation of the production process into a table divided into two axes.", the production axis has been clustered into two groups, namely equipment supplier selection and service supplier selection. In the vertical axis, the access pipelines are listed, namely web service platform, asset provider, and service provider (Table 4).

Concerning the equipment supplier selection, the DC has been identified in the platform in its first step since it's through its web services that the customer can upload its requirements. The population of the catalogue with the possible assets or manufacturing capabilities will depend on the manufacturers themselves. At the same time, the matchmaking performances will rely on the platform capabilities

**Table 4** Decision Centers (DCs) identification

| | Service supplier selection | | | Equipment supplier selection | | |
|---|---|---|---|---|---|---|
| | Customer searches for the most suitable application | Supplier populates catalogue | Matchmaking | Customer enters product category | Supplier populates catalogue | Matchmaking |
| Platform | DC1 | | DC3 | DC4 | | DC6 |
| Asset provider | | | | | DC5 | |
| Service provider | | DC2 | | | | |

themselves. Concerning the service supplier solution, the DCs allocation is specular to the equipment one, with the only difference of the catalogue population, which depends on the service supplier.

## 4.2 *Phase 1: Objectives' Assignment*

This phase aims to determine the objectives of each identified DC, which will go over in three sub-sections BMN, objectives identification and split up diagram. In this section, the BMN framework is applied for all the actors, analysing the changes concerning the previous status quo. Via using the web service platform, these changes are going to be highlighted and explained. In this case, four main actors and users that take part in the various transactions and phases of the platform procedure have been considered: Customer, Service Provider, Asset Provider, Platform Provider.

Figure 3 depicts the customer, which is involved in the changes, especially for the methodology of how the sale procedure is conducted. More specifically, the use of the Platform itself represents a significant change in the methodology; in fact, the whole information flow from the suppliers to the customer is wholly virtualized and enables enhanced decision-making. This enhancement results in a better value chain since the platform makes it possible to be in contact with multiple actors of the value chain in an immediate and pervasive way. Furthermore, the value for all customers who are using the platform is higher compared to regular business processes as the search and comparison of production equipment is more fluid and faster, because of the implemented advanced user interaction means.

For the suppliers (service provider and asset provider), both have a different way and methodology of interacting with the client, hence there is a different "how", but for both the groups the "how" is increased since there is a pervasive web presence of their products and services on a web-portal, which makes it possible to have an enhanced user experience, increasing the visibility towards global users.

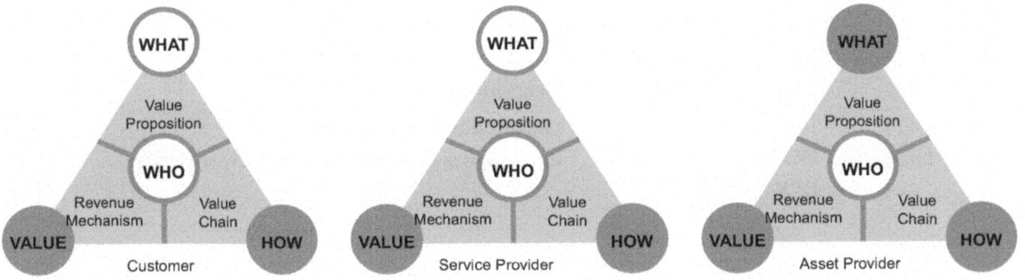


**Fig. 3** Business Model Navigator (BMN) implementation

**Table 5** Business Objectives (BOs)

| BOs ID | BOs name | Description |
|---|---|---|
| BO1 | Shorter time-to-buy | The platform will reduce the purchase time of assets and services for the end-users |
| BO3 | Enhance customer care services | The platform will ease the communication between the technical departments of the customer and the supplier |
| BO4 | Friendly purchasing experience | The platform will ease the purchase of assets and services for the end-users |

In the suppliers' case, the "value" is also enhanced, since all suppliers can support the customers in the whole equipment lifecycle, from the selection and contracting to the equipment commissioning and after-sales. The suppliers have a large quantity of data regarding the customer at their disposal, hence they have an advantage in being able to give value to their proposal and product for the customer. Regarding the asset provider, also the "what" factor is highlighted mainly because the matching between the asset provider and the customer is provided by the platform. This kind of link did not exist before; this means that previously the object of the transaction (assets) was not being directly sold to the customer. This translates into an enrichment of the assets and services sold, thanks to the use of the platform.

Based on the analysis performed in the BMN, the BOs to strengthen the performance of the platform were also determined, share of each domain is: Metal domain 8 BOs, Plastic domain 5 BOs, and High-Tech domain 4 BOs.

To show and explain the implementation of the methodology introduced in Sect. 2, the focus of this paper will be on showing an example of the application of this method, so only three out of eight BOs mentioned in Table 5 will be further examined.

In the next step to create split up diagram, FOs should be determined which the only function that includes all three aforementioned objectives is as follows (Table 6):

A diagram highlighting the influence of the FOs on the BOs is depicted in Fig. 4, as it is mentioned in the previous paragraph, the focus of this paper to show an example of methodology will be on FO4.

**Table 6** Function Objectives (FOs)

| FOs ID | Related DCs | Related BOs | FOs name | Description |
|---|---|---|---|---|
| FO4 | DC3, DC6 | BO1, BO3, BO4 | Support feedbacks | During the matchmaking phase, the platform supports the data exchange between the two parties |

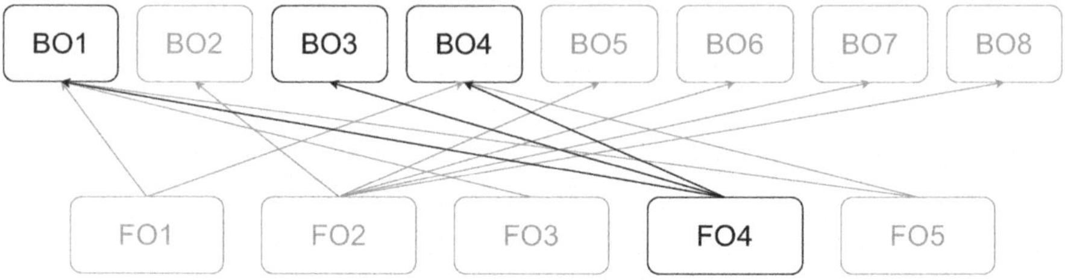


**Fig. 4** Split up diagram

**Table 7** Drivers' identification

| Driver ID | Related FO | Driver name | Description |
|---|---|---|---|
| $D_{ex.}$ | FO4 | Feedbacks | The platform will support the transfer of files of different sizes and formats in a secure way |

$D_{ex}$: this driver is introduced primarily for data security and privacy purposes; in this regard, to support feedback provisions during the matchmaking process, to exchange data between the two parties, the platform will support secure file transfer of various sizes and formats

## 4.3 Phase 2: Drivers' Identification

This phase is dedicated to the introduction of drivers related to DCs and FOs, which in this section, in accordance with the explanations given in Sect. 3.2, the driver related to FO4 will be explained (Table 7).

## 4.4 Phase 3: KPIs Identification

This phase is dedicated to determining the Key Performance Indicators to calculate the performance of the platform in accordance with the drivers specified in the previous section. Therefore, the KPIs that are introduced in accordance with the mentioned driver (D) or with the steps of the BPMN (S) are explained in Table 8 (where KPI4 is the one related to $D_{ex}$ and has been hence renamed to $KPI_{ex}$).

**Table 8** KPIs identification

| KPI ID | Related Driver | Type | KPI name | Description |
|---|---|---|---|---|
| KPI1 | D1 | Boolean | Availability | Webservice or mobile app to unify the access by the customers |
| KPI2 | D2 | Numeric | Subscribers | Minimum number of companies registered to the platform and uploading their catalogues of products and services |
| KPI3 | D3 | Numeric | Expected time to receive technical design | Reduction of the time for the final customer to receive a technical design |
| $KPI_{ex}$ | D4 | Numeric | File size | Ability of the platform to transfer big size files |
| KPI5 | D5 | Numeric | Expected time to sign contract | Reduction of the contract signing time |
| KPI6 | S1 | Numeric | Machines in Catalogue | Number of machines populating the catalogue |
| KPI7 | S1 | Numeric | Services in Catalogue | Number of services populating the catalogue |
| KPI8 | S2 | Numeric | Queries for searching machine | Number of successful queries searching machines |
| KPI9 | S3 | Numeric | Queries for searching service | Number of successful queries searching services |
| KPI10 | S4 | Numeric | Time between equipment selection and first response | At the customer side, mean time between the entry of the requirements and the first response received |
| KPI11 | S4 | Numeric | Time between service selection and first response | At the customer side, mean time between the entry of the requirements and the first response received |

*$KPI_{ex.}$*: in order to support data exchange between the two parties during matchmaking, as mentioned in $D_{ex.}$, the platform will support the transfer of files of different sizes and formats in a secured way. The KPI, which is determined in this section, is "File size", since often CAD files are characterized by cumbersome sizes. To handle this issue, the platform should be able to transfer large-size files

## 4.5 Phase 4: Final Testing

To test the indicators identified in phase 3, in this phase the actual value of each KPIs is determined and compared with a target (expected value), and the purpose of this section is to test and analyse indicators to find the gaps and improve them. For this reason, in Table 9, how to perform the test for the KPI specified in phase 3 ($KPI_{ex.}$) is defined.

$T_{ex}$: in order to support information exchange between customers and suppliers and to measure file size, the demo version of the platform will be used to understand the dimension of a PDF/CAD file successfully transferred through the platform pipeline.

**Table 9** Test

| ID | Related KPI | Methodology | Description | Actual Value | Expected Value |
|---|---|---|---|---|---|
| $T_{ex.}$ | $KPI_{ex.}$ | Demo | Dimension of a PDF/CAD file successfully transferred through the platform pipeline (from service SUPPLIER to end-users) | 100 MB | 100 MB |

**Table 10** Summary of results

| Domains | N. KPIs | N. DCs | N. BOs | N. FOs | N. Drivers |
|---|---|---|---|---|---|
| Metal | 11 | 6 | 8 | 5 | 5 |
| Plastic | 10 | 6 | 5 | 5 | 5 |
| High-tech | 13 | 9 | 4 | 6 | 6 |

# 5 Conclusion

In this paper, an adaption of the traditional ECOGRAI methodology, tailored to the multi-stakeholder scenario has been implemented to evaluate the performances of an industrial-devoted marketplace. In this digital marketplace, three application scenarios have been defined (Metal, Plastic, High-Tech domains). For each domain, all phases mentioned in this paper were implemented (total number of KPIs, DCs, BOs, FOs, and Drivers are listed in Table 10).

Since some KPIs have been the same in all three domains, after performing different phases in each one, it is a remarkable result that certifies the effectiveness of the introduced methodology. In addition, since the core of the project is to address the development of a software platform and to assess the KPIs, this procedure has been applied to its different business scenarios. In case of any change in the business model of the platform, the methodology should be repeated. Since the method introduced in this paper is used to identify KPIs to better understand the advantages of business, can be also adequate for production KPIs in addition to developing project management ones.

Furthermore, the integration of BPMN analysis in the definition of the objectives has demonstrated in the implementation phase a smooth approach in the identification of the interactions among different actors (DCs). The current trends of manufacturing-related research, focused on the interaction of human actors with informative systems and automated machinery, offer a wide range of possible application cases for this methodology, which in future researches will need to adapt to this new human-centric paradigm with a deeper level of granularity.

## References


1. Maretto, L., Faccio, M., & Battini, D. (2023). The adoption of digital technologies in the manufacturing world and their evaluation: A systematic review of real-life case studies and future research agenda. *Journal of Manufacturing Systems, 68*, 576–600. https://doi.org/10.1016/j.jmsy.2023.05.009
2. Doumeingts, G., Clave, F., & Ducq, Y. (1995). *ECOGRAI — A method to design and to implement Performance Measurement Systems for industrial organizations—Concepts and application to the Maintenance function.* https://doi.org/10.1007/978-0-387-34847-6_39.
3. Lookman, K., Pujawan, N., & Nadlifatin, R. (2023). Innovative capabilities and competitive advantage in the era of industry 4.0: A study of trucking industry. *Research in Transportation Business & Management, 47*, 100947. https://doi.org/10.1016/j.rtbm.2023.100947
4. Wongsansukcharoen, J., & Thaweepaiboonwong, J. (2023). Effect of innovations in human resource practices, innovation capabilities, and competitive advantage on small and medium enterprises' performance in Thailand. *European Research on Management and Business Economics, 29*(1), 100210. https://doi.org/10.1016/j.iedeen.2022.100210
5. Popkova, E. G., Bogoviz, A. V., Ekimova, K. V., & Sergi, B. S. (2023). Will Russia become a blueprint for emerging nations' high-tech reforms? Evidence from a 26-countries dataset. *International Journal of Innovation Studies, 7*(4), 294–306. https://doi.org/10.1016/j.ijis.2023.05.001
6. Cavallo, A., Burgers, H., Ghezzi, A., & van de Vrande, V. (2021). The evolving nature of open innovation governance: A study of a digital platform development in collaboration with a big science Centre. *Technovation*, 1–53. https://doi.org/10.1016/j.technovation.2021.102370
7. Porter, M. E., & Heppelmann, J. E. (2015). How smart, connected products are transforming companies. *Harvard Business Review, 93*(10), 96–114. https://doi.org/10.1017/CBO9781107415324.004
8. Acerbi, F., Polenghi, A., Quadrini, W., Macchi, M., & Taisch, M. (2022). Fostering circular manufacturing through the integration of genetic algorithm and process mining. In D. Y. Kim, G. von Cieminski, & D. Romero (Eds.), (A c. Di) *Advances in production management systems. Smart manufacturing and logistics systems: Turning ideas into action* (pp. 407–414). Springer Nature. https://doi.org/10.1007/978-3-031-16411-8_47
9. Zizic, M. C., Mladineo, M., Gjeldum, N., & Celent, L. (2022). From industry 4.0 towards industry 5.0: A review and analysis of paradigm shift for the people, organization and technology. *Energies, 15*(14), Articolo 14. https://doi.org/10.3390/en15145221
10. Rüßmann, M., Lorenz, M., Gerbert, P., Waldner, M., Justus, J., Engel, P., & Harnisch, M. (2015). Industry 4.0: The future of productivity and growth in manufacturing industries. *Business and Information Systems Engineering*. https://doi.org/10.1007/s12599-014-0334-4
11. Sassanelli, C., Pezzotta, G., Pirola, F., Rossi, M., & Terzi, S. (2019). The PSS design GuRu methodology: Guidelines and rules generation to enhance PSS detailed design. *Journal of Design Research, 17*, 125–162. https://doi.org/10.1504/jdr.2019.10026968
12. Pezzotta, G., Sala, R., Pirola, F., Campos, A. R., Margarito, A., Correia, A. T., Fotia, S., & Mourtzis, D. (2016). Definition of a PSS engineering environment: From the theoretical methodology to the platform implementation. *Proceedings of the Summer School Francesco Turco, 13–15-Sept*, 97–101.
13. Rosa, P., & Terzi, S. (2021). *New business models for the reuse of secondary resources from WEEEs (P. Rosa & S. Terzi, A c. Di; SpringerBr)*. Springer. https://doi.org/10.1007/978-3-030-74886-9
14. Quadrini, W., Negri, E., & Fumagalli, L. (2020). Open interfaces for connecting automated guided vehicles to a fleet management system. *Procedia Manufacturing, 42*(2019), 406–413. https://doi.org/10.1016/j.promfg.2020.02.055
15. Macedo, H. D., Sassanelli, C., Larsen, P. G., & Terzi, S. (2021). Facilitating model-based design of cyber-manufacturing systems. *Proceedings of the 54th CIRP Conference on Manufacturing Systems 2021*. https://doi.org/10.1016/j.procir.2021.11.327.

16. Sassanelli, C., & Terzi, S. (2022). The D-BEST based digital innovation hub customer journey analysis method: Configuring DIHs unique value proposition. *International Journal of Engineering Business Management, 14*, 18479790221124634. https://doi.org/10.1177/18479790221124634
17. Kerssens-Van Drongelen, I. C., & Bilderbeek, J.. (s.d.). *R&D performance measurement: More than choosing a set of metrics*.
18. De Carolis, A., Macchi, M., Negri, E., & Terzi, S. (2017). Guiding manufacturing companies towards digitalization. *23rd ICE/IEEE International Technology Management Conference*, 503–512. https://doi.org/10.1109/ICE.2017.8279925
19. Sassanelli, C., Rossi, M., & Terzi, S. (2020). Evaluating the smart maturity of manufacturing companies along the product development process to set a PLM project roadmap. *International Journal of Product Lifecycle Management, 12*(3), 185–209. https://doi.org/10.1504/IJPLM.2020.109789
20. Rossi, M., & Terzi, S. (2017). CLIMB: Maturity assessment model for design and engineering processes. *International Journal of Product Lifecycle Management, 10*(1), 20. https://doi.org/10.1504/IJPLM.2017.082998
21. Maas, R., Shevtshenko, E., & Karaulova, T. (2023). Supply chain quality improvement based on customer compliance. In L. M. Camarinha-Matos & F. Ferrada (Eds.), (A c. Di) *Technological innovation for connected cyber physical spaces* (pp. 230–242). Springer Nature. https://doi.org/10.1007/978-3-031-36007-7_17
22. Stephens, S. (2001). Supply chain operations reference model version 5.0: A new tool to improve supply chain efficiency and achieve Best practice. In *Information systems Frontiers* (Vol. 3). Kluwer Academic Publishers.
23. Ahn, H., Clermont, M., & Hesping, J. (2021). The unit effect from a performance management perspective. *International Journal of Productivity and Performance Management, 71*(5), 1895–1915. https://doi.org/10.1108/IJPPM-03-2020-0115
24. Shahin, A., & Mahbod, M. A. (2007). Prioritization of key performance indicators: An integration of analytical hierarchy process and goal setting. *International Journal of Productivity and Performance Management, 56*(3), 226–240. https://doi.org/10.1108/17410400710731437
25. Lobna, K., Mounir, B., & Hichem, K. (2013). Using the ECOGRAI method for performance evaluation in maintenance process. In *2013 international conference on advanced logistics and transport, ICALT 2013* (pp. 382–387). https://doi.org/10.1109/ICAdLT.2013.6568489
26. Mouafo Nebot, G. V., & Wang, H. (2022). Port terminal performance evaluation and modeling. *Logistics, 6*(1), Articolo 1. https://doi.org/10.3390/logistics6010010
27. Quadrini, W., & Fumagalli, L. (2022) Impact of Learning Factories over sustainable production. *Proceedings of the Summer School Francesco Turco*..
28. Rhouzali, A., Nsiri, B., & Abid, M. (2018). Modeling and performance evaluation of the skills production systems: Using the ECOGRAI method. *WSEAS Transactions on systems and Control*, 1–10.
29. Chinosi, M., & Trombetta, A. (2012). BPMN: An introduction to the standard. *Computer Standards and Interfaces*. https://doi.org/10.1016/j.csi.2011.06.002
30. Weinberger, M., Bilgeri, D., & Fleisch, E. (2016). IoT business models in an industrial context. *At-Automatisierungstechnik*. https://doi.org/10.1515/auto-2016-0054

# Method of Minimax Terminal Program Control of Enterprise Product Output for Digitalization of Decision-Making Processes

**Andrey F. Shorikov**

**Abstract** The article examines the problem of Minimax (optimization of a guaranteed result) terminal program control of enterprise product output with a vector objective function and risks. To model the dynamics of such process, a new economic-mathematical model—a system of linear discrete-time recurrent equations—is used. Its basic parameters are its phase vector of the controlled object (the enterprise), demand vector, control action vector (control), and the vector that describes a priori uncertain risks (disturbances) that arise in production. The article formalizes the problem under consideration and proposes a constructive solution method, which can serve as the basis for developing a numerical algorithm and creating a computer software application. The results presented in the paper can be used in the digitalization of decision-making processes at manufacturing enterprises.

**Keywords** Minimax program control · Vector objective function · A priori uncertain risks · Digitalization of decision-making processes

## 1 Introduction

The article discusses the problem of optimizing a guaranteed result—the Minimax approach [1–3] to managing the product output of an enterprise with a vector objective function in the case of a priori uncertain risks (disturbances). To model such dynamics, a new economic-mathematical model—a system of linear discrete-time recurrent equations—is used. The basic parameters of this system are the phase vector of the controlled object (the enterprise), the control action vector (the control subject), the demand vector, and the vector that describes a priori uncertain risks (disturbances) that arise in production. The control action vector (the control) takes only a finite set of values in each time period, and the phase vector of the model, the demand vector, and the risk vector are limited by convex compact polyhedrons (with

A. F. Shorikov (✉)
Institute of Economics of the Ural Branch of the Russian Academy of Sciences, Ekaterinburg, Russian Federation
e-mail: shorikov.af@uiec.ru



A. Appolloni et al. (eds.), *The Future of Industry*, Lecture Notes in Information Systems and Organisation 70, https://doi.org/10.1007/978-3-031-66801-2_32

a finite number of vertices) in the corresponding finite-dimensional vector spaces. As a quality criterion for implementing the process under consideration, a vector terminal objective function is used, depending on the implemented vector functions of control and risks (for fixed demand), and its values are determined at the final states of the phase vector of the controlled object.

For the initial issue, a mathematical formalization is proposed in the form of a multi-step problem of Minimax terminal program control [3] of enterprise product output with a vector objective function and risks. The article describes a constructive technique for solving the problem under consideration, based on the *general recurrent algebraic method* [3, 4] for constructing reachability sets (predictive sets) of linear discrete-time controlled dynamical systems, and discusses the possibility of its implementation as a corresponding computer application. The obtained results are based on [3–6] and can be used to solve practical problems of economics, mathematical models of which are presented in, e.g., [7–23].

## 2 Literature Review

Looking into managing the production of a manufacturing enterprise requires developing an appropriate dynamical economic and mathematical model. First of all, a model of the dynamics of the managed object under consideration (an enterprise) is required which will allow predicting its state in a specific period. The basic elements of such a model are: the phase vector of the controlled object, containing the main parameters describing its state; the demand vector characterizing the volume of demand for the enterprise's products; the control action vector (the control) of that is managed by the subject of management, and the vector of a priori uncertain risks (disturbances) that affect the dynamics of the object. A key task for managers of a manufacturing enterprise is developing methods for optimizing production management in order to achieve the best (optimal) values for the generated target function (functions) which is selected as a criterion (criteria) for the quality of its implementation. To solve this issue, a computer software system for information support and management is necessary at the enterprise, which allows predicting the state of the process under consideration and supporting management decisions. Notably, in real-life situations, production risks are inevitable; various disturbances have a significant impact on production, and such a system must take these into account. For this, a dynamical economic and mathematical model is needed for optimizing the management of product output for given (predicted) demand in case several objective functions and risks (disturbances) are present.

Various studies look into problems of optimally managing product output. The paper [18] describes an algorithm for such optimal management using a linear mathematical programming model. Based on it, a computer software application was developed to automate management decision-making. The study [23] examines the management of a medical institution and the possibility of optimizing corporate social responsibility. This paper formalizes the problem under consideration within the framework of a nonlinear mathematical programming model. The developed model is matched with a linearized model within which the authors created an iterative heuristic algorithm that allows eliminating repetitive computational operations. The article also describes the computational procedure and a computer experiment, which yielded an acceptable result for solving the problem under consideration. Szopa and Marczyk [24] study multicriteria optimization of managing the production of ceramic bearings at a manufacturing plant. To solve this problem, a linear mathematical programming model is proposed, on the basis of which various options for feasible solutions are analyzed and a compromise solution is found. The study [25] considers multicriteria optimization of enterprise production management. Here, scalarization of the vector objective function is used by transforming the original problem into a canonical linear mathematical programming problem. The results of the numerical experiment are implemented in the MatLab environment and presented in the work.

Olanrele et al. [26] looked into the optimal management of enterprise costs for a given production output. A linear discrete-time economic-mathematical model was developed, and a modification of the dynamic programming method was used, which is presented in [27]. For optimizing production planning in the case of a convex objective function, David et al. [11] describe a differential model that uses the Cobb-Douglas production function. The necessary optimality conditions are analyzed in the form of Pontryagin's maximum principle. The study [16] presents the discrete-time dynamical model of a "digital twin" of a manufacturing enterprise created by the authors (using the example of a television equipment assembly plant). This paper proposes a combined approach based on hybrid techniques of agent-based and discrete-event simulation modeling. The article also describes the proposed digital model based on which computer software was implemented in the AnyLogic simulation environment. A discrete-time dynamical model of product output by a manufacturing enterprise with a priori uncertain demand was studied in [28]. To solve the problem of optimizing the adaptive management of the process under consideration, a specialized genetic algorithm was developed that minimizes the objective function. In [8–10, 12, 15–17, 19, 22, 23], models and methods of simulation and agent-based modeling of production systems management are widely presented. Dynamical economic and mathematical models for managing socio-economic processes were studied in [13, 14, 20, 21].

The brief overview of the most typical works related to the present study allows drawing the following conclusions:

1) the tasks of economic and mathematical modeling of managing dynamical processes of industrial enterprises are relevant and complex;
2) static models of linear mathematical programming and various versions of the simplex method are widely used to develop numerical methods for solving problems of optimal management of production;
3) when using static models of nonlinear mathematical programming, various schemes for linearization of the original model were developed to form an

approximate numerical solution already within the framework of the corresponding linear mathematical programming models;

4) issues of optimally managing dynamical production processes in the case of technical and economic conditions and restrictions are most often studied using linear or nonlinear discrete-time and differential economic and mathematical models, on the basis of which the search for optimal solutions is carried out using dynamic programming, Pontryagin's maximum principle, agent-based modeling, etc.

## 3 Methodology

Modeling the dynamics of managing objects in production systems and solving issues of the corresponding processes require special economic and mathematical tools that take into account the characteristics of the objects and processes under consideration.

Developing economic and mathematical models of managing complex multifactor dynamical systems is carried out within two main directions—stochastic and deterministic. Stochastic models and methods demand following strict requirements and conditions for their implementation (see [29]). At the same time, studies of managing socio-economic and production systems reveal that these requirements and conditions are most often impossible to meet.

The deterministic Minimax approach (optimization of a guaranteed result) for modeling management of production systems required satisfied conditions on sets that limit the permissible values for the parameters used in the model. Such conditions are not burdensome and are usually reduced to acceptable properties of sets in finite-dimensional vector spaces (see [1, 3]).

For the issue studied in the present work, the methodology of the Minimax approach presented in [1–3] is used, which allows taking into account a priori uncertain risks (disturbances). To simulate the dynamics of the process under consideration, a new dynamical model was developed in the form of a system of linear discrete-time recurrent equations. It contains the phase vector that describes the key parameters characterizing its state, the control action vector controlled by the controlled subject, the demand vector, and the vector that describes a priori uncertain risks (disturbances) that arise in production. The control vector takes only a finite set of values in each period, and the phase vector of the model, the demand vector, and the risk vector are limited by convex compact polyhedrons (with a finite number of vertices) in the corresponding finite-dimensional vector spaces. The quality of implementing the process under consideration is assessed using a vector terminal objective function that depends on the sets of implementations of vector control functions, and risks (for fixed demand) on a given integer time interval, and its values are determined in the final states of the phase vector of the controlled object.

For the initial issue, an economic and mathematical formalization is proposed in the form of a multi-step problem of Minimax terminal program control [3] of enterprise product output with a vector objective function and risks. The paper describes the proposed constructive method for solving the problem under consideration, based on the general recurrent algebraic method [3, 4] for constructing reachability sets (prediction sets) of linear discrete-time controlled dynamical systems, and discusses the possibility of its implementation as a corresponding computer application. The obtained results are based on [3–6] and are adjacent to works [1, 2, 7, 14, 20, 21, 30–32].

# 4 Results

## 4.1 *Forming a Discrete-Time Dynamical Model for Managing the Production of an Enterprise in Case of Risks*

Below is the formalization of a discrete-time controlled model, which describes the dynamics of the main parameters of the production system and the existing limitations in the process under consideration.

Let us consider managing the product output of an enterprise on a given integer time interval (hereinafter, a time interval)$\overline{0,T} = \{0, 1, \ldots, T\}$ ($T \in \mathbf{N}$, hereinafter,$\mathbf{N}$ is the set of all natural numbers). Then, using the results of [3, 5], it is possible to form the following new system of linear discrete-time recurrent equations which describes the dynamics of the process under consideration, taking into account the volume of demand for the enterprise's products, control influence, and risks (a priori uncertain disturbances)

$$\begin{cases} x(t+1) = H(t)x(t) + \overline{u}(t) - \overline{s}(t) + \omega^{(1)}(t)\left(\varepsilon^{(1)}(t)\right)', \\ x(0) = x_0 = \mathbf{0}_{\overline{n}},\ \overline{s}(0) = \overline{s}_0, \\ z(t+1) = R(t)z(t) + v(t) - \overline{A}(t)\overline{u}(t) + \omega^{(2)}(t)\left(\varepsilon^{(2)}(t)\right)',\ z(0) = z_0, \\ k(t+1) = \gamma(t)k(t) + \\ +\alpha \cdot \left(\langle c(t), \overline{s}(t)\rangle_{\overline{n}} - \langle q(t), l(t)\rangle_m - \langle p(t), x(t)\rangle_{\overline{n}} - \langle d(t), z(t)\rangle_m\right) - \\ -\beta(t) \cdot G + \omega^{(3)}(t)\varepsilon^{(3)}(t), \\ k(0) = k_0 = G + G_0, \\ Z(t+1) = Z(t) + \langle q(t), l(t)\rangle_m + \langle p(t), x(t)\rangle_{\overline{n}} + \langle d(t), z(t)\rangle_m + \\ +\beta(t)G + \omega^{(4)}(t)\varepsilon^{(4)}(t), \\ Z(0) = \langle p(0), x(0)\rangle_{\overline{n}} + \langle d(0), z(0)\rangle_m,\ t \in \overline{0, T-1}, \end{cases} \tag{1}$$

where $\overline{n}$ is the total number of finished products types of the enterprise ($\overline{n} \in \mathbf{N}$); $m$ is the total number of types of resources for the given product ($m \in \mathbf{N}$); $x(t) = (x_1(t), x_2(t), \ldots, x_{\overline{n}}(t))'$ is the vector of volumes of finished product left and stored in enterprise warehouses during the period $t \in \overline{0, T}$, $x(t) \in \mathbf{R}^{\overline{n}}$ (hereinafter, for $\delta \in \mathbf{N}$, $\mathbf{R}^{\delta}$ is the $\delta$-dimensional vector space of column vectors, even if written in a row to save space); $\mathbf{0}_{\overline{n}} = \Big(\underbrace{0, 0, \ldots, 0}_{\overline{n}}\Big)' \in \mathbf{R}^{\overline{n}}$; $z(t) = (z_1(t), z_2(t), \ldots, z_m(t))'$ is the vector of volumes of remaining production resources stored in enterprise warehouses during the period $t \in \overline{0, T-1}$, $z(t) \in \mathbf{R}^m$; $\overline{A}(t) = \left\|\overline{a}_{ij}(t)\right\|_{\substack{i \in \overline{1,m} \\ j \in \overline{1,\overline{n}}}}$ is the matrix of norms for resource consumption in the period $t \in \overline{0, T-1}$ of dimension $(m \times \overline{n})$, ($\overline{a}_{ij}(t)$is the amount of $i$-th type resources required for the $j$-th type of production unit, ($i \in \overline{1, m}, j \in \overline{1, \overline{n}}$); $\overline{u}(t) = (\overline{u}_1(t), \overline{u}_2(t), \ldots, \overline{u}_{\overline{n}}(t))'$ is the vector production intensity in the period $t \in \overline{0, T-1}$, $\overline{u}(t) \in \mathbf{R}^{\overline{n}}$; $v(t) = (v_1(t), v_2(t), \ldots, v_m(t))'$ is the vector of warehouse resources replenishment intensity during the period $t \in \overline{0, T-1}$, $v(t) \in \mathbf{R}^m$; $\varepsilon(t) = ((\varepsilon^{(1)}(t))', (\varepsilon^{(2)}(t))', \varepsilon^{(3)}(t), \varepsilon^{(4)}(t))'$ is the vector of risks (uncontrollable disturbances) in the system during the period $t \in \overline{0, T-1}$, $\varepsilon(t) \in \mathbf{R}^{\overline{n}+m+2}$; $\omega(t) = ((\omega^{(1)}(t))', (\omega^{(2)}(t))', \omega^{(3)}(t), \omega^{(4)}(t))'$ is the given vector in the period $t \in \overline{0, T-1}$, $\omega(t) \in \mathbf{R}^{\overline{n}+m+2}$; $\overline{s}(t) = (\overline{s}_1(t), \overline{s}_2(t), \ldots, \overline{s}_{\overline{n}}(t))'$ is the given (predicted) vector of demand for finished products of the enterprise produced in the period $t \in \overline{0, T-1}$, $\overline{s}(t) \in \mathbf{R}^{\overline{n}}$; $\overline{s}(0) = (\overline{s}_1(0), \overline{s}_2(0), \ldots, \overline{s}_{\overline{n}}(0))' = \overline{s}_0$ is the vector of the initial volume of demand for finished products during management in the initial period (at $t = 0$), $\overline{s}_0 \in \mathbf{R}^{\overline{n}}$; $z(0) = (z_1(0), z_2(0), \ldots, z_m(0))' = z_0$ is the vector of the initial production resources volume during management in the initial period (at $t = 0$), $z_0 \in \mathbf{R}^m$; if at the beginning of the period $t \in \overline{0, T-1}$ stocks of finished products in warehouses were in the quantity $x(t)$, by the end of this period only a part of it will be suitable for sale, equaling $H(t)x(t)$, where $H(t) = \left\|h_{jj}(t)\right\|_{j \in \overline{1,\overline{n}}}$ is the diagonal matrix of dimension$(\overline{n} \times \overline{n})$, characterizing the "aging" of products for this period; for the reserves of production resources described by the vector $z(t)$, by the end of the period $t \in \overline{0, T-1}$, only a part of them will be suitable for use in production, equaling $R(t)z(t)$, where $R(t) = \|r_{ii}(t)\|_{i \in \overline{1,m}}$ is the diagonal matrix of dimension($m \times m$), characterizing the "aging" of products for this period; the enterprise intends to form financial resources for investing in production expansion in the initial period of management (at $t = 0$) based on a bank loan in the amount $G$ and its own financial resources $G_0$ deducted from net profit and directed to expand production; $k(t)$ is the number of financial resources available at the beginning of the period; $t \in \overline{0, T-1}$; $\gamma(t)$ is the numerical coefficient ($0 \leq \gamma(t) \leq 1$) characterizing "unforeseen costs" of financial resources for the period $t \in \overline{0, T-1}$; $\alpha$ is the coefficient of tax deductions from profits; $\beta(t) = r/100 + \beta_{\partial}(t)$, here $r$ is he annual interest rate for the loan, $\beta_{\partial}(t)$ is the share of the paid loan during the period $t \in \overline{0, T-1}$; $c(t) = (c_1(t), c_2(t), \ldots, c_{\overline{n}}(t))'$ is the vector of real purchase prices for sold products manufactured by the enterprise during the period $t \in \overline{0, T-1}$, $c(t) \in \mathbf{R}^{\overline{n}}$; $q(t) = (q_1(t), q_2(t), \ldots, q_m(t))'$is the vector of real prices for production resources necessary for the enterprise to manufacture products in the period $t \in \overline{0, T-1}$, $q(t) \in \mathbf{R}^m$; $p(t) = (p_1(t), p_2(t), \ldots, p_{\overline{n}}(t))'$is the vector of the enterprise's costs for storing finished product left in warehouses during the period $t \in \overline{0, T-1}$, $p(t) \in \mathbf{R}^{\overline{n}}$; $d(t) = (d_1(t), d_2(t), \ldots, d_m(t))'$ is the vector of the enterprise's costs for storing the remaining production resources in warehouses during the period $t \in \overline{0, T-1}$, $d(t) \in \mathbf{R}^m$; the vector $l(t) = \left(\left\langle \overline{a}_1^{(1)}(t), \overline{u}(t) \right\rangle_{\overline{n}}, \left\langle \overline{a}_2^{(1)}(t), \overline{u}(t) \right\rangle_{\overline{n}}, \ldots, \langle \overline{a}_m^{(1)}(t), \right.$ $\left. \overline{u}(t) \rangle_{\overline{n}}\right)' \in \mathbf{R}^m$; the vector $\overline{a}_i^{(1)}(t) = (\overline{a}_{i1}(t), \overline{a}_{i2}(t), \ldots, \overline{a}_{i\overline{n}}(t))' \in \mathbf{R}^{\overline{n}}$, $i \in \overline{1, m}$, $t \in \overline{0, T-1}$; $Z(t)$ are the total costs of the enterprise for $t$ periods, $t \in \overline{0, T-1}$.

Notably, the parameters $\overline{A}(t)$, $H(t)$, $R(t)$, $\omega(t)$, $\overline{s}(t)$, $c(t)$, $q(t)$, $p(t)$, $d(t)$, $\alpha$, $\beta(t)$, $\gamma(t)$, $t \in \overline{0, T-1}$, $x_0$, $z_0$, $k_0$, $G$, $G_0$ in the system (1) are to be known in advance (for example, formed based on the available statistical data on the process under consideration, technical and economic forecasts, and other sources, by applying methods for assessing data and identifying the parameters of the system under consideration).

Let the vector $y(t) = (x_1(t), x_2(t), \ldots, x_{\overline{n}}(t), z_1(t), z_2(t), \ldots, z_m(t), k(t), Z(t))' = (y_1(t), y_2(t), \ldots, y_n(t))'$ be the *phase vector* for the system (1) in the period $t \in \overline{0, T}$, $y(t) \in \mathbf{R}^n$, where $n = \overline{n} + m + 2$, the coordinates of which characterize the state parameters of the enterprise under consideration—Object I; the vector $u(t) = (\overline{u}_1(t), \overline{u}_2(t), \ldots, \overline{u}_{\overline{n}}(t), v_1(t), v_2(t), \ldots, v_m(t))' = (u_1(t), u_2(t), \ldots, u_p(t))'$ is the *control action vector (the control)* for the system (1) in the period $t \in \overline{0, T-1}$, $u(t) \in \mathbf{R}^p$, where $p = \overline{n} + m$, which is controlled by the business entity—Agent $E$; the vector $s(t) = \left( \overline{s}_1(t), \overline{s}_2(t), \ldots, \overline{s}_{\overline{n}}(t), \underbrace{0, 0, \ldots, 0}_{m+2} \right)' = (s_1(t), s_2(t), \ldots, s_n(t))'$ is the *demand vector* for the enterprise's products for the system (1) in the period $t \in \overline{0, T-1}$, $s(t) \in \mathbf{R}^n$ and is assumed given; the vector $\varepsilon(t) = ((\varepsilon^{(1)}(t))', (\varepsilon^{(2)}(t))', \varepsilon^{(3)}(t), \varepsilon^{(4)}(t))' = (\varepsilon_1(t), \varepsilon_2(t), \ldots, \varepsilon_n(t))'$ is the *vector of a priori uncertain risks (disturbances)* for the system (1) during the period $t \in \overline{0, T-1}$, $\varepsilon(t) \in \mathbf{R}^n$.

Therefore, the system (1), which models the dynamics of the considered production by the enterprise—Object I, can be represented in the form of a vector-matrix linear discrete-time recurrent equation.

$$y(t+1) = A(t)y(t) + B(t)u(t) - s(t) + \omega(t)(\varepsilon(t))', y(0) = y_0, \quad t \in \overline{0, T-1}, \quad (2)$$

where $A(t)$ and $B(t)$ are real matrices of dimensions $(n \times n)$ and $(n \times p)$, respectively; their elements are formed from the system (1), and are described in detail in [5]; $\omega(t) = (\omega_1(t), \omega_2(t), \ldots, \omega_n(t))'$ is the given vector that characterizes the *influence of risks* on the dynamics of the considered production by an enterprise during the period $t \in \overline{0, T-1}$.

Below it is assumed that for the fixed $\delta \in \mathbf{N}$ and corresponding finite-dimensional vector space $\mathbf{R}^\delta$, the symbol $\mathbf{\Sigma}(\mathbf{R}^\delta)$ denotes *the set of all finite subsets* of this space, and the symbol $\mathbf{\Omega}(\mathbf{R}^\delta)$ denotes *the set of all convex compact polyhedrons (with a finite number of vertices)* contained in this space, for example, *the set of all parallelepipeds* (the definition assumes that single-element sets in the finite-dimensional vector spaces under consideration are convex compact polyhedron).

It is assumed that the parameters of the recurrent Eq. (1) must satisfy *the following specified restrictions*:

$$\forall t \in \overline{0,T} : y(t) \in \mathbf{Y}_*(t) \in \boldsymbol{\Omega}(\mathbf{R}^n); \tag{3}$$

$$\forall t \in \overline{0,T} : s(t) \in \mathbf{S}_*(t) \in \boldsymbol{\Omega}(\mathbf{R}^n); \tag{4}$$

$$\forall t \in \overline{0,T-1} : u(t) \in \mathbf{U}_*(t) = \left\{u^{(1)}(t), u^{(2)}(t), \ldots, u^{(K_t)}(t)\right\} \in \boldsymbol{\Sigma}(\mathbf{R}^p); \tag{5}$$

$$\left(\forall t \in \overline{0,T-1}\right) \wedge \left(u(t) \in \mathbf{U}_*(t)\right) : \varepsilon(t) \in \mathbf{E}_*(t; u(t)) \in \boldsymbol{\Omega}(\mathbf{R}^n). \tag{6}$$

Notably in (3), (4) and (6), for each period $t \in \overline{0,T}$ sets $\mathbf{Y}_*(t)$, $\mathbf{S}_*(t)$ and $\mathbf{E}_*(t; u(t))$, $u(t) \in \mathbf{U}_*(t)$, can be specified, for example, as corresponding multidimensional parallelepipeds in the space $\mathbf{R}^n$.

In the process under consideration, Agent *E* knows for each fixed period of time $\tau \in \overline{1,T-1}$ (based on the measurements taken): the phase vector $y(\tau) = y_\tau$ of Object I in the period $\tau(y(0) = y_0 \in \mathbf{Y}_{*0})$; $s_\tau(\cdot) = \{s_\tau(t)\}_{t \in \overline{\tau,T-1}}$ is the demand vector function$\left(\forall t \in \overline{\tau,T-1} : s_\tau(t) \in \mathbf{S}_*(t)\right)$ predicted over the time interval $\overline{\tau,T}$. It is also assumed that systems of Eqs. (1) and (2) describing the dynamics of the model of Object I, and restrictions (3)—(6) are known as well.

## 4.2 Formalizing the Issue of Minimax Terminal Program Control of Enterprise Product Output

Let us introduce a number of definitions necessary for the strict mathematical formalization of the aforementioned issue; here, the dynamics of the control object and restrictions on the phase vector, action control vector, demand vector, and risk vector are described by an economic-mathematical model (1)—(6).

For any sets *X* and *Y*, the set $X \times Y$ is the product of *X* and *Y*, i.e., the set of all pairs $\{x \times y\}$ such that $x \in X$, $y \in Y$ (a similar notation is used for a larger number of sets).

Hereinafter, for $k \in \mathbf{N}$ and the integer interval $\overline{i,j}$ $(i, j \in \mathbf{Z} : i \leq j$; $\mathbf{Z}$ is the set of all integers), the symbol $\Xi_k\left(\overline{i,j}\right)$ will denote the metric space of functions $\sigma : \overline{i,j} \to \mathbf{R}^k$ of an integer argument in which the metric $\rho_k$ is given by the relation

$$\rho_k(\sigma_1(\cdot), \sigma_2(\cdot)) = \max_{t \in \overline{i,j}} \|\sigma_1(t) - \sigma_2(t)\|_k, \{\sigma_1(\cdot), \sigma_2(\cdot)\} \in \Xi_k\left(\overline{i,j}\right) \times \Xi_k\left(\overline{i,j}\right)$$

(hereinafter, for any vector $a \in \mathbf{R}^k$, the symbol $\|a\|_k$ denotes the value of the Euclidean norm of this vector in the space $\mathbf{R}^k$).

For the fixed period $\tau$ $\left(\tau \in \overline{0,T-1}\right)$, based on constraint (4), *the set* $\mathbf{S}\left(\overline{\tau,T}\right) \subset \Xi_n\left(\overline{\tau,T-1}\right)$ *of admissible demand vector functions* (all possible *scenarios for implementing the function)* is defined over the time interval $\overline{\tau,T}$ by the following relation

$$\mathbf{S}\left(\overline{\tau,T}\right)=\left\{s_\tau(\cdot):s_\tau(\cdot)\in\Xi_n\left(\overline{\tau,T-1}\right),s_\tau(\cdot)=\{s_\tau(t)\}_{t\in\overline{\tau,T-1}},\forall t\in\overline{\tau,T-1},s_\tau(t)\in\mathbf{S}_*(t)\right\}. \tag{7}$$

Further, for the fixed period $\tau$ $\left(\tau\in\overline{0,T-1}\right)$, based on constraint (5), *the finite set* $\mathbf{U}\left(\overline{\tau,T}\right)\subset\Xi_p\left(\overline{\tau,T-1}\right)$ *of admissible program controls of Agent E* (all possible *scenarios for implementing the function*) is defined over the time interval $\overline{\tau,T}$ by the following relation

$$\mathbf{U}\left(\overline{\tau,T}\right)=\left\{u_\tau(\cdot):u_\tau(\cdot)\in\Xi_p\left(\overline{\tau,T-1}\right),u_\tau(\cdot)=\{u_\tau(t)\}_{t\in\overline{\tau,T-1}},\forall t\in\overline{\tau,T-1},u_\tau(t)\in\mathbf{U}_*(t)\right\}. \tag{8}$$

For the fixed period $\tau\in\overline{0,T-1}$ and for the control $u_\tau(\cdot)\in\mathbf{U}\left(\overline{\tau,T}\right)$ of Agent $E$, fixed over the time interval $\overline{\tau,T}$, based on constraint (6), the set $\mathbf{E}\left(\overline{\tau,T};u_\tau(\cdot)\right)\subset\Xi_n\left(\overline{\tau,T-1}\right)$ of *admissible risk vector functions* $\varepsilon_\tau(\cdot)\in\Xi_n\left(\overline{\tau,T-1}\right)$ (all possible *scenarios for implementing the function*) is defined over the time interval $\overline{\tau,T}$, corresponding to the program control $u_\tau(\cdot)$, by the following relation:

$$\mathbf{E}\left(\overline{\tau,T};u_\tau(\cdot)\right)=\left\{\varepsilon_\tau(\cdot):\varepsilon_\tau(\cdot)\in\Xi_n\left(\overline{\tau,T-1}\right),\varepsilon_\tau(\cdot)=\{\varepsilon_\tau(t)\}_{t\in\overline{\tau,T-1}},\forall t\in\overline{\tau,T-1},\right.$$
$$\left.\varepsilon_\tau(t)\in\mathbf{E}_*\left(t;u_\tau(t)\right)\right\}. \tag{9}$$

Let us name the set $w(\tau)=\{\tau,y(\tau),s_\tau(\cdot)\}=w_\tau\in\overline{0,T}\times\mathbf{R}^n\times\Xi_n\left(\overline{\tau,T-1}\right)$ $(w(0)=\{0,y_0,s_0(\cdot)\}=w_0)$ *$\tau$-position of the discrete-time controlled dynamical system* (1)–(6), or simply*$\tau$-position of the system*$\left(s_0(\cdot)=\{s_0(t)\}_{t\in\overline{0,T}}\right)$. For each $\tau\in\overline{0,T}$ let us define the set $\mathbf{W}(\tau)=\{\tau\}\times\mathbf{Y}_*(t)\times\mathbf{S}\left(\overline{\tau,T}\right)$ $\left(\mathbf{W}(0)=\mathbf{W}_0=\{0\}\times\mathbf{Y}_{*0}\times\mathbf{S}\left(\overline{0,T}\right)\right)$ of all *admissible $\tau$-positions* of the system under consideration.

Next, let $y(\cdot)=\psi_{\overline{\tau,T}}(\cdot;y_\tau,u_\tau(\cdot),s_\tau(\cdot),\varepsilon_\tau(\cdot))=\{y(t)\}_{t\in\overline{\tau,T}}$ be the phase trajectory of Object I, admissible over the time interval $\overline{\tau,T}\subseteq\overline{0,T}$and corresponding to the admissible set $\{y_\tau,u_\tau(\cdot),s_\tau(\cdot),\varepsilon_\tau(\cdot)\}\in\mathbf{R}^n\times\mathbf{U}\left(\overline{\tau,T}\right)\times\mathbf{S}\left(\overline{\tau,T}\right)\times\mathbf{E}\left(\overline{\tau,T};u_\tau(\cdot)\right)$ $(w(\tau)=\{\tau,y_\tau,s_\tau(\cdot)\}=w_\tau;w(0)=\{0,y_0,s_0(\cdot)\}=\{0,y_0,s_0(\cdot)\}=w_0)$, if $\forall t\in\overline{\tau,T}$: $y(t)=\psi_{\overline{\tau,T}}(t;y_\tau,u_\tau(\cdot),s_\tau(\cdot),\varepsilon_\tau(\cdot))\in\mathbf{Y}_*(t)$, $y(\tau)=y_\tau$, where $\psi_{\overline{\tau,T}}:\mathbf{R}^n\times\Xi_p\left(\overline{\tau,T-1}\right)\times\Xi_n\left(\overline{\tau,T-1}\right)\times\Xi_n\left(\overline{\tau,T-1}\right)\to\Xi_n\left(\overline{\tau,T}\right)$ is the operator of the right side of the Eq. (2), acting in the time interval $\overline{\tau,T}$ and such that each set $\{y_\tau,u_\tau(\cdot),s_\tau(\cdot),\varepsilon_\tau(\cdot)\}\in\mathbf{R}^n\times\Xi_p\left(\overline{\tau,T-1}\right)\times\Xi_n\left(\overline{\tau,T-1}\right)\times\Xi_n\left(\overline{\tau,T-1}\right)$ is associated with the phase trajectory $y_\tau(\cdot)=\{y_\tau(t)\}_{t\in\overline{\tau,T}}=\psi_{\overline{\tau,T}}(\cdot;y_\tau,u_\tau(\cdot),s_\tau(\cdot),\varepsilon_\tau(\cdot))\in\Xi_n\left(\overline{\tau,T}\right)$ of Object I based on the following formula:

$$\forall t \in \overline{\tau, T-1} : y_\tau(t+1) = A(t)y_\tau(t) + B(t)u_\tau(t) - s_\tau(t) + \omega(t)(\varepsilon_\tau(t))', y_\tau(\tau) = y_\tau.$$

It is believed that over the time interval $\overline{\tau, T} \subseteq \overline{0, T}$ for all admissible implementations of the sets $\{w(\tau), u_\tau(\cdot), \varepsilon_\tau(\cdot)\} \in \mathbf{W}(\tau) \times \mathbf{U}(\overline{\tau, T}) \times \mathbf{E}(\overline{\tau, T}; u_\tau(\cdot))$, $w(\tau) = \{\tau, y(\tau), s_\tau(\cdot)\} = \{\tau, y_\tau, s_\tau(\cdot)\} = w_\tau \in \mathbf{W}(\tau)$ ($w(0) = \{0, y(0), s_0(\cdot)\} = \{0, y_0, s_0(\cdot)\} = w_0 \in \mathbf{W}_{*0}$), *the quality of the considered production by an enterprise* is assessed by *the vector terminal objective function* $\mathbf{F}_{\overline{\tau,T}} = \left(\mathbf{F}^{(1)}_{\overline{\tau,T}}, \mathbf{F}^{(2)}_{\overline{\tau,T}}, \ldots, \mathbf{F}^{(r)}_{\overline{\tau,T}}\right)$ *of Agent E*, which consists of $r$ ($r \in \mathbf{N}$) *terminal objective functions* $\mathbf{F}^{(i)}_{\overline{\tau,T}} : \mathbf{W}(\tau) \times \mathbf{U}(\overline{\tau, T}) \times \mathbf{E}(\overline{\tau, T}; u_\tau(\cdot)) \rightarrow \mathbf{R}^1$, $i \in \overline{1, r}$, the values of which for the admissible implementations of sets $\{w(\tau), u_\tau(\cdot), \varepsilon_\tau(\cdot)\} \in \mathbf{W}(\tau) \times \mathbf{U}(\overline{\tau, T}) \times \mathbf{E}(\overline{\tau, T}; u_\tau(\cdot))$ assess the quality of control of the process under consideration and are determined through the values of the corresponding *convex terminal functionals* $\lambda^{(i)} : \mathbf{R}^n \rightarrow \mathbf{R}^1$ based on the following formulas:

$$\mathbf{F}^{(i)}_{\overline{\tau,T}}(w_\tau, u_\tau(\cdot), \varepsilon_\tau(\cdot)) = \lambda^{(i)}\left(\psi_{\overline{\tau,T}}(T; y_\tau, u_\tau(\cdot), s_\tau(\cdot), \varepsilon_\tau(\cdot))\right) = \lambda^{(i)}(y(T)),$$
$$i \in \overline{1, r}, \tag{10}$$

where $y(T) = y_\tau(T) = \psi_{\overline{\tau,T}}(T; y_\tau, u_\tau(\cdot), s_\tau(\cdot), \varepsilon_\tau(\cdot))$, $\forall t \in \overline{\tau+1, T}$: $y_\tau(t) = \psi_{\overline{\tau,T}}(t; y_\tau, u_\tau(\cdot), s_\tau(\cdot), \varepsilon_\tau(\cdot)) \in \mathbf{Y}_*(t)$, $y_\tau(\tau) = y_\tau$.

It is assumed that each convex terminal functional $\lambda^{(i)}$, $i \in \overline{1, r}$, *has continuous partial derivatives on the coordinates of the phase vector* $y$ of Object I.

Based on the vector objective function $\mathbf{F}_{\overline{\tau,T}} = \left(\mathbf{F}^{(1)}_{\overline{\tau,T}}, \mathbf{F}^{(2)}_{\overline{\tau,T}}, \ldots, \mathbf{F}^{(r)}_{\overline{\tau,T}}\right)$, introduced by the relation (10), *to assess the optimization of managing the processes under consideration*, let us regard *the convex scalar objective function* $\mathbf{\Phi}_{\overline{\tau,T}} : \mathbf{W}(\tau) \times \mathbf{U}(\overline{\tau, T}) \times \mathbf{E}(\overline{\tau, T}; u_\tau(\cdot)) \rightarrow \mathbf{R}^1$, the values of which over the time interval $\overline{\tau, T}$ for admissible implementations of the sets $\{w(\tau), u_\tau(\cdot), \varepsilon_\tau(\cdot)\} \in \mathbf{W}(\tau) \times \mathbf{U}(\overline{\tau, T}) \times \mathbf{E}(\overline{\tau, T}; u_\tau(\cdot))$, where $w(\tau) = \{\tau, y(\tau), s_\tau(\cdot)\} = \{\tau, y_\tau, s_\tau(\cdot)\} = w_\tau \in \mathbf{W}(\tau)$ ($w(0) = \{0, y(0), s_0(\cdot)\} = \{0, y_0, s_0(\cdot)\} = w_0 \in \mathbf{W}_{*0}$), *are determined on the basis of convex terminal functionals* $\mathbf{F}^{(i)}_{\overline{\tau,T}}$, $i \in \overline{1, r}$, according to the following formula:

$$\Phi_{\overline{\tau,T}}(w_\tau, u_\tau(\cdot), \varepsilon_\tau(\cdot)) = \sum_{i=1}^{r} \mu_i \cdot \mathbf{F}^{(i)}_{\overline{\tau,T}}(w_\tau, u_\tau(\cdot), \varepsilon_\tau(\cdot)) =$$

$$= \sum_{i=1}^{r} \mu_i \cdot \lambda^{(i)}\left(\psi_{\overline{\tau,T}}(T; y_\tau, u_\tau(\cdot), s_\tau(\cdot), \varepsilon_\tau(\cdot))\right) = \sum_{i=1}^{r} \mu_i \cdot \lambda^{(i)}(y(T)) =$$

$$= \lambda(y(T)) = \lambda\left(\psi_{\overline{\tau,T}}(T; y_\tau, u_\tau(\cdot), s_\tau(\cdot), \varepsilon_\tau(\cdot))\right),$$

$$\forall i \in \overline{1,r} : \mu_i \geq 0, \sum_{i=1}^{r} \mu_i = 1, \tag{11}$$

where $y(T) = y_\tau(T) = \psi_{\overline{\tau,T}}(T; y_\tau, u_\tau(\cdot), s_\tau(\cdot), \varepsilon_\tau(\cdot))$ ; $\lambda : \mathbf{R}^n \to \mathbf{R}^1$ is the *convex terminal functional.*

Note that the terminal objective function $\Phi_{\overline{\tau,T}}(w_\tau, u_\tau(\cdot), \varepsilon_\tau(\cdot))$ is *a convex scalar convolution* of the original vector terminal objective function $\mathbf{F}_{\overline{\tau,T}} = \left(\mathbf{F}^{(1)}_{\overline{\tau,T}}, \mathbf{F}^{(2)}_{\overline{\tau,T}}, \ldots, \mathbf{F}^{(r)}_{\overline{\tau,T}}\right)$, i.e. it is formed in accordance with *scalarization of vector objective functions* (see, for example, [30]), with non-negative scalar weighting coefficients$\mu_i$, $i \in \overline{1,r}$, which *can be determined, for example, by expert means or based on knowledge of statistical information* about the history of implementing the main parameters which describe the considered processes of the enterprise and external influences.

Thus, the dynamical system (1)—(11) is *the economic-mathematical model* for the process under consideration in the case of a vector objective function and risks.

Within the formed economic-mathematical model (1)—(11), which describes with the relations (1)—(6) and over the considered integer time interval $\overline{0,T}$ the dynamics of the phase vector of Object I—a set of basic parameters of the enterprise characterizing its state, the implementation restrictions of the phase vector of Object I, control vector of Agent *E*, demand vector, and risk vector, the auxiliary elements introduced by relations (7)—(9), as well as the scalar convex objective function $\Phi_{\overline{\tau,T}}$, the values of which are determined on the basis of the original vector objective function $\mathbf{F}_{\overline{\tau,T}} = \left(\mathbf{F}^{(1)}_{\overline{\tau,T}}, \mathbf{F}^{(2)}_{\overline{\tau,T}}, \ldots, \mathbf{F}^{(r)}_{\overline{\tau,T}}\right)$ according to formulas (10), (11), one can formulate *the following multi-step problem of Minimax terminal program control of enterprise product output with a vector objective function and risks.*

**Problem 1** Over the time interval $\overline{0,T}$ $(T \in \mathbf{N})$ for the multi-step process of managing the output of an enterprise, described by a discrete-time controlled dynamical system (1)—(6), for the given period $\tau \in \overline{0,T-1}$, $\tau$-position of the system $w(\tau) = \{\tau, y(\tau), s_\tau(\cdot)\} = \{\tau, y_\tau, s_\tau(\cdot)\} = w_\tau \in \mathbf{W}(\tau)$ $(w(0)=\{0, y(0), s_0(\cdot)\}= =\{0, y_0, s_0(\cdot)\} = w_0 \in \mathbf{W}_{*0})$ and for the generated terminal objective function $\Phi_{\overline{\tau,T}}$ which is the scalar convolution of the given vector terminal objective function $\mathbf{F}_{\overline{\tau,T}} = \left(\mathbf{F}^{(1)}_{\overline{\tau,T}}, \mathbf{F}^{(2)}_{\overline{\tau,T}}, \ldots, \mathbf{F}^{(r)}_{\overline{\tau,T}}\right)$, its values are determined according to formulas (10), (11) based on convex terminal functionals$\lambda^{(i)}$, $i \in \overline{1,r}$, forming a convex terminal functional $\lambda$ which has continuous partial derivatives on the coordinates of the phase vector $y$ of Object I, Agent $E$ needs to find the set $\mathbf{U}^{(e)}_{\mathbf{\Phi}_{\overline{\tau,T}}}(\overline{\tau,T},w_\tau) \subseteq \mathbf{U}(\overline{\tau,T})$ of admissible program controls $u_\tau^{(e)}(\cdot) \in \mathbf{U}(\overline{\tau,T})$ of Agent $E$ over the time interval $\overline{\tau,T}$, and the number $\mathbf{\Phi}^{(e)}_{\overline{\tau,T}} = c_\lambda^{(e)}(\overline{\tau,T},w_\tau)$ both satisfying the following *Minimax condition:*

$$
\begin{aligned}
&\mathbf{U}^{(e)}_{\mathbf{\Phi}_{\overline{\tau,T}}}(\overline{\tau,T},w_\tau) = \{u_\tau^{(e)}(\cdot) : u_\tau^{(e)}(\cdot) = \left\{u_\tau^{(e)}(t)\right\}_{t\in\overline{\tau,T-1}} \in \mathbf{U}(\overline{\tau,T}),\\
&\mathbf{\Phi}^{(e)}_{\overline{\tau,T}} = \mathbf{\Phi}_{\overline{\tau,T}}\left(w_\tau, u_\tau^{(e)}(\cdot), \varepsilon_\tau^{(e)}(\cdot)\right) = \max_{\varepsilon_\tau(\cdot)\in\mathbf{E}\left(\overline{\tau,T};u_\tau^{(e)}(\cdot)\right)} \mathbf{\Phi}_{\overline{\tau,T}}\left(w_\tau, u_\tau^{(e)}(\cdot), \varepsilon_\tau(\cdot)\right) =\\
&\quad= \min_{u_\tau(\cdot)\in\mathbf{U}\left(\overline{\tau,T}\right)} \max_{\varepsilon_\tau(\cdot)\in\mathbf{E}\left(\overline{\tau,T};u_\tau(\cdot)\right)} \mathbf{\Phi}_{\overline{\tau,T}}(w_\tau, u_\tau(\cdot), \varepsilon_\tau(\cdot)) =\\
&\quad= \min_{u_\tau(\cdot)\in\mathbf{U}\left(\overline{\tau,T}\right)} \max_{\varepsilon_\tau(\cdot)\in\mathbf{E}\left(\overline{\tau,T};u_\tau(\cdot)\right)} \lambda\left(\psi_{\overline{\tau,T}}(T; y_\tau, u_\tau(\cdot), s_\tau(\cdot), \varepsilon_\tau(\cdot))\right) =\\
&\quad= \max_{\varepsilon_\tau(\cdot)\in\mathbf{E}\left(\overline{\tau,T};u_\tau^{(e)}(\cdot)\right)} \lambda\left(\psi_{\overline{\tau,T}}\left(T; y_\tau, u_\tau^{(e)}(\cdot), s_\tau(\cdot), \varepsilon_\tau(\cdot)\right)\right) =\\
&\quad= \lambda\left(\psi_{\overline{\tau,T}}\left(T; y_\tau, u_\tau^{(e)}(\cdot), s_\tau(\cdot), \varepsilon_\tau^{(e)}(\cdot)\right)\right) = c_\lambda^{(e)}(\overline{\tau,T},w_\tau),\\
&\forall t \in \overline{\tau+1,T} : y_\tau^{(e)}(t) = \psi_{\overline{\tau,T}}\left(t; y_\tau, u_\tau^{(e)}(\cdot), s_\tau(\cdot), \varepsilon_\tau^{(e)}(\cdot)\right) \in \mathbf{Y}_*(t),\\
&y(0) = y_0 \in \mathbf{Y}_{*0}\},
\end{aligned}
\tag{12}
$$

*by implementing a finite sequence of only one-step operations that allow their algorithmization.*

Let us call $\mathbf{U}^{(e)}_{\mathbf{\Phi}_{\overline{\tau,T}}}(\overline{\tau,T},w_\tau)$ the set of *Minimax program controls* of Agent $E$, and the number $\mathbf{\Phi}^{(e)}_{\overline{\tau,T}} = c_\lambda^{(e)}(\overline{\tau,T},w_\tau)$ *the optimal guaranteed result* or *the Minimax value of the objective function* $\mathbf{\Phi}_{\overline{\tau,T}}$ *for the problem of Minimax terminal program control of enterprise product output with a vector objective function and risks* on a given time interval $\overline{\tau,T}$ for the multi-step discrete-time controlled dynamical model (1)—(11) relative to its $\tau$-position $w(\tau) = w_\tau$ ($w(0) = w_0$).

Taking into account the finiteness of the set of program controls $\mathbf{U}(\overline{\tau,T})$ of Agent $E$, admissible over the time interval $\overline{\tau,T}$, the properties of the multi-step discrete-time dynamical model (1)—(11), and the Minimax condition in (12), it can be shown, similarly to the way it is described in [3], that the solution for the formulated task exists.

### 4.3 Constructive Technique for Solving the Problem of Minimax Terminal Program Control of Enterprise Product Output with a Vector Objective Function and Risks

Notably, Problem 1, described by the economic-mathematical model (1)—(12), cannot be solved by enumerating acceptable options for the risk vector $\varepsilon(t)$ since in each period $t \in \overline{0, T-1}$, for each control $u(t) \in \mathbf{U}_*(t)$ of Agent $E$, the corresponding set $\mathbf{E}(\overline{\tau, T}; u(t))$ appearing in constraint (6) and limiting its permissible values, in the general case, is a convex compact polyhedron (with a finite number of vertices) in the space $\mathbf{R}^n$, i.e., is an infinite set.

For any convex compact polyhedron$X$(with a finite number of vertices) in the space $\mathbf{R}^\delta$ ($\delta \in \mathbf{N}$), let us useV - rep$\{X\}$ to denote the set of all its vertices [12]. Then the convex hull of the setV - rep$\{X\}$ coincides with$X$, i.e., $\mathrm{co}_\delta$(V - rep$\{X\}$) $= X$. The symbol H - rep$\{X\}$ denotes such a finite system of linear algebraic equations and inequalities that the set of its solutions coincides with $X$, i.e., $\mathrm{Sol}_\delta$(H - rep$\{X\}$) $= X$.

Thus, the set V - rep$\{X\}$ and the finite system of linear algebraic equations and inequalities H - rep$\{X\}$describe a convex compact polyhedron (with a finite number of vertices) $X$using the dual operationsV - rep and H - rep.

Further, for the given period $\tau \in \overline{0, T-1}$ and $\tau$-position of the system $w(\tau) = \{\tau, y(\tau), s_\tau(\cdot)\} = \{\tau, y_\tau, s_\tau(\cdot)\} = w_\tau \in \mathbf{W}(\tau)$ $(w(0)=\{0, y(0), s_0(\cdot)\} = \{0, y_0, s_0(\cdot)\}= =w_0 \in \mathbf{W}_{*0})$, the symbol $\mathbf{Y}(\cdot; \overline{\tau, T}, y_\tau, u_\tau(\cdot), s_\tau(\cdot))$ denotes *the tube of all permissible phase trajectories* $y_\tau(\cdot) = \psi_{\overline{\tau,T}}(\cdot; y_\tau, u_\tau(\cdot), s_\tau(\cdot), \varepsilon_\tau(\cdot))$ of Object I [2], [3] on the time interval $\overline{\tau, T}$, corresponding to the set $\{y_\tau, u_\tau(\cdot), s_\tau(\cdot)\} \in \mathbf{R}^n \times \times \mathbf{U}(\overline{\tau, T}) \times \mathbf{S}(\overline{\tau, T})$, i.e., this is the set of all admissible phase trajectories of Object I, which is determined by the following formula:

$$\mathbf{Y}(\cdot; \overline{\tau, T}, y_\tau, u_\tau(\cdot), s_\tau(\cdot),) = \Big\{ y_\tau(\cdot) : y_\tau(\cdot) = \{y_\tau(t)\}_{t \in \overline{\tau,T}} \in \Xi_n(\overline{\tau, T}),$$
$$y_\tau(\cdot) = \psi_{\overline{\tau,T}}(\cdot; y_\tau, u_\tau(\cdot), s_\tau(\cdot), \varepsilon_\tau(\cdot)),$$
$$\forall t \in \overline{\tau, T}, y_\tau(t) \in \mathbf{Y}_*(t), \varepsilon_\tau(\cdot) \in \mathbf{E}(\overline{\tau, T}; u_\tau(\cdot)) \Big\}, \tag{13}$$

and $\mathbf{Y}(t; \overline{\tau, T}, y_\tau, u_\tau(\cdot), s_\tau(\cdot))$ denotes its section in the period $t \in \overline{\tau, T}$ $(\mathbf{Y}(\tau; \overline{\tau, T}, y_\tau, u_\tau(\cdot), s_\tau(\cdot)) = \{y_\tau(\tau)\} = \{y_\tau\})$.

For the period $t \in \overline{\tau + 1, T}$, let us call the set $\mathbf{Y}(t; \overline{\tau, T}, y_\tau, u_\tau(\cdot), s_\tau(\cdot))$ *the forecast set*, or the *reachability set* [1], [3] of Object I in this period, which is the set of all admissible phase vectors $y_\tau(t)$ of Object I, corresponding to the admissible implementation of the set $\{y_\tau, u_\tau(\cdot), s_\tau(\cdot)\}$, i.e. this is the set of those and only those phase vectors $y_\tau(t)$ of Object I, that admissible implementations of risk vector functions $\varepsilon_\tau(\cdot) \in \mathbf{E}(\overline{\tau, T}; u_\tau(\cdot))$ exist, for which the following is true: $y_\tau(t) = \psi_{\overline{\tau,T}}(t; y_\tau, u_\tau(\cdot), s_\tau(\cdot), \varepsilon_\tau(\cdot)) \in \mathbf{Y}(t; \overline{\tau, T}, y_\tau, u_\tau(\cdot), s_\tau(\cdot))$.

It can be shown (similar to the reasoning in [3]) that for the dynamical system under consideration (1)—(6), each forecast set$\mathbf{Y}\big(t; \overline{\tau, T}, y_\tau, u_\tau(\cdot), s_\tau(\cdot)\big)$, $t \in \overline{\tau, T}$, *is a convex compact polyhedron (with a finite number of vertices)* in the space $\mathbf{R}^n$.

Then, taking into account the results of [3], [6], the constructive technique for solving formulated multi-step Problem 1 can be represented as the implementation of the following *only one-step actions*.

1. For the multi-step process of managing the output of an enterprise, considered over the time interval $\overline{0, T}$ ($T \in \mathbf{N}$) and described by the discrete-time controlled dynamical system (1)—(6) and the given period $\tau \in \overline{0, T-1}$, the $\tau$-position of the system $w(\tau) = \{\tau, y(\tau), s_\tau(\cdot)\} = \{\tau, y_\tau, s_\tau(\cdot)\} = w_\tau$ ($w(0) = \{0, y(0), s_0(\cdot)\} = \{0, y_0, s_0(\cdot)\} = w_0$) is formed. Then, if $w_\tau \in \mathbf{W}(\tau)$, Action 2 is performed; if $w_\tau \notin \mathbf{W}(\tau)$, the conditions of Problem 1 are violated, and the search for a solution stops.
2. Based on the given vector terminal objective function $\mathbf{F}_{\overline{\tau,T}} = \left(\mathbf{F}^{(1)}_{\overline{\tau,T}}, \mathbf{F}^{(2)}_{\overline{\tau,T}}, \ldots, \mathbf{F}^{(r)}_{\overline{\tau,T}}\right)$, the corresponding scalar convex terminal objective function$\mathbf{\Phi}_{\overline{\tau,T}}$ is formed which evaluates the quality of implementing the $r$ processes under consideration over the time interval$\overline{\tau, T}$, the values of which are calculated using formulas (10), (11) based on *convex terminal functionals* $\lambda^{(i)}$, $i \in \overline{1, r}$, which form the convex terminal functional $\lambda$ that has continuous partial derivatives on the coordinates of the phase vector $y$ of Object I.
3. Using constraint (5) and formula (8), the finite set $\mathbf{U}\big(\overline{\tau, T}\big) = \big\{u^{(k)}_\tau(\cdot)\big\}_{k \in \overline{1, L_\tau}}$ is formed consisting of $L_\tau$ admissible program controls of Agent $E$ over the time interval $\overline{\tau, T}$, $L_\tau \in \mathbf{N}$ (*realized by implementing a finite sequence of algebraic operations on vectors in space* $\mathbf{R}^p$).
4. For the formed $\tau$-position of the system $w_\tau = \{\tau, y_\tau, s_\tau(\cdot)\} \in \mathbf{W}(\tau)$($w_0 = \{0, y_0, s_0(\cdot)\} \in \mathbf{W}_{*0}$), the following is assumed:$\widetilde{\mathbf{U}}\big(\overline{\tau, T}\big) := \varnothing$; $k := 1$; $M_\tau := 0$.
5. For the admissible program control $u^{(k)}(\cdot) \in \mathbf{U}\big(\overline{\tau, T}\big)$, the problem of forming the forecast set $\mathbf{Y}\big(T; \overline{\tau, T}, y_\tau, u^{(k)}_\tau(\cdot), s_\tau(\cdot)\big)$ of Object I in the period $T$ is solved which corresponds to the known set $\big\{y_\tau, u^{(k)}_\tau(\cdot), s_\tau(\cdot)\big\}$ and is determined by formula (13) on the basis of the tube $\mathbf{Y}\big(\cdot; \overline{\tau, T}, y_\tau, u^{(k)}_\tau(\cdot), s_\tau(\cdot)\big)$ of all admissible phase trajectories of Object I over the time interval $\overline{\tau, T}$, and containing the set of all admissible final phase vectors $y(T) = \psi_{\overline{\tau,T}}\big(T; y_\tau, u^{(k)}_\tau(\cdot), s_\tau(\cdot), \varepsilon_\tau(\cdot)\big)$ of phase trajectories $y^{(k)}_\tau(\cdot) = \big\{y^{(k)}_\tau(t)\big\}_{t \in \overline{\tau,T}} = \psi_{\overline{\tau,T}}\big(\cdot; y_\tau, u^{(k)}_\tau(\cdot), s_\tau(\cdot), \varepsilon_\tau(\cdot)\big)$ of Object I over the time interval $\overline{\tau, T}$, corresponding to the sets $\big\{y_\tau, u^{(k)}_\tau(\cdot), s_\tau(\cdot), \varepsilon_\tau(\cdot)\big\}$, $\varepsilon_\tau(\cdot) \in \mathbf{E}\big(\overline{\tau, T}; u^{(k)}_\tau(\cdot)\big)$, and $\forall t \in \overline{\tau, T}$ the phase constraint (3) must be met: $y^{(k)}_\tau(t) = \psi_{\overline{\tau,T}}\big(t; y_\tau, u^{(k)}_\tau(\cdot), s_\tau(\cdot), \varepsilon_\tau(\cdot)\big) \in \mathbf{Y}_*(t)$, $y^{(k)}_\tau(\tau) = y_\tau \in \mathbf{Y}_*(\tau)$ $\big(y^{(k)}_\tau(0) = y_0 \in \mathbf{Y}_{*0}\big)$; if $\mathbf{Y}\big(T; \overline{\tau, T}, y_\tau, u^{(k)}_\tau(\cdot), s_\tau(\cdot)\big) = \varnothing$, the transition to action 6 is performed; if $\mathbf{Y}\big(T; \overline{\tau, T}, y_\tau, u^{(k)}_\tau(\cdot), s_\tau(\cdot)\big) \neq \varnothing$, i.e., if there is at least one phase trajectory of Object I, consisting of phase vectors each satisfying the

constraint (3), this set is a convex compact polyhedron (with a finite number of vertices) in space$\mathbf{R}^n$ [3] (by definition, it is assumed that the only vector of the space $\mathbf{R}^n$ is one with a single vertex) the following is supposed: $\widetilde{\mathbf{U}}(\overline{\tau,T}):=\widetilde{\mathbf{U}}(\overline{\tau,T}) \cup \{u_\tau^{(k)}(\cdot)\}$ ; $M_\tau$: $=$ $M_\tau$+1 (implemented by applying *the general recurrent algebraic method for constructing reachability sets (predictive sets)* of linear multi-step discrete-time controlled dynamical systems [3] and carried out by implementing a finite recurrent sequence of solutions to one-step linear mathematical programming problems, solutions to finite systems of linear algebraic equations and inequalities, a finite sequence of one-step algebraic operations on vectors and convex compact polyhedrons (with a finite number of vertices) in the spaces $\mathbf{R}^n$ and $\mathbf{R}^p$, i.e., by *implementing a finite recurrent sequence of only one-step operations that allow their algorithmization*).

6. Assuming $k := k + 1$, then if $k \leq L_\tau$, the transition to Action 5 is carried out; otherwise, Action 7 is performed.
7. If $M_\tau$=0, it is concluded there is not a single admissible program control $u_\tau^{(k)}(\cdot) \in \mathbf{U}(\overline{\tau,T}), k \in \overline{1,L_\tau}$, such that $\mathbf{Y}(T;\overline{\tau,T},y_\tau,u_\tau^{(k)}(\cdot),s_\tau(\cdot)) \neq \varnothing$, therefore, Problem 1 has no solution, and the search for it stops; otherwise, Action 8 is performed.
8. As a result, the finite set $\widetilde{\mathbf{U}}(\overline{\tau,T}) = \left\{\widetilde{u}_\tau^{(k)}(\cdot)\right\}_{k\in\overline{1,M_\tau}} \subseteq \mathbf{U}(\overline{\tau,T})$ of admissible program controls of Agent $E$ over the interval$\overline{\tau,T}$ is formed, consisting of $M_\tau$ ($M_\tau \leq L_\tau, M_\tau \in \mathbf{N}$) elements such that for each $\widetilde{u}_\tau^{(k)}(\cdot) \in \widetilde{\mathbf{U}}(\overline{\tau,T}), k \in \overline{1,M_\tau}$, the set $\mathbf{Y}\left(T;\overline{\tau,T},y_\tau,\widetilde{u}_\tau^{(k)}(\cdot),s_\tau(\cdot)\right) = \widetilde{\mathbf{Y}}_\tau^{(k)}(T) \neq \varnothing$ and is described by the set of all its verticesV-rep$\left\{\widetilde{\mathbf{Y}}_\tau^{(k)}(T)\right\}$ for which the following is true: $\widetilde{\mathbf{Y}}_\tau^{(k)}(T) =$ $= \mathrm{co}_n\left(\text{V-rep}\left\{\widetilde{\mathbf{Y}}_\tau^{(k)}(T)\right\}\right)$.
9. Assuming: $k := 1$.
10. For the admissible program control $\widetilde{u}_\tau^{(k)}(\cdot) \in \widetilde{\mathbf{U}}(\overline{\tau,T})$, the operation is performed of transforming the description of the forecast set $\widetilde{\mathbf{Y}}_\tau^{(k)}(T)$ in the form of V-rep$\left\{\widetilde{\mathbf{Y}}_\tau^{(k)}(T)\right\}$ into the corresponding finite system of linear algebraic equations and inequalities H-rep$\left\{\widetilde{\mathbf{Y}}_\tau^{(k)}(T)\right\}$ (for example, the algorithm from [3] is used, which is based on the results of [31]), and for the set of solutions of which the following is true: $\mathrm{Sol}_n\left(\text{H-rep}\left\{\widetilde{\mathbf{Y}}_\tau^{(k)}(T)\right\}\right) = \widetilde{\mathbf{Y}}_\tau^{(k)}(T) =$ $= \mathbf{Y}\left(T;\overline{\tau,T},y_\tau,\widetilde{u}_\tau^{(k)}(\cdot),s_\tau(\cdot)\right)$ (carried out by *implementing a finite sequence of one-step algebraic operations on vectors in the space* $\mathbf{R}^n$).
11. For the admissible program control $\widetilde{u}_\tau^{(k)}(\cdot) \in \widetilde{\mathbf{U}}(\overline{\tau,T})$, the following numerical value is calculated from the solution of *the convex mathematical programming problem*

$$\lambda_{\overline{\tau,T}}\left(y_\tau,\widetilde{u}_\tau^{(k)}(\cdot)\right)=\max_{\widetilde{y}_\tau^{(k)}(T)\in\mathrm{Sol}_n\left(\text{H-rep}\left\{\widetilde{\mathbf{Y}}_\tau^{(k)}(T)\right\}\right)}\lambda\left(\widetilde{y}_\tau^{(k)}(T)\right)=$$

$$=\max_{\widetilde{y}_\tau^{(k)}(T)\in\widetilde{\mathbf{Y}}_\tau^{(k)}(T)}\lambda\left(\widetilde{y}_\tau^{(k)}(T)\right)=$$

$$=\max_{\varepsilon_\tau(\cdot)\in\mathbf{E}\left(\overline{\tau,T};\widetilde{u}_\tau^{(k)}(\cdot)\right)}\lambda\left(\psi_{\overline{\tau,T}}\left(T;y_\tau,\widetilde{u}_\tau^{(k)}(\cdot),s_\tau(\cdot),\varepsilon_\tau(\cdot)\right)\right)=$$

$$=\max_{\varepsilon_\tau(\cdot)\in\mathbf{E}\left(\overline{\tau,T};\widetilde{u}_\tau^{(k)}(\cdot)\right)}\mathbf{\Phi}_{\overline{\tau,T}}\left(w_\tau,\widetilde{u}_\tau^{(k)}(\cdot),\varepsilon_\tau(\cdot)\right) \quad (14)$$

(the solution to *the convex mathematical programming problem* is found, for example, using *the Zoutendijk gradient method* (see [30]), i.e., by *implementing only one-step algebraic operations on vectors in the space* $\mathbf{R}^n$).

12. Assuming: $k := k + 1$; then if $k \le M_\tau$, the transition to Action 10 is carried out; otherwise, the next action is performed.
13. The following set is formed

$$\widetilde{\mathbf{U}}^{(e)}_{\mathbf{\Phi}_{\overline{\tau,T}}}\left(\overline{\tau,T},w_\tau\right)=\left\{\widetilde{u}_\tau^{(e)}(\cdot):\widetilde{u}_\tau^{(e)}(\cdot)=\left\{\widetilde{u}_\tau^{(e)}(t)\right\}_{t\in\overline{\tau,T-1}}\in\widetilde{\mathbf{U}}\left(\overline{\tau,T}\right),\right.$$

$$\lambda^{(e)}_{\overline{\tau,T}}=\lambda_{\overline{\tau,T}}\left(y_\tau,\widetilde{u}_\tau^{(e)}(\cdot)\right)=\lambda_{\overline{\tau,T}}\left(y_\tau,\widetilde{u}^{\left(k^{(e)}\right)}(\cdot)\right)=\min_{k\in\overline{1,M_\tau}}\lambda_{\overline{\tau,T}}\left(y_\tau,\widetilde{u}_\tau^{(k)}(\cdot)\right)=$$

$$\left.=\widetilde{c}_\lambda^{(e)}\left(\overline{\tau,T},w_\tau\right)=\widetilde{\mathbf{\Phi}}^{(e)}_{\overline{\tau,T}}\right\} \quad (15)$$

(implemented by *solving a one-step finite discrete optimization problem*).

14. The set $\widetilde{\mathbf{U}}^{(e)}_{\mathbf{\Phi}_{\overline{\tau,T}}}\left(\overline{\tau,T},w_\tau\right)$ and the number $\widetilde{\mathbf{\Phi}}^{(e)}_{\overline{\tau,T}}=\widetilde{c}_\lambda^{(e)}\left(\overline{\tau,T},w_\tau\right)$ are displayed in the form suitable for use by Agent $E$

Taking into account the constructions made and the relations (10)—(15), similar to the proof given in [3], the following statement is true.

**Statement 1** For the multi-step process of managing the output of an enterprise considered over the time interval $\overline{0,T}$ ($T \in \mathbf{N}$) and described by the discrete-time controlled dynamical system (1)—(6), the given period $\tau \in \overline{0,T-1}$, $\tau$-position of the system $w(\tau) = \{\tau, y(\tau), s_\tau(\cdot)\} = \{\tau, y_\tau, s_\tau(\cdot)\} = w_\tau \in \mathbf{W}(\tau)$ ($w(0)=\{0, y(0), s_0(\cdot)\} = \{0, y_0, s_0(\cdot)\} = w_0 \in \mathbf{W}_{*0}$) and the formulated terminal objective function $\mathbf{\Phi}_{\overline{\tau,T}}$ which is the scalar convolution of a given vector terminal objective function $\mathbf{F}_{\overline{\tau,T}}=\left(\mathbf{F}^{(1)}_{\overline{\tau,T}},\mathbf{F}^{(2)}_{\overline{\tau,T}},\ldots,\mathbf{F}^{(r)}_{\overline{\tau,T}}\right)$, and its values are determined according to formulas (10), (11), based on the convex terminal functionals $\lambda^{(i)}$, $i \in \overline{1,r}$, forming the convex terminal functional $\lambda$, having continuous partial derivatives with respect to the coordinates of the phase vector $y$ of Object I, for the admissible program controls $\widetilde{u}_{\tau}^{(e)}(\cdot) \in \mathbf{U}(\overline{\tau, T})$ of Agent $E$ during the time interval $\overline{\tau, T}$, formed as a result of the implementation of the proposed constructive technique, for the set $\widetilde{\mathbf{U}}^{(e)}_{\mathbf{\Phi}_{\overline{\tau,T}}}(\overline{\tau, T}, w_{\tau}) \subseteq \mathbf{U}(\overline{\tau, T})$, and the number $\widetilde{\mathbf{\Phi}}^{(e)}_{\overline{\tau,T}} = \widetilde{c}_{\lambda}^{(e)}(\overline{\tau, T}, w_{\tau})$ the following equalities are valid:

$$\widetilde{\mathbf{U}}^{(e)}_{\mathbf{\Phi}_{\overline{\tau,T}}}(\overline{\tau, T}, w_{\tau}) = \mathbf{U}^{(e)}_{\mathbf{\Phi}_{\overline{\tau,T}}}(\overline{\tau, T}, w_{\tau}); \widetilde{\mathbf{\Phi}}^{(e)}_{\overline{\tau,T}} = \widetilde{c}_{\lambda}^{(e)}(\overline{\tau, T}, w_{\tau}) = \\ = c_{\lambda}^{(e)}(\overline{\tau, T}, w_{\tau}) = \mathbf{\Phi}^{(e)}_{\overline{\tau,T}}, \quad (16)$$

i.e., they are a solution to Problem 1.

At the same time, the description of the constructive technique for the proposed solution to Problem 1 means that the calculation of sets $\widetilde{\mathbf{U}}^{(e)}_{\mathbf{\Phi}_{\overline{\tau,T}}}(\overline{\tau, T}, w_{\tau})$ and of the number $\widetilde{\mathbf{\Phi}}^{(e)}_{\overline{\tau,T}} = \widetilde{c}_{\lambda}^{(e)}(\overline{\tau, T}, w_{\tau})$ is carried out *by implementing a finite recurrent sequence of solutions to one-step problems of linear and convex mathematical programming, solutions to finite system of linear algebraic equations and inequalities, the finite sequence of one-step algebraic operations on vectors and convex polyhedra-compacts (with a finite number of vertices) in the spaces* $\mathbf{R}^n$*and* $\mathbf{R}^p$, *as well as solving a one-step finite discrete optimization problem that allows their algorithmization.*

Thus, by virtue of equalities (16), the formed set $\widetilde{\mathbf{U}}^{(e)}_{\mathbf{\Phi}_{\overline{\tau,T}}}(\overline{\tau, T}, w_{\tau})$ and the number $\widetilde{\mathbf{\Phi}}^{(e)}_{\overline{\tau,T}} = \widetilde{c}_{\lambda}^{(e)}(\overline{\tau, T}, w_{\tau})$ form a solution to Problem 1—*Minimax terminal program control of enterprise product output with a vector objective function and risks.*

Notably, the proposed constructive technique for solving Problem 1 can serve as a basis for developing numerical algorithms and, on their basis, creating computer applications that support managers of manufacturing enterprises in making decisions.

## 5 Discussion

This paper investigates the problem of developing an economic-mathematical model for multi-criteria optimization of a guaranteed (Minimax) result of managing the production of a manufacturing enterprise in case of risks (disturbances).

The analysis identified the main features of the management object—a manufacturing enterprise; these are to be taken into account when developing the appropriate economic and mathematical model: (1) the object is dynamic; (2) to describe the state of the object, it is necessary to take into account a significant number of parameters, i.e., it is multi-parameter; (3) the dynamics of the process under consideration is significantly influenced by risks (disturbances); (4) there is an economic entity—the agent capable of managing the object (a production enterprise); (5) the management agent has several target functions for assessing the quality of implementing the process under consideration; (6) there is no statistical information sufficient for stochastic modeling, yet it is sufficient for restricting the implementation of the values of the parameters describing the process under consideration.

The identified features of the controlled object and the analysis of available scientific sources led to the conclusion that the process under study is a complex system for economic and mathematical modeling and data on the developed models of such system have not been identified in the scientific literature.

This article, to formally describe the dynamics and management optimization of production, uses the system approach, economic and mathematical modeling, and the Minimax approach to optimize the guaranteed result for the process under study. Technologies for the development of automated and intelligent management decision support systems for complex multifactor production systems are based on economic and mathematical models of the objects and processes under consideration. At the same time, it is only possible to use stochastic models for multiparameter systems if there are very strict conditions concerning the data on the parameters and concerning the implementation of the processes under study. Therefore, the required economic and mathematical model was developed in this paper within the deterministic Minimax approach. This approach does not require the availability of large amounts of statistical data on the parameters of the control process under consideration and on meeting strict requirements for its implementation.

The model developed in the given article is deterministic; the dynamics of the control object—the production enterprise—are described by a new system of discrete-time recurrent equations. To solve the problem under study, a constructive technique is proposed for finding the solution by implementing only one-step operations that allow their algorithmization.

The results presented can serve as the basis for further research and development of specific economic and mathematical models that take into account real conditions and features of production by manufacturing enterprises. Based on such models, it is proposed to develop a computer intelligent system to support management decision-making in a specific production enterprise.

## 6 Conclusion

For the initial problem of optimizing product output management at a manufacturing enterprise, an economic and mathematical formalization is proposed in the form of a multi-step problem of Minimax terminal program control with a vector objective function and risks. The article describes a constructive technique for solving the problem under consideration, which is based on the general recurrent algebraic method for constructing reachability sets (predictive sets) of linear discrete-time controlled dynamical systems and is carried out by implementing a finite sequence of one-step operations that allow their algorithmization. The method proposed for solving the Minimax problem can serve as the basis for digitalization of decision-making processes at manufacturing enterprises.

The results obtained in the article are based on [3–6], are adjacent to the results of [1, 2, 7, 14, 20, 21, 30, 31], and can be used in computer modeling and creation of intelligent information systems to support management decision-making for complex socio-economic processes operating under conditions of risk and uncertainty. Mathematical models of such processes are presented, for example, in [7–23].

**Acknowledgments** The study was carried out in accordance with the Research Plan of the Institute of Economics of the Ural Branch of the Russian Academy of Sciences.

## References

1. Krasovskii, N. N. (1968). *Theory of motion control*. Nauka.
2. Krasovskii, N. N., & Subbotin, A. I. (1988). *Game-theoretical control problems*. Springer.
3. Shorikov, A. F. (1997). *Minimax estimation and control in discrete-time dynamical systems*. Publishing House of the Ural State University.
4. Tyulyukin, V. A., & Shorikov, A. F. (1988). On algorithm for constructing the reachability sets of linear control system. *Non-smooth optimization problems and control, Sverdlovsk, UB AS USSR* (pp. 55–61).
5. Shorikov, A. F., & Rassadina, E. S. (2013). Dynamic optimization of complex adaptive management of the structure of the product range of the enterprise. *Economy of Region, 2*(34), 176–184.
6. Shorikov, A. F. (2022). Forecasting and Minimax estimation of the state of a production system in the presence of risks. *Applied Informatics, 17*(4(100)), https://doi.org/10.37791/2687-0649-2022-17-4-97-112.
7. Akberdina, V. V., & Romanova, O. A. (2021). Regional aspects of industrial development: A review of approaches to the formation of priorities and regulatory mechanisms. *Regional Economy, 17*(3), 714–736.
8. Aksyonov, K., Bykov, E., Aksyonova, O., Goncharova, N. & Nevolina, A. (2017). A. Multi-agent simulation of the resource conversion processes with the sample application to the logistical problem. In *UKSim-AMSS 11th European Modelling Symposium on Mathematical Modelling and Computer Simulation. Manchester, England* (pp. 177–181). https://doi.org/10.1109/EMS.2017.39.
9. Barbati, M., Bruno, G., & Genovese, A. (2012). Applications of agent-based models for optimization problems: A literature review. *Expert Systems with Applications, 39*(5), 6020–6028. https://doi.org/10.1016/j.eswa.2011.12.015
10. Billari, F. G., Fent, T., Prskawetz, A., & Scheffran, J. (2006). *Agent-based computational modelling: Applications in demography, social, economic and environmental sciences (contributions to economics)*. Physica-Verlag. https://doi.org/10.1007/3-7908-1721-X
11. David, S. A., Oliveira, C., Derick, D., & Quintino, D. D. (2012). Dynamic model for planning and business optimization. *Modern Economy, 3*(4), 384–391. https://doi.org/10.4236/me.2012.34049
12. Emelyanov, A. A., Vlasova, E. A., & Duma, R. V. (2014). *Simulation modeling of economic processes*. Finance and Statistics.
13. Kleiner, G. B., & Rybachuk, M. A. (2017). *Systemic balance of the economy*. Scientific Library.

14. Lotov, A. V. (1984). *Introduction to economic and mathematical modeling*. Nauka.
15. Madejski, J. (2007). Survey of the agent-based approach to intelligent manufacturing. *Journal Of Achievements In Materials and Manufacturing Engineering, 21*(1), 67–70.
16. Makarov, V. L., Bakhtizin, A. R., Beklaryan, G. L., & Akopov, A. S. (2021). Digital plant: Methods of discrete-event modeling and optimization of production characteristics. *Business Informatics, 15*(2), 7–20. https://doi.org/10.17323/2587-814X.2021.2.7.20
17. Makarov, V. L., Bakhtizin, A. R., & Sushko, E. D. (2017). Regulation of industrial emissions based on an agent-based approach. *Economic and Social Changes: Facts, Trends, Forecast, 6*(54), 42–58. https://doi.org/10.15838/esc.2017.6.54.3
18. Margineanu, C., & Lixandroiu, D. (2021). Optimization of industrial management processes. *IOP Conf. Ser.: Mater. Sci. Eng*, 1009, 012039, 1–9.
19. Novikova, T. S., & Tsyplakov, A. A. (2020). Social policy in a multi-industry agent-oriented model. *Economic and Social Changes: Facts, Trends, Forecast, 13*(3), 129–142. https://doi.org/10.15838/esc.2020.3.69.9
20. Propoi, A. I. (1973). *Elements of the theory of the optimal discrete processes*. Nauka.
21. Ter-Krikorov, A. M. (1977). *Optimal control and mathematical economics*. Nauka.
22. Wooldridge, M., & Jennings, N. (1995). Intelligent agents: Theory and practice. *Knowledge Engineering Review, 10*(2), 115–152.
23. Zhang, Q., Chen, Y., Lin, W., & Chen, Y. (2021). Optimizing medical enterprise's operations management considering corporate social responsibility under industry 5.0. *Discrete Dynamics in Nature and Society, 9298166*, 1–13. https://doi.org/10.1155/2021/9298166
24. Szopa, R., & Marczyk, B. (2011). Optimization of production problems using mathematical programming. *Polish Journal of Management Studies, 4*, 231–238.
25. Cheng, W., & Xiao-Bing, L. (2013). Integrated production planning and control: A multi-objective optimization model. *Journal of Industrial Engineering and Management, 6*(4), 815–830. https://doi.org/10.3926/jiem.771
26. Olanrele, O. O., Olaiya, K. A., Aderonmu, M. A., Adegbayo, O. O., & Sanusi, B. Y. (2014). Development of a dynamic programming model for optimizing production planning. *International Journal of Management Technology, 2*(3), 12–17.
27. Wagner, H. M., & Whitin, T. M. (2004). Dynamic version of the economic lot size model. *Management Science, 50*(12), 1770–1774. https://doi.org/10.1287/mnsc.1040.0306
28. Qing, Q., Shi, W., Li, H., & Shao, Y. (2016). Dynamic analysis and optimization of a production control system under supply and demand uncertainties. *Hindawi Publishing Corporation: Discrete Dynamics in Nature and Society, 2016*, 6823934. https://doi.org/10.1155/2016/6823934
29. Landau, I. D., Lozano, R., M'Saad, M., & Karimi, A. (2011). *Adaptive control: Algorithms, analysis and applications*. Springer.
30. Bazaraa, M. S., & Shetty, C. M. (1979). *Nonlinear programming: Theory and algorithms* (2nd ed.). Wiley Publ.
31. Chernikov, S. N. (1968). *Linear inequalities*. Nauka.
32. Windrum, P., Fagiolo, G., & Moneta, A. (2007). Empirical validation of agent-based models: Alternatives and prospects. *Journal of Artificial Societies and Social Simulation, 10*(2), 8. https://doi.org/10.1017/9781108227278.009

# Risk Evaluation in the Strategic Planning of Industrial Regions' Development Within Industry 5.0

**Daria S. Laskova**

**Abstract** Progressive socio-economic development of regions is an urgent task for governments around the globe. This is particularly significant for a federally organized state, whose industrial development is directly linked to the headway of its territories. There is a relationship between digital instrumental and analytical trends, regional development strategies, and associated risks, as evidenced by the literature review in the paper. The study sheds light on how to track the impact of risk events on the development scenario and what methodology should be used to measure the degree of this impact on the region and the country's industrial policy. The paper presents a mechanism developed by the author for assessing risk elements. They are the most likely manifestations of a threat to regional strategizing. The methodology of using the GRETL software product to identify the causal relationship between risks and indicators of strategizing is also shown. The author has formulated recommendations to support the regional strategy in the implementation of the country's course towards the transition to Industry 5.0.

**Keywords** Regional strategies · Risk assessment · Digital tools · Industry 5.0 · Socio-economic development · Industrial policy

## 1 Introduction

In the modern digital realities of the economic space associated with the global Industry 5.0 paradigm, there is a need for accelerated integration of state into digital technical and technological world processes. Considering information trends in the sustainable development of industry and industrial market conditions is essential in creating and maintaining the innovation and competitiveness of the Russian economic system, in which the efficiency of activities of any level of economic entities is high. The vector of progress is formed in the transition of the Russian Federation

D. S. Laskova (✉)
Southern Federal University, Rostov-on-Don, Russian Federation
e-mail: laskova@sfedu.ru



A. Appolloni et al. (eds.), *The Future of Industry*, Lecture Notes in Information Systems and Organisation 70, https://doi.org/10.1007/978-3-031-66801-2_33

to Industry 5.0 based on the inclusion of advanced digitalization solutions in the system measures of strategizing the development of industrial policy at both the macro and meso levels [1]. Such solutions use high-tech technologies associated with high application risks [2]. To overcome them, it is necessary to find a tool that ensures their resistance and consider the methodology of its use. It is possible to lay this in a broad assessment of the risk events of the development strategies of each region of the state, in which industrial policy is incorporated for its implementation.

Economic and social life in Russia is actively developing as the priority field of a new round of industrial evolution. It is useful to explore options for achieving such a transition in the rapidly developing regions of the state, which are typical representatives of dynamic multi-industrialization. According to the rating of Russia's most efficient regions at the International Industrial Exhibition INNOPROM-2023, the Rostov region was characterized as an average region with the accelerated socio-economic development rate within of Industry 5.0 [3]. This makes the Rostov region a universal object of research.

Since the planning of the prospects for the effective development of the country is carried out at the federal and regional levels of government, problematic aspects of determining the instrumental basis of strategizing appear. Strategizing is the process of creating future progress and evaluating the effectiveness of the development measures taken. The strategizing cycle cannot be carried out without the use of analytical tools and indicators. The tools form the fundamental component of the construction of socio-economic strategies. They determine the specifics of the data for study, organize consensus analysis, and interpret the results. Indicators suggest the rates, the pursuit of which lies in the purpose of the document itself. Together, they represent a methodological element of strategy that substantiates the processes of strategic planning and management: economic and mathematical models, methods of strategic management, various statistical and econometric analyses, a wide range of business indicators and ratings, etc. However, regional peculiarities and the intensity of the ongoing changes in each territorial entity affect the range of strategizing tools and indicators used in the development of measures.

One of the methods of strategizing in the regions is risk assessment through the prism of their impact on the indicators planned in the strategic document. Therefore, the objectives of the article are to study the risk assessment method as a tool for the formation of regional socio-economic development strategies and to make recommendations to improve the effectiveness of the strategy for the implementation of the transition of the state to Industry 5.0. In the study, it is implemented based on the Strategy of Socio-economic Development of the Rostov region until 2030, which focuses on sustainable development. The aim is to demonstrate the possibilities of using a risk assessment tool to develop a set of measures to improve socio-economic strategizing. The results of the study will leave it new and relevant as long as there is a practice of creating and implementing regional development strategies.

## 2 Literature Review

A review of publications in the selected subject field on digitalization and information trends, sustainable development and strategizing, identification of strategic risks, and methods of working with them allows us to reveal the interrelationships of all concepts. Among the analyzed publications, several main areas of research can be identified.

The global vision of the interaction of informatization, sustainable development, and related risk situations is gaining popularity in a variety of scientific papers. For example, researchers Zhou Zhiyia and Zhang Hongye [4] draw attention to the possibilities of long-term effective use of digital trends in the strategic development of enterprises. The paper presents a model of the mechanism of the influence of digital opportunities on organizations' sustainable development with the inclusion of uncertain risks. In the publication by Popkova et al. [5], the analysis of the links of sustainable development institutions through the prism of the use of digital technologies demonstrates the threats from the newly emerging risks for such a model.

Simon Hollis [6] sees the strategy and risk events of natural disasters as an inseparable block in the process of area's development. Regional management of non-man-made risks is presented in the strategic plans of organizations whose interest is due to national security and global norms. The onset of such risks is determined by modern realities and digital tools.

Saleh and Saad [7] describe the direct impact of information technology on strategic risk management using SPSS and Smart PLS for data analysis and hypothesis testing. Hall et al. [8] present the methodology of using digital tools in the search for strategizing risks. The authors utilize the infrastructure model "system of systems" that is designed to predict successful long-term solutions in the interdependent infrastructure systems of the region.

There is also a large body of works devoted to specific methods of determining the risks of strategic development in global, state, and organizational contexts and plans for their management [9, 10, 11]. These works relate to such fields as economics, business, medicine, and political sciences (Fig. 1).

In particular, Shang Ying-qiu [12] states that the symbiosis of research on the identification of risk events from the process of strategizing the exogenous and endogenous conjuncture and on the development of measures for predicting consequences allows one to competently develop a strategy for sustainable development. From the standpoint of informatization, ensuring the operation of such a symbiosis is entrusted to digital tools.

Thus, from the general array of works revealing various interrelations between information trends, development strategies, and the risks associated with them, it is possible to distinguish those aimed at identifying risk situations in global or business-strategic research. At the same time, to date, the problem of analyzing risks using the capabilities of digital technologies and measures to manage them in regional strategies to ensure sustainable development has not been sufficiently worked out. The current study is aimed at bridging this gap.

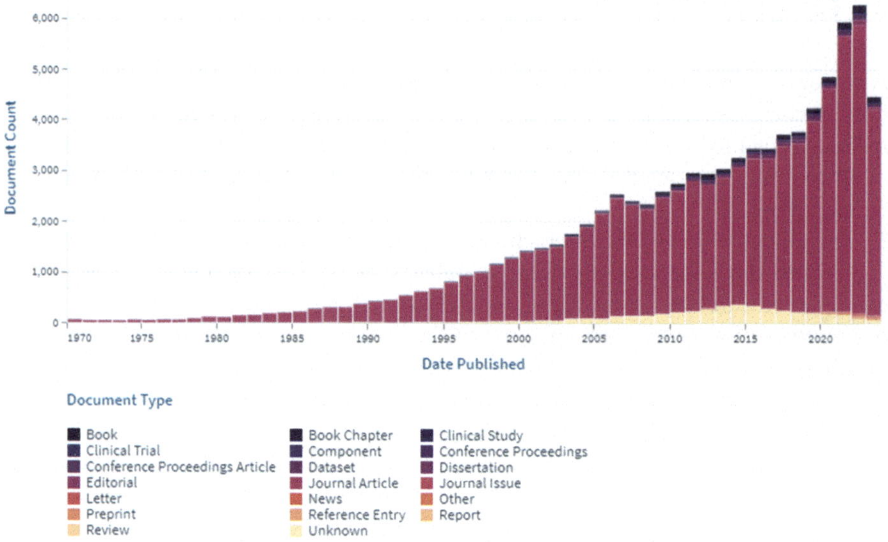


**Fig. 1** Scientific papers on the risks of strategizing over time according to the data LENS.ORG

## 3 Material and Methods

The theoretical basis of the research consists of materials in the fields of globalization sustainable development, digitalization trends in planning and management of regional strategic development, concepts of analytical tools for strategizing, work on the practice of strategic measures developed since this toolkit emerged.

To check whether there is a relationship between digitalization issues and information trends, sustainable development and strategizing, identification of strategic risks, and methods of working with them, an analysis of the relevant literature was conducted. Using the database LENS.ORG, articles and keywords published from 2011 to 2022 were selected. Then, 1550 of the most relevant articles on each of the topics were picked. The selection criteria were compliance with the topic and the abstract. Based on the analysis, a query was formed, and a search for scientific papers in the database was carried out. A total of 21 articles were found, of which six publications were selected that most closely corresponded to the subject of the study. A content analysis was conducted on the publications.

To identify the roles of risk elements in strategizing, expert risk assessment methodology is used. The risk assessment process consists of three milestones that are consistently implemented:

1. risk identification: on the basis of relevant and up-to-date information, variants of risk situations and their potential consequences are determined;

2. risk situation analysis: the analysis tools in the form of various coefficients, cost indicators, one of the variants of the risk map or matrix are used to study the list of risk situations and their qualitative and quantitative characteristics.

In order to analyze the risks, one needs to use a statistical method. It measures risk based on the collected statistics of indicators within the framework the average expected value and the fluctuation of the possible result by variance or coefficient of variation.

The expert judgment method is necessary for selecting statistical indicators of risks. It is formed using an expert survey algorithm that defines expert stances on various types of risk. The methodology of expert judgments is visualized using a matrix. This is a list of identified risk situations arranged in a readable tabular form. To build a risk matrix, it is necessary to use the specified scales for assessing the probability and scale of the consequences of the corresponding risk situations. When a group of experts assesses several risks, the matrix includes an aggregated mark for a specific position, which determines the collective judgment of the level of a risk event [13];

3. establishing the degree of influence of the risk element: interpretation of estimates, identification of the impact of risk events on the timing and strength of the decision-making.

To analyze the impact of risks on socio-economic development, the causal interaction of Granger on stationary time series was used. The stationarity of time series indicates their stability. Therefore, when studying time series, stability testing is required. This is done by evaluating the main coefficient of the equation of the autoregressive process of the time series for equality to one, which is called the existence of a unit root. The presence of a single root indicates the confidence level, that is, the $P$-value. It is also necessary to understand the values of deviations from standard stationarity in order to adjust econometric models with time series. The Augmented Dickey-Fuller test (ADF test) evaluates the presence of fundamental assumptions in time series modeling simultaneously through the test statistics of deviation from standard stationarity and the $P$-values for the probability of non-stationarity in the time series. The methodology of this variant of the statistical test allows for the correct implementation of both results with less time and research resources required [14].

## 4 The Role of Risk Element Assessment in Region Strategizing

At the stage of strategy scripting, the definition of risky events begins, which, with some probability, will be able to influence the expected picture of regional development. As soon as the identification process of performance indicators ends in all types of scenarios, possible future changes are considered. They entail violations of the achievement of the set progress indicator [15]. But the identified risks remain relevant for no more than 6 months or a year, since the variability of global components is of a daily nature. In this regard, a constant review of the impact of risky events on regional development is required.

A risky event is generated by the very concept of risk as a property of possible danger, organically inherent in any activity. The onset of risk creates development alternatives that differ in the method used to manage it [16]. If the tactic of accepting the level of the risk element becomes the chosen one, then among the methods one can single out the transfer of the risk situation to a later time of making a management decision or the implementation of risk transfer. The direction of changing the probability of a risk event includes methods aimed at limiting the source of risk and compensating for the manifestations of the risk element. Dissipation leads to a reduction in the impact of risk through distribution among many those who may be affected by risk consequences and various diversification options.

But for the right managerial choice of direction in risk management, it is necessary to assess risk events [17]. As a result of the risk assessment, the tactics for managing the most probable risk situations are formed, according to which specific measures are proposed. They allow achieving the mission and purposes of the strategy and minimizing the negative manifestations of risk elements.

With regional strategizing of the Rostov region, the process of identifying and including risks is carried out once at the beginning of the next stage of the scenario implementation. After the event, no adjustments are made and current risks are not considered, which affects the speed and usefulness of the strategy implementation. Therefore, the introduction of new risk elements through risk assessment in the terms of the changed exogenous and endogenous conjuncture of the country is a problem area of regional strategizing in the region that requires improvement.

## 5 Determining the Impact of Risk Elements on the Regional Strategy Development

The problem zone of under-inclusion of new risk conditions in the process of strategizing can be exhausted by identifying risks that are significant for the indicators embedded in the scenario of the strategic document. Then a modified forecast of indicators is created, taking into account risk elements, and proposals are made with adjustments to the forces and measures of action to achieve the necessary values of the indicators [18].

Significant newly formed risks for the prospect of implementing the second stage until 2025 were identified during the study of the Rostov region's Strategy and the given implementation plan. Among them, it is possible to identify the risks of restructuring financing into production facilities for the military-industrial activities, breach of the ecological balance, and others. The latter were formed due to the geopolitical and international economic and social situation of 2022, which seriously affects the medium- and long-term state of the region.

To single out from the multitude of risky events only those that are significant for socio-economic development, an analysis of expert judgments is performed. The experts are employees of the Regional Management Center, specialists of the Strategic Planning Department and the Department of Economic Analysis and Forecasting of the Ministry of Economic Development of the Rostov region, and the Sector of Consolidated Budget Planning of the Ministry of Finance of the Rostov region. Experts rank risks according to Table 1 item "Danger of a risk event" on a scale from 0, when the risk element is insignificant, to 100, when the impact of the risk is extremely high. Herewith, experts' consistency should not differ by more than fifty points. The probabilities of risk occurrence predicted by experts are reflected in the paragraph "Probability of a risk event". The overall risk level is calculated by taking the arithmetic mean of the product of the danger and the likelihood of risk occurrence for each of the expert opinions.

According to the average expert judgment, all risks identified by the Strategy are characterized as likely to occur in the future. But those to which experts have assigned more than 50 points are considered potentially dangerous. Therefore, further analysis of the impact of risk elements on the planned indicators in the strategic document of the Rostov region will be carried out for such risk events.

To describe the risk events of high migration growth, reorientation of finances to military-industrial needs, unfavorable policy of own production of previously imported goods and new widespread diseases, based on the data from the Federal State Statistics Service and its territorial body, indicators for 2008–2022 were selected: migration growth (Migrrost), the index of public-private partnership investments in the manufacturing industry region (iInvestvobrabprom), product turnover within the framework of import substitution (Oborotimportozam), and the index of primary diagnoses according to information provided from regional health organizations (iKolvopervdiagnoz). To find out to what extent a probabilistic event affects the corresponding indicator of the socio-economic situation of a subject in the Russian Federation, correlation and causal relationship analyses are conducted according to the Granger testing procedure using the GRETL software product.

The strategic indicator is provided in the action plan for implementing the Development Strategy of the Rostov region until 2030—the number of potential jobs for the permanent population (Kolvorabmest)—was not planned taking into account the threat of the risk component [15]. But despite the increased expert judgment of the risk of migration growth, it is necessary to consider the relationship between the migration growth indicator and the planned indicator (Fig. 2).

The relationship between the indicators is statistically significant. On the Cheddock scale, it is considered noticeable. Negativity indicates the opposite. For professionally logical reasons, the migration increase causes a decrease in potential places in the labor market for the permanent population. You can check whether the values of Migrrost improve or worsen the predictions of Kolvorabmest values through Granger testing. It is possible to track the effect using this method for

**Table 1** Risk matrix of strategizing in the Rostov region

| Expert opinion | Danger of a risk event | Probability of a risk event | Risk event level |
|---|---|---|---|
| *High migration growth* | | | |
| 1 | 75 | 0.80 | 71,124 |
| 2 | 95 | 0.83 | |
| 3 | 89 | 0.91 | |
| 4 | 84 | 0.79 | |
| 5 | 78 | 0.89 | |
| *Redirection of financial resources to the military-industrial complex* | | | |
| 1 | 67 | 0.68 | 58,104 |
| 2 | 72 | 0.70 | |
| 3 | 76 | 0.85 | |
| 4 | 83 | 0.87 | |
| 5 | 75 | 0.77 | |
| *Unfavorable import substitution policy* | | | |
| 1 | 62 | 0.62 | 53,096 |
| 2 | 73 | 0.67 | |
| 3 | 88 | 0.78 | |
| 4 | 79 | 0.81 | |
| 5 | 65 | 0.70 | |
| *Violation of the security contour of social facilities* | | | |
| 1 | 64 | 0.46 | 35,124 |
| 2 | 75 | 0.49 | |
| 3 | 69 | 0.47 | |
| 4 | 77 | 0.50 | |
| 5 | 70 | 0.55 | |
| *New mass diseases* | | | |
| 1 | 75 | 0.83 | 61,742 |
| 2 | 70 | 0.77 | |
| 3 | 87 | 0.80 | |
| 4 | 80 | 0.79 | |
| 5 | 83 | 0.72 | |
| *Increasing social conflicts* | | | |
| 1 | 55 | 0.46 | 29,156 |
| 2 | 62 | 0.45 | |
| 3 | 53 | 0.49 | |
| 4 | 61 | 0.55 | |
| 5 | 57 | 0.58 | |
| *Violation of transport infrastructures* | | | |
| 1 | 78 | 0.59 | 47,214 |
| 2 | 76 | 0.53 | |
| 3 | 68 | 0.64 | |
| 4 | 75 | 0.67 | |
| 5 | 80 | 0.70 | |

(continued)

**Table 1** (continued)

| Expert opinion | Danger of a risk event | Probability of a risk event | Risk event level |
|---|---|---|---|
| *Consequences of environmental disasters* | | | |
| 1 | 40 | 0.47 | 19,216 |
| 2 | 36 | 0.40 | |
| 3 | 47 | 0.48 | |
| 4 | 43 | 0.42 | |
| 5 | 42 | 0.53 | |

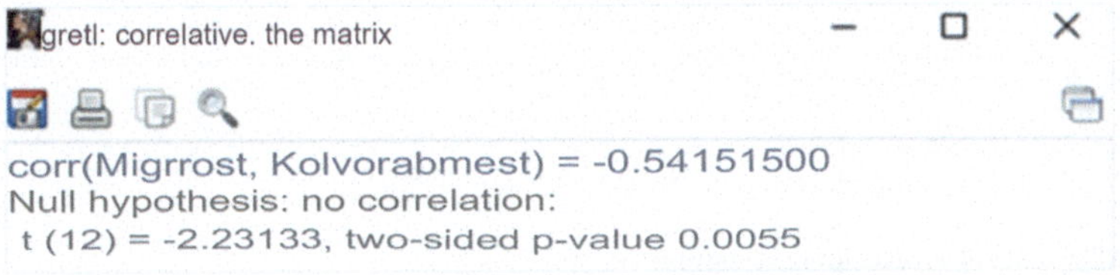


**Fig. 2** Linear dependence of migration growth on the number of potential jobs for the permanent population

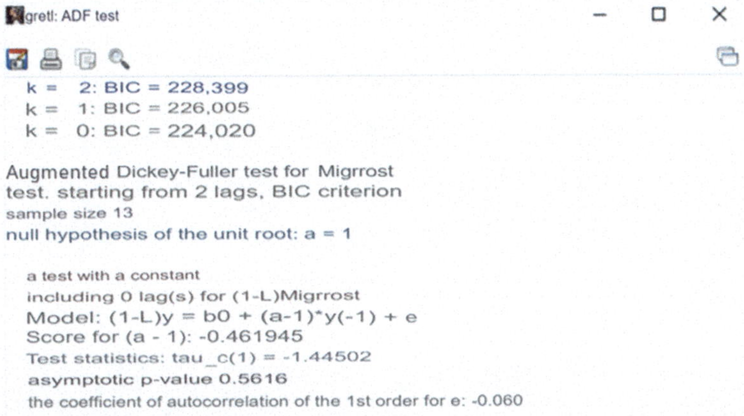


**Fig. 3** ADF test for Migrrost values

stationary time series, so the data are checked by a specialized unit root test (Figs. 3 and 4).

The obtained *p*-values of more than 5% indicate the need to accept the hypothesis $H_0$ of the Augmented Dickey-Fuller test about the non-stationarity of time series. In this case, for the correct study of the data, they address the definition of cointegration. It testifies the acceptance of the hypothesis of a single root for individual variables and the rejection of this hypothesis for regression residuals, so as not to lose important information about the long-term equilibrium of indicators (Fig. 5).

```
gretl: ADF test

  k = 2: BIC = 228,211
  k = 1: BIC = 226,769
  k = 0: BIC = 224,649

Augmented Dickey-Fuller Test for Kolvorabmest
test. starting from 2 lags, the BIC criterion
sample size 13
null hypothesis of the unit root: a = 1

  a test with a constant
  including 0 lag(s) for (1-L)Kolvorabmest
  Model: (1-L)y = b0 + (a-1)*y(-1) + e
  Score for (a - 1): -0.757283
  Test statistics: tau_c(1) = -2.65233
  asymptotic p-value 0.08257
  coefficient of autocorrelation of the 1st order for e: -0.013
```

**Fig. 4** ADF test for Kolvorabmest values

```
Cointegration regression -
LSM, observations 2008-2022 were used (T = 15)
Dependent variable: Kolvorabmest

                ratio         art. error     t-statistics     p-value
  ------------------------------------------------------------------
  const        41627,4        1800,31          23,12         2,55e-011   ***
  Migrrost     -0,566767      0,254004         -2,231        0,1455

The average is frozen. changes 38934.86   St. off. It's frozen. perem: 5713,001
sq. m. Amount residues         3.00e+08   St. model error               4998.985
R-squared                      0.293238   Fixed. The R-square is        0.234342
Lov, the likelihood is        -138.0239   Crit. Akaike                  280.0479
Crit. Schwartz                 281.3260   Crit. Hennan-Quinn            279.9296
rho parameter                  0.279756   Stat. Darbin-Watson           1.275144
pay attention to the abbreviations of statistics

Step 4: testing the unit root for uhat

Augmented Dickey-Fuller Test for uhat
test. starting from 2 lags, the BIC criterion
is the sample size of 13
the null hypothesis of the unit root: a = 1

  a test without a constant
  including 0 lag(s) for (1-L)uhat
  hodel: (1-L)y = (a-1)*y(-1) + e
  score for (a - 1): -0.720244
  Test statistic: tau_c(2) = -2.86752
  asymptotic p-value 0.0452
  coefficient, 1st order autocorrelation for e: 0.043
```

**Fig. 5** The cointegration relationship of Migrrost and Kolvorabmest

Model 1: LSM, observations 2013-2021 (T = 9)
Dependent variable: d_d_d_Kolvorabmest
Standard errors of US, bandwidth 1 (Bartlett Core)

| | ratio | art. error | t-statistics | p-value | |
|---|---|---|---|---|---|
| const | 3048,53 | 1971,91 | 1,546 | 0,1970 | |
| d_d_d_Migrrost_1 | -0,508548 | 0,334155 | -1,522 | 0,2027 | |
| d_d_d_Migrrost_2 | -1,29625 | 0,445138 | -2,912 | 0,0436 | ** |
| d_d_d_Kolvorab~_1 | -1,28512 | 0,240571 | -5,342 | 0,0059 | *** |
| d_d_d_Kolvorab~_2 | -1,01230 | 0,335824 | -3,014 | 0,0394 | ** |

| | | | |
|---|---|---|---|
| The average is frozen. changes | 1096.222 | St. off. It's frozen.perem | 24008.30 |
| Amount of sq. m. residues | 7.08e+08 | St. model error | 13302.15 |
| R-squared | 0.846506 | Fixed. R is the square of | 0.693012 |
| F (4, 4) | 29.00094 | P is the value (F) | 0.003259 |
| Log. likelihood | -94.58239 | Crit. Akaike | 199.1648 |
| Crit. Schwartz | 200.1509 | Crit. Hennan-Quinn | 197.0367 |
| rho parameter | -0.429874 | h-Darbin statistics | -1.863094 |

pay attention to the abbreviations of statistics

Excluding the constant, the largest p-value is obtained for the variable 18 (d_d_d_Migrrost_1)

**Fig. 6** Granger causality for migration growth in the region

However, when evaluating the cointegration regression, Migrrost does not affect the long-term equilibrium of the indicator of the Strategy for Testing Residues. Therefore, a transition is made to differences for converting time series into stationary ones. After that, the presence of a causal relationship is checked. The least squares method is used to assess the validity of the hypothesis that regional migration growth is responsible for the change in the number of potential jobs for the region's permanent population. It is determined that the parameter with a lag of two Migrrost is significant. This indicator is the Granger reason for Kolvorabmest values (Fig. 6).

Causality is also checked in terms of the number of potential jobs for the permanent population (Fig. 7). The analysis shows that the parameters for Kolvorabmest lags are insignificant. The risk of the region's high migration growth is exposed by the reverse impact on potential jobs for the permanent population. This means that it has an impact on the situation in the labor market.

Similar procedures are carried out with respect to three more risky elements and lead to the following results:

- the indicator of the volume of shipped goods of own production, works, and services of the manufacturing industry performed by own forces from the Strategy is most likely affected by the risk of transferring part of state financing to the military-industrial complex. This is observed in the trend of reducing investment in many industrial sectors, except for the IT sector. The results of the causal relationship analysis prove that the risk event is not the root cause of the indicator change. It is possible that the connection will be established on a deeper level of the analysis, for example, correlation relations. However, it cannot be argued that for the region, the non-obvious causality of a risk event can lead to serious consequences that cannot be dealt with at the current moment of managerial

Model 2: LSM, observations 2013-2021 (T = 9)
Dependent variable: d_d_d_Migrrost
Standard errors of US, bandwidth 1 (Bartlett Core)

| | ratio | art. error | t-statistics | p-value | |
|---|---|---|---|---|---|
| const | -648,024 | 1817,55 | -0,3565 | 0,7394 | |
| d_d_d_Kolvorab-_1 | 0,324165 | 0,217158 | 1,493 | 0,2098 | |
| d_d_d_Kolvorab-_2 | 0,318777 | 0,405018 | 0,7871 | 0,4753 | |
| d_d_d_Migrrost_1 | -1,11809 | 0,369513 | -3,026 | 0,0389 | ** |
| d_d_d_Migrrost_2 | -0,751473 | 0,522866 | -1,437 | 0,2240 | |

| | | | |
|---|---|---|---|
| The average is frozen. changes | -369.77778 | St. off. It's frozen.perem | 20250.74 |
| Amount of sq. m. residues | 5.17e+08 | St. model error | 11364.85 |
| R-squared | 0.842524 | Fixed. R is the square of | 0.685047 |
| F (4, 4) | 369.2845 | P is the value (F) | 0.000022 |
| Log. likelihood | -93.16578 | Crit. Akaike | 196.3316 |
| Crit. Schwartz | 197.3177 | Crit. Hennan-Quinn | 194.2035 |
| rho parameter | -0.411571 | h-Darbin statistics | NA |

pay attention to the abbreviated notation of statistics

Excluding the constant, the largest p-value was obtained, but for the assigned 21 (d_d_d_Kolvorabmest_2)

**Fig. 7** Granger causality for the number of potential jobs for the permanent population of the region

decision-making. Therefore, it is impractical to introduce additional strategic measures for this risky element;

- for an indicative strategic indicator of the GRP, the risk of an unfavorable import substitution policy is quite noticeable. This is also confirmed by Granger testing, where a significant lag of the Oborotimport indicator demonstrates the causality of the import substitution policy in relation to GRP, just as GRP itself is the cause of variability in the turnover of import-substituted products. As a result, the risk element and the strategizing indicator form a bidirectional causal relationship;
- speaking about the risk of new mass diseases, experts mean a surge in primary diagnoses of a new type of disease. Therefore, to study its impact on the labor productivity index, the iKolvopervdiagnoz index is also included in the Strategy. However, the causal relationship between the indicators is one-sided: the diagnosis of a new disease previously not in the region's population is a very significant factor in changing the productivity of the region.

## 6 Proposals to Improve the Measures of Socio-Economic Development Strategies Considering Risk Events

The analysis of the assessed risks identified three areas of strategic measures for the Rostov region. For them, recommendations should be produced for the prosperous unfolding of the action plan of the development strategy [19]:

1. In the strategic document of the region, the target indicator of the socio-economic development scenario is the gross regional product. It is not adjusted for the resulting unfavorable import restrictions. To consider such a risk, it is possible to coordinate the measures on the policy of import substitution of the Ministry of Economic Development of the Rostov region with the objectives of the economic policy of the Strategy until 2030 in the production areas with the largest shares in the GRP of the region, as follows:

   - inclusion of livestock farms in the list of "100 Governor's Investment Projects" for the production of import substitution products;
   - subsidizing part of the costs of modernization and the purchase of warehouses and specialized equipment for agricultural products;
   - assistance with investment projects of regional industrial enterprises in obtaining federal support;
   - protection of regional companies producing domestic products under the voluntary certificate "Made on Don";
   - allocation of subsidies for the creation and production of new industrial goods by participants in industrial clusters in the region.

2. Smoothing the risk of high migration growth in the Rostov region is necessary to reduce the possible sharp increase in unemployment among the permanent population of the region. Such a thesis gives two different outcomes:

   - bringing under the control of the Ministry of Labor and Social Development of the region an increase in the plan for creating new jobs both in traditionally specialized areas for the subject and in new industries. Including high-tech ones, the formation of which was included in the number of strategic tasks of Russia's economic development until 2020. Also, consider the training plans of potential employees among those permanently residing in the region when considering the labor market. New qualifications generate ranges of new professions and jobs. The primary applicants for these new jobs are permanent residents who have received specialized education in the region. Thus, they displace possible migrants from such places in the labor market;
   - the impact of the region's migration service and the region's employment centers in the sense of the distribution of potentially unpopular vacant jobs among the permanent population among the migration influx. This is done based on collecting information on professional skills and distributing the migration flow through logistical communication with migration services and employment centers of all subjects of the Russian Federation on a common database of jobs in the country.

3. The Ministry of Labor and Social Development of the Rostov Region is also engaged in tracking labor productivity in the subject of the Russian Federation. Since the beginning of the current decade, it has highlighted the diagnosis of primary new diseases in the region's population and subsequent long-term sick leave, aggravating post-painful syndromes, or even the facts of the deaths of workers as a special risk for the most productive areas of the economic and social

block. Reducing such a risk involves measures contributing to 100% accessibility of primary health care and improving the provision of specialized, high-tech medical care. The proposed activities for these tasks are grouped into two categories:

- acquisition, installation, and equipping of medical organizations with the latest technologies in the field of medicine;
- provision of training, advanced training, and professional retraining programs for medical and pharmaceutical personnel.

However, in order to neutralize the high threshold of danger of such a risk, a comprehensive solution should be developed in the areas of informing citizens about the possibilities of obtaining high-quality medical care in all regions and improving the diagnostic procedures of the population. Interaction with the media will contribute to the formation of a conscious attitude among citizens towards checking their health quality. The use of mobile laboratories for the analysis of biological materials makes it possible to quickly respond to any suspected diagnosis. More frequent implementation of measures for routine medical diagnostics in organizations will reduce the spread of the disease and the identification of many primary diagnoses among employees.

Having studied the possibility of risk events and the associated indicators of the strategic document for the development of a region, it is possible to draw up a program of recommendations for a detailed strategy of socio-economic development of a territory in different parts of the world [20].

## 7 Conclusion

The analytical tools for assessing the risks of forming and implementing the region's socio-economic development strategies were studied. It is advisable to use them repeatedly in the development and improvement cycle of the strategic document. When creating scenarios of regional progress, it is important to exclude underestimation of possible damages as constantly labile factors. The methodology for incorporating risk elements into the preparation of socio-economic development strategies is universal and easily adaptable to the conditions of any country, enabling it to accommodate their strategic goals. It involves the following steps:

1. Expert judgment of risk events (identification of risks, analysis of the consequences and probability of risk events, determination of the degree of strength of the risk element);
2. Investigation of the impact of risk events on the indicators of the effectiveness of the implementation of the strategic document laid down in the target scenario of the subject's development;
3. Adjustment or creation of new activities in the action plan to ensure the successful accomplishment of the indicators of the development strategy.

The limitations of this methodology may include the availability of qualified personnel in the field of governmental activities and risk assessment. It also requires a database of strategic initiatives with growth indicators at the macro and micro levels, as well as software that supports the procedural packages of causal relationships. Finally, it demands coordination of actions for the development of region nationwide.

These steps were tested during the study of the of the Rostov Region's Development Strategy until 2030 to determine the direction for improving measures. The recommendations from the paper were also used for the implementation of the strategic document to achieve the planned progress of Russia's subject.

## References


1. Babkin, A. V., Fedorov, A. A., Liberman, I. V., & Klachek, P. M. (2021). Industry 5.0: Concept, formation and development. *Russian Journal of Industrial Economics, 14*(4), 375–395. (in Russ.).
2. O'zdemir, V., & Hekim, N. (2018). Birth of industry 5.0: Making sense of big data with artificial intelligence, "the internet of things" and next - generation technology policy. *Journal of. Integrative Biology, 22*(1), 65–76. https://doi.org/10.1089/omi.2017.0194
3. Expo.innoprom. (2023). *The rating of regions with effective implementation of industrial policy was presented at INNOPROM-2023.* (n.d.). https://expo.innoprom.com/tpost/7huz7t40g1-na-innoprom-2023-prezentovali-reiting-re. (in Russ.)
4. Zhiyi, Z., & Hongye, Z. (2023). Digital capability and sustainable development of enterprises: The role of long-term competitive advantage. *Academic Journal of Business & Management, 5*(14), 71–75. https://doi.org/10.25236/ajbm.2023.051413
5. Popkova, E. G., De Bernardi, P., Tyurina, Y., & Sergi, B. S. (2022). A theory of digital technology advancement to address the grand challenges of sustainable development. *Technology in Society, 68*(C), 101831. https://doi.org/10.1016/j.techsoc.2021.101831
6. Hollis, S. (2015). *The role of regional organizations in disaster risk management.* Palgrave Macmillan UK eBooks. https://doi.org/10.1057/9781137439307
7. Saleh, M. A., & Saad, M. (2023). Digital transformation impact on agility and strategic risk management. *Journal of Business and Management Sciences, 11*(1), 63–82. https://doi.org/10.12691/jbms-11-1-5
8. Hall, J. W., Thacker, S., Ives, M. C., Cao, Y., Chaudry, M., Blainey, S., & Oughton, E. J. (2017). Strategic analysis of the future of national infrastructure. *Proceedings of the Institution of Civil Engineers, 170*(1), 39–47. https://doi.org/10.1680/jcien.16.00018
9. Albukhitan, S. (2020). Developing digital transformation strategy for manufacturing. *Procedia Computer Science, 170*, 664–671. https://doi.org/10.1016/j.procs.2020.03.173
10. Bencsik, A. (2020). Challenges of Management in the Digital Economy. *International Journal of Technology, 11*(6), 1275–1285.
11. Drăgan, F., Ivașcu, L., & Ardelean, B. (2022). Trends for manufacturing industry: A strategic roadmap toward industry 5.0. In *Sustainability and innovation in manufacturing enterprises* (pp. 275–292). https://doi.org/10.1007/978-981-16-7365-8_11
12. Ying-qiu, S. (2011). *Strategic risk identification model construction.* Technoeconomics & Management Research.
13. Sinyavskaya, T. G., & Tregubova, A. A. (2015). *Economic risk management: Theory, organization, methods.* Publishing and printing complex of RSEU (RINH). (in Russ.).

14. Kosolapova, N. A., Mukhanova, Z. Z., & Laskova, D. S. (2022). Russian practice of regional planning: Implementation of data science in strategic planning. *State-Humanitarian Research, 43*(5), 154–157. (in Russ.).
15. Pechkina, E. V. (2016). Methods and tools of strategic planning of regional development. *Issues of Economics and Management, 4*(6), 78–80. (in Russ.).
16. Lyukevich, I., Agranov, A., Lvova, N. A., & Guzikova, L. (2020). Digital experience: How to find a tool for evaluating business economic risk. *International Journal of Technology: IJ Tech, 11*(6), 1244–1254. https://doi.org/10.14716/ijtech.v11i6.4466
17. Morton, J., Wilson, A. D., & Cooke, L. (2020). The digital work of strategists: Using open strategy for organizational transformation. *The Journal of Strategic Information Systems, 29*(2), 101613. https://doi.org/10.1016/j.jsis.2020.101613
18. Novoselov, A. S., Itsenkov, O. O., & Ubozhenko, E. V. (2021). Economic problems of regions and industry complexes. *Problems of Modern Economy, 1*(77), 115–119. (in Russ.).
19. The official portal of the Government of the Rostov region. (2023). *The strategy of socio-economic development of the Rostov region for the period up to 2030.* https://www.donland.ru/activity/2158/#pril1. (in Russ.)
20. Trufanova, S. A. (2021). Methodology and evaluation of key performance indicators (KPIs) as a tool for improving the level of regional governance. *Problems of Management Theory and Practice, 6*, 76–87. (in Russ.).

# Implementation of the Windows of Opportunity in the Investment Sector of Industry of Russian Regions in the Context of Digitalization

**Pavel Ivanov and Tatyana Altufeva**

**Abstract** The transition of the world economy to Industry 5.0 and the sanctions pressure on the Russian economy create "the windows of opportunity" to achieve a technological breakthrough in the Russian industry. An important factor in the implementation of the opening "windows of opportunity" is the formation of an effective system of tools of state support and investment attraction in large, medium, and small-sized industrial enterprises. The purpose of the article is to identify the key problems of underinvestment in the industry of Russian regions, to study the existing tools for attracting investment in industrial enterprises in Russia's federal constituent entities, and to formulate directions for their improvement and digitalization in order to implement new "windows of opportunity" opened in the context of sanctions. The article studies the investment industrial infrastructure in terms of its constituent tools, constraints, and promising directions for development as exemplified by developed regions of the Volga Federal District (VFD) in comparison with the Sverdlovsk region, an industrially developed region of the Ural Federal District (UFD). Based on the Data Envelopment Analysis model (DEA), the efficiency of investment resources utilization in the studied regions of the VFD and the UFD has been assessed. Promising directions for improving the efficiency of investment infrastructure activities in order to timely implement "windows of opportunity" to attract investment in the industry of the Republic of Bashkortostan and other Russian regions, including digital ones, have been proposed.

**Keywords** Investments · Small and medium-sized business · Windows of opportunity · Industry · Institutions of development · Digital transformation

P. Ivanov (✉) · T. Altufeva
Institute of Social and Economic Researches – Subdivision of the Ufa Federal Research Centre of the Russian Academy of Sciences, Ufa, Russian Federation



A. Appolloni et al. (eds.), *The Future of Industry*, Lecture Notes in Information Systems and Organisation 70, https://doi.org/10.1007/978-3-031-66801-2_34

## 1 Introduction

At present, under the transformation of the existing world order, trends towards the policy for strengthening the technological sovereignty of states (this topic is relevant for modern European studies [1]) based on the support of their own (domestic) industrial production [2], development of advanced innovative technologies and digitalization, are increasing. The issues of protectionism are raised in the European Union [3] and the United States [4], where each party tries to use its advantages (lower energy costs and tax benefits in the United States, proximity of consumers and subsidies in the EU) to attract resources for the development of industry in its territory.

The active introduction of digital technologies in various areas of activities, increased costs on research and development activities, and increased innovation activities of enterprises ensure the formation of "the Windows of Opportunity" for the transition to Industry 5.0, which stimulates investment in the development of modern high-tech industrial production all over the world, including Russia. In this regard, the relevance of studying the sufficiency of the existing measures and tools to support the industry from the viewpoint of increasing investment activities in modern conditions increases. Since the industry of any country consists of regional production operations, it is important to examine the investment infrastructure of industrial support in the regions. In view of the above, the purpose of the article is to identify the key problems, analyze the existing tools of investment attraction in large, medium, and small-sized industrial enterprises of the constituent entities of the Russian Federation, and formulate avenues for their improvement as one of the most important directions to implement "the Windows of Opportunity".

## 2 Literature Review

A significant number of publications by both Russian [5–7] and foreign authors [8–10] are devoted to the issues of effective use of "the Windows of Opportunity" in the economy. The concept of "the Windows of Opportunity" was first proposed in the late 1980s by Perez and Soete [11], who noted that after the opening of the Windows of Opportunity, as the technological system developed, an economic entity would need a growing flow of investment to maintain its leadership. This indicates the critical importance of ensuring a sufficient level of investment, especially at the early stages of the life cycle of products and technologies (including industry) for the formation of interconnected technological systems as the basis for sustainable development of the territory within a certain technical and economic paradigm (technological mode).

To develop the ideas of Perez and Soete, Lee and Malerba [10] identified the following factors opening "the Windows of Opportunity" for catching-up development: the creation of a new technology or the introduction of radical innovation ("the

Windows of Technology"), the formation of an appropriate consumer demand for the advantages provided by the new technology ("the Demand Window"), the implementation of public policy and the conditions of the institutional environment that provide a certain level of protection for domestic companies ("the Institutional Window"). The first two factors can be realized because of the fact that the leading company chooses a strategy of profit extraction based on the assumption of maintaining its dominant position in the market by only modernizing its current technologies and reluctance to invest in new technologies, the payback of which is highly uncertain.

Due to the fact that companies differ in their reaction to the emerging Windows of Opportunity and the interconnection of factors in their opening (technology, demand, institutions), Davy and Hansen [8] suggest using an approach based on taking into account, in addition to industry characteristics (knowledge, networking, technology, institutions), individual configurations of opportunities of specific companies in terms of determining their ability, firstly, to implement the opening Windows of Opportunity and, secondly, to analyze the potential benefits and costs before making a final decision. This approach contributes to a better understanding of the relevance of the Window of Opportunity for a particular company, the cause-and-effect relationship between the Windows of Opportunity and the mechanisms of their successful implementation by companies that have chosen the path of catching-up development.

In other research papers, the Windows of Opportunity are considered as a way to level the technological gap [12, 13], to increase the competitiveness of enterprises based on their innovative [14, 15], digital [16, 17] development, and the use of international experience [18].

In the context of isolation of the Russian economy from Western markets, which entails significant restrictions in the use of economic advantages of globalization and country specialization of labor, the relevance of applying the concept of "the Windows of Opportunity" in the field of investment attraction in the industry of Russia's constituent entities is increasing. For example, Mitrofanov [19] considers the Windows of Opportunity as potentials of possible events. "The Windows of Opportunity" or "Critical Window" can be interpreted as an interdisciplinary concept, the specificity of which is largely determined by a particular area of economic activities. Thus, in business, it is a relatively short time period during which investments in certain technologies and types of innovative products will be particularly productive and significant.

The algorithm for assessing new "Windows of Opportunity" for enterprises in the region includes the following stages. At the first stage, the urgent needs of the region in import substitution of products by small, medium-sized and large enterprises are identified, and these needs are compared with the technical projects available in "the Investment Portfolio" of the region, forming a list of projects ready for investment. The next stage consists in studying the operational capability and readiness of the region's enterprises to implement import substitution projects, in particular, based on analyzing their innovation activities. At the last stage, by comparing the region's needs for import substitution of products and technologies (stage 1) and the readiness of its enterprises to invest in them (stage 2), the optimal timing and duration of opening "the Windows of Opportunity" for the implementation of investment projects that meet the region's needs are determined [20].

Under the conditions of the new world order, the ability of industrial enterprises of all sizes to take advantage of the opening "Windows of Opportunity" in connection with the mass withdrawal of foreign brands from the Russian market is conditioned by the potential admissibility of catching a specific period of time, favorable for making investments in the production of import substitution products and industrial technologies, organizational innovations, etc., while eliminating the risks of possible complications [11, 21].

Methodologically, the determination of the moment of opening "the Window of Opportunity" is based on the definition of the most favorable correlations of starting positions for the technological breakthrough of industrial enterprises, firstly, with the long-wave patterns of technological development (within the framework of the concept of Industry 5.0) and secondly, with the increasing degree of disruption of international logistics chains, the shortage of imported raw materials, components and ingredients [22, 23].

## 3 Materials and Methods

The methods of statistical, comparative and factor analysis, as well as linear programming have been used as research methods.

Among the methods of statistical analysis, statistical observation has been applied in the form of analyzing the structure of investment and value added of the industrial sector of the most developed constituent entities of the Russian Federation, which made it possible to identify the specificity of the studied collection of regions in terms of investment and production activities. In the process of statistical analysis of time series, the dynamics of the studied indicators of investment in the fixed capital and the level of socio-economic development for 2010–2021, which affected the change in their structure, has been explored. The specific techniques of statistical comparative analysis have been used, which allowed identifying the features of specific objects by comparing them with their environment. The factor analysis helped to establish the factors that caused the investment superiority of the Republic of Tatarstan and the Sverdlovsk region in the field of industrial development. The analytical method of benchmarking has been applied as a development of linear programming methods for comparing multi-parameter objects in terms of performance efficiency, termed as the DEA (Data Envelopment Analysis). This method was applied to assess the comparative efficiency of industrial investments in the regions due to the absence of the need to determine their relative importance a priori [24, p. 268]. Due to the fact that the approach belongs to the group of methods of benchmarking, it allows assessing the relative efficiency of investments in regional industry by comparing the characteristics of the object studied with the indicators achieved by other objects that are homogeneous with the studied ones.

Let us consider the last of the methods described in detail. The output-oriented DEA (Data Envelopment Analysis) model has been used [25, P. 34], which allows assessing the potential for growth of the result ($z$) at the current level of resource utilization (1):

$$z_0 = \max z + \varepsilon \left( \sum_{i=1}^{m} s_i^- + \sum_{r=1}^{s} s_r^+ \right) \tag{1}$$

under the following restrictions:

$$\sum_{j=1}^{n} \lambda_j x_{ij} + s_i^- = x_{io}$$

$$\sum_{j=1}^{n} \lambda_j y_{rj} - s_r^+ = z y_{ro}$$

$$\lambda_j \geq 0$$

$j = 1..n$; $r = 1..s$; $i = 1..m$.where $y_{rj}$ is the $r$-th output of the $j$-th object; $x_{ij}$ is the $i$-th input of the $j$-th object; $s$ is the number of outputs; $m$ is the number of inputs; $s_i^-$, $s_r^+$ are slacks (leftovers); $z_0$, $\lambda_j$ are required parameters.

The criterion of object efficiency according to the DEA method is the achievement of the Pareto optimum when the following conditions are met:

1) none of the output parameters of the object can be increased without decreasing other ones or increasing at least one input parameter;
2) none of the input parameters of the object can be reduced without increasing other ones or decreasing at least one output parameter.

When $z_0^* = 1$ and zero leftovers (the so-called slacks), the object is considered efficient. Furthermore, in case of $z_0^* > 1$ object is not efficient, i.e., there is a solution that allows achieving a higher result at the same level of resource consumption. The DEA model allows forming a "reference" region for a particular region, by calculating the weighted sum of positive $\lambda_j^*$.

The degree of depreciation of fixed assets in industry (In_1) and the investment volume in the fixed capital per one employee (In_2) by region have been proposed as input indicators. The resulting indicator was the turnover of industrial enterprises per one employee (Out_1). Assuming an investment lag of 1 year, the investment volumes by region for the model calculations were taken at the level of 2020 (other indicators were for 2021). The input and output parameters of the model have taken into account statistical data on all types of enterprises—small, medium-sized and large.

The information base of the research was official statistical data of the Federal State Statistics Service in Russia (Rosstat) [26].

## 4 Results

*The first result.* Assessment of investment provision of industrial economic activities of the studied regions based on statistical analysis of the dynamics and structure of investments and value-added of their industrial enterprises (Table 1).

In 2010–2021, the share of investments in industrial production in Russia increased by 3.1 percentage points. This had a positive impact on the dynamics of the share of industries in GRP, which increased by 2.0 percentage points to 34.7% at the end of the period. At the same time, within the industry, the change in the structure of investment and gross value added is in favor of the extractive sector (Inv 15.1% ÷ 19.3%, GRP 10.4% ÷ 14.4%) rather than the manufacturing sector (Inv 14.2% ÷ 17.2%, GRP 17.1% ÷ 17.7%), which has a higher value added. There is quite a significant differentiation by region: two times in terms of the share in investments and 1.5 times in terms of the share in the GRP. As a result, the investment volume per 1 person employed in the industry (excluding small business entities) in 2021 fluctuated from 224 rubles in the Sverdlovsk region to 605 rubles in the Perm Krai, which correlates with the data on the Inv indicator presented in Table 1.

In the modern context, the main force for investments in the Russian economy is large business [27]. The investment activities of small and medium-sized business (SMB) in the industry is lower both due to the still underdeveloped SMB sector in Russia as a whole (the share of SMB in the country's GDP in 2021 was 20.3%, compared to 50–70% in developed countries) and the dominance of activities with a high asset turnover rate (in 2020, the share of small wholesale and retail trade enterprises in the total revenue of small enterprises amounted to 47.6%) and more stable demand (for example, investments in construction and real estate operations accounted for more than 1/3 of all investments of small enterprises). In addition, SMB investments are limited due to their insufficient involvement in the supply chains of large holding structures. In comparison with large and medium-sized enterprises, SMB entities on average in Russia invest 3 times less in industrial

**Table 1** Share of the industrial sector of the economy in fixed capital investment (Inv) and gross regional product (GRP) of Russian regions, %

| | 2010 | | 2015 | | 2020 | | 2021 | |
|---|---|---|---|---|---|---|---|---|
| Region | Inv | GRP | Inv | GRP | Inv | GRP | Inv | GRP |
| Russia, including | 39.2 | 32.7 | 41.0 | 31.9 | 44.6 | 30.9 | 42.3 | 34.7 |
| Perm region | 63.1 | 47.1 | 73.8 | 49.1 | 68.8 | 50.8 | 70.8 | 56.1 |
| Republic of Tatarstan | 50.0 | 41.7 | 64.3 | 43.2 | 56.3 | 40.4 | 52.9 | 50.7 |
| Nizhny Novgorod region | 48.2 | 35.5 | 40.5 | 34.7 | 59.1 | 31.8 | 51.3 | 30.2 |
| Samara region | 57.9 | 42.0 | 65.4 | 44.0 | 51.5 | 38.2 | 50.9 | 45.5 |
| Republic of Bashkortostan | 41.8 | 40.4 | 58.0 | 35.8 | 48.6 | 32.2 | 49.1 | 37.8 |
| Sverdlovsk region | 51.7 | 38.2 | 53.3 | 36.0 | 35.8 | 38.7 | 36.7 | 38.9 |

*Source:* the authors' calculations based on Rosstat data [26]

**Table 2** Investments of large, medium, and small-sized enterprises in industry per 1 employed person in 2020, thousand rubles

| Region | Large and medium-sized enterprises | Small enterprises |
|---|---|---|
| Republic of Bashkortostan | 372 | 169 |
| Republic of Tatarstan | 585 | 206 |
| Perm region | 616 | 106 |
| Nizhny Novgorod region | 517 | 132 |
| Samara region | 317 | 199 |
| Sverdlovsk region | 258 | 93 |

*Source:* the authors' calculations based on Rosstat data [26]

**Table 3** Source and calculated data for the DEA method

| Region | In_1 | In_2 | Out_1 | DMU efficiency | Target Out_1 |
|---|---|---|---|---|---|
| Republic of Bashkortostan | 53.2 | 0.35 | 6.7 | 1.265 | 8.5 |
| Republic of Tatarstan | 52.4 | 0.54 | 9.9 | 1.000 | 9.9 |
| Perm region | 55.2 | 0.56 | 5.9 | 1.765 | 10.4 |
| Nizhny Novgorod region | 54.8 | 0.46 | 5.2 | 1.839 | 9.5 |
| Samara region | 60.3 | 0.30 | 5.9 | 1.495 | 8.8 |
| Sverdlovsk region | 47.8 | 0.24 | 7.0 | 1.000 | 7.0 |

Note: In_1 is a degree of depreciation of fixed assets in industry, %; In_2 is investment volume in the fixed capital per one employee, million rubles; Out_1 is turnover of industrial enterprises per one employee, million rubles
*Source* Authors' calculations based on the Rosstat data [26]

development per one employee (604 thousand rubles vs. 188 thousand rubles) (Table 2).

If in the structure of investments in fixed capital of large and medium-sized enterprises the industrial sector occupies 44.6%, in the structure of investments in small enterprises it is 15.8%. This share varies by region from 9.2% in the Republic of Bashkortostan to 20.1% in the Nizhny Novgorod region. This indicates the underinvestment of industrial SMB entities (primarily in the form of fast-growing innovative companies and small technology companies) as a promising direction for the implementation of the opening "Windows of Opportunity" under the sanctions pressure. According to the survey of the NAFI Research Center, conducted in June 2022, 62% of Russian entrepreneurs consider sanctions as "good opportunities" [28, p. 20].

*The second result.* The regions of the best practice (from among the researched ones) in the field of return on investments in industry by the DEA method have been identified. The source and calculated data of this task are presented in Table 3.

According to the results of the DEA model calculations, with the source data used for the calculation, only the Republic of Tatarstan and the Sverdlovsk region can be recognized as efficient constituent entities of the RF (efficiency equals to 1). The values of Decision Making Units (DMUs) for the rest of the regions are more than 1, which, with the output-oriented DEA method, means that they are inefficient. In this respect, all the regions have zero slack values, which indicates the absence of leftovers and full allocation of resources to obtain the target values of the modeled result. The reference region for the Republic of Bashkortostan is a hypothetical region obtained based on a weighted sum of the Republic of Tatarstan (weighted 0.31) and the Sverdlovsk region (weighted 0.77). Implementation of the best practice of these regions in the Republic of Bashkortostan would allow, at the current level of depreciation of fixed assets and the volume of investments, to ensure the growth of turnover of industrial enterprises per one employee by 27% (up to 8.5 million rubles).

On the one hand, these values can be considered as a reference point, potential opportunities ("the Windows of Opportunity"), rather than a direct guide to action, since the model result is formed from the best combination of weighted sums of values by different regions. On the other hand, the results obtained allow paying closer attention to the experience of the regions that have demonstrated more efficient utilization of investment resources as promising directions to implement "the Windows of Opportunity".

*The third result.* The main types of state support of industrial enterprises by federal and regional institutions of such support have been studied. Due to the large number of such institutions in Russia and the impossibility to consider all of them within a single article, the most significant of them have been selected as follows:

- The Industrial Development Fund is the key institution for industrial development in the Russian Federation, whose support includes nine main programs (development projects, components, labor productivity, vehicle components, leasing, marking of goods, formation of a component and resource base, priority projects in manufacturing and environmental projects) and four joint programs implemented with regional industrial development funds (development projects, components, labor productivity, forestry development projects). The volumes of support range from five million rubles to five billion rubles under the main programs at the rate of 1–5% for the term of 2–10 years, under joint programs—from 20 up to 200 million rubles at the rate of 1–3% for the term of 3–5 years.
- Within the framework of the Project Finance Factory project, VEB.RF State Corporation provides support for high-tech industries through loans, guarantees and sureties, participation in authorized capitals, financial and guarantee support for exports.
- The Ministry of Industry and Trade of the Russian Federation has been carrying out an industrial mortgage program for the SMB since 2022 (loans for the acquisition or modernization of production facilities secured by real estate). The following figures prove its demand: at the beginning of the program implementation, the Government of the Russian Federation allocated 300 million rubles, but in 6 months, the volume of applications for participation from business amounted to 17 billion rubles. Due to budget constraints, the Government of the Russian Federation has allocated additional financing for only one billion rubles. Another tool, i.e., a special program of preferential loans for manufacturers of priority industrial products, has been implemented since February 2023,

but also on a limited scale (one billion rubles to subsidize interest rates on loans). Additionally, the industry is supported through various budgetary subsidies, special economic zones and territories of advanced social and economic development tax and customs privileges, leasing of land plots without bidding, reduced rates of social contributions, etc. are applied in them), industrial parks, special investment contracts (the possibility of obtaining the status of a sole supplier for enterprises within the framework of public procurement), public private partnerships (concessions). For the convenience of choosing the most appropriate support measures for a particular enterprise, the Ministry has formed a special navigator, which systematizes more than 2000 support measures [29].

- The Federal Corporation for the development of medium-sized and small business (SMB Corporation) provides support to innovative SMB entities, fast-growing high-tech companies ("gazelles"). Since 2019, the SMB Corporation together with the Ministry of Economic Development of the Russian Federation and the Bank of Russia have been implementing a preferential investment-lending program (Program "1764", 633.2 billion rubles issued in 2022). The Bank of Russia also implements a program to stimulate lending (in abbreviated form: PSL, 232.2 billion rubles issued in 2022). The SMB entities engaged in manufacturing industries can also participate in these programs (in 2022, every fourth loan was issued under the PSL program in this area). Due to sanctions, most of the loans in 2022 were issued as working capital loans (up to 3 years). However, in 2023, the focus was on lending (for up to 10 years) to investment projects to implement "the Windows of Opportunity" for import substitution. For this purpose, support was planned to be in the format of "1764" + PSL. In addition, the SMB Corporation provides guarantee support to the SMB entities and issues umbrella guarantees (215 billion rubles in 2022). On the platform of МСП.РФ (MSP.RF), "the Center for Support of Investment Lending" was created to simplify the obtaining of loans by the SMB entities [30].
- The Innovation Promotion Fund, within the framework of the "Development" program provides grant support (15–30 million rubles for 1–2 years, co-financing at the expense of own funds in the amount of at least 15% of the grant amount is required) to small technology companies to conduct R&D for the production of innovative products. Grants (up to 50 million rubles) are also allocated for solving problems in the field of artificial intelligence. The Fund is a participant in the mechanism of seamless integration of support measures, which ensures the exchange of information between development institutions to reduce the time required to collect information for making decisions on financing.

In addition to federal support, regional development institutions operate in various constituent entities of the Russian Federation as follows: regional industrial development funds, development corporations, innovation funds, agencies for the development of small and medium-sized business, etc.

*The fourth result.* The current level of application of digital financial assets (DFA) in the studied leading regions has been established. A distinctive feature of development institutions in the leading regions (the Republic of Tatarstan and the

Sverdlovsk region) is the promotion of active development of the crowdlending market using digital financial assets. In October 2023, in the Sverdlovsk region, the investment platform "VDelo" created by the regional authorities and the Sverdlovsk Regional Fund for Entrepreneurship Support for the first time to attract investment, DFAs have been used (for the amount of ten million rubles with a yield for investors of 17% per annum), which have been booked by investors within half an hour after their placement [31].

In the Republic of Tatarstan, the practice of using DFA for financial support of small enterprises is also spreading. In March 2024, the Small Business Leasing Company of the Republic of Tatarstan on the digital platform of Alfa-Bank issued DFA at 19% per annum for 18 months [32] (the placement has been recognized by the platform operator as having taken place, with the amount of 1 DFA (token) amounting to 1 thousand rubles, and the minimum declared amount to recognize the placement as having taken place was equal to one million rubles, and the maximum—120 million rubles), which is higher than the current rates on bank deposits. These attractive conditions caused a high interest in investments in DFA on the part of individuals.

***The Fifth Result*** The factors that ensured the leadership of the Republic of Tatarstan and the Sverdlovsk region in terms of investment activities in industry have been identified. The leading positions of the Republic of Tatarstan and the Sverdlovsk region as efficient regions in the field of attracting investments in the industry are to some extent associated with the existing fundamental economic conditions that create opportunities for supporting the industry (Table 4).

Deterrents to growth for the majority of regions are lower values of budget sufficiency (the volume of tax and non-tax revenues of the consolidated budget of the region per capita) of the territories as a whole in comparison with the leading regions, which reduces the potential opportunities of regional authorities to create favorable conditions for attracting investments [34], allocation of budgetary funds to

**Table 4** Financial and budgetary factors in supporting the industrial sector of the regions in 2021, thousand rubles

| Region | Budget sufficiency per capita | Volume of loans issued to industrial enterprises per one employee | GRP per capita |
|---|---|---|---|
| Republic of Bashkortostan | 50.5 | 589.9 | 499.0 |
| Republic of Tatarstan | 86.4 | 796.8 | 888.0 |
| Perm region | 77.4 | 592.4 | 677.8 |
| Nizhny Novgorod region | 70.1 | 1043.7 | 597.4 |
| Samara region | 75.4 | 312.2 | 675.3 |
| Sverdlovsk region | 84.5 | 868.3 | 710.4 |

*Source:* the authors' calculations based on data from Rosstat [26] and Bank of Russia [33]

subsidize interest rates on priority investment projects, affecting the volume of business lending.

In addition, the insufficient level of implementation of digital technologies in production as compared to the leading regions also negatively affects the competitiveness of enterprises and the investment attractiveness of territories in general. For example, in 2022 the share of enterprises using special software for: (1) automation of industrial processes in the Sverdlovsk region amounted to 22.3%, in the Republic of Tatarstan—15.1%, in the Republic of Bashkortostan—10.5%; (2) financial settlements in electronic form—53.2%, 42.4% and 37.2%, respectively.

## 5 Discussion

Based on the results of the studies and global and Russian experience, the authors consider it expedient under sanctions for the implementation of "the Windows of Opportunity" in the regions of the Russian Federation and, in particular in the Republic of Bashkortostan in the medium-term perspective to stimulate the state growth of investments in the following types of economic activities by different types of industrial enterprises:

- for large and medium-sized companies—to unmanned aviation, chemical industry, production of liquefied natural gas, etc.;
- for small companies (including in cooperation with large and medium-sized businesses)—in the production of electronic and radio-electronic products, pharmaceutical production, development of digital solutions based on artificial intelligence (in particular, in the field of computer vision).

The tools proposed for this purpose are currently little used in Russian regions:

- implementation of offset contracts (public procurement), which allow industrial enterprises to ensure guaranteed demand for their products in the future in exchange for investment commitments to the state for the output of products with prescribed properties, volumes and delivery dates. The economic benefit for the regions from the implementation of offset contracts consists in attracting investments to their territory, creating new jobs, increasing tax revenues to the budget and saving budget funds, acquiring new competencies by the territories. The economic effect of the leading region in the Russian Federation by the number of contracts with cross investment obligations, including 17 offset contracts—Moscow, for 10 years will amount to more than 340 billion rubles with the number of new jobs created, that is 6500 units. Expected savings under the offset contract in St. Petersburg for the production and supply of pharmaceuticals (3 years—construction, 7 years—production and supply) at a contract price of 8.7 billion rubles—20.6 billion rubles with investments of at least 2.3 billion rubles. The first offset in the machine-building industry in Russia (production of new trolleybuses), implemented in the Republic of Bashkortostan, will have an effect of at least one billion rubles in investments and the Republic will receive 45 low-floor trolleybuses with autonomous driving and dynamic recharging;

- return the norm on irrevocability of state guarantees of Russia's constituent entities to the RF Budget Code, since currently this type of capital attraction is not considered by loan organizations as a reliable tool for loan support. The effect of the return proposed will allow lending organizations to free up capital to increase lending to highly reliable borrowers, which, in turn, will simplify the implementation of effective transformational economic projects of regional development;
- deployment of the support system for fast-growing high-tech industrial enterprises and small technology companies in Russia:

***In Terms of Fast-Growing Companies*** To form a digitized register of potential fast-growing companies (FGCs) in the Russian Federation from among small and medium-sized enterprises through their standardized selection (based on the volume of R&D costs, the number of available inventions, patents, utility models and other scientific and technological achievements, as well as the priority directions of development proposed by the applicants for the implementation of the current "Windows of Opportunity");

To introduce the mechanism of "gradient cultivation" of new technology-oriented FGCs in the regions to develop key technologies in order to overcome the consequences of sanctions pressure;

To create the Ufa zone of economic and technological development in the Republic of Bashkortostan, specialized in the cultivation of technology-oriented FGCs based on convergence processes of Internet technologies, Big Data and artificial intelligence with industrial technologies;

To find a possibility of long-term direct financing from the budgets of the constituent entities of the Russian Federation of a selected group of enterprises/applicants for the FGC status, supported by the state concierge service, carried out in the interests and at the request of these enterprises;

To provide additional support by regions to high-tech FGCs in the form of subsidies for technological innovations (R&D) and free-of-charge specialized training programs for technical personnel.

The economic effect of supporting fast-growing high-tech industrial enterprises, especially in combination with digital transformation, will be the creation of more jobs per unit of revenue growth, which will provide the constituent entity of the Russian Federation with a significant number of new jobs (quite highly qualified) in the medium term. At the same time, FGCs will partially cover those needs that had previously been covered by Western sources of financing, including project financing, to ensure technological development.

***In Terms of Small Technological Companies*** To develop tools of state support for innovation activities of small technology companies;

To create a register of small technology companies of the Republic of Bashkortostan;

To observe federal and establish regional privileges on payment of taxes, fees, insurance contributions established by the legislation of the Russian Federation on taxes and fees, and on payment of customs duties in accordance with the customs legislation of the Customs Union within the EAEU and the legislation of the Russian Federation on customs procedures;

To provide assistance to small innovative, high-tech companies of the regions in terms of implementing their advanced developments at the sites of large industrial enterprises and at all stages of the life cycle of their products.

The economic effect of supporting small technology companies in cooperation with medium-sized and large enterprises of the Russian Federation and its constituent entities should be expected in the development of "critical technologies", i.e., industry technologies that are critically needed in the context of geopolitical tension to produce the most important types of high-tech products and create high-tech services to solve socio-economic problems and ensure the technological sovereignty of Russia and its territories.

## 6 Conclusion

Thus, the following conclusions can be drawn based on the results of the study of investment activities and investment infrastructure in the industry of Russian regions:

1. Economic sanctions against Russia and the transition of the world economy to Industry 5.0 have opened "the Windows of Opportunity" for Russian industrial enterprises in the field of import substitution, development of digital and innovative technologies as promising directions for improving the competitiveness of their business. At the same time, one of the key problems of the manufacturing industry in Russian regions in general is underinvestment as compared to the extractive sector. Increasing the investment activities of small business in the industry requires special attention and support. It is necessary to create conditions for the state to boost investments by small industrial enterprises per one employee, the volume of which is currently three times lower as compared to large businesses. Due to the higher predisposition of small enterprises to innovations, as evidenced by the experience of developed countries, strengthening their support in Russia, according to the authors, will contribute to more effective implementation of the windows of opportunity in the industry. One of the key tools for attracting investment in the industrial sector of Russian regions is the creation of special economic zones and technoparks equipped with modern digital infrastructure. Such zones provide investors with more detailed and quicker access to privileges and benefits, which, in turn, stimulates investment attraction to the territory.
2. Based on the DEA method, the best practice regions showing the highest level of return on investment in industry (the Republic of Tatarstan and the Sverdlovsk

region) have been identified. It was found that the main factors of leadership of these regions are higher levels of socio-economic development (GRP per capita) and digital maturity (share of enterprises using specialized software tools), fiscal capacity and loan support for industry as compared to other territories.

3. The analysis of the activities of the main development institutions of industrial enterprises shows that with a rather large number of them and a variety of support programs offered by them, the deterrent, especially for the development of new promising directions, is the insufficient coordination and comprehensiveness of the support provided, which would allow ensuring the production and disposing industrial goods within their full life cycle.

In general, stop factors of investment in promising directions of industrial development are general economic uncertainty, relatively high lending rates (limited budgetary funds for subsidizing interest rates), shortage of production personnel, insufficient state support, especially for small industrial enterprises, weak cooperative ties between large corporations and small and medium-sized enterprises.

**Acknowledgements** The research was performed within the framework of the state assignment of the Ufa Federal Research Centre of the Russian Academy of Sciences (UFRC RAS) No. 075-00570-24-01 for 2024 and for the planned period of 2025 and 2026 years.

## References

1. Edler, J., Blind, K., Kroll, H., & Schubert, T. (2023). Technology sovereignty as an emerging frame for innovation policy. Defining rationales, ends and means. *Research Policy, 52*(6), 104765. https://doi.org/10.1016/j.respol.2023.104765
2. Mikhail Mishustin took part in the Moscow Financial Forum. (2023). http://government.ru/news/49623/
3. Blenkinsop, P. (2023). Fears of European industry exodus to U.S. may be overdone. https://www.reuters.com/business/fears-european-industry-exodus-us-may-be-overdone-2023-03-03/
4. European industry pivots to US as Biden subsidy sends 'dangerous signal'. (n.d.). https://www.ft.com/content/59a8d135-3477-4d0a-8d12-20c7ef94be07
5. Samarina, V., Skufina, T., Savon, D., & Kudryavtseva, S. (2021). Technological windows of opportunity for Russian Arctic regions: Modeling and exploitation prospects. *Journal of Risk and Financial Management, 14*(9), 400. https://doi.org/10.3390/jrfm14090400
6. Topoleva, T. (2023). Decomposition of factors of innovative development of regional-oriented production systems. *Vestnik of The Kazan State Agrarian University, 18*(3), 193–201. https://doi.org/10.12737/2073-0462-2023-193-201
7. Zelentsova, L., & Spesivtseva, M. (2022). Mechanism to detect windows of opportunities for implementing new technical and technological solutions for the purpose of industrial organizations sustainable development. *Vestnik Universiteta, 8*, 68–76. https://doi.org/10.26425/1816-4277-2022-8-68-76
8. Davy, E., & Hansen, U. (2023). A firm-level perspective on windows of opportunity. *Technology in Society, 75*(2). https://doi.org/10.1016/j.techsoc.2023.102374
9. Giachetti, C., & Mensah, T. D. (2023). Catching-up during technological windows of opportunity: An industry product categories perspective. *Research Policy, 52*(2), 104677. https://doi.org/10.1016/j.respol.2022.104677

10. Lee, K., & Malerba, F. (2017). Catch-up cycles and changes in industrial leadership: Windows of opportunity and responses of firms and countries in the evolution of Sectoral systems. *Research Policy, 46*(2), 338–351. https://doi.org/10.1016/j.respol.2016.09.006
11. Perez, C., & Soete, L. (1988). Catching up in technology: Entry barriers and windows of opportunity. In G. Dosi (Ed.), *Technical change and economic theory* (pp. 458–479). Columbia University Press and Pinter.
12. Kwak, K., & Yoon, D. (2020). Unpacking transnational industry legitimacy dynamics, windows of opportunity, and latecomers' catch-up in complex product systems. *Research Policy, 49*(4), 103954. https://doi.org/10.1016/j.respol.2020.103954
13. Peng, X., He, L., Ma, S., & Lockett, M. (2023). Windows of opportunity, Alliance portfolio and catch-up of latecomer firms: A longitudinal case study of sunny from 1984 to 2018. *Nankai Business Review International.* https://doi.org/10.1108/NBRI-01-2023-0001
14. Guo, L., Zhang, M. Y., Dodgson, M., Gann, D., & Hong, C. (2016). Windows of opportunity, technological innovation and globalization: A framework of Huawei's global Catchup. *Academy of Management: Annual Meeting Proceedings, 2016*(1). https://doi.org/10.5465/ambpp.2016.66
15. Hamdali, Y., & Skade, L. (2023). When the time is made right: Constructing windows of opportunity for innovation in practice. *Academy of Management Proceedings, 2023*(1). https://doi.org/10.5465/AMPROC.2023.174bp
16. Guo, H., Li, X., & Wang, C. (2023). When the window of opportunity opens: How does open search impact the business model design of digital startups? *Asia Pacific Business Review, 29*(4), 1–24. https://doi.org/10.1080/13602381.2023.2191451
17. Xiong, J., Wang, K., Yan, J., Xu, L., & Huang, H. (2021). The window of opportunity brought by the COVID-19 pandemic: An ill wind blows for digitalization leapfrogging. *Technology Analysis and Strategic Management, 35*(8), 586–598. https://doi.org/10.1080/09537325.2021.1979212
18. Garrido, E., Giachetti, C., & Maicas, J. P. (2023). Navigating windows of opportunity: The role of international experience. *Strategic Management Journal, 44*(8), 1911–1938. https://doi.org/10.1002/smj.3485
19. Mitrofanov, A. (2015). Windows of opportunity. https://www.razumei.ru/lib/article/2652
20. Dunlap, D. R., Santos, R. S., & Latham, S. F. (2023). A window of opportunity: Radical versus repurposing innovation under conditions of environmental uncertainty and crisis. *IEEE Transactions on Engineering Management*, 1–13. https://doi.org/10.1109/TEM.2023.3282803
21. Shinkevich, A. I., Shinkevich, M. V., & Zaraichenko, I. A. (2010). Technological "windows of opportunity": Managing transaction costs of innovative development. *Bulletin of Kazan Technological University, 3*, 207–214.
22. Dementyev, V. E. (2009). Catching up development through the prism of the theory of "long-wave" technological dynamics: The aspect of "windows of opportunity" in crisis conditions. *Russian. Economic Journal, 1-2*, 34–48. EDN: PJIOPN.
23. Glazyev, S. Y. (2018). Leap into the future. Russia in new technological and world economic structures. In *Series "collection of the Izborsky Club"*. Book World.
24. Frants, M. V., & Shmakova, M. V. (2023). Effectiveness of healthcare expenditures in the republic of Bashkortostan: Assessment based on the DEA approach. *Journal of Altai Academy of Economics and Law, 10-2*, 267–273. https://doi.org/10.17513/vaael.3022
25. Zhu, J. (2014). *Quantitative models for performance evaluation and benchmarking* (p. 414). Springer International Publishing. https://doi.org/10.1007/978-3-319-06647-9
26. Rosstat. (n.d.). https://rosstat.gov.ru
27. Altufeva, T. Y., Ivanov, P. A., & Sakhapova, G. R. (2019). Financing the development of municipal entities at different life cycle stages: Public and private resources. *Proceedings of the RAS Ufa Scientific Centre, 3*, 53–60. https://doi.org/10.31040/2222-8349-2019-0-3-53-60
28. Expert Report "Small and Medium-Sized Business as a Form of National Identity". (2022). https://disk.yandex.ru/i/M6xoJvnYky-xog
29. Navigator of support measures for industrial enterprises. (n.d.). https://gisp.gov.ru/nmp/

30. MSP (SMB) Digital Platform. (2023). https://xn%2D%2Dl1agf.xn%2D%2Dp1ai/services/antikrizisnye-mery/kakuyu-podderzhku-malyy-i-sredniy-biznes-mozhet-poluchit-v-korporatsii-msp_/
31. In the Sverdlovsk Region, The First Transaction using Digital Financial Assets Took Place on The "VDelo" Investment Platform. https://oblgazeta.ru/industry-and-economy/enterprise/2023/10/20884/.
32. On the Wave of FinTech Innovations: Debut Issue of Digital Financial Assets of The Small Business Leasing Company of The Republic of Tatarstan. (2024). https://ivfrt.ru/news/novosti-fonda/na-volne-fintech-innovatsiy-debyutnyy-vypusk-tsifrovykh-finansovykh-aktivov-lkmb-rt/
33. Bank of Russia. https://www.cbr.ru/statistics/bank_sector/sors/.
34. Ivanov, P. A. (2021). Theoretical and methodological aspects of assessing the investment activity of regions. *Ars Administrandi, 13*(4), 495–515. https://doi.org/10.17072/2218-9173-2021-4-495-515

# Integration of the Sustainability Aspects into the Evaluation of the Export Potential of High-Tech Companies

**Anastasia Y. Nikitaeva, Anna S. Deynichenko, and Olga I. Dolgova**

**Abstract** In order to increase the efficiency of industrial structures' foreign economic activity, an adequate evaluation and expansion of the export potential of the Russian high-tech complex are required. The introduction of the Industry 5.0 concept, accompanied by the humanization of technologies and economic resilience, as well as ensuring sustainability, into the production of high-tech products, can bring the Russian high-tech complex to a new level of development. This study defines the concept of export potential and provides approaches to its evaluation. The authors conducted a scientometric analysis, which showed a low number of research into the relationship between the sustainability and the export potential of high-tech companies. At the same time, there is an increase in the number of publications on the sustainable development, which makes this area relevant for the study. Correlation analysis helped identify the factors closely interrelated with the export of high-tech products, among which the indicator "production and consumption waste generation" turned out to be significant. Based on these and other arguments from the paper, the authors propose to introduce a sustainability contour into the assessment of the export potential of high-tech industrial enterprises.

**Keywords** High-tech sector · Export capacity · Sustainable development · Export potential evaluation · Industry 5.0

## 1 Introduction

In the context of the new industrial revolution and large-scale digital transformations, countries with significant industrial potential found themselves faced with the need to find new mechanisms for economic development and ensuring competitiveness. Russia is one of such countries facing new opportunities and challenges in industrial development in a global context. The development of non-primary

A. Y. Nikitaeva · A. S. Deynichenko · O. I. Dolgova (✉)
Southern Federal University, Rostov-on-Don, Russian Federation
e-mail: aunikitaeva@sfedu.ru; pavliukevich@sfedu.ru; oldolgova@sfedu.ru



A. Appolloni et al. (eds.), *The Future of Industry*, Lecture Notes in Information Systems and Organisation 70, https://doi.org/10.1007/978-3-031-66801-2_35

non-energy exports is one of the key objectives of Russia focused on technological sovereignty and sustainable economic growth. The creation of new industries and the modernization of the existing high-tech industries can increase the efficiency of the Russian industrial complex. Investing in full innovative high-tech cycles (development of high technologies, their introduction into the production process at the expense of internal resources, obtaining finished high-tech products) can increase the competitiveness of the Russian high-tech complex and its export potential. Under the current conditions, the structure of Russia's foreign economic relations has undergone changes. Many multinational corporations have withdrawn from the Russian market, and import and export restrictions have been imposed on the Russian economy. At the same time, there is a reorientation of Russia's foreign trade relations with new countries; the role, composition of participants, and functionality of BRICS are expanding. This gives an additional incentive to the development of the export potential of the Russian high-tech sector. However, identification of directions and ways of development and capacity building requires a preliminary study and evaluation.

According to the experience of industrially developed countries, large-scale production poses an increased threat to the environment and human health. In this regard, the trend of the world's advanced high-tech industries is sustainable development, which is closely related to the quality of human life, environmental safety, and the effective economy. The integration of high-tech and sustainability trends is implemented within the Industry 5.0 concept. A sustainable economy is aimed at improving the quality of the environment, rational use of natural resources, and the introduction of innovations (including green innovations) into the production process. In this regard, the evaluation of the export capacity of the high-tech industry needs to take into consideration the introduction of sustainable development technologies into the production process.

With that said, this study is aimed at solving three interrelated tasks: analyzing the essence and existing methods for assessing export potential considering the imperatives of Industry 5.0; identifying the relationship between indicators of export potential and sustainable development; and, based on the results obtained, substantiating the expediency and possibility of integrating the sustainability contour into the assessment of the export potential of the high-tech industry.

## 2 Literature Review

An analysis of the literature has shown that the issues of export potential and its assessment have become the subject of study for many scientists.

The export potential of the high-tech industry is a set of means and capabilities of the national high-tech complex for the production and export of high-tech goods. For example, Andreeva and Malysheva [1] distinguish between two approaches to understanding export potential: process and resource. From the viewpoint of the process approach, the export potential is a set of abilities and opportunities for the development of an economic entity (high-tech industrial enterprise). Raisberg [2] argues that export potential is the ability to create and export manufactured products. Fokina [3] understands export potential as the ability of an economic entity to adapt to constantly changing environmental conditions. According to Karachaev [4], the export potential includes three components: the implementation of activities in the foreign market, the ability of an economic entity to successfully develop in the world market, and the ability to maximize profits in the foreign market.

Within the resource approach, Savinov [5] defines export potential as the ability to produce products that are competitive on the foreign market with the use of innovative factors of production. Savikov [6] interprets the export potential as a set of resources available to an entrepreneur and the possibilities of their effective use. Nikitaeva and Deynichenko [7] consider export potential to be a set of sub-potentials that make up it: innovative, institutional, infrastructural, financial, scientific, resource, and production, which form the conditions for the development of export potential as a whole.

Despite a sufficient number of definitions of export potential proposed by the scientific economic community, this concept lacks a unified interpretation. Further research is required, since the content of the concept determines the possibilities and methods of its evaluation and development. The existing approaches and methods do not fully take into account the framework of sustainable development, which is becoming increasingly important in the transition to Industry 5.0. Industry 5.0 represents an innovative approach to industrial production, the key feature of which is human orientation and the introduction of the latest technological achievements [8]. Unlike previous industrial revolutions, Industry 5.0 is focused on people's cooperation, flexibility, and individualization [9], as well as sustainable development, resilience, and humanization of technologies.

The term "resilience" in relation to enterprises means that a company has the potential to regulate its activities before, during, and after changes so that it cannot only withstand accidents but also continue to perform its functions [10].

The evolutionary transition to Industry 5.0 is mainly due to the need to disclose the role of man in cyber-physical systems. In the process of developing Industry 4.0 technologies, it was forgotten that technologies should only be a tool to achieve the goal but not the goal itself. That is why humanization of technologies aimed at achieving a symbiosis between humans and new technologies is one of the key factors in Industry 5.0 [11].

It is important to consider not only the potential benefits of exporting products but also the risks to the environment that an increase in the production and export of high-tech products carries. This concerns the increase in waste, emissions of harmful substances, water, and electricity consumption, not only in the production process but also in transportation. In addition, requirements related to various manifestations of sustainable development are laid down by many countries as mandatory conditions for the import of products, which affects the opportunities and volumes of Russian exports.

**Table 1** Content of the evaluation of export potential in scientific research

| Authors | Estimated indicators | Evaluation methods |
|---|---|---|
| Wang & Du | Indicators of foreign trade | Gravity model, factor analysis |
| Izutina | Volume of products manufactured | Index of revealed comparative advantages (RCA index), product space model, "open forest" index |
| Zhi Yuan Lü & Mu Zhang | Efficiency of financial investments, technical efficiency | Data envelopment analysis |
| Sergienko & Zubarev | Foreign trade indicators | Analysis of the dynamics of indicators, expert evaluation in point terms |
| Eliseeva | Indicators of foreign trade, infrastructure development | Analysis of the dynamics of indicators |
| Fedina | Indicators of foreign trade per capita | Expert assessment, point ranking |
| Gaponenko | Export opportunities of the region's subjects, factors influencing exports | Analysis of the dynamics of indicators, factor analysis |
| Silvaa, Borré, Castillo, Castro, & Varelae | Export activity of the company | Methods of intellectual analysis: The method of synthetic resampling of the minority, K-means clustering, a generalized regression neural network, a neural network of direct back propagation, a support vector machine, a decision tree and a naive Bayesian algorithm. |
| Sukhyh & Katz | Competitiveness of export products, the efficiency of the enterprise, after-sales service, logistics system and the level of qualification of personnel | "Branded" methodology, expert assessment |
| Moseyko & Azmina | Opportunities for the company to enter foreign markets, indicators of the company's foreign trade | Analysis of the dynamics of indicators, expert evaluation |

*Source*: constructed by the authors according to [12–20]

Due to the lack of a universally recognized definition of export potential, a similar situation is observed with respect to methods of its evaluation. The characteristics of various methods of export potential evaluation are given in Table 1.

Wang and Du [12] and Izutina [13] evaluate the export potential of the high-tech industry at the state level. The authors consider the export potential of the high-tech complex as a whole. Wang and Du [12] apply a gravity model to determine the factors affecting China's foreign trade with third countries. Izutina [13] uses the index of revealed comparative advantages (RCA index), the product space model, and the open forest index to determine the projected volume of exports of high-tech products.

Zhi and Zhang, Sergienko, Zubarev, Eliseeva, Fedina, and Gaponenko consider the export potential of the region. Zhi and Zhang [14] evaluate the effectiveness of financial incentives for the high-tech sector from the standpoint of the activities of specific enterprises and regions. Eliseeva [15] evaluates the export potential through the calculation of a function that includes the index of development of foreign trade in the regions, the index of proximity to the end-user market, the index of development of transport infrastructure, and the index of state support for exports in the region.

Fedina [16] and Gaponenko [17], in assessing the export potential, pay special attention to the following performance indicators: exports per capita, the number of export partners, the number of exporters, the number of residents of priority development territories, the number of small and medium-sized businesses, the number of year-round checkpoints, the number of implemented tools of the Regional Export Standard 2.0, the share of the region in the foreign trade turnover of the country, the share of the region in the total volume of the country's exports, the region's foreign trade turnover per capita, and the export of the region's products per capita.

Silva et al. [18], Katz and Sukhoi [19], Moseyko and Azmina [20] consider the export potential of high-tech companies. Silva et al. [18] propose data mining methods for predicting a company's export activity. Artificial neural networks showed 85.7% of the ability to distinguish and classify companies in accordance with their competitive profile. Katz and Sukhoi [19] consider the assessment of export potential in the context of the enterprise. The authors propose analyzing alternately the internal and external export potentials of the enterprise, calculating the indicators of competitiveness of export products, indicators of the efficiency of the enterprise, and the efficiency of production of export products using an expert assessment of the significance of each indicator.

Moseyko and Azmina [20] evaluate the export potential in the context of small and medium-sized enterprises in the region. The multifactorial assessment of the export potential is based on an expert assessment of the possibilities of an enterprise entering foreign markets, an analytical assessment of the export potential of enterprises based on conceptual and logical models, the formation of an information and analytical system, a comparison of the results of the study, and the opinion of a group of experts.

Thus, the evaluation of the export potential of the high-tech industry is carried out by various researchers at the levels of the state, region and high-tech companies. For analysis, scientists use indicators reflecting production capacity as well as performance indicators. The existing approaches and methods for assessing export potential are focused mainly on technological, innovative, and foreign trade components without sufficient consideration of the framework of sustainable development. Therefore, the authors of this study propose to evaluate the export potential of the high-tech industry, taking into account the integration of the sustainability contour into such an assessment. The relationship between the export potential of high-tech production and sustainable development will be demonstrated in the following sections of this study.

## 3 Materials and Methods

To reveal the place that sustainable development occupies in the structure of scientific research on export potential, keywords for selected publications were analyzed. Since two generally accepted terms are widely used to determine export potential—"export potential" and "export capacity", – it was decided to scrutinize the main directions of export potential research taking into account the variability of the terms.

The international Lens database (lens.org), containing more than 263.4 million scientific papers from open libraries of well-known universities and large scientific resources of open access, was used as the main database of scientific works. In a schematic form, the methodology for selecting articles is presented in Fig. 1.

**Fig. 1** Selection of publications on "export potential" and "export capacity" in the Lens.org database. Source: compiled from the materials of the study

| **Export potential** | |
|---|---|
| **Export potential** | **Export capacity** |
| *Number of mentions in scientific papers* | |
| 136,063 publications | 65,693 publications |
| *In the title, annotation, keywords or scientific field* | |
| 44,533 publications | 17,031 publications |
| *Type of publication – journal article* | |
| 26,271 publications | 9,370 publications |
| *Research area – Economics, Business* | |
| 11,112 publications (1,893 *keywords*) | 4,740 publications (836 *keywords*) |
| *Minimum number of appearances* | |
| at least 5 times | at least 3 times |
| *Exclusion of irrelevant words* | |
| 15 *keywords* | 12 *keywords* |
| *Final sample* | |
| 95 *keywords* | 73 *keywords* |

According to the selected publications, keywords were chosen and used to build the network map. To ensure the comparability of network maps, a different value of the minimum frequency of keyword usage was selected for the queries "export potential" and "export capacity", allowing for the total number of unique keywords for the selected publications.

To check the relationship of various indicators with the volume of exports of high-tech products, the indicator "the share of high-tech goods in total exports" was used as a dependent variable. Correlation analysis was applied to select independent variables. Statistica software was used to perform calculations. The data were retrieved from open sources: the Russian Federal State Statistics Service [21], the Unified Interdepartmental Statistical Information and Statistical System [22], and the statistical collection "Digital Economy: 2023" [23]. Export potential is influenced by various types of factors; therefore, 18 indicators related to different spheres were selected as independent variables for analysis (Table 2).

The structure of the selected indicators is shown in Fig. 2. As indicators of sustainability, the following were chosen: "Production and consumption waste generation" and "Utilization and neutralization of production and consumption waste by type of economic activity".

For variables x2, x3, x15, and x16, the data were calculated based on the OKVED codes for high-tech enterprises. Since different agencies are responsible for the placement of different indicators, there is a wide variation in the periods for which data are provided, which makes it difficult to conduct statistical analysis. The time period from 2018 to 2020 was chosen as the observation period, the data for which were published for all the variables under consideration (Table 3).

Since the number of observations was the minimum possible for correlation analysis, the conditions for selecting variables corresponding to the significance level $p > 0.5$ for three observations were quite strict. Consequently, the number of variables that could be classified as significant was limited. Prior to the analysis, the data was normalized to allow comparison of indicators with different units of measurement.

It is important to note the limitations of correlation analysis. Firstly, its results do not allow us to determine the cause-and-effect relationships. Correlation cannot be used to conclude that one variable causes changes in another. Secondly, correlation analysis makes it possible to evaluate only the linear relationship between the indicators. The result of the analysis may be distorted if the relationship between the indicators is nonlinear. Thirdly, in order to get the most accurate results, a large sample is needed to reduce possible errors.

The main limitation of the developed model is the small sample size caused by the lack of public data. In this model, the risk of getting erroneous data is compensated by using a high-level $p$-value. The sample size used allows us to draw preliminary conclusions about the relationship between the variables.

**Table 2** Analyzed variables

| | Indicator | Unit of measurement |
|---|---|---|
| y | The share of high-tech goods in total exports | % |
| x1 | The share of high-tech goods in total imports | % |
| x2 | The index of production by high-tech activities | % |
| x3 | The share of high-tech and knowledge-intensive industries in the gross domestic product | % |
| x4 | The share of machinery and equipment in the total volume of fixed assets for high-tech activities (excluding small businesses) | % |
| x5 | The share of investments aimed at reconstruction and modernization in the total volume of investments in fixed assets (by organizations that are not related to small businesses in high-tech activities) | % |
| x6 | Index of the physical volume of investments in machinery and equipment carried out during reconstruction and modernization (by organizations that are not related to small business entities in the context of high-tech activities) | % |
| x7 | Advanced manufacturing technologies used | Units |
| x8 | Developed advanced production technologies | Units |
| x9 | The proportion of organizations that implemented technological innovations in the total number of surveyed organizations | % |
| x10 | The level of innovation activity of organizations | % |
| x11 | The share of domestic research and development costs in GDP | % |
| x12 | The number of organizations that have carried out research and development | Units |
| x13 | Expenditures on civil science from the federal budget | % |
| x14 | Total number of researchers | Units |
| x15 | Production and consumption waste generation | Thousands of tons |
| x16 | Utilization and neutralization of production and consumption waste by type of economic activity | Thousands of tons |
| x17 | The number of personal computers in the surveyed organizations | Thousand units |
| x18 | Internal costs of organizations for the creation, distribution and use of digital technologies and related products and services | Billions of rubles |

*Source*: constructed by the authors according to data [21–22]

## 4 Results

Based on the analysis of keywords found in scientific publications on the subject of "export potential", a network map was built using VOSviewer software (Fig. 3).

Based on the constructed network map, four main directions of research in the field of export potential, presented in the form of clusters of different colors in Fig. 3, were defined.

1. The largest cluster is highlighted in red; it includes the most frequently used keywords. This cluster is the most interdisciplinary one, as it includes many

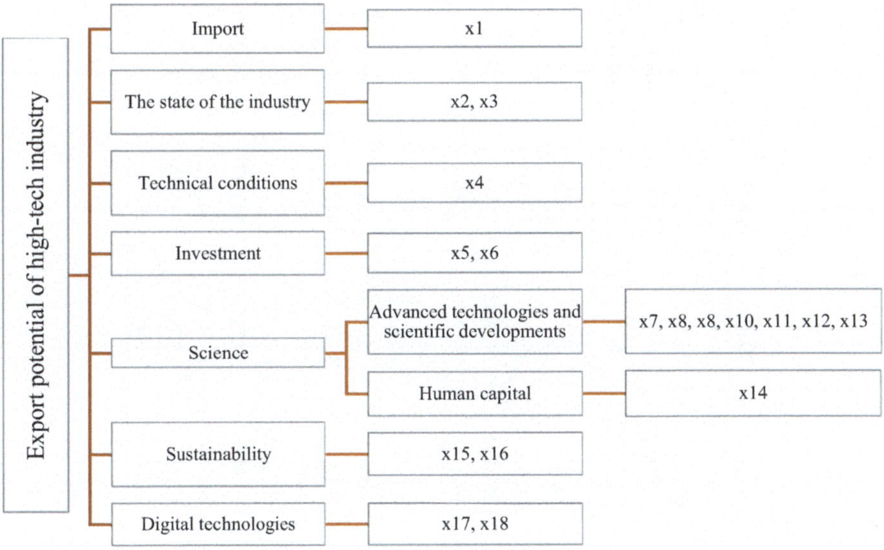


**Fig. 2** Structure of the selected indicators. *Source*: compiled by the authors based on the research materials

different concepts. In general, the work of this group is devoted to the issues of ensuring *economic security in international trade*.

2. The next cluster highlighted in green includes publications dealing with socio-economic issues. The main topic is *demography and the labor market*.
3. The smallest group (yellow) consists of keywords related to the characteristics of a *human as an object of socio-economic research*.
4. The fourth cluster (colored blue) is *sustainable economic development*. This area includes publications devoted to research into sustainability and conservation of natural ecosystems.

This demonstrates the high interest of researchers in the concept of sustainability as one of the key factors influencing export potential [24, 25]. The analysis of the popularity of the use of keywords by year showed that the topic of sustainable development has become of active interest to scientists since 2020. At the same time, issues of the influence of the demographic component on export potential were actively investigated back in the 1990s. A network map on the subject of "export capacity" was also built (Fig. 4).

Since the sample size for this query was much smaller than for the previous one, the variety of keywords used by scientists was significantly lower. Despite the fact that practically all the keywords were used by the authors both in publications on the subject of "export potential" and on the subject of "export capacity", the main directions of research in the field of "export capacity" were somewhat different. In total, five main areas of research were identified.

**Table 3** Initial data

| Year | 2013 | 2014 | 2015 | 2016 | 2017 | 2018 | 2019 | 2020 | 2021 | 2022 |
|---|---|---|---|---|---|---|---|---|---|---|
| y | 10.2 | 10.0 | 12.8 | 14.5 | 13.6 | 10.8 | 9.1 | 26.2 | | |
| x1 | 62.4 | 61.2 | 58.7 | 61.3 | 68.3 | 67.2 | 65.5 | 75.3 | | |
| x2 | | | 96.3 | 98.4 | 107.9 | 100.7 | 104.4 | 107.1 | 110.0 | 95.6 |
| x3 | 21.0 | 21.6 | 21.1 | 21.3 | 21.8 | 21.3 | 22.2 | 25.0 | 23.9 | 22.6 |
| x4 | | | | | 54.5 | 57.1 | 59.2 | 55.6 | 57.0 | 58.4 |
| x5 | | | | | 16.3 | 17.4 | 16.2 | 16.7 | 12.5 | |
| x6 | | | | | | 140.4 | 78.6 | 85.7 | 116.0 | |
| x7 | | | 218,018 | | | 254,927 | 262,645 | 242,931 | | |
| x8 | | | 1398 | 1534 | 1402 | 1565 | 1620 | 1989 | 2186 | 2621 |
| x9 | | | 8.3 | | | 19.8 | 21.6 | 23.0 | | |
| x10 | | | 9.3 | | | 12.8 | 9.1 | 10.8 | | |
| x11 | 1.03 | 1.07 | 1.10 | 1.10 | 1.11 | 1.00 | 1.04 | 1.10 | 1.00 | 0.94 |
| x12 | 3605 | 3604 | 4175 | 4032 | 3944 | 3950 | 4051 | 4175 | 4175 | 4195 |
| x13 | 3.19 | 2.95 | 2.81 | 2.45 | 2.30 | 2.52 | 2.69 | 2.41 | 2.53 | 2.51 |
| x14 | | | 564,801 | | | 682,580 | 682,464 | 679,333 | | |
| x15 | | | | 25,601 | 42,744 | 51,012 | 49,199 | 59,215 | 182,939 | 161,041 |
| x16 | | | | 11,389 | 23,180 | 20,786 | 24,880 | 28,058 | 50,247 | 56,133 |
| x17 | 11,438 | 11,741 | 11,992 | 12,422 | 12,766 | 13,256 | 13,817 | 15,791 | 17,226 | 18,081 |
| x18 | | | | | 1739 | 1953 | 2453 | 2262 | 2947 | |

*Source*: constructed by the authors according to data [21–22]

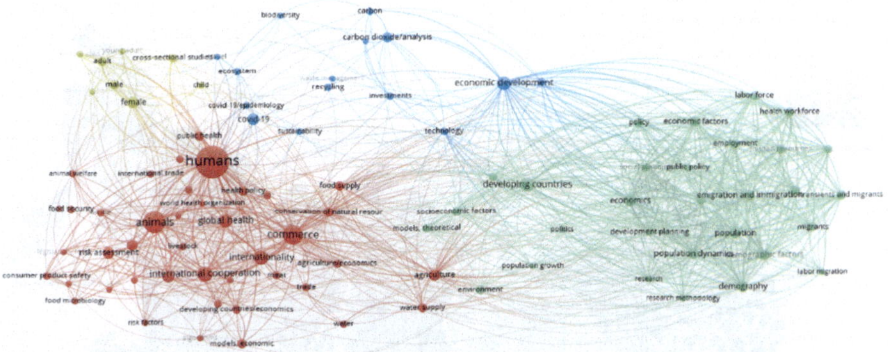


**Fig. 3** Network map of keywords on the subject of "export potential" contained in selected publications. *Source*: compiled by the authors according to the materials of the study

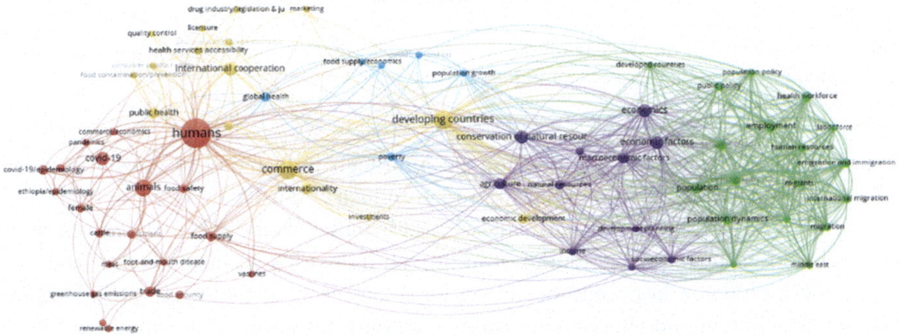


**Fig. 4** Network map of keywords on the subject of "export capacity" contained in selected publications. Source: compiled by the authors based on research materials

1. The cluster of studies dedicated to ensuring sustainability and economic security is represented in red.
2. The direction dedicated to international relations is highlighted in green.
3. Keywords related to socio-economic research are colored yellow.
4. A block of keywords dedicated to demography and employment is highlighted in blue.
5. The purple color represents the direction of research in the context of the impact on the export potential of global problems of humanity, such as poverty, overpopulation, etc.

It is worth noting that the active discussion of the issues of transitioning to renewable energy sources and waste management was started by scientists in 2020.

The study of export potential within the concept of sustainable development has gained researchers' attention only a few years ago, while the number of such works is still quite small. At the same time, very few scientific publications are devoted to

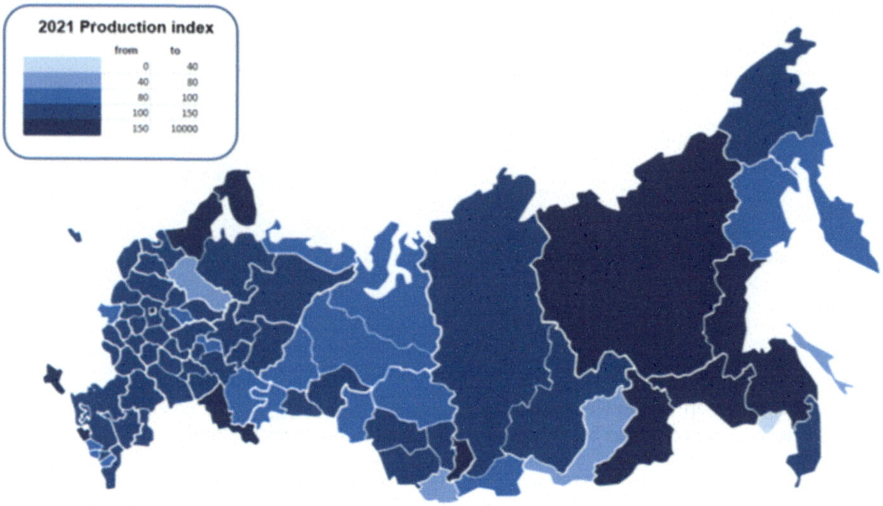


**Fig. 5** Climate map of the production index of high-tech activities by Russian regions for 2021. Source: built by the authors according to [22]

the analysis of the export potential of the high-tech industry (124 journal articles based on request "export potential high-tech industry" in the Lens database in the subject area of "Economics and Business"). This indicates the relevance of research on establishing the export potential of high-tech industries within Industry 5.0.

Russia includes a large number of regions, and each of them has an individual investment climate and special conditions for doing business. Therefore, the development of the high-tech industry is heterogeneous: in some regions, there are a large number of high-tech enterprises whose activities bring high revenue, while in others there are a small number of enterprises that reduce output every year. To assess the dynamics of the high-tech industry development in Russia, a climate map was made according to the average production index of high-tech activities for 2021 (Fig. 5).

Despite the problems with the supply of imported components, the volume of output of high-tech products has increased in more than half of the regions, but there is still a fairly large number of the RF subjects where there is a negative trend in the production of high-tech products.

Figure 6 presents a graph indicating the change in the production index of high-tech products by type of activity. This chart allows us to see a significant increase in the production of medicines and medical devices during the coronavirus pandemic. The remaining activities are mostly stable during the observation period, although there are small fluctuations in production activity. In 2022, a decrease in the growth rate of production is visible. Probably, this is largely due to the current economic and political situation. The production of motor vehicles is worth special attention. This industry decreased significantly in 2020 due to the global shortage of conductors, and it was also severely affected by the economic sanctions of 2022.

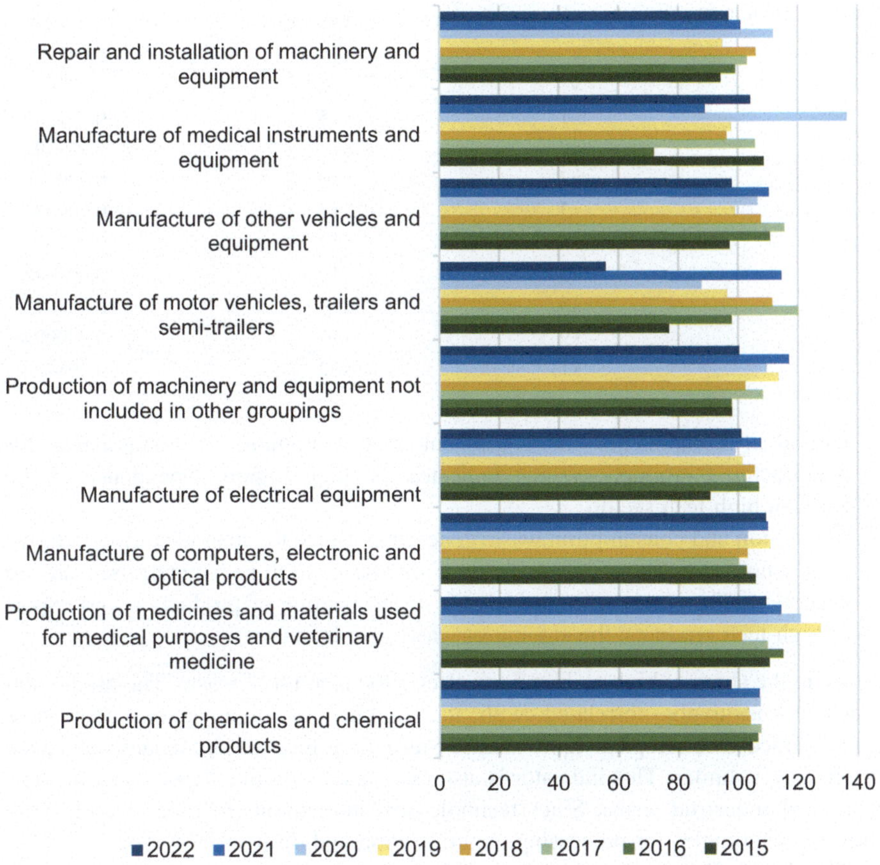


**Fig. 6** Dynamics of the production index of high-tech products by type of activity. Source: constructed by the authors according to [22]

Correlation analysis was used to establish what factors are associated with the share of exports of high-tech products (y), as well as what relationships exist between the indicators that affect it. Due to the small sample size, the requirements for the correlation value to be recognized as significant were very strict.

Table 4 presents the results of the paired correlation analysis of the studied variables. The variables that are significant at a given level of significance and the number of observations are highlighted in red. As can be seen in the figure, variables with a correlation value of 0.996 and higher were classified as significant.

The correlation analysis showed that the following indicators are closely interrelated with the share of exports of high-tech products:

1. The share of high-tech imports. The manufacturing of high-tech products requires special manufacturing equipment. Which is often not produced in Russia. So companies need to purchase such equipment abroad. This also applies to

**Table 4** Significant pair correlations

| Indicator 1 | Indicator 2 | Correlation |
|---|---|---|
| y | x1 | 0.99771 |
| y | x15 | 0.99697 |
| x1 | x15 | 0.99995 |
| x2 | x9 | 0.99979 |
| x2 | x16 | 0.99980 |
| x3 | x17 | 0.99973 |
| x4 | x13 | 0.99963 |
| x5 | x10 | 0.99964 |
| x5 | x18 | −0.99809 |
| x9 | x16 | 0.9999998 |
| x11 | x12 | 0.99843 |

individual components for equipment and a number of components for manufactured products. Which indicates the high import dependence of the Russian high-tech sector.

2. Production and consumption waste generation. Since the manufacturing industry as a whole generates a huge amount of waste. high-tech enterprises are no exception. Therefore. with an increase in the volume of production and export of high-tech products. the amount of waste also increases.

A rise in the share of high-tech imports affects the amount of waste. The production index is positively correlated with the number of organizations that have implemented technological innovations. Since they help to significantly enhance production volumes. This indicator is also associated with the disposal and neutralization of industrial waste. Since technological innovations include, among other things, technologies for processing, neutralization and disposal of waste.

The share of products of high-tech industries in GDP shows a positive relationship with the number of personal computers in organizations. Which is associated with the need to implement many tasks of high-tech companies using software and personal computers. The level of provision of enterprises with machinery and equipment in the total volume of fixed assets shows the presence of correlations with the costs of scientific research. For high-tech research carried out by state order or within the framework of state projects. it is necessary to have a large amount of equipment. Investments aimed at reconstruction and modernization are positively associated with the level of innovation activity of organizations. Since a large number of ongoing innovations are technological. Moreover. the amount of investment in modernization and reconstruction is negatively affected by the increase in the costs of creating, distributing and using digital technologies. This is due to the fact that most companies cannot afford to simultaneously make high investments in equipment modernization and digital technologies. The share of organizations that have implemented technological innovations is also related to the amount of waste disposed. Which is explained by the need to use special technologies for waste disposal and recycling. The number of organizations that have carried out research and development is closely related to the share of internal research and development

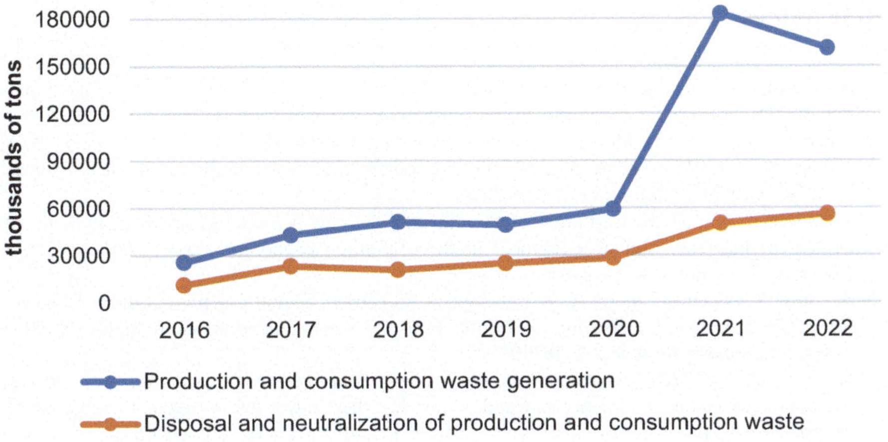


**Fig. 7** Dynamics of waste generation and disposal by high-tech industries. *Source*: constructed by the authors according to [21]

costs in GDP. since the more organizations invest in research and development. The higher the share of costs in GDP.

Thus, the relationship between export potential and sustainable development is confirmed. The transition to green technologies and circular business models is extremely relevant for the high-tech industry since waste generation in Russia significantly exceeds their utilization (Fig. 7).

## 5 Conclusion

Today, while the new Industry 5.0 paradigm is being formed. The issues of humanization of technologies, resilience and ensuring the sustainability of not only production processes but also of all supply chains are particularly acute. Due to the ubiquitous process of digitalization. The demand for high-tech products is growing. Which makes their production and export extremely relevant. At the same time. The production and export of high-tech goods can have a negative impact on sustainable development. According to the results of the correlation analysis. One of the key factors closely related to the export of high-tech goods in Russia is the formation of production and consumption waste. In this regard, it is advisable to include a sustainability contour in the assessment of the export potential of the high-tech industry. This suggests that the assessment of export potential should take into account not only the maximization of its components for increasing production but also factors in resource efficiency. Waste recycling and the introduction of circular economy models. In this case, sustainable development acts as a certain limiting contour in the methodology for assessing export potential. and the relevant indicators taken into account allow us to talk about both quantitative and qualitative characteristics of export potential.

## References

1. Andreeva, E. L., & Malysheva, E. V. (2020). Theoretical approaches to the study of the export potential of the national economy. *Journal of Economic Theory, 17*(2), 265–275.
2. Raisberg, B. A. (2012). *Modern economic dictionary*. INFRA-M.
3. Fokina, D. A. (2017). The essence of the export potential of RCP enterprises. *Actual Problems of Aviation and Cosmonautics, 3*, 966–968.
4. Karachev, I. A. (2015). Definition of the category "export potential of an enterprise" in the context of the formation of a regional model of foreign economic activity. *Bulletin of the Financial University., 4*, 24–37.
5. Savinov, Y. A., Oreshkin, V. A., & Lebedev, A. A. (2013). Export potential of the industry for the development and marketing of information and communication technologies. *Russian Foreign Economic Bulletin., 6*, 28–40.
6. Savikov, O. V. (2010). *Assessment of the foreign economic activity potential of small and medium-sized business structures.* Cand. econ. sci. diss. https://www.dissercat.com/content/otsenka-potentsiala-vneshneekonomicheskoi-deyatelnosti-malykh-i-srednikh-predprinimatelskikh
7. Nikitaeva, A. Y., & Deynichenko, A. S. (2021). Development of high-tech industry in the south of Russia: Opportunities for increasing export potential. *Natural Sciences and Humanities Research Magazine, 38*(6), 254–261.
8. Gupta, K. K., Saha, S., Sahoo, S. K., & Goswami, S. S. (2023). Revolutionizing healthcare industry 5.0: Exploring the potential of Blockchain Technology for Medical Applications. *Journal of Technology Innovations and Energy., 2*(3), 76–93. https://doi.org/10.56556/jtie.v2i3.610
9. Aheleroff, S., Huang, H. X., & Zhong, R. Y. (2022). Toward sustainability and resilience with industry 4.0 and industry 5.0. *Frontiers in Manufacturing Technology, 2*, 951643. https://doi.org/10.3389/fmtec.2022.951643
10. Sepehr, P., Sepehr, A., Rezaee, R., & Samimi, K. (2020). Safety culture and resilience in a petrochemical industry. *Archives of Occupational Health, 4*, 870–875. https://doi.org/10.18502/aoh.v4i4.4513
11. Grabowska, S., Saniuk, S., & Gajdzik, B. (2022). Industry 5.0: Improving humanization and sustainability of industry 4.0. *Scientometrics, 127*, 3117–3144. https://doi.org/10.1007/s11192-022-04370-1
12. Wang, J., & Du, Y. (2017, June 16–18). A study of China's high-tech products trade flow and export potential based on gravity model. In *International Conference on Services Systems and Services Management.* Dalian. China. https://doi.org/10.1109/ICSSSM.2017.7996280.
13. Izutina, T. A. (2022). Application of the "open forest" index to assess the export potential of Russia. *Moscow Economic Journal., 4*, 278–297.
14. Zhi, L., & Zhang, M. (2021). Evaluation on financial support efficiency of new generation high-tech industry in China. *Journal of the Information Technology and Quantitative Management., 199*, 254–261. https://doi.org/10.1016/j.procs.2022.01.031
15. Eliseeva, M. V. (2022). Methodology for assessing the export potential of the subjects of Russia. *The World Economy, 213*, 201–207. https://doi.org/10.14451/1.213.201
16. Fedina, E. V. (2023). Modification of the assessment of the export potential of territories in order to formulate the strategy of industrial development of Russia. *Innovative Investments., 4*, 423–426.
17. Gaponenko, Y. V. (2013). The level of development of the export potential of the region and methodological aspects of its assessment. Socio-economic innovations. *Bulletin of the Volgograd State University 10, 2*(9), 16–20.
18. Silvaa, J., Borré, J., Castillo, A., Castro, L., & Varelae, N. (2019). Integration of data mining classification techniques and ensemble learning for predicting the export potential of a company. *Procedia Computer Science, 151*, 1194–1200.

19. Katz, V. M., & Sukhoi, D. G. (2015). Methods of assessing the export potential of the enterprise. Russian experience. *Bulletin of Siberian Science., 2*(17), 62–74.
20. Moseyko, V. O., & Azmina, Y. M. (2012). Multifactorial assessment of the export potential of small and medium-sized enterprises in the region. Regional economy. *Bulletin of the Volgograd State University. 3, 2*(21), 63–71.
21. Federal State Statistics Service. (2023, September 17). https://rosstat.gov.ru/
22. Official statistical indicators. (2023, September 25). https://fedstat.ru/
23. Abdrakhmanova, G. I., Vasilkovsky, S. A., & Vishnevsky, K. O. (2023). *Digital economy 2023: A brief statistical collection. National research.* Higher School of Economics University.
24. Debbarma, J., Choi, Y., Yang, F., & Lee, H. (2022). Exports as a new paradigm to connect business and information technology for sustainable development. *Journal of Innovation & Knowledge., 7*, 4. https://doi.org/10.1016/j.jik.2022.100233
25. Xu, J., Yu, Y., Zhang, M., & Zhang, J. Z. (2023). Impacts of digital transformation on eco-innovation and sustainable performance: Evidence from Chinese manufacturing companies. *Journal of Cleaner Production., 393*. https://doi.org/10.1016/j.jclepro.2023.136278

# Impact of Digitalisation on the Technological Development of Industry: Russian Experience

**Olga Smirnova and Lyudmila Chesnyukova**

**Abstract** The pursuit of technological independence in the modern information society where digital technologies are becoming increasingly important is becoming critical for developing countries. The study is devoted to assessing the impact of digitalisation on the technological development of the Russian industry towards achieving technological independence. The article provides the indicators for assessing the impact of digitalisation on the technological development of industry, namely, production-related, socio-economic, environmental and technological indicators. A theoretical model for the technological development of industry is presented, which may include blocks comprising innovations and investments, digitalisation, education and human resources, environmental sustainability and state support. The paper explores the role of industrial digitalisation in the context of the formation of technological independence. The results of the article can serve as a basis for the development of strategies aimed at supporting industrial digitalisation and strengthening technological independence.

**Keywords** Industrial complex · Digital technologies · Digital transformation of industry

## 1 Introduction

Industry represents one of the most important sectors of the Russian economy, which strives for constant development and progress. In recent years, modern digital technologies have been playing a key role in this development. The integration of

O. Smirnova (✉)
Institute of Economics of the Ural Branch of the Russian Academy of Sciences, Ekaterinburg, Russia

Ural Federal University, Ekaterinburg, Russia
e-mail: smirnova.op@uiec.ru

L. Chesnyukova
Ural State University of Economics, Ekaterinburg, Russia



A. Appolloni et al. (eds.), *The Future of Industry*, Lecture Notes in Information Systems and Organisation 70, https://doi.org/10.1007/978-3-031-66801-2_36

new digital technologies in the production and logistics sectors provides an opportunity to optimise production processes. All this contributes to the economic growth and sustainable development of digital technologies in the Russian industry.

One of the main elements in charge of competitiveness is the integration of digital technologies into the production processes of the country's industrial complex.

Currently, industrial enterprises are actively applying various available digital solutions that contribute to the achievement of significant economic advantages, unlocking additional potential for profit, and development of new business models. However, the results achieved through digitalisation are not predetermined and depend on the innovation and investment strategy of all involved parties. Technological advancement may cause significant changes in industrial production; the competition for technological independence has been present for many years and is likely to continue in the future.

However, the COVID-19 pandemic predetermined the importance of digital technology and infrastructure for due sustainability of industrial enterprises, especially at times of crisis. The active implementation of digital infrastructure in Russia has played a crucial role in the country's ability to cope with the isolation and respond efficiently to COVID-19 challenges.

Thus, digital gaps can pose threats to technological independence and industrial resilience in case of a crisis regardless of its nature.

Russia's industry is currently undergoing transformation processes. State digitalisation programmes such as Digital Economy and Industrial Development and Increasing Its Competitiveness are actively implemented. The country also has significant scientific and technological potential and human resources that can be used for the successful implementation of these programmes. The choice of the research object is based on the strategic importance of assessing the impact of digitalisation on Russia's industry technological development and the need to ensure its technological independence and development potential.

The purpose of the research is to assess the impact of digitalisation on the technological development of the Russian industry towards achieving technological independence.

The methodological basis of the study includes the results of academic economists' research on the problems of technological independence and digitalisation of the industrial complex.

## 2 Literature Review

The problem area addressing the impact of digitalisation on the technological development of Russian industry towards achieving technological independence is a relevant subject of research. Lately, the issues of ensuring the technological independence of industry have been widely discussed in the scientific and economic literature.

Modern studies by a number of Russian scientists—Andreeva [1], Afanasiev [2], Efimov and Tikhonovskova [3], Konstantinov and Konstantinova [4], Neklyudov and Livshits [5]—analyse the concept of technological development and elaborate a strategy for its achievement in Russia.

The issues of the interrelation of sectoral markets and technological development are raised in the works by Gushchina et al. [6], Moiseychik and Faradzhov [7]. The studies by Bauer et al. [8], Herter and Ovtcharova [9], Meissner et al. [10] and Schlaepfer et al. [11] are devoted to assessing the impact of digital technologies on the development of enterprises. The authors conclude that the digitalisation of industry in Russia helps to increase productivity and optimise production processes. However, some problems with cybersecurity and the need to retrain personnel with regard to new technologies should be addressed.

The works by Smirnova et al. [12], Abdrakhmanova and Vishnevsky identify the regions with different levels of digital maturity: high, medium and low. The research results presented by Akberdina and Romanova [13–15], Nabatova and Plotnikov [16], and Stepanov [17] have contributed to the development of tools for assessing the level of digital transformation of the Russian industrial complex.

Technological development is an important element of national security and is related to the ability of the state to generate or use critical technologies necessary for its functioning [1, 2, 18, 19].

## 3 Materials and Methods

The theoretical model of the technological development of industry towards the achievement of technological independence is presented in Fig. 1. In terms of the processes contributing to the achievement of technological independence, the country's industrial, scientific, and technological complexes play a key role [20]. The industrial complex, with regard to all production factors (raw materials, equipment, staff, technologies, infrastructure), is in charge of the commercialisation of scientific developments, while the scientific/technological complex is aimed at their creation (Fig. 1) [21]. It is necessary to note that the technological development of industry should include an inflow of investments in innovations promoting continuous improvement of advanced technologies at a high level regardless of external factors. This implies a system of incentives and alignment of stakeholders' interests.

The theoretical model of technological development of Russian industry may include several key elements: 1. Innovation and investment: Stimulating innovations in industry plays an important role in technological development. This may include support for research and development and the creation of innovative infrastructure and financing mechanisms for start-ups. 2. Digitalisation: The adoption of digital technologies such as the Internet of Things (IoT), artificial intelligence (AI), big data and factory automation can improve the efficiency and competitiveness of industrial enterprises. 3. Education and human resources: Training a skilled human resource

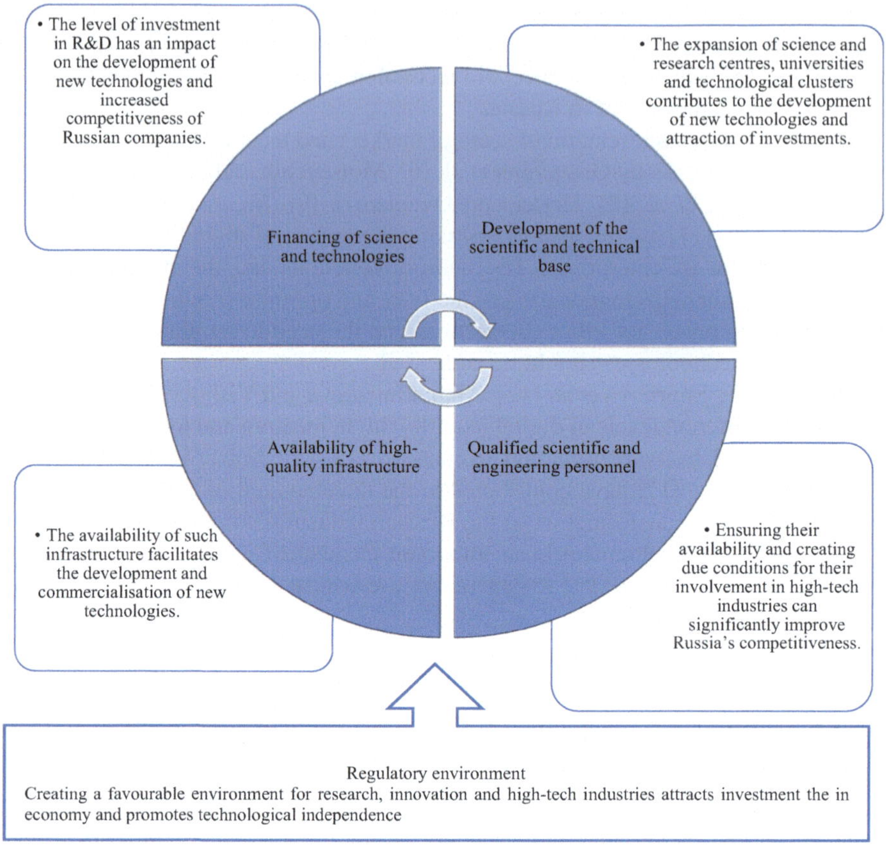


**Fig. 1** Theoretical model of Russian industry technological development towards achievement of technological independence [4, 22]

capable of working with new technologies is a key to successful technological development. This may include updating educational programmes, staff training, and support for research and development projects. 4. Environmental sustainability (infrastructure): Given the growing emphasis on environmental sustainability, the industrial development model should take into account environmental aspects such as reducing emissions and improving energy efficiency. 5. Government support (regulatory environment): Government policies and support programmes can promote technology development in industry through tax incentives, grants, subsidies and other instruments.

The technological development model for the Russian industry takes into account these other factors as well (Fig. 2) to ensure stable and sustainable growth of the industry.

The list of indicators to assess the impact of digitalisation on the technological development of the Russian industry towards the achievement of technological

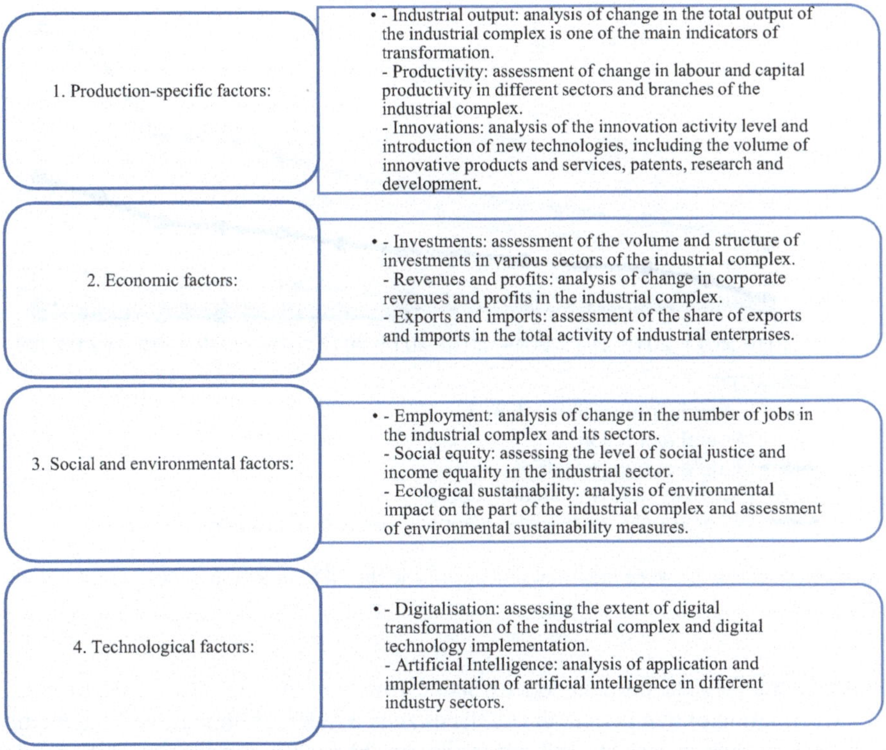


**Fig. 2** System of indicators for assessing the impact of digitalisation on the technological development of Russian industry towards achieving technological independence [22–29]

independence was compiled on the basis of the available regular statistical data provided by the Russian Federal State Statistics Service; it includes industrial, socio-economic, environmental, and technological factors (Fig. 2) [22–29].

The impact of digitalisation on the technological development of Russian industry was assessed using qualitative, quantitative methods and regression analysis. The use of a regression approach will make it possible to assess the statistical significance of the interrelation of variables such as the digitalisation level, productivity, innovation activity and other indicators influencing the technological development of industry (Fig. 2).

## 4 Results and Discussion

The high level of socio-economic development and the efficiency of the industrial complex have been confirmed for a long time. This can be seen in Fig. 3, which shows the relationship between the gross domestic product (GDP) and industrial production volumes.

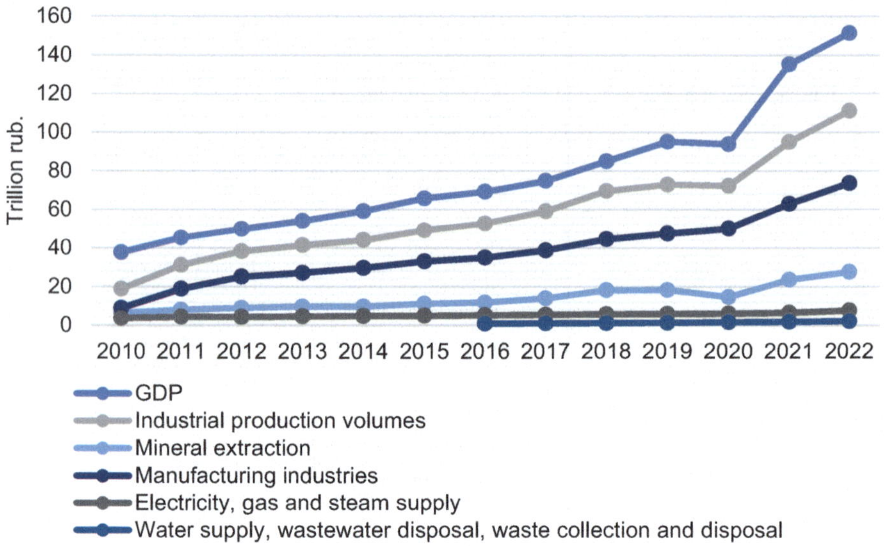


**Fig. 3** Relationship between industrial production and the GDP in Russia in 2010–2022, trillion rub [22–29]

Analysing the data, one can notice a stable growth of the GDP from 2010 to 2022. At the beginning of that period, the GDP equalled 37,687.7 billion rubles, but by the end of the period increased to 135,295.0 billion rubles. This is indicative of the stable economic growth and development of the country. At the same period, an increase in industrial production could also be observed. At the beginning of the period, the industrial output amounted to 18,763.8 billion rubles, increasing to 94,888.3 billion rubles by the end of the period. This is evidence of the active development of the industrial complex and the increase in production capacities. The mineral extraction industry also showed steady growth from 2010 to 2022. A significant increase from 6,226,603 units in 2010 to 27,615,365 units in 2022 was observed. The manufacturing industries also show steady growth over the period under review. A significant increase from 8,871,976 units in 2010 to 73,698,348 units in 2022 is observed. Thus, the analysis of indicators makes it possible to conclude on the growth of the GDP and the industrial production volume in the period under review, as well as on the positive dynamics in the mining and manufacturing industries. In general, the data reflect the positive trends in the development of Russia's industrial complex and testify to its importance for the country's economy.

Analysing the data presented in Fig. 4, one can identify the following trends in the development of industry at that period. In 2010–2022, steady production growth was clearly observed, followed by a slight decline in 2020. This development points to a gradual increase in productivity in the industrial complex. The spending on innovative research and development was also increasing: within the period from 2010 to 2020, it rose from 400.8 billion rubles to 2134.1 billion rubles. This is

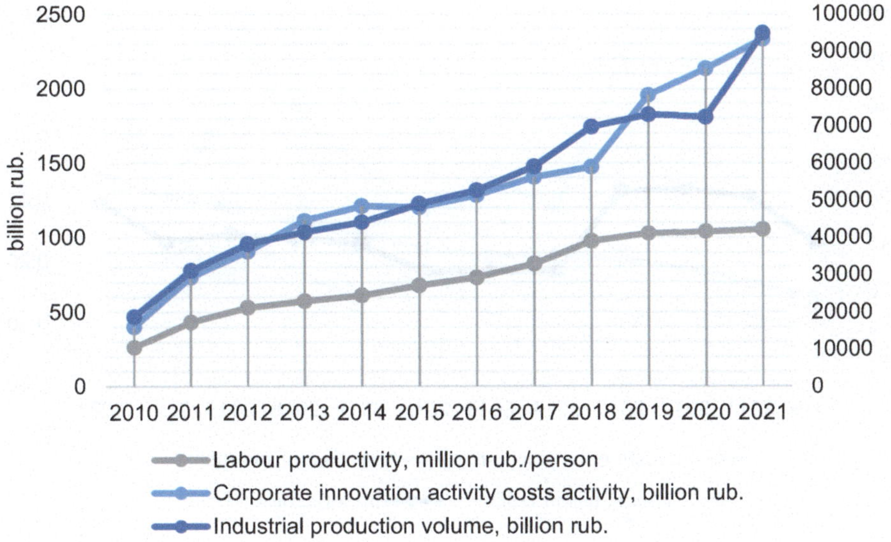


**Fig. 4** Dynamics of production performance in 2010–2021, billion rub [22–29]

evidence of the growing interest of corporate entities in applying new technologies. Thus, one can conclude that the period under consideration is characterised by the increase in the production output, labour productivity, and innovation activity costs. These trends are indicative of positive technological development and the corporate entities' desire to improve efficiency and competitiveness.

During the period under review, the investment in the industry gradually increased (Fig. 5).

Since 2010, the investment volume reached its maximum in 2021 and totalled 22,945.4 billion rubles. This is evidence of the growing interest in the development of the industrial complex and the improvement of the investment environment. The profit indicator also shows a positive trend with some temporal variation. After falling in 2014, it increased significantly and reached a high level in 2021, totalling 33,915.8 billion rubles. This can be attributed to the increased production efficiency and improved financial performance of industrial enterprises. Some trends can also be viewed with regard to exports and imports. The export of Russian industrial goods showed some fluctuations within that period but generally demonstrated positive dynamics. After declining in 2014, the exports gradually increased, reaching \$493.1 billion in 2021. Meanwhile, the imports also showed certain growth with minor fluctuations. It peaked in 2021, reaching \$293.5 billion. This evidences the importance of international trade relations and the Russian market's need for imported goods.

Thus, the period under review shows some positive trends—the increase in investments, profit markup, and development of foreign trade. These data are important for assessing the efficiency and prospects of the country's industrial complex development.

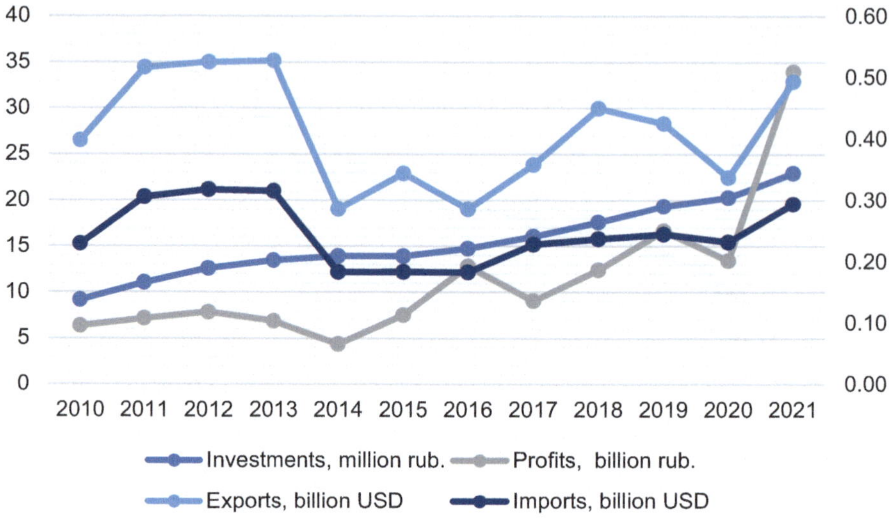


**Fig. 5** Dynamics of economic performance in 2010–2021 [22–29]

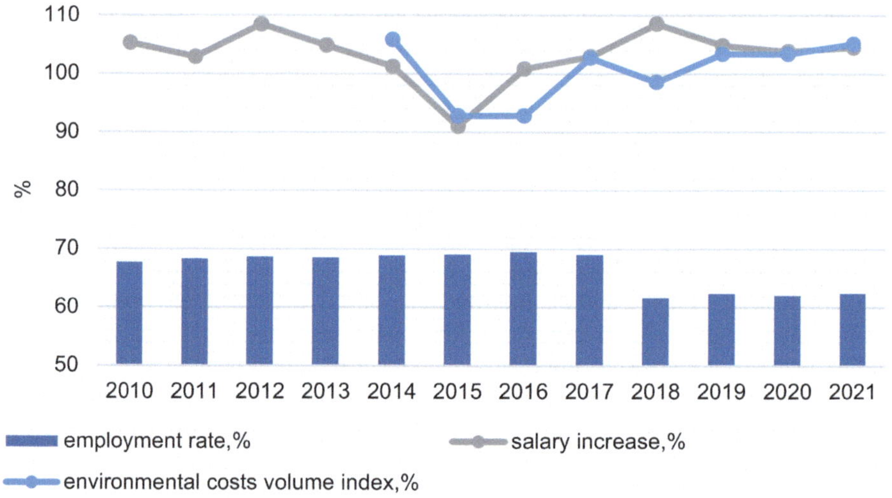


**Fig. 6** Dynamics of social factors in 2010–2021, % [22–29]

Employment in Russia's industrial complex remained relatively stable from 2010 to 2021, ranging from 61.6% to 69.5% (Fig. 6). However, from 2018 onwards, the employment rate started to decline, possibly due to the automation of production and changes in the structure of industries. The wages in the industrial complex were growing moderately from 2010 to 2012, followed by some fluctuations; however, the overall positive trend was maintained. However, a decline in wages took place in

2015, being especially sensitive in 2016. After that, the wages started to rise gradually and by 2021 reached the level exceeding the initial value by 4.5%. This fluctuation may be explained by economic factors and changes in qualification requirements and labour productivity.

The environmental sustainability index of the industrial complex, which reflects the nature protection costs, shows unstable dynamics from year to year (Fig. 6). A particularly significant decline was recorded in 2015; however, after that, the index began to recover. Such fluctuations may be accounted for by the change in priorities and approaches to environmental policy as well as by investments in ecological technologies. As a result, Russia's industrial complex faced some challenges in 2010–2021 related to the changes in the labour market, including the decline in employment. However, it also shows positive wage dynamics and some signs of recovery of environmental sustainability. The assessment of these trends and their impact on industry can be useful in developing industrial development and sustainability strategies.

The extent of the realisation of digital technologies in the Russian industrial complex can be characterised by the following indicators [30] (Fig. 7): (1) The use of personal computers. The share of organisations working with personal computers remained quite stable in the period of 2010–2019, ranging from 93.8% to 94%. However, in 2020, a significant decrease in this proportion to 80.7% was registered; in 2021 it increased slightly to 81.8%. The use of personal computers has decreased slightly in recent years. (2) The use of servers. The share of organisations using servers showed significant fluctuations from 2010 to 2021. This percentage increased from 2010 to 2013, reaching a peak in 2013 (73.4%). However, the share of corporate entities using servers decreased within the period of

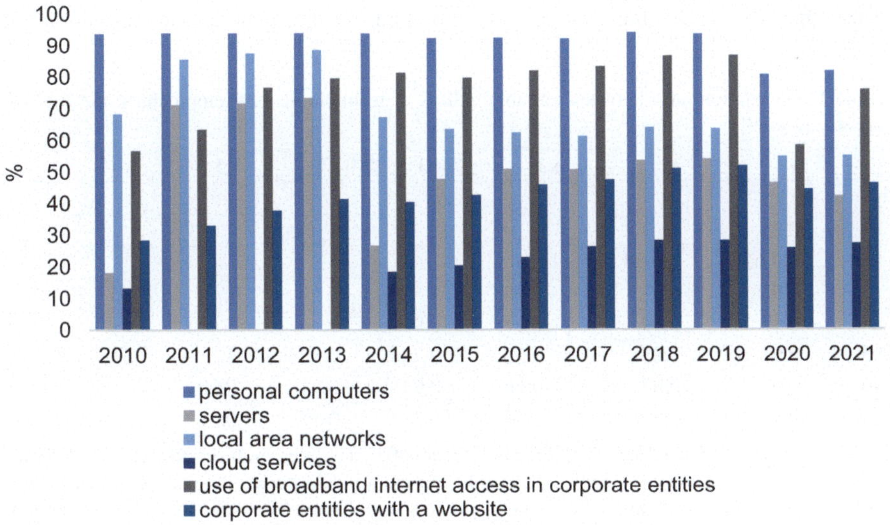


**Fig. 7** Dynamics of technological performance in 2010–2021, % [23–30]

2014–2021, stabilising around 42%. Thus, one cannot talk of significant growth in the use of servers in the Russian industrial complex. (3) The use of local area networks. The share of companies using local area networks shows dynamics similar to the use of servers. From 2010 to 2013, this indicator was growing, reaching its maximum in 2013 (88.7%). However, from 2014 to 2021, the share of corporate entities using local area networks was decreasing, approaching the 55% level. Thus, the use of local area networks also does not show due growth within the Russian industry. (4) The use of cloud services. Access to cloud services is a relatively new technology in the industry. The share of corporate entities using cloud services grew from 2010 to 2017, reaching a peak in 2017 (28.1%). However, this figure has been remaining relatively stable since 2017, fluctuating around 25–27%. Thus, the introduction of cloud services in Russia's industrial complex does not show any significant growth. (5) The use of broadband internet access. From 2010 to 2019, the share of organisations that had access to broadband internet was growing, peaking in 2019 (86.6%). However, a sharp decline in this indicator to 58.1% was registered in 2020, but further, it rose to 75.6% in 2021. Thus, access to broadband internet in Russian industrial organisations is still a challenge.

To carry out the factorial analysis, let us build a correlation matrix (Table 1).

The table reflects the correlation between different indicators related to industrial transformation. The GDP is positively correlated with the industrial production volume (0.981), corporate innovation activity costs (0.950), per capita investments in fixed capital (0.974), and the extent of use of information and communications technologies (0.986). The average annual number of employed persons has a negative correlation with the GDP (−0.613). The spending on corporate innovation activity is correlated with the GDP (0.950), which demonstrates that the level of innovations in organisations increases with the growth of GDP. The fixed capital investment per capita is also correlated with the GDP (0.974), which may demonstrate that the GDP increase is accompanied by an increase in fixed capital

**Table 1** Correlation ratio between variable indices of technological development in the Russian industry [23–29]

| | y | x1 | x2 | x3 | x4 | x5 | x6 | x7 |
|---|---|---|---|---|---|---|---|---|
| y | 1 | | | | | | | |
| x1 | 0.98 | 1 | | | | | | |
| x2 | −0.61 | −0.58 | 1 | | | | | |
| x3 | 0.95 | 0.97 | −0.68 | 1 | | | | |
| x4 | 0.97 | 0.99 | −0.67 | 0.99 | 1 | | | |
| x5 | 0.91 | 0.83 | −0.52 | 0.78 | 0.83 | 1 | | |
| x6 | 0.99 | 0.97 | −0.60 | 0.95 | 0.97 | 0.90 | 1 | |
| x7 | 0.18 | 0.22 | −0.04 | 0.31 | 0.27 | 0.01 | 0.23 | 1 |

Note: y—GDP, million rubles; x1—Industrial production volumes, million rubles; x2—Average annual number of employed people, thousand persons; x3—Corporate innovation activity costs, million rubles; x4—Fixed capital investments per capita, million rubles; x5—Profit, million rubles; x6—Use of information and communications technologies (share of companies having a website), %; x7—Use of electronic document flow,%

investment. The profit figures correlate with the GDP with a factor of 0.912, indicating a positive relationship between the profits and the GDP. The use of information and communications technologies is also correlated with the GDP (0.986), which may mean that GDP growth is accompanied by the development of information technologies. The use of electronic document management has a weak positive correlation with the GDP (0.178), which may mean that better-developed countries use electronic document management more actively.

In general, these results show that there is a relationship between the GDP and other indicators such as industrial output, innovations, investments, and ICT use. The average annual number of employed workers has a negative relationship with the GDP, which may be an interesting subject for further research.

Let us make a regression equation to determine the change in GDP depending on the technological development factors in the industry towards achieving technological independence (Table 2).

The regression equation has the form:

$$Y = 361{,}988{,}543.1 + 1.5x1 + 4557x2 + 13x3 + 914.8x4 + 1070.5x5 + 282{,}058x6 + 178{,}455.4x7$$

This equation shows that GDP growth is strongly influenced by investment, employment rate, and the use of information and communications technologies.

The determination coefficient, R-square, shows the share of variation (dispersion) of the dependent variable (yt) relative to its mean. R2 = 0.997543 means that 99.7% of the variation yt—GDP is explained by the selected factors (Table 3).

The formation of an efficient industrial policy that would provide financial and institutional support becomes a key tool for stimulating investments in industry. Flexibility and adaptability of industrial policy instruments are necessary for the

**Table 2** Data for the regression equation describing the technological development of the Russian industry [23–29]

| Year | y | x1 | x2 | x3 | x4 | x5 | x6 | x7 |
|---|---|---|---|---|---|---|---|---|
| 2010 | 37.7 | 18.8 | 71.5 | 0.4 | 64.1 | 6.3 | 28.5 | 61.0 |
| 2011 | 45.4 | 31.1 | 71.9 | 0.7 | 77.2 | 7.1 | 33.0 | 61.9 |
| 2012 | 49.9 | 38.2 | 72.2 | 0.9 | 87.9 | 7.8 | 37.8 | 61.9 |
| 2013 | 54.1 | 41.4 | 72.2 | 1.1 | 93.7 | 6.9 | 41.3 | 81.7 |
| 2015 | 59.2 | 44.1 | 72.1 | 1.2 | 95.2 | 4.3 | 40.3 | 81.7 |
| 2015 | 65.8 | 49.1 | 72.4 | 1.2 | 94.9 | 7.5 | 42.6 | 62.7 |
| 2016 | 69.3 | 52.7 | 72.1 | 1.3 | 100.6 | 12.8 | 45.9 | 66.1 |
| 2017 | 74.8 | 59.1 | 71.8 | 1.4 | 109.1 | 9.0 | 47.4 | 66.1 |
| 2018 | 85.0 | 69.6 | 71.6 | 1.5 | 121.1 | 12.4 | 50.9 | 68.6 |
| 2019 | 95.1 | 72.9 | 71.1 | 2.0 | 131.6 | 16.6 | 51.9 | 70.0 |
| 2020 | 93.8 | 72.4 | 69.6 | 2.1 | 138.6 | 13.4 | 58.1 | 70.0 |
| 2021 | 135.3 | 94.9 | 70.8 | 2.3 | 157.3 | 33.9 | 75.6 | 70.0 |

Note: y—GDP, trillion rubles; x1—Industrial output, trillion rubles; x2—Average annual number of employees, million people; x3—Corporate innovation activity costs, trillion rubles; x4—Fixed capital investment per capita, billion rubles; x5—Profit, billion rubles; x6—Use of information and communications technologies (share of organisations having a website), %; x7—Use of electronic document flow, %

**Table 3** Regression statistics for the technological development of the Russian industry [23–29]

| | Coefficients | Mean-square error | t-statistics | P-value | Lower 95% | Top 95% | Lower 95.0% | Upper 95.0% |
|---|---|---|---|---|---|---|---|---|
| Y- intersection | 361.989 | 253.843 | 0.000 | 0.000 | −342.792 | 1066.770 | −342.792 | 1066.770 |
| Variable X 1 | 0.000 | 0.000 | 0.000 | 0.000 | 0.000 | 0.000 | 0.000 | 0.000 |
| Variable X 2 | −0.005 | 0.003 | 0.000 | 0.000 | −0.014 | 0.005 | −0.014 | 0.005 |
| Variable X 3 | 0.000 | 0.000 | 0.000 | 0.000 | 0.000 | 0.000 | 0.000 | 0.000 |
| Variable X 4 | −0.001 | 0.001 | 0.000 | 0.000 | −0.003 | 0.001 | −0.003 | 0.001 |
| Variable X 5 | 0.001 | 0.000 | 0.000 | 0.000 | 0.000 | 0.002 | 0.000 | 0.002 |
| Variable X 6 | 0.282 | 0.506 | 0.000 | 0.000 | −1.122 | 1.686 | −1.122 | 1.686 |
| Variable X 7 | 0.178 | 0.213 | 0.000 | 0.000 | −0.413 | 0.770 | −0.413 | 0.770 |

| Indicator | Value |
|---|---|
| Multiple R | 0.99760 |
| R-square | 0.99521 |
| Normalised R-square | 0.98683 |
| Mean-square error | 3,113,419 |
| Observations | 12 |

Note: y—GDP, million rubles; x1—Industrial production volumes, million rubles; x2—Average annual number of employed people, thousand persons; x3—Corporate innovation activity costs, million rubles; x4—Fixed capital investments per capita, million rubles; x5—Profit, million rubles; x6—Use of information and communications technologies (share of companies having a website), %; x7—Use of electronic document flow, %

successful adaptation of the industrial complex to modern challenges involving competitiveness and innovative development. Owing to increasing financial and institutional support, Russian industrial enterprises would be able to improve their competitiveness, enter international markets, and develop innovative products. This will also help to solve the infrastructure problems, increase the efficiency of governmental programmes, and promote industrial development.

## 5 Conclusion

The study shows that the introduction of digital technologies is a key factor in the technological development of Russian industry towards achieving technological independence. Digitalisation plays a key role in the technological development of industry, and Russia's experience in this area confirms this. Owing to the introduction of digital technologies into production processes, Russian enterprises are becoming more competitive in the global market and contribute to increased labour productivity. The application of digital solutions makes it possible to optimise production processes, improve labour efficiency, and increase sectoral industries' competitiveness. However, the successful realisation of the technological development of industry towards the achievement of technological independence requires financial support and the development of policy instruments meeting modern economic requirements in the competitive environment. The implementation of systemic measures of governmental support, such as the provision of loans, subsidies and tax advantages, as well as the improvement of infrastructure and education, will contribute to technological independence and stable economic growth. By integrating new digital technologies into production processes and their due management, countries may strengthen their economies, improve competitiveness and ensure balanced development. However, successful digitalisation requires not only attention to technological aspects but also efforts to ensure adequate training, infrastructural development and the creation of a favourable ecosystem for innovation. In this way, countries will be able to ensure their technological independence and become leaders in the digital era.

**Acknowledgements** The article was prepared under the research plan for the Institute of Economics of the Ural Branch of the Russian Academy of Sciences.

## References

1. Andreeva, O. V. (2014). Technological and financial sovereignty of The Russian Federation: Problems, contradictions, implementation mechanism. *Journal of Economic Regulation, 5*(4), 126–135.

2. Afanasiev, A. A. (2022). Technological sovereignty as a scientific category in the system of modern knowledge. *Economics, Entrepreneurship and Law, 12*(9), 2377–2394. https://doi.org/10.18334/epp.12.9.116243
3. Efimov, A. V., & Tikhonovskova, S. A. (2022). Technological sovereignty of Russia in the context of strategic goals of regional economic development. *Drucker, 4*(48), 165–172. https://doi.org/10.17213/2312-6469-2022-4-165-172
4. Konstantinov, I. B., & Konstantinova, E. P. (2022). Technological sovereignty as a strategy for future development of Russian economy. *Bulletin of the Volga Region Institute of Administration, 22*(5), 12–22. https://doi.org/10.22394/1682-2358-2022-5-12-22
5. Neklyudov, A., & Livshits, I. (2016). Import phaseout or technological sovereignty? *Connect, 9*.
6. Gushchina, E. A., Makarenko, G. I., & Sergin, M. Y. (2018). Measures to ensure governmental information and technological sovereignty in the conditions of digital economy development. *Pravo.by, 6*(56), 59–63.
7. Moiseychik, G. I., & Faradzhov, T. I. (2015). Financial and technological sovereignty issues as the main subject of the 21st-century economic science. *Oikonomos: Journal of Social Market Economy, 2*(3), 47–67.
8. Bauer, H., Patel, M., & Veira, J. (2016). *The internet of things: Sizing up the opportunity*. McKinsey & Company. http://www.mckinsey.com/industries/high-tech/ourinsights/the-internet-of-things-sizing-up-the-opportunity/
9. Herter, J., & Ovtcharova, J. (2016). A model-based visualization framework for cross discipline collaboration in industry 4.0 scenarios. *Procedia CIRP, 57*, 398–403. https://doi.org/10.1016/j.procir.2016.11.069
10. Meissner, H., Ilsena, R., & Aurich, J. C. (2017). Analysis of control architectures in the context of industry 4.0. *Procedia CIRP, 62*, 165–169. https://doi.org/10.1016/j.procir.2016.11.069
11. Schlaepfer, R. C., Koch, M., & Merkhofer, P. (2015). *Challenges and solutions for the digital transformation and use of exponential technologies*. Deloitte.
12. Smirnova, O. P., Averina, L. M., & Ponomareva, A. O. (2020). Transformation of industries in the conditions of new technological challenges. *Advances in Systems Science and Applications, 20*(3), 36–49. https://doi.org/10.25728/assa.2020.20.3.851
13. Akberdina, V. V. (2018). Transformation of the Russian industrial complex in the conditions of digitalisation of economy. *Journal of the Ural State University of Economics, 19*(3), 82–99. https://doi.org/10.29141/2073-1019-2018-19-3-8
14. Akberdina, V. V., & Romanova, O. A. (2021). Regional aspects of industrial development: A review of approaches to the formation of priorities and regulatory mechanisms. *Economy of Region, 17*(3), 714–736. https://doi.org/10.17059/ekon.reg.2021-3-1
15. Akberdina, V. V. (2023). Efficiency of digital transition in industry: Russian experience. *Intellect Innovations. Investments, 1*, 10–18. https://doi.org/10.25198/2077-7175-2023-1-10
16. Nabatova, N. Y., & Plotnikov, V. A. (2021). Innovations, informatisation, industry: Structural analysis of the macroeconomic dynamics in The Russian Federation. *BENEFICIUM, 1*(38), 90–99. https://doi.org/10.34680/BENEFICIUM.2021.1(38).90-99
17. Stepanov, E. V. (2022). Digital transformation of industrial enterprises on the basis of creative solutions within the concept "industry 4.0". *Vestnik of Samara University. Economics and Management, 13*(1), 49–55. https://doi.org/10.18287/2542-0461-2022-13-1-49-55
18. Afanasiev, A. A. The mechanism for formation of Russian industrial policy in the system of strategic planning. *Economics, Entrepreneurship and Law, 3*. https://doi.org/10.18334/epp.13.3.117203
19. Grant, P. (1983). Technological sovereignty: Forgotten factor in the 'hi-tech' razzamatazz. *Prometheus, 1*(2), 239–270.
20. Prikhodko, I. I. (2022). Theoretical aspects of the technological sovereignty concept. *Scientific Notes of V.I. Vernadsky Crimean Federal University. Economics and Management, 4*. https://cyberleninka.ru/article/n/teoreticheskie-aspekty-kontseptsii-tehnologicheskogo-suvereniteta

21. Afanasiev, A. A. Technological sovereignty: Main policy directions towards its achievement in modern Russia. *Issues of Innovative Economy, 4*, 2193–2212. https://doi.org/10.18334/vinec.12.4.116433
22. Smirnova, O. P., & Ponomareva, A. O. (2020). Methodological approach to assessing the efficiency of regional industrial policy. *Economic Analysis: Theory and Practice, 19*(8), 1431–1457. https://doi.org/10.24891/ea.19.8.1431
23. Russian Federal State Statistics Service (Rosstat). (2012). *Regions of Russia. Socio-economic indicators. 2012: statistics digest.* Moscow.
24. Russian Federal State Statistics Service (Rosstat). (2014). *Regions of Russia. Socio-economic indicators. 2014: statistics digest.* Moscow.
25. Russian Federal State Statistics Service (Rosstat). (2016). *Regions of Russia. Socio-economic indicators. 2016: statistics digest.* Moscow.
26. Russian Federal State Statistics Service (Rosstat). (2018). *Regions of Russia. Socio-economic indicators. 2018: statistics digest.* Moscow.
27. Russian Federal State Statistics Service (Rosstat). (2019). *Regions of Russia. Socio-economic indicators. 2019: statistics digest.* Moscow.
28. Russian Federal State Statistics Service (Rosstat). (2020). *Regions of Russia. Socio-economic indicators. 2020: statistics digest.* Moscow.
29. Russian Federal State Statistics Service (Rosstat). (2022). *Regions of Russia. Socio-economic indicators. 2022: statistics digest.* Moscow.
30. Sukharev, O. S. (2021). Digitalisation and thrusts of technological modernisation of the Russian industry. *Journal of New Economy, 22*(1), 26–52. https://doi.org/10.29141/2658-5081-2021-22-1-2

The manufacturer's authorised representative in the EU is Springer Nature Customer Service Centre GmbH, Europaplatz 3, 69115 Heidelberg, Germany. If you have any concerns regarding our products, please contact ProductSafety@springernature.com

Printed and bound by CPI Group (UK) Ltd, Croydon, CR0 4YY
01/10/2026
02225911-0018